The many Faces of Crime for Profit
and
Ways of Tackling it

Petrus C. van Duyne

Jackie Harvey

Georgios A. Antonopoulos

Klaus von Lampe

The many Faces of Crime for Profit and Ways of Tackling it

Petrus C. van Duyne, Jackie Harvey, Georgios A. Antonopoulos,
Klaus von Lampe (eds.)

ISBN: 9789462404366

This volume contains a selection of peer reviewed papers based on the presentations of the authors at the sixteenth Crossborder Crime Colloquium, hosted by the Northumbria University 26-28 June 2016, Newcastle upon Tyne, United Kingdom.

This project was supported by the Teesside University.

The Cross-Border Crime Colloquium is an annual event since 1999. It brings together experts on international organised (economic) crime to discuss the latest developments in empirical research, legislation and law enforcement, with a special geographical focus on Western, Central, and Eastern Europe.

The Colloquia aim at building bridges in three respects: between East and West Europe, between scholars and practitioners, and between old and young. The Cross-border Crime Colloquium, so far, has been organised fifteen times:

2016 Newcastle upon Tyne, UK
2015 Prague, Czech Republic
2014 Sarajevo, Bosnia & Herzegovina
2013 Cambridge, UK
2012 Manchester, UK
2011 Tilburg, the Netherlands
2009 Gent, Belgium
2008 Belgrade, Serbia
2007 Prague, Czech Republic

2006 Tallinn, Estonia
2005 Sarajevo, Bosnia and
Herzegovina
2004 Berlin, Germany
2003 Ainring, Germany
2002 Ljubljana, Slovenia
2001 Bratislava, Slovakia
2000 Budapest, Hungary
1999 Prague, Czech Republic

Copies can be ordered at:
Wolf Legal Publishers (WLP)
P.O. Box 313
5060 AH Oisterwijk
The Netherlands
www.wolfpublishers.com
E-Mail: sales@wolfpublishers.nl

cover design: The Colloquium Group

Table of contents[1]

---

[1] General footnote: throughout this volume the writing of numbers will be 'normal European': the commas are for the decimals and the dots the thousands.

Table of contents

List of authors

Georgios A. Antonopoulos
Professor of Criminology, Teesside University, UK.

Abdullahi U. Bello
Ag. Head, Forensic Accounting and Financial Investigation, Economic and Financial Crimes Commission, Nigeria.

Deborah Booth
Researcher, Northumbria University, UK.

Anna Di Ronco
Lecturer, University of Essex, UK.

Alan Doig
Visiting Professor, Newcastle Business School, Northumbria University, UK.

Petrus C. van Duyne
Visiting professor, Northumbria University, UK, and Utrecht University, The Netherlands.

Filippo Espinoza
Doctoral student, University of Trento, Italy.

Doron Goldbarsht
PhD Candidate, Faculty of Law at the University of New South Wales in Sydney, Australia.

Jackie Harvey
Professor, Northumbria University, UK.

Rob Hornsby
Senior Lecturer, Northumbria University, UK.

Tjalling J. van Koningsveld
Director, Offshore Knowledge Centre, The Netherlands.

Anita Lavorgna
Lecturer, University of Southampton, UK.

Argyro Elisavet Manoli
Lecturer in Sports Marketing and Communication, Loughborough University, UK.

Anna Markovska
Senior Lecturer in Criminology, Anglia Ruskin University, UK.

Christopher Michaelsen
Associate Professor of Law, University of New South Wales in Sydney, Australia.

Kenneth Murray
Head of Forensic Accountancy, Police Scotland, UK

Radu Nicolae
Centre for Legal Resources, Romania and adjunct lecturer at the National School of Political Science and Public Administration (SNSPA), Romania.

Georgios Papanicolaou
Reader in Criminology, Teesside University, United Kingdom

Joschka J. Proksik
Research fellow and programme coordinator, Department of Politics and Administration, University of Konstanz, Germany.

Nicholas Ryder
Professor in Financial Crime, University of the West of England, United Kingdom

Alexey Serduyk
Deputy Head of Scientific Research Laboratory of Crime Enforcement, Kharkiv National University of Internal Affairs, Ukraine.

Dina Siegel
Professor of Criminology, Willem Pompe Institute, Utrecht University, The Netherlands.

Toine Spapens
Professor of Criminology, Tilburg University, The Netherlands.

Nadya Stoynova
Analyst, Center for the Study of Democracy, Bulgaria.

Klaus von Lampe
Associate Professor, John Jay College of Criminal Justice in New York, USA.

Aleksandra Zurakowska
Doctoral student, European University Viadrina, Frankfurt (Oder), Germany.

Introduction: Truths and the many faces of crime

Alternative truths

What about truth? It is at once a lofty and banal concept. We cannot live without truth: that is an existential axiom. Nevertheless, throughout human history or in one's lifetime, one cannot fully live with it either: we live a fair part of our lives with untruths if not outright lies, from 'white lies' to pitch-black ones. And we survive by this duplicity. For that ambiguity we have a whole dictionary of excuses (Vrij, 2008). The White House Cabinet even upgraded the concept of 'untruth' to 'alternative facts' and downgraded unwelcome truths to 'fake news' though there are also 'genuine' fake news. Is there a new trend, a kind of 'truth-relativism', navigating through the various shades of true and false statements? If that is correct, there could be a new genuine search for truth. Maybe, but be cautious: dealing with 'truths' is also a kind of art of deception, masterly exploited by conmen (Kabki, 2014; Van Duyne and Kabki, 2016) as well as statesmen. Those who lack this skill of juggling in the political world of 'alternative facts' may resort to a defensive ham-handed simplification, if not distortion of reality. An example of this is the way climate science has been heavily handled by the present US administration.

While such gross simplifications and distortions are easy to reject, with 'truth relativism' we may feel more uncomfortable. Often times we realise that there are nuances or multiple faces of truth while our cognition says there should be only one. A kind of uneasy ambiguity that make us waver just because the concept of truth has a positive existential value even in absolute terms. People were prepared to go to the stake because of some absolute truth, not for some nuance. For example Bruno was burnt in 1600 for his heretical cosmological theories in accordance with the then novel Copernican model. That was not for a nuance, as his successor scientist Galileo experienced three decades later. These are extreme cases and for our purpose connected to the extra aureole of truth: science. Science is the contradiction of anything fake and evokes the image of dedicated and impartial scholars sifting through raw material and weighing documents of colleagues and predecessors to find coveted 'pearls of truth'. The verb 'to find' may be incorrect because it is too passive: scholars work hard to extract or construct truths from other building blocks as the most plausible explanation of a phenomenon. Has this any relation to Trumpian 'alternative' truths? Beware! Ideally such a quest for truth should be an unselfish undertaking for its own sake. This fits in the serene picture of science. However, this is only an ideal image hiding other faces of that quest for truth. Apart from breaches of integrity in science, ranging from cooking the statistics to inventing data, pressure may be exerted to colour in the most 'favourable face of truth', often within the 'mainstream'. This created discontent and unrest. The ways in which the Environmental Protection Agency was treated by president Trump ignited this discontent and drove scientists in the USA and other countries to a rare demonstration of protest. In many countries they took to the streets and not only because the new US administration curtailed climate research funding.

There is indeed a genuine and justified concern of being pressured or nudged to outcomes which are mainly comfortable to principals of research projects. However, there are many alternative drivers for researchers that make them susceptible to the pressure against which they recently protested: *e.g.* citation rates. This may have more impact on researchers' conduct than the truth value of their publications. Or getting research grants: think of research on health care ('Big Pharma' and Gøtzsche, 2014), humanities, political science or criminology, they all depend on funds from third party stakeholders. These are the Lords of the Grants and Subsidies who determine the agenda of truth finding and its funding, which give scholars a place to work.

Apart from that, real science consists of a chain of falsifications, not of truth confirmations (Popper, 1969). That is uncomfortable: psychologically, refutations do not feel good. This goes to the depth of our nervous system: reaction times to sentences with denials are always longer than to confirmations while classical reasoning experiments show that subjects test logical statements by looking for confirmations instead of falsification (Johnson-Laird and Wason, 1972). This makes an 'alternative truth' so much easier to sell than the nuances of multi-faceted truths. This may also apply to the scientific publishing practice: negating research is less popular. This socio-psychological context may explain why Trump can safely launch his 'alternative truths': they linger on because rejection costs more effort and is less accepted.

This volume is about a selection of the many faces of crime and related authorities. As much criminality is intended to remain hidden, the authors intend to present disguised or distorted faces of 'true crime'.

Corruption

For good reasons this volume starts with corruption, characterised by stapling pretence on pretence while hiding the exchange of advantages for illegally obtained decisions (Van Duyne, 2001). Or, in our discourse, mixing up alternative truths which become the more entangled the higher one comes, till one cannot tell one from the other. That happens on all levels, distorting not only the daily relevant decision making, ranging from getting a parking ticket waved to obtaining preferential treatment in the hospital to corrupting the tax administration for skimming the national till. This is not just a local matter of a corrupt policeman or local doctor; it affects international relations, for example, when donor countries suspect their development aid is returning through underground channels to the real estate market of Manhattan or West London (Doward, 2017). Naturally, this is a matter of on-going concern. *Alan Doig* describes in his chapter on corruption how this concern stretches back half a Century, while indicating that there are more 'faces' to this crime than simply a moral one. He underlines this by drawing on an article of 50 years ago by Colin Leys who wrote that corruption was a functional rather than a moral issue. The focus of his and Doig's elaboration is the region of *Sub-Saharan Africa* with its long-term intertwined problems of failing democracy and economic development, and corruption. In this combination corruption has a 'functional' place. If that is the case, how can we move forward to reduce it? The question is raised whether economic growth leads to more democracy and consequently to less corruption. Many countries in the region have experienced economic growth, but failed in democratisation and in reducing corruption or saw their democratic institutions captured by a corrupt elite. For donors this results in a development aid agenda with different ambiguous trajectories: should one begin with promoting economic growth and democracy or fighting corruption first? If one cannot tackle the three problems at the same time, addressing one may lead to a solution for the other two problems, though with some delay. It is a problem of choices which cannot be solved by moral arguments against corruption only. This level of corruption may be too high for morality alone. A realistic or cynical conclusion or rather a recognition of the various faces of corruption?

Naturally, at a national level corruption has various faces, depending on its usefulness in running a criminal enterprise. *Nadya Stoynova* guides us into the world of Bulgarian human trafficking and related corruption which is functional in guarding and furthering the criminal business, both locally as well as cross-border. Actually, Zhang and Pineda (2008) detected a correlation between corruption and human trafficking. Stoynova describes how in a quarter of a Century human trafficking (for sexual services) has evolved alongside 'functional' corruption. Some functions became obsolete. Thus, the free movement of people and capital in Europe implied less corruption at the borders. In addition, the increased pressure in Bulgaria to do more against corruption entailed perhaps less, but certainly other *modus operandi* of corruption: corrupt deals became less direct and more through intermediaries forming a network for exerting influence on political decision makers. These are called 'black lawyers', networks of 'strongmen' with the capacity pull strings. This ranges from local to the national level to influence investigations, prosecutions and even court decisions. It is of interest that this more or less unstructured corruption network survived the demise of many high-ranking criminals and shifts in the human trafficking market. Resilience of corruption was (as in Sub-Saharan Africa) not weakened by the growth of democracy and economic development. It may even be their derivative of that development: while the essence of corruption remains the same, it has altered its appearance.

The multi-faceted nature of corruption also emerges in the sport sector: international as well as local, where corruption scandals abound, often in the football sector. Specific results become the subject of bets placed worldwide. Such betting outcomes should be the result of fairness: good insight, intuition or just (statistical) luck. As clairvoyance is a rare talent (if existing at all), and control is preferred above the uncertainties of fortune, there is a motivation to influence the outcome of betting by bribing all (or strategically situated) participants. Football is one of the sports being susceptible to such 'match fixing' by bribing players, referees or the whole football club by colluding with its corrupt president. The reader will be aware of the worldwide corruption in the international football organisation: the scandal of the FIFA top officials who after many years of rumours and denials were indicted. *Argyro Elisavet Manoli* and *Georgios A. Antonopoulos* present a picture of the corrupt football sector in Greece. The authors project their findings of corrupt conduct against a broader business landscape of degeneration of tax fraud and mismanagement. Not only the public and honest betters are deceived, but also the licencing and tax authorities: the corruption of the match goes hand in hand with ticket tampering and fraudulent management of the clubs themselves. It is not only personal greed but also a policy intended to keep the club from insolvency: the 'higher aim' as driver or excuse. Of course, measures have been taken to tackle corruption and fraud, but these are based on the assumption that the abuse is an aberration from the norm. However, as the authors make clear, the corruption in the Greek football industry is not a matter of aberration of its values and norms, but the 'new normal'.

The confusing faces of crime-money

Banking has always been a matter of trust that funds will always be returned, whether from the view of the customer (depositor) or the bank (as lender). Over the past 25 years this simple trust relationship has been overtaken by another concern: the criminal origin of money. Banks must trust that the money it receives for further processing is 'clean'. That has become a global political issue from 1990 onwards underpinned by a general concern of potential erosion of trust in the financial system as a whole. Whether that is due to money laundering itself or to its broader embeddedness in a surrounding political or criminal landscape remains a debated question (Van Duyne *et al.*, forthcoming). The possibility of a criminal entrepreneurial landscape should certainly be taken seriously as is the case in Ukraine as described by *Anna Markovska* and *Alexey Serduyk*. They explain how money laundering has become part of a criminalised economy. This has its roots in the socialist times with its denial of criminality, also concerning financial crime against the banks. In the Soviet Union these were centrally directed but with the collapse of the socialist regime banks had to become independent resulting in many small undercapitalised banks. The need to attract capital made them susceptible to shady funds becoming instrumental in their laundering. Otherwise the banks operated in a criminal financial landscape that had changed little over the last decades: organised crime groups, shady entrepreneurs and corrupt officials comprised the banks' customers (Osyka, 2001). The banks' independence became a Potemkin village with senior officials determining the policy behind the screens enabled by weak laws and enacted by crony legislators. It is of interest to note that Ukraine adopted all the anti-money laundering recommendations of the FATF, being complimented for this 'achievement' by removal from the FATF 'black list' of non-compliant states. Meanwhile, it was obvious that 'on the ground' the 'laundering mills' of a multitude of small banks remained in operation. Many went bankrupt with great loss of savings for the account holders. "*The tragedy of the Ukrainian banking system is a tragedy of the modern Ukraine, willing and corrupt insiders coupled with significant political pressure*", as the authors observe. With so much opacity and (non)truths put upside-down, a wise Ukrainian keeps his money under the mattress.

If the American savers had also heeded this advice, the impact of the 2007 credit crisis would have been much less or may not even have happened. But the American drama was not about saved but 'created' money by means of credits with bad or fabricated collateral. It appeared that the financial institutions and their top management operated unethically if not outright criminally: the system was corrupt and rotten, though different from that of Ukraine with its broader criminalised economy (Markovska, 2007). Nevertheless, the authorities were to blame: there were early warnings but these were not heeded. This enabled fraudsters such as Madoff to continue their criminal schemes without hindrance. *Nicholas Ryder* describes how the authorities responded when the credit bubble burst and the shockwaves reverberated worldwide. If laws can be compared with guns and supervisory and law enforcement institutions with gunners, a full broadside could have been fired. There are the SEC, FBI and Department of Justice and the Commodity Futures Trading Commission. And there are the various laws, like barrels pointed at the wrongdoers. The relevant laws to tackle fraud in various ways were available: the Mail Fraud Statute that popular with prosecutors because of its wide range; the equally broad Wire Fraud Statute; Bank Fraud Act was extended by the Financial Institutions Reform; Recovery and Enforcement Act 1989; the Major Fraud Act 1988. What was achieved with this full battery? The author observes that lot of small fry was hit (mainly related to mortgage fraud) but none at the centre or at the top of the largest financial institutions. This contrasts with the SEC which succeeded in imposing sky-high administrative penalties of up to $ 550 million (*e.g.* Goldman Sachs). But no criminal convictions of 'Wall Street': most unethical but for criminal law too elusive?

The elusiveness of shady funds becomes stronger and more difficult to penetrate when it is maintained by a worldwide corporate financial secrecy industry operating in offshore centres. This appeals to the imagination and for good reasons: the Panama leak illustrates how the rich and famous, crooks and Prime Ministers alike seek and enjoy the discrete services of offshore financial consultancy firms. It is inherent to the nature of the discrete services that the wealth of these customers remains hidden which implies that estimates about the volume of offshore monies remains a matter of guess work. As it is politically very tempting to make tough statements about these hidden monies wild estimates circle around, upheld by respected authorities, such as the IMF, World Bank and the United Nations (Schneider, 2016). But the wilder the estimates, the more elusive the phenomenon becomes, as is set out in the chapter by *Petrus C. van Duyne* and *Tjalling J. van Koningsveld*. Moreover, what is an offshore centre? A sunny island with blue lagoons, white beaches and palm trees? Abstracting from this popular image, the authors line up a variety of current definitions, most of them very imprecise (Van Koningsveld, 2015). Naturally this inaccuracy is no basis for estimation. Instead they raise the question of the whereabouts of all this wealth. Stashed in the vaults of the offshore banks? Or floating around somewhere? To approximate an answer to this question the authors analysed the data of the Bank of International Settlement, to find indications of cross-border bank claims between countries: bank country A holding bank accounts in country B. Country A is then offshore and country B onshore. It appears that offshore banks have huge accounts in banks in *onshore* countries. About 25% of the worldwide cross-border bank claims are from offshore banks to onshore banks. If world leaders raise the alarm about the huge hidden wealth they may be advised to look within their own national financial industry: the so-called hidden wealth floats through their own banks where a higher yield may be produced than in the offshore centres. The authors looked subsequently at the offshore own real estate in the Netherlands suspecting that part of the offshore hidden wealth is likely to find its way to this destination. Other studies have indicated that the real estate sector is susceptible for abuse though the scope of research was limited to two cities only (Unger and Ferwerda, 2011). To get the national picture the authors analysed the full database of the Dutch Land Registry for 2014 and 2015 as far as *offshore* ownership is mentioned: fully owned or burdened with a mortgage. They found that the assessed offshore owned real estate is about 2.500 million Euro: that is 0,13% of the national property value (2015), within which abuse is to be located as a subset. The main offshore ownership countries proved to be the 'usual suspects': Switzerland, Luxembourg and Delaware, a thriving offshore centre in the heart of the most important champion of the anti-laundering policy. These countries were also the most important mortgage holders. As the Land Registry has no 'suspiciousness variable', nothing could be concluded about *suspicious* funds. Did the outcomes match the popular face of the offshore world? Unfortunately, the picture of hidden wealth remains wrapped in fog: the findings are too broad for such a match, but also give no reason for panic.

Though that may sound reassuring, policy makers will not easily allow themselves to be soothed. With so much fog around there is always something 'at risk' requiring additional supervisory vigilance: if you do not know the criminal face of your opponent, be prepared! This is how pressure is maintained and justified on the whole chain of AML policy: from the FATF downwards to the compliance officers and professions tasked with this policy. However, this is not a simple linear chain of command, because the regulated money making institutions are also the principals who employ these compliance officers, but who are not 'real' money makers. This means that these officers can experience pressure from two sides. And both sides can be unreasonable in the pressure they exert. To address this problem *Abdullahi U. Bello* developed an interesting 'self-protecting theory' and carried out interviews with present and former compliance staff. He found that compliance officers must often defend their decisions to both sides: a tough regulator and the banks and customers who may be equally tough. That is comparable what Sandulescu (2016) calls the integration of compliance in the banking culture. Psychologically this is an interesting balancing act, creating a distance between both sides rather than putting the required energy in preventing money laundering. The author pleads for a middle course approach of *independence* of the compliance officer and *fairness* of pressure. The author acknowledges this theory needs further sharpening and provides an interestingly broader angle through its possible an applicability in hospitals.

Handling these and other varieties of vague faces is a serious matter which should not be waved as a kind of pedantic pettiness. Indeed, maintaining vagueness often serves the purpose of usurping power and influence, while transparency, a 'sharp fact', safeguards the basic means of democratic control and rule of law. This is a serious lesson which can be deduced from the chapter written by *Doron Goldbarsht* and *Christopher Michaelsen*. Though the authors write about the Australian norm-development, the moral of their elaboration goes far beyond this region. The authors describe the dual approach to tackle money laundering: the road of legality through treaties and (UN) conventions and the road of informality chosen by the G-7 in 1989 through an informal policy advisory club: the Financial Action Task Force on money laundering (FATF). This had the advantage of circumventing the formalities of traditional international approaches which requires democratic voting procedures. For the USA, the initiator and leading force in this field, formal approach was not an attractive option (Wechsler, 2001). Not only because the built-in uncertainty of outcome, but also because the formal treaty road would bind only signatory countries. At present, irrespective of signatures, about 180 countries have implemented the 40 FATF Recommendations, though the FATF has only 37 members. Also, in its standard setting and the enforcement of implementation the FATF remained unhindered. The authors point at the circumstance that the FATF has arrogated an enforcement authority which is at odds which the prevailing rule of law principles in the civilised world. The FATF investigates whether a country is compliant, it determines the seriousness of non-compliance, gives a judgement and is its executioner. This differs fundamentally from the prevalent "*international law and governance in which state consent and sovereignty constitute key defining principles*". While this reflects a serious encroachment of the separation of powers, few seem to care. The warnings by Stessens (2000; 2001) and Wechsler (2001) failed to engender debate of this fundamental matter. Therefore, it is important that the authors bring this issue again to the fore. And what about the national democratic 'watchdogs', the parliaments? As far as Australia is concerned they observe that "*this process of norm-development reduces domestic parliaments to rubber stamping institutions*" brow-beaten by the stern face of the FATF. In view of the FATF's uncontested global reach and its Principal, the semi-closed ring of 'rich countries', the G-7, alias G-20, this most probably does not only apply to Australia. It should be a concern to all democracies where no sound of debate can be heard.

Faces of 'true crime': look at the differences

Where there are so many half disguised, half open faces, one should not be surprised that clarity through striving at generalisations will equally be impeded where it concerns predicate offences. This is not as bad as it looks like. In experimental psychology there is a classical rule 'not to generalise light-heartedly over borders of domains': rather a limited hypothesis tested than launching a grand generalisation. So looking at the subject of the next chapter we heed this admonition of modesty. What do the authors say?

First, we are guided by *Toine Spapens* to the world of cannabis and money. It is an interesting and detailed tour in a region the author knows very well (Spapens, 2016): he begins by guiding us through the scenery of a thriving flexible industry in a provincial town (Tilburg) and its surrounding region in the Brabant, a southern province of the Netherlands. Then the reader is led through the many attempts to obtain a proper sight on the 'how much' issue and, finally, of what criminals do with their ill-gotten wealth.

It is no surprise that the estimations of criminal production are as nebulous as that of most crime-money estimates such as issued by the UNODC (2011).

The reader may be inclined to leaf through quickly, which may make him overlook an interesting issue: the alleged overproduction relative to the Dutch user market and the assumed exportation to neighbouring countries. This assumption is important as it is used against the proposed legalisation of the cannabis industry: national legalisation would not make much difference as the main cannabis growing is for export. This argument has been stated for decades and it is true: the Netherlands are selling drugs to a continuous flow of drug tourists. This is not enough for an explanation of the imbalance between production and user estimations. Nor are there sufficient large interceptions at the border or further abroad to fill the gap. So, where does all that cannabis production remain? Are the estimations realistic; nothing overlooked? Naturally, when the production quantum is doubted the estimation of the revenues must follow suit: is there really so much crime money in this sector? "There should be", but as soon as that is said the picture is obscured. First, as in the legitimate economy, there are large income and wealth differences (Van Duyne, 1999; Van Duyne and Soudijn, 2010). Second, where one would expect some sophisticated 'criminal money management' (as a better phrase for money laundering), the author presents an interesting 'true crime' description of spending and spilling in which every cliché becomes reality (Van Duyne and Levi, 2005): horses, cars and women, and, of course, all extremely expensive. Nevertheless, some criminals succeed in rising beyond that shallow criminal socio-economy by obtaining local influence in the town or community administration. But that is risky by itself: some become too cocky, attracting undue attention leading to exposure and downfall. The best survival rule in the organisation of crime is to keep an elusive face.

Next we go from southern Netherlands to organised crime in Scotland as set out by *Kenneth Murray*. He discerns in the central belt of Scotland organised crime groups with more or less territorial borders, while further up north there are fewer local barriers to entry. For both groups their *raison d'être* is participation on the hard drug market. This is no real revelation, nor the finding that local and international trade are necessarily connected, together with the handling of the flow of cash, from retail level and up the chain of hierarchy. At every level we meet other professional handlers and the adaptation of the organisation to the tasks at that level, according to the general principle: organisation follows task execution. A new aspect is the introduction of the concept of 'rhizomes'. This is a relationship which goes beyond a mere symbiosis: *"it extends to become a unity that is multiple in itself, able to connect any point in the system to any other point"*. That ambiguous 'unity that is multiple' is not some kind of riddle but a formidable strength: cohesion while retaining the flexibility to move around in a wide space where networks of such relationships exist. The author characterises this as a 'nomadic' market conduct, which makes the Scottish organised crime groups just as elusive as the ones described in the Dutch Brabant cannabis scene.

With the narrative of the cyber criminals in Romania, as described by *Radu Nicolae*, we move closer to meeting almost real nomadic criminals. Or is the author's metaphor of the flock of crows being together, dispersing and uniting again, a better one? Both apply: nomads have to pitch up their tents and crows have to come to the ground for foraging and both disperse as soon as there is danger. And that is what the author found in the 30 Romanian cyber crime cases analysed: a restless bunch of criminals who could not defraud worldwide by remaining at their screens but rather, had to move. If they have a 'bite' mobility sets in: they have to move to withdraw money from the bank accounts in any other place to where they operate and preferably abroad; or to place devices in ATMs abroad to get bank pass codes or manipulate the machine; or exchange the stolen money into goods, *etc*. In short, it is 'off and on the ground': digital, feet on the earth (e.g. manipulating ATM), digital again and finally return home. While working globally, these crime groups consisted mainly of Romanians with a few Bulgarians and range from 3 to 27 participants. That is substantial and requires a smooth organisation and coordination in task determined networks (Morselli, 2009) in view of the high-speed mobility with which the hacked bank accounts were emptied before discovery. Identities could be stolen in Germany and within 24 hours sold further up and down a number of time zones, returning to the command post at home for settling accounts. These were profit oriented rationally organised crime groups with only one case of ideologically motivated hacking. They worked according to identifiable business models (fake e-bay auctions, phishing, skimming and identity theft) belying the usual organised crime clichés: no violence, power struggles with other groups, cooperation and just one case of bribery. That is also one of the faces of organised crime: an almost normal enterprise.

Crime can show a very pleasing face when it satisfies the demand or fulfils the hopes of many who remain dissatisfied by the mainstream legal supply of goods and services. One of these services can be called the alternative 'health and hope industry' with a broad legal twilight zone of useless products against 'aging', vitamin shortage or energy boosting. Let us say 'legal deception unless proven otherwise'. There is also an outright 'criminal desperation exploitation': criminal deception, fraud and outright dangerous criminal quackery. That is the criminal supply side. But what about the demand side of the numerous believers who prop up this practice and view their health crooks as gifted gurus? This demand side was researched by *Anita Lavorgna* and *Anna Di Ronco*. One may wonder whether this is a criminal phenomenon at all: believers and gurus are naturally convinced of their legal alternative medical interaction. The authors avoid this discussion by deliberately selecting three convicted medical gurus who despite their convictions continued with their prohibited health service. Their next question concerns the support for this criminal practice extended by the believers, sometimes forming sect-like chat groups on the internet contributing to the continuation of these harmful criminal practices. The authors studied one of the most popular online fora to identify discussion threads in the online community. It is interesting to observe that guru-followers with serious diseases did not feel themselves victimised. If they felt victimised, it was by the medical establishment ('Big Pharma') and not by the ineffective alternative medicines and treatments often worse than placebos. Nevertheless, they are victims but at the same time contributing to the scam by their supporting statements and complaints against 'them', the recognised medical professionals and authorities. It is a hideous face of crime: the medical criminal and his victimised desperate believers and collaborators.

Authorities: shaping faces and a capsized 'flagship'

It goes without saying that the many faces of crime are not shaped by criminals alone as most want to remain unknown. The authorities play a more prominent role in shaping the face of crime in which they are not impartial. The face they present must serve a policy function: it does not need to be true as long as it is accepted as such. It also does not need to be sharply defined: some vagueness in defining can serve a purpose allowing the absorption of 'alternative truths', all according to political or budgetary needs. This can have consequences for all involved. Victims of certain offences may be recognised or 'defined away', interventions expanded or halted and budgets dried up. "What is in the name?" Much: it determines the 'face of the crime' the authorities present to the public and the choice of the subsequent response (Spencer, 2008). This has been interestingly clarified in the chapter of *Rob Hornsby*, *Jackie Harvey* and *Deborah Booth* about trafficked, smuggled and exploited children which they present as a 'hidden victim population' due to misclassification. There is not much insight into this category of victims due to frequent 'misclassification' as emerged from the extensive interviews of 17 respondents of 14 difference organisations. What field workers recognised as child trafficking for exploitation, particularly inland instead of 'organised cross-border' did frequently not get over the 'recognition threshold': *e.g.* domestic servitude, child begging, swapping children between families for benefit fraud, *etc.* They *"dropped off the radar"*, and were thus not labelled as 'trafficking'. Consequently with too few cases, the responsible agencies could not develop expertise for investigation. Withdrawal of funds led to further under-reporting. One can say that the trafficking of children within the UK did not get the 'ugly face' required for higher prioritising.

"To label or not to label": the impact of labelling by the authorities can be severe, certainly when there are suspicions of a deliberate political mislabelling leading to serious social and economic harm. This has been set out by *Dina Siegel* in her chapter on the misfortunes of the sex workers in the Dutch town of Utrecht. What was the problem? As in many other states in Europe, prostitution, or, rather commercial sex service, is no longer prohibited. So there should have been a neutral label and corresponding benign policy. However, that is not the case. From left and right, from feminism to Christian moralists, the concept of prostitution is surrounded by negative moral associations: "it should not be there". It has also a strong criminal association: human trafficking for sexual exploitation is always looming large. For the authorities that is a strong energising label and easily connected to the 'organised crime' label: a formula forcing them 'to do something' publicly. It is also a convenient justification for a repressive and 'preventive' intervention against prostitution, as has been the case in the Zandpad ("Sandpath"): a road along a canal to which barges were anchored.

A large number of sex workers had an orderly and rather safe place for their licensed enterprises. This was not to the liking of the Mayor and Councillors who reacted on a rumour of 'women trafficking' at the Zandpad by withdrawing all licenses from the operators of the prostitution windows. The (soft) information was kept secret (for 'privacy' reasons), the sex workers were not consulted and there were no arrests or prosecutions. Worse, there was no contingency plan to accommodate the sex workers in replacement facilities. In short, they lost their place of work and income and were scattered to unsupervised, unsafe shady places. While the authorities said they acted for 'safety reasons', the women ended in more risky working conditions. It was not the first time intended moralist concern and protection led to economic harm to the sex workers (Verhoeven, 2017). A result of malicious labelling? Though the author does not use this qualification, the reader may feel to have glanced on an unreliable face.

One can say that the Mayor and Councillors of Utrecht harmed the sex workers, but from a well-intended, 'lofty righteousness' they acted on behalf of 'the general good'. The general good as perceived by politicians can become so prevailing (or a convenient excuse), that the authorities even condone or collude with law breaking. There are many examples of such opportunistic collusions: in 1943 the invading US army in Sicily turned to the local strong men, who were actually Mafiosi, to keep order; the US was allegedly involved in the drug trade during the Vietnamese war to keep local tribes in the mountains happy; the drug policy in Latin America in the1980s knew many opaque upper- underworld intertwining (McCoy, 2003). In the same vein the Chinese government condoned organised violation of intellectual property rights, but seems to take no effective action at present. In these cases there was a silent understanding between local illegal traders and the authorities. Going somewhat further back in time, to the 1920s, *Georgios Papanicolaou* and *Filippo Espinoza* describe how the Italian local government operated similarly in their newly acquired colony: the *Dodecanese*, a group of twelve islands in the South-eastern Aegean Sea. For the then governor, the stability of the social and economic life in the new colony and the local support was of primary importance. Given the meagre economic resources of the islands and their dependence on the informal (smuggling) economy, the new colonial rule adopted a policy of tolerance via the condonation of illicit markets and the dodging of regulations. This was to the benefit of the economic elite which was allowed to maintain its dominant position (if remaining loyal). The authors raise the question whether illegal markets play a role in a state's conscious strategies and efforts to establish and reproduce order. Their answer is positive even if one may think this a perverse and corrupt public policy.

Is this a reason to adopt a cynical attitude to authorities? It must be admitted that under the cloak of higher interests, or the 'general good', many alternative truths may be hidden to be used at an opportune moment. That evokes images of dark conspiracies which must usually be taken with more than a pinch of salt as reality may be rather disorderly and in human terms sometimes 'flat' for conspiracies. A 'flat' but in this case orderly law enforcement arrangement is presented in the chapter by *Klaus von Lampe* and *Aleksandra Zurakowska* on the German-Polish border cooperation. Despite an unhappy shared history, the police cooperation along the shared Oder-Neisse frontier between Germany and Poland has developed in a fruitful way. The institutions and arrangements for exchange of information and common investigations have proved to be effective against the cross-border crime in both directions. The crime rate has dropped, though that may be due to a general reduction in crime in a greying industrial society, for which law enforcement likes to take credit. Nevertheless, Joint Investigation Teams dismantled some gangs operating cross-border. Alongside information exchange, the informal friendly relationships contributed to efficiency in by-passing the usual bureaucratic hurdles. It appears that there is a geographic distance factor: the same institutional arrangements function better when supported by the informal network along the border compared to police stations further inland. A simple human truth, as is the language factor: given the asymmetric economic advantages, there are more Poles who speak German than the other way round.

Amidst the many waves of European negativity this is a happy story with a positive EU-face we should cherish. Unfortunately, there are many sad EU-stories attracting more attention than the successful ones. The EU handling of the legal support project in Kosovo is one of the sadder stories, which is elaborated in the last -but not least- chapter by *Joschka J. Proksik*. After the ill-fated United Nations mission for helping to establish a rule of law (project name UNMIK), the EU took over in 2008 with the mission to assist the Kosovo authorities in criminal as well as other legal matters: it was called the European Union Rule of Law Mission in Kosovo (EULEX). It was intended to be a 'flagship mission' for the price of for the price of € 100 million per year and 2.800 staff (later reduced). The EULEX mission entered a landscape of clan-wise organised crime and corruption under a thin icing of a public administration trusted by few citizens. Within a dysfunctional justice system, Kosovo was at risk to become a "*black hole*" in the EU's immediate neighbourhood. To prevent this EULEX was entrusted with wide powers to act independently from the local law enforcement. With this equipment it was assumed to do more than just 'filling black holes'. So it was the EU's firm determination to restore the rule of law in an unruly country. The author looked behind this firm face at various aspects of the implementation of this mission, in particular its effectiveness and efficiency. Unfortunately, there are no output data to determine anything about these potential outcomes. The effects on the intended institution building (*e.g.* police, prosecution and courts) is euphemistically called "limited". The prosecution and verdict average output of the EULEX legal staff also proved to be meagre, in particular concerning the kind of prioritised types of criminality: organised crime (0,007 cases per judge per year), trafficking humans and corruption (1,05). High-level corruption and organised crime investigations and trials were rare and understandable against the background of insufficient protection against threats and pressure. Unsurprisingly opinion surveys revealed that the trust of the population in the judiciary remained low. The author concludes that it is not to be expected that "Kosovo's rule-of-law institutions will be 'seaworthy' on the day the EU's 'flagship mission' is finally scrapped." A logical conclusion in view of the fact that the flagship itself has capsized and long-since sunk.

References

Doward, J., The dark side of Britain's gold rush: how corruption crept into our suburbs. *The Guardian*, 14 January 2017

Duyne, P.C. van, 'Will Caligula go transparent?' Corruption in acts and attitude. *Forum on Crime and Society*, 2001, vol. 1, *no. 2*, 73-98

Duyne, P.C. van and A. Kabki, Investment and long firm fraud. Local and cross-border. In: P.C. van Duyne *et al.*, *Narratives on organised crime in Europe. Criminals, corrupters and policy.* Wolf Legal Publishers, Oisterwijk, 2016

Duyne, P.C. and M. Soudijn, Crime-money in the financial system: what we fear and what we know. In: M. Herzog-Evans (ed.), *Transnational Criminology Manual, Volume 2*, Nijmegen, Wolf Legal Publishers, 2010

Duyne, P.C. van and M. Levi, *Drugs and money. Managing the drug trade and crime-money in Europe*. London, Routledge, 2005

Duyne, P.C. and Miranda, H., The emperor's cloths of disclosure: hot money and suspect disclosures. *Crime, Law and Social Change*,1999, *no. 3*, 245-271

Gøtzsche, P.C., *Deadly medicines and organised crime. How Big Pharma has corrupted healthcare*. Radcliffe Publishing Ltd, 2014

Johnson-Laird, P.N. and P. Wason, *The psychology of reasoning. Structure and content*. Batsford, London, 1972

Kabki, A., *Fraude ontrafeld. Een studie naar de werkwijzen en drijfveren van fraudeurs*. Boom|Lemma Uitevers, 2014

Koningsveld, T.J. van, *De offshore wereld ontmaskerd*. Kerckebosch, Zeisty, 2015

Markovska, A., The bitter pill of a corrupt heritage. Corruption in Ukraine and developments in the pharmaceutical industry. In: P.C. van Duyne, A. Maljevic, M. van Dijck, K. von Lampe and J. Harvey (eds.), *Crime business and crime money in Europe. The dirty linen of illicit enterprise*. Nijmegen, Wolf Legal Publishers, 2007 (pp. 1-14)

McCoy, A.W., *The politics of heroin: CIA complicity in the global drug world*. Lawrence Hill Books, 2003

Morselli, C., *Inside criminal networks*. Springer Science + Business Media, 2009

Osyka, I., Organised economic crime problems in the Ukraine. In: P.C. van Duyne, V. Ruggiero, M. Scheinost and W. Valkenburg (eds.), *Cross-border crime in a changing Europe*. Huntington, Nova Science Publishers, 2001

Popper, K.R., *Conjectures and refutations. The growth of scientific knowledge*. Routledge and Kegan Paul Limited, London, 1969

Sandulescu, M., *Integrating Anti-money laundering compliance duties into the banking culture*. Unpublished dissertation, Lugano, 2016

Schneider, F., The financial flows of transnational crime and tax fraud in OECD countries: some empirical facts. In: G.A. Antonopoulos (ed.), *Illegal entrepreneurship, organised crime and social control*. Springer, New York, 2016

Spapens, T., North Brabant: a brief history of a hotbed of organised crime. In: G.A. Antonopoulos (ed.), *Illegal entrepreneurship, organised crime and social control*. Springer, New York, 2016

Spencer, J., Media constructing organised crime concepts in an extended Europe: trafficking women for sexual exploitation. In: P.C. van Duyne, J. Harvey, A. Maljevic, K. von Lampe and M. Scheinost (eds.), *European crime-markets at cross-roads. Extended and extending criminal Europe.* Nijmegen, Wolf Legal Publishers, 2008

Stessens, G., *Money laundering: a new international law enforcement model.* Cambridge, Cambridge University Press, 2000

Stessens, G., The FATF 'Black List' of Non-Cooperative Countries and Territories. *Leiden Journal of International Law*, 2001, 199-208

Unger, B. and J. Ferwerda, *Money laundering in the real estate sector. Suspicious properties.* Edward Elgar, Cheltenham UK, 2011

UNODC, (2011), *Estimating illicit financial flows resulting from drug trafficking and other transnational organized crime.* Vienna

Verhoeven, M.,*Government policies and sex work realities: human trafficking in the regulated sex industry.* Doctoral Dissertation, Free University Amsterdam, 2017

Vrij, A., *Detecting lies and deceit. Pitfalls and opportunities.* Wiley, New York, 2008

Wechsler, W.F., Follow the money. *Foreign Affairs*, July/August 2001, 40-57

Zhang, S.X. and S.L. Pineda, Corruption as a causal factor in human trafficking. In: D. Siegel and H. Nelen (eds.), *Organised crime, culture, markets and policies.* Springer, New York, 2008

Is there a continuing problem with corruption?
Deviant trajectories, competing agendas and state development

Alan Doig[1]

Introduction: Leys and the functionalist approach to corruption

This chapter derives from Colin Leys' much-referenced article – "What is the Problem About Corruption?" – published in the *Journal for Modern African Studies* (Leys, 1965). Focusing primarily on Sub-Saharan Africa (SSA), Leys[2] took a functional approach to corruption, rejecting an absolutist ethical approach and arguing for a relativist rather than a moral stance against corruption that avoided labelling corruption as morally 'bad' in all countries and all contexts. Leys was concerned that the approach ignored societal and cultural contexts, and allowed for its negative use to criticize political opponents. He suggested that addressing corruption did not in itself ensure an 'efficient and socially useful administration' which would, for example, reduce inequality and benefit the poor. As he put it: *"this is not to say that all kinds of inequality promoted by all kinds of corruption are beneficial from the point of view of development; it is merely to challenge the assumption that they are invariably bad"* (Leys, 1965: 220-221).

In discussing whether all corruption was both 'bad' and, in development terms, significant he argued that *"neither attitudes nor material conditions in these countries are focused on the support of a single concept of the national interest or of the official purposes of state and local officers and institutions which would promote that inter-*

Visiting Professor, Newcastle Business School, Northumbria University.
[2] Colin Leys is emeritus professor of politics at Queen's University, Canada, and an honorary professor at Goldsmiths University of London. He has worked for many years on the political economy of development in Africa and Britain, and most recently on health policy in England. He published the article when he was Professor of Politics, School of Social Studies, University of Sussex, Brighton, England.

19

est" (Leys, 1965: 224). Poised between achieving public morality of the western nation-state and the disappearing public morality of traditional society, developing countries were prone to corruption both as a means to engage with an alien and punitive state as well as public officials seeing private benefit as much more normal than adhering to imported rules on public conduct.

While it was possible to develop economically without an 'effective public morality', the emergence of western state morality, at least in its refined and detailed forms, would take time. Meanwhile corruption in developing countries could only be addressed through a shift in the behaviour of the ruling elites or through a piecemeal widening of the concept of the public interest. There was, he suggested, some form of transitional state during this shift, from an acceptance of private benefit from public office being made at the expense of the public welfare to one where private benefit from public office occurred while providing services to citizens. These would be demanded, he argued, by what he termed 'puritans', the economically independent professional and middle classes.

While the article has, as expected of its time, many conceptual and empirical flaws, it does raise some interesting issues about the primacy of corruption as an issue, about time needed to achieve levels of western state morality (if that is the preferred developmental goal), about the possibility of a transitional state, about citizenry capable of demanding reform and, indeed, about the priorities and sequencing of the developmental process that would lead to western state morality. At its core lies the issue of whether corruption is a functional consequence of development, rather than to argue that corruption as morally wrong, and whether its presence is more about countries having 'a different social, economic and political system, and a different historical experience' (Leys, 1965: 217). The chapter asks if, in taking the initiatives they have, donors have ignored some of the issues raised by Leys and, in so doing, helped ensure that corruption is likely to continue to be a problem, fifty years after Leys' article.

The end of functionalism: corruption as the core inhibitor of development

Leys' perspectives on corruption were not alone. A number of other academics took a similar functionalist approach to corruption in developing countries. Nye argued that "*corruption in developing countries is too important a phenomenon to be left to moralists*" particularly when "corruption can provide the solution to several of the more limited problems of development" (1967: 427). Scott stated that "*cor-*

ruption . . . can work important changes in government policy" (1969: 340) while Leff suggested that "*preoccupation with corruption can itself become an impediment to development*" (1964: 13). However, the functionalist perspectives on corruption were short-lived. In 1983 Simcha Werner was reflecting a newer orthodoxy in describing functionalist views as "*reckless generalisations and logical inconsistencies*" and corruption as threatening "*the very pillars of the democratic experience*" (1983: 152). By the end of the millennium the orthodoxy prevailing among both academic and practitioner literature argued that corruption was

> "*not just a development problem but a central issue in development policy*" (Johnston, 1998: 88) and that "corruption is bad for development" because it undermines governments' "*ability to enact and implement policies in areas in which government intervention is clearly needed—whether environmental regulation, health and safety regulation, social safety nets, macroeconomic stabilisation, or contract enforcement*" (World Bank, 1997: 8).

While donors and others were slow to insist on democratisation and not averse to working with military, one-party and authoritarian states (see Ezrow and Frantz 2011), global economic shocks, debt crises, and domestic policy failures gave the multilateral donor institutions the leverage to push for a developmental trajectory toward the western nation-state with economic liberalisation and '*standard liberal democratic practices and norms – representative and responsible government, the rule of law, and the absence of corruption*' (see Bevir, 2004: 2; Alence, 2009). Within this context, and as corruption was considered a core impediment to development, so democratisation toward the liberal democratic model became regarded as the "*best facilitators of development*" and "*a pre-condition for economic growth*" (Marquette, 2003: 7; Bellamy and Barry, Jones 2000: 207). Indeed some have considered that a commitment to democracy should be mandatory requirements for aid (Diamond, 1999: 277)[3]. Later efforts to address failed states have underlined efforts to achieve this rapidly and comprehensively through a donor-inspired governance approach to collectively address the "*capacity of government, the private sector, and civil society organisations to exercise political, economic, and administrative authority to manage a nation's affairs*" (United Nations Department of Economic and Social Affairs and United Nations Development Programme, 2007: 14; see also Brinkerhoff, 2005 and Doig and Tisne, 2009).

The rhetoric that encompassed democratisation as the ideological development vehicle also considered it not only as the necessary political and state

---

3   See, for example, the Millenium Challenge Account [MCA] funding criteria on corruption and good governance – the latter term often used by multilateral institutions instead of democracy to avoid being seen to being interfering with internal politics by imposing a specific political ideology (Hoogvelt, 2001: 185).

framework for economic progress but also through which corruption should be addressed. Corruption was explicitly stated as inhibiting democratisation and thus its role in promoting economic and social development; "*not only subverting economic prosperity but harming health, economic equality, social trust, political legitimacy, and people's subjective well-being*" (Uslaner and Rothstein, 2012: 3). Democracy in turn was seeing as providing "*a more conducive environment for market-led economic growth and because it carries the potential for more efficient and accountable government*" (Luckham and White, 1996: 284). In relation to democracy and corruption, the orthodoxy essentially saw the democratisation process as leading to the main checks such as "*the rule of law, and the civil and political rights of citizenship*" (Whitehead, 2002: 117) and the rise of "*political competition, with the electorate holding politicians accountable through the ballot box*" (Marquette, 2003: 57-58). Further, democracy is seen a requirement for economic progress, and not the other way around (see Marangos, 2009).

Since Leys: Overview of contemporary Sub-Saharan Africa

The out-turn for this approach is mixed for SSA countries, highlighting many of the issues raised by Leys 50 years ago. 28 SSA countries remain among the most under-developed countries, with increasing disparities between those in poverty and the beneficiaries of economic growth and limited redistribution of state resources and continuing levels of state corruption (see Mungiu-Pippidi 2013a). In terms of corruption SSA countries currently take up nearly 50% of the bottom quartile of Transparency International's Corruption Perception Index (and of those only 10% had shown any improvement over the past decade according to the WBI 'Control of Corruption' Indicator). 25 SSA countries occupy the bottom 25% of the 2014 Failed States Index (Messner, 2014). The 2014 World Justice Project's assessment of corruption relating to judiciary, the military and police, and the legislature, placed all 19 SSA countries in the survey in the lower half of its rankings, with corruption "*prevalent in all branches of government and in the police and the military*" and "*no significant improvement in reducing the levels of corruption throughout the entire region*" (World Justice Project, 2014: 41).

In terms of political development and democratisation, SSA countries have been one of the main beneficiaries of what has been termed the third wave of democratisation: "*in the African case the regional wave of democratisation not only removed the surviving African one-party states, but also virtually annihilated what had for decades been the world's largest bodies of military regimes*" (Brooker, 2000: 191). On the other hand, the linearity and effectiveness of the democratisation process has been less than successful. In terms of the established presence of democracy most SSA countries fall within the lowest quartile of the World Audit survey (www.worldaudit.org/) and, although military interventions have dropped as elections have increased, "*many elections are still rigged. Progress in democracy in the region has been slow and uneven, but nevertheless continues*" (Economist Intelligence Unit, 2013: 24).

In macro-economic development terms, on the other hand, SSA countries are seen as generally successful, despite arguments that the cost of corruption was a key reason why SSA countries remain underdeveloped in terms of democratisation and economic development relative to other continents (Osinibi, 2011: 223; see also Handley et al., 2009; World Bank, 2010). While many SSA countries were assessed as having shadow economies of 30% or higher (Schneider *et al.*, 2010), the World Bank's overall economic forecast for SSA argues that "*GDP grew 4,7 percent in 2013 led by robust domestic demand, and is set to continue to rise. Despite emerging challenges, the medium-term outlook remains positive. Supported by investment in the resource sector, public infrastructure, and agriculture, GDP growth is projected to remain stable at 4,7 percent in 2014 and to rise to 5,1 percent in 2015 and 2016*" (World Bank, 2014: 77; see, similar arguments from the IMF [IMF, 2014]).

What does this mixed picture tell us not only about Leys' perspectives on corruption and development but also about the efforts of donors and others to shape a development agenda that has placed an emphasis on addressing corruption as a serious and important inhibitor to development and on a straight democratisation trajectory toward the western nation-state and its notions of the public interest and public morality? Moreover, what does this mixed picture say about Leys' view that, the SSA context, a society without an effective public morality would be highly unlikely to develop economically?

Since Leys: Issues in contemporary Sub-Saharan Africa

First, democratisation has not been fully embedded and functioning effectively. Prevailing perspectives suggest that the failures lie with political leadership's lack of commitment to the public good (Afegbua and Adejuwon, 2012), a reluctance to relinquish political office, and a primacy on competition for the control of, and misuse of, state resources for maintaining power (see van Wyk, 2007 and Timamy, 2005). More importantly, leadership has been blamed for ensuring limited political and financial accountability, weak parliamentary oversight and penetration of the administrative sectors with wider implications for economic and political development (see Owoye and Bissessar, 2014; Agbude and Etete, 2013; Dasandi, 2014).

Most democratising states can still *"be characterised as neopatrimonial where power and political relations are reliant upon informal patronage systems and clientelism. Poor governance includes weak formal institutions and rule of law, poorly designed and implemented policies, inadequate service delivery, lack of accountability to citizens and high levels of corruption"* (Handley *et al.,* 2009: 34; see also Blundo and de Sardan, 20060; Timamy, 2005). This has been compounded by a democratisation process where corruption does not fund its development but the process itself, including party funding and post-election spoils of office arrangements, promotes corruption and precludes principles of good governance (see International Institute for Democracy and Electoral Assistance, 2007: 128-129; see also Lekvall, 2013).

Public sector reform – either in terms of Leys' transitional state or the public morality of the western nation state - has not been considered generally successful in SSA (see, for example, Maphunye, 2009; Fgba, 2013; Amadi and Ekekwe, 2013; Engida and Bardill, 2013). Tatile and Adejuwon, 2010; Ahere has been some limited work on the development of public sector ethics and accountability in SSA which, while this does note the general presence of the formal procedures and requirements, also emphasises a failure to implement them, train civil servants in their use and relevance, and to monitor their effectiveness (see, for example, UN Department of Economic and Social Affairs, 2001). A detailed study of public administration in four of the larger African economies noted a

"lack of political and bureaucratic commitment, lack of ownership of the reform process, politicisation resulting in breakdown in the merit system, inability to hire and retain

senior officials, weak systems of accountability, poor and wrong diagnosis and prognosis" (Economic Commission for Africa, 2010: xii).

There is also little evidence that that economic growth and an expanding middle class would initiate anti-corruption demands (see ADB 2011; see also Ncube and Shimeles, 2012; Ncube and Lufumpa, 2015; Visagie, 2013; Ndletyana, 2014 and Schatz, 2013 on expectations of civil society). Given that the development of the private sector has in part been the consequence of privatisation, often through companies linked to the political elites, and where concepts of corporate governance appear as limited as those of public ethics (see Gumede, 2012; Ndikumana, 2013) there is no evidence that an expanded private sector may support an independent middle class. Indeed, that expansion may reflect a rise in crony capitalism *where politicians happen to have the same interests, or to be the same people, as the entrepreneurs*" (Booth et al., 2014: viii).

Overall, and comparing IMF data over the past decade to that of the Transparency International Corruption Perception Index and the World Bank Institute's 'Control of Corruption Indicator, as well as citizens' perceptions for the Africa Barometer, the mixed picture would appear to suggest that, in ignoring some of the issues raised by Leys, and pursuing their own approaches to the centrality of addressing corruption and committing to democratisation but without thinking through questions of priorities, sequencing and timescales, "the apparent obsession of international agencies with reforming the *state* along what are assumed to be 'Western' lines may be somewhat misplaced" (Theobald, 1999: 500). It may also have developed a deviant developmental trajectory for state development which in turn could also be susceptible to newer agendas emerging from multilateral and bilateral donors.

So why is corruption a continuing problem and what are the consequences?

The decades-long donor agendas have had a number of consequences in terms of state development. There is an increasing possibility that the failure to prioritise, sequence and integrate democratisation and anti-corruption reforms may have significant impact at country level. This failure to progress manipulates and embeds the realities of state power, corruption, clientelism and a patrimonial state under the veneer of democratisation, creating 'hollowed out' democracies whose rhetoric and institutions are often developed to please or placate donors, but continue to be weak enough to maintain the existing order (see Diamond,

1997 and Robinson, 1998). In other words, one of the consequences of the developmental trajectory, and democratisation and anti-corruption initiatives within that trajectory, is that SSA countries may also comprise hollowed-out democracies (or broken-back democracies; see Rose *et al.*, 1998) which are economically improving but which remain – and likely to continue to be – both corrupt and susceptible to capture and control by elite groups for several reasons.

First, the capture of the processes and procedures of democratisation by elite groupings and sectional interests means that the use of elections by mass movements to facilitate meaningful change and to place a premium on policy agendas is secondary to their use as a legitimising and controlling mechanism, ushering in what has been termed hybrid regimes such as competitive authoritarianism: *"civilian regimes in which formal democratic institutions exist and are widely viewed as the primary means of gaining power, but in which incumbents' abuse of the state places them at a significant advantage vis-à-vis their opponents. Such regimes are competitive in that opposition parties use democratic institutions to contest seriously for power, but they are not democratic because the playing field is heavily skewed in favour of incumbents"* (Levitsky and Way, 2010: 5).

Second, continuing political dominance of the state and political penetration of the public sector by those controlling the state and exercising political power not only denies both the rule of law and the development and delivery of state functions and services in the public interest but also ensures their use to maintain patronage networks and the particularistic politics that pervades, politicalises and skews the formal state in favour of elites and interests (see (Menocal *et al.*, 2008; Maaß *et al.*, 2014).

Third, competitive authoritarianism as a deviant development trajectory may be difficult challenge or redirect. This is in part because the welding of the trappings of democratisation and the persistence of elite control reflect a natural synergy; *"our (admittedly far from cheering) conclusion is that there prevails in Africa a system of politics inimical to development as it is usually understood in the West"* (Chabal and Daloz, 1999: 162). This also in part because of the *"social and economic realities and the disconnection between societal values and the values of formal public institutions"*, where the *"failings of public trust leads to communitarian solidarity-networks within a state, which strive for the common good of particular social collectives rather than the national public good"* (Hellsten and Larbi, 2006: 135). It is debatable, therefore, how far this could be seen as a transitional state favoured not just be Leys but also developmentalists among whom *"sequencing – the idea that democracy should wait until socioeconomic development was substantially accomplished –*

was widespread, as was a preference for a political strong hand" (Carothers, 2010: 15; see also Leftwich, 1994; 1996).

Fourth, a further consequence of persisting with the prevailing developmental trajectory sought by donors, is how far this embeds and reinforces a deviant developmental trajectory. The persistence of corruption, poor leadership, and government inability to address corruption, as countervailing influences against an established external enthusiasm for democracy and improvements in public services, continue to have significant developmental implications (see Asunka 2013; Richmond and Alpin, 2013; Bratton and Houessou, 2014). It is also debatable how far donor agendas are amenable to change or how far the dynamism of other agendas will only serve to complicate the reform process or discussions of alternative approaches.

50 years and beyond: corruption as a continuing problem?

Overall, the outcomes of 50 years' of donor approaches – and specifically in relation to corruption - appear to underline the argument that "*our treatment of the phenomenon has not moved very far beyond the insights offered by Leys. That is to say, in spite of the implicit recognition in much writing on corruption that the West's historical experience is distinctive, unique and unrepeatable, this experience continues to provide the model of the 'modern' state to which pre-modern or less developed forms must aspire*" (Theobald, 1999: 471). There is little evidence of any substantive engagement in a review, refinement or revision of current iterations of the overall approach, or even any significant understanding of why these have been less than successful: "*donor understanding of the forms and drivers of corruption – and with it, ability to provide genuine guidance on AC – has been limited*" (NORAD, 2011a: 68). For fragile states, "*donor understanding of the dilemmas and dynamics of corruption and integrity in state building is beset by a lack of knowledge and the absence of systematic analysis of what works or not, why and under which conditions*" (OECD DAC Network on Governance – Anti-Corruption Task Team, 2009: 31). In part this relates to unfulfilled assumptions about aid directly intended for anti-corruption initiatives: "*a range of donor-supported reforms are aimed at improving governance in general and reducing corruption in particular . . . (and) have often had rather disappointing effects on corruption*" (Kolstad *et al.*, 2008: ix).

It may also be an issue of the focus and context of aid, particularly if it is for the wrong purpose and given in weak governance environments: "*as the record shows, without good institutions, aid is likely to have a detrimental impact on the quality of governance in a recipient developing country*" (Abuzeid, 2009: 23; see also Brautigam and Knack, 2004; Asongu and Jellal, 2013). It could also be because donors haven't developed robust enough approaches; DFID has not "*developed an approach equal to the challenge, nor has it focused its efforts on the poor. While some programmes show limited achievements, there is little evidence of impact on corruption levels or in meeting the needs of the poor*" (Independent Commission for Aid Impact, 2014: 1). At the same time many donors have not yet embraced the idea that effective changes are less the consequence of 'specific policies' (Vaz Mondo, 2011) than a consequence of a range of country-specific, intended and unintended, direct and indirect configurations: "*there is no global success case of anti-corruption as promoted by the international anti-corruption community. Successful countries followed paths of their own*" (NORAD, 2011b: 82). Even with the attempts to improve donor coordination and cooperation, as well as encourage countries to lead on priorities, the 2011 review of the implementation of the Paris Declaration noted that, while the 'free-for-alls' of competitive, uncoordinated and donor-driven activities were now unusual, partner country governments still were not devoting "*higher political priority and more focused action to further reducing the most stubborn development challenges of poverty, exclusion and corruption*" (Wood *et al.*, 2011: xviii).

This failure to appreciate the impact of the macro-level approach is one that also raises some interesting questions about how to address corruption in the future. Reviews both of evidence-led policy (Hanna *et al.*, 2011) or on effective monitoring and review of policies (U4, 2011; U4, 2012; Kolstad, 2008) seems to suggest a paucity of innovation or willingness to break away from existing portfolios of initiatives within the general trajectory sought by both multilateral and bilateral donors although access to comprehensive information on donor programmes in terms of costs, consultants and evaluations, has remained confidential or opaque or under-researched (see, for example, Independent Commission for Aid Impact, 2011; see also U4, 2011 and U4, 2012).

The anti-corruption discourse now argues the most effective policy approach for anti-corruption interventions from a number of perspectives. These range from the need for the 'norms of universalism' (Mungiu-Pippidi, 2006: 87), the 'Big Bang' approach currently espoused by Rothstein (2011; see also Holmberg and Rothstein, 2012) to a Collective Action approach (Persson *et al.*, 2010; 2013 – a concept discussed decades earlier, see [IRIS, 1996]). It includes discussion on the importance of embedded democracy and associated levels of genuine political competition, and respect for political and civil rights (von Soest, 2013), as well as the more limited 'good enough governance' stance proposed for, for example, fragile states. Even here there also continues to be divergence over the institutions or cultures to be to the focus of reform.

Some suggest that only a necessary combination of four factors – values, social capital, civil society and civic culture – would enable countries to "*overcome competing tendencies toward violence, cronyism, and social hierarchy and to generate normative constraints that empower ethical universalism*" (Mungiu-Pippidi, 2013b: 104). Others argue that that "an instalment of the Freedom of Information Acts (FOIA) can, in the presence of an active civil society and attentive opposition to the governing structures, significantly decrease levels of corruption in a country" (Loncaric, 2011: 7). Still others argue that initiatives such as anti-corruption authorities, civil service reforms or the use of corruption conditionality in aid allocation decisions are much less effective that "*two types of interventions: public financial management (PFM) reforms and supreme audit institutions (SAIs)*" (U4, 2012: iv). Other arguments focus on methods or levels of delivery include integrating anti-corruption work with other donor initiatives, the use of third party organisations for fund dispersal or an preference for decentralisation (see, for example, U4, 2013; Public Accounts Committee, 2015; Crawford and Hartmann, 2008), the importance of the professionalisation of the administration (see Heywood and Meyer-Sahling, 2013), or a permutation or version of the new puritans among leaders and citizens to sustain incremental reform for themselves or the wider good (see for example, Johnston, 1997 and Schatz, 2013).

50 years and beyond: a continuing problem exacerbated by emergent agendas?

The problem with the discourse on what to do about corruption is, like the approach to democratisation, are based on variations of past iterations of the same overall assumptions about the necessity of addressing both as both moral and, often, the only options. They also are being made at a time when deviant developmental trajectories may be leading to state types that are even less amenable to reform or re-direction. Indeed, it could even be argued that reform may have to return to the basics in understanding the drivers and circumstances underpinning the roles and purposes of, for example, corruption before asking: "*what functions does corruption serve as well as what obstacles exist to eradicating it? Arguably, without answering the first question, one cannot begin to adequately answer the second*" (Marquette and Peiffer, 2015: 11).

Answering that question even within the current discourse, however, may find itself further down developed countries' agendas as they prioritise other concerns. These could have implications not only in terms of regulatory and enforcement arrangements in developing countries but also how far they are concerned about the type of regime or state they need to work with. At the same time, the exclusivity that came with the primacy of western states in determining the multilateral and bilateral donor agendas is itself changing, first, as emergent economies also seek economic and other relationships with developing countries and, second, as continuing shifts and trends in existing donor approaches place the emphasis on developing states to lead on decisions on capacity, commitment and even donor partners. These are leading to a number of consequences.

First, the dynamics of globalisation agendas and of approaches to anti-corruption mean the increased relevance of the conduct of emergent economies in international trade, particularly in relation to mineral and other resources and delivering capital projects. This introduces new international actors alongside traditional multilateral and bilateral agencies. Here is some evidence that these non-western developmental partners or international corporations may be more amenable to ignore international standards or national governance arrangements, to be less than committed to, for example, anti-corruption extractive initiatives (see Global Witness, 2012; 2013a and 2013b). They may be willing, as in the case of China, *"adapt their strategies to suit the particular histories and geographies of the African states with which they engage"*, including *"clientelism with African state elites, proxy force and other power elements, both soft and hard"* (Carmody, 2011: 75; for related issues for oil see Shaxson, 2007 and Yates, 2012).

Second, corruption is increasing seen as a facilitator or medium for a number of illicit activities, including tax evasion, drugs and human trafficking, and organised crime, with developed countries pushing for increased state regulatory and anti-corruption reforms. Developed countries *"spend an inordinate amount of time, energy, and attention trying to control"* the illicit flows of goods and funds from deviant globalisation, whether toxic waste dumping, illicit logging or trade in mineral resources, flows facilitated by state weakness, poor regulatory environments and the propensity to corruption (Gilman *et al.*, 2011: 276).

Third, emerging threats may invoke responses that may be different or not aligned with existing donor approaches. Recently, for example, *"it is becoming increasingly evident that internationally sponsored terrorist networks have found a permanent home in sub-Saharan Africa and within the hearts and minds of its people, which poses significant challenges for the international community, given the region's patchwork of failed states, where terrorists can easily hide and thrive"* (Howard, 2010: 960). In the case of organised crime there is a growing concern over the juxtaposition of organised crime and weak states: "*of note, a remarkable 80 per cent of all pronouncements of the Security Council on organised crime relate to conflicts in Africa*" (Shaw *et al.*, 2014: 20). Further, of more significance in SSA countries, it is not simply the ineffectual nature of law enforcement and the levels of corruption involved but also "*a reformulation of politics and crime into networks that transcend the state/non-state boundary in ways that are hardly subsumed in standard concepts of organized crime*" which will see state actors, business elites and organised crime groups operating in ways that make it difficult to disentangle illegal from legal business activity (Ellis and Shaw, 2015: 505; see also UNODC, 2013). Finally there is the potential of external organised crime interacting with local gang cultures which in turn have low-level corruptive and political relations with law enforcement and political groups (see Andvig and Barasa, 2014).

Fourth, such agendas generate different responses in terms of demands made of developing countries by external actors. The 2014 Basel AML Index reported that "*the Sub-Saharan region has the highest average risk score worldwide*" with a number of countries vulnerable to money laundering and terrorist financing not only because of inadequate procedures but also because of weak law enforcement and high rates of corruption (International Centre for Asset Recovery, 2014: 6). Of significance here is the focus of the increasing intervention of FATF and other international agencies (see FATF, 2011; Van der does de Willebois *et al.*, 2011; OECD/StAR, 2012) in part because of the rising anti-money laundering and terrorist financing agendas in developed countries (see Marshall, 2013; Demas, 2011) and in part because they do have sanctions and intend to use them. Thus the 2013 FATF methodology for the Fourth Round evaluations now requires assessors to report on contextual factors that might significantly influence the effectiveness of a country's anti-money laundering and combatting the financing of terrorism (AML/CFT) measures, including a country's levels of, and approaches to addressing, corruption (FATF, 2013: 6).

Fifthly, there is the question not only of what is to be required of developing countries but also where the primary benefit lies when those requirements are made. The issue for SSA countries in relation to the FATF is not only that negative reports may have serious adverse implications for the stability and growth of developing countries' financial and banking services but also that the actions called for may have less to do with democratisation and state development than with the importance of enhancing the robustness and integrity of the international financial and banking systems as determined by developed countries.

This and other agendas also increase the actors and agencies involved in promoting specific anti-corruption measures that are primarily focussed on addressing money laundering, counter-terrorist finance, tax evasion and asset tracing without assessing its place within the range of anti-corruption reforms or its role to address domestic corruption (see, for example, the emphasis on illicit enrichment legislation in Muzila *et al.*, 2012). For these agendas, often undertaken outside the scope of and detached from the mainstream donor approaches, the pressure from developed countries may become prescriptive; "*governments must apply consistent pressure, coupled with the credible threat of consequences, on Sub-Saharan African countries to increase the accountability of their public officials and implement a rule of law*" (Demas, 2011: 365). On the one hand that prescription may be more relevance to the developed countries than their developing counterparts: for example, "*foreign governments and organisations that support combating organised crime in West Africa have tended to focus on measures aimed at alleviating the impact of organised crime in their home countries rather than their effect on the economy, polity and society at large of West African countries*" (Alemika, 2013: 14; see also Sharman and Chaikin, 2009).

One specific consequence is that developed countries are, collectively, becoming more interested in issues that affect them – terrorism, trafficking, organised crime, tax evasion, and so on – and are increasingly more likely to push developing countries toward necessary robustness and resourcing of institutions to address these as 'global' issues. Thus corruption, for example, may be pushed down the international agenda; Transparency International had already noted in 2015 that in relation to the Organisation for Economic Co-operation and Development's (OECD's) Anti-Bribery Convention there were 41 signatory countries were responsible for approximately two-thirds of world exports and almost 90 per cent of total foreign direct investment outflows but only four of the signatories were active in enforcement[4]. A more general consequence for state development is, as has happened elsewhere in the world, 'where western powers have countervailing economic or strategic interests at stake, autocratic governments often possess the bargaining power to ward off external demands for democracy by casting themselves – and regime stability – as the best means of protecting those interests" (Levitsky and Way, 2010: 41).

---

[4] See
http://www.transparency.org/whatwedo/publication/exporting_corruption_prog
ress_report_2015_assessing_enforcement_of_the_oecd

Conclusions

Just over 50 years ago Colin Leys wrote an article arguing that corruption was a functional rather than a moral issue; it may not have been as important as some suggested. Corruption occurred as a consequence of change, rather than a cause of inhibiting change. Western-style public morality would diminish corruption but, given the long timescales involved, it was possible that a transitional state could have been contemplated where corruption still operated alongside improved public services and functions – narrowing the space for self-interest and widening that of public interest and thus encouraging citizens to demand further reforms. Reform, whether gradualist or through revolution, was achievable but Leys believed that, in the SSA context, "*a society without an effective public morality cannot develop economically*" (Leys, 1965: 228).

In practice the evidence, although not entirely one-sided, would suggest that SSA countries have not moved substantively toward functioning representative democracies, or to a welfare-distributive state model (a definable characteristic of a western liberal democrat model) despite economic growth. There does not appear to have been a concomitant development of a culture of public ethics that acknowledges and represents public service and public interest as core drivers of the model. Further, although there is a rising middle class, they have not yet been a vehicle for demanding reform and no evidence of policy-driven, citizen-focused democratic politics. Corruption remains a presence at all levels in SSA countries. On the other hand, economic development has occurred and a number of SSA countries demonstrate year-on-year progress in terms of GDP, foreign investment and a rise in the standards of living of specific societal groups in each country, often linked to ruling groupings.

In terms of donor involvement, the insistence that corruption was a core inhibitor for progress to democratisation – and addressing it evidence of a commitment to progress – may have missed the point about corruption. In also urging rapid democratisation toward a western-style public morality donors may have side-stepped the transitional state favoured by some developmentalists. They may also, by focussing more on the repressive side of anti-corruption rather than on prevention and public ethics as well as spending little time and resources promoting the management of economic growth, have missed the opportunities for state-building, empowering citizens and creating clear distinctions between public and private space. Donors may have also misunderstood the issues of priorities, timescales and sequences. The upfront attention to, but failure to deliver on, corruption and democratisation has seen the former continue to be pervasive and entrenched and the latter vulnerable to control and manipulation by existing political and business elites. One consequence is the emergence of countries where economic growth is matched by significant levels of corruption and democratic and other institutions influenced by elite groupings and sectional interests, suggesting deviant trajectories less amenable to future reform.

Thus, within such a dynamic continuum, there is the question of whether the developmental trajectory of economic growth alongside persisting levels of corruption, will negate the consolidation of democratisation and the dividend it should bring in terms of the provision of public benefits and rights. Inequitable economic growth combined with a failure to institutionalise the democratic dividend will lead to a general distrust of reform while encouraging elite groupings' grip on political power, penetration of the administrative sphere and an asymmetrical relationship with citizens. Moreover organised crime, terrorism and other illicit aspects of global agendas are more likely to want to work with such regimes which want to remain without demanding reform as a condition of cooperation. They are also more likely to provide resources to deliver on the agendas. One example of an emerging agenda focus, is that of illicit financial flows (IFFs) and their sources. It is interesting to note from the 2015 *Report of the High Level Panel on Illicit Financial Flows from Africa* commissioned by the AU/ECA Conference of Ministers of Finance, Planning and Economic Development, where corruption fits into such an agenda. However, it is not seen as the primary source of IFFs, and nor is it seen as significant in terms of other threats and criminality (African Union Commission/United Nations Economic Commission for Africa, 2015).

At the same time, while it is clear that anti-corruption efforts continue to be essential to donor agendas and to their wider objectives based on assumptions of correlations between democratisation and a diminution of corruption and between economic liberalization and growth, and a diminution of corruption, the discourse seems unable to agree on what to do about the failings to date in either effectively addressing corruption and embedding democratization. In other words, to return to Leys' basic arguments, is there room in the discourse to assess whether democratisation and economic growth lead to a diminution in corruption or does addressing corruption promote democratisation and economic growth and a diminution in corruption or is a developmental state required to promote economic growth to encourage the demand for anti-corruption and in turn promote democratisation? Until such a debate takes place, then it is likely that corruption will continue to be a problem for another 50 years.

References

Abuzeid, F., Foreign Aid and the "Big Push" Theory: Lessons from Sub-Saharan Africa. *Stanford Journal of International Relations,* 2009, XI, 1: 16-23

ADB (African Development Bank), *The Middle of the pyramid: dynamics of the middle class in Africa.* Abidjan: ADB, 2011

Afegbua, S.I. and K.D. Adejuwon, The challenges of leadership and governance in Africa. *International Journal of Academic Research in Business and Social Sciences,* 2012, 2, 9: 141-157

African Union Commission/United Nations Economic Commission for Africa (AUC/ECA), 2015. *Illicit Financial Flow: Report of the High Level Panel on Illicit Financial Flows from Africa.* Addis Ababa: ECA

Agba, M.S., G.E. Ochiena and Y.I. Abubakar, Public service ethics and the fight against corruption in Nigeria: A critical analysis. *International Journal of Public Administration and Management Research,* 2013, 2, 1: 113-118

Agbude, G.A. and P.I. Etete, Ethical leadership, corruption and irresponsible governance: rethinking the African dilemma. *Mediterranean Journal of Social Sciences,* 2013, 4, 6: 481-488

Alemika, E.E.O. (ed.), *The impact of organised crime on governance in West Africa.* Ajuba: Friedrich-Ebert-Stiftung, Regional Office Ajuba, 2013

Alence, R., Democracy and development in Africa. *Journal of the International Institute; University of Michigan International Institute,* 2009, 16, 2: 4-5

Amadi, L. and E. Ekekwe, Corruption and development administration in Africa. *African Journal of Political Science and International Relations,* 2014, 8, 6: 163-174

Asongu, S.A. and M. Jelal, *On the channels of foreign aid to corruption.* AGDI Working Paper Research Department. Yaounde, Cameroun: African Governance and Development Institute, 2013

Asunka, J., *What People Want From Government Basic Services Performance Ratings, 34 Countries.* http://www.afrobarometer.org, 2013

Bellamy, R. and B.J. Barry Jones, Globalisation and democracy – an Afterword in B. Holden (ed.), *Global Democracy: key debates.* London: Routledge, 2000

Bevir, M., *Democratic Governance, Working Paper 2004: 5.* Berkeley CA: University of California, Institute of Governmental Studies, 2004

Blundo, G. and O. de Sardan, Everyday corruption in West Africa in Blundo, G. and O de Sardan with N.B. Arifari and M.T. Alou. *Everyday corruption and the state: citizens and public officials in Africa.* London: Zed Books, 2006

Booth, D., B. Cooksey, F. Golooba-Mutebi and K. Kanyinga, *East African prospects: An update on the political economy of Kenya, Rwanda, Tanzania and Uganda*. London: Overseas Development Institute, 2014

Bratton, M. and R. Houessou, *Demand for democracy is rising in Africa, but most political leaders fail to deliver*. www.afrobarometer.org, 2014.

Brautigam, D. A. and S. Knack, Foreign aid, institutions, and governance in Sub-Saharan Africa', *Economic Development and Cultural Change,* 2004, 52, 2: 255-285

Brinkerhoff, D.W., Rebuilding governance in failed states and post-conflict societies: core concepts and cross-cutting themes. *Public Administration and Development,* 2005, 25, 1: 3-14

Brooker, P., *Non-democratic regimes: theory, government and politics*. Basingstoke: Macmillan Press Ltd, 2000

Carmody, P., *The new scramble for Africa*. Cambridge: Polity Press, 2011.

Carothers, T., Democracy support and development aid: the elusive synthesis. *Journal of Democracy,* 2010, 21, 4: 12-26

Chabal, P. and J-P. Daloz, *Africa works: disorder as political instrument*. Oxford and Bloomington: James Currey and Indiana University Press, 1999

Crawford, G and C. Hartmann (eds.). *Decentralisation in Africa*. Amsterdam: Amsterdam University Press, 2008

Dasandi, N., *The politics-bureaucracy interface: impact on development reform*. Developmental Leadership Program; wwwdlprog.org, 2014. Accessed 12 January 2015

Demas, R.R., Moment of truth: development in Sub-Saharan Africa and critical alterations needed in application of the Foreign Corrupt Practices Act and other anti-corruption Initiatives. *American University International Law Review,* 2011, 26, 2: 315-369

Diamond, L., *Developing democracy*. Baltimore: The John HopkinsUniversity Press, 1999

Diamond, L., *Is the third wave of democratisation over? An empirical assessment*. Working Paper #236. Indiana: Kellogg Institute, 1997

Doig, A. and M. Tisne, A candidate for relegation? Corruption, governance approaches and the (re)construction of post-war states**.** *Public Administration and Development*, 2009, 29, 5: 374-386

Economic Commission for Africa. *Innovations and best practices in public sector reforms: the case of civil service in Ghana, Kenya, Nigeria and South Africa*. Addis Ababa: Economic Commission for Africa, 2010

Economist Intelligence Unit. *Democracy Index 2013*. London: Economist Intelligence Unit, 2013

Ellis, S. and M. Shaw, Does organized crime exist in Africa?. *African Affairs,* 2015, 114, 457: 505-528

Engida, T.G. and J. Bardill, Reforms of the public sector in the light of the new public management: A cases of Sub-Saharan Africa, *Journal of Public Administration and Policy Research,* 2013, 213, 5, 1: 1-7

Ezrow, N. and E. Frantz, E. *Dictators and dictatorships.* London: Continuum, 2011

FATF. *Laundering the proceeds of corruption.* Paris: FATF/OECD, 2011

FATF. *Methodology for assessing technical compliance with the FATF Recommendations and the effectiveness of AML/CFT Systems.* Paris: FATF/OECD, 2013

Fatile, J. O. and K. Adejuwon, Public sector reform in africa: issues, lessons and future directions. *Journal of Sustainable Development in Africa,* 2010, 12, 8: 145-157

Gilman, N., J. Goldhammer and S. Weber, *Deviant globalisation: black market economy in the 21st Century.* New York: Continuum, 2011

Global Witness. *Financing a parallel government?* London: Global Witness, 2012.

Global Witness. *Logging in the Shadows.* London: Global Witness, 2013a

Global Witness. *Rubber Barons.* London: Global Witness, 2013b

Glynn, P., S.J. Kobrin and M. Naim, The Globalisation of Corruption. In K.A. Elliott (ed.). *Corruption and the global economy.* Washington, DC: Institute for International Economics, 1997

Gumede, W., *FPC briefing: corruption fighting efforts in Africa fail because root causes are poorly understood.* London: Foreign Policy Centre, 2012

Handley, G., K. Higgins, B. Sharma, K. Bird and D. Cammack, *Poverty and poverty reduction in Sub-Saharan Africa: an overview of key issues.* Working Paper 299. London: Overseas Development Institute, 2009

Hanna, R., S. Bishop, S. Nadel, G. Scheffler and K. Durlacher, *The effectiveness of anti-corruption policy: what has worked, what hasn't, and what we don't know – a systematic review.* Technical report. London: EPPI-Centre, Social Science Research Unit, Institute of Education, University of London, 2011

Hellsten, S. and G.A. Larbi, Public good or private good? The paradox of public and private ethics in the context of developing countries. *Public Administration and Development,* 2006, 26,2: 135–145

Heywood, P. and J-H. Meyer-Sahling, Danger zones of corruption: how management of the ministerial bureaucracy affects corruption risks in Poland. *Public Administration and Development,* 2013, 33, 3: 191-204

Holmberg, S. and B. Rothstein, *Good government.* Cheltenham: Edward Elgar, 2012.

Hoogvelt, A., 2001. Globalisation and the PostColonial World. Basingstoke: Macmillan

Howard, T., Failed states and the spread of terrorism in Sub-Saharan Africa. *Studies in Conflict and Terrorism*, 2010, 33, 11: 960-988

IMF. *Regional economic outlook. Sub-Saharan Africa.* Washington: International Monetary Fund, 2014

Independent Commission for Aid Impact. *The Department for International Development's approach to anti-corruption.* London: ICAI, 2011

International Centre for Asset Recovery. *Basel AML Index.* Basel: ICAR, 2014

International Institute for Democracy and Electoral Assistance (IDEA). *Political Parties in Africa: Challenges for Sustained Multiparty Democracy.* Stockholm: IDEA, 2007

IRIS (Centre for Institutional Reform and the Informal Sector, University of Maryland). *Governance and the Economy in Africa: Tools for Analysis and Reform of Corruption.* Maryland: IRIS, 1996

Johnston, M., Public Officials, Private Interests, and Sustainable Democracy: When Politics and Corruption Meet in Elliott, K. A. (ed). *Corruption and the Global Economy.* Washington DC: Institute for International Economics, 1997

Kolstad, I., V. Fritz and T. O'Neil, *Corruption, anti-corruption efforts and aid: do donors have the right approach?* Working paper 3; Research project (RP-05-GG) of the Advisory Board for Irish Aid. London: Overseas Development Institute, 2008

Leff, N., Economic development through bureaucratic corruption. *American Behavioural Scientist,* 1964, 8, 3: 8-14

Leftwich, A., Governance, the State and the Politics of Development. *Development and Change,* 1994, 25, 2: 363-386

Leftwich, A., (ed.). *Democracy and development.* Cambridge: Polity Press, 1996

Lekvall, A., *Development first, democracy later.* Stockholm: IDEA, 2013

Leys, C., What is the problem about corruption? *Journal of Modern African Studies,* 1965, 3, 2: 215-230

Levitsky, S. and L.A. Way, *Competitive authoritarianism: hybrid regimes after the Cold War.* New York: Cambridge University Press, 2010

Loncaric, M., *Beyond good governance: performance of the international anticorruption institutional arsenal put to the test.* Berlin: Hertie School of Governance, European Research Centre for Anti-Corruption and State-Building, 2011

Luckham, R. and G. White, Conclusion: Democratisation in the South: the Jagged Wave. In R. Luckham and G. White (eds.), *Democratisation in the south: the jagged wave.* Manchester: Manchester University Press, 1996

Maaß, S., T. Richter, C. von Soest and R. Bratu, *A comparative assessment of regional trends and aspects related to control of corruption in the Middle East and North Africa, Asia and the Pacific, Sub-Saharan Africa, Latin America and the Caribbean, and the former Soviet Union.* Anti-Corr Work Package: WP3, Corruption and governance improvement in global and continental perspectives. Berlin: Hertie school of Governance, 2014

Maphunye, K., *Public administration for a democratic developmental state in Africa: prospects and possibilities.* Research report 114. Johannesburg: Centre for Policy Studies, 2009

Marangos, J., What happened to the Washington Consensus? The evolution of international development policy'. *The Journal of Socio-Economics,* 2009, 38:1. 197-208

Marquette, H., *Corruption, politics and development: the role of the World Bank.* Basingstoke: Palgrave Macmillan, 2003

Marquette, H. and C. Peiffer, *Corruption and collective action.* Research Paper 32. Birmingham: Developmental Leadership Program/Bergen: U4, 2015

Marshall, A., *What's yours is mine: asset recovery in global corruption cases.* CGD Policy Paper 018. Washington DC: Center for Global Development, 2013.

Menocal, A.R., V. Fritz and L. Rakner, Hybrid regimes and the challenges of deepening and sustaining democracy in developing countries. *South African Journal of International Affairs,* 2008, 15, 1: 29-40

Messner, J.J., (ed.), *The Fragile States Index.* Washington: The Fund for Peace, 2014

Mungiu-Pippidi, A., Corruption: diagnosis and treatment. *Journal of Democracy,* 2006, 17, 3: 86-99.

Mungiu-Pippidi, A. *Global comparative trend analysis report.* Berlin: Hertie School of Governance, 2013a

Mungiu-Pippidi, A. Controlling corruption through collective action. *Journal of Democracy,* 2013b, 24, 1: 101-115.

Muzila, L., M. Morales, M. Mathias and T. Berger, *On the take: Criminalizing illicit enrichment to fight corruption.* Washington DC: World Bank, 2102

Ncube, M. and C.L. Lufumpa, *The emerging middle class in Africa.* Abingdon: Routledge, 2015

Ncube, M. and A. Shameless, *The making of the middle class in Africa.* Abidjan: African Development Bank, 2102

Ndikumana, L., *The private sector as culprit and victim of corruption in Africa.* Amherst: University of Massachusetts Political Economy Research Institute, 2013

Ndletyana, M., Middle-class in South Africa: significance, role and impact. *BRICS Academic Forum*. Brazil: Rio de Janeiro, March 10, 2014, NORAD. *Joint Evaluation of Support to Anti-Corruption Efforts Tanzania Country Report* Report 6/2011. Oslo: NORAD, Evaluation Department, 2011a

NORAD. *Contextual choices in fighting corruption: lessons learned report 4/2011.* Oslo: NORAD, Evaluation Department, 2011b

Nye, J., Corruption and political development: a cost-benefit analysis. *American Political Science Review,* 1967, 61, 2: 417-427

OECD DAC Network on Governance – Anti-Corruption Task Team. *Integrity in state building: anti-corruption with a state building lens.* Paris: OECD, 2009

OECD/StAR. *Identification and quantification of the proceeds of bribery.* Paris/Washington DC: OECD/World Bank, 2012

Osinibi, O.M., The political economy of rising Asian interests in Africa: problems, prospects and challenges. In T. Falola and J. Achberger. *The political economy of development and underdevelopment.* New York: Routledge, 2013

Owoye, O. and N. Bissesar, Corruption in African countries: a symptom of leadership and institutional failure. In G.M. Mudacumura and G. Morcol (eds.), *Challenges to democratic governance in development countries.* Cham: Springer International, 2014

(PAC). Public Accounts Committee. *Oversight of the Private Infrastructure Development Group.* 33rd Report of Session 2014-15. London: TSO, 2015

Persson, A., B. Rothstein and J. Teorell, *The failure of anti-corruption policies: a theoretical mischaracterisation of the problem.* QoC Working Paper Series 2010: 19. The Quality of Government Institute: University of Gothenburg, 2010

Persson, A., B. Rothstein and J. Teorell, Why anticorruption reforms fail— systemic corruption as a collective action problem. *Governance,* 2013, 26,3: 449-471.

Richmond, S. and C. Alpin, *Governments Falter in Fight to Curb Corruption.* www.afrobarometer.org, 2013

Robinson, G.E., Defensive democratisation in Jordan'. *International Journal of Middle East Studies,* 1998, 30, 3: 387-410

Rose, R., W. Mishler and C. Haerpfer, *Democracy and its alternatives.* Polity Press, 1998.

Rothstein, B., Anti-corruption: the indirect 'big bang' approach. *Review of International Political Economy,* 2011, 18, 2: 228-250

Schatz, F., Fighting corruption with social accountability: a comparative analysis of social accountability mechanisms' potential to reduce corruption in public administration. *Public Administration and Development,* 2013, 33, 3: 161-174

Scott, J.C., The analysis of corruption in developing countries. *Comparative Studies in Society and History,* 1969, 11, 3: 315-341

Schneider, F., A. Buehn and C.E. Montenegro, *Shadow economies all over the world new estimates for 162 Countries from 1999 to 2007.* Washington: The World Bank Development Research Group Poverty and Inequality Team & Europe and Central Asia Region Human Development Economics Unit, 2010

Sharman, J.C. and D. Chaikin, Corruption and anti-money-laundering systems: Putting a luxury good to work. *Governance,* 2009, 22, 1: 27-45.

Shaw, M., T. Reitano and M. Hunter, *Comprehensive assessment of drug trafficking and organised crime in West and Central Africa.* Addis Ababa: African Union, 2014

Shaxson, N., Oil, corruption and the resource curse. *International Affairs,* 2007, 83, 6: 1123–1140

von Soest, C., Persistent systemic corruption: why democratisation and economic liberalisation have failed to undo an old evil. *Zeitschrift für Vergleichende Politikwissenschaft,* 2013, 7, 1:57-87

Theobald, R., So what really is the problem about corruption? *Third World Quarterly,* 1999, 20, 3: 491-502

Timamy, K., African leaders and corruption. *Review of African Political Economy,* 2005, 104, 5: 383-393

U4. *How to monitor and evaluate anti-corruption agencies: Guidelines for agencies, donors, and evaluators.* Bergen: U4, 2011

U4. *Mapping Evidence Gaps in Anti-Corruption: assessing the state of the operationally relevant evidence on donors' actions and approaches to reducing corruption.* Bergen: U4, 2012

U4. *Donor Anticorruption Strategies: Learning from Implementation.* Bergen: U4, 2013

UN Department of Economic and Social Affairs. Public service ethics in Africa. In R. Hodess, J. Banfield and T. Wolfe, T. (eds.), *Global Corruption Report 2001.* Berlin: Transparency International, 2001

United Nations Department of Economic and Social Affairs and United Nations Development Programme. *The Challenges of Restoring Governance in Crisis and Post-Conflict Countries.* New York: United Nations, 2007

UNODC. *Transnational Organised Crime in West Africa: a threat assessment.* Vienna: UNODC, 2013

Uslaner, E.M. and B. Rothstein. *The roots of corruption: mass education, economic inequality and state building.* APSA Annual meeting. New Orleans, Aug/September, 2012 van der Does de Willebois, E., E.M. Halter, R.A. Harrison, J.W. Park and J.C. Sharman, *The Puppet Masters*. Washington DC: World Bank, 2011

Van Wyk, J-A., *Political leaders in Africa: presidents, patrons or profiteers?* Occasional Paper Series: volume 2, number 1. Durban: The African Centre for the Constructive Resolution of Dispute, 2007

Visagie, J., *Race, gender and growth of the affluent middle class in post apartheid South Africa*. Biennial Conference Of The Economic Society Of South Africa, University Of The Free State. Bloemfontein: South Africa, 25-27 September, 2103

Vaz Mondo, B., *Control of corruption: the road to effective improvement – lessons from six progress cases*. Berlin: Hertie School of Government, 2011

Werner, S., New directions in the study of administrative corruption. *Public Administration Review,* 1983, 43, 2: 146-154

Whitehead, L., *Democratisation*. Oxford: Oxford University Press, 2002

Wood, B., J. Betts, F. Etta, J. Gayfer, D. Kabell, N. Ngwira, F. Sagasti and M Samaranayake. *The Evaluation of the Paris Declaration, Final Report*. Copenhagen: Danish Institute for International Studies, 2011

World Bank. *Helping countries combat corruption: the role of the World Bank*. Washington DC: World Bank, 1997

World Bank, *Africa Development Indicators 2010*. Washington: World Bank, 2010

World Bank, *Global economic prospects: Sub-Saharan Africa*. Washington: World Bank, 2014

World Justice Project. *Rule of Law Index 2014*. Washington: The World Justice Project, 2014

Yates, D.A., *The scramble for African oil*. London: Pluto Press, 2012

Corruption mechanisms, actors and significance for human trafficking: Evidence from Bulgaria

Nadya Stoynova[1]

Introduction

Trafficking in human beings (THB) for sexual exploitation is a criminal business of transnational nature, ranking third after narcotics and arms trafficking (United Nations Office on Drugs and Crime (UNODC), 2011a) in generating huge illegal profits, with an estimated annual revenue of $99 billion worldwide (International Labour Organisation (ILO), 2014). A conservative estimate puts the revenue generated from trafficking for sexual exploitation in Europe at €2,5 billion (UNODC, 2014a). THB in all its manifestations is a harmful crime that results in significant psychological, emotional, financial and often physical harm to victims, representing a serious violation of human rights. Despite the seriousness of the crime, law enforcement and criminal justice authorities across the world encounter various problems in investigating and punishing perpetrators. According to the UNODC (2014b: 13) "impunity prevails" with regard to THB. This fact and the estimated considerable scale of trafficking indicate the specific challenges in tackling this crime. One important barrier is corruption, which – as with other criminal enterprises – is a significant facilitating mechanism (UNODC, 2011b). However, while the importance of corrupt practices for THB is discussed in many academic papers, relatively little is known about the specific roles of corrupt actors or the mechanisms utilized.

This chapter examines the role that corruption plays in the process of trafficking victims for sexual exploitation from Bulgaria and sheds new light on this important phenomenon. The first two sections explore the methodology of the research project and the theoretical background with regard to human trafficking and corruption, followed by the main findings of the research. The emer-

---

[1] The author is an analyst at the Security Program of the Center for the Study of Democracy, a leading public policy research institute, based in Sofia, Bulgaria.

gence and subsequent development of the process of trafficking in the country and of the criminal groups, which control this criminal enterprise is outlined together with the current state of affairs. The major criminal actors involved are identified with their preferred modus operandi with regard to trafficking and corruption mechanisms.

Methodology

The findings in the present chapter are based on triangulation of methods including desk review of secondary data (both academic and grey literature) as well as primary research carried out in Bulgaria. In-depth semi-structured interviews were carried out, covering a wide array of stakeholders involved either in countering THB or in the crime itself including law-enforcement officers, judicial investigators, lawyers, prosecutors, pimps and sex workers. Furthermore, an analysis of media reports regarding key cases and perpetrators of THB was carried out to cross-check the main findings from the interviews and to uncover any possible additional information on how corruption mechanisms are used in practice. Based on the reports and the interviews several illustrative cases have been selected and presented in more detail.

Last but not least, a review of court cases on trafficking for the period 2012-2015 was carried out in order to identify any references to corruption in THB trials. Furthermore, the review also has the aim of tracing the verdicts usually given in trafficking cases for this serious crime. The review focused on cases from three cities (Pleven, Pazardhik and Sliven) known for being significant sources of victims as well as from the Specialized Criminal Court, which is tasked with presiding over cases of organised criminal activities and other serious crimes. The examination was undertaken through the database of the Supreme Judicial Council, which includes verdicts and motives of the court. While no complete coverage of THB cases can be guaranteed, as courts do not always publish their whole sentence, all available cases under the relevant Criminal Code provisions[2] from the designated courts were inspected.

---

2   The following Bulgarian Criminal Code articles were taken in account: Section IX Human Trafficking (includes arts. 159a-c) and art. 156 (abducting a person to be used for lewd acts).

Definitions

The definition of human trafficking, adopted for the purpose of this report is, the one laid down in Art.3 of the Protocol to Prevent, Suppress and Punish Trafficking in Persons, especially Women and Children (Palermo Protocol) supplementing the Convention of the United Nations against Transnational Organised Crime:

> *"the recruitment, transportation, transfer, harbouring or receipt of persons, by means of the threat or use of force or other forms of coercion, of abduction, of fraud, of deception, of the abuse of power or of a position of vulnerability or of the giving or receiving of payments or benefits to achieve the consent of a person having control over another person, for the purpose of exploitation"* (United Nations (UN), 2000)

The intended exploitation (referred to as the objective of trafficking) is defined as including, at a minimum, *"the exploitation of the prostitution of others or other forms of sexual exploitation, forced labour or services, slavery or practices similar to slavery, servitude or the removal of organs"*. The offence is subject to two qualifying circumstances. First, the consent of a victim of trafficking is irrelevant where any of the means listed above are present. Secondly, when the victim is a child (any person under eighteen years of age) the offence shall be considered as trafficking even if it does not involve any of those means.

Corruption has been recognised as an important facilitator of many criminal activities, including trafficking in human beings. Corruption is a complex phenomenon, referring to a number of different criminal activities. In order to encompass the full range of corrupt behaviours, the widely adopted definition put forward by Transparency International (2016) – *"abuse of entrusted power for private gain"* – will be used in this report. Corruption can be classified as grand, petty and political, depending on the impact it has, the money lost as a result and where it occurs and how many persons are involved (*Ibid*).

Theoretical framework

Theories and models of human trafficking

Despite being such a pressing and widespread problem, human trafficking has not been theorised very systematically. Still, different social scientific fields and theoretical strands have been used in explaining this crime. Individual involvement in trafficking can be looked at from the perspective of different criminological theories such as for example rational choice and neutralisation theory (Organisation for Security and Cooperation in Europe (OSCE), 2011). Routine activities theory, on the other hand, focuses on situational factors which upon convergence can result in crime – trafficking can occur when there is a coming together of motivated offenders, suitable victims and lack of capable guardians (Albanese, 2008).

Theories from other social scientific fields have also been utilized to explain the phenomenon. Usman (2014) has illustrated the value that international relations theories can have in explaining the different aspects in trafficking, looking at feminism (generally divided in two camps, one adopting a position condoning prostituion as a genuine occupation and the other an absolutist position condemning both protistution and trafficking), constructivism with regards to policy making and norm diffusion between the domestic and the international level and *vice versa*. Yet other authors have chosen to resort to theory integration, combining (parts of) different models, concepts and theories to explain human trafficking. Lutya and Lanier (2012) incorporate rational choice theory, demand theory, victimology, constitutive theory and economic theory in their exploraiton of human trafficking.

However, the phenomenon has mostly been theorised as a business enterprise both in migration studies and in economic analysis. The market forces of supply and demand for particular goods and services and cost-benefit calculations on the side of the traffickers involved are key to understanding and measuring trafficking. Nevertheless, theoretical models on trafficking are generally few. Some have been designed to capture human *smuggling* as well, such as the model designed by Tamura (2010), who looks at the starting point of exploitation once the desired destination has been reached. This model allows for the co-existence of subsequent exploitation of the newly arrived migrant (when the smugglers deems this to be profitable) with non-exploitative smuggling. Wheaton *et al.* (2010) view traffickers as intermediaries, who connect employers looking for illegal labour and migrants (in terms of their potential skills) who seek illegal passage to the destination country. The model focuses on traffickers, which behave as monopolistic firms, calculating the costs of the activity and adjusting actions accordingly. Decreases in demand and costs for the traffickers will result in decrease in trafficking. Akee *et al.* (2011) also see the traffickers as intermediaries but allow for a domestic market for the victims – traffickers decide whether to engage in trafficking and which market to serve. The domestic and international markets become linked and anti-trafficking policies of the two countries might complement or offset each other. The model developed by

Dessy *et al.* (2005) is focused on child trafficking and takes the investment of the government and parents in child protection as a main deterrent for traffickers.

Mahmoud and Trebesch's (2009) model takes trafficking to be an inevitable side of mass migration. Areas with high emigration rate have higher trafficking rates and increased risk of exploitation of migrants due to an agglomeration effect and negative self-selection. The agglomeration effect arises due to large scale emigration, which lowers the costs for recruitment that traffickers face and leads to the creation of economies of scale and concentration of traffickers and actors involved in supporting services in such areas. Negative self-selection is explained by the fact that large scale out-migration is usually connected to significantly disadvantaged areas leading persons to be more desperate to leave and willing to take larger risks in order to do so. The two effects reinforce each other and illegal migration increases trafficking risks.

None of these models pay much attention to corruption per se. However, considering the general focus on the costs and profits underpinning the models, it is likely that the corruption will be considered as a business cost, as it is largely a factor that re-directs part of the profits generated from the criminal activity towards other actors.

The link between trafficking and corruption

The link between corruption and trafficking has been posited by academics (*e.g.* Lyday, 2001; Bales, 2005) and international organisations (UNODC, 2011; Organisation for Economic Co-operation and Development (OECD), n.d.). Despite limited evidence about the nature of the connection, the link between these two criminal activities is often mentioned as a matter of fact. For example, the UNODC (2011b: 8) recognises corruption as "possibly the main cost factor" in human trafficking which can occur in all stages of the trafficking process – recruitment, transportation, exploitation. However, understanding is scarce both regarding the relationship between the crimes and in terms of the types of corruption mechanisms used and actors involved at different stages of the process.

Lyday (2001) finds a strong correlation between the score given to a country according to the US Department of State Trafficking in Persons Report and Transparency International's Corruption Perceptions Index (CPI). Countries considered to be fully compliant with the US Trafficking Victims Protection Act's (TVPA) minimum standards (Tier 1 countries) all but one have low CPI scores. Furthermore, some researchers state to have found a 'causal link' between levels of corruption and human trafficking (Zhang and Pineda, 2008).

According to Zhang and Pineda (2008), is corruption among the most important factors behind THB and the most corrupt countries which are the ones that consistently fail in tackling trafficking. Indeed, compliance with anti-trafficking policies appears to diminish strongly as corruption increases (Cho, Dreher and Neumayer, 2014; Van Dijk and Van Mierlo, 2010). Generally, compliance with what Cho, Dreher and Neumayer (2014) call 'prosecution policy' (which they define as criminalisation of trafficking) is highest across all countries. However, this is a legalistic proposition: criminalisation is one thing, successful prosecution and punishment of traffickers is another thing and hardly taken into account. The correlation between corruption and trafficking appears to be most significant when it comes to source countries. Bales (2005; 2007) finds government corruption to be the most important factor predicting trafficking from a country. Significant source countries for THB such as Brazil, where it is identified as a causal factor (Studnicka, 2010), and strong evidence of links from Thailand (Sakdiyakorn & Vichitrananda, 2010) and Nigeria (Agbu, 2003) confirm the importance of corruption for THB. Corruption in destinations is also important but ranks second in predicting trafficking with a lower statistical significance than the third and second factors influencing THB from a country (Bales, 2007).

Other research supports the conclusion that the place that a country occupies in the trafficking chain matters with regard to the type of corruption which criminals need to use. Corruption in destination countries is more often related to administrative procedures: for example, the issuing of residence permits, allowing the operations of brothels in zones where they are prohibited (*e.g.* in the Netherlands) (Gounev and Bezlov, 2010). On the other hand, source countries are more prone to corruption at various levels of law enforcement, the judiciary and government (*Ibid.*). These distinctions are a matter of degree, however. Destination countries are not immune to law enforcement, judiciary and political corruption but they are more limited to lower levels of institutions. When large scale, organised corruption schemes are uncovered such as the scandal in Germany in 2007 (Holmes, 2009), they seem to be more of an exception rather than the rule (Gounev and Bezlov, 2010). In addition, the distinctions between countries with regard to the stage of trafficking should not be seen as fixed categories as there is significant overlap: many countries are destinations, sources and transit countries of which the status can be altered with time. Furthermore, all countries experience a certain measure of domestic traffic. Nevertheless, considering the findings of the available studies, measureable differences seem to exist regarding corruption practices employed, which are connected to the position of a country on the continuum between source of and destination for victims of trafficking.

Trafficking in Bulgaria

The following sections present the main findings of the study. First, the legislative framework regulating this type of crime is explored briefly with a focus on how it has changed in response to higher rates of trafficking.

Legislative framework

Bulgarian legislation distinguishes between types of exploitation, thus allowing for the collection of differentiated data. Considering the main goal of trafficking is sexual exploitation, it is important to address the legal status of prostitution as sex workers who are especially susceptible to become victims. In Bulgaria the commercial provision of sexual services is not itself a criminal offence, but all other related activities are illegal: pimping, running brothels, providing premises for lewd acts etc. Even though prostitution is not illegal, charges for living off funds earned in an illegal or immoral way or for lacking identification documents are often brought against sex workers (Dobreva, 2013). In 2013, an attempt was made to stem demand for prostitution by criminalising the use of victims of trafficking for 'lewd' acts. However, this provision of the Criminal Code has rarely been used (*Ibid*).

Recognising the extent of the problem of trafficking, Bulgaria has expanded and sharpened its legislation in 2002, when amendments to the Criminal Code were adopted adding a new section on human trafficking criminalising both national and trans-border trafficking in human beings as a separate offence. Parallel to expanding and introducing more detailed criminal law regulations on human trafficking, legislation and policies aiming to enhance protection of victims of trafficking were developed and implemented. Furthermore, Bulgaria developed a specialised institutional infrastructure for countering THB. The main body is the National Commission for Combating Trafficking in Human Beings (NCCTHB) at the Council of Ministers of the Republic of Bulgaria. It is acting as an equivalent mechanism to a national rapporteur to the European Commission on trafficking in Bulgaria, as well as a national anti-trafficking coordinator. It coordinates the work of the national Mechanism for Referral and Support to Trafficked Persons (Kozhuharova *et al.*, 2010) which was first implemented in 2008-2010. Furthermore, the Commission is responsible for the annual development of a national program for preventing and combating human trafficking and protecting victims (NCCTHB, 2015).

Emergence and development

In order to understand trafficking from Bulgaria and the role of corruption, it is necessary to address the historical context of the emergence and evolution of the criminal structures involved in it. The development of THB in Bulgaria can roughly be divided in three periods. The first one is from the fall of the Soviet bloc to the removal of visa requirement for Bulgarian citizens entering Schengen (1990-2001). The second period is up until the entry of Bulgaria in the European Union (2001 – 2007) and the third encompasses the years from 2007 to now. It is important to note that every stage in the evolution of THB has had influence in shaping current corruption channels and mechanisms.[3]

During much of the 1990s, Bulgaria was in a state of permanent political, societal and economic crisis. The country's political class and institutions were unprepared for transitioning and functioning into a market economy. Thus, the poorly handled process of privatisation, together with the outdated legal framework could not fulfil the expectations of Bulgarian society for a fair transition towards a stable democracy. In addition, during the first months of 1990 large numbers of law enforcement and judiciary personnel exited institutions and for the rest of the decade the police, prosecution and the court system barely functioned. As a result of this situation, in the middle of the decade sizable criminal organisations emerged, such as VIS-2, SIC, Apollo Balkan, Corona Ins. *etc.*, which undermined and eventually took over state monopoly on violence through the sale of protection and forced insurance. These sizable OCGs managed to subdue whole regions to their control and in some cases even acquired national significance. As they were already involved in contraband, stolen cars and drugs trafficking, these criminal associations were well placed to engage in THB as well. They established control over the market for sex services through ownership of hotels, night clubs and bars in big cities and resorts. Each of these OCGs had its own chain of brothels which became reservoirs of women and later expanded and developed into a system of connected city reservoirs (CSD, 2007).

---

[3] The conclusion is made on the basis of a number of interviews with high ranking law enforcement officials (BG-P1, BG-P2, BG-P6, BG-P8, BG-P13, BG-P17, BG-P18)

During the first period, the closed borders of Western European countries were a key factor in determining destinations. Bulgarian citizens still had free access to the states of Central Europe and therefore, in the beginning the export of women was largely pragmatic as victims were brought to easy to reach countries in that region. Hotels and night clubs in the big cities of Central European countries such as Poland, the Czech Republic and Hungary together with small towns close to the borders of Germany and Austria became half-way destinations (BG-P1, BG-P3, BG-P17). With time, stable channels developed between the different nodes of the network of reservoirs as women would be stationed in Central Europe and later transported further to EU countries such as Greece, Italy, Germany and the Netherlands (BG-P1, BG-P8, BG-P9).

The barriers to reaching lucrative sex markets meant that very few Bulgarian sex workers in Western Europe worked outside the control of criminal networks. Apart from mass violence, corrupt practices became one of the key methods supporting the operation of THB (BG-P1, BG-P2, BG-C3). Gradually, whole corrupt complexes emerged involving Bulgarian border guards, officials from the migration and passport services, local police chiefs, officials from the special police bodies tasked with fighting organised crime, magistrates on different levels and even politicians (BG-P2, BG-P19). This system was complemented by the involvement of Western European administrators who secured visas, residence permits, rent registrations *etc.* (CSD, 2007; Rusev, 2013).

In Bulgaria the link between organised crime and prostitution originated in the early 1990s. Research by NGOs and other experts, suggest that in the late 1990s and early 2000s about 95% of prostitution was controlled by organised crime (Ibid). Later estimates show a decrease but nevertheless still significant OCG involvement in prostitution and trafficking (CSD, 2012). Different assessments put the proportion of Bulgarian GDP connected to prostitution in and outside of the country between 3,6 % and 7,2 % (CSD, 2007). Both criminal activities are highly lucrative businesses of international and even global nature, generating huge amounts of illegal profits. Bulgarian organised crime, generates an estimated 1,46 billion euro annually from trafficking and the extent of the problem, data released by the Bulgarian Prosecution indicates that only 16% of all cases of crimes committed by organised criminal groups that reached trial phase in 2013 involved charges of human trafficking (PORB, 2013). From the cases that do reach courts, it appears that the majority are concluded by a settlement. Suspended sentences predominate and when effective sentences are given, they are under or close to the minimum foreseen for this crime, despite the presence of aggravating circumstances in many cases.

During the second phase, after the requirement for Schengen visa for Bulgarians was lifted in 2001, a significant rise in THB occurred. Sociological studies show that prostitution emerged as a mass profession in many Bulgarian cities (Mediana Agency, 2008a; Mediana Agency, 2008b). Sex workers could hardly escape OCG control and work in the sex services industry outside of the country continued to be possible only through the criminal structures for 80-90% of them (BG-P1, BG-P2, BG-P14, BG-C3). In two to three years, Bulgaria became third, and in some Western European states second, country of origin for THB victims. Organised crime developed a particular infrastructure at all stages of the trafficking process incorporating the system of reservoirs and developed solutions to the barriers they encountered. For example, the restriction of three month stay for tourists in Schengen countries gave rise to the model of weekly shuttles, which transported sex workers from Bulgaria to other cities in the EU and back after the allowed period. In the first years after 2001, the large organised criminal groups were still predominant and simultaneously controlled networks of pimps in several Western European countries. The criminal groups benefited significantly from the large number of women willing to service the sex market. The financial resources generated by OCGs was used to ensure the smooth running of the THB operations (BG-P1, BG-P3, BG-P17). Police officers were bribed to hide information, to ignore signals by concerned relatives of recruited women, to ignore outside requests for cooperation in investigations and to withhold information about victims that are returned to the country. Border guards and passport services were paid to falsify documents for traffickers and victims extradited from the EU and in cases of travel bans (BG-P14, BG-P16, BG-P17, BG-C2, BG-C4). During this period THB cases began reaching the desks of local prosecution and courts. Thereupon OCGs started to put more effort into avoiding the initiation of court procedures and the delay of decisions. This was done by directly bribing magistrates or through the use of intermediaries (BG-P16, BG-P17, BG-P21, BG-P22, BG-C1).

The third period can be described as a phase of adaptation (BG-P1, BG-P3, BG-P17, BG-P18, BG-P21). The rise in number of Bulgarian victims, prompted a reaction by law enforcement and judicial institutions in Western Europe and the first important international investigations took place. With the upcoming accession of Bulgaria in the European Union, Bulgarian institutions increased pressure on the criminal organisations including the ones linked to THB for sexual exploitation. The violent period subsided at the turn of the Century and many of the big criminal holdings passed through a processes of legalisation and were eventually replaced by looser criminal networks (BG-P1, BG-P3, BG-P14). Their main strategy for adaptation involved a transformation into a small business type with a simple structure which came to predominate the market for sex services. Use of physical violence was reduced to a minimum and only applied as a last resort and traffickers employed more subtle tactics to entice victims such as the lover boy method. The goal was to represent prostitution as the willing choice of the women (BG-P1, BG-P3, BG-P14, BG-P21, BG-P22, BG-C1, BG-C2, BG-C3).

Criminal networks also had to adjust to the new situation where the control over the victims became more elusive and difficult to exert (BG-P1, BG-P14). The chance to study at European universities with low tuition fees and to work legally in part of EU countries has forced criminal networks to change their approach. This has been the case with the rise of the internet and mobile phones, which gave more freedom to sex workers to work independently, but at the same time also gave criminals more opportunities for control (BG-P1, BG-P4, BG-P6, BG-C1, BG-C2, BG-C5, BG-C6).

Though the environment has changed, the enduring importance of OCGs in THB should not be underestimated. The conducted interviews suggest that criminal networks continue to play an important role in the trafficking process and provide a number of much needed market and security services. Women that attempt to work independently in Western Europe are often exposed to violence by clients or other criminal groups and have difficulties in finding work places that provide enough clientele.[4] Similarly, the way technology has changed prostitution markets appear to remain off the radar of the Bulgarian law enforcement and justice institutions. With Bulgaria's accession to the EU, corrupting border police and passport services has become obsolete (Rusev, 2013). Avoiding prosecution came to the forefront as the most important protection that OCGs needed and efforts were directed in two main avenues. Firstly, securing significant influence over political actors meant that police and specialised agencies could be prevented from interfering with recruitment of women. Secondly, corruption of the judicial system allowed criminal networks to avoid charges being brought, to significantly slow down court procedures and to minimize the number of guilty verdicts (BG-P1, BG-P17, BG-P21).

It is important to note that a certain core structure resting on enduring relations between members of the old criminal organisations remains essential to the successful operation of THB. Local criminal groups turn to this core for support when they are a target of police investigations and court proceedings and repay by providing local support with regard to investments, elections and political campaigns. The starkest and most frequently observed cases of obstruc-

---

[4]   Several studies based on interviews with sex workers and pimps, carried out by the CSD in the period 2006-2014.

tion of prosecution are made possible by the ability of the old criminal 'authority'[5] to influence public officials, politicians and political formations (BG-P1, BG-P17). Such examples will be examined in further detail in the next sections.

Current organisation of THB

The evolution of THB and other core OCG activities in Bulgaria over the last 25 years determined the specifics of the criminal networks which are currently involved in it. As already mentioned, many of the present networks are fragments of the so called violent entrepreneurship prominent in Bulgaria, Russia and other states in Eastern Europe during the nineties (CSD, 2007; Volkov, 2002). However, the radical change in environment experienced after 2007 resulted in a division in two distinct groups.

The first one is connected to the traditional criminal 'holdings' and in addition to prostitution and THB are still involved in other criminal activities like drug smuggling, auto theft, card skimming *etc.*

The second group is also connected to the old criminal organisations since they pay in order to operate and to use the old infrastructure of source and destination reservoirs to recruit women. Furthermore, the old criminal core is approached for assistance in cases of problems with authorities.

The main difference between the first and second group is that the latter views the offer of sexual services as a purely *business oriented activity* and eschews involvement in other risky illegal enterprises. The second group employs three main models for export of sex services to the EU countries, including Switzerland, Turkey and Norway (BG-P1, BG-P3, BG-P10, BG-P12, BG-P17, BG-P18, BG-P20, BG-C1, BG-C3, BG-C7, BG-C8).

The model of direct involvement

This model is characterised by decentralisation and active participation of the same criminals at all stages of the trafficking process, from recruitment to the

---

[5] An avtoritet is a prominent violent entrepreneur, leader of an important criminal group. Established avtoritets have a reputation which allows them to control and support criminal activities without getting directly involved. The avtoritet's name and reputation are the group's trade mark and carry important connotations of influence when used. Independent criminal groups cannot operate in the same territory without the approval of the avtoritet and payment to his group (Volkov, 2002).

everyday running of the business. The pimp finds a woman in Bulgaria[6] or outside of the country, offers her a work place in one of the reservoir cities and brings her there once she agrees. The main function of the pimp is to protect the sex worker, to find customers and to solve logistic hurdles such as finding a place to live, securing a residence permit *etc*. As the internet and social media have grown in importance, the pimp also takes part in communicating with clients. In order to effectively protect the sex worker, the pimp works in cooperation with friends and other Bulgarians. In case he wants to expand the enterprise, the pimp can find a second and a third woman. During the recruitment process, the first sex worker is left under the protection of friends from the network and the pimp returns the favour when needed. Generally, this model is successfully hidden from the police provided there are no conflicts. In reality however, rifts occur frequently due to reasons such as competition for control over better work places or over the women with highest earnings (BG-P1, BG-P3, BG-P7, BG-P10, BG-P12).

The model of differentiation and specialisation

This model is characterised by the existence of vertical chains of command and differentiation of tasks among those engaged in the activity. Specialisation begins with the recruitment of women. The first group of recruited women is tasked with cruising malls, clubs and other establishments, browsing Facebook, WhatsApp and other popular social media sites to find other women that they can enlist for work in prostitution. Once a potential victim is found, she is brought to the managers —experienced pimps with connections who can supply profitable workplaces. They offer a deal depending on the available work places and the wishes of the woman. The new sex worker is taken outside of the country and to the destination city by one of the initially recruited women. The new sex worker is then taken over by another participant in the network who protects her, manages her and collects dues from her. Usually these are Bulgarian nationals from the same city, who cooperate between each other inside of their own network and under the control of the manager. The main condition for the successful operation of the scheme is again *absence of conflict*. Once there is a problem with a certain pimp or a sex worker, the network cuts ties with him/her. In addition, problematic individuals often receive some sort of compensation such as a work place outside of the territory controlled by the network and a sum often agreed on forehand. The goal is to avoid any alerts to the police, prosecution or NGOs. Despite such efforts, however, conflicts arise

---

[6]   Due to demographic changes often outside of his own reservoir.

frequently, which necessitates the existence of a crisis-response mechanism. This is where the role of lawyers in and outside Bulgaria is in the centre of the enterprise (BG-P1, BG-P3, BG-P10, BG-P12).

The family model

This model is usually characterised by couples, where the wife/girlfriend works and the husband/boyfriend assists. Under this type of configuration, the couple pays for the services they use, such as the premises where the sex worker works, but also keeps all profits for themselves. Such small arrangements usually function independently from the Bulgarian criminal networks in their day-to-day activities. They are mostly free of conflict and racketeering. On the other hand, they are often vulnerable to violence (BG-P1, BG-P3, BG-P10, BG-C7, BG-C8).

Despite differences between the models, all traffickers are dependent on the developed infrastructure of the reservoir and on the new opportunities offered to them by large criminal entrepreneurs. These criminal bosses rent or acquire premises in Western and Central Europe such as night clubs, rooms in red light districts, escort websites and agencies that offer such services in the fashion and IT industries (BG-P1, BG-P3, BG-P10,BG-C1, BG-C3). With regard to corruption mechanisms, the first two models use the same tactics and avenues which the old criminal holdings developed in the late 1990s and early 2000s. For the third model, on the other hand, the use of corruption schemes "in the initial stages of the process is practically not needed in contrast to the middle and end stages" (BG-P1), as there is almost no risk with regard to recruitment. For the family model, use of corruption practices becomes necessary in foreign markets where problems with the local bureaucracy or police might occur. Conflicts that arise are solved by payment to the "those in control of the infrastructure" (BG-C1, BG-P3, BG-P4), the first group which is close to the criminal core. Corruption payments become much more necessary in cases of incidents, complaints by the family partner and initiation of investigations. The other two models also buy corruption services from the first group. It is nevertheless unclear if the corruption payments that this second group has to make are higher or lower in comparison to the first one. On the one hand, the second group faces fewer risks due to the different role of the women and their pimps. On the other hand, as outsiders to the system they need to pay more (as they do not bribe directly) in order to ensure their problem free operation (BG-P1, BG-P11, BG-P21).

Corruption mechanisms and actors

Direct Influence

Large economic structures with national presence and influence at all levels of public institutions

As elaborated above, at the turn of the Century, criminal organisations were increasingly becoming a target of police investigations and court procedures and as a result many of them laundered the accumulated criminal proceeds and transformed their crime-enterprises into legitimate business holdings. It is widely recognised that many of these currently legitimate business structures were indeed connected to large scale criminal activities during the nineties. Moreover, even after legalising their proceeds and moving into the legal economy, their owners kept a portion of their criminal structures. Their significant financial capabilities allowed them to invest in responding to pressures from law enforcement, which is tantamount to 'preventive corruption'. Ultimately they succeeded in establishing corrupt relationships with officials from practically all institutions which undertook actions against them (BG-P1, BG-P16, BG-P17). Thus these holdings had influence all the way to the highest levels of power. Most significantly, the political influence that these organisations enjoyed, helped them evade police investigations and consequent court procedures for significant periods of time. Through the use of political corruption, the costs of investigations and prosecutions which could not be avoided were nevertheless minimized and reached only low level players or particular individuals from criminal organisations. Evidence presented by the prosecution has often been discredited or outright ignored by the courts, witnesses have withdrawn their testimonies etc. (BG-P1, BG-P16, BG-P17). An illustrative example in this regard is the case of the 'The Tender Octopus', which was brought to the public's attention in 2010 (see Case Box 1).

Case Box 1: The Case of the 'Tender Octopus'

One of the most notorious examples of the corruptive reach of OCGs with national coverage is the case of the Tractor and his associate Mitko the Policeman (BG-P16, BG-P17, BG-P18)[7]. The Tractor[8] is a former Minister of Interior offi-

---

[7]   The authors of the current analysis will use nicknames with which the persons that have not been convicted of a crime in court are known to the public. It should,

cial and an employee of the predecessor of State Agency for National Security (SANS) as well as of the agency itself after it was reformed and therefore enjoyed strong political support. The Bulgarian prosecution initiated two court cases against him including one for THB, named the 'Tender Octopus'. After becoming the leader of a criminal network involved in prostitution and THB in 1998, his venture expanded until in 2010 it was targeted by both MoI and SANS. The crisis in the Tractor's holding began when the boss became engaged in actively supporting the politicians that had protected his operations, placing him at odds with the political opposition, which won the 2009 elections.

In the period 2008-2009 when the Tractor was in the height of his political influence, his criminal operations proceeded practically undisturbed by law enforcement. The network controlled between half and two thirds of the market for sex services in Sofia (BG-P1, BG-P16) including night clubs in two of the biggest resorts in the country. Similarly, the criminal group exported women for sexual exploitation to almost all EU countries with significant markets.

The Tractor case allows for the observation of clientelism and corrupt relations with individuals from the highest levels of government (members of political parties and the Supreme Judicial Council (SJC) all the way down to lowest level of police officers and tax officials (BG-P16, BG-P18)). The Internal Security Directorate of MoI discovered that an officer from the Drugs Division of the Sofia Metropolitan Police had, in return for payment, informed of upcoming raids on clubs, and on which members of the group special investigative means were in use (Kadiiska, 2014). Other employees from the agency tasked with employing special investigative means at MoI also had "for years been on the payroll" (BG-P4) of the Tractor.

In response to arrests, the Tractor's group initiated a media attack with compromising materials on almost all key officials on various political levels[9], including

---

however, be kept in mind that final convictions in key cases are still scarce. Only parts of the activities of large criminal organisations have been proven in court. To focus only on cases where criminal activities have been proven indisputably in court would unnecessary limit the scope of the report and would lead to paucity in understanding of the corruption practices OCGs use.

8 He is a co-owner of a large gathering of legal companies involved in a variety of industries such as trade and real estate. The holding further includes one of the largest insurance and taxi companies in the country. According to the police and prosecution, however, the Tractor's enterprises include large criminal structures involved in auto theft and prostitution.

9 The substantial financial resources of the group together with the influence in law enforcement gave the Tractor and his associates the opportunity to acquire compromising materials against their biggest critics and to circulate them in the media. The Tractor took advantage of the confrontation in the country and assisted the rivals of the governing politicians. Due to the unwillingness of established political parties to be associated with the Tractor's group, he attempted to create new political formations. He supported financially and organisationally the street protests against the government in January-February 2013. Subsequently, when the newly

against the Minister of the Interior, the Director of the Directorate General Combatting Organised Crime (DGCOC) deputies and magistrates.[10]

Cases against different segments of the structure controlled by the Tractor stalled with the rising political instability. Many of the police officers working on the case, along with the prosecutor and the judge were replaced, raising further suspicions. In the fall of 2015, an attempt was made to start the trial in court. However, from a total of forty-three defendants, charges against nine are dropped due to the expiration of legally prescribed procedural periods. Investigators interviewed point to inside help as the most important factor (experts made 'mistakes', documents disappeared etc.[11]) along with pressure on witnesses to retract testimonies (BG-P4). At the same time, law enforcement did not manage to stop the financial flows to the criminal organisation and their business continued. As a result of such sustained solvency, opportunities to influence witnesses, experts, MoI officials and magistrates went unabated.

Small criminal groups with political influence on the national level

Small criminal groups with influence on the national level are involved in elite prostitution and operate mostly in the capital. Up to ten people comprise such organisations including owners, organisers, recruiters and security personnel (BG-P1, BG-P4). Due to the fact that they provide sex services to sensitive clients, such as influential individuals in politics and the economy, these OCGs have been able to evade police attention for more than twenty years (BG-P17). Even though the sex workers under their control receive substantial remuneration, there are reasons to assume that they are frequent victims of cross-border trafficking, because they acquire a portion of their income from full or part time work abroad. There are numerous witness accounts of women being coerced, even of systematic use of violence, to work in the elite prostitution market (BG-P1).

---

formed government also faced protests, the Tractor became involved in the organisation of contra-protests. With the return of the political rivals of the Tractor in power in November 2014, actions against him and his group were limited. Political commentators presume that a compromise was reached on a political level.

[10] According to information from interviews with police officers, one of the most important instruments for securing leverage was the use of recordings made in striptease bars, brothels and by sex workers themselves of compromising video materials involving politicians, magistrates and other influential individuals (BG-P2, BG-P6).

[11] Different loopholes in the Bulgarian Criminal Procedural Code give the defense the opportunity to stall the process. According to an interview with BG-P18 part of the chances that the defence gets are a result of corruption relations between investigators and lawyers

Investigations into this market, took place in the period 2010-2012 (undertaken for political reasons) but were hindered by political protection and a legal framework carefully crafted so as to deliver evidence of criminal offences well-nigh impossible. Regardless of the form of elite prostitution in Bulgaria, from fashion agencies, music companies to night clubs and striptease bars, the existence of work contracts for the women constitutes a serious barrier for police and prosecutors as it makes proving illegal activities difficult. In some cases, elite sex workers active in foreign markets have well drafted contracts which also regulate work outside of Bulgaria in order to avoid problems (BG-P21, BG-C1).

The main difference between the large and small criminal organisations with influence on the national level, however, is that it is more difficult for the latter to stop an investigation once it has been initiated. In order to ensure the suspension of law enforcement activities, sustained effort on the political level is necessary. This is evident in the development of court cases against such criminal groups. In three of the four important cases started in Sofia the court found evidence of crimes. After a change of governments in 2013, however, all investigations in this area have practically ceased. The specialized police agency for combatting organised crime, the DGCOC was taken out of MoI and moved under SANS, operational cases were archived, the specialized prosecution was terminated and no charges were pressed against those arrested.

Case Box 2: The case of Scandal VIP Club

The owner of the Scandal VIP Club in Sofia was a former European champion in weight lifting and Sofia a municipal council member from one of the leading political parties. He was arrested at the Sao Paolo airport, Brazil in October 2011, during an attempt to transport 7,2 kg of cocaine. In May 2012 he was sentenced to nine years and four months in prison by the federal court in Brazil. In January 2013 GDCOC entered his Scandal VIP Club in Sheraton hotel, Sofia and arrested five people for involvement in an OCG engaged in THB and prostitution. In the case materials it is claimed that the owner of the establishment is in fact the leader of the group, who owns the bar since 2006. Witnesses for the prosecution included some of the people working in the establishment and a victim that was trafficked to the Netherlands. The specialized prosecution took into account the fact that the Scandal VIP owner was already serving a sentence in Brazil and at the time did not press charges. In October 2013, he was mysteriously released from prison and came back to Bulgaria. No charges of drug smuggling were pressed against him despite the fact that the investigation showed that the cocaine was destined for Bulgaria. Similarly, no charges were pressed for the participation in an OCG involved in THB and prostitution. The media speculated that his release was secured by influential Bulgarian politicians against whom the Scandal VIP owner has compromising materials. Currently, the club is back in business and despite not being the official owner, the former boss is still effectively in charge. It is claimed that he even expanded his business to Spain (Naidenova, 2013).

Criminal structures with regional influence

In Bulgaria, not only commercial establishments can function as reservoirs. Certain district cities have developed themselves into significant sources of victims for THB, drawing women and girls from surrounding towns and villages. They are subsequently transferred by criminal networks to other places in the country or outside of Bulgaria. In cases of internal traffic, the most common destinations are the four largest cities (Sofia, Varna, Bourgas and Plovdiv). On the other hand, victims transported abroad are usually brought to specific places where the criminal network has an already established presence. Therefore, women from different localities are trafficked to service specific markets in Western Europe.

There are differences in the organisation of these district reservoirs stemming from the criminal groups involved, the degree of co-option of law enforcement institutions in the localities, and seasonal variations. In the three biggest cities except for Sofia – Plovdiv, Varna and Bourgas, the sex services market works under specific principles. Varna and Bourgas are dependent on seaside tourism and thus the market for sexual services grows exponentially during the summer. In Plovdiv, like in Sofia, during the same period activities decline as sex workers migrate to seaside resorts.

Case box 3: The Varna Municipal Councillors' Case

In 2009 three of Varna's municipal councillors, Hristo Danov, his father Veselin Danov and Ivan Slavkov were sentenced for leading an OCG involved in money laundering, THB and extortion. According to experts interviewed (BG-P13, BG-P17), the three defendants together with the former police officer Veselin Jekov managed to secure a monopoly over prostitution in Varna and the region including nearby resorts Constantine, Helena and Golden Sands (BG-P11, BG-P16, BG-P17). In media interviews Veselin Danov admitted to be one of the originators of the violent entrepreneur structures in Varna, which offered protection to businesses in return for payment. His entry in the sex services market occurred in the mid-nineties (Afera, 2008). Besides relying on a large criminal organisation Veselin Danov also took advantage of the position of his father, who is one of the most renowned Bulgarian jurists. During the period 1990-1991, Hristo Danov was the Minister of the Interior and in 2002-2003 held a position at the Bulgarian Constitutional Court. Owing to his father's reputation, Veselin Danov was not investigated by the police after 1990 and had access to high ranking police officers and magistrates. It is claimed that in 2000 Hristo Danov was forced by the then Prosecutor General Filchev to influence the Constitutional court on the legality of the procedure for the appointment of Prosecutors General in order to avoid a trail against his son (Nikolov, 2002).

Based on information from media interviews with Veselin Danov, different schemes of cooperation between the large national criminal organisations and the regional groups (SIK, Apollo Balkan and VIS-2) can be distinguished. Agencies like SANS and its predecessor offered Danov protection from criminal investigations. It appears that the SANS advisor and alleged boss of a large OCG the Tractor promised Danov full retraction of charges and release from jail[12]. Danov claims that in return the Tractor demanded that the Varna councillor sends him an individual, who the criminal leader was to make his personal broker in the Varna division of SANS. The Tractor also promised Veselin Danov to employ his son at SANS and "to appoint for a deputy director of SANS a person who I will recommend" (Gospodinova, 2012). Despite these efforts, however, the three municipal councillors were sentenced. According to witnesses on the case, the defendants had managed to establish a monopoly over around thirty night clubs and brothels in Varna and the Constantine and Helena and Golden Sands resorts (BG-P17, BG-P23).

In comparison to the biggest cities, smaller municipalities (50-150.000 residents), lack a local sex services market (excluding highway prostitution). Therefore, local criminal networks are mostly involved in the control over sex workers in the largest cities, resorts and those working abroad (BG-P3, BG-P11, BG-P12). In terms of cooperation of law enforcement on the regional level, there are problem towns for OCGs such as Sliven and Pazardzhik, where the police is active in investigating and pressing charges.[13] However, in the trial phase these proceedings are disrupted, most likely by intermediaries influencing the prosecution (BG-P3, BG-P8, BG-P14), a practice addressed in more detail in subsequent sections. This impression is strengthened by roughly equal num-

---

[12] The prosecutor in charge of the case against Danov admits that attempts have been made to influence the proceedings on part of the Tractor.

[13] The differentiation is provisional and is based on reports by national police, GDCOC, the prosecution and media accounts

ber of first instance court cases in Pleven and Sliven[14], after adjustment for the fact that Sliven is smaller in terms of population and has a lot less registered victims of trafficking .

Problem cities, however, are few, with the exception of among other Sliven and Pazardzhik. Instead, quiet cities predominate where the police and intelligence services fail to gather operational data or collect it only sporadically and incompletely. In quiet cities prostitution and THB are thus rarely investigated. Due to the general absence of a market for sex services in these localities, police authorities often claim they have not come in contact with the respective criminal groups and individuals (BG-P2, BG-P8). The main risk to OCGs in such quiet towns and cities stems from local law enforcement seeking assistance from foreign police forces or if a national investigation is initiated. Otherwise it can be argued that quiet towns are characterised by the existence of a protective umbrella which shields OCGs and is present on all levels of MoI, including in local structures (BG-P1, BG-P3, BG-P14, BG-P15). According to previous CSD studies and the experts interviewed, this protection can be classified as "active and passive".[15] Passive protection involves payment when there are problems for the criminal network. Police officers on all levels consider this to be a good source of income for those involved in an investigation. Active protection is practically a police protection racket and entails law enforcement's extortion of bribes from OCGs.[16] A regular 'peace tax' is collected where the amount can be determined per time period, sex worker or pimp. If despite such payments there are signals against them, OCGs withhold a portion of the amount of protection monies as 'fines' for disruptions of the established system of protection.

The peace tax and the fines can be both cash or in kind payments. The latter were much more frequently mentioned by interviewees. With regard to smaller OCGs bribes there is mention of delivering sex services for police officers or gifts (mobile phones, designer clothing). Big OCGs presiding over a lot of sex

---

[14]   Based on a sample of trafficking cases gathered by the authors for the period 2012-2015 from the regional courts of first instance Sliven, Pazardzhik, Pleven and the Specialized Criminal Court.

[15]   According to an official at the Internal Security Directorate of MoI (BG-P14) due to the fact that most criminal organisations are involved in other crimes as well such as drug trafficking, racketeering etc., and these crimes are investigated but the THB and prostitution are often missed. Illustrative is the fact that when stemming drug trafficking comes to the forefront on the national level and operations are undertaken, only charges of drug trafficking are pursued and any evidence and witness testimonies for THB and prostitution discovered in the process are 'forgotten'

[16]   The operational information received is not registered officially but is kept for personal use or for leverage to the group (BG-P2).

workers usually bribe with money, cars[17] and when it comes to high ranking officials even apartments (at seaside resorts, in Sofia and Plovdiv or sometimes also outside of the country).

There is an important caveat however, which is valid for all district cities (BG-P2). If an international investigation is initiated regarding Bulgarian OCGs participating in THB, police and special services cooperate actively with their foreign colleagues. It became clear from the interviews that there were many examples, where sizeable amounts of money and property were offered but despite that the investigations were not suspended at the level of MoI (BG-P2, BG-P3, BG-P7). Unfortunately, there have been failures in such instances by the prosecution and courts but generally magistrates consider them to be of high reputational risk and not susceptible to corruption pressure (BG-P1, BG-P2, BG-P14). This assertion is supported by the court cases on trafficking in the regional cities of Sliven, Pazardzhik and Pleven. While court settlements, where guilt is admitted in exchange for a lower sentence are frequent, there have been no acquittals and a majority of the persons have been convicted regardless of the type of sentence (suspended or effective) for their involvement in cases of international human trafficking.

Pleven is a good illustration of a district city where OCGs enjoy protection on all levels. Despite being among the cities with the highest prevalence of THB to Western Europe, police investigations are rare. Even in cases where other serious crimes such as murder by means of an explosion or a shooting against a judge who later turned out to have links to pimps were involved, no charges were pressed. There is evidence to suggest that high ranking police officers have not only stopped all investigative work on THB but there is evidence to suggest that they were even involved in criminal activities themselves, such as recruiting women (BG-P14, BG-P6, BG-C3). Similarly, there have been cases where the police has discouraged victims and their families from filing a complaint. One example involved a Roma clan that had trafficked up to hundred women to Bremen in 2012. The Pleven police had been aware of the crimes and their perpetrators but were of the opinion that those were actually poor Roma families that would once in a while engage in street prostitution (BG-P14). Once the German police opened an investigation, the Pleven police was fully cooperative (with the criminal clan), prompting the protectors of the

---

[17] Money is returned to the country and laundered through the purchase of designer clothing on sale, electronics and most often second hand cars. Real estate is another investment often made by criminal leaders and pimps. Many of them own construction companies and would build apartment complexes on the Black sea and winter resorts and big cities. In the last years there are many instances of construction in Greece, Cyprus, and even in Spain, Italy, and Germany.

criminal group to seek to influence the prosecution. The regional prosecutor tried to persuade a colleague responsible for the case not to demand a stricter punishment. The case gained notoriety due to the complaint that followed from this personal conflict within the local prosecution (Kolev, 2015).

Indirect corruption schemes – the intermediary system

After the beginning of Bulgaria's accession negotiations with the EU, direct influence over public institutions became more difficult and OCGs were forced to adapt to the new environment. A key element in this adaptation is the emergence of intermediaries (BG-P1, BG-P21). The system of brokers offering services for organisations and entrepreneurs in the black and grey markets (CSD, 2007; CSD, 2012) arose already at the beginning of Bulgaria's democratic transition. However, the established criminal organisations of the era did not make intensive use of it until the late nineties[18] since violence or direct corrupt channels would usually be used to settle problems. The abatement of the economic and political crisis in 2000, however, led staff of law enforcement agencies and the judiciary to strengthen control over their employees and to a significant restriction of opportunities for violent settlement of disputes between private parties. Consequently, criminal networks began establishing contacts with the networks of intermediaries which had already developed in the spheres around privatisation, restitution and the grey economy (construction, trade, tourism, entertainment industry etc.) and who had access to politicians, magistrates and high ranking public administration officials. The brokers work for their own or for their group's interest and are not dependent on specific criminal/business networks or on public officials (BG-P1, BG-P23).

All established criminal activities requiring protection on multiple levels within different institutions necessitate the involvement of several intermediaries. The data collected suggests that even influential brokers with access to the highest levels of the executive, legislative and judicial power cannot alone ensure enough influence. Thus, in order to attain the desired outcome, coordina-

---

[18] The genesis of the intermediary system can be traced the exodus of law enforcement and judiciary personnel in the beginning of the nineties, when around nineteen thousand employees were fired or resigned from the police and the security services. A large proportion of them entered the private sector and sought employment in private security firms or became lawyers and started cooperating with criminal groups and violent entrepreneurs. Similar developments can be observed among prosecutors and judges most of whom became lawyers. Both groups retained connections with their former colleagues. In the beginning of the nineties these intermediaries worked largely with police and security services. Later in the decade protection from the judiciary became a crucial service for criminal groups.

tion between multiple persons is needed as exemplified in statements such as "a couple of people called me about him" (BG-P6) or "it is not yet clear who is going to do the job" (BG-P3) etc.

Roughly four types of intermediaries can be distinguished, based on their background, the services they provide and the level on which they operate. At the lowest, *local level*, brokers influence the police regarding investigations and other operational activities. During interviews, 'black lawyers'[19] were mentioned frequently but often former local police officers have become intermediaries as well.[20] Due to their connections they can inform members of OCGs if an investigation is initiated against them and can supply information about criminal competitors to their former colleagues. Black lawyers usually operate in the city or locality where their network is best developed and lobby for their clients to officials or when needed redirect them to a colleague from the network who knows the responsible investigator, police chief or in some cases prosecutor (BG-P23). Clients are aware of this service and often actively inquire for it. Furthermore, the network of black lawyers can mediate in order to ensure important obstructions of the investigation, influencing for example police officers from other police units, experts appointed on the case, results from a medical expertise *etc.* (BG-P15, BG-P21, BG-P22).

Case box 4: The case of the Club 777 boss

The case against the boss of the violent entrepreneur organisation Club 777 in the town of Sliven, which was involved in extortion, racketeering and debt collection is indicative of obstruction of trial proceedings by brokers. With the waning of the market for protection, the criminal leader and his associates became involved in prostitution and THB. Initially, the Club 777 boss enjoyed protection from the local police but after foreign law enforcement agencies initiated investigations such involvement became too risky. However, despite international efforts information about the police inquiry continued to leak to the criminal leader and the local district prosecutor did not press charges. Eventually, as a result of the media attention the case received, and the requests for investigation and cooperation from law enforcement authorities in the EU, the case was brought to court for trial. The first instance court convicted the criminal leader and sentenced him to 12 years in prison, subsequently reduced to 9 years on

---

[19] Black lawyers are lawyers who usually defend persons from criminal circles. Their aim is to disrupt the investigation and trial procedure by seeking to influence officials involved at all levels through corruption or through the use of clientelist relations (CSD, 2007).

[20] There is a certain overlap between the two groups as there are examples of former police officers who have become lawyers.

second instance. The Supreme Court of Cassation, however returned the case to the court of first instance with the bizarre argument that the judge had harassed the wife of one of the defendants. The experts interviewed explain this turn of events with the influence of the so called black lawyers and intermediaries and point to the fact that the judge is a senior (70 years old) and that such an argument coming from the Supreme Court is puzzling (BG-P15, BG-P18). The aim on the side of the criminal network and its affiliates is that such a delay the process will lead to a suspension of the case due to legally mandated time constraints (BG-P18, BG-P21).

The second group of more influential intermediaries can deliver a range of services such as supplying information regarding agents and witnesses, closing of case files and ensuring the suspension of investigations. Compared to black lawyers whose activities and network are usually known, the successful operation of these insider brokers depends on remaining hidden (BG-P1, BG-P2). These brokers are an amorphous group with a more diverse background. They are variably referred to as "*managers*" or "*strongmen*" (BG-P1, BG-P13, BG-C3) and can be chiefs of police, former employees of the Communist State Security, former customs officials and prosecutors turned businessmen *etc.*

The third group of intermediaries emerged after 2003-2004 and is comprised of *politicians*, who are part of the local political party organisations. They often are local council members or deputy candidates placed on positions at the regional lists that are unlikely to ever get them elected. Usually these individuals have criminal ties or past. Some of them have convictions from Bulgarian or even foreign courts, which prevent them from entering politics on national level. Such brokers act locally, securing their political party a certain amount of votes in national and local elections. Their positions in the local power structure justify contacts with police chiefs, tax administration officials, prosecutors and judges. Respectively, they provide brokerage services and their efforts carry significant weight as they have the opportunity to influence personnel decisions in the police, public administration and the judiciary (BG-P7, BG-P16).

Case box 5:   The Snotnose Case

Snotnose is a Roma leader from Dobrich, who is known for his involvement in the export of sex workers for EU countries and Norway and in schemes for buying votes from local Roma communities. In 2007 he was a leader of the list of the Movement for Rights and Freedoms (MRF) party. In 2014 he was arrested along with his son on charges of unlawful export of precursors to the EU. From the interviews conducted it is evident that there have been numerous cases of political interference with his criminal cases leading to the suspensions of investigations targeted at Snotnose (BG-P16). The Roma leader would on his part provide mediation services regarding investigations of different individuals involved in THB.

The fourth group of brokers operates on *national level*. Their networks include magistrates, politicians, policemen, and leading officials in the public administration. Most often these are renowned lawyers and legal firms who have influence over legislative amendments in the country and access to magistrates at the appellative and cassation level. The cases of Vasil Telbizov, the Club 777 boss (See Case Box 4) and Vanko 1 (see Case Box 6) demonstrate how this systemic influence is applied on different levels. The process already begins at the stage: when the court considers the detention in custody of persons from big criminal network who can afford the services of these national intermediaries. Avoiding detention gives the opportunity at an early stage to influence witnesses, destroy or hide evidence *etc*. The black lawyers with national influence can also ensure the support of magistrates at the appellative court level. There are cases where smaller criminal networks manage to acquire the services of national level intermediaries only at the cassation level such as in the Club 777 (See Case Box 4) case.

Case box 6: The Vanko 1 Case

The case of the second most popular rap artist in the country is illustrative of the ability of influential brokers to sway national institutions such as the High Court of Cassation and the Parliament. Vanko 1 used his clubs and bars in Plovdiv to recruit women from among his fan base, who were afterwards trafficked to France, Italy and Spain. The criminal network was hierarchically controlled and used violence towards victims which caught the attention of the French police, which collected substantial amounts of evidence, including many testimonies by victims.

Vanko 1 was convicted by a second instance court for THB and received a twelve year sentence. However, the case reached the High Court of Cassation, where the decision was overturned and returned to a court of appeals. While the new case was underway, the governing coalition lobby proposed amendments in the Criminal Code that lowered the punishment for inducement to prostitution to five years. The law was passed and in the end Vanko 1 was released after only a year in prison (Sega, 2006). Despite the ensuing media scandal and the clear understanding of the seriousness of this crime, no subsequent alterations to the Criminal Code have been made. The controversial change in criminal law went down in history as the Vanko 1 Amendment (Ibid).

Conclusion

In conclusion, corruption is one of the key instruments adopted by organised criminal groups to avoid detection and obstruct counter-trafficking efforts – together other serious crimes which are tackled. Although the use of corruption is often mentioned along with human trafficking, few studies have empirically explored the factors and mechanisms behind this nexus. This chapter fills this gap its findings being based on research of primary and secondary data and explores in addition key aspects of the link between human trafficking and corruption. The research findings shed light on key aspects of the link between corruption and trafficking.

The research shows that once changes in the environment take place, criminal organisations adjust accordingly, including the ways they utilize corruption. With the removal of restrictions on movement and residence for Bulgarians in the European Union, corruption of border guards and for obtaining forged documents became practically obsolete. Similarly, due to increases in awareness about THB, the methods employed and the fact that especially when it comes to women they willingly and knowingly went to work in the sex industry, corruption to assist in recruitment or to this stage of the process, also became largely unnecessary. The decline in the need for such specialized services, implied that the entry to the market was lowered and it was possible for smaller criminal organisations to get involved. Coupled with more enforcement pressure, the success in laundering criminal profits and exit of some criminal bosses from black markets led to the disintegration of the large scale criminal conglomerates. Nevertheless, due to their extensive networks the criminal core retains its importance, as it controls much of the infrastructure needed to operate. The role of corruption in avoiding prosecution, obfuscating investigations and court trials already underway became essential, for example for minimising punishments. However, since influencing law enforcement and the judiciary was seen as risky for members of these institutions, direct corruption declined in importance and was replaced by the use of intermediaries. Corruption thus became an investment in protecting partly or fully the whole operation – a necessary cost in periods of increased prosecution and law enforcement activity.

References

Agbu, O., Corruption and organised crime: The Nigerian case. *West Africa Reivew 4*, 2003, 1-13

Akee, R.B. *et al.*, *Transnational trafficking, law enforcement and victim protection: A middleman trafficker's perpesctive.* Bonn: Institute for the Study of Labor, 2011

Albanese, J., Risk assessment in organised crime. *Journal of Contemporary Criminal Justice vol. 24*, 2008, 263-272

Bales, K., *Understanding global slavery: A reader.* Berkley: University of California, 2005

Bales, K., What predicts human trafficking. *International Journal of Comparative and Applied Criminal Justice 31*, 2007, 269-279

CSD, *Organized Crime in Bulgaria: Markets and Trends.* Sofia: Center for the Study of Democracy, 2007

CSD, *Serious and organised crime threat assessment 2010-2011.* Sofia: Center for the Study of Democracy, 2012

Cho, S.-Y., A. Dreher and E. Neumayer, determinants of anti-trafficking policies: Evidence from a New Index. *The Scandinavian Journal of Economics 116*, 2014, 429-454

Dessy, S.M., *The economics of child trafficking (part II).* Montreal: Department of Economics Université du Québec à Montréal, 2005

Dobreva, N., *Protecting the rights of trafficked persons in Bulgaria: A Human rights based approach.* Sofia: Animus Association Foundation, 2013

Gospodinova, N. (2012, March 12). *Veselin Danov: I see the City Council in prison clothes.* Retrieved January 14, 2016, from DarikNews: http://dariknews.bg/view_article.php?article_id=873436

Gounev, P. and T. Bezlov, *Examining the links between organized crime and corruption.* Sofia: Center for the Study of Democracy, 2010

Holmes, L., Human trafficking & corruption: triple victimisation. In C. Friesendorf, *Strategies against human trafficking: the role of the security sector* (pp. 83-114). Geneva: DCAF, 2009

ILO, *Profits and poverty: the economics of forced labour.* Geneva: ILO, 2014

Kadiiska, M. (13 October 2014), *A police officer supplied information to the policeman's group.* Retrieved January 11, 2016, from Monitor: http://www.monitor.bg/article?id=446399

Kolev, N. (21 April 2015). *Ivo Radev's defence: Personal relations are at the foundation of the charge against the District Prosecutor.* Retrieved Decemer 12, 2015, from DarikNews: http://dariknews.bg/view_article.php?article_id=1422342

Kozhuharova, N, *et al.*, *National mechanism for referral and support to trafficked persons.* Sofia: NCCTHB, 2010

Lutya, T. A., *An integrated theoretical framework to describe human trafficking of young women and girls for involuntary prostitution.* Rijeka: Intech, 2012

Lyday, C., The shadow market in human beings: an anti-corruption perspective. *10th International Anti-Corruption Conference.* Prague: Transparency International, 2001

Mahmoud, T.O., *The economic drivers of human trafficking: micro-evidence from five Eastern European countries.* Kiel: Kiel Institute for the World Economy, 2009

Naidenova, M. (2013, October 26). *Mitko the policeman three copies of sex recoding of MPs, police officers and even EU Officials.* Retrieved December 17, 2015, from Blitz: http://www.blitz.bg/news/article/229783

NCCTHB, *National Program for Combating Traffic in Human Beings and Victims Protection for 2015.* Sofia: NCCTHB, 2015.

Nikolov, Y. (2002, March 30). *The Constitutional Court conserved Filchev.* Retrieved December 15, 2015, from Capital: http://www.capital.bg/politika_i_ikonomika/bulgaria/2002/03/30/214522 _konstitucionniiat_sud_konservira_filchev/

OECD, *Background Paper: Developing a Framework for Combatting Corruption Related to Trafficking in Persons.* Paris: OECD, n.d.

OSCE, *Analysing the business model of trafficking in human beings to better prevent the crime.* Vienna: OSCE, 2011.

Sakdiyakorn, M., and S. Vichitrananda, Corruption, human trafficking and human rights: the case of forced labor and sexual exploitation in Thailand. *NACC Journal July,* 2010, 54-66

Studnicka, A.C., Corruption and human trafficking in Brazil: findings from a multi-modal approach. *European Journal of Criminology 7,* 2010, 29-43

Tamura, Y., Migrant smuggling. *Journal of Public Economics 94,* 2010, 540-548

UN, *United Nations Convention against Corruption.* New York: United Nations, 2003

UNODC, *Estimating illicit financial flows from drug trafficking and other transnational organized crimes.* Vienna: UNODC, 2011a

UNODC, *Issue Paper: The role of corruption in trafficking in persons.* Vienna: UNODC, 2011b

UNODC, *Trafficking in persons to europe for sexual exploitation.* Vienna: UNODC, 2014a.

UNODC, *Global report on trafficking in persons.* Vienna: UNODC, 2014b

Van Dijk, J. and F.K. Van Mierlo, *Indicators of corruption: further explorations of the link between corruption and implementation failure in anti-trafficking policies.* Lastrada, 2010

Volkov, V., Violent entrepreneurs: The use of force in the making of Russian capitalism. Ithaca, Cornell University Press, 2002

Wheaton, E. *et al.*, Economics of human trafficking. *International Migration 48*, 2010, 114-142

Zhang, S. and S. Pineda, Corruption as a causal factor in human trafficking. In D. Siegel and H. Nelen (eds), *Organised Crime: Culture, Markets and Policies* (pp. 41-55). New York: Springer, 2008

Corrupt practices in Greek football: Are they inevitable?

Argyro Elisavet Manoli and Georgios A. Antonopoulos[1]

Introduction

Numerous reports by Greek government institutions as well as by international organisations and NGOs have demonstrated that corruption levels in Greece are extraordinarily high for the country's level of development (Transparency International, 2016). Transparency International's overall Corruption Perception Index score for Greece have consistently been closer to those of Central and Eastern European countries in transition than to those of Western Europe (see Antonopoulos and Tagarov, 2012). Some have pointed to cultural explanations. According to Bull and Newell, when the Modern Greek state was formed in the mid-nineteenth Century, "*corruption was . . . encouraged by an inherited culture of 'rousfeti', a system of bribery widely practiced in the Ottoman Empire*" (Bull and Newell, 2003: 25). Similar arguments have been put forward with respect to the whole post-Ottoman period by some authors like Polychroniou (2008), who has argued that "*graft and corruption have always been an integral part of Greece's political culture*". Others, such as Lambropoulou (2012), argue that corruption is neither an issue of morals nor of embedded cultural attitudes. It is the result of serious social and organisational problems that exists in the country.

While accepting that corruption is a significant factor in Greek society in general (a phenomenon that is facilitated by non-existent, weak or half-hearted measures to "fight" corruption), it manifests itself as an inevitable aspect of Greek football too. From the late 1990s corrupt practices in Greek football have been considered as a serious problem for and threat to the integrity of the sport in the country. To a great extent these practices were initially associated with the existence of the 'paranga' (literally, 'The Shanty'), which refers to a mechanism for fixing games by selecting specific referees for specific games in order

[1] Argyro Elisavet Manoli is Lecturer in Sports Marketing and Communications at Loughborough University, UK (e.a.manoli@lboro.ac.uk). Georgios A. Antonopoulos is Professor of Criminology at Teesside University, United Kingdom (g.antonopoulos@tees.ac.uk).

for particular clubs to benefit. The ultimate goal of the 'paranga' was for a particular club to win the Greek league title as this is associated with significant
income from Champions' League games and television rights (Kapranos, 2002).

Following the exposure of fixed matches in Greece in 2011, also known as
Koriopolis (a pun name on the Italian scandal *Calciopolis* and the Greek word
'korios' or phone-tap), detailed information about numerous matches played in
the 2008/09, 2009/10 and 2010/11 seasons that attracted UEFA's attention
were brought into the public eye (Eleftherotypia 2011). Greek football has also
attracted considerable attention from UEFA in light of other scandals including
'shady' football club owners' imprisonment (Homewood, 2015), which led the
national and international media to portray Greek football as a 'mafia-type'
organisation, especially after the former president of the Hellenic Football Federation was accused of being involved in a 'criminal organisation' that was allegedly directed by the current President-Owner of Olympiakos (Rumsby,
2015; de Quetteville, 2003; Hill, 2010).

In response to these events, both the national governing bodies of the sport
and the Ministry of Culture and Sport have introduced a number of schemes
and measures in 2013 *in addition* to the existing relevant national legislation
(such as the Law 2725/1999 on 'Amateur and Professional Sports') and international legal frameworks (such as the UN Convention Against Corruption and
the UN Convention Against Transnational Organised Crime) (see European
Commission, 2012). These include educational workshops delivered to young
players that will be discussed in some more detail in a section that follows.

The measures taken to tackle corruption have been introduced and implemented in the top tiers of professional football and were met originally with
enthusiasm since they were seen as an effective way to protect and enhance the
'product' (see Mason, 1999) of Greek football. However, it can be argued that
there has been no success in stamping out corrupt practices in Greek football
and this is exemplified primarily –and among others – by a continuous discussion about how integral match-fixing in the country has been[2], a discussion that
now has spilled outside the country (see, for example, The Guardian, 2014) as
well as an enduring distrust among football fans towards the 'product' itself and
the authorities that supposedly regulate and promote it. Mplounas' (2014) study
shows that the Greek public is not interested in Greek football since they think
that the image of Greek football is 'bad' and that the quality of the sport in the
country is 'low'. The public considers that the factors that contribute to the

---

[2] It is perhaps interesting to note that there is a *weekly* TV show in a major national
network (SKAI) focusing on football match-fixing as well as other corrupt practices in Greek football.

negative image and low quality of Greek football are among other things, the systematic bias of the organisers of football leagues towards specific clubs (91,5%), and the tolerance of the government to criminal and corrupt practices in football (86, 5%). In addition, the public considers that a significant number of football matches' results in Greece are a product of match-fixing, while it has a negative perception of referees who are considered an integral part of the match-fixing process (Mplounas, 2014).

This negative perception appears to be the case among players too and this is highlighted not only by reactions to match-day injustices suffered by specific football clubs but also by a recent report that reveals that 12,8% of Greek football players interviewed admitted that they had been approached to 'fix' a match within the past year, and 64% of them said they were confident that matches in their league were fixed (Kovac, 2014).

The aim of this chapter is to show why corruption in Greek football is inevitable by offering a detailed account of a number of football-related corrupt practices and highlighting their contextual parameters (see Brooks *et al.*, 2013) as well as juxtaposing them against the set of measures implemented against football corruption in the country. Through the analysis of the data collected, three major areas of football-related corruption were identified: match-fixing; ticket 'tricks'; and tax evasion through fake tax and insurance certificates. Although this is hardly an exhaustive list of corrupt practices in Greece, these issues were selected because they have either received considerable media attention, or because they have been identified as 'normal' practices in the working of the Greek football clubs that have been the context of our empirical research. This is why doping, for instance, is beyond the scope of our study. In our endeavour, and for the purposes of this chapter, we use Gorse and Chadwick's (2010: 40) definition of sports corruption: "*any illegal, immoral or unethical activity that attempts to deliberately distort the result of a sporting contest for the personal material gain of one or more parties involved in that activity*".

Our goal is neither to offer a systematic analysis of the causes of football corruption in Greece, nor to provide an account of every type of football-related corruption in the country. Moreover, we do not have the objective of evaluating the measures implemented against football corruption in Greece. On the contrary, our aim is to examine the three selected corrupt practices in detail, along with the measures against them, while highlighting the factors that suggest that corruption is an integral and almost inevitable aspect of Greek football.

Methods and data

The primary source of information for this chapter is ethnographic research that the first author of this chapter conducted while being employed on a full-time basis in two football clubs in Greece. One of the clubs is one of the major and most popular clubs in country, and part of the *Super League* (first division), whereas the other is a historic club in the second division (also known as *'Football League'* in Greece). The ethnographic work offered the researcher the opportunity to study individuals who seldom offer themselves for examination, and a unique opportunity for exploration. This part of the research required immersion in the field for a significant amount of time (from August 2008 to February 2011 and from April 2011 to April 2013), and participation in activities that were not related to the collection of data *per se*. Within the context of the ethnographic research, additional information on the issues at stake was obtained through interviews with informed actors from the realm of Greek football.

Secondly, with regards to match-fixing in particular, we used the telephone conversations that were available as the result of wiretapping by the National Intelligence Agency (*EYP*) in relation to the latest football match-fixing scandal (2011). These wiretapped conversations disclosed an abundant amount of information about the broad range of actors and groups involved, and identify patterns of social organisation across a number of cases many of which were related to one another. Finally, we collected, examined and analysed published media sources which allowed us to obtain information not only on the process behind corrupt practices within football clubs, but also on the key actors involved, while triangulating the data collected through the first two methods.

The chapter is structured as follows: initially, a presentation of the measures against corruption that have been introduced in Greek football over the past years is offered followed by an examination of three major types of corrupt practices that takes place, in an attempt to highlight the key actors and underlying structures that support them. We finish with a discussion of our findings.

Tackling corruption in Greek Football

The measures against corruption that have been introduced in Greek football in recent years (following the latest match-fixing scandal exposure in 2011) include educational programmes and tighter regulations in both financial control and match-fixing detention, which will be described in more detail below. Presenting them will allow for a thorough understanding of the response to corruption to be achieved, while simultaneously highlighting the actors and areas they have been focused on.

Two educational programmes were designed and ran by the Greek Super League and the Hellenic Football Federation: The first is the scheme "*Staying on side: How to stop Match-Fixing*" (Transparency International, 2013), an educational workshop delivered to young players (playing in Under 17 and Under 20 national championships) who are urged to care for "[their] team, [their] career, [their] responsibility" (according to the programme's motto), has been introduced by the Greek Super League. This programme ran for the duration of a season and aimed at raising awareness on the effects match-fixing can have on the future of the sport and each individual player's career. More than 800 players and coaches attended the workshop and were informed on the above mentioned repercussions of match-fixing, based on the principle that *ethics* and *integrity* can be taught and as a result key actors can be trained to support fair play and reject corruption, leading to a better future for football (see Segal, 2013). The programme was sponsored by 'Transparency International', which aims at addressing corruption in all aspects of modern life (Transparency International, 2013).

The second set of programmes consists of educational courses run throughout the last few seasons, promoting *fair play* and *ethical conduct* in football to high school students (Super League Greece, 2013). Through these courses, the students were informed of the idea of fair play in football and were given the opportunity to appreciate the benefits of following such practices in regards to enjoying the sport and protecting its future. The programme was supported by the major football clubs of the country that urged their players to deliver some of the courses themselves. These courses were delivered in schools around the capital of the country and were welcomed by the local authorities and the Ministry of Education.

Both 'Staying on side' and the fair play programmes were run in conjunction with the European Professional Leagues Association (EPFL) and aimed at educating potential key actors in order to prevent match-fixing and non-fair play behaviour in general. By educating these individuals on the effects their decisions can have, and enabling them to visualise the repercussions of their actions, prevention of corruption can be achieved (see also Haberfeld and Sheehan, 2013).

The basis on which the programmes were designed follows the INTERPOL-FIFA Anti-Corruption Training Initiative, which started in May 2011 with "*the overall objective of tackling sport corruption in football, with a principal focus on illegal and irregular betting and match fixing, through providing various training programmes to improve key individuals*" (Abbott & Sheehan, 2013: 282). According to the Anti-Corruption Initiative protecting the *integrity* of football can be supported by three pillars; training, education, and prevention. All three pillars entail raising awareness on the phenomenon of match-fixing and the ways in which each individual actor can resist and report match-fixing, as well as how information on match-fixing can be shared between international organisations, in order that *transparency* of new updates on the phenomenon to be ensured (see Abbott & Sheehan, 2013).

Additional measures on addressing corruption on a European level including Greece focused on the appropriate governance of the sport, which as Jones (2013) suggests, resembles the way in which problems would be dealt with in the corporate world. These measures included the introduction of tighter *financial regulations on the clubs*, which was supported by UEFA's financial fair play guidelines (UEFA, 2015a; b), and the establishment of firmer control on key events, such as match-days, through each league's 'independent official auditors'. The financial regulations imposed called for additional transparency on the accounts of each club, while ensuring that any money owed to either companies and individuals or the country would be paid in order for the clubs to be permitted to participate in the season's championship. Introducing a centrally controlled electronic tax system would allow for each club's ticket issue (one of the key income sources) to be managed and regulated more closely, while eliminating the room for individual errors or favouritism (see also Dimitropoulos, 2006). Appointing 'independent official auditors' to each club on a match-day would then ensure that detailed reports on these key events would be provided to the pertinent governing bodies, tax authorities and the police.

Finally, a tighter control on betting was regarded as a priority, having been identified as a major factor for corruption in football. The additional and firmer control was assisted by the introduction of the UEFA Betting Fraud Detection System (BFDS) (UEFA, 2014). The system allows for all legal betting activities world-wide to be monitored, in order for any irregularities to be noticed. These irregularities include unexpectedly high activity on significantly favourable odds for rather unanticipated results before and especially during a match. The system allows for these activities to be identified and for the betting system supporting them to be blocked. The system has also been used in order for matches that have already been concluded to be reviewed thoroughly, especially when suspicion was raised due to unexpected events taking place within their duration. The BFDS enables the analysis team to examine these matches carefully and decide whether they can be considered 'questionable' or 'exceptionally questionable'. Once a match has been classified in any of these two categories, the national football association is informed in order for an investigation to begin. Interestingly enough, 41 Super League and Football League matches played between 2008 and 2011 were considered to be 'exceptionally questionable', according to the system, probing the Hellenic Football Federation to investigate them further (see Proto Thema, 2010). It is worth noting that a significant number of Greek matches are being reported as 'questionable' or 'exceptionally questionable' by UEFA each season (UEFA, 2015a). All matches reported are being investigated by the Hellenic Football Federation, which has so far deemed only those 41 matches as 'exceptionally questionable' and disregarded all other reports.

Football-related corrupt practices in Greece

As mentioned earlier, through the analysis of the data collected, three major examples of corrupt football practices can be identified:

- match-fixing;
- ticket 'tricks'; and
- tax evasion through fake tax and insurance certificates.

These examples will be discussed here in some detail, with a focus on the individuals and structures that have not been addressed by the corruption prevention schemes presented above.

Match-fixing

The match-fixing web revealed through the official case files of the *Koriopolis scandal*, appears to comprise a complex figuration of a number of actors, participating willingly or unwillingly in order for the events and final results of particular matches to be set according to pre-arranged agreements. The actors involved in match-fixing range from those individuals who initiate the process to unwilling members who participate under the threat of physical harm. As the following analysis will show, only a few of these individuals have been involved in the prevention programmes, with the initiators of the whole process, in particular remaining not yet addressed.

As was presented earlier in the study, the educational prevention programmes have targeted young players and potential managers, while neglecting the professional footballers currently playing in the top tier of Greek football. Yet, due to their role as key constituents in the process that can secure a desired result for a match, players have been participating in match-fixing willingly or unwillingly. It has often been suggested that their involvement was a result of intimidation or fear imposed on them by the owners or presidents of the clubs. However, while threats have been recorded as a successful means of ensuring collaboration in match-fixing, additional evidence suggests that players' involvement in the process can in reality be an informed and even calculated decision. In fact, this was argued by a player on one of the many occasions when one of the authors was present.

> "I had to do it [ensure a particular result was achieved]. All five of us [pointing to an additional four players] were in. We got some good money out of it and it was so easy. They're not paying us enough, so we have to find another way to make money."

Footballers may well be aware of the repercussions their actions can have, but they choose to neglect these in order for 'easy and quick' profit to be gained. However, closer scrutiny of the transcripts provided by EYP suggests that the Presidents (owners or chairmen) of the clubs are the individuals who initiate the process of match-fixing and ultimately ensure that the agreed result of each match will be achieved.

According to the transcripts of recorded conversations, the Club Presidents, after being informed of a favourable betting rate for a match involving the club which they own or lead, will attempt to reach an agreement on the required result that would secure them that rate. This agreement is either reached with the President of the club they are playing against, the referee, or the players of either or both clubs. This mechanism whereby an agreement is reached entails either the promise of reward (*"I'll give you the number of my booker and you can bet a few grand on it and get a little something for yourself"*), or the threat of harm to someone's career or physical health (*"if you don't do it, my boys will break your legs and you won't be able to kick a ball ever in your life"*). The Presidents are also in charge of ensuring that the desired result is achieved and are, therefore, in regular contact before and throughout each match with those individuals who are involved in the agreement.

Another category of key actors that have not been addressed by the new measures is one that was involved in one of the biggest scandals in Greek football in the early 1990s, namely *referees*. The referees' role entails executing, rather than initiating, the match-fixing agreement. Their power depends on exerting significant influence on the final result of a match through the decisions they make. Based on this power and on the fact that their decisions cannot in practice be disputed, a pre-arranged result can be achieved through referees' collaboration. The first highly documented match-fixing scandal in Greece in the 1990s was in fact structured around a mechanism of fixing matches by selecting specific referees for particular matches in order for the outcomes of those matches to be decided. A number of referees have in fact faced legal action against their involvement in both recent match-fixing scandals. As the data show, referees have agreed to influence the course of matches in order for desired results to be attained, by making wrong decisions or turning a blind eye at key moments during matches. Once again, the evidence suggests that both rewards and threats have been used to convince referees to participate in match-fixing.

Finally, bookmakers or illegal agents have also been identified as key actors in match-fixing, since they provide the incentives that primarily and predominantly create the need for this phenomenon (see Skokas, 2012). Whether legally or illegally, the betting rates they set and promote act as inducements and rewards for any of the above mentioned actors who decide to fix a match. Even though tighter control measures have been implemented by both international and national governing bodies (FIFA, UEFA, the Greek Super League) and local betting providers (OPAP), as was discussed earlier in this paper, betting still remains widely uncontrollable.

As the above analysis of match-fixing has demonstrated, the individuals involved in the process include groups that are not currently addressed by the strategies and structures that have been introduced. Indeed, the structure of this complex web is not even sufficiently examined for the true underlying issues to be identified. Additionally, even within groups that the current programmes have captured, the element of intention behind their choice to participate in match-fixing is not addressed.

Ticket tricks

Football clubs rely heavily on income from match-day ticket sales, particularly in lower divisions where the agreements about sponsorship and TV rights are not very lucrative (Triandafyllou, 2012). However, compared with the other sources of income, ticket sales have also been considered the least controlled income stream since the actual transaction is completed when the exchange of money for a paper ticket takes place, without any additional paper trail. In order for this income source to be more closely monitored, additional measures have been introduced that have included detailed reporting of the tickets sold and the appointment of 'official league auditors' for each match (see Kathimerini, 2012).

The process of selling and reporting the tickets sold (through which the taxable income is also calculated) is further problematic by the existence of an additional match-day ticket category to which most people do not have access. This category, known as *season (card exchange) tickets*, was originally created in order for an account to be kept of the number of season ticket holders that attend each match, while allowing for the income generated through the season tickets to be distributed throughout each season. According to this process, the tax authorities would then rely on each club to report the exact number of season card exchange tickets validated at each match, representing the number of season ticket holders who had attended, which is then used to calculate the income tax liability of the club for each match. The process would require each season ticket holder to visit the ticketing office before entering the stadium, in order for him or her to get an additional paper exchange ticket. The validation of these tickets would then take place when entering each stadium, and would be overseen by both security staff and the league's 'official auditors'.

The way in which this process takes place in practice, however, deviates from the original plan. The league's 'official auditors' rarely oversee the validation process in detail, and instead prefer a more indirect method of calculation. At the end of each match, the auditors provide the ticket officers of the home club with a rough estimate of the number of season ticket holders who have entered the stadium, in order for the corresponding exchange tickets to be 'validated'. This estimate is based on the auditors' vague guess of the number of season ticket holders, as well as their predisposition towards the home club. Since validating the exchange tickets using an actual validation machine would be rather 'impractical' at this point, the 'validation' that takes place involves manually shredding the tickets that should have been given to the season card holders before entering the stadium.

Interestingly, the estimated number suggested by the 'auditors' is rarely undisputed. On the contrary, this number becomes a negotiation topic between the auditor and the head of the ticketing department of the club who aims to reach agreement on the lowest number possible. The auditor is often asked to be understanding and lower the number substantially and this is regularly achieved. The final number agreed is then documented in the official reports of the match which are then signed by the auditor and submitted to the tax service, the local police and the league's governing body. These reports will be also used by the club accountants in order for the tax liability to be calculated. It is worth noting that this negotiation is anticipated by both parties and even encouraged by higher league officials. On one of the many occasions when one of us was present, an auditor admitted that he was planning to be understanding towards a particular club, since one of the vice-presidents of the league in which the club was playing had personally asked him to.

However, requesting the auditors' consent to disobey the laws is not limited to the above mentioned negotiation. A more complex and demanding negotiation process can also take place on the occasion of a club being unable to issue an adequate number of match-day tickets caused either by financial problems (lack of tax or insurance certificates, for example, as discussed below) or a simple miscalculation of likely demand. The auditors are then asked to agree to 'turn a blind eye' in order for unofficial tickets to be used, thereby allowing for an exchange of money to take place without any paper trail. The process that they are in fact agreeing to overlook involves the selling of unofficial tickets that have not been issued by the relevant governing body or stamped by the local police and tax service. The result is untraceable and therefore un-taxable income for the club. In other words, the auditors are asked to sign the official reports stating that no additional tickets were sold while unofficially allowing non-ticket holders to enter the stadium.

Surprisingly enough, this complex negotiation has proved successful and has even been encouraged by the league's administration. It is worth noting that on one occasion when one of the authors was present, a vice-president of the league in which a particular club was playing joined the auditor and the head of the ticketing department before the negotiation began and told the auditor to "*look after those guys as best as [he] can*". The head of the ticketing department was thus encouraged to ask for a further reduction of the 'estimated' number of season ticket holders during the negotiation that followed.

Fake tax and insurance certificates

On the basis of the additional control measures introduced by the governing bodies of the sport, in collaboration with the Ministry of Culture and Sport and the Ministry of Finance, more thorough procedures were gradually introduced for football clubs. As a result, and in order to complete key tasks, such as signing a new player, getting permission to participate in the championship or even issuing tickets for the next home match, an additional step has had to be taken. A tax certificate or an insurance certificate has to be obtained from the local tax authority or employees' trust fund (see Dimitropoulos, 2006). A *tax certificate* can be issued when the club has settled any tax liabilities owed to the government, by either paying the debt off or by agreeing to a repayment scheme. Similarly, an *insurance certificate* is issued when the club has settled any outstanding debt regarding the employees' national insurance contributions, by paying it off or by reaching a settlement with the trust fund. By making one or both of these documents compulsory the governing bodies have ensured that the clubs should be kept 'on a short leash' regarding their payments to the government and the employees' insurance contribution.

However, Greek football clubs have succeeded in discovering creative ways to avoid this additional hurdle and continue their 'questionable' practices with significant short-term success. Firstly, securing a number of consecutive settlement agreements can 'buy' a club some valuable time, ranging from one to two months *i.e.* from the moment an agreement is reached to the moment it collapses at which point the next agreed payment becomes overdue. This short time window can allow for the certificates required to be issued and tasks in hand to be completed (while these temporary certificates are valid), without any additional payments being made to either the tax or the national insurance debt.

Secondly, using personal connections in the local tax service or the local employees' trust fund office in order for exceptions to be made regarding the club, has been a popular practice, especially on the part of football clubs located in provincial areas of Greece. Favouritism, or simply asking employees to turn a blind eye when a club has been unable to obtain a new tax or insurance certificate, has proved to be particularly successful in Greek football, with a number of smaller clubs succeeding in completing various crucial tasks, such as issuing tickets for the majority of the matches of the season, without a valid certificate having been issued. This practice is *gradually* being abandoned by the clubs, since the newly introduced online countrywide filing system does not allow for individual employees to alter or omit any of the required steps, making it increasingly difficult if not impossible for favouritism to succeed (see Siomopoulos, 2013).

Thirdly, a rather risky and even more creative way of avoiding this additional hurdle was invented: this is the production of *fake tax and insurance certificates*. This practice attracted considerable attention, when a number of first division clubs, currently facing charges and possible relegation for their actions, were caught using fake certificates in order for new players to be signed and tickets for home matches to be issued (Livanios, 2014). Regardless of the attention this practice has received, however, creating and using a fake certificate is still one of the most successful and common ways to overcome the additional controls in Greek football. According to this practice, a fake tax or insurance certificate is created by the employees of a club, who ensure that the final product looks identical to an authentic tax or insurance certificate. The only thing that differs from the prototype used is the protocol number, which is updated accordingly, in order for the tax office employees receiving the document to be convinced. This fake document is then filed along with the other necessary documentation, depending on the task in hand. On the odd occasion when the fake certificate has to be delivered in person, for example in order for match tickets to be approved by the local tax service, the person in charge of presenting the document is offered additional advice on how to behave ("*act natural*", "*say that you don't know anything about it*") and what to do if the fake document is identified ("*call the President in case something goes wrong*").

Finally, a documented way of avoiding the additional controls, which is often used when all the above described practices fail, is the use of personal political connections by the Presidents of the clubs. On such occasions, it is not the employees of the club asking local tax employees to turn a blind eye to a missing paper; it is the Presidents of the club asking similar favours from political figures who are then requested to use their power over the local or national authorities and down to the administrators, so that the favours can be granted.

Given the secrecy surrounding this method, little information exists as to the identities of the individuals involved, or the actual discussions that take place between them. What can be presented, however, is an overview of how this method works. Once an unexpected problem occurs, the President of the club is notified and is provided with details about the issue. The President then approaches a well-known politician who is often a close personal contact, in order to request a favour for 'overcoming this obstacle'. Since this approach takes place privately and often involves a single phone call from one party to the other, little information exists on the identity of the politicians engaged in the process. What has been observed, however, is the third step in this method, namely the result of the political figure's influence. Depending on the nature of the problem, the politician makes the relevant authority (for example, the local tax service) aware of his or her personal interest and ensures that the particular authority stops the process. This step often entails a personal phone call made by the politician to the person blocking this progress (*e.g.* the director of the local tax service) who is then asked to "turn a blind eye" in his or her favour. Even though information on the actual content of this phone call cannot be obtained, this method has proven to be particularly successful in Greek football. As a director of a local tax service confided to a club's employee during our research:

> "I shouldn't really be doing this for you [signing the document that allowed the club to issue match tickets without a tax certificate)], but I am. I personally don't mind what happens with the club. But if he [referring to the politician and pointing at the phone] comes through, then I am happy. I want to keep him happy, because I don't want to be stuck here for long. He is a good connection to have and I want him to be happy with me".

Discussion

Corruption in Greek football has significant negative repercussions for the sport. The measures that have been introduced to deal with corrupt practices in Greek football are, of course, positive developments. However, they tend to ignore important aspects, not least the *actors* and *processes* that are *integral* to the commission of corrupt practice. The educational programmes focus on players and prospective players while overlooking important actors that are instrumental in the commission of corrupt practices such as presidents of the clubs, referees and betting agents. Specifically, the individuals involved in the role of the President of each club have attracted considerable attention because they included people with dubious legal or even criminal past and equally 'questionable' motives (Dabilis, 2011). It is worth noting that although a *Fit and Proper* test has been a legal requirement of the Greek law since 1999 (Law 2725/1999) (Efimerida Kyverniseos, 1999); in reality, it has never been actively applied.

Similarly, despite the numerous promises that the appointment and training of referees through the Hellenic Football Federation will become a transparent and closely controlled process, this has not been the case. Moreover, with regards to betting, one of the key drawbacks of the BFDS is that the system can examine and control the *legal* betting activities world-wide, however, it cannot trace and, therefore, assist to restrain any of the numerous *illegal* betting practices (UEFA, 2014). Unfortunately, as it was underlined by UEFA (2014), these practices account for 70% of the overall betting activities globally. The existence of illegal betting agents often located in Asian countries and, therefore, operating under different regulations have allowed for betting to remain a key lucrative incentive for match-fixing.

Even though tighter financial regulations were introduced gradually throughout the country and are now implemented in professional Greek football, a number of creative solutions have been invented in order to avoid situational constraints. The way in which these measures have been put in operation in Greek football has not stopped corruption. On the contrary, it has created the need for more elaborate or resourceful ways to maintain or even increase the level of corruption within it (see Jones, 2013) while exposing *cultural* and *economic* conditions that are conducive to corruption, as well as the general half-heartedness in dealing with the phenomenon.

An important indigenous cultural condition favouring football-related corruption in Greece is politics. As Dimitropoulos (2010) has noted in his work, Greek politicians have been unjustifiably favourable towards football clubs either in a direct or an indirect manner, in fear of the significant political cost entailed in possibly denying them extravagant favours. As a result, the role political figures have held in this practice has not been addressed, allowing for this method to remain successful in overcoming any problems created in any of the above mentioned measure against corruption (Eleftherotypia, 2013a). Perhaps unlike other contexts, what happens in Greece is that the clubs participating in corruption are in essence protected against any significant punishment by the politicians of the locality the clubs are based in. The level of interconnectedness between football and politics in Greece is – among other – exemplified by the fact that the current mayor of Piraeus (hometown of Olympiakos FC), Yiannis Moralis, who was elected in 2014, was formerly the vice-chairman of Olympiakos (Kathimerini, 2015).

Measures implemented also ignore or overlook the *financial* football-related context in the country, which is, of course, an extension of the general financial and entrepreneurial landscape in Greece. Firstly, since the beginning of the 1980s when the sport became 'professionalised' and football clubs in the first, second and third division were transformed into companies, football has been used as a platform of action for extremely powerful individuals who use clubs and the popular support for them not only as an income source *per se* (season tickets, advertisements, merchandise, *etc.*) which is particularly the case for big clubs, but also as a vehicle for tax evasion and money laundering, as a protection shield against the state, and as leverage towards securing state bids. From the moment football clubs are companies that are to be protected as 'investments', sport itself becomes a secondary concern.

Moreover, the 'paranga' mechanism mentioned earlier in this study ('referee fixing') facilitated corrupt practices in primarily two ways: firstly, it consolidated the extremely high 'outcome certainty' within the Greek football causing significant competitive imbalance among the clubs (see Eleftherotypia, 2013b). This imbalance did not only lead to the creation of 'big' and 'small' teams, as Szymanski and Kesenne (2004) suggest, but also to the formation of 'rich' and 'poor' clubs. As Schmidt and Berri (2001) note, since the performance on the field in professional competitive sports has a direct impact on their financial income, the gap between these two groups is affected by the competitive balance or imbalance of the league. The high outcome certainty in Greek football has arguably led to high levels of competitive imbalance within the professional leagues of the sport. This has led to the creation of 'rich' and 'poor' clubs, with the gap between these two categories being widened year after year as the clubs' financial records show (Direction Business Reports, 2015).

Another way to underline this competitive imbalance within the league would be to examine the level of probability of determining the winner of the league (see Buzzacchi *et al.*, 2004). Taking into consideration that the Greek Championship has been won by the same club 17 times within the last 19 years, outcome certainty has reached an extreme high level in Greek football, with the Super League often being characterised as a 'monopoly' (see Eleftherotypia, 2013b), with all the financial implications this entails. This also meant that no other major clubs in the country were able to profit from such an achievement creating a condition in which even major football clubs face deteriorating finances[3]: a situation that could have been avoided with participation in Champions' League and the resulting income from basic allocation and performance bonuses from UEFA, and TV revenue.

In addition, the 'paranga' was instrumental in corruption becoming widespread in Greek football in the presence of self-governance and autonomy of the Greek football in which state monitoring is virtually absent. It created an environment of distrust in which most clubs had to 'pick sides' if they wanted to guarantee preferential treatment, better positioning in play-offs, avoidance of relegation, increased chances of promotion or playing in European competitions *etc*.

This pervasive corruption in the world of Greek football has been demonstrated to basically act as providing a comparative advantage to those structures which do not operate according to officially established rules. Inevitably, some corrupt activities such as match-fixing in this endemically corrupt environment, have become viable, rather short-term solutions for many football clubs. Moreover, it is a way of making sure that money is being made under the enormous financial pressure that most Greek football clubs face in the current entrepreneurial and financial landscape of the country. Reasons for the financial hardship of football clubs (see also Spapens and Olfers, 2015) include the continuous reduction in clubs' income especially after 2009, the reduced attendance in Greek stadia with an average of 4.328 spectators per Super League match, and the general low commercial value (brand finance) of the Greek football (Siemos, 2014). Corruption lowers the stimulus for quality which does not go unnoticed by the public.

Though these data may not be precise, for the methodological reasons given in this paper, the order of magnitude is likely to be about right: it gives an idea of the scale of the 'real' problem, which naturally has severe financial repercussion for individual players. In fact, the way in which footballers are treated in modern Greek football in terms of finances has led to numerous official complaints issued to the international governing bodies of the sport. This in turn

---

[3]   One of the top and most popular Greek clubs, AEK, was a casualty of this situation declaring bankruptcy and seeking relegation to third division in 2013.

resulted in the International Federation of Professional Footballers (FIFPro) issuing an official announcement, advising footballers to avoid signing contracts with Greek clubs because there is some type of personnel mismanagement and bad leadership not inspiring integrity (FIFPro, 2013). Within the formation of this financial imbalance among clubs that we mentioned above, corrupt practices within football clubs are very much the product of the pre-emptive fear of the club 'not making it' and losing their position in the football industry.

Conclusion

The measures implemented ignore that corruption in the Greek football business world is not any more an aberration, a temporary anomic diversion from an industry guided by good values, or a set of immoral actions taken by individuals that 'hide' behind the rules in order to disconnect from any moral responsibility. Morals have been relocated from the core to the margins to act as a guide to individuals and entities such as football clubs who compete hard in the football business environment (see Hall, 2012). With such a powerful amoral injunction at the core of the Greek football industry, and failure punished by the threat of extinction from the football scene, it is unsurprising that many will resort to largely undetected unethical or criminal means (see also Hobbs, 2013). Corrupt practices in the Greek football are not the intrusion of 'anomie' (normlessness) at the core of an industry displacing traditional values and norms but the *new norm* (see Hall, 2012).

The measures implemented give the false impression of being able to accommodate ethical sociability. This neglect the bitter reality of Greek football: clubs must continue to make profits or 'die'. In difficult circumstances such as these mentioned earlier, ethical restraints can easily be overridden. As financial pressures intensify in Greece in general, and the Greek football industry in particular, ethical restraints for a range of actors associated with football clubs are under pressure by corrosive forces that are imposed on the football industry by the economy's pathogenic core (Hall, 2012; see also Hall and Antonopoulos, 2016). Aggressive neoliberal political economy that has spread to Greek football now present us with corrupt practices as the 'only game in town'.

References

Abbott, J. and D. Sheehan, The INTERPOL approach to tackling match-fixing in football. In M. Haberfeld and D. Sheehan (*ed.*) *Match-fixing in international sports.* (pp.263-288) London: Springer, 2013

Antonopoulos, G.A. and N. Tagarov, Greece: The politics of crime. In P. Gounev and V. Ruggiero (eds.), *Corruption and Organised Crime in Europe: Illegal Partnerships.* (pp.125-143) Oxford: Routledge, 2012.

Brooks, G., A. Aleem and M. Button, *Fraud, corruption and sport.* Basingstoke: Palgrave Macmillan, 2013

Bull, M. and J. Newell. *Corruption in Contemporary Politics.* London: Palgrave, 2003

Buzzacchi, L., S. Szymanski and T. Valletti, Equality of opportunity and equality of outcome. *Journal of Industry, Competition and Trade*, 2004, 3(3), 167-186.

Dabilis, A., 'Greek Football Turns Ugly', *Southeast European Times*, November 21, 2011

de Quetteville, H., ''Godfathers' of Greek football face crackdown', *The Telegraph*, February 2, 2003.

Dimitropoulos, P., 'The Financial Performance of the Greek Football', *Choregia*, 2010, 6(1), 5-28

Direction Business Reports, *Football Clubs' revenue 2013/14*, Athens: Direction Business Network, 2015

Efimerida Kyverniseos, 'Law 2725/1999/A-121 Amateur-Professional Sports', *FEK A'* 121/17-6-1999

Eleftherotypia, 'Krataei xronia afti i...mpoxa', *Eleftherotypia*, March 13, 2011.

Eleftherotypia, 'Afxanonde k plithinonde oi katigoroumenoi gia ta stimena', *Eleftherotypia*, May 19, 2013a

Eleftherotypia, 'Greek «monopoly»', *Eleftherotypia,* March 12, 2013b.

European Commission, *Match-Fixing in Sport: A Mapping of Criminal Law Provisions in EU-27.* Brussels: European Commission, 2012

FIFPro, 'FIFPRO warns players of clubs' non-payment', *FIFPro*, 2013, accessed on September 29, 2015. Available online at:
http://www.fifpro.org/en/news/fifpro-warns-players-of-clubs-nonpayment

Gorse, S. and S. Chadwick, Conceptualising corruption in sport. *European Business Review*, 2010, July/August, 40-45

Haberfeld, M. and D. Sheehan (eds.), *Match-fixing in international sports.* New York: Springer, 2013

Hall, S., *Theorising crime and deviance.* London: Sage, 2012

Hall, S. and G.A. Antonopoulos, Troika, austerity and the reluctant resort to criminality in Greece'. In D. Whyte and J. Wiegratz (eds.) *Neoliberalism and the Moral Economy of Fraud*. London: Routledge, 2016.

Hill, D., *The Fix: soccer and organised crime*. London: McClelland & Stewart, 2010

Hobbs, D., *Lush life*. Oxford: OUP, 2013

Homewood, B., 'Olympiakos Champions League spot safe for now', *Reuters*, June, 30, 2015 accessed on September 29, 2015, available at http://uk.reuters.com/article/2015/06/30/uk-soccer-uefa-greece-idUKKCN0PA21120150630

Jones, K.L., Compliance mechanism as a tool of prevention. In M. Haberfeld and D. Sheehan (eds.) *Match-fixing in international sports*. (pp.199-228) London: Springer, 2013

Kapranos, D., 'O 'Theios', o 'Kokkaliaris' kai o 'Periergos'', *Kathimerini,* April 7, 2002

Kathimerini, 'Kathimerini appeals for Supreme Court reversal', *Kathimerini,* September 5, 2003

Kathimerini, 'Pos dianemondai i eisprakseis kai pou kataligoun ta esoda', *Kathimerini*, January 29, 2012

Kathimerini, 'Volos Mayor, Beos, among 85 to face trial over match-fixing', *Kathimerini*, July 30, 2015.

Kovac, A., Europe's football battlefield', *International Policy Digest*, 2014, September 26

Lambropoulou, E., Myths and realities about corruption in public administration and its discourse in Greece. *Amsterdam Law Forum*, 2012, 4(3), 77-96

Livanios, S., Vasileio paranomias, *Eleftherotypia*, September 17, 2014.

Mplounas, T., Apaksiomeno to Elliniko Podosfairo', *Kathimerini,* November 11, 2014.

Polychroniou, C., Political culture and corruption in Greece: A synergistic relationship, *Online Journal*, 2008 http://onlinejournal.com/artman/publish/article_2911.shtml

Proto Thema, 'Sti fora ta ypopta pexnidia', *Proto Thema*, April 26, 2010

Rumsby. B., 'Match-fixing case in Greece just adds to sense of Greek chaos', *The Telegraph*, July 15, 2015

Schmidt, M. and D. Berri, Competitive balance and attendance, *Journal of Sports Economics*, 2001, 2(1), 145-167

Segal, L., The role of the academe in sports integrity: the objectives and shape of a sports integrity training course. In M. Haberfeld and D. Sheehan (eds.) *Match-fixing in international sports*. (pp.303-330) London: Springer, 2013

Siemos, V., Epaggelmatiko Podosfairo & I Syneisfora tou stin Elliniki Econo-mia. Presentation to *Greek Super League*, Athens, February, 2014

Siomopoulos, D., To sxedio gia tin katapolemisi tis diafthoras se efories kai teloneia. *To Vima*, May 10, 2013

Skokas, I., Epaggelma, Paranomos Book. *To Vima*, October 21, 2012

Spapens, T. and M. Olfers, Match-fixing: The current discussion in Europe and the case of the Netherlands, *European Journal of Crime, Criminal Law and Criminal Justice,* 2015, 23(4), 333-358

Super League Greece, *Annual Report*. Athens: Super League Greece, 2013

Szymanski, S. and S. Kesenne, Competitive balance and gate revenue sharing in team sports. *Journal of Industrial Economics*, 2004, 52(1), 165-177

The Guardian, 'Sixteen Reportedly Charged in Greek Match-fixing Allega-tions', *The Guardian*, December 4, 2014

Transparency International, *Staying on side*. Berlin: Transparency International, 2013

Transparency International, *Greece*. Accessed on 30 September 2016, available at: www.transparency.org/country#GRC

Triandafyllou, A., 'Erevna: ta esoda ton omadon tis Superleague', *Goal*, Sep-tember 9, 2012

UEFA, *Sports betting monitoring and fraud detection systems*. The Hague: UEFA, 2014.

UEFA, 'Financial fair play', *UEFA*, 2015a. Accessed on 29 September 2015, available at www.uefa.com/community/news/newsid=2064391.html

UEFA, 'Disciplinary updates', *UEFA*, 2015b. Accessed on 9 October 2015, available at www.uefa.org/disciplinary/index.html

Banking in Ukraine: The self-created monster of the financial industry?

Anna Markovska and *Alexey Serduyk*[1]

> The truth is that all men having
> power ought to be distrusted
> *James Madison*

Introduction: Who can live well in Ukraine? Robber barons!

The Avizo case

Almost a quarter of a Century ago a huge bank robbery in Ukraine took place: no arms, no break-in but an old-fashioned teletype machine was used. Between June and October 1993, illegal teletype equipment in Ukraine issued false Bank Orders, with all the required passwords and keys, in order to transfer funds from The Central Bank to at least seven Ukrainian banks. The total sum transferred was 153.130.600.000 krb. Almost all funds were immediately cashed or transferred outside of Ukraine. The official exchange rate in 1993 was $1=4.539 krb, so the total amount was $33.736.638 (Vitrenko, 2005). In the early 1990s, long before computerisation of the banks, banks required bank order to issue payments (called Avizo). From 1993-1994, most of the Avizos's legal bank orders were sent via a teletype service. The key to the success of these illegal transactions was in obtaining the password for the codes of this teletype service. Banks transferred the money almost immediately, but checked the Avizo's payments only once a month. This system allowed criminals to collect, and

[1] Dr. Anna Markovska is Senior Lecturer in Criminology, Department of Humanities and Social Sciences, Faculty of Arts, Law and Social Sciences, Anglia Ruskin University, Cambridge. Dr. Alexeye is Deputy Head of Scientific Research Laboratory of Crime Enforcement of the Kharkiv National University of Internal Affairs, Ukraine. The authors would like to acknowledge the financial support of the Department of Humanities and Social Sciences, Anglia Ruskin University.

subsequently conceal, the procedes of crime. During 1993-1994 these criminal transfers became known as 'the 3 billion affairs' after the losses calculated. Everyone was surprised by the scale of this fraud. The actors involved were highly professional, as was their knowledge of the operational technologies and structure of the banking system in Ukraine. The criminals managed to get access to all the required key information for the teletype codes within the country. This knowledge was concealed by the National Bank of Ukraine. More than 100 criminal cases followed. However, only three individuals were arrested and one car was confiscated, although the investigation into this case lasted for over 6 years and 160 volumes of information were collected. Kiev City Court heard the case for more than three years, and none of the accused pleaded guilty, arguing that they were compromised by the others. Furthermore, in the years that followed, most of the accused received political or financial sector promotions within Ukraine (Vitrenko, 2005). The funds stolen were state funds, belonging to the people of Ukraine, so the general population suffers rather those who keep the keys and passwords to the state budget.

Very early in the years following independence, Ukrainian officials learned that the best way to get rich is to rob their own country. In the 25 years that followed, numerous scams were created by party officials, members of parliament and industry representatives to defraud the country. The examples include laundering embezzled state subsidies aimed to help mining industry (Zabyelina, 2015; Forbes Ukraine, 2013), to setting up counterfeit vodka production on a national level (Anticor, 2016). We observe that the safest way to commit fraud in Ukraine is to defraud the state.

Do ordinary people trust politicians? The simple answer is no. Bekeshkina (2015) reported that in 2015 Ukrainians generally trust voluntary organisations and the church, and put much less trust in politicians, judges, police and security services. There is a reason for that. The Orange revolution in 2004 and in Maidan 2013- 2014 have failed to significantly reduce the level of corruption. Kurkov (2014) notes that, in 2014, Ukrainians spent *"only the first eight days of their protest fighting for the choice of Europe. After that, the mass protests were about a rogue state that featured an incredibly high level of corruption and a lack of respect for human rights."* Fighting corruption in politics in 2015 proved to be as difficult as finding the guilty for the *Avizo scam* in 1993 (elaborated later) athough anti-corruption legistation has been extended. In 2006 Ukraine joined the Group of States Against Corruption, and in 2011 established the National Anti-Corruption Committee. In May 2014, an Anti-Corruption Initiative was established. Under a corrupt president such as Yanukovych, these measures seemed to have little effect, and corruption charges seemed to be filed mainly against political opponents. Would things change after the Maiden revolution? According to the 2016 Transparency International Corruption Perception Index, the improvement is small: from 25 in 2013 to 27 in 2015 (ranking is from 1-100, with 1 the most corrupt). With that score Ukraine is just above Nigeria but under Timor-Leste. Clearly more transparency is needed and one of the measures is the declaration of wealth by politicians and high officials. What would help to reveal this?

The 31st October, 2016 was the deadline for Ukrainian MPs to hand in their wealth declarations. They are now obliged to declare their income and assets in a public database for the first time (Euronews, 2016). These declarations resulted in significant public anger. For example, the Prime Minister, Voldymyr Groysman, declared that he and his wife had a total of 1,2 million dollars in bank accounts and 460.000 euros in cash, and a collection of luxury watches. On the basis of these declarations Reuters (2016) estimated that "the 24 members of the Ukrainian cabinet together have nearly \$7 million, just in cash".

Just a few weeks before MPs declared their wealth, the results of the poll by the International Republican Institute's (IRI) Centre for Insights in Survey Research were published. According to this study, 72% of Ukrainians think that "the country is going into the wrong direction". The poll also uncovered pessimism about the economy: "a combined total of 74% saying the economic situation in Ukraine has either 'worsened somewhat' or 'worsened a lot'." (*Ibid.*). This poll also suggested that 18% of Ukrainians need to save money to buy food, and an additional 35% report they need to save to buy clothing and shoes (IRI, 2016). People do not trust politicians (they never did) and ordinary people are busy surviving by all means, as always.

The role of trust and social capital

Trust is an important part of building an effective state and a financial system. Why for example, did the MPs not tend to keep their money in the banks? Is that an indication of general untrustworthiness of the Cabinet, the way to avoid taxes or something else? Though eyebrows may be raised at his wealth, the Prime Minister and his Cabinet members are not alone in keeping their money in cash. In fact, many prefer to keep their cash outside of the banking system which radiates anything but trust, the foundation of any financial system.

The efficient functioning of the modern economies is dependent on social trust. Economists consider trust as a carefully calculated long-term interest, which brings different groups of people together and results in voluntary contracts. It has been argued that the level of the economic development reflects the level of trust in the society. Fukuyma (2001) finds a possible explanation of corruption in a system with a narrow radius of social trust, where different standards of behaviour would apply to different groups of people. In such system, the 'transaction cost', the cost of legal agreement, can be substantial. Thus, Ukraine has weak voluntary associations because people do not trust each other. When the level of social trust is low, the ability of people to co-operate is reduced, and long-term co-operation may not be possible.

Discussing different types of trust from sociological perspective, Anheier and Kendall (2000: 9) point that "*non-profit organisations become trustworthy intermediaries, located between supply and demand.*" Researchers note that many non-profit organisations are religious institutions, and 'thus' they are more likely to be trusted. Naturally that should not be taken for granted, as the sexual abuse scandals in the Catholic church has demonstrated. However, it is intersting to note that non-profit organisations and especially the volunteering sector and the church represent sectors that people in 2016 Ukraine trust more than any official institution (Bekeshkina, 2016).

Modern societies consist of many different groups interacting with each other to provide the wide spectrum of social trust, and thus economic and political benefits. Fukuyma (2001) considers the economic function of social capital and argues that it reduces the transaction cost associated with formal co-ordination mechanisms such as contracts and bureaucratic rules. It is argued that if the level of social trust is low, the ability of people to co-operate is reduced, and the danger of state interference in all sectors of life is particularly high. Greenwald and Stiglitz (1987) and later Bossone (2002) note that asymmetric information exist where one side of the market has better information than the other on options and incentives, and the less informed side is aware of the informational disadvantage. In Ukraine, asymmetric information advantage is used by the powerful elite to defraud the state to which should be added that many of them are at the same time a functionary. One can say that the state fosters its own asymmetry.

It is important to note, that in an attempt to restore trust on government institutions and to satisfy the demands of the Maidan protesters, on 16 October 2014, Ukraine has introduced a new law on Lustration (the Law of Ukraine on Lustration). The Organised Crime Observasory (OCO, 2015) notes that the Law prohibits the holding of public offices for the persons (i) "who worked from the 25th of February 2010 to the 22nd of February 2014 and by their decisions, acts or omissions, promoted the usurpation of power by the President

Yanukovich, sapped the foundations of national security, defense and territorial integrity of Ukraine resulting in violation of human rights and freedoms and (ii) the persons who held managerial positions at the Communist Party of the Soviet Union, Ukraine or the Republics of the Soviet Union". While on paper it can be considered a step forward to improve the rule of law, some observers note that this is a judicial 'purge' that will leave Ukraine in a situation of absent judicial leaders. OCO (2015: 70-71) also notes that "the lustration in itself does not cope with corruption through any rule of law, but merely applies an extra-judicial political process, which in turns reinforces the dependence of Justice on the political power". In reality Ukraine has to deal with a dangerously politicised war on corruption of which it is uncertain whether it contributes to raising trust.

So, given the fact that hoarding cash at home is also risky, why do MPs generally not trust the banking sector in Ukraine? Answering this question directly may not be possible and feasible for this chapter. Instead, this chapter aims to discuss the main stages in the development of the banking industry in Ukraine against the background of trust. In order to do this, we will briefly review criminality in the banking industry in two distinctive periods: starting from the 1950s to the end of the Soviet period; and from 1991-2016, the period of independent Ukraine. We argue that the transition from the 'mono-bank' system in Soviet times to the independent commercial banking in Ukraine has after a quarter Century not yet been completed fully. This casts doubt on the integrity of the stakeholders involved. During Soviet times banks were centrally controlled by the state, similarly; but who controls the banks in the era of independence?

The development of banking criminality in Ukraine

Surveying the banking criminality in Ukraine, we can identify four distinctive stages in the proliferation of criminal activity in this sector.

The first stage, *criminality against banks*, can be recognised during the Soviet period. The characteristic feature of this stage is personal corruptive links between criminals and bank officials. It is fair to say that in the middle of the 20th Century the issue of criminality within the banking industry in the USSR was not the priority of the research agenda. This allowed it to grow unnoticed. Given that any agenda was dictated by the central socialist system, the main aim was to improve legality and develop mechanisms to prevent crimes against socialist property in different industries.

Osenin and Pozdnyakov (1951) identified five main types of banking criminality in the 1950s. The first one is to do with the *cash deposits* accepted from the members of the public. The second type is about *illegal use of the payments* within the bank. The third type is to do with the stealing from the *government bonds* payments. *Pension* and *social payments fraud* is the fourth type. The fifth type concerns the illegal cash payments from the funds of the Central State Bank of the USSR. The authors comment that 95% of crimes within the banks in the USSR were committed using forged documents. It is interesting to observe that despite the fact that the typology was developed in the 1950s, some of the crimes still exist today in a slightly modernised form. Crimes committed within the banking sector during Soviet times had two features: the essential role of insiders and the ability to falsify the documents. Even by the 1990s, in the first few years of Independence, forging bank stamps led to the billions in criminal profit (see the case of Avizo discussed later in the chapter).

The second stage is about *organised criminal groups operating against banks*. By the end of the Soviet period, when the banks were beginning to position themselves as the independent players in the financial market, this independence was abused by the organised criminal groups in order to set up money laundering schemes. Popovich (1998) argues that the first traces of victimisation of the banking industry could be found in the practice of so-called 'zcehoviki', or 'shadow' entrepreneurs in the USSR. Who are they?

Zcehoviki were people who "made the impossible possible". It was impossible during the Soviet times to establish a private company to produce and sell goods. However, the demand for goods was not met by the official structure. So, zcehoviki created their solutions: they either produced 'unofficial' goods using state enterprise's equipment and sold the goods on the black market; or they produced goods using shadow enterprises, but distributed the goods through official channels. To ensure success of their business, zcehoviki had good connections with the party officials, police and state inspection (Popovich, 1998; Rawlinson, 2010). So, the main aim of zcehoviki was to use legal structures for illegal gains, something that will be observed on a bigger scale while considering criminality within banking.

Analysing banking in Soviet times, Hofer (2004) describes how banks were centrally administered and did not direct money flows or credit. Banking "lacked business skills", and banks "operated mainly as bureaucratic institutions". By the end of the 1980s the USSR has started restructuring on a colossal scale. The so-called 'perestroika', liberalisation of the economy, legalisation of the private sector as well as building up co-operatives all this preceded the col-lapse of the Soviet Union. The first co-operative banks appeared in the USSR in 1989. As a result of reforms in 1989-1991 the financial system has changed a lot and moved away from the total monopoly of the state bank of the USSR. The banking industry had to change from a "*banking sector simply as an arm of the state and part of the government bureaucracy*" to a commercial industry with strate-gies in place (Hofer, 2002).

The first task of reform was to create commercial banks out of the previous 'mono-bank system'. Three critical issues should have been addressed by Ukraine (Hofer, 2002): First, "a two-tiered system that divorces the central bank from making commercial credit decisions". Second, the need to establish "a clear legal and supervisory framework that regulates banking activities". Third, the need "to find ways to deal with bad debts and ensure that banks are adequately capitalized". These three tasks presented significant challenges for the country.

In the first few years of the 1990s, a large number of small, undercapitalized banks were established in the country. 76 banks were registered in 1991, and by 1995 the number reached 230 banks (*Ibid.*). Many of these banks were often too small to operate at the required level of efficiency, but most importantly, many "*were directly controlled or owned by the directors of the state-owned enterprises or newly privatised, previously state-owned enterprises*" (Hofer, 2002). Significant struc-tural changes within the financial industry failed to trigger corresponding changes within the legal system. As a result, the commercialisation of the bank-ing industry and the positioning of the banking system as an independent actor in the financial market was abused by those who aimed at legalising criminally gained capital.

Was only money laundering at stake? Many see a broader picture and argue that almost the whole Ukrainian economy was criminalised which could only be made possible with the collaboration from the political and financial upper-world (Osyka, 2002; Markovska and Serduyk, 2015, Kosak, 2016). During the first few years after the collapse of the Soviet Union, the political upper class in Ukraine has found itself in the situation of political independence (for the first time in years not controlled from Moscow). Regrettably, this independence was used not to set up a series of reforms for the benefit of nation, but to safe-guard the criminal profit of the minority who just happened to be within the power structure (Kravchuk, 2016). Markovska and Serdyuk (2011) argued that most profitable organised criminality in Ukraine is the one that is embedded within the structure of the government and dealing with the state budget and natural resources.

What was the extent of this criminality? As Figure 1 below suggests, it is very difficult to analyse the available statistics on crimes in banking sector. The main reason is ever developing regulatory regime, changing legislation and introduction of new categories to count crime, and new definitions of crimes.

Figure 1.
Crimes commited in the banking industry, 1996–2009
(number of crimes recorded).

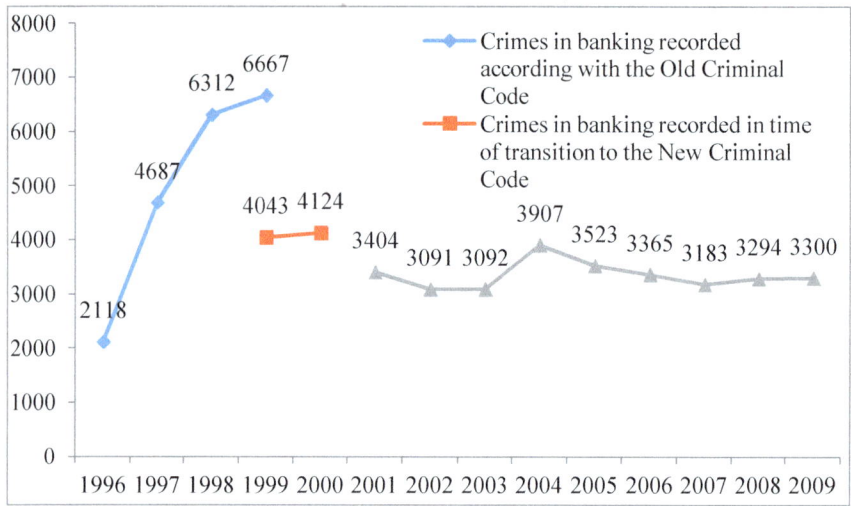

Source: Ministry of Interior of Ukraine official statistics (http://www.mvs.gov.ua)

Larichev (1993) developed a typology of criminality within banking to single out four stages of banking criminality in the early 1990s: 1) at the stage of the bank formation; 2) payment stage; 3) credit operations; 4) foreign currency exchange. Credit fraud, tax evasion and money laundering were the most profitable crimes in the period from 1993-1996 (Popovich, 1998). As a consequence, by the late 1990s, bad debt had become a significant issue for most of the banks in Ukraine.

In the second half of the 1990s, criminality within banking moved from simply opportunistic to strategically and intellectually advanced. Banks were beginning to be used more as legal enablers of criminal activity rather than random cover for a variety of opportunities. The case of *Avizo* described in the introduction is symbolic of this time.

In the third stage, organised criminal groups were beginning to set up their own banks, the so-called 'pocket banks' (in-house banks). By the end of the 1990s, organised criminal structures were allowed to get full access to the activities of the financial industry. Pocket banks became useful tool in facilitating criminal activity (Osyka, 2002; Williams and Picarelli, 2002). Hoffer (2004: 4) notes that many of these banks were "*directly controlled or owned by the directors of the state-owned enterprises or newly privatised previously state-owned enterprises*". Pocket banks are often small banks that are established with one aim, to obtain profit by legal and illegal means (*Ibid.*). These banks can function legitimately, but there is always a hidden agenda (*ibid.*). For example, these banks tend to attract customers by offering the interest rate of 20%; banks offer money laundering services and suspicious loans (Zaderei, 2006).

This is the stage where the criminal underworld and the criminal upperworld began to mix more openly. By the beginning of the 21st Century, the banking system in Ukraine improved its position as service provider for organised money laundering and illegal state credit operations. Most perpetrators could operate without state intervention. Despite this wide spread criminality of the politicians and entrepreneurs, the only well-known figure who ended up in jail in the USA on charges of money laundering was Former Prime-Minister Lasarenko. Lasarenko was Prime Minister of Ukraine from June 1996 until the summer of 1997. In his positions as Minister of Energy and then Prime Minister he had sent millions of dollars overseas using a wide variety of offshore companies and bank accounts. The Organised Crime Observatory (2015) notes that during his time in office Larenko "*was able to provide contracts, permits, licenses, or government guarantees. The transactions that figured in the U.S. trial allegedly netted Lazarenko approximately $114 million over 2 years, although his overall profits may have been considerably larger*" (OCO, 2015: 57). Lazarenko fled to the USA in 1999 to seek political asylum. However, the US authorities indicted him on 53 counts of money laundering, conspiracy to commit money laundering, wire fraud, and interstate transportation of stolen property (OCO, 2015). He remained under the house arrest from 2004-2006. In June, 2009 Mr Lasarenko was tried and sentenced to "97 months in prison, ordered to pay a $9 million fine and forfeit $22.851.000 and various specified assets resulting from his money laundering convictions" (FBI, 2009). According to OCO (2015), only Switzerland returned some $20 mln of stolen money to Ukraine.

The scale of involvement of politicians in banking has been highlighted in 2002 with the bankruptcy of the Ukraina Bank. The Ukraina Bank had supported agro-industrial complex and "*made virtually no loans of any size without political approval*" (Hofer, 2004: 8). "*Many of the loans were made under circumstances that would, in a more regulated environment, be classified as fraud. All parties involved in the process – bankers, borrowers and political intermediaries – knew that the prospects of repayment ranged from questionable to non-existent*" (KP News, 2002, as quoted in Hofer, 2004).

Figure 2 presents statistics in crimes committed within the banking sector in the first 15 years of the new millennium. It is interesting to note that while general criminality within banking sector was on the rise, specific crimes of money laundering were officially declining. One way to understand the decline in the number of money laundering offences is to understand the fourth stage of the development of criminality, more specifically, the political criminal nexus of the first 15 years of this Century. In this network of criminals and politicians, enforcement becomes corrupt and the legal framework is used to support criminality rather than punish.

Figure 2
Crimes commited within the banks, 2001-2015.

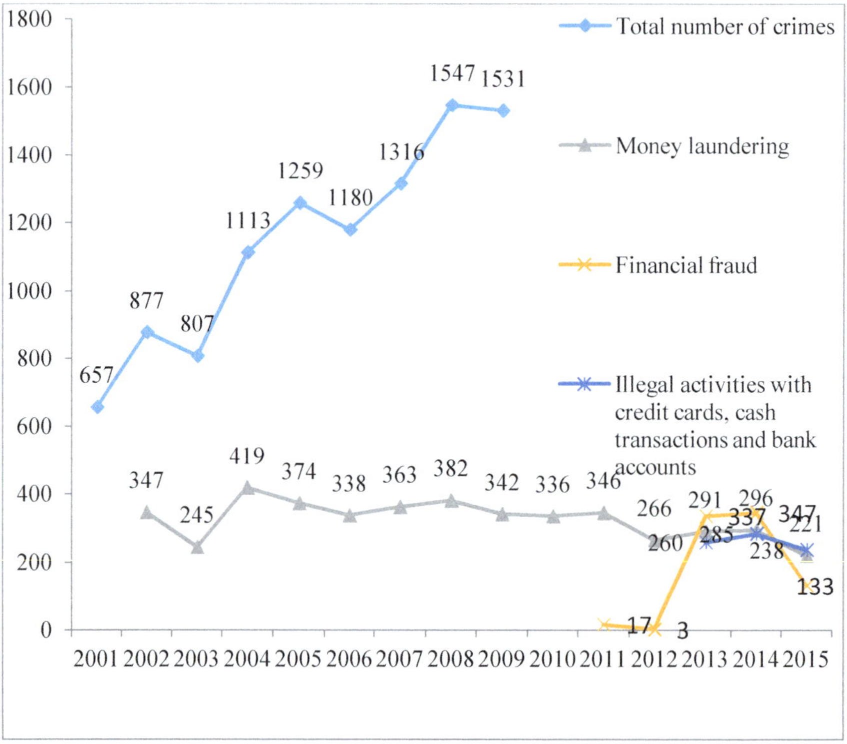

Source: Ministry of Interior of Ukraine official statistics http://www.mvs.gov.ua)

This fourth and final stage is about *organised criminals and state officials working together* using banks as a tool that enables criminality at the highest level of Ukrainian society. Criminal banking enables corrupt state officials to launder money and to siphon off funds from the country. What is more important, they can deliver it all within the established legal framework.

There are at least two well-known schemes to defraud the state by making the banks to conduct required transactions. First, there is the so-called fictitious bankruptcy. The bank management who is committed to criminal conduct, allowed to transfer cash from the bank, and receive re-financing from the state budget. The second scheme is to organise activities that can lead to bankruptcy. In these cases, organised criminals worked together with the state and enforcement officials. The case of the Brokebusiness bank is an interesting illustration for the fourth stage.

In 1991 The Arendbank of the USSR was renamed as Brokerbusiness Bank. The main strategy of the bank was to improve privatisation and develop services to deal with the privatisation vouchers. 23 years later the bank is purchased by Mr Kurchenko (at the time close associate of President Yanukovich). Interestingly, six months later the bank was bankrupt. The statutory capital of the Brokebusiness was the largest in the country. This is important! According to the national legislation the National Bank of Ukraine can provide re-financing of the minimum statutory funds to any bank. Brokebusiness transferred all funds from The National Bank to another bank, The Real Bank (another bank owned by Sergei Kurchenko). That was a suspicious move because by February 2014 it appeared that 12 bln HRV or about $1,5 bln was stolen from the state and laundered abroad (in official language used it was not about 'state loss', but 'state re-financed'). The attempts to recover the 'loot' are still ongoing in 2017.

We argue that this type of criminality will remain invisible in the official statistics unless, depending on political opportunities, certain players will need to be named. It is interesting to note the rise in the number of recorded crimes in 2004 (see Figure 3 below), the year of Orange revolution and the short lived 'cleansing' of the system.

The official data presented in Figure 3 also suggests the inability of enforcement agencies to capture grand fraud and corruption in banking, the highly politicised nature of the recording and the legislative system that is used to help criminals.

Graph 3.
Recorded organised groups and criminal organisations, 2002-2012.

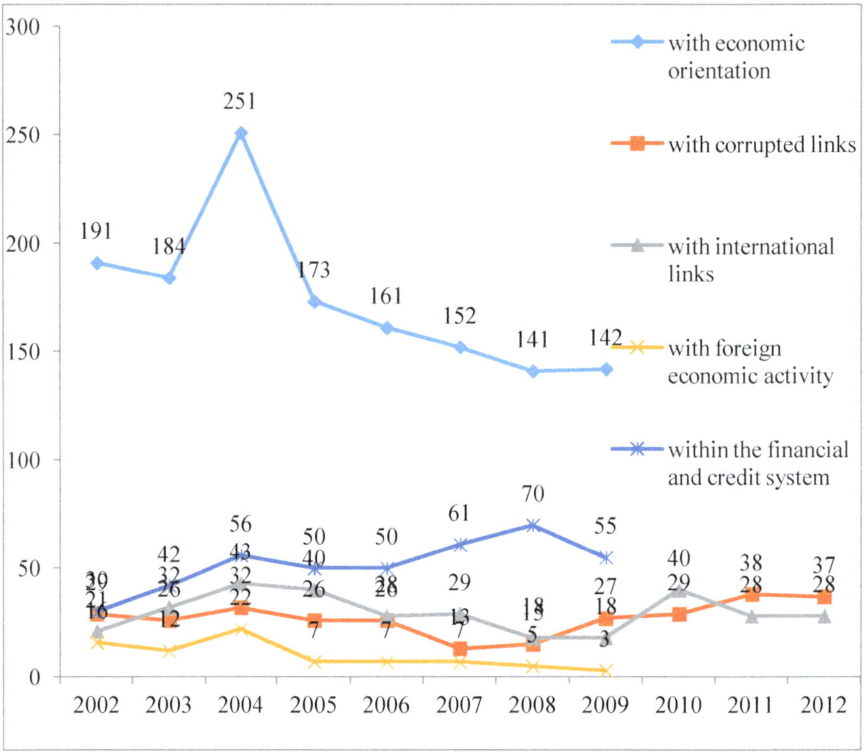

Source: Ministry of Interior of Ukraine official statistics
(http://www.mvs.gov.ua)

The journey of the legal background

The transnational banking activity has been seen as a core of the economic foundation of globalisation. It is important for the international community to regulate this area to ensure it works safely (Levi, 1991; 1998). In the last fifteen years a number of reforms were suggested for the implementation in Ukraine. Starting from 1991, establishing an appropriate regulatory regime has been seen as an important strategy to develop a reliable banking sector. However, the reality of banking shows a different story. While analysing the most corrupt years of the development within Ukrainian banking, different narratives can be gathered from key regulators. For example, in 2011 the Financial Action Task Force (FATF) suggests that "*Ukraine has made progress by taking a number of meas-ures aimed at improving its level of compliance with the FATF standards, and in particu-*

lar the 2003 FATF core recommendations. It comments on the adoption in 2014 of a new AML/CFT Law which introduces the key elements of the 2012 FATF standards which is also considered as a signal that the Ukrainian authorities remain committed to the implementation of the global standards".

The Council of Europe (2015: 6) has listed the following legal developments:

- The Law "On the prevention and counteraction to legalisation (laundering) of proceeds from crime or terrorism financing and the financing of proliferation of weapons of mass destruction" adopted on 14 October 2014;
- a resolution on "Issues of organisation of the national risk assessment legalisation (laundering) of proceeds from crime and terrorist financing";
- 2015 Government Resolution № 299 on "Some issues of Unified Information system on prevention and counteraction to legalisation (laundering) of proceeds from crime, terrorist financing and the financing of proliferation of weapons of mass destruction";
- 2014 Act "on Amendments to Certain Legislative Acts of Ukraine regarding the determination of the ultimate beneficial owner of legal persons and public figures" № 1701-VII;
- the law "On principles of state anti-corruption policy in Ukraine (Anti-corruption Strategy) for 2014 – 2017",
- the law on "The National Anti-Corruption Bureau of Ukraine", which entered into force on 25 January 2015; and
- the law on "prevention of Corruption" which entered into force on 26 April 2015.

The FATF (2011) concludes that "Ukraine is therefore no longer subject to FATF's monitoring under its on-going global AML/CFT compliance process".

The Council of Europe Committee (2015) reported that although significant changes can be identified in the legislation the number of investigations, prosecutions and convictions in cases of money laundering "appears to show a consistent decrease in 2013 and in 2014". For example the number of cases under investigation in 2012 was 410, and in 2015 the number was 77. According to the Ukrainian authorities this is due to the ongoing task of training judges and financial investigators (Council of Europe, 2015: 8-9). The report has observed that the number of suspicious transactions recorded by banks in 2014 was 486.564. The number of cases received by the Financial Investigation Units (FIU) in 2014 was 780.234. The report argued that although the suspicion based approached has been introduced into practice, the actual result is difficult to establish. One of the deficiencies noted by the report is the inadequacy of the mechanisms for "*confiscation of property of corresponding value, as well as confiscation of income, profits or other benefits from the proceeds of crime, in the context of a ML offence*" (p. 22).

While not perfect, and still with a number of deficiencies, a significant progress has been made in Ukraine to set up the regulatory framework for financial institutions. What the example of Ukraine has identified, is that setting up the framework is only one step towards success. Halliday, Levi, and Reuter (2014: 32-33) assessed the regimes to control money-laundering and argue that "*formal compliance and program implementation with an AML regime can be adopted by virtually all countries (although in fact many countries had not put in place even the legal building blocks), in practice the fundamental objectives of an AML regime cannot or will not be attained effectively by large numbers of countries because they are either unwilling or unable to do so*". This statement reflects the developments in banking in Ukraine and the willingness/unwillingness of the authority to improve the real practice. It is also the case of the willingness /unwillingness of international players to acknowledge the realities of Ukraine. Implementation in real practice proved to be tortuous, as demonstrated by the law on insolvency.

The case of the insolvency law

Tytych (2016) discusses an interesting example of the development of insolvency legislation in Ukraine. In 2004, Ukraine has adopted the Commercial Code, which "provided clarification of substantive norms in insolvency procedures, [and] became an important development in the reform of bankruptcy law." However, Tytych noticed that the law was developed by American consultants and "was not duly mesh [harmonised] with the existing legislative system, containing legal constructions which had been unknown in Ukrainian legislation and did not take into account the legal practice. Accordingly, many gaps and inconsistencies of the Law were [to be] settled by case-law, and with information letters and interpretations of higher courts". Tytych (2016) argues that "*this state of the regulation, coupled with the significant growth of corruption in the judiciary of Ukraine led to [the situation] that the proceedings in the bankruptcy cases in fact became a procedure for legitimising crimes in the economic sphere and a tool for dispossession of participants in economic relations*".

The new version of the Law "On Restoring the Debtor's Solvency or Recognising it Bankrupt" came into force on 01-19-2013. Tytych (2016) notes that this Law was not the first attempt to establish a European model. The problem was the reluctance and unwillingness of the MPs to improve the system. "After the MPs' 'improvements' to this version of the law, there were no conceptual innovations remaining in it. In reality, the structure of the text was slightly changed and the number of articles was increased by reducing their size, but without significant change of the main provisions of the law. In addition, some new provisions worsen the regulating of insolvency relationships when compared to the previous version of the law." Apparently uncooperative and self-minded politicians and a corrupt judiciary still present a significant threat to the development of reliable and transparent financial system.

The banking tragedy

In the last few years Ukraine has been experiencing an ongoing 'banking catastrophe' (Kosak, 2016). "Don't feel sorry for the 82 banks we shut last year [2015]. These were not real banks. 20 banks out of 82 were used simply to launder money, and the remaining 62 simply had no active capital: the banks simply stole money from the clients", Mrs Gontareva, The Head of the National Bank of Ukraine said (Gontareva, 2016).

According to Ukrainian associations representing banks, insurers and financial institutions operating in Ukraine, "between 2014-2016, as a result of the recognition of 77 Ukrainian banks as insolvent, banking industry lost UAH 435bn in assets" (Kosak, 2016). This is the equivalent of 22% of Ukraine's GDP (*ibid*.). Kosak (2016) calculated that "enterprises in the real economy lost UAH 82bn of their current assets in the bankrupt banks, corresponding to 25 per cent of all the business assets deposited in Ukrainian banks (as of January 1st, 2016)". Taking into account the state of the liquidated banks, most of this amount has been lost forever, "disappeared", is the favourite description of the banking crime. Due to the wave of bank failures "insurance companies lost a further UAH2bn which threatens to spread the crisis of the banking sector to the insurance sector. Investment funds and non-state pension funds lost UAH1bn. The UAH25bn that local governments invested in the bankrupt banks is also lost" (Kosak, 2016).

According to Rozhkova (2017), in 2014, a total of 32 banks were liquidated and in 2015 a further 33. In 2016, 15 Ukrainian banks, with UAH9bn of savings of individuals, have already gone bankrupt (Kosak, 2016). The Guarantee Fund of Deposits of Individuals (GFDI) paid UAH7.3bn in compensation to the victims. The total payments for clients of all the banks that have gone bankrupt since 2014 amount to almost UAH 79bn, or $ 3bn (*Ibid*.). The main problem is that in order to fulfill its obligations the Guarantee Fund has to take money from the state budget (Rozhkova, 2017, Kosak, 2016). At the beginning of 2017, despite the manyfold bankruptcies, there are still 102 banks operating on the Ukrainian market.

Naturally, this chain of bankruptcies in the financial sector led to a free fall of trust in Ukrainian banks. Therefore the national cash hoarding tendency: stash your money at home! As remarked earlier, unsurprisingly, the Ukrainian MPs are not the only one who keep cash at home. Ordinary Ukrainians have withdrawn UAH70bn and $16bn from the banks in order to rescue their savings (Kosak, 2016).

The tragedy of the Ukrainian banking system is a tragedy of the modern Ukraine, willing and corrupt insiders coupled with significant political pressure. Nadia Savchenko, the helicopter pilot who spent two years in Russian prison, famously commented on MPs declaration of wealth in 2016, "*No wonder the IMF is so interested in this money since it's likely to be from their previous loans from Ukraine*" (Fitzwilliam, 2016). What remains to be the question is the role of international organisations in stopping the abuse of power and resources in Ukraine. To a certain extent it can be argued that Ukrainian politicians out smarted the international anti-corruption and anti- money laundering organisation.

Starting shortly after independence, the banking sector in Ukraine has become "*a battleground of the struggle of politicians for economic influence*" (Novak, 2016, quoted in Kosak, 2016). As such, the banking sector has become an enabler of the criminality of the political elite in the country. Corrupt judiciary and an ever evolving, muddled, legislation provided some fertile ground on which to establish large-scale state enabled fraud where the banks have become the 'enablers' of the criminal activity of elite.

Many bankruptcies in Ukraine were artificially induced. However, the Central Bank, the national regulator acted on behalf of corrupt politicians and oligarchs to enable completion of criminal transactions. When banking becomes the platform for the conflict between the oligarchs, legislation and regulatory standards are ignored. In this context, it is extremely difficult to assess the way any country deals with financial regulation: proposed regulatory compliance and reality have become different worlds. On one hand, the legislative framework has been constantly under development, producing encouraging results (FATF, 2011). However, on the other hand, these are not changes "on the ground": the reality of banking is that the sector is still highly corrupt. While crime data is collated on the low level criminality within the sector, the extraordinary tales of bankruptcies and illegal enrichment remain outside of the enforcement agenda and within the purview of investigative journalists. In the last twenty years, the evolving legal framework has been highjacked by the criminal elite who used it to enable specific tasks/crimes within Ukraine. This is why, the criminality of the powerful elite is often impossible to classify as crimes, because the legal framework tends to be used to help the powerful to avoid the label of criminality. By constantly changing this legal basis, officials remain the priority holders of key information used for legislative decision making. In this function they constantly redefine 'rights' and 'wrongs' in their interests.

Conclusions

This chapter considers the important issue of trust and finances. Many argue that, in Ukraine, this concept of trust has been as seriously eroded as a medieval statue in acid rain. The regulatory mechanisms and legislative surroundings often change unpredictably, agreements and guarantees are often disregarded, judicial system is under political influence and parties are often prepared to violate agreements. It is a general characteristic which Ukraine shares with other countries infested with corruption, such many adjacent Eastern European countries or Italy.

A number of paradoxes can be observed in Ukraine. The two-tiered banking system used in Ukraine includes both the first tier, where banks generally comply with all the regulations, and the second tier where the regulation is abused for the advantage of a selected number of officials. In this system, the more you change the regulation and create confusion, the more advantage there is for the corrupter.

To ensure legitimate co-operation, international organisations tend to work with government officials, who they trust with the anti-money laundering implementation strategy. This appeaers naïve or at least formalistic. However, during the years since Ukraine was removed from the 'black list' of FATF, Ukrainian banks and senior officials continued to engage in criminal conduct and use banks to siphon off illegally-gained resources. This happened under the allegedly watching eye of the anti-money laundering organisations. Ukraine is not an exception when considering the lack of successful prosecutions of criminal officials. It shares this with many other countries in Eastern Europe (Russia, Moldova, Serbia or Montenegro) where there seems to be the silent 'policy' that being prosecuted is a function of losing political clout or having the wrong friends. It is understandable that in such a political swamp outsiders (from the international community) have no real power to fight corruption in Ukraine, while elite insiders even after two revolutions have no intention to change themselves or colleagues.

We argue that the transition from the 'mono-bank' system of Soviet times to the independent commercial banking in Ukraine has, after a quarter Century, not yet been completed. This casts doubt on the integrity of all the parties involved. During Soviet times banks were centrally controlled by the state. Similarly, since independence, the criminal political elite of Ukraine has established control over the banking sector. The surface has changed, the roots remaining. As long as this lasts, Ukrainians are advised to keep their savings under their mattresses.

References

Anheier, H.K. and J. Kendall, Trust and voluntary organisations: Three theoretical approaches Civil Society. Working Paper 5. [On-line]. Available at: http://eprints.lse.ac.uk/29035/1/CSWP5web-version.pdf, 2000

ANTICOR, "Ukrspirt" is at the center of scandal yet again. [Укрспирт снова в центре скандала]. [On-line]. Avaialbale at: http://ANTIKOR.COM.UA/ARTICLES/131903-UKRSPIRT_SNOVA_V_TSENTRE_SKANDALA, 2016

Bekeshkina, I., Survey: The trust of Ukrainians to the officials has decreased significantly. [Опрос: Доверие украинцев к властям резко ухудшилось]. [On-line]. Available at: http://politrada.com/news/opros-doverie-ukraintsev-k-vlastyam-rezko-ukhudshilos/, 2015

Bureau of International Narcotics and Law Enforcement Affairs, 2015 International Narcotics Control Strategy Report (INCSR). [On-line]. Available at: https://www.state.gov/j/inl/rls/nrcrpt/2015/vol2/239110.htm, 2015

Council of Europe, Committee of Experts on the Evaluation of Anti-Money laundering measures and the Financing of Terrorism (MONEYVAL), Ukraine: Written analysis by the Secretariat of Core and Key Recommendations1. [On-line]. Available at: http://www.coe.int/t/dghl/monitoring/moneyval/Evaluations/Progress%20reports%202y/MONEYVAL(2015)2_UKR_3rdProg_Analysis_en.pdf, 2015

Euronews, Vast wealth declared by Ukrainian politicians causes shock and anger. [On-line]. Available at:
www.euronews.com/2016/10/31/vast-wealth-declared-by-ukraine-politicians-causes-shock-and-anger, 2016

FATF Outcomes of the Plenary meeting of the FATF, Paris, 27-28 October 2011
[On-line]. Available at:
www.fatf-gafi.org/publications/fatfgeneral/documents/outcomesoftheplenarymeeting ofthefatfparis27-28october2011.html, 2011

FBI, Press Release: Former Ukrainian Prime Minister Sentenced to 97 Months in Prison Fined $9 Million for Role in Laundering $30 Million of Extortion Proceed. [On-line]. Available at:
https://archives.fbi.gov/archives/sanfrancisco/press-releases/2009/sf111909a.htm, 2009

Forbes Ukraine, The organisation of kopanka business [Как устроен бизнес на «копанках»]. [On-line]. Available at:
http://forbes.net.ua/magazine/forbes/1351902-kak-ustroen-biznes-na-kopankah, 2013

Fukuyama, F., Differing disciplinary perspectives on the origins of trust. *Boston University Law Review*, June, 2001

Greenwald, B., and J., Stiglitz, Imperfect information, credit markets and unemployment. *European Economic Review*, 1987, vol. 31 (1-2), 1987

Hofer, T., *A tale of two nations*. [On-line]. Available at:
https://www.uwsp.edu/busecon/Special%20Reports/2000-2009/2002/A%20Tale%20of%20Two%20Nations-Commerical%20Banking%20in%20Poland%20and%20Ukraine.pdf, 2004

IRI, Ukraine Poll: Continued Dissatisfaction with Government and Economic Situation.[On-line]. Available at: http://www.iri.org/resource/ukraine-poll-continued-dissatisfaction-government-and-economic-situation, 2016

Kosak, M., Bank failures in Ukraine ruin citizens and hit the economy. Central European Financial Observer. [On-line]. Available at:
http://www.financialobserver.eu/cse-and-cis/ukraine/bank-failures-in-ukraine-ruin-citizens-and-hit-the-economy/, 2016

Kravchuk, S., *Economic crimes in Ukraine*. [On-line]. Available at:
http://uchebnikonline.com/ekonomika/ekonomichna_zlochinnist_v_ukrayini_-_kravchuk_sy/sutnist_ekonomiko-kriminologichnoyi_transformatsiyi_ekonomichnoyi_zlochinnosti.htm, 2016

Markovska, A. and A., Serduyk, Ukrainian underworld: from street gambling games to the games of politics and big business. In: G. Antonopoulos *et al.* (eds.) *Usual and unusual organising criminals in Europe and beyond: profitable crimes, from underworld to upper world.* Apeldoorn: Maklu, 2011

Markovska, A., and A. Serduyk, Black, grey or white? Finding the new shade of corruption in Ukraine. In: P.C. van Duyne *et al.* (eds.) *The relativity of wrongdoing: corruption, organised crime, fraud and money laundering in perspective.* Oisterwijk: Wolf Legal Publishers, 2015

Ministry of Interior of Ukraine, Official statistics. [On-line]. Available at: www.mvs.gov.ua, 2016

OCO, Ukraine and the EU: Overcoming criminal exploitation toward a modern democracy ?
[On-line]. Available at:
www.o-c-o.net/wp-content/uploads/2013/11/Ukraine-and-the-EU-Overcoming-criminal-exploitation-toward-a-modern-democracy.pdf, 2015

Osenin, V.Y. and A.M. Pozdnyakov, *Investigating fraud within banks.* Moscow: Gosyurizdat, 1951

Osyka, I., Organised economic crime problems in Ukraine. In Petrus C. van Duyne, Vincenzo Ruggiero, Miroslav Scheinost, Wim Valkenburg (eds.), *Cross-border crime in a changing Europe.* Huntingdon, New York: Nova Science Publishers, 2001

Popovich, V.M., *Shadow economy as a subject of economic criminology.* Kiev: Pravovi Dzherela, 1998

Rawlinson, P., *From fear to paternity: a Russian tale of crime, economy and modernity.* London: Pluto Press, 2010

Repich, A., The fraud of the Century. *Zakon*, No. 5, issue 5, 2010

Rozhkova, Bankopad in Ukraine. [On-line]. Available at:
http://vlasti.net/news/243141, 2017

Sergi, A., Mafia and politics as concurrent governance actors. In: P.C. van Duyne et al (eds.) *The relativity of wrongdoing: corruption, organised crime, fraud and money laundering in perspective.* Oisterwijk: Wolf Legal Publishers, 2015

Williams, P. and J. Picarelli, *Organized crime in Ukraine: challenge and response.* Available at: www.ncjrs.gov/pdffiles1/nij/grants/198321.pdf, 2002

Zabyelina, Y., Mine control: Conflict and crime threaten Ukrainian coal mining. *Jane's Intelligence Review*, October 2, pp. 44-47, 2015

Zaderei, N., *Small banks in Ukraine.* [Мелкие банки Украины: Биография].
www.prostobank.ua/depozity/stati/melkie_banki_ukrainy_biografiya, 2006

The 2008 financial crisis and financial crime: A critial analysis of the response in the United States

Nicholas Ryder[1]

Introduction

The purpose of this chapter is to critically reflect on the response in the United States of America (US) towards financial crime originating from the 2008 financial crisis. The chapter briefly outlines the initial policy and legislative responses to the financial crisis introduced by President George Bush and President Barak Obama. The chapter then appraises the regulatory responses towards financial crime deriving from the financial crisis. This involves a detailed analysis of the relevant enforcement by the Securities and Exchange Commission (SEC), the Federal Bureau of Investigation (FBI), the Commodities Futures Trading Commission (CFTC) and the Department of Justice.

Policy and Legislative Response

The initial policy response to the financial crisis was jointly led by the Federal Reserve and the Department of Treasury, who were concerned with providing economic assistance to maintain the financial stability of the US economy. These actions were supported by the enactment of the Economic Stimulus Act 2008, which aimed to stimulate the US economy by providing tax rebates, encouraging businesses to invest in qualifying property and by increasing the loan limits for Fannie Mae, Freddie Mac and the Federal Housing Administration. The Emergency Economic Stabilisation Act 2008, authorised the US government to purchase and insure certain types of troubled assets. The most significant aspect of this Act was the creation of the Troubled Asset Relief

---

[1] Professor in Financial Crime, University of the West of England.

Programme, a Department of Treasury fund, which injected $700bn into the financial services sector, by purchasing the troubled assets and equity from financial institutions. The Housing and Economic Recovery Act 2008 had two important objectives: to improve the levels of regulation for Fannie Mae and Freddie Mac and to provide additional funding to prevent the foreclosure of properties (Reiss, 2009: 340). The foundations of the legislative responses from President Barak Obama are to be found in the American Recovery and Reinvestment Act 2009, which aimed to both generate and protect jobs (Moye, 2010: 29). The Fraud Enforcement and Recovery Act 2009, was a direct response to financial crime crime that *"contributed to the . . . economic collapse"* (Lover, 2012: 1129). The Act was a reaction to what he described as *"economic calamity . . . ostensibly combating the type of chronic misconduct which may have helped foster economic instability rather than merely combating the acute symptoms of such instability"* (Reidy, 2010: 318). The Act contained five important provisions.

1. it provided a significant increase in the funding for the Department of Justice and FBI to combat fraud;
2. it made some important amendments to fraud and money laundering legislation;
3. the Act increased the penalites for those convicted of mortgage fraud;
4. the Act extended the definition of financial institutions to include private mortgage lending businesses and mortgage brokers;
5. the Act increased the supervision of the Troubled Asset Relief Programme (TARP).

Additionally, the Act contained measures to tackle healthcare fraud, it established the Financial Crisis Inquiry Commission, extended the protection afforded to fraud related whistleblowers and amended the False Claim Act 1986. The Fraud Enforcement and Recovery Act, 2009 was welcomed by the Department of Justice who stated that it *"would provide federal investigators and prosecutors with significant new tools and resources, both civil and criminal, with which to combat mortgage fraud, securities and commodities fraud and related offenses"* (United States Department of Justice, 2009).

The Fraud Enforcement and Recovery Act, 2009 represents an attempt by President Barak Obama to redress some of the imbalances created by President George Bush, who wrongly prioritised the 'war on terror' at the expense of mortgage fraud. The Act has allowed the Department of Justice and the FBI, to pursue white collar criminals who have contributed toward the financial crisis. This is demonstrated by the significant increase in mortgage fraud convictions and ongoing investigations by the FBI.

Regulatory and law enforcement response

The regulatory response of the US has been heavily influenced by the introduction of legislation that specifically acknowledged the link between the financial crisis and financial crime. This led to the creation of *another* task force to tackle financial crime emanating from the financial crisis. The response of the SEC, FBI and Department of Justice and the Commodity Futures Trading Commission (CFTC) are now judiciously appraised.

The SEC

The SEC (Securities and Exchange Commission, n/d) was established as a result of the Wall Street Crash and Great Depression and was initially designed to act as an *"economic watchdog"* (Huynh, 2010: 108). Its mission is to protect *"investors, maintain fair, orderly, and efficient markets, and facilitate capital formation"*. The SEC is *"responsible for the enforcement and regulation of the US and securities market . . . it is charged with regulating all companies that hold and trade public stock"* (Huynh, 2010: 108). During the last two decades the SEC became more involved and committed to enforcing the provisions of the Securities Act, 1933 and the Securities Exchange Act, 1934 (*ibid.,* 109). The Division of Enforcement undertakes investigations for alleged breaches of securities legislation and prosecutes the SEC's civil suits. Common remedies pursued includes injunctions, financial penalties and the suspension or prohibition from people acting in certain positions. The SEC is also permitted to provide compensation for the victims of fraud and generate administrative proceedings before an SEC Administrative Law Judge. There are several different categories of proceedings that the SEC could pursue against wrongdoers including a cease and desist order, a disgorgement order, the revocation of a licence or registration or even suspension. The Division of Enforcement seeks to support and advise the SEC in *"executing its law enforcement function by recommending the commencement of investigations of securities law violations, by recommending that the Commission bring civil actions in federal court or as administrative proceedings before an administrative law judge, and by prosecuting these cases on behalf of the Commission"* (Securities and Exchange Commission, n/d). The SEC investigates a wide range of financial crime activities including allegations of misrepresentation, market manipulation, insider trading and selling unregistered securities. The SEC has an extensive array of civil enforcement powers, and it has imposed a record number of financial sanctions since the onset of the financial crisis. However, it has *no* authority to instigate criminal proceedings and its effectiveness has been questioned (Maher, 2013: 463).

Huynh, citing Black, stated that only ten percent of the cases originally investigated by the SEC are referred to the Department of Justice for further examination (2010: 108). Maher stated that *"there is no indication that the Department of Justice plans to indict any of these executives for their actions"* (Maher, 2013: 463). It is important to note that this position *must* be contrasted with that of the United Kingdom's Financial Conduct Authority, who has the ability to commence criminal proceedings (Ryder, 2017). Despite having an arsenal of enforcement powers the regulatory performance of the SEC during the financial crisis has been overshadowed and perhaps permanently tarnished as a result of the actions of Bernard Madoff. Pontell *et al.* stated: *"another way to meaningfully gauge the regulatory response or lack thereof in the current crisis is to consider the SEC's indifference to Bernard Madoff"* (2014: 3). Bernard Madoff's Ponzi scheme illustrates how the SEC failed to protect investors on numerous occasions. In 2008, Bernard Madoff was arrested by federal agents after being accused of orchestrating one of the largest Ponzi frauds ever encountered in the US. The impact of the fraud was extensive, as noted by Nunziato: *"it* [the fraud] *is estimated that thousands of investors lost somewhere between $20bn and $65bn . . . Madoff purported to invest the savings of some four thousand clients . . . who spanned across forty-eight of the fifty states, as well as throughout Europe, Latin America, and Asia"* (2010: 603-604). Bernard Madoff established his firm 'Bernard L Madoff Securities' in 1960, and operated a secret investment company, which was not registered with the SEC until 2006 (Hurt, 2009: 952). In 2009, Bernard Madoff pleaded guilty to wire fraud, securities fraud, money laundering, mail fraud and perjury was sentenced to 150 years imprisonment. Judge Chin rejected the defence's recommendation for twelve year custodial sentence and described Madoff's crime as "extraordinary evil" that justified the maximum sentence as it would act as a deterrent and also for the harm he had caused to his victims (Smith, 2009).

One of the most significant questions that must be considered is how was Bernard Madoff able to avoid detection for so many years? The first reason lies with the ineffective regulatory stance of the SEC, which was described by Klock as an *"alarming level of incompetent examinations . . .* [the SEC] *is not capable of providing adequate protection for the integrity of our financial markets"* (2010, 784). Furthermore, it has been argued that the SEC *could* have prevented the Ponzi scheme on several occasions (*ibid*: 789-904). For example, the SEC received numerous warning from many informants that Madoff's *"returns **defied** market realities"* (Valukas, 2010). Valukas criticised the SEC who *"had no interest in* *investigating successful funds whose investors were delighted with their returns. It therefore made only cursory investigations of Madoff's funds. Opportunities to expose his blatantly illegal practices were overlooked because of his very success*" (*ibid*). Bernad Madoff's ponzi scheme was identified by Harry Markopolos, who had reported this to the SEC on several occasions. The full extent of the fraud was outlined in his infamous memo sent to the SEC in 2005 entitled "*The World's Largest Hedge Fund is a Fraud*" (Securities and Exchange Commission, 2005). Bernard Madoff was able to avoid detection for several decades due to his "*ability to cultivate notable relationships with key market regulators*" (Colesanti, 2012: 528). For example, he was a member of the Financial Industry Regulatory Association's Board of Governors, a member of the SEC's Advisory Committee on Market Information; he was Chairman of the NASDAQ in the 1990s, a member of the board of the Securities Industry and Financial Markets Association and a member of the Securities Traders Association of New York. Another reason why Madoff was allowed to deceive investors and regulators was due to his reputation as a "*trusted titan of Wall Street*" (*ibid*: 527). Indeed, Nichols argued *that* "*Madoff was held in high esteem in the securities industry by regulators and other market participants*" (2011: 644-645). This led Hiznay to assert that "*critics have at least implicitly blamed Madoff's investors for permitting the frauds proliferation*" (2009: 421).

The regulatory failings of the SEC were highlighted by the SEC Office of Inspector General (2009). The Office of Inspector *General* "*revealed a surreal tale of anonymous tips, unheeded red flags and corroboration never sought, all commencing with a 1992 complaint about Madoff's unregistered activities*" (*ibid*: 78-82, 95-96, 143, 149-150, 158, 234, 411-412). This is a view supported by Nichols, who stated that the SEC could have discovered the Madoff fraud on no less than ten separate occasions (2011: 661-666). Harris noted that "*more than ample information was received by the SEC over the years to warrant an investigation into Bernard Madoff's activities . . . but none of the five examinations and investigations initiated by the SEC was thoroughly or competently performed*" (2010: 33). Other commentators such as Hiznay stated that "*critics are primarily targeting the SEC, the flinging disapproval towards what many view as the agency's generally inadequate regulatory system*" (2009: 417). The failings of the SEC illustrate a break down of communications and failings of the regulatory agency that was established to protect investors from white collar criminals like Bernard Madoff. The counterargument is that SEC has failed to detect the extensive ponzie fraud due to lack of resources or that it was understaffed. However, such arguments are unfounded as the SEC's ability to detect fraud was described as that "*they couldn't find ice cream in a Dairy Queen*" (Markopolis, 2009).

The FBI

The FBI has been the most active law enforcement agency towards financial crime associated to the financial crisis. For example, investigations by the FBI in 2011 resulted in 1.223 indictments and 1.082 convictions for mortgage fraud (FBI, 2011). Furthermore, due its investigations the FBI has secured $1,38bn in restitution, acquired fines totalling £116,3m, approximately $16m has been seized and $7,3m has been forfeited (*ibid.*). These actions has been influenced by the enactment of the Fraud Enforcement and Recovery Act 2009, which resulted in the FBI being granted additional funding to tackle mortgage fraud. However, the benefits and impact of this funding has been questioned. For example, Black took the view that due to the large volume of referrals the FBI received it *"can investigate only a tiny percentage of criminal referrals for mortgage fraud"* (2012: 998). Furthermore, according to statistical data published in September 2013 there has been a significant fall in the number of financial crime prosecutions brought by the FBI (TRAC, 2013). The report also illustrates that the total number of annual financial crime prosecutions have fallen from approximaltey 5.500 in 1993 to approximately 2.500 in 2013 (*ibid.*).

Nonetheless, the ability of the FBI to investigate and tackle mortgage fraud prior to the financial crisis was affeted by the decision of President George Bush to instigate the 'War on Terror', at the expense of financial crime. This decision has been correctly criticised by many commentators and the FBI themselves, who forewarned the Bush Administration of the threat posed by mortgage fraud in 2004, before the financial crisis. Chris Swecker, the former Assistant Director of the FBI stated that the *"potential impact of mortgage fraud on financial institutions and the stock market is clear. If fraudulent practices become systemic within the mortgage industry and mortgage fraud is allowed to become unrestrained, it will ultimately place financial institutions at risk and have adverse effects on the stock market"* (FBI, 2004). This warning was followed by a request for *"more investigators to address fraud in the mortgage industry"* (Ramirez, 2013: 876). These were ignored by President George Bush.

The FBI established the National Fraud Mortgage Team (NFMT), with the objective of improving already existing affiliations with mortgage providers and the originate new mechanisms to detect mortgage fraud (Black, 2011, 640). The FBI stated that the NFMT would *"assist field offices in addressing the financial crisis, from the mortgage fraud problem and loan origination scams to the secondary markets and securitization . . . [it would also] provide tools to identify the most egregious mortgage fraud perpetrators, prioritizes investigative efforts, and provides information to evaluate resource needs"* (2008). Additionally, the FBI is a key member of several mortgage fraud task forces and working groups (*ibid.*). For example, the FBI is also a member of the Department of Justice National Mortgage Fraud and National Bank Fraud Working Groups and the Financial Fraud Enforcement Task Force (FBI, 2009).

The Department of Justice

The Department of Justice has "*investigated and held accountable those responsible for financial fraud*" during the financial crisis (2012a). For example, it has "*prosecuted some of the most significant financial crimes* [. . .] *bringing to justice* [. . .] *numerous individuals across the country who perpetrated investment, securities and other fraud schemes*" (*ibid.*). This view is supported by Henning, but he noted that "*the cases are local in nature and do not involve large financial institutions*" (2012 95). One of the first measures introduced by the Department of Justice was the Financial Fraud Enforcement Task Force, which is one of several similar task forces established by the Department of Justice to tackle financial crime. Other examples include the Corporate Fraud Task Force, the Enron Task Force and the National Procurement Fraud Task Force. The Financial Fraud Enforcement Task Force replaced the Corporate Fraud Task Force, which aimed to "*provide direction for the investigation and prosecution of . . . related financial crimes committed by commercial entities*" (Podgor, 2011: 301). The Corporate Fraud Task Force was created to "*restore market confidence and cut down on corporate fraud*" (Arogeti, 2006: 430) and it secured over 1.200 fraud related convictions (Johnson, 2007). The Financial Fraud Enforcement Task Force would assist the Department of Justice to "*investigate and prosecute significant financial crimes and other violations relating to the current financial crisis*".[2] The objectives of the Financial Fraud Enforcement Task Force is to:

> "provide advice . . . for the investigation and prosecution of [significant] cases of bank, mortgage, loan, and lending fraud; securities and commodities fraud; retirement plan fraud; mail and wire fraud; tax crimes; money laundering; False Claims Act violations; unfair competition; discrimination; and other financial crimes and violations".[3]

In order to achieve these objectives, the Task Force prioritised fraud that is direclty associated with the financial crisis. For example, this includes for mortgage fraud, securities and commodities fraud, the distribution of

---

[2]   Exec. Order No. 13519, 74 FR 60123, 2009 WL 3848641 (Pres.).

[3]   Exec. Order No. 13,519, 74 FR 60123, 2009 WL 3848641 (Pres.) as cited *Ibid.*.

government funds via the American Recovery and Reinvestment Act and TARP.[4] The Task Force would result in "*increased coordination and cooperation among the different federal and state authorities involved in the regulation of the financial markets*" (Brotman and Dougherty, 2011: 19). However, the structure of the Financial Fraud Enforcement Task Force is very similar to that adopted by the Corporate Fraud Task Force. The latter of of which consisted of the Department of Justice, the SEC, the Commodities Future Trading Commission and the Federal Energy Regulatory Commission (Arogeti, 2006: 427). Nonetheless, Corporate Fraud Task Force did result in the Department of Justice and SEC forming a closer working relationship towards tackling financial crime. The Department of Justice would use its criminal enforcement powers while the SEC would compliment these by using its wide reaching civil powers (*ibid.*: 427-428).[5] The Financial Fraud Enforcement Task Force is an attempt by President Barak Obama to improve the response towards financial crime by adopting an coordinated response (Sheppard and Dougherty, 2012, 20). One of the highest profile actions of the Task Force has been its 'Distressed Homeowner Initiative', which was launched in 2011 (FBI, 2012). The aim of this measure was to concentrate on fraud that targets homeowners who have fallen into arrears on their mortgage repayments. In such cases, the fraudster will approach the homeowner and promise them that they will be able to prevent the repossession or foreclosure of their property for a large fee. The fraudster promises that investors will purchase the homeowners mortgage or in some cases will ask them to transfer the home ownership to the fraudulent investors (Department of Justice, 2012). In 2012, the Department of Justice reported that the scheme resulted in "*530 criminal defendants charged, including 172 executives, in 285 federal criminal indictments or informations filed* [. . .] *these cases involved more than 73.000 homeowner victims and total losses by those victims estimated by law enforcement at more than $1bn*" (*ibid.*).

At first instance, the actions and results of the Distressed Homeowner Initiative appear to be very impressive. However, the figures were questioned by a Bloomberg report that suggested that the statistics incorporated investigations and actions two years prior to Barak Obama being elected President (Mattingly and Schoenberg, 2012). As a result of this investigation, the statistics were corrected and restated by the FBI (*ibid.*). The report also suggested that the publication of the results was politicially motivated as they were published a month before the 2012 presidential elections.

---

4   *Ibid*, at 2.4.
5   *Ibid.*, at 428-429.

Another important measure that was utilised by the Task Force was 'Operation Broken Dreams', which was launched in October 2010. The purpose of this initiative was to "*target mortgage fraudsters throughout the country and was the largest collective enforcement effort ever brought to bear in confronting mortgage fraud*" (Department of Justice, 2011). It has been described as the "*government's largest mortgage fraud takedown to date*" (FBI, 2010). By June 2010, Operation Stolen Dream identified 1.215 defendants, 486 arrests had been made, there were 673 indictments, there had been 135 complaints, 336 convictions, estimated losses of $2,3bn and over $10m has been seized (*ibid*). Additionally, civil cases had been instigated against 400 defendants and the total number of civil enforcement actions was 191. After announcing these results, the Attorney General stated that that "*mortgage fraud ruins lives, destroys families and devastates whole communities, so attacking the problem from every possible direction is vital . . . we will use every tool available to investigate, prosecute and prevent mortgage fraud, and we will not rest until anyone preying on vulnerable American homeowners is brought to justice*" (Department of Justice, 2010).

It has been claimed that the creation of the Financial Fraud Enforcement Task Force clearly illustrates that the "*the investigation and prosecution of financial and investment fraud is a primary concern* [for the Obama Administration]" (Saladrigas, 2012: 464).

Enforcement Response

The SEC has used its civil enforcement sanctions against violaters of securities and fraud legislation, while the Department of Justice and FBI have attempted to commence criminal prosecutions against white collar criminals. The civil enforcement response has generated a superabundance of high profile, record breaking, headline grabbing and media friendly financial sanctions. Likewise, the criminal enforcement response has resulted in numerous low level prosecutions, especially those relating to mortgage fraud. The response to the most recent financial crisis can be contrasted to that adopted towards the Savings and Loans Crisis (Black, 2011: 988). The next part of the chapter review the use of criminal sanctions against those white collar criminals during the financial crisis.

Criminal Sanctions

US law enforcement agenices have a considerable collection of legislative provisions at their disposal to tackle financial crime associated with the financial crisis. The prevention of fraud is an essential part of many criminal statutes (Podgor, 1999: 760). For example, the Mail Fraud Statute criminalises mistreating the post office in continuance with any fraudulent activity. Prosecutors must prove that the defendant intended to create a scheme to defraud the post office and it is not obligatory for the false representation to be communicated by mail, only that the mail system was to be used to conduct the fraudulent activity (Weintraub, 1987: 524). The Mail Fraud Statute has become one of the most popular fraud statutes with prosecutors and it has even been described as a launch pad for money laundering prosecutions. The law has become the most important and powerful fraud prosecutorial tools. The Act has been amended and extended by the Anti-Drug Abuse Act, 1988 and the Violent Crime Control and Law Enforcement Act, 1994. Therefore, the Mail Fraud Statute *now* "*covers a full range of consumer frauds, stock frauds, land frauds, bank frauds, insurance frauds, and commodity frauds, but [also] areas as blackmail, counterfeiting, election fraud, and bribery*" (Greenwood, 2008: 719). The Mail Fraud Statute is often used in conjunction with the Wire Fraud Statute and it provides prosecutors with a broad range of measures (Blumel, 2005: 678). The courts have expanded the application of the Wire Fraud Statute to an ever increasing number of methods of communication and it also applies to a wide range of fraudulent activities (*ibid.*).

The Bank Fraud Act was a reaction to a large number of fraudulent schemes that targeted financial institutions (Madia, 2005: 1445) and the Supreme Court's decision in *Williams v United States*,[6] which resulted in the Department of Justice abandoning many fraud related prosecutions. Therefore, Congress responded by enacting the Bank Fraud Act which criminalises schemes that intend to deceive or obtain finances from federally insured financial institutions (Biskupic, 1999: 382). The Act criminalises cheque forging, credit card fraud, student loan fraud, mortgage fraud and false financial transactions between offshore shell banks and domestic banks. The scope of the Bank Fraud Act was extended by the Financial Institutions Reform, Recovery and Enforcement Act, 1989, to include the 'financial kingpin crime', which imposes a life sentence for defendants who manage so called financial crime enterprises. The Major Fraud Act, 1988 was instituted to tackle procurement fraud, but its scope is limited to frauds that exceed $1m (MacKay, 1992: 8). As a result of the infa-

---

[6]   458 US 279.

mous collapse of Enron and WorldCom the Sarbanes-Oxley Act 2002 with the objective of improving the level of regulation by accountants and to dissuade fraudulent and unethical behaviour (Saksena, 2009: 37). The Act increased the maximum penalty for wire and mail fraud from five years to twenty years imprisonment.

Therefore, US law enforcement agencies and prosecutors have a vast array of legislative tools at their disposal to tackle white collar criminals associated with the financial crisis. According to Creseney *et al.* "*federal regulators and law enforcement agencies, eager to demonstrate they are acting to uncover criminal activity, have responded to the credit crisis by opening a substantial number of investigations*" (2009: 235). Podgor added that "*prosecutors understandably feel the necessity to show the public that there will be punishment for criminal conduct*" (2010: 216). However, the response of prosecutors in the US must be questioned because there have been no successful prosecutions of high-profile contributors to the financial crisis. Pontell *et al.* stated that "the offences that have been prosecuted thus far remain relatively minor compared to the mind-boggling felonies perpetrated by those at the centre or at the top of the largest financial institutions" (2014: 3). Morgenson and Story stated that "*whether prosecutors and regulators have been aggressive enough in pursuing wrongdoing is likely to be a subject of debate. All say they have done the best they could in difficult circumstances*" (2011). However, the latter argument can be questioned. For example, the Fraud Enforcement and Recovery Act 2009 provided additional funding for federal prosecutors and law enforcement agenices to tackle crime associated with the financial crisis. Despite the increase in funding the Department of Justice refused to create a specific mortgage task-force and the FBI reduced the number of agents investigating allegations of mortgage fraud (*ibid.*). Prosecutors have also been criticised because they sometimes "*resort to **shortcut charges** to demonstrate a quick response to the criminal conduct*" (Podgor, 2010: 217). Eric Holder, the former Attorney General, defended the prosecutors and stated that "*our record of success* [on fraud] *has been nothing less than historic*" (Department of Justice, 2012a). The accuracy of this statement must be queried given the robust response of the Department of Justice toward the Savings and Loans crisis related frauds and the swift reaction of the Corporate Fraud Task Force to the collaspe of Enron and WorldCom. However, Eric Holder did point out that "*we've found that much of the conduct that led to the financial crisis was unethical and irresponsible. But we also have discovered that some of this behaviour – while morally reprehensible – may not necessarily have been criminal. Believe me, I understand – and I often hear about – the public desire to, as one pundit put it, see the handcuffs come to Wall Street*" (*ibid.*). This is a view supported by Abramowitz and Sack who stated that "the very depth and breadth of the recent financial crisis makes it difficult to separate criminal behaviour from business misjudgement and mistake" (2013: 2).

The Department of Justice and FBI did investigate the alleged criminal activities in several banks and by September 2008, 24 banks were under investigation (Jordan, 2008). In February 2009, the number of major firms under investigation by the FBI increased to 38 (Ryan, 2009). Nonetheless, not one individual in any of these institutions has been held criminally accountable since the start of the financial crisis. The only banker who has been convicted in relation to the financial crisis was Kareem Serageldin (United States Attorney's Office, 2013).

However, the Department of Justice has secured the conviction of Rajat Gupta for insider trading, the conviction of several executives of General Electric, the mortgage fraud related conviction of Shawn Portmann, the conviction of Joseph Braas for his role in the collapse of the Bank of Lancaster County, the conviction of Peter Madoff and the several indictments for other fraud related activities. However, it is important to note that the SEC, unlike the FBI and Department of Justice, has been able to utilise its enforcement powers against some of these financial institutions. For example, Bank of America agreed to pay $150m to settle SEC charges over its having "*failed to properly disclose employee bonuses and financial losses at Merrill Lynch before shareholders approved the merger of the companies in December 2008*" (Securities and Exchange Commission, 2010). Furthermore, Angelo Mozilo, the former CEO of Countrywide agreed to settle SEC charges and paid a $22,5m penalty for "*misleading investors as the subprime mortgage crisis emerged. The settlement also permanently bars Mozilo from ever again serving as an officer or director of a publicly traded company*" (*ibid.*). The highest profile enforcement action brought by the SEC is against Goldman Sachs who agreed to pay a record financial penalty of $550m. The former Goldman Sachs Vice President Fabrice Tourre has was hold liable for faud regarding his part in a synthetic collareralised debt obligation that was linked to subprime residential mortgages. The jury concluded that Fabrice Tourre was liable for six of the seven securities law violations and that he has assisted an alleged fraud by Goldman Sachs (Baer *et al.*, 2013). Another reason for the lack of criminal proceedings is the adverse effect that financial crimes have on the stock market. Dooley and Radke stated that "*because of the market's sensitivity to any hint of financial impropriety, the misstatement of financial information by publicly-listed companies, or a corporate scandal, any such revelations are likely to trigger a shart and significant stockprice drop*" (2010: 639).

A graphic illustration of this occurred following the Enron scandal that resulted in the downfall of Arther Anderson, which was then regarded as one of the "Big Five" accountancy firms, surrending its practicing licence and eventual liquidation. Furthermore, it is necessary to emphasise that investigations and prosecutions in the area of financial crime are notoriously complex and difficult (Creseney *et al.*, 2009: 235). The prosecution is furher complicated by the sophisticated mechanisms used by white collar criminals to disguise their illegal activities and that the appearance of the proceeds of crime can often appear to be legitimate (Bell, 2007, 1627). It has been argued that prosecutors could utilise the *responsible corporate officer* doctrine to support the prosecution of instances of mortgage fraud (Schuck, 2010: 372-373). The responsible corporate officer doctrine provides that "*individuals can be held criminally liable if they fail to prevent fraud from occurring despite having the authority and capacity to do so*" (*ibid.*). Schuck recommended that "*there are two possibilities exist to expand the doctrine to mortgaeg fraud. First, courts can expand the doctrine by applying it to mortgage fraud prosecutions. Alternatively, Congress can amend a state already used to prosecute mortgage fraud to include 'responsible corporate officers'*" (2010: 388). Anothter scheme that could be used by prosecutors is to compel companies to cooperate with them by threating to instigate criminal proceedings against them. Wray and Hur argued that an indictment "*often amounts to a virtual death sentence for business entities, a corporate prosecution provides a government an opportunity for deterrence on a massive scale*" (2006: 1096). By employing such a tactic the government can been accussed of creating an enforcement culture that seeks to avoid prosecuting corporations. This is further supported by the increased use of non-proseuction agreements of deferred prosecution agreements.

Civil Sanctions

It has been extremely difficult for law enforcement agencies to prosecute those who contributed to the financial crisis. Therefore, the most frequently imposed sanction on the culprits of the financial crisis has been the imposition of civil sanctions. These have been imposed by the Department of Justice, the CFTC and the SEC. Montagano took the view that "*in the wake of the Great Recession, the SEC, like countless other federal and state agencies, is using every tool at its disposal to restore confidence in US markets in hopes of restoring the economy*" (2012: 577). In 2007, the SEC commenced 776 investigations, imposed 262 civil actions and approximately 400 administrative proceedings. These enforcement activities were for a broad range of issues including "*financial fraud, abusive backdating of stock options, insider trading, violations by broker-dealers, and fraud related to mutual funds*" (Securities and Exchange Commission, 2007). Additionally, the enforcement activities of the SEC resulted in $1,6bn of disgorgement and penalties (*ibid:*, 2). In 2008, the SEC instigated 671 enforcement activities which illustrated a 25% increase in the number of insider trading cases and a 45% rise in market manipulation cases (Securities and Exchange Commission, 2008). Additionally, the SEC refunded $1bn to damaged investors (*ibid.|:* 17). In 2009, the SEC was able to redistribute a proportion of $843m to approximately 250.000 failed investors of AIG (Securities and Exchange Commission, 2009: 29). It is very intersting to note that in 2009, the SEC spent $980m to enforce the federal securtities laws (*ibid.*: 28). In 2012, the SEC announced that it had filed 734 enforcement actions . . . [it had] requiring the payment of more than $3bn in penalties and disgorgement for the benefit of harmed investors. It represents an 11 % increase over the amount ordered last year. In the past two years, the SEC has obtained orders for $5,9bn in penalties and disgorgement" (Securities and Exchange Commission, 2012). Additionally the SEC has taken enforcement action against many Ponzi related fraud schemes since the onset of the 2008 financial crisis (Securities and Exchange Commission, n/d).

The Commodities Futures Trading Commission (CFTC) has been heavily involved in the LIBOR scandal and has imposed several financial sanctions on banks. For example, in June 2012 the CFTC fined Barclays $200m for its attempted manipulation and false reporting of LIBOR and Euribor. Furthermore, CFTC fined UBS $700m for its attempted manipulation and false reporting of LIBOR and Euribor (Commodities Futures Trading Commission, 2012). In February 2013, the CFTC fined RBS $325m for its manipulation, attempted manipulation and false reporting of Yen and Swiss Franc LIBOR (Commodities Futures Trading Commission, 2013a). In September 2013, the CFTC fined ICAP Europe Limited $65m civil monetary penalty for the market manipulationipulation of LIBOR (Commodities Futures Trading Commission, 2013b). More recent examples include Deutshce Bank agreeing to pay an $800m penalty for the manipulation of LIBOR and Citibank paying a $175m penalty (Commodities Futures Trading Commission, 2015).

Additionally, the Department of Justice played a key role in obtaining the largest settlement ($25bn) for robo-signing (Department of Justice, 2012a), it also acquired the largest fair lending settlement ($335m) with Countrywide Financial Corporation (Commodities Futures Trading Commission, 2012), and the second largest fair lending settlement ($125m) against Wells Fargo Bank (Commodities Futures Trading Commission, 2012). In relation to the manipulation of LIBOR the Department of Justice reached an agreement with Barclays Bank that it would pay $160m penalty for its actions. In December 2012, the Department of Justice announced that UBS Securities Japan, a subsidiary of UBS pleaded guilty to wire fraud and its role in manipulating LIBOR (Commodities Futures Trading Commission, 2012d). The company has entered into an agreement with the DoJ which required them to pay a $100m fine. Additionally, its parent company UBS AG, entered into a non-prosecution agreement which resulsted in the payment of a further $400m fine (*ibid.*). Additionally, in February 2013 the Department of Justice announced that RBS Securities Japan Limited, a subsidiary of RBS had pleaded guilty to wire fraud and manipulation as part of the Japense Yen LIBOR as part of a deferred prosecution agreement (Department of Justice, 2013). However, the largest civil penalty imposed by the Deparement of Justice was $16.65bn on Bank of America for fraud in July 2014 (Department of Justice, 2014).

Conclusions

The response towards the financial crisis and financial crime in the US has been largely led by the Department of Jusice, the FBI, the SEC and the CFTC. Each of these agencies has attempted to adopt a robust stance to the illegal activities within their law enforcement regulatory remit. Barak Obama introduced the Fraud Enforcement and Recovery Act 2009 which resulted in the rebalancing the amount of federal funding for financial crime related agencies including the FBI, SEC and Department of Justice. This has contributed towards a significant increase in the number of investigations, arrests and mortgage fraud related convictions secured by the FBI.

However, the results of this additional funding must be questioned when compared to the response to the Savings and Loans crisis which resulted in approximatley 800 fraud related convictions. The results since the financial crisis have been tainted in the eyes of several commentators because there has not been one high profile bank related conviction despite the FBI instigating numerous investigations. President Barak Obama also created the Financial Fraud Enforcement Task Force to direclty tackle financial crime including securities and mortgage fraud emitting from the financial crisis. This resulted in immediate action from the Task Forces and its members. Thereore, the response by President Barak Obama to the financial crisis and financial crime can be categorised as *predictable* as similar responses were made to the threat of corporate bribery in the 1970s, the Savings and Loans Crisis in the 1980s, securities fraud, the corporate scandals in the 1990s – so called 'mega frauds' – and the collapse of Enron and WorldCom. For example, in response to the collapse of Enron and WorldCom President George Bush introduced the Sarbanes-Oxley Act in 2002. This measure was supported by the creation of the Corporate Fraud Task Force, who in conjunction with the Department of Justice obtained nearly 1.300 corporate fraud convictions.

The SEC has been the most active regulatory agency since the start of the financial crisis. However, all of the enforcement activities instigated by the SEC are of a civil nature and either amount to the imposition of a financial sanction or a prohibition order. The SEC has imposed a number of high profile financial sanctions on firms who have breached their rules and regualtions. The SEC does not have the ability to instigate criminal proceedings and it is exclusively reliant on the referrals it makes to the Department of Justice. The SEC must be criticised for its weak response to financial crime associated with the financial crisis. The clearest example of its ineffective approach related to the ponzi fraud scheme instigated by Bernard Madoff, who the SEC could and should have stopped on numerous occasions. Nonetheless, the SEC has continued to instigate an enforcement strategy that that seeks to continuously impose financial sanctions on on firms who have breached its regulations. This stance has also been followed by the Department of Justice and the CFTC, who have imposed large financial sanctions on firms since the start of the financial crisis. For example, the CFTC and Department of Justice has imposed record financial penalties on banks who have manipulated LIBOR, and an identical stance to regulatory bodies around the world responding to the LIBOR scandal.

US authorities have a plethora of criminal legislative provisions that could have been used since the financial crisis. A vast majority of the criminal proceedings instigated since 2007 by the Department of Justice and the FBI have generally targetted people involved in mortgage fraud. As outlined earlier in this chapter, the FBI has conducted numerous investigations into banks following the financial crisis. However, the FBI has failed to successfully convict any member of Wall Street associated with the alleged misconduct prior or during the financial crisis. It is extremely difficult to secure financial crime related convictions and in many investigations the conduct discovered by law enforcement agencies was irresponsible and unethical, but not necessarily criminal. It appears that US law enforcement agencies have created an enforcement culture that seeks to avoid prosecuting corporations.

References

Arogeti, J. How much cooperation between government agencies is too much? Reconciling United States v Scrushy, the corporate fraud task force, and the nature of parallel proceedings' (2006) *Georgia State University Law Review*, Winter, 23, 427-453

Baer, J., C. Bray and Eaglesham, 'Fab Trader Liable in Fraud', 2 August 2013, available from http://online.wsj.com/article/SB10001424127887323681904578641843284450004.html, accessed 7 October 2015.

Bell, S., Criminal procedure within the firm. *Stanford Law Review*, 2007, 59, 1613-1670

Biskupic, S., Fine tuning the bank statute: a prosecutor's perspective'. *Marquette Law Review*, 1999, 82, 381-403

Black, W., Neo-classical economic theories, methodology, and praxis optimize criminogenic environments and produce recurrent, intensifying crises. *Creighton Law Review*, 2011, 44, 597-645

Black, W., The Department of Justice 'chases mice while lions roam the campsite': why the department has failed to prosecute elite frauds that drove the financial crisis. *UMKC Law Review,* 2012, Summer, 80, 987-1019

Blumel, R., Mail and wire fraud. *American Criminal Law Review*, 2005, 42, 677-698

Brotman, E. and E. Dougherty. Blue collar tactics in financial crime. *Champion*, 2011, September, 35, 16-20

Colesanti, J., Another Madoff masquerade? Questioning 'securities fraud' in the crime and its clean-up. *Saint Louis University Law Journal*, 2012, 56, 521-565

Commodities Futures Trading Commission (2013a) 'CFTC Charges ICAP Europe Limited, a Subsidiary of ICAP plc, with Manipulation and Attempted Manipulation of Yen Libor', 25 September 2013, available from http://www.cftc.gov/PressRoom/PressReleases/pr6708-13, accessed 25 September 2013

Commodities Futures Trading Commission (2013b) 'CFTC Orders The Royal Bank of Scotland plc and RBS Securities Japan Limited to Pay $325 Million Penalty to Settle Charges of Manipulation, Attempted Manipulation, and False Reporting of Yen and Swiss Franc LIBOR', 6 February 2013, available from http://www.cftc.gov/PressRoom/PressReleases/pr6510-13, accessed 12 August 2013

Commodities Futures Trading Commission (2012) 'CFTC Orders UBS to Pay $700 Million Penalty to Settle Charges of Manipulation, Attempted Manipulation and False Reporting of LIBOR and Other Benchmark Interest Rates', 9 December 2012, available from www.cftc.gov/PressRoom/PressReleases/pr6472-12, accessed 12 August 2013.

Commodity Futures Trading Commission (2015) 'Deutsche Bank to Pay $800 Million Penalty to Settle CFTC Charges of Manipulation, Attempted Manipulation, and False Reporting of LIBOR and Euribor', April 23 2015, www.cftc.gov/PressRoom/PressReleases/pr7159-15 accessed 28 November 2016

Creseney, A., E. Eng Gordon and S. Nuttal, Regulatory investigations and the credit crisis: the search for villains. *American Criminal Law Review*, 2009, Spring, 46, 225-273

Department of Justice (2014) 'Bank of America to pay $16.65bn in historic Justice Department Settlement for financial fraud lending up to and during the financial crisis', 21 August 2014, available from www.justice.gov/opa/pr/bank-america-pay-1665-billion-historic-justice-department-settlement-financial-fraud-leading, accessed 28 November 2016.

Department of Justice (2013) 'RBS Securities Japan Limited Agrees to Plead Guilty in Connection with Long-Running Manipulation of Libor Benchmark Interest Rates', February 6 2013, available from www.justice.gov/opa/pr/2013/February/13-crm-161.html, accessed 13 August 2013

Department of Justice (2012a) 'Attorney General Eric Holder Speaks at Columbia University Law School on Preventing and Combating Financial Fraud', 23 February 2012, available from http://www.justice.gov/iso/opa/ag/speeches/2012/ag-speech-120223.html, accessed 6 October 2013

Department of Justice (2012b) 'Financial Fraud Enforcement Task Force Members Reveal Results of Distressed Homeowner Initiative', 9 October 2012, available from www.justice.gov/opa/pr/2012/October/12-ag-1216.html, accessed 1 August 2013

Department of Justice (2011) 'Coinciding with One-Year Anniversary of "Operation Stolen Dreams," Three Loan Officers and a Title Agent Charged in $2.5 Million Reverse Mortgage and Loan Modification Scheme', 6 July 2011, available from www.justice.gov/opa/pr/2011/July/11-civ-884.html, accessed 1 August 2013

Department of Justice (2010) 'Financial Fraud Enforcement Task Force Announces Results of Broadest Mortgage Fraud Sweep in History', 17 June 2010, available from www.justice.gov/opa/pr/2010/June/10-opa-708.html, accessed 1 August 2013

Department of Justice (2009) *Letter to The Honorable Patrick J. Leahy Chairman, Committee on the Judiciary*, Arpril 1 2009, available from www.justice.gov/ola/views-letters/111-1/040109-s386-fraud-enforcement-recovery-act.pdf, accessed June 20th 2013

Dooley, D. and M. Radke, Does severe punishment deter financial crimes? *Charleston Law Review Spring*, 2010, 4, 619-659

Federal Bureau of Investigation (2009) '2009 Mortgage Fraud Report', n/d, available from http://www.fbi.gov/stats-services/publications/mortgage-fraud-2009, accessed 8 August 2013

Federal Bureau of Investigation (2004) 'Chris Swecker, Assistant Director, Criminal Investigative Division, Federal Bureau of Investigation, Before the House Financial Services Subcommittee on Housing and Community Opportunity', 7 October 2004, available from www.fbi.gov/news/testimony/fbis-efforts-in-combating-mortgage-fraud, accessed 8 August 2013

Federal Bureau of Investigation (2011) 'Financial Crimes Report to the Public - Fiscal Years 2010-2011', 2011, available from www.fbi.gov/stats-services/publications/financial-crimes-report-2010-2011/financial-crimes-report-2010-2011#Mortgage, accessed 8 August 2013

Federal Bureau of Investigation (2012) 'Inside the FBI – Podcast', 11 October 2012, available from www.fbi.gov/news/podcasts/inside/distressed-homeowner-mortgage-fraud.mp3/view, accessed 14 October 2013

Federal Bureau of Investigation (2010) 'Operation Stolen Dreams Hundreds Arrested in Mortgage Fraud Sweep', 17 June 2010, available from http://www.fbi.gov/news/stories/2010/june/mortgage-fraud-sweep, accessed 1 August 2013

Harris, J., Getting over Madoff: how the SEC must restore its credibility. *Company Lawyer*, 2010, 31(2), 33-34

Henning, J., Making sure the buck stops here: barring executives for corporate violations. *University of Chicago Legal Forum*, 2012, 91-128

Hiznay, H., How the Bernard Madoff scandal exposed weaknesses in asset management regulation. *Review of Banking and Financial Law*, 2009, Spring, 28, 413-425

Hurt, C., Evil has a new name (and a new narrative): Bernard Madoff. *Michigan State Law Review*, 2009, Winter, 947-987.

Huynh, D., Pre-emption v. punishment: a comparative study of financial crime prosecution in the United States and the United Kingdom. *Journal of International Business and Law*, 2010, Spring, 9, 105-135

Johnson, C. 'U.S. Promotes Its Record on Corporate Crime', 18 July 2007 www.washingtonpost.com/wp-dyn/content/article/2007/07/17/AR2007071701767.html, accessed 31 July 2013.

Jordan, L., FBI Investigating Companies At Heart Of Wall St Crisis', 23 September 2008, www.huffingtonpost.com/2008/09/23/fbi-investigating-compani_n_128759.html, accessed 27 September 2013

Klock, M., Lessons learned from Bernard Madoff: why we should partially privatise the Barney Fifes at the SEC. *Arizona State Law Journal*, 2010, 42, 783-835

Lover, C., The Fraud Recovery Enforcement and Recovery Act of 2009 and the expansion of the liability under the False Claims Act. *Utah Law Review*, 2012, 1129-1154

MacKay, S., Major fraud against the United States. *Army Lawyer*, 7-14 September, 1992

Madia, M., The bank fraud act: a risk of loss requirement? *University of Chicago Law Review*, 2005, 72, 1445-1471

Maher, C., Crisis not averted: lack of criminal prosecutions leave limited consequences for those responsible for the financial crisis. *New England Journal on Criminal and Civil Confinement*, 2013, 39, 459-476

Markopolis, H. 'Testimony before the US Senate Banking, Housing and Urban Affairs Committee', 4 February 2009, available from www.banking.senate.gov/public/index.cfm?FuseAction=Files.View&FileStore_id=a157968b-2c5f-4477-a9d6-7042fec46593, accessed 14 October 2013

Mattingly, P. and T. Schoenberg. U.S. Mortgage Group Forced to Correct Initiative Stats', 9 August 2013, www.bloomberg.com/news/2013-08-09/u-s-mortgage-group-forced-to-correct-initiative-stats.html, accessed 14 October 2013

Montagano, C., The global crackdown on insider trading: a silver lining to the great recession. *Indiana Journal of Global Legal Studies*, 2012, 19, 575-598

Morgenson, G. and L. Story, 'In financial crisis, no prosecutions of top figures', 14 April 2011, available from www.nytimes.com/2011/04/14/business/14prosecute.html?pagewanted=al l&_r=0, accessed 27 September 2013

Moye, J., Are we bulletproof?: a defensive business strategy to protect health care companies from False Claims Act litigation and corporate integrity agreements. *University of Baltimore Law Forum*, 2010, Fall, 41, 24-42

Nichols, C., Addressing inept SEC enforcement efforts: lessons from Madoff, the hedge fund industry, and title IV of the Dodd-Frank Act for the US and global financial systems. *North-western Journal of International Law and Business*, 2011, 31, 637-698

Nunziato, M., Aiding and abetting, a Madoff family affair: why secondary actors should be held accountable for securities fraud through the restoration of the private right of action for aiding and abetting liability under the federal security laws. *Albany Law Review*, 2010, 73, 603-643

Podgor, E., Criminal fraud. *American University Law Review*, 1999, 48, 729-768

Podgor, E., Financial crime and the recession: was the chicken or egg first? *University of Chicago Legal Forum*, 2010, 205-222

Podgor, E., Introduction: examining financial crime with trifocals. *Fordham Urban Law Journal*, 2011, December, 39, 299-308

Pontell, H., W. Black and G. Geis, Too big to fail, too powerful to prosecute? On the absence of criminal prosecutions after the 2009 financial meltdown. *Crime, Law and Society*, 2014, August, 61, 1

Ramirez, M., Criminal affirmance: going beyond the deterrence paradigm to examine the social meaning of declining prosecution of elite crime. *Connecticut Law Review*, 2013, February, 45, 865-931

Reidy, J., The problem of proceeds in the era of FERA. *American Journal of Criminal Law*, 2010, Summer, 5, 295-323

Reiss, D., The role of the Fannie Mae/Freddie Mac duopoly in the American housing market. *Journal of Financial Regulation and Compliance*, 2009, 17(3), 336-348.

Review, 45, 717–740

Ryan, J., Fraud 'Directly Related' to Financial Crisis Probed', 11 February 2009, http://abcnews.go.com/TheLaw/Economy/story?id=6855179&page=1, accessed 27 September 2013.

Ryder, N., The financial crisis and financial crime in the United Kingdom: a critical analysis of the response by Financial Regulatory Agencies. *Company Lawyer*, 2017, 38(1), 4-14

Saksena, P., The Sarbanes-Oxley Act and occupational fraud: does the law effectively tackle the real problem. *International Company and Commercial Law Review*, 2009, 20(2), 37-43

Saladrigas, C., Corporate criminal liability: lessons from the Rothstein debacle. *University of Miami Law Review*, 2012, Winter, 66, 435-469

Schuck, M., A new use for the responsible corporate officer doctrine: prosecuting industry insiders for mortgage fraud. *Lewis & Clark Law Review*, 2010, 14, 371-395

Securities and Exchange Commission (2010) 'Goldman Sachs agrees pay record $550m to settle SEC charges related to subprime mortgage CDO', 15 October 2010, available from www.sec.gov/news/press/2010/2010-123.htm, accessed October 7 2013

Securities and Exchange Commission (n/d) 'SEC Enforcement Actions Against Ponzi Fraud Schemes', n/d, available from: accessed 28 November 2016

Securities and Exchange Commission (2012) 'SEC's Enforcement Program Continues to Show Strong Results in Safeguarding Investors and Markets', 14 November 2012, available from www.sec.gov/News/PressRelease/Detail/PressRelease/1365171485830, accessed 11 August 2013

Securities and Exchange Commission (2007) *2007 Performance and Accountability Report* (Securities and Exchange Commission: Washington DC, 2007)

Securities and Exchange Commission (2008) *2008 Performance and Accountability Report* (Securities and Exchange Commission: Washington DC, 2008)

Securities and Exchange Commission (2009) *2009 Performance and Accountability Report* (Securities and Exchange Commission: Washington DC, 2009)

Securities Exchange Commission (2005) 'The World's Largest Hedge Fund is a Fraud', 7 November 2005, available from www.sec.gov/news/studies/2009/oig-509/exhibit-0293.pdf, accessed October 13 2013

Sheppard, M. and E. Dougherty, Tapping into Wall Street - the government employs tougher tactics against money crimes. *Criminal Justice*, Winter, 26, 20-29

Smith, A., Madoff sentenced to 150 years, CNN, June 30 2009, available from http://money.cnn.com/2009/06/29/news/economy/madoff_prison_senten ce/index.htm, accessed 17 August 2012.

TRAC Reports 'Slump in FBI financial crime prosecutions', September 24 2013, http://trac.syr.edu/whatsnew/email.130924.html, accessed 17 October 2013

United States Attorney's Office 'Former Credit Suisse Managing Director Pleads Guilty In Connection With Scheme To Hide Losses In Mortgage-Backed Securities Trading Book', 12 April 2013, available from www.justice.gov/usao/nys/pressreleases/April13/SerageldinKareemPleaPR.php, accessed September 27 2013.

Valukas, A.R. , Examiner In re Lehman Brothers Holding Inc., Report, Chapter 11 Case No. 08-13555, United States Bankruptcy Court for the Southern District of New York, www.distressedvolatility.com/2010/03/fullexaminer –

Weintraub, L., Crime of the Century: use of the mail fraud statute against authors. *Boston University Law Review*, 1987, 67, 507-549

Wray, C. and R. Hur, Corporate criminal prosecution in a post-Enron world: the Thompson memo in theory and practice. *American Criminal Law Review*, 2006, 43, 1095-1188

The offshore world: nebulous finances

Petrus C. van Duyne and *Tjalling J. van Koningsveld*[1]

Introduction

Sundays are supposed to be days of leisure and relaxation. However, on Sunday 3 April 2016 many woke up after a restless night and with a head full of worries because disturbing news about the Panama consultancy firm Mossack and Fonseca. The reason of their state of mind was the publication of what was called the *Panama papers* and the fear of the mentioning of their company, their addresses or even family name. Due to a leak at the mentioned firm, which provides a unique sight on the offshore world, they found themselves unexpectedly involved in a worldwide scandal. Against the background of the recent history of (financial) information safety breaches, it was another example of the fact that in principle no digital information storage is safe. Anybody having for whatever reason spread his or her commercial or financial interests over one or more jurisdiction could have known that leak-proof hidden financing is no longer of this world.[2] The history of financial leakage incidents shows that the veil of bank secrecy was regularly lifted by (ex-)employees or hackers compromising the institutions' integrity reputation in the eye of secrecy seekers. Naturally, supervising and regulatory institutions have another idea of institutional integrity: there task is to see to it that banks should stay away from shady monies and methods to hide the identity of their owners. Instead, suspicious transactions should be reported to authorities to prevent money laundering, tax evasion (or both) or other suspicious financial conduct. From this view on integrity, law enforcement and tax authorities have no qualms in taking advantage of

---

[1] Prof. Petrus C. van Duyne is visiting professor at Northumbria (UK) and Utrecht University (Netherlands). Dr. Tjalling J. van Koningsveld is director of Offshore Knowledge Centre.
   The authors want to thank the Dutch Land Registry for its open and valuable support and the access to its database.

[2] Since the leak of the KB Bank Luxembourg there have been seven other leaks damaging among others the UBS Bank and HSBC Switzerland.

stolen financial information, a stand underpinned by the Courts of Cassation in various countries.[3]

There are good reasons for the authorities to make use of any information enabling the detection of hidden assets or methods and techniques of keeping these illegally out of reach of the tax administration. It is a generally accepted claim that a very large portion of the wealth of countries remains outside the reach of the governments: *i.e.* wrongly untaxed (see table 2). While there are no reliable data to determine the exact volume of the hidden wealth, impressive estimates abound, which all have the same weakness: their empirical and theoretical foundations are questionable. The United Nations (2011) speak of an "IMF consensus range" according to which hidden proceeds from crime amount to 2-5% of the GDP, worldwide. This sounds authoritative, but the nature of that consensus (between whom?) or the empirical sources of the estimate, are shrouded in clouds. About two decades ago, the President of the IMF, Camdessus, launched this estimate, but without any reference: a kind of 'alternative fact' *avant la lettre*. Despite that, it became a kind of socio-political tenet buttressed by his authority and IMF publications (Tanzi, 1996; Quirke, 1996) and that of other international bodies, such as the UN and OECD. Nevertheless, it is still a matter of belief or of 'alternative truth'. Believers got ample scholarly support to maintain that consensus, particularly from estimation studies on money laundering (Unger and Rawlings, 2006; Unger, 2007). Unfortunately these studies were loaded with fuzzy concepts, ambiguous definitions, unproven assumptions and unreliable methodology (Van Duyne *et al.*, 2005). The fuzzy concepts concern what should be considered as the criminal, black, grey or informal economy and related money laundering, among others. Schneider and Enste (2000) and Schneider and Windischbauer (2008) provided a taxonomic map or typology of criminal, black and grey economy, but problems arise as soon a proper demarcations must be made or operational definitions have to be coined. This has consequences for assessing the size of the phenomenon in financial terms: a change of definition or assumptions can entail a sizeable change in estimated volume. This allows much politically opportunistic representations usually leaning towards the higher ranges of the estimates: words or definitions do matter. They can influence national prioritisation contributing to lack of coherence between countries' policy: using similar terms does not imply aiming at the same objectives. This impedes the determination of the effectiveness of the various policies.

---

[3] See case KB Lux, ECLI:NL:HR:2006:AX7471. The information stolen from Luxembourg or Swiss banks can now be exchanged between EU tax authorities.

The problem is further compounded if we realise that the static 'volume question' disregards the dynamism inherent to the management of financial assets. Knowledge of this dynamism is a pre-condition for targeted policy making. 'Crying wolf' with big figures is not enough. Therefore, we should also look at how much illegal wealth is in circulation, deposited or withdrawn again to be eventually enjoyed. Most of the monetary assets travels continuously, not physically but from account to account and from country to country. And most obviously, a large part of that mobility is cross-border. This financial mobility is served by a multitude of enterprises specialised in offering financial discretion or –less euphemistically– secrecy. They reside at numerous jurisdictions enabling such services. Though the latter are also named tax haven or -paradise, we prefer to use the more neutral denotation: offshore (financial) centre. As we will see, it is a cliché to link them to the proverbial sunny palm-tree white beach islands. Offshore centres exist also on mainland, like the states of Delaware, Utah, Nevada, South Dakota and other emerging 'offshore states' in the USA (World Bank, 2011; Financial Times, May 8, 2016).

Given their importance, we will examine in this chapter how these offshore centres and/or offshore companies are defined, and what the available data can tell us about the flows of moneys through these offshore jurisdictions and their use in one particular asset category: real estate in the Netherlands. In short: knowing and mapping the offshore centres or companies and their money flows and their place in the real estate market.

What are offshore centres and offshore companies?

Despite the political importance attributed to the phenomenon of offshore businesses, the way in which the term 'offshore' is used is very loosely. We have offshore banks, accounts, jurisdictions being used by offshore companies, but there is still not a universal objective definition of what an offshore company or tax haven or Offshore Financial Centre should be. Every organisation or author has his own definition and criteria and therefore has own lists with different number of companies/jurisdictions. Unsurprisingly Koningsveld (2015; Ch. 2) identified 15 definitions, most rather loosely formulation, of which we can only present a few examples. It is interesting to observe that the way of formulation can reflect a particular commercial or political interest. For example, a US corporate service provider describes in his Offshore Money Book offshore as:

"*An international term meaning not only out of your country (jurisdiction), but possibly out of the tax reach of your country of residence, domicile, or citizenship.*"[4]

It looks like an advertisement to attract customers.

The International Tax Glossary description is more elaborate, but looks also directed at customers in need of fiscal safety:

"*[A] term usually applied to a company registered in a country (often a tax haven) other than the country in which it carries on its business activities. (. . .) Certain tax haven countries have legislation specifically designed to make the use of offshore companies registered in their jurisdiction attractive.*"[5]

Not surprisingly the IMF gives a description with an implicit reproach deduced from its task to guard financial stability and transparency:

"*An OFC is a country or jurisdiction that provides financial services to non-residents on a scale that is incommensurate with the size and the financing of its domestic economy*".[6]

The element of "incommensurate with the size" etc. is rather moralistic and judging than a part of a formal definition of 'offshore': what is 'incommensurate'? Important is the key element of 'services to non-residents'.

The Bureau for International Narcotics and Law Enforcement Affairs defines an offshore financial centre as:

"*Usually a low-tax jurisdiction that provides financial and investment services to nonresident companies and individuals. Generally, companies doing business in offshore centres are prohibited from having clients or customers who are resident in the jurisdiction. Such centres may have strong secrecy provision or minimal identification requirements.*"[7]

The emphasis is here on low tax and secrecy, implicitly also pointing at tax avoidance, if not evasion. What the element 'usual' means in a formal definition remains unspecified.

We are of the opinion that these and similar definitions have some suitable elements but are otherwise burdened by irrelevant opinions or morals. The simplest description is provided by the OECD:

A legal entity incorporated in a foreign jurisdiction and usually only conducts economic activities outside the country in which it was incorporated."[8]

---

[4] Cornez 2000, p. 267.
[5] International Tax Glossary 2001, p. 248.
[6] IMF 2007, p.7. according to its definition there would be 49 countries qualifying as offshore centres.
[7] INCRS 2015, p. vii. International Narcotics Control Strategy???
[8] OESO 2009, p. 24.

This is a proper formal definition, unfortunately spoiled by the unspecified adverb 'usually'. According to the definition of Van Koningsveld (2015, p. 78), the dividing line is much more stringent: "*an offshore corporation is not allowed to be commercially active in the place of registration while its ultimate beneficial owner resides in another country*". At the country of residence its only acts consist of the payments of fees for registration or other services: very welcome to pay, but not to stay. All the other attributes are more or less extra features as a consequence of commercial and fiscal advantages, such as tax exemption and attractive secrecy laws, which makes the country of registration into an attractive offshore centre. That can be any country as Sikka (2003; p. 4) observed:

> "*The term offshore is not necessarily restricted to tiny or remote islands. It can also be applied to any location (e.g. New Jersey, Delaware, City of London) that seeks to attract capital from non-residents by promising low/no taxes, low regulation, secrecy and confidentiality.*"

It cannot be denied that many small island states are offshore financial centres, which has a perfect historical and legal background. Decades ago after becoming independent or getting autonomy they were encouraged into the financial service market by the same industrialised world and international financial institutions (IMF, World Bank, OECD) which later became worried by the success of the same offshore centres. After a change of policy, the mentioned financial institutions pursued an active policy against 'unfair' tax competition and secrecy laws which may hinder the fight against money laundering: "*In particular, we agree (. . .) to take action against (. . .) tax havens. The era of bank secrecy is over*".[9] As recent EU steps against various tax dodging multinationals demonstrate, the big financial interests did not only concern money laundering, nor some tropic islands but also special tax arrangements made within the industrialised world, for example in Ireland and the Netherlands.[10]

As mentioned repeatedly in many descriptions of offshore financial centre, (OFC) the provision of secrecy, rather anonymity, is an important service. For many persons and companies it is an essential element for considering establishing a company in an OFC in the first place. The legislation of most OFCs (mainly previous British colonies) allow legal arrangements through trust offices and International Business Companies. Abstracting from the local legal technicalities, the core of these arrangements consists of *nominee services*. Stripped from

---

[9]   Statement of G20 during the meeting in London, 2 April 2009, point 15.
[10] For example, see the cases of Apple, Starbuks and See: OECD 'Library Briefing of the European Parliament', 2009, p. 3; Communication of the EC of 30 August 2016 concerning illegal state support by Ireland, Netherlands and Luxembourg (http://europa.eu/rapid/press-release_IP-16-2923_nl.htm)

all legal technicalities, these are legalised *straw man services*: the professional in the OFC can act as a nominated director or shareholder such that the real beneficial owner (director or shareholder) remains hidden. The local service provider, *e.g.* an attorney or staff of the local trust office gets an annual fee and otherwise indemnifies himself against all third-party liabilities or claims. In short, a trusted, professional and perfect straw man service. The nominee director or share-holder do not need to know their principal or ultimate beneficial owner. In the first place, the latter can be hidden behind a string of offshore companies spread over a multitude of OFCs. In second place, one does not need to travel person-ally to the OFC, as registration by e-mail with a copy of a passport is in many cases also possible. This is not only the case in 'far-away islands', but also right within the international financial centre: the UK, allegedly rated as the most anti-laundering compliant country (Van Koningsveld, 2015: Ch. 3.4.).

The geographical spread of offshore centres

As we indicated above, OFCs can be located anywhere. So in order to get a proper survey we first addressed the local Chambers of Commerce of 40 juris-dictions falling under our offshore definition. The return from this source was not complete whereupon the International Narcotics Control Strategy reports and the Company Formation Survey were consulted. This search was directed at jurisdictions with a specific legislation for International Business Companies. There are also jurisdictions with no specific offshore company legislation but they serve non-resident legal persons in comparable ways, such as with tax ex-emption ('zero-tax companies'). Table 1 presents the results of this search.

Table 1
Offshore companies registered and established in 2013

Jurisdiction	Total registered 2013	Newly established 2013
Anguilla	13.236	4.353
Aruba	282	3
Bahamas	35.544	3.056
Belize	140.747	12.761
Bermuda	13.297	2.572
British Virgin Islands	1.130.190	53.329
Cayman Islands	78.070	8.428
Cyprus[11]	272.157	10.847
Dutch Antillen/Curaçao	15.202	697
Gibraltar	30.017	1.589
Isle of Man	20.072	2.452
Guernsey	18.707	1.648
Jersey	32.479	2.517
Liechtenstein	5.997	n.a.
Madeira	1.640	146
Malaysia / Labuan	9.487	779
Malta	39.858	2.869
Mauritius	20.493	2.196
Nauru[12]	59	n.a.
Panama[13]	88.775	n.a.
Seychelles[14]	140.000	20.747
St. Lucia[15]	2.935	487
St. Vincent & Grenadines	21.888	969
Turks & Caicos Islands	14.548	1.453
Total	**2.145.680**	**133.898**

It should be noted that this picture is not complete: No data were available from 16 countries: Antigua & Barbuda; Barbados; Brunei; Cooks Island; Dominica; Grenada; Niue; St. Kitts & Nevis; Samoa; Vanuatu; Hong Kong; Ireland; Luxembourg; Marshall Islands; Delaware; Switzerland. This absence is not just 'a bit awkward': the missing countries veil important examples of global non-transparency in international finances. For example, the missing data of Delaware and Hong Kong are surprising. Though we know how many com-

---

[11] For Cyprus no differentiations could be made of the number of companies actually used for offshore purposes.
See: www.nauruoffshore.com. and Mutual Evaluation Report july 2012: www.apgml.org.
[13] Panama has a territorial tax system. Only revenues obtained in the country itself are taxed. De Hoon 2006, p. 227.
[14] www.atcoffshore.com.
[15] CFATF Mutual Evaluation Report November 2008, p. 130.

panies are registered in both jurisdictions (879.000 (2010) respectively 1.067.434 (2013)), there is no differentiation according to an offshore status. According to the Financial Secrecy Index, Delaware has a high degree of secrecy index, while the World Bank found out that Delaware Corporations have a high prevalence in corruptions investigations (World Bank, 2011). Obviously, the US government, in pursuit of global transparency, foreign corruption and money laundering has something to explain.[16]

Despite this incomplete picture, the distribution of the number of offshore companies is not proportionally spread over the jurisdictions. The British Virgin Islands appear to dominate the scene in absolute numbers: it had 53% of all known registered offshore International Business Companies (IBC) worldwide. The country has experienced a remarkable growth since 1990: the yearly registered number of IBCs rose from 36.000 by more than 1.000.000, though levelling off in the last two years. The British Virgin Islands is followed at some distance by Belize, Cyprus and Seychelles: together they account for 78% of the total known offshore companies, however, not all of them are active.

As is the case with all public figures, they know many caveats. We pointed already at the missing data of 16 jurisdictions. This may be related to the negative attention to the offshore phenomenon which may have made countries wary of bringing statistics to the open: 10 of these jurisdictions did not show missing data in 2007, when we made a first query. There are also indications that some of the countries record only *active* companies thereby keeping 'sleeping' companies out of the statistics.

These statistics provide a rough indication of the volume of the offshore service industry, but do not say much about potential abuse or the location of assets which assumed to be hoarded in these territories. There is no direct relationship between the number of registered offshore companies in a particular OSC and involvement in serious criminal money flows. Jurisdictions with only a small number of offshore companies may nevertheless harbour serious offenders. For example, Antigua & Barbuda had only 3.255 registered offshore companies (2007; more recent data were not available), one of which belonged to Stanford International Ltd of the mega investment fraudster Alan Stanford.[17] Tiny Nauru was connected to an alleged large money laundering operation by Russian customers in the late 1990s.[18] These rough frequencies should therefore

---

[16] Tax Justice Network, Financial Secrecy Index 2015; Narrative Report on USA

[17] Stanford misappropriated about $ 7-8 billion of about 350 customers. He was found guilty and sentenced to 110 years imprisonment. (March 2012). Department of Justice, 14 June 2012.

[18] Allegedly there were 87.000 electronic transactions with a total value of $ 15 billion. Palan (2010), p. 74-75.

not be taken as an indication of the size of managed (or hidden) assets. The registered companies are often just a name and number in the local Company Registrar, with bank accounts anywhere in the world. As we will see, most often in the industrialised world.

Indications of the volume of offshore assets

How serious is the hide-and-seek of hidden monies across so many jurisdiction worldwide? The previous section underlined that even approximating the 'how much' question will be difficult. The 'how much' does not only concern the volume of the hidden moneys and its potential laundering: due to lack of valid data this is per definition unanswerable even if of continuing interest. But there are other quantitative questions for which there should be data for answering them. For example: the transactions between countries and the related money flows; registered unusual or suspicious cross-border transactions; investments or purchases by offshore companies. In 2010, an important question concerning the ultimate beneficiary at the end of the transaction chain has been prioritised politically. Despite solemn policy papers and recommendations from the FATF, the yield relating to the new chase of the beneficiary owner has remained less than modest thus far. Despite this depressing data scarcity the 'how much' question continues to rankle and to satisfy this thirst for figures we will take stock of some of the available data, though aware of the many caveats built in every database: reason for cautious interpretation.

Giving figures in such a fluid world as international offshore finances has the built-in risk of presenting stability where the real world is all the time in motion: a quantitative picture is a still of what is all the time moving. Nevertheless, for the sake of recognisability we start with the still from various sources, as depicted in Table 2, next page.

As can be observed, the range between the estimates is large, between the estimating institutions as well as across years. This is not surprising as the essential definitions, assumptions and methodology are not the same. The methodology is not always properly accounted for, often consisting of a mixture of public data (*e.g.* the Bank of International Settlement (BIS), but not always the same tables) and interviews with 'experts'. For example, the concept of bank account: is every foreign bank account considered as 'off-shore'? Adding the two is inflationary. While it is tempting to take some middle figure as a tentative plausible estimate, say 6.000 billion dollars, it still remains uncertain what the denotation of the terms 'wealth' or 'assets' covers: only bank accounts, shares and bonds or also property and moveable valuable possessions such as cars and boats or personal valuables?

Table 2
Estimates of offshore assets

Source	Billions $	Scope	Year
BCG[19]	9.800	Managed monetary assets	2015
Own research[20]	5.565	Bank balance (BIS)	2013
Zucman[21]	4.300	Bank accounts households	2013
Tax Justice Network[22]	21.000	Bank Balance	2012
OECD[23]	5-7.000	Offshore wealth	2007
McCann Offshore Fin.[24]	6.500	Offshore wealth	2006
Oxfam[25]	6-7.000	Offshore assets	2000
IMF[26]	4.600	Cross-border assets	1999

It is equally tempting to equate the offshore wealth to tax evasion if not money derived from other law breaking and therefore money laundering. This is the assumption of *Tax Justice Network* which arrives at the highest offshore estimate: $ 21.000 billion, mainly owned by "High Net Value Individuals": 92.000 individuals owning about $ 9.800 in billions.[27] According to Zucman about 80% of all the offshore bank accounts are not declared to the local tax authorities of the jurisdiction where the owner is living (Zucman, 2015: 59).

---

[19] Boston Consultancy Group. *Global Wealth Report 2015*. Their definition of wealth includes cash deposits, the net amount of listed securities held either directly or indirectly through managed funds, and life and pension assets. Property, business ownership and objects of values have been left out.

[20] T.J. van Koningsveld, 2015.

[21] G. Zucman, The missing wealth of nations, *The quarterly Journal of Economics*, 9 April 2013, p. 1321-1364

[22] James S. Henry, *The Price of Offshore revisited*. www.taxjustice.net/cms/upload/pdf/Price_of_Offshore_Revisited_120722.pdf.

[23] OECD, Towards a level playing field, Assessment by the Global Forum on Taxation, 2007.

[24] McCann, 'Offshore Finance', 2006.

[25] Oxfam, Taxhavens: 'Releasing the hidden billions for poverty eradication', 2000.

[26] IMF, Offshore Financial Centres, International Monetary Fund Background paper, 2000.

[27] http://www.taxjustice.net/cms/upload/pdf/Price_of_Offshore_Revisited_120722.pdf. TJN has a very wide definition of offshore comprising all cross-border depositing, also from Belgium to England or France.

There are good reasons to take a look at these rich or even superrich ("Upper High Net Worth") as these have the motivation and the interest to be financially mobile. However, the methodology of data collection – as far as publicly accounted for – is such that the statements about these groups must be cautiously interpreted. The *Capgemini* global wealth investigation (2013) is based on questionnaires collected from 4.400 affluent individuals (>1 million dollars assets). The outcomes reveal that indeed, the rich get richer and their number is increasing: from 2009 onwards the average wealth of HNW individuals increased from $10 million to $15,4 million in 2015 with a correspondent total wealth increase of $39.000 trillion to 58,7 trillion dollars. The Boston Consulting Group came to 17 million HNW *households* in 2014 owning 41% of the global private wealth. While this is an interesting development, fully underlining Piketty's (2015) observation about the unequal division of wealth, the Capgemini investigation does not address the question of the proportion of wealth placed in on- or offshore financial centres. Boston Consulting Groups provides such an estimate, though without disclosing its methodology. The outcome is presented in the following Figure 1:

Figure 1
Inflow of capital into the off-shore world

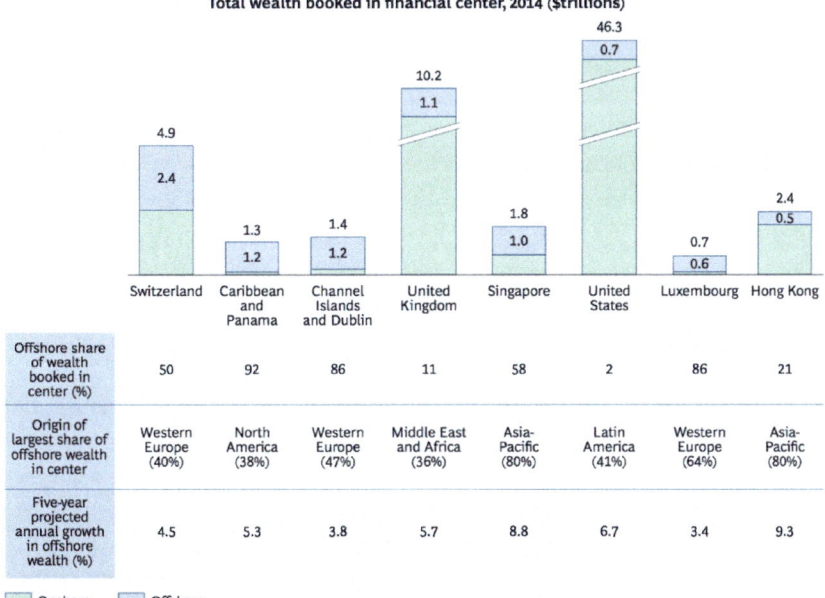

EXHIBIT 5 | Switzerland Remained the Largest Offshore Center but Hong Kong Is Poised for the Strongest Growth

Total wealth booked in financial center, 2014 ($trillions)

	Switzerland	Caribbean and Panama	Channel Islands and Dublin	United Kingdom	Singapore	United States	Luxembourg	Hong Kong
Offshore share of wealth booked in center (%)	50	92	86	11	58	2	86	21
Origin of largest share of offshore wealth in center	Western Europe (40%)	North America (38%)	Western Europe (47%)	Middle East and Africa (36%)	Asia-Pacific (80%)	Latin America (41%)	Western Europe (64%)	Asia-Pacific (80%)
Five-year projected annual growth in offshore wealth (%)	4.5	5.3	3.8	5.7	8.8	6.7	3.4	9.3

Onshore   Offshore

Source: BCG Global Wealth Market-Sizing Database, 2015.
Note: Offshore wealth is defined as private financial wealth booked in a country where the household is not resident. For further details, please refer to the Methodology section of the report.

As the Figure of BCG suggests, Western Europe and Asia and Pacific remain the main outflow regions of capital into the offshore world. In line with the observation in previous years: the US was with 0,7 trillion dollars not the main contributor of capital to offshore centres. Still, 38% of the offshore capital in the Caribbean and Panama came from the US. But there is also an inverse movement of capital to 'onshore': the lion's share of offshore capital in the US came from Latin America (with again a methodological warning of a too broad definition of offshore). We will discuss these reverse streams in a later section.

While it cannot be denied that the volume of offshore wealth is large, the present databases lack the precision to determine the total size, let alone to identify within that hypothetical total the subset attributable to identifiable types of law breaking, whether of criminal offences or tax crimes. The indications of profit oriented law breaking we have consist mainly of a string of anecdotes; meaningful in itself, but no substitute for a systematic assessment. One of the anecdotes is the Panama leak: very instructive for shedding light on the global functioning of *one* offshore service provider in one jurisdiction and the many "High Net Worth" individuals (and corporations) it serves.

The Panama Papers: 11,5 million documents of a Panamanian law firm

The leak of the Mossack Fonseca's administration was inconvenient to many, to say the least. It was most inconvenient to the many anti-laundering institutions, headed by the Financial Action Task Force on money laundering (FATF), guarding the integrity of the global financial system as well as to the hundreds of people mentioned in the thousands of documents. Regarding the FATF, after a long monitoring of Panama because of "strategic deficiencies", the Task Force declared in 19 February 2016 that Panama had "made significant progress in improving their regimes to combat money laundering and terrorist financing and will therefore no longer be subject to the FATF's monitoring process". Two month later it appeared that the FATF had taken a Potemkin Village for a real one.

Mossack Fonseca is one of the many corporate service providers with a worldwide clientele whose financial interests were managed, among others by putting some 214.000 shell companies in place. To put matters in perspective: some documents date from the 1970s and many of the documents show nothing but normal "prudent financial management". Apart from that, the papers give an insight into the "who is who" of many High Net Worth Individuals: twelve current or former political office holders, 128 other public officials and politicians in addition to hundreds of other members of the elites, literally worldwide: from the Prime Minister of Iceland, to a picture gallery of kleptocrats in Russia (but not Putin himself), and (no surprise) the leadership of FIFA (Guardian, 6 April 2016). In his time at the UEFA the present chairman of the FIFA, Infantino, may have been implicated in exclusive broadcast right contracts with Cross-trading in Argentina,

---

which sold these right for three times the price to Ecuador (*NRC.nl*, 5 April 2016). In this FIFA case there were also a Dutch company involved, Torneos & Traffic Sports Marketing BV.

Apart from these high-up corruption cases were also indirect links through two alleged launderers to the infamous drug king Guzmán. In addition there were 7 'drug mentions' in the papers but not directly implicating M&S..

Apart from the rich, famous and wealthy or who for one reason or another surfaced from the documents, it is the geographical reach of the Mossack & Fonseca's services which is interesting. It had branches outside Panama, among others two in the US, and was itself served by other law firms or banks who referred their customers to M&F: from the Caribbean basin to the Pacific, Niue and Samoa, and over the Gulf States back to Panama. The creation of shell companies appears to be the most mentioned service and indeed, technically, M&F were basically shell firm wholesalers: over the years it managed over 300.000 shell firms with 80.000 active in 2009.

M&F was not only waiting for customers to knock on its door. It was actively searching for or directly creating opportunities for offshore services. For example in 1996 it addressed the tiny Pacific state of Niue to help it to create tax haven facilities, and even proposed drafting the required legislation. For Niue it was a fair deal (cashing the fees per registered enterprise) if it were not for the US being worried about money laundering. When in 2001 various US banks blacklisted Niue, the island let the contract with M&F expire. Samoa was also seduced to establish companies and trusts.

Though M&F provide global services, it does not mean that it hoards hidden monies in vaults of institutions in Panama. As a matter of fact it served its customers to get their assets best placed: *e.g.* by assisting in establishing offshore companies in other jurisdictions, such as the British Virgin Islands or the Seychelles, which are instrumental for opening bank accounts in other jurisdictions.

As the Boston Consulting Group suggests, most offshore depositors prefer financial services in nearby offshore centres. M&F provided such services as well, albeit the staggering volume of its services does not say anything about total *financial* volume or the locations of wealth which may be managed by other service providers.

We remind the reader that this is only an example of one corporate service provider in one country, Panama. How many of such firms are operating in other jurisdictions and how much money do they manage or how many customers and firms do they advise to keep the money rolling without being observed? Thus far this question has not been addressed systematically, apart from our research and that of Zucman (2008) and Johannesen and Zucman (2013).

Floating monies

The observations of the last section suggests that the offshore centres are not necessarily the places of the bank accounts of the registered offshore companies. For example, a German client as ultimate beneficial owner who has a firm in Panama which is the holding company of another company in the Seychelles with a local nominee director and a bank account in Switzerland. So that bank account is registered as belonging to the Seychelles company and not as Panamanian, let alone German. However, the German beneficiary is mandated to the Swiss account, but that mandate is not registered. Indeed, it is inherent to the offshore system that the statistical data connections are of a 'one-step depth': from accounts to the nearest accountholders only. With this in mind we should look at the cross-border bank data with caution: they provide plausible indications of offshore bank balances but are far removed from any solid proof of the heated claims that half or three quarter of the worldwide wealth is 'hoarded' offshore. How to extract more insight from these cross-border bank data? We will see how far we can get.

The Bank of International Settlement (BIS), established in Basle (Switzerland), provides data which can be used to approximate the movement of money related to offshore centres. One of the main tasks of BIS, which is not a real bank handling deposits and loans, is fostering discussion and facilitating collaboration among central banks for which it collects data. One of the instruments is the analysis of international money flows based on reports of national central banks. For our purpose we made use of the 'Locational Banking Statistics' of the BIS. One of the (quarterly) statistics concerns claims and liabilities of account holders of *offshore* commercial banks to foreign *onshore* banks: *e.g.* a Cayman Island firm having a bank account in London (claim). Or the reverse, the London bank having money in its account from the Cayman Islands (liability).

The Central Banks of 43 countries take part in this locational specific statistics for each quarter of the year.[28] One of the subsets of this group of countries consists of the offshore centres for which the BIS uses the following definition: "*countries with banking sectors dealing primarily with non-residents and/or in foreign*

---

[28] Australia, Austria, Bahamas, Bahrain, Belgium, Bermuda, Brazil, Canada, Cayman Islands, Chile, Chinese Taipei, Curacao (2010), Cyprus, Denmark, Finland, France, Germany, Greece, Netherlands, Netherlands Antilles, Norway, Panama, Portugal, Singapore, South Africa, South Korea, Spain, Sweden, Switzerland, Turkey, the United Kingdom and the United States. We found no specification of the selection criteria. There are some curiously missing countries, such as Russia, China, Argentina, India or Italy.

currency on a scale out of proportion to the size of the host economy". The last sentence part ("on a scale out of proportion . . .") is for a formal definition a fuzzy and therefore wrong component: there is no reference to a standard to measure 'proportionality'. The BIS may have adopted this inaccuracy from the IMF. Nevertheless, applying this definition the BIS qualified 21 countries as offshore from where in 2014 offshore companies had together $ 3.998.305 million in accounts in the *on*shore BIS reporting countries. However, this finding is defi-nition-biased, demonstrating that the seemingly rhetoric question "what is in the name" does matter. Under our definition of offshore centre there are 40 relevant offshore countries that in 2014 had onshore bank balances to the amount of $ 5.440.836 million ("claims") which is 26% of all cross-border claims (onshore and offshore) between countries (under the BIS calculation 18%).

Table 3 on the next page first informs us of the bank claims of offshore centres in onshore BIS counties which provides a valuable, but limited view. The BIS statistics encompass 46 countries which matter financially, but what happens financially outside this sample is not covered statistically. BIS denotes 21 countries as offshore, while Van Koningsveld's definition encompasses 40. Further, the figures are aggregated and do not allow a country-to-country analysis. Another limitation to an adequate interpretation is the geographical spread of financial institutions and their local branches which facilitates a smooth transfer of bank accounts from one offshore country to another. Thus, major banks like UBS or Credit Suisse can transfer customers' balances to their branches in other offshore centres which leads to a reduction of offshore capital in Switzerland but not to a reduction of the total offshore capital of the relevant banks: a financial waterbed effect. Nevertheless, the only figures we have, those of BIS, cannot be neglected.

Table 3
Deposits of offshore companies in onshore countries (claims)
2008 and 2014 (in million dollars)

Land	2008	%	2010	%	2012	%	2014	%
Aruba	1.522	0,0	1.125	0,0	1.122	0,0	1.223	0,0
Bahamas	494.158	7,8	352.555	6,0	284.641	5,3	172.634	3,8
Barbados	20.437	0,3	26.208	0,4	39.642	0,7	53.033	1,0
Belize	9.518	0,1	9.957	0,8	13.483	0,3	13.389	0,3
Bermuda	68.579	1,0	71.451	1,2	72.156	1,4	93.744	1,7
Brunei	4.346	0,1	3.940	0,07	5.649	0,1	3.707	0,1
Cayman Isl.	1.872.984	27,2	1.835.324	31,0	1.455.474	27,2	1.737.965	31,9
Cyprus	48.608	0,7	47.131	0,8	49.307	1,0	36.478	0,7
Curaçao	-		109.158	1,85	78.182	1,5	38.651	0,7
Dominica Rep	218	0,0	289	0,00	291	0,0	289	0,0
Dutch Antill.[29]	141.495	2,0	7	0,00	-		0	
Gibraltar	18.451	0,3	15.297	0,3	13.839	0,3	19.228	0,4
Grenada	182	0,0	164.084	0,00	56	0,00	102	0,0
Guernsey	188.582	2,7	100	2,8	145.436	2,7	112.028	2,0
Hong Kong	551.186	8,0	441.028	7,5	434.953	8,1	462.762	8,5
Ireland	526.814	7,7	467.977	7,9	487.732	9,1	500.111	9,2
Isle of Man	76.927	1,1	77.751	1,3	68.653	1,3	57.739	1,1
Jersey	478.378	6,9	371.814	6,3	326.628	6,1	297.040	5,5
Liechtenstein	34.734	0,5	22.166	0,4	20.665	0,4	16.403	0,3
Luxembourg	780.374	11,3	643.380	10,9	706.226	13,2	695.685	12,8
Malaysia/Labu.	18.557	0,3	23.004	0,4	28.889	0,5	33.915	0,6
Malta	17.721	0,3	20.834	0,4	20.603	0,4	17.625	0,3
Marshall Isl.	7.396	0,1	10.948	0,2	12.192	0,2	11.559	0,2
Mauritius	14.722	0,2	16.586	0,3	17.034	0,3	21.689	0,4
Nauru	11	0,0	12	0,0	11	0,0	40	0.0
Panama	102.679	1,5	86.401	1,5	84.066	1,6	77.184	1,4
Samoa	6.257	0,1	7.996	0,1	9.846	0,2	12.689	0,2
Seychelles	4.559	0,1	6.090	0,1	8.598	0,2	9.739	0,2
St. Lucia	409	0,0	494	0,0	404	0,0	399	0,0
St. Maarten	0		8	0,0	655	0,0	221	0,0
St. Vincent	3.431	0,1	2.599	0,0	2.747	0,1	1.965	0,0

[29] The Kingdom of the Netherlands has per October 2010 another structure of government: the original Dutch Antilles were abolished: Curaçao and St. Maarten became autonomous countries within the Kingdom.

Switzerland	1.160.338	16,8	845.667	14,3	703.441	13,2	664.197	12,2
Turks/Caicos	1.870	0,0	2.163	0,0	1.508	0,0	1.465	0,0
Vanuatu	519	0,0	419	0,0	446	0,0	454	0,0
W. Indies UK[30]	232.617	3,4	226.609	3,8	255.562	4,8	275.484	5,0
Total offshore claims on BIS-onshore[31]	6.888.579		5.910.572		5.350.137		5.440.836	
All cross-countries claim (on-& onshore)	24.467.447		23.312.871		21.769.796		20.717.324	
% Offshore / all countries	28%		25%		25%		26%	

Source: BIS, Table 7A of the Quarterly Dec. 2008 and 2014 recalculate according to Van Koningsveld 2014. The figures concerns only bank balances and not other assets, such as shares, bonds, property or vessels

As the first year of observation we took 2008, the year of the financial bubble and the credit crisis. Naturally this is somewhat arbitrary: during the prosperous years since 2000 we see a more than tripling of bank claims from offshore centres to onshore countries from $ 2.162.827 to $ 6.888.579 million. After 2008 a decline sets in and the offshore balances in onshore countries appear to follow the same global downward trend. Hence, from a top of $ 24.467.447 million balances between BIS countries (onshore and offshore) in 2008, we observe a decrease of 15%. Within this total of cross-border bank claims we have also the subset of bank claims of offshore centres on BIS onshore countries: together these offshore centres reveal the same downward trend of their onshore balances from 2008 to 2014, though less steep, namely 11% with a stabilisation from 2012 onwards.

Between the offshore centres substantial differences can be observed: 11 offshore centres showed an increase of onshore claims, ranging from 363% (Nauru) to only 4% (Gibraltar). However, the share of these rising offshore centres in the total of offshore to onshore bank claims is modest: about 10% (2014). Should this be conductive to financial instability, as the IMF claims?

---

[30] Including the British Virgin Islands, Anguilla, Antiqua and St Kitts.
[31] There were no data of the Cook Islands, Niue and Madeira. The figures of the US were not included as there was no differentiation between single states.

There is no documentation to underline this hypothesis: from these figures no such hypothesis can be deducted.

The 20 offshore centres with decreases of bank claims in onshore countries differed also substantial, geographically as well as in terms of the volume of claims. The biggest negative change of 65% was observed in the Bahamas and Curaçao, however, with a very difference bank claim volumes: from $494.158 (2008) to $172.634 million in the Bahamas versus $109.158 (2010) to $38.651 million in Curaçao (2014).[32] In general there was not much correlation between the size of the offshore centres in terms of onshore bank claims and the drop in percentage. 'Big' Luxembourg with an onshore bank claim of $780.374 million (2008) had a decrease of 11%, but the bigger player Switzerland with an onshore claim of $ 1.160.338 experienced a decrease of 43%: $664.197 million, both in the time span 2008-2014. As remarked, such a decrease can be compensated by a transfer to branches of Swiss banks in other offshore centres. Two other offshore centres, the small Vanuatu ($454 million) and the even smaller Grenada ($102 million) also experienced a decrease of 13% respectively 44%.

From our perspective the relevant question is: "Where did the money go?" Unfortunately the BIS statistics cannot answer this question because of the mismatch between increase and decrease across all BIS countries. The volume of onshore plus offshore claims worldwide decreased with $3.750.123 million while the offshore claims on onshore countries decreased with $1.447.743 million. We do not know how much capital 'evaporated' due to the credit crises or was withdrawn from the financial system (converted into cash or other valuables) or returned fully to the offshore centres where the account holding offshore corporations formally reside. In the latter case the bank balances of the offshore centres should have increased substantially. That would result in an accumulation of capital which should be expected to find its way to the capital market onshore: the outflow of surplus capital for investment. After all, the onshore financial sector remains an important receiver for its offshore counterparts. This kind of mobility has thus far not been investigated systematically.

Apart from the reduction in the offshore bank claims due to the financial crisis in 2008, the emergence of more cross-border tax regulations (sharing of bank details between jurisdictions) may also have played a role, though difficult to determine exactly. For some jurisdictions it is plausible that international pressure and multilateral tax information exchange agreements led to a reduction in offshore-to-onshore bank balances. But was the money repatriated to the onshore beneficiary? To shed light on this question Johannesen and Zucman (2014) investigated the effect of bilateral information exchange treaties

---

[32] No data available of Curaçao for 2008.

on bank balances in 'tax havens'. They also used BIS data and bilateral information of debts and claims between countries. They concluded that the information exchange treatises led to a transfer of funds: *e.g.* Frenchmen having accounts in Switzerland withdrew 11%. However, the money did not go "home": instead it was moved to (offshore) countries with which France did not have such treatises. It suggests that money keeps moving and does so in a more rational way than the mainstream statements of the IMF suggests. In whatever way we look at the available evidence we do not see the irrational volatility as suggested by Tanzi (1996) and Quirke (1996) and the authors following in their footsteps.

Looking at these data we are of the opinion that claims of the threat of offshore capital accumulations should reconsidered. Much money is held onshore from offshore corporations residing elsewhere. The BIS group of countries 'West Indies UK' with its leading offshore territory the British Virgin Islands is a good example. It has in absolute numbers the highest registered number of offshore corporations, but the share of this group in the total of onshore bank claims in 2014 is 5%. Is the remaining money stored in the BVI? That seems unlikely: according to Reuters's Business News (28 January 2014) BVI "welcomed $92 billion of foreign cash in 2013, according to preliminary figures compiled by the U.N. trade and economy think tank UNCTAD" but much of that money "is transferred quickly in and out of the country or cash moved through the treasury accounts of large firms which UNCTAD terms 'transnational corporations' or TNCs."[33]

We have not found the offshore '*Treasure of Ringelungen*', which would be the wrong metaphor: it is large but not solid. It is fluid and there are clear indications that much of it is elsewhere, onshore.

Offshore ownership of real estate in the Netherlands

If it is plausible that the hidden wealth may be onshore it looks as if we just have to 'look around ourselves' to identify suspicious assets. That may seem easy, which is not the case. The part of the wealth consisting of moveable valuables are what they are: moveable until they are used or – if proceeds – seized (and eventually forfeited) in a criminal recovery procedure. Most moveable assets concern a lifestyle objects such as cars and boats. The unmovable part, real

---

[33] Reuters *Business News*, Top tax haven got more investment in 2013 than India and Brazil: U.N. 28 January, 2014. Accessed 26-2-2017.

estate seems to be exempt from much of this instability, if we abstract from the boom and crash in 2008 and the depression in the housing market in the years after this crisis. In addition, land and building registry is assumed to be reliable, as it is a public database for other legal deeds, such as mortgaging. Also given the popular assumption that real estate is a favoured outlet or investment for monetary wealth, part of which assumed to be 'shady', we decided to have a closer look at the database of the Dutch Land Register (Kadaster) from our angle of offshore possessions: how much property is according to the Land Register owned legal persons established in foreign jurisdictions which are according to our definition 'offshore'.

To support us with our research the Land Register   provided us with databases of real estate owned by a legal person residing in the designated jurisdictions of which we used the following:
1. a database comprising records of ownership of *one property* and one purchase price: the 'one-to-one database';
2. a database consisting of ownership of *more properties* of which one total purchase price was recorded in the notary deed;
3. a database comprising acquired property burdened with a *mortgage*.[34]

The raw data are taken from the notaries deeds and are considered to reflect (legal) 'reality': date of acquisition, the purchase/selling price, the ownership information, the number of properties, whether or not burdened with a mortgage, the official usage of the premises and the surface in square metres. We had no access to natural personal data which implies that multiple personal ownership or nationality could not be identified. This is an important limitation, given the finding from other laundering research in the real estate market that individuals may own more properties, or properties are in the name of more persons (Van Duyne *et al.*, 2009).

This is the ultimate public knowledge foundation of 'legal real estate reality'. We realise that this may hide much unrecorded or falsely recorded 'underworld reality' that blends in as a kind of subset (Ferwerda and Unger, 2011).

These databases were not united into one whole database because of differences between some of the variables. In the 'one-to-one database' the use of the property is mentioned (dwelling, business or agriculture), which is omitted in

---

[34] The database in which no purchase price was recorded still had to be cleaned and processed at the time of writing.

the 'more-properties database', as the various properties bundled into one trans-action could have different application: for example a dwelling plus a piece of land for agriculture or an adjacent shed with a different registration number. These were not converted into a connected string of variables. In the 'mortgage database' the mortgage figure was mentioned instead of the purchase price. The mortgage could also cover more objects and rights as collateral, which were not differentiated.

These databases concerned the year 2014 and 2015. Each year consists of two stock takings: on 1 January and 31 December. These double stock takings could not be added, as that would result in double counting for those properties which were owned through-out the year which are then recorded at both ob-servation moments. As we wanted a database per year, we harmonised this double stock taking by discarding the January count if the same property was also recorded in the December count. We did not unite the two years which implies that property recorded in 2014 may also be recorded in 2015 if it was not sold meanwhile. Hence, there is an overlap in ownership between the two years, while the difference consists of property sold or new purchase taking place after December 2014. This implies that the information of the following tables concerns the ownership *status* and not transactions. However, the data-bases also provide information about the year of purchase which may give an impression of the stability or changeability of the offshore property ownership.

Table 4

Year of acquisition of properties (in intervals) by offshore companies:
Acts of one and more properties in two registration years

	1 object 2014	1 object 2015	>1 object 2014	>1 object 2015
Purchase year	%	%	%	%
1987–2000	21	15	30	25
2001–2005	13	12	8	8
2006–2010	26	20	28	25
2011–2014/15	40	53	34	42
Total = 100%	202	189	112	115

As presented in Table 4, the databases 'one property' and 'more properties' broken down by year of purchase, shows that some the ownership data goes as far back as 1987. More than half of the properties have been acquired before 2010; a sizeable part of around 20% even as long as 20 years ago. This raises the question about the often mentioned 'threat of volatility' of the off-shore floating money. Without proper measurement standards for volatility in the property market we could just as well say that these data reflect a relative stability.

Naturally, of equal interest is the money involved, in view of the fear that through offshore centres offshore companies might contaminate the licit financial system and markets such as the real estate market. We referred already to the many caveats as soon as the 'volume question' of the hidden (criminal) finances is raised. The financial figures are presented in the next Table, together with the time variable.

Table 5
Year and mean price of properties: acts with one and more properties

Purchase year	1 object 2014 Mean €	1 object 2015 Mean €	>1 object 2014 Mean €	>1 object 2015 Mean €
1987–2000	259.018	289.318	907.772	945.206
2001–2005	1.161.158	1.339.220	370.661	329.476
2006–2010	1.622.186	1.844.210	12.659.875	13.820.531
2011–2014	1.839.411	3.622.365	4.391.903	5.414.123
Median	273.000	350.000	400.000	410.743
Total absolute €	275.575.974	470.169.491	516.106.882	602.629.523

As can be observed, the average purchase price has increased over time but a look at the medians shows that a few extremely high maximum prices inflates the mean substantially: these were in the range between 20-80 million euros.

For the database with one property the prices for 2014 and 2015 were differentiated according to the type of use. As mentioned before, the database of more properties per purchase the category of application of the property was not indicated.

Table 6
Type of use and price per object 2014 and 2015: 1 property purchase

Type of use	N	2014 Mean	2014 Median	N	2015 Mean	2015 Median
Agro	2	77.750	77.750	4	1.945.750	135.250
Business	68	3.481.669	771.426	66	6.137.044	1.387.500
Dwelling	114	329.323	241.386	105	383.187	255.932
Unknown	18	62.457	25.000	14	1.221.923	35.000
Total	202	1.364.237	273.000	189	2.487.669	350.000

Table 6 demonstrates again that the frequency distribution is skewed upwards resulting in a much higher mean than the median. There are indeed some extremely expensive purchases of 31 and 88 million Euros but these concerned the business category. For 50% the offshore ownership is in the highest price range, certainly where it concerns business property. Most property was bought for the purpose of dwelling with a median price of around € 250.000 (mean about € 350.000) which means less extreme figures than with business property. Though we have no official national median price indexes for these categories, according to the National Statistical Office, the general *mean price* of dwellings in the Netherlands is around € 210.000 for 2014/15 (with variations). This is below the mean of the set of offshore owned dwellings as shown in Table 6.

The next question concerns the identification of important offshore centres from where offshore companies own property in the Netherlands and for what amount? Given that the frequencies are unequally spread, the following Table focuses on the offshore countries with the highest number of properties and highest purchase prices for the years 2014 and 2015. The other centres are collected in the 'other'.

Table 7

**Top offshore countries: ownership of one or more properties:
percentages and sum purchase price per country**

	One property				More properties			
	2014		2015		2014		2015	
Offshore country	%	Sum €	%	Sum €	%	Sum €	%	Sum €
Aruba	7	4.741.749	6	3.850.323	7	2.837.000	6	2.152.000
Brit. Virgin Isl.	7	3.394.780	7	3.394.780	12	3.424.365	13	4.871.365
Cayman Islands	4	45.825.500	3	33.938.000	5	105.201.390	4	105.201.390
Cyprus	5	3.340.516	4	2.499.500	6	2.407.500	4	1.757.500
Guernsey/Jersey	-	–	-	–	7	97.870.022	7	97.870.022
Luxembourg	24	169.442.974	30	262.247.865	21	107.665.822	24	193.077.094
Panama	4	3.721.387	4	3.687.522	1	242.500	2	1.092.500
Seychelles	4	2.649.000	4	4.124.000	5	1.020.431	4	1.020.431
Switzerland	20	15.072.816	15	12.311.991	18	125.805.169	16	122.591.724
USA/Delaware	11	12.125.659	12	125.947.894	13	67.719.425	15	72.062.786
Other centres	14	15.261.593	14	18.167.616	5	1.413.258	5	932.712
Total	202	275.575.974	189	470.169.491	112	515.606.882	115	602.629.524

This table gives a fair impression of the prominent offshore centres where the offshore companies-owners have their domicile. As can be observed four countries are leading: Luxembourg, Switzerland, Delaware and, in the category of more properties, British Virgin Islands. In each database they account for more than half of the offshore legal persons. The table also shows that the frequencies and prices of some offshore centres changed considerably. This was the case with Luxembourg for both databases: jumping up with almost 100 million. It is also the country with the highest offshore owned property value in the Netherlands for 'one-property' and 'more property' cases. Next comes Delaware of which the offshore companies saw a tenfold increase in the 'one-property' database only. The purchase prices of 'more properties' are in both years the highest for offshore companies in: Switzerland, Luxembourg, the Cayman Islands and Delaware. The figures of the Cayman Islands appear to be determined by a small number of offshore companies (particularly in the 'more' database) while the figure of Guernsey/Jersey is determined by one 'more property' case with a purchase value of € 90.350.000 showing how easily the picture can be biased by one or a few extreme values.

Table 8
Number of properties in the notary acts per corporation: 2014–2015

Offshore country	2014			2015		
	N corp	N property	Median €	N corp	N property	Median €
Aruba	8	24	126.000	7	22	–
Brit. Virgin Isl.	13	37	310.839	15	44	310.839
Cyprus	6	10	465.000	4	6	465.000
Cayman Islands	5	26	7.940.000	5	26	7.940.000
Guernsey/Jersey	8	122	472.738	8	122	472.738
Luxembourg	23	60	315.900	28	93	552.850
US/Delaware	15	36	344.000	17	40	428.000
Switzerland	20	74	336.695	18	69	336.695
Other countries	14	33	250.000	13	31	250.000
Total: N & €	112	422	515.606.882	115	453	602.629.524

Table 8 presents the summary of the 'more properties' database: the countries with at least five mentioned corporations, the remainder low frequencies grouped to 'other'. The number of properties ranged from two to 104 (purchase 1997 for five million Euros by Guernsey offshore), with fifteen cases with more than five properties which points at a rather flat distribution. Without identification of the nature of the properties such numbers are difficult to interpret. The total median value is € 313.370 against an average of € 4.608.097 confirming the skewed distribution we noticed earlier. The very high median of Cayman Islands is due to the finding that half of the cases are above seven million euros, all acquired in 2007.

The third database of offshore property in the Netherlands concerns the purchases of properties 'burdened' with a mortgage. As remarked earlier, the mortgage can be higher or lower than the price actually paid and can also comprise other collaterals than the building.

Table 9
Mortgaged properties 2014 and 2015

Offshore Centre	December 2014			December 2015		
	N cases	Sum €	N objects	N cases	Sum €	N Objects
Aruba	7	16.077.572	70	5	9.127.572	38
Brit. Virgin Isl.	4	2.280.670	5	6	92.165.670	8
Cayman Island	21	687.662.500	43	9	283.475.000	16
Luxembourg	19	308.785.890	33	19	510.592.690	42
Panama	2	264.135	2	3	763.293	20
Seychelles	2	2.055.000	2	2	2.055.000	2
USA/Delaware	20	1.020.711.958	93	17	509.833.556	22
Switzerland	16	62.132.198	131	13	45.013.686	75
Other countries	5	2.780.000	7	7	3.206.890	11
Total	96	1.015.132.509	386	81	1.456.233.357	234

To analyse the mortgage for each year we deleted the doubles (mentioned in January *and* December). As remarked before, the establishment of a mortgage by a notary act covers more properties or rights, as can be deduced from Table 8. The mortgage figures should not be equated with purchase prices. Also, at the time of purchase the full amount of the allowed credit does not need to be used: if for the exploitation or repair of the building more funds are required, of which the amount is not yet clear, a higher mortgage than the purchase price may be agreed for later used. The database does not have such variables or data about who provided the loan, which can be a financial institution, a private person or a combination in the Netherlands or abroad residing in another country than the country of the offshore company.

In both years Switzerland has the highest number of properties per notary act (131 and 75) followed by Delaware (2014) and Luxembourg (2015). There is no description of the nature of the property: it can be a villa, a residence or office block, separate parking boxes or a meadow. As in many transactions more properties are covered by one summed-up mortgage figure, no further statistics about mean or median for the objects can be calculated.

Though mortgages are mostly long-term stable contracts, we still observe some variability: see the steep rise or decline of mortgages of the offshore owners in the British Virgin Islands, Cayman Island, Luxembourg and USA/Delaware. The largest changes were caused by mortgages for: a Delaware corporation of € 350.500.000; a Luxembourg one of € 114.000.000 and a British Virgin Island mortgage of € 90.000.000 (rounded figures) which shows that the range of the loans is very large.

Otherwise there is no further information about these mortgages which makes interpretations concerning hidden or laundered monies speculative. For example, there may be *loan-back* constructions in these mortgage cases, but these data are not adequate for testing such suspicions. Moreover such constructions are only a subset within the total set of registered mortgages: roughly 90 registrations per year.

When we look at the offshore jurisdictions where most legal persons are registered we observe that Luxembourg, Delaware and Switzerland have the highest frequencies; the latter having the lowest mortgage sums.

Taken together, the offshore real estate ownership in the Netherlands is not insignificant: adding the available data for 2015 being the most recent year we arrive at a rounded figure of about € 2.000.000.000. To this the small database with lacking purchase prices should added, that may – speculatively – heighten then total to a value of around € 2,5 billion. That represents only the circumference of the offshore property market within which dubious offshore investments must be identified. Given the fact that about a third of the properties has been acquired more than ten years ago, attributing such suspicions to cases or subsets of offshore ownerships in the real estate market, requires that we should have to go far back in time. We will also have look at the geographical spread: the ownership appears to be concentrated in a limited number of offshore countries.

It is of interest to compare the Dutch data with that of the Land Register of the UK comprising foreign ownership – with all due warnings of the caveats which such a comparison implies. The method of recording is different, the variables differ and there are many missing data (around 30%). The database was found on the internet from an organisation called *Private Eye* (www.private-eye.co.uk/registry). In September 2015, they published a database of properties in England and Wales owned by offshore companies at the end of 2014. The information was coming from the Land Register and contains about 100.000

land titles. After we had cleared the file duplicates we analysed this database. However, the price variable appeared to be polluted, for which reason we only looked at the country of residence of the proprietor and singled out the major offshore countries.

Table 10
Offshore ownership of property in the UK 2014

Country/territory	N	In % of N
all for. countries	61.856	100%
Of which offshore	53.934	87
Major offshore countries		
British Virgin Islands	16.453	30,5
Guernsey	7.736	14,3
Island of Man	7.932	14,7
Jersey	9.510	17,6
Luxembourg	1.124	2,1
Total	42.755	79,2

Comparison with the Dutch Land Register shows that in both countries foreign ownership by legal persons is concentrated in a limited number of offshore countries: five offshore countries account for 80% of the number of the offshore owned properties. For these transactions the (ultimate) beneficial owners were registered in nearby or known territory: either close at home in the waters around Britain or in the apparently popular British Virgin Islands. For the really expensive real estate there was a preference for Luxembourg as we also found in the Dutch Land Registry. Though the Dutch database clearly identifies Delaware as an offshore resident state, the UK database lacked such state differentiation. It is a guess how many of the 523 proprietors registered in the USA are in reality offshore USA corporations registered in Delaware, Utah or Wyoming. Unfortunately, there is no US-'state' variable for further differentiation. In view of the prominent place of Delaware offshore companies in the Dutch Land Registry statistics the omission of American offshore states is a serious deficit.

Conclusion

We started with the mainstream representation of the enormous amounts of wealth of legal or criminal origin finding a 'refuge' against the (tax) law or financial insecurity in a variety of offshore centres. 'Going offshore' is to be found in all layers of society, though must attention is at present devoted to the commercial and political 'elite', at present a negative buzzword. This image found support in the context of the leaked Panama papers of the firm Mossack and Fonseca. It also seems to confirm the adage that "one percent owns 99 percent" of global wealth. This is followed by the claim that offshore centres are instrumental in hiding or even laundering much these funds whose beneficial owners go a long way to evade taxation. Did the Mossack and Fonseca leaked documents not 'prove' that? After all, this is only one firm while there are thousands of similar firms spread worldwide.

Though these Panama papers present a meaningful illustration, one may wonder what is exactly proven, given the defectively defined phenomenon of 'offshore'. There are fifteen definitions of this concept which are of a various degree of 'fuzziness' when it comes to properly delineating the field of application. Many definitions contain value terms allowing to expand the coverage. No surprise that this state of affairs combined with a debatable methodology led to a wide range of assessments of the offshore hidden assets: from 5.000 to 21.000 billion dollars.

With a sharper definition we identified 40 offshore centres of which 25 had sufficient data for our analysis. This subset was quantitatively dominated by one player: the British Virgin Islands, accounting for 53% of all globally registered offshore corporations. So, is that the place where all the assumed hidden funds are stashed? This question implies a too simple assumption, namely that the place of registration of an offshore company is not the same as the place of hiding. If that were the case, then –with only a few major players this murky world of offshore finances– this problem could be easily solved: by sending the proverbial (diplomatic) gunboat to a few hot spots. However, that would fail because there is no necessary direct connection between the place of residence of the offshore corporations and the location of the funds. The idea of offshore centres functioning as a kind of 'hoarding place' with assets figuratively 'stacked' against the wall in the 'banks' vaults' is not real.

If the offshore centres do not keep the deposited money, where does it go? We found out that the data of the bank of International Settlement (BIS) reveals that huge amounts of funds of offshore corporations are in banks in *onshore* countries. It suggests that the offshore country function rather as a registration address with the bank accounts in the countries where they are needed. Comparison of the registration frequencies of corporations in the offshore centres with the bank accounts held in onshore countries showed that there is little correlation. For example, the 78.000 offshore corporations in the Cayman Island held $ 1.737.965 million in foreign onshore bank accounts against the

1.130.000 British Virgin Islands corporations having 'only' $275.484 million in onshore bank accounts (2014).

Public data provide no explanation for these differences. Therefore, one should be cautious to jump to further speculative conclusions: a British Virgin corporation can have a bank account in the Cayman Islands which has a connected account in the UK which counts as onshore from the Cayman Islands and not the British Virgin Islands. That is what the Panama Leaks make clear: an offshore country can just be a springboard to further offshore locations from which the important last landing may take place in the onshore countries, maybe the same countries from where these monies originated. That would be a strong indication of money laundering though that is just a hypothesis.

Hiding assets has no purpose if it cannot be used in one's place of living and if there is no massive move of beneficial owners to 'their' offshore countries to enjoy their assets on site, the money has to repatriate. We tried to approximate this assumed repatriation by looking at real estate in the Netherlands as far as it was owned by legal persons established in offshore countries. It appears that the property was mainly bought by offshore corporations partly nearby: established in Switzerland, Luxembourg, the Channel Islands or in Delaware. There are outliers: Cayman Islands, with a very high purchase value, look more like the 'usual' offshore country with a modest number of registered offshore corporations (78.000). Nevertheless, it has in the Netherlands € 140 million property in ownership by only ten offshore corporations. How to interpret such finding? This point at a limitation: further breaking down, *e.g.* along the time or another variable will result in too low frequencies for further statistical analysis. The extent of the phenomenon may statistically not be big enough.

Data of the British Land Register also show concentration of offshore ownership in a handful 'favoured' offshore countries/territories, reflecting per chance a UK preference for the Channel Islands and the Island of Man, in addition to the popular British Virgin Islands and Luxembourg for the real pricey properties. If the British authorities want to shed light of this phenomenon they do not need to travel far.

Discussion

What do these findings tell us about the offshore wealth against the background of the many claims of the seriousness of *hidden* or *laundered* offshore wealth. There are many caveats to go from official statistics to a broader interpretation within a law enforcement frame work. A study of police and court data showed that the top of Dutch organised criminals used offshore centres to move their monies, particularly for their villas, or a portfolio of properties (Van Duyne and Soudijn, 2009; Van Duyne, 2009; Van Koningsveld, 2015). For example, 'renting' a dwelling at home while the owner/landlord is an offshore shell corporation with a straw man director nominated by the service provider in the offshore country (Van Koningsveld, 2015), while the 'tenant' is the actual beneficial owner and silently in control of the offshore corporation which formally made the purchase or provided the mortgage. The collections of such cases are valuable, but still are rather single stamp collections and no substitute for integrated research on this phenomenon.

It is surprising that the ways offshore operate in onshore countries has not been an object of systematic empirical analysis. While the relevance of the phenomenon is recognised, the data remain poor. Ferwerda and Unger (2013), researched misuse in the real estate sector in the Netherlands, but of the 17 indicators none referred to the use of offshore facilities for law breaking: the word 'off-shore' is missing.

The FATF in its typologies reports on money laundering through real estate (2007), the report on the misuse of corporate vehicles and service providers (2006) and the update report on trust and company service providers (2010).[35] The functioning of offshore corporations is in these reports clearly brought to the fore. However, given their primary educational and informative intention, the presentations of the short case descriptions constitute no bridge to the broader quantitative panorama, as we attempted in this chapter. On the other hand, this broader panorama has the disadvantage of being not specific enough when it comes to assessing misuse. It allows little more than speculations in answering the 'how-much' abuse question if not placed in a proper formulated framework: the whole sum of properties and what abuse can be identified within this set. The broad perspective of the Dutch real estate in terms of total national value is 2.000.000 million Euro of which the assessed offshore owned real estate is about 2.500 million Euro: that is 0,13%, within which abuse is to be located. Is this little more than a minuscule statistical part of the whole?

While within the whole the share offshore possessed properties in the Netherlands may be small, from the law enforcement perspective it is considered significant. Not only because of its size and value (well above the national average), but also because of its seeming separation of offshore corporation, funds

---

[35] FATF 2006: The misuse of corporate vehicles, including trust and company service providers. FATF 2007: Money laundering & terrorist Financing through the real estate sector. FATF 2010: Money laundering using trust and company service providers.

and ultimate beneficial ownership. That makes this field shrouded in fog as was also noted in a report of Transparency International and Thomson Reuters (2017) who analysed the London land titles in possession of foreign companies. They observed among others that 91% of the identified foreign companies were registered in 'secrecy jurisdiction', though mainly in British waters! Their outcomes underline our attempt to carry out sharper database analyses to be complemented by a qualitative research of law enforcement findings. If the concerns about the (mis)use of foreign corporations and real estate is genuine, we have to go beyond the usual lamentations or the FATF stamp collections.

References

Boston Consulting Group, *Global wealth report 2016*

Cornez, A.L., *The offshore money book. How to move assets offshore for privacy, protection and tax advantage.* Edison 2000.

Duyne, P.C. van, M. Soudijn and T. Kint, Bricks don't talk. Searching for crime money in real estate. In: P.C. van Duyne, S. Donati, J. Harvey, A. Maljevic and K. von Lampe (eds.), *Crime, money and criminal mobility in Europe.* Nijmegen, Wolf Legal Publishers, 2009

Duyne, P.C. van, M. Soudijn, Gebakken stenen en gebakken lucht. In: *Tijdschrift voor Compliance.* No. 3, Jaargang 9, mei/juni, 2009.

Duyne, P.C. van, M.S. Groenhuijsen and A.A.P. Schudelaro Balancing financial threats and legal interests in money-laundering policy. *Crime, Law and Social Change*, 2005, vol. 43, *no 2-3*, 117-147

FATF 2006: The misuse of corporate vehicles, including trust and company service providers.

FATF 2007: Money laundering & terrorist Financing through the real estate sector.

FATF 2010: Money laundering using trust and company service providers.

Ferwerda, J. and B. Unger, Detecting money laundering in the real estate sector. In: B. Unger and D. van der Linde (eds.), *Research handbook on money laundering.* Cheltenham, Edward Elgar, 2011

Hoon, I. de, Belastingparadijzen: handleiding voor de fiscale wereldreiziger. Roul Arta Books, 2006

Johannesen, N. and G. Zucman, The end of bank secrecy? An evaluation of the G20 tax haven crackdown. *American Economic Journal: Economic Policy*, 2014, 6(1): 65–91

OESO, Towards a level playing field, Assessment by the Global Forum on Taxation, 2007.

Palan, R., *Tax Havens: How Globalization Really Works,* Cornell University Press London, 2010.

Piketty, J. *Capital in the 21ˢᵗ Century (Le Capital au XXI Century),* Harvard University Press, 2014

Quirk, P., *Macroeconomic implications of money laundering*. IMF Working Paper, WP/96/66, Monetary and Exchange Affairs Department, IMF, Washington, DC, 1996

Reuters, Th., *London property: a top destination for money launderers.* Reuters/Andrew Winnings/Transparency International, 2017

Tanzi, V., *Money laundering and the international financial system*. Washington: International Monetary Fund, 1996.

Tax Justice Network, *Financial Secrecy Index 2015*; *Narrative Report on USA.*

Schneider, F. and U. Windischbauer, Money laundering: some facts. *European Journal of Law and Economics*, 2008, 26 (4), pp. 387-404

Schneider, F. and D. Enste, Shadow economies: size, causes, and consequences. *The Journal of Economic Literature*, 2000, 38 (1), 77–114.

Sikka, P., *The role of offshore financial centres in globalisation.* Essex University, Accounting Forum, December 2003

Tax Justice Network, *Financial Secrecy Index 2015*

UNODC, *Estimating illicit financial flows resulting from drug trafficking and other transnational organized crime.* Vienna, 2011

Unger, B. and G. Rawlings, *The amounts and effects of money laundering*. Report for the Ministry of Finance. Utrecht School of Economics, Utrecht, 2006

Unger, B., *The scale and impacts of money laundering*. Cheltenham, Edward Elgar Publishing, 2007

Zucman, G., The missing wealth of nations, *The quarterly Journal of Economics*, 9 April 2013, p. 1321-1364

Self-protecting in organisational life: a case study of Money Laundering Reporting Officers

Abdullahi U. Bello[1]

Introduction

There are several theories in organisational studies that deal with the relationship between various stakeholders in an organisation. Agency theory, for example, deals with the conflict of interest between two parties while stakeholder theory explains the relationship between an organisation and others that affect and are affected by it. In this chapter, I will introduce another theory called the 'self-protecting theory' (Bello, 2017) that also explains the relationship between stakeholders in an organisation. I will also give an example of how the theory is applicable in hospitals.

The self-protecting theory differs from agency theory by suggesting that it may not be possible to always align the interest of conflicting parties, as such, and that a new approach is needed to accommodate the differences. The theory was discovered from research into the behaviours of Money Laundering Reporting Officers (MLROs) in UK banks (Bello, 2014, 2017). It extends the stakeholder theory by introducing the concept of fairness and independence in managing the relationship between various stakeholders. The theories mentioned in this section will be discussed below, but before then it is important to present a brief background of money laundering and the justification for the research in order to provide a context for the self-protecting theory.

Money laundering is a global problem that has been around for a long time (Unger, 2013). It is the process of hiding the source of illegal money so it will appear to come from a legitimate source (Reuter and Truman, 2004). Because of its effect on the economy (Barone and Masciandaro, 2011), several institutions have tried to tackle the problem by implementing laws and policies to deal with it. The Financial Action Task Force (FATF) is at the forefront of the fight

---

[1] The author is Ag. Head, Forensic Accounting and Financial Investigation at Economic and Financial Crimes Commission, Nigeria.

against money laundering. They developed 40 recommendations in 1989 (Shehu, 2005) and in 2012 a more comprehensive review was made to include recommendations on the proliferation of weapons of mass destruction and to integrate the 9 recommendations on terrorism (FATF, 2012). The United Nations is also at the vanguard of the fight. The UN Convention against the Illicit Traffic in Narcotic Drugs and Psychotropic Substances introduced in 1988 was the first international initiative that was issued to deal with money laundering (Ryder, 2008; Shehu, 2005). The World Bank, IMF and the EU are also some of the major institutions that are fighting money laundering.

I decided to conduct the research on money laundering because most research on AML is descriptive and conceptual while there are insufficient theoretical studies in the field (Demesis, 2010). Some are also based on opinions while others are on typologies of money laundering. "... *While these typological examinations remain useful for practitioners, academic research ought to be grounded on a theoretical level and assist in drawing the implication to practice*" (Demesis, 2010: 36).

MLROs were selected as participants for the research because of the key role they play in AML. MLROs are designated officers in banks who are responsible for coordinating AML activities and liaising with Financial Intelligence Units, which can be part of law enforcement which depends on the jurisdiction. The essence of having this role is to prevent money launderers from using the financial system to launder their ill-gotten wealth (Broek, 2011). Their main function is to receive internal suspicious activity reports from within the banks and then report them to law enforcement for the purpose of preventing money laundering. They also assist in implementing various provisions of AML regulations.

Organisational theories

There are several theories in organisation studies dealing with various aspects of organisational life (Eisenhardt, 1989). There are however two theories that are relevant to the discussion in this paper; the *agency theory* and the *stakeholder theory*. This is because both theories deal with conflict between parties which is also at the heart of the self-protecting theory to be elaborated later. I will now look at the two theories and later show how the self-protecting theory expands the two theories.

Agency theory

Agency theory is a theory about the conflict of interest between two parties. "*It deals with the relationship that develops when an individual in a transaction (the principal) grants authority to another (an agent) and the welfare of the principal becomes affected by the decision of the self-interested agent*" (Wright and Mukherji, 1999: 297). The core of the theory is therefore the *"goal conflict inherent when individuals with differing preference engage in cooperative efforts*" (Eisenhardt, 1989: 63).

Since the inherent assumption in agency theory is that an agent is self-interested among others (Bosse and Phillips, 2016), the relationship should be structured to ensure that the agent is actually working for the best interest of the principal. There are, however, costs to the agency relationship. The main costs, according to Jensen and Meckling, (2008) are monitoring costs, bonding costs and residual costs. According to them, monitoring costs are expenses of the principal to ensure that the agent is working on his behalf, while bonding cost is a cost the agent incur to convince the principal that he will act on his behalf. Residual cost on the other hand is the reduction in welfare as a result of the action of the agent.

There is however some that challenged the traditional assumption of the agency relationship. The assumption of self-interest, opportunistic behaviour and the concept of the economic man of the agency theory, according to (Wright and Mukherji, 1999), is leading to increasing cost and risk to the relationship. They proposed a socioeconomic approach as an alternative that would reduce costs and minimise risks. The alternative is based on the assumption of enlightened self-interest, trustworthy behaviour and the concept of the non-economic man. Similarly, Bosse and Phillips, (2016) introduced the concept of bounded self-interest as a modification to the self-interest assumption to help explain other manifestation of the agency relationship.

Stakeholder theory

Stakeholder theory on the other hand deals with the relationship of an organisation with others that have an interest in the organisation. Donaldson and Preston, (1995) provided a detailed explanation of the theory, it uses and misuses and the main areas of its strength. They argued that the theory is descriptive, instrumental, and managerial but that it is fundamentally a normative theory. They also argued that the stakeholder theory is better than the alternative shareholder theory in explaining the relationships in an organisation. Similarly, Freeman, (2010) agrees with Donaldson and Preston, (1995) on the usefulness of the theory in explaining the relationship of organisations with its stakeholders. He defines stakeholders as ". . . *any group or individual who can affect or is affected by the achievement of the organisation's objectives*" (Freeman, 2010: 46). Examples of stakeholders are suppliers, customers, employees and owners in addition to environmentalist, consumer advocates, media and government among others.

Identifying and managing these stakeholders is therefore important for the effective functioning of an organisation. Freeman, (2010) mentioned the classification grid as a way of identifying stakeholders and the level of their power and stake in an organisation. This is similar to the stakeholder mapping by Mendelow, (1991), in which stakeholders are grouped based on their power and interest. According to him, minimal effort should be used to manage stakeholders with low power and low interest, while stakeholders with high power and high interest are key players. Similarly, those with low power, but high interest should be kept informed while those with high power but low interest should be kept satisfied.

Although the stakeholder theory has been gaining momentum over the years, Beaver (1999), is of the opinion that it is an untenable theory given the events of the last few decades. According to him, the series of hostile takeovers, mergers and downsizing, executive compensation and the power of institutional investors have shifted the focus of managers from stakeholders to shareholders who wield enormous power over organisations. Nwanji and Howell (2007), however, tried to combine the two approaches. They argued that by adopting a stakeholder approach an organisation is invariably adopting shareholder approach.

Overview of the Self-protecting theory

Self-protecting theory was 'discovered' during research on the behaviour of Money Laundering Reporting Officers (MLROs) or compliance officers within the UK banking industry (Bello, 2014). To understand the AML system, I focused on MLROs. I wanted to find out about their concerns and how they are dealing with them. I decided to use the classical grounded theory approach to conduct the study because it aligns with my philosophical position and the objective of the research. Classical grounded theory, as will be explained later, is an approach that is about discovering the concerns of participants and generating a theory that explains how the participants are dealing with the concerns (Glaser, 2011).

At the end of the research I discovered the main concerns of MLROs to be unfair pressure from both banks and regulators and I then generated the self-protecting theory that explains how they are resolving the concern. The theory states that the more *unfair pressure* is exerted on MLROs the more they *discharge* their responsibilities to *protect* themselves rather than *comply* with regulations to *prevent* money laundering.

The theory is therefore a theory of behaviour in an organisation, as such, it is within the ambit of sociology and psychology. The concepts of *culture* and *ethics* derived from the research, for example, are present in the social theory of legitimacy where, according to Tyler, (2006, p. 270), "*people's motivation to cooperate with others, in this case legal authorities, is rooted in social relationships and ethical judgments, and does not primarily flow from the desire to avoid punishments or gain rewards*". Similarly, *belief* a key concept in self-protecting theory also featured prominently in legitimacy theory. According to Hyde (1983: 382) for example, legitimacy is "*a state of widespread belief; namely, the belief that an order is obligatory or exemplary. Moreover, the belief is a reason for action*". Other social theories related to the self- protecting theory are the social learning theory (Sutinen and Kuperan, 1999) which states that peer pressure and social influence determines compliance behaviour just as unfair and fair pressure determine behaviour in self-protecting theory.

Although the self-protecting theory is more a sociological theory as explained above, and given that the grounded theory methodology used for the research has its roots in sociology (Glaser and Strauss, 1967), the theory is also an economic theory because of the two key concepts of *reward* and *punishment* discovered in the research, which are essential part of the deterrence model of regulation espoused by (Becker, 1968). The framework derived from the self-protecting theory is also closely related to game theory, an economic theory of regulation (Scholz, 1984).

Self-protecting theory is also a psychological theory because of the focus on the behaviour of MLROs. The theory emphasises the place of morality in compliance behaviour (Sutinen and Kuperan, 1999), for example, is linked with the concept of *personal ethics* of the self protecting theory.

The self preservation theory (Karni and Schmeidler, 1986) and the protection motivation theory (Rogers, 1975) are also some of the theories in psychology that are linked to the self protecting theory. The self-preservation theory is related to the self protecting theory since it was the in vivo codec (a word borrowed from participants) of self-preservation that gave rise to the protecting concept. The two theories are however different because the self preservation theory is an evolutionary theory that is concerned with survival (de Catanzaro,

1991), while the self-protecting theory is about regulatory behaviour (Bello, 2017). The protection motivation theory (PMT) is also similar to the self protecting theory regarding the factors influencing behaviour. PMT is however, more concerned with resolving the fear appeal rather than *pressure* of the self protecting theory. Rogers, (1975: 93), in explaining the PMT, for example, states that a change in attitude result from the "(*a) the magnitude of noxiousness of a depicted event; (b) the probability of that event's occurrence; and c) the efficacy of the protective response*". Therefore, while the self protecting theory is concerned with the conflict of interest between parties (Bello, 2014), the PMT is a "*general theory of persuasive communication*" (Boer and Seydel, 1996: 95).

The self protecting theory also relates to theories of fraud in criminology. The fraud triangle in which pressure, rationalisation and opportunity formed the edges of the triangle (Turner *et al.*, 2003) , for example, is related to the self protecting theory since pressure corresponds to *unfair pressure* and rationalisation corresponds to *justifying*– a concept of *self-protecting*. An important addition to the fraud theory is the distinction between fair and unfair pressure. While *pressure* in fraud triangle predicts a certain behaviour that results from having an opportunity, the behaviour resulting from pressure in self protecting theory depends on the type of pressure. A fair pressure will lead to a positive action while an unfair pressure will lead to a negative action (Bello, 2017).

Methodology

Deciding on the methodology to use in the research that led to the self-protecting theory was a systematic process. It started with the establishment of the philosophical position for the study since philosophy determines how research is conducted (Collier, 1994; Collins and Hussay, 2013). Based on the recommendation that for a quality research, a researcher should start with understanding his philosophical inclination, I reflected on the nature of reality (ontology) and the process of how to understand it (epistemology). Ontology and epistemology, according to Guba, (1990), are two of the most important concepts that determines the philosophical position of a researcher.

My reflection resulted in identifying Peirce Pragmatism as the philosophical position that closely mirrored my thought on the nature of reality and how to understand it. Peirce Pragmatism has an objective ontology, where reality is independent, and subjective epistemology, where a person's experience and knowledge affects how he understands the objective reality (Peirce, 1905, 1908). A detailed discussion of philosophy is beyond the scope of this chapter, but this introduction will hopefully highlight what informed the choice of my methodology.

Following from this reflection, the classical grounded theory approach of Braney Glaser[2] appeared to be the best methodology that suits my philosophical position. Other methodologies reviewed did not match the ontological and epistemological position I took for the research. The Strauss and Corbin approach to grounded theory, for example, is more suited to the subjective ontological position (Bryant, 2009; Kelle, 2005) while phenomenology is clearly a subjective methodological approach (Oberg and Bell, 2012; Sadala and Adorno, 2002).

Classical grounded theory approach was therefore adopted for the research. In this approach, a researcher is required to go to the field with as little preconception as possible (Glaser, 2008) to identify the concerns of participants and how they are dealing with the concerns through a process of concurrent data collection and analysis. The procedures of the approach include data collection, substantive coding and theoretical coding. Others are theoretical sampling, memoing and sorting, all vital and necessary procedures in grounded theory (Glaser, 1978).

Sixteen interviews where conducted during the research. Those interviewed included serving MLROs from investment banking, building societies, private banking, wholesale banking, universal banking and commercial banking. Others interviewed were former MLROs within the banking industry.

These interviews were conducted based on the principle of theoretical sampling, a procedure in which data collection is based on analysis of previous data. In the word of Glaser: "*Theoretical sampling is the process of data collection for generating theory whereby the analyst jointly collects, codes, and analyses his data and decides what data to collect next and where to find them, in order to discover his theory as it emerges*" (Glaser and Strauss, 1965). For example, when discussing with the MLRO of an investment bank, he mentioned specific concerns of MLROs in big commercial banks, which then led to the interview of MLROs of some commercial banks to understand the concerns from their own perspective. Similarly, analysis and further data collection pointed to the plight of small and private banks. Furthermore, former MLROs were selected because they are accessible and they do not have the same inhibitions as employed MLROs. Besides, most of them have worked in various capacities in the banking industry as MLROs giving them a unique experience. The first participant, however, was selected purposely to start the process, but "*decisions about which data should*

---

[2]   There are two main approaches to grounded theory; the Glaserian approach and the Straussian approach (Jones and Noble, 2007)

be collected next are determined by the theory that is being constructed." (Suddaby, 2006: 634).

In addition to interviews, secondary data was also collected and analysed, again based on theoretical sampling. Four documents were analysed to support the interviews conducted. The first document was on the case between Shah and HSBC (Shah V HSBC Private Bank Limited and Division, 2012) while the second was a case against Standard Chartered Bank by the US government (New York District Attorney, 2012). The first document was analysed to understand the frustration of an MLRO who had to endure court appearances resulting from performing his reporting obligation while the second was analysed to further understand the concept of conspiracy that was prominent in the data. The third was a transcript of an interview with a deputy MLRO from a previous unrelated research while the fourth was a 168 page government document (Financial Services Authority, 2011) that highlighted some of the issues with AML compliance.

Other procedures used in the research are substantive coding, theoretical coding, memoing, and sorting (Glaser, 1978). Substantive coding is divided into open and selecting coding. In open coding, the data collected is analyse line by line to generate concepts from the data. It is called "*running the data open*" (Glaser, 1978: 56). As data are analysed, memos are written to describe the relationship between the concepts being generated, to record examples from the data and to record gaps for further data collection.

In selective coding, analysis of data is sustained, but unlike in open coding where all data are analysed to identify patterns, in selective coding, analysis is focused on the emerging theory being developed. In other words, further data collection and analysis are focused on the core categories discovered during open coding (Corbin and Strauss, 1990; Glaser, 1978; Jones and Noble, 2007).

The final procedure in the coding process is theoretical coding, where the core concepts and categories are integrated according to a theoretical code. Theoretical codes are theoretical frameworks that are used to generate a theory (Glaser and Holton, 2005). The 'degree family', for example, are theoretical codes that denote range, extreme, intensity, extent and polarity (Glaser, 1978). An example of the use of a degree theoretical code is "*the more that is spent on policemen, court personnel, and specialized equipment, the easier it is to discover offenses and convict offenders.*" (Becker, 1968: 174).

The next stage of the process is sorting. This is the process of arranging concepts and categories to discover theoretical codes and also integrate the concepts and categories to form a theory according to the theoretical code selected (Glaser, 2012). It is done when saturation is almost completed. Saturation occurs when further data collection and analysis seem unnecessary (Suddaby, 2006) or when concepts are developed enough to form a theory (Glaser and Strauss, 1967). During analysis, memos are written to explain what is going on in the data. The memos are then stored in a memo bank where memos from different analysis are combined together. Sorting is conducted by taking out the memos from the bank and arranging them according to the theoretical code selected for the research.

After conducting the interviews over a period of 1 year from April 2012 to March 2013, reviewing secondary data and applying the core techniques discussed above, I was able to generate a theory that explains how MLROs are dealing with their concerns and from the theory developed a framework of compliance behaviour. The next section presents the summary of my findings.

Findings

The main concern I found out from the research was *unfair pressure* exerted on MLROs from the regulators on the one hand and the banks on the other. In doing their jobs, regulators exert a lot of pressure on banks, and since MLROs are the faces of the banks, they bear most of the brunt of regulations. One of the concerns of MLROs is *defective regulations* enforced by regulators. One of such regulations is the 'consent regime' where compliance officers are obliged to report transactions they consider suspicious, and wait for the approval of law enforcement before they allow the transactions to go through (POCA, 2002). Whenever there is a delay in approval, compliance officers face a lot of pressure from customers who want to complete their transactions. What makes it even worst is that compliance officers are not allowed to inform their customers of the reason for the delay (POCA, 2002). Another regulation that they consider defective is the *risk-based approach*. They agree that in principle the risk based approach is good but in practice it is not effective. They complained mostly on the ownership of assessment. An MLRO may decide that a transaction is not suspicious based on his own objective assessment, but regulators may consider the transaction suspicious based on their own assessment

Another concern is the constant *shifting expectation* of regulators. These involve the constant changes in regulations. The complaint is mainly about the speed and amount of regulation which most often increase the cost of compliance. The expectations of regulators sometimes might not even be covered by any regulation, but based on the assessment of regulators. The number of suspicious activity reports (SARs) that is expected from a big bank, for example, may not be the same for a small bank. This is not minding that a big bank that has an effective AML controls and an effective reporting mechanism may report less number of SARs than a small bank that reports everything. It may also be because money launderers prefer to transact with smaller banks because of the bureaucratic nature of big banks.

Other concerns relate to the *damage to the reputation* of compliance officers. Compliance officers have seen how their colleagues are sanctioned for infringing money laundering laws, and they have also seen how their colleagues are smeared on the pages of newspapers. They also fear the loss of their jobs and even prosecution for unintentional breaches of AML regulations.

MLROs also complain about the *naivety of regulators*. They complain that regulators sometimes do not understand how banks operate, and that they sometimes employ inexperienced and unskilled employees to supervise the banks. Furthermore, they complain that regulators sometimes issue blanket regulations not minding the different types of banks in the industry. An investment bank, for example, is different from a retail bank, so also is a small bank different from a big bank with international operations.

Compliance officers also face pressure from their banks. *Lack of enough resources* to perform their duties was the main concern raised by the officers. They need resources to buy software for monitoring and assessing transactions, and resources to employ staff to assist them in the job. The other concern relates to the difficulty they face in managing employees that are not under their direct control. I called this *marginal management* since the employees report to managers in other departments that have different objectives than that of compliance officers. A marketer, for example, is more concerned with bringing businesses to the bank while a compliance officer is more concerned about the nature of the businesses. The behaviour of the compliance officer may result in turning away businesses from the bank.

To deal with these concerns, compliance officers adopt various strategies. The common strategy is to *discharge* their responsibility to *protect* themselves rather than *comply* with regulations to *prevent* money laundering. This strategy is mainly adopted when dealing with regulators. Their *assessing* and *reporting* is mainly to ensure that they comply with the letter, but not necessarily the spirit of the law. For example, a compliance officer will look at a suspicious transaction and ask himself: what will happen if I report or fail to report this transaction? Is the bank going to be angry with me for reporting a valued customer or are the regulators going to sanction me for not reporting the customer?

Therefore MLROs are *assessing* the impact of transactions on themselves rather than *assessing* whether transactions are money laundering activities. It is a *balancing* act: they weigh the cost and benefit to themselves and then *use their discretion* when *assessing* transactions.

Furthermore, MLROs *play safe* when *reporting* transactions based on the cost / benefit analysis of reporting. After deciding to report or not to report, they then vigorously defend their judgments. When they report a valued customer, for example, they try to convince the banks that it is necessary to report the customer to the regulators. Other strategies for dealing with pressure from regulators are *learning, automating* and *complaining*. To deal with constant changes in regulation, MLROs attend conferences and seminars to update their knowledge. They also attend networking events to find out how other MLROs are dealing with the challenges of the work. Similarly, they rely on software tools to *automate* assessing and reporting activities.

The strategy for dealing with banks is, however, different. Compliance officers are constantly *justifying* their actions; *justifying* the need for resources and the decision to report a customer. They are also constantly engaging in *dialogue* with management and other employees to obtain what they want. They do that by *negotiating* for resources and *coordinating* with different departments and other officers in different locations. At times, they even *threaten* both employees and management to get the resources and attention they need to perform their duties. They also deal with the *unfair pressure* from both banks and regulators by *complaining* about it to whosoever cares to listen. The core category of *protecting*, therefore, has two sub-core categories called *discharging* and *communicating*. Under *discharging* are comprised: *assessing, reporting, learning, automating* and *complaining* while *dialogue* comprises: *justifying, threat* and *complaining* are the categories of *communicating*.

MLROs, however, *align* with either banks or regulators depending on their *interests* in terms of *punishment* and *reward*, and *belief* in terms of *culture, conviction* and *personal ethics*. *Reward* and *punishment* are similar to the concepts of reward and punishment in the economic approach to regulation (Becker, 1968), while *culture* is related more to organisational culture which, in essence, is the "*shared beliefs and values guiding the thinking and behavioural styles of members*" (Cooke and Rousseau, 1988: 245). Similarly, the concept of *ethics* of the research is more related to virtue theory of ethical behaviour (Aristotle, 1962) since it was discovered that the 'character of MLROs' strongly influences their behaviour, while conviction is the commitment of a person to his belief (Bello, 2014).

The more either party satisfies their interest, for example, the more they align with the party, but their belief also strongly moderates their alignment. From the research, it was discovered that most MLROs in the UK align with the banks mainly because of the reward from the banks despite the threat of punishment from the regulators. The *belief* and *conviction* of some compliance officers of being targeted rather than targeting the actual money launders also make them to align with the banks, though there are some whose personal ethics makes them to tilt towards the regulators. It is this alignment that determines the nature of protecting behaviour of MLROs. By *aligning* with the banks the unfair pressure is mostly originating from the regulators and vice versa.

Following from applying the procedures of classical grounded theory, theoretical coding was used to integrate the various concepts into a theory. As discussed earlier, theoretical coding is the process of integrating concepts and categories into a theoretical code that fits the data being collected and analysed. There are several theoretical codes to choose from, but the ones that closely match the data were the 'degree family' and the 'binary code'. The degree family are codes that deals with a range of features: extreme, intensity and polarity, while the binary code belongs to the 'paired opposite family' of theoretical codes (Glaser, 1978). For example, unfair pressure belongs to the degree family of theoretical codes, since the intensity of the concept determines the behaviour of the compliance officer i.e. whether he is *preventing* money laundering or *protecting* himself. The polarity between *preventing* and *protecting* represents the paired opposite theoretical code. Similarly, *discharging* and *complying*, *communicating* and *cooperating* are other examples of the paired opposite code.

From these theoretical codes and based on the procedures of classical grounded theory, the self-protecting theory was discovered. In its most basic form, the theory as depicted below states that the more there is unfair pressure on MLROs (a person) the more he protects himself rather than prevents money laundering.

Figure 1

Self-protecting theory

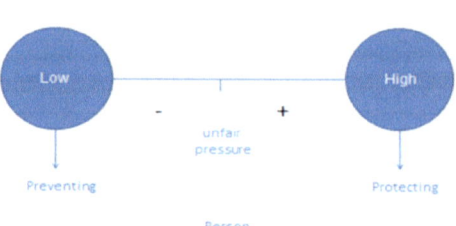

180

The finding in the research as discussed earlier, however, shows that there are two ways of *protecting* oneself. *Protecting* oneself from the regulators or *protecting* oneself from the banks. When the *unfair pressure* is mostly from the regulators and the MLROs are *aligned* with the bank, then they are just *discharging* their responsibilities to *protect* themselves rather than *complying* with regulations to *prevent* money laundering. This scenario is represented as follows:

Figure 2

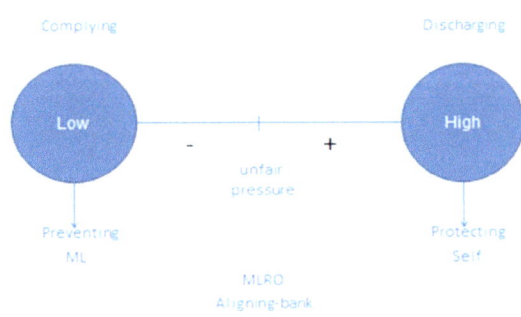

Source: Author, (Bello, 2014, 2017)

The theory then says that the more unfair pressure is exerted on MLROs by the regulators the more they *discharge* their responsibilities to *protect* themselves rather than *comply* with regulations to *prevent* money laundering. Since the *unfair pressure* is from the regulators then the concerns are *defective regulations*, *naïve regulators*, *shifting expectation* and *damage to reputation*, and since they are protecting themselves from the regulators, they do so by *using their discretion* when assessing transactions, *playing safe* and making defensive reporting among other *discharging* behaviours.

If, however, the *unfair pressure* is mostly from the banks and the MLROs are aligned with the regulators, then the MLROs are *communicating* with the banks to *protect* themselves rather than *cooperating* with the banks to *prevent* money laundering. This scenario is represented as follows:

Figure 3

Self-protecting theory

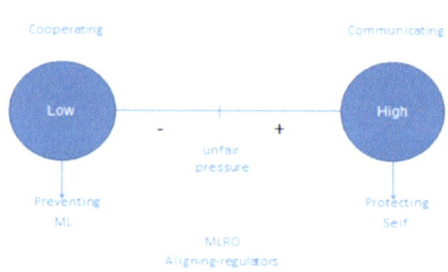

Source: Author, (Bello, 2014, 2017)

The theory then says that the more *unfair pressure* is exerted on MLROs by the banks the more they are *communicating* with the banks to *protect* themselves rather than *cooperating* with the bank to *prevent* money laundering. Since the *unfair pressure* is from the banks then the concerns are *lack of resources* and *marginal management*, and since they are protecting themselves from the banks they do so by *negotiating* for resources, engaging in *dialogue*, *justifying* their decisions and even *threatening* the staff of the banks who fail to cooperate.

Since most of the *unfair pressure* is coming from the regulators and the compliance officers are mostly aligned with the banks, the first scenario where MLROs are *discharging* their responsibilities to *protect* themselves rather than *complying* with regulations to *prevent* money laundering is more applicable to the UK AML environment. Other jurisdictions or industries may however be different depending on the source of pressure and the alignment of compliance officers.

The self-protecting framework

Having generated the theory, a framework was developed based on the concepts discovered in the research. It was observed that the four main concepts of *discharging, communicating, complying* and *cooperating* corresponds to *weak regulation, tough regulation, smart regulation* and *self regulations* respectively. These concepts together with the concern of *unfair pressure* and the two subcategories of *aligning* i.e. *belief* and *interest* formed the self-protecting theory as shown and described below.

Figure 4

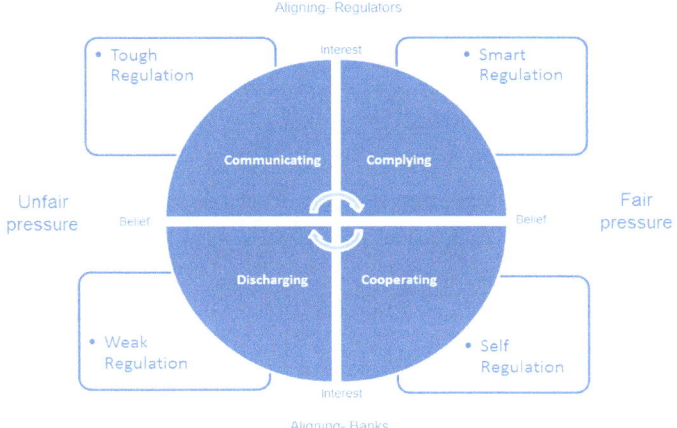

Source: Author, (Bello, 2014, 2017)

The framework suggests four regulatory environments depending on the behaviour of compliance officers in the environments. *Tough* regulation is where compliance officers are aligning with regulators because of unfair pressure from banks while *weak regulation* is where the compliance officers are *aligning* with the banks because of the *unfair pressure* from the regulators. With *tough regulation*, banks may be complying to some extent, but it is more a compliance to the rules rather than to the principals of AML. In *weak regulation*, the compliance with regulations is not as much as in the tough regulatory environment because of the protecting behaviour of compliance officers. Similarly, in *self-regulation* there is fair pressure from the regulators and the compliance officers are aligned with the banks, while in *smart regulation* there is fair pressure from the banks and the compliance officers are aligning with the regulators.

Self regulation is therefore desirable, but there is the potential problem of capture where organisations take advantage of regulation for their own benefit (Ayres and Braithwaite, 1992). *Smart regulation* is also desirable, but the cost of enforcement to regulators can be prohibitive (Bello, 2017).

The AML regulatory environment in the UK is therefore *weak* since, as discussed earlier, most compliance officers are *discharging* their responsibilities to *protect* themselves rather than *complying* with regulations to *prevent* money laundering.

The middle–course approach

It is not enough to present a theory and a framework that explains how participants in a study are resolving their main concerns. Equally important is to suggest a solution that would allay the concerns of participants. The *middle course approach* is, therefore, a recommendation that seeks to provide a solution for the dysfunctional self-protecting behaviours of compliance officers.

What is interesting about the approach is that it was also discovered from the research.[3] Even though *smart regulation* and *self regulation* are better forms of regulations than *weak* and *tough regulation*, the best form of regulation that emerged from the research is in the middle between *smart regulation* and *self-regulation* (the middle course approach).

Smart regulation may be effective for regulators because banks are complying, but it may not be efficient because of the amount of resources required to enforce compliance. *Self-regulation* on the other hand may be efficient for the regulators because it is the banks that shoulder the responsibility for enforcement, but it may not be effective since the banks may be working in their own self-interest (Bello, 2017).

The *middle course approach* will, therefore, deal with the problem of cost of compliance associated with *smart regulation* and the problem of capture associated with *self-regulation*. The approach recommends that compliance officers should be as *independent* as possible and the pressure on them should be *fair*. This will result in a regulatory environment that is effective and more efficient for regulators as well as effective and more efficient for banks. The following show the position of middle course approach on the framework.

---

3 For details of how the approach was discovered see (Bello, 2017).

Figure 5

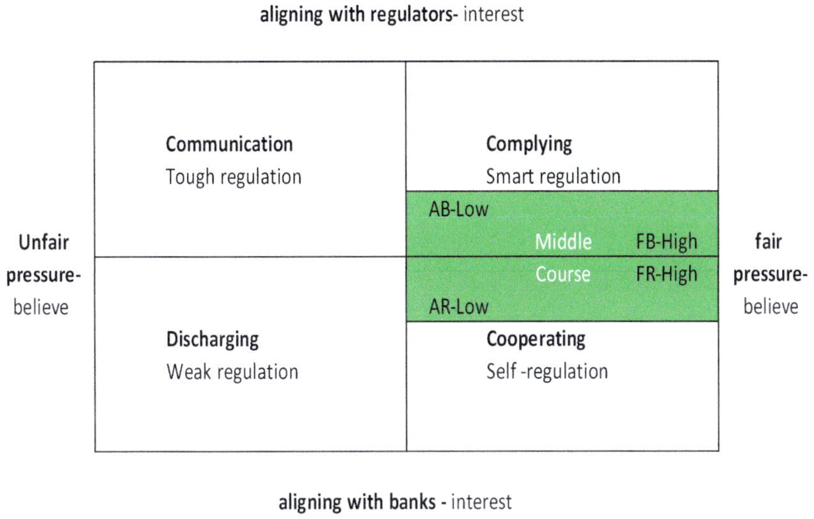

aligning with regulators- interest

aligning with banks - interest

Independence was derived from the framework because compliance officers are neither aligned with the banks nor are they aligned with the regulators, but they sit in the middle where aligning with both banks and regulators is low. *Fairness* on the other hand is already part of the framework since both *smart regulation* and *self-regulation* are characterised with fairness as against *weak* and *tough* regulations that are characterised with unfairness. The suggestion of *independence* and *fairness* of the *middle course approach* is therefore a result that combines the best of *smart regulation* and the best of *self-regulation*

What is fair and what constitutes independence is however subject to further research. From the research, however, fairness can be seen as the opposite of unfairness. The consent regime of suspicious activity reporting, for example, is unfair according to the participants. So removing the provision that makes MLROs to be under undue pressure will be considered fair. MLROs are required to delay a transaction that they reported until they receive an approval from law enforcement within a certain period of time. They are also not allowed to inform the customer about the reasons for the delay which will be considered a breach of the tipping off provision. This puts the MLROs under intense pressure from customers who want to complete their transactions.

Independence, on the other hand, as suggested by one participant, can take the form of sharing the burden of remunerating MLROs between the banks and the regulators. Further research may, however, identify other forms of independence and fairness that may ensure a more effective and efficient AML compliance.

The contribution of the self-protecting theory to organisational studies

We have seen earlier that agency and stakeholder theories are similar to the self-protecting theory since they all deal with conflict of interest between parties to a relationship.

In agency theory the solution to an agency problem is to align the interests of both the principal and the agent (Bosse and Phillips, 2016). This may work in some situations, but not always. The self-protecting theory suggests that in a situation where you have a conflict of interest that is difficult to align, a third party (MLROs in AML) is needed to resolve the difference. This is similar to the concept of having a judge to adjudicate in cases between two parties or the position of an arbitrator in a dispute. It is also similar to republican tripartism suggested by Ayres and Braithwaite, (1991) where they recommended engaging a public interest group, an external third party, in the regulatory decision making. In self protecting theory, however, the third party works within the system. In AML, for example, MLROs are employees of banks, but they have certain responsibilities that makes them accountable to the regulators. Similarly, internal auditors work for an organisation, but they have a reporting line to the board of directors (Basel Committee on Banking Supervision, 2012). What is required is to treat the third parties fairly and give them a level of autonomy that would allow them to do their jobs independently. The concept of fairness in an agency relationship was also the focus of a paper by Bosse and Phillips, (2016) where they argued that although actors seek to maximise their self-interest, they do so within the bound of fairness. This is consistent with the self-protecting theory (Bello, 2014, 2017).

Another aspect of the theory is that the relationship between banks and MLROs as well as the relationship between MLROs and the regulators are agency relationships. Since the interest of the banks and that of the MLROs on the one hand and the MLROs and the regulators on the other hand are not as conflicted as between the relationship between the banks and the regulators, it is easier for the MLROs to align the interests of the banks and the regulators. MLROs are not as conflicted because they have dual functions in AML. They are employees of banks so they owe some allegiance to the banks, but their main function is to ensure that AML regulations are complied with by the banks so they serve the interest of regulators. For the banks, complying with AML regulation come with a cost (compliance cost) while for the regulators not complying with the regulation comes with a cost (cost of money laundering activity to the society). MLROs, therefore, aim to ensure that the cost of compliance is as low as possible while the effect of money laundering is kept to the minimum possible.

In *stakeholder theory*, the main issue for the management is how to deal with various stakeholders each having a different objective. As discussed earlier, one of the strategies for dealing with stakeholders is to identify them and determine their power and interest in an organisation. Once this is done, a strategy should then be adopted for dealing with each.

The implication of the Mendelow Matrix (Mendelow, 1991) to focus attention on key players, though a good strategy, may not be the ideal for both the key players and the company. This is because when the key players exert *unfair pressure* on management, the management may respond by *protecting* themselves rather than working to improve the performance of the company. The contribution of the self-protecting theory through the middle-course approach, therefore, is that key players should realise that it is only by exercising their powers fairly and allowing the management some level of autonomy that they can maximise the benefits from the organisation. This also applies to other stakeholders of an organisation.

Application of the Self-protecting Theory in Hospitals

The self-protecting theory is a theory that was derived from studying the behaviours of MLROs, but it has general application in organisations that are characterised by conflict. One of the examples of this is hospitals, where government works through managers, doctors and patients: the three main parties to the tripartite relationship. The agency and stakeholder theories are also applicable since hospitals are organisations with stakeholders that have conflicting objectives.

Doctors are like MLROs, they sit in the middle between a government that is more concerned with efficiency of care and the patients who are more concerned with the effectiveness of care. In the UK, for example, this relationship between the trio has been deteriorating from the time when there was an "implicit compact" (Ham and Alberti, 2002, p.838) between the three in which the doctors have autonomy and independence to carry out their functions, the patient are passive recipients of care while the government tacitly empowers doctors to do their jobs.

The introduction of the NHS in 1948 did not substantially alter the implicit agreement (Ham and Alberti, 2002). The agreement is such that the government funds health care for all citizens, the doctors deliver the care and the public pay taxes for the use of health care services. Managers were then allowed to administer the system on behalf of the government.

But the implicit compact subsequently weakened when patients became more active and in some instances, standards were compromised (Ham and Alberti, 2002). This resulted in the gradual decline in doctor's autonomy and increasing calls for accountability (Edwards, 2003). Finally, in 1997, the implicit compact was broken with patients becoming less deferential to doctors and more demanding (Ham and Alberti, 2002).

The concern of doctors on pay, increased workload and the erosion of clinical autonomy made the conflict between managers, representing the government, and doctors to increase (Edwards, 2003). Some of the main areas of concerns included the issue of accountability and the diminishing power of the doctors to decide how to provide care (Richard Smith, 2001). In addition, the litigation culture in the UK and the increased involvement of government in health care provision increased pressure on doctors (Doran, Fox, Rodham, Taylor, and Harris, 2016).

The unfair pressure for both MLROs and doctors therefore mainly revolves around defective regulation, under-resources and shifting expectation. The government was increasingly introducing policies and regulations in health care that seems to erode the autonomy of doctors (Reasbeck, 2008) and undermine the relationship between managers and doctors (Rimmer, 2016). Successive governments have also introduced reforms, according to (Ham, 2014) that are major distractions. Under resources is manifested in terms of increased workload and stagnating pay (Edwards, 2003). In addition, the expectations of both patients and government have been increasing. The government expects better care with fewer resources (efficiency) while patients expect flawless care no matter the cost (effectiveness).

These concerns of doctors were aptly summarised by (Doran et al., 2016) in which they found out that many General Practitioners (GPs) are leaving their jobs because they are under-valued and under-appreciated among others. Furthermore, doctors are increasingly asked to perform administrative tasks that take them away from face to face contact with patients (Doran et al., 2016). These concerns are strikingly similar to the concerns on MLROs discussed earlier. In the case of money laundering officers, the unfair pressure comes from banks on the one hand and regulators on the other hand, while in the case of doctors the unfair pressure comes from the government on the one hand and patients on the other.

The ways doctors and MLROs deal with their concerns are also similar. Doctors protect themselves by practicing defensively and by following the tick box approach (Doran et al., 2016), a key concern in AML (Killick and Parody, 2007). They stay late in the hospitals, take work home and change their appointments to deal with the concerns over work overload (Doran *et al.*, 2016).

Since the concerns are similar, the solution should also be similar. The solution lies in finding a middle course between the desire of government for efficiency and the desire of patients for effectiveness. The middle-course approach introduced earlier may therefore serve the health care industry as well because it is a recommendation for dealing with the effectiveness and efficiency dilemma.

Doctors should, therefore, be treated fairly by both the government and the patients, and they should be given a level of independence required to perform their duties. It may not be possible for them to get the level of autonomy they used to enjoy (Edwards, 2003), but the control over the provision of care should be relaxed. This is because doctors, like MLROs, are the experts; they have both the qualification and experience to provide health care to patients. The details of what should be a fair pressure and the kind of independence required is however beyond this paper. Further research is required to find out the best way to reduce unfair pressure on them and to identify the specific measures to take to guarantee their independence.

Conclusion

Conflict is at the heart of the relationship between stakeholders in an organisation. The agency theory describes the relationship between parties that have conflicting interest while stakeholder theory describes the relationship between various stakeholders in an organisation. The self- protecting theory is another addition to theories in organisational studies that also deals with conflict. It was discovered that *unfair pressure* was the main concern of MLROs within the UK banking industry. To deal with the concern, MLROs employ various strategies depending on the source of the pressure. When the pressure is coming from the regulators, they protect themselves by engaging in *defensive reporting, assessing* transactions based on the risk to themselves rather than the risk of money laundering among other strategies. If, however, the pressure is coming from the banks, they negotiate with management to obtain resources to do their work and in some instances threaten other staff in order to make them comply with AML regulations. A framework was also developed that present the regulatory environment that results from MLROs' behaviour. Finally, the *middle course approach* was recommended as an approach that will ensure effective and efficient AML compliance. The approach introduced the concept of *fair pressure* and *independence* in dealing with compliance officers. When compliance officers are given the required level of *independence* and are treated *fairly*, they work to ensure that both banks and regulators benefit in the fight against money laundering.

The self-protecting theory, therefore, expands the agency theory by suggesting that a third party is needed to help resolve the difference between parties with conflicting and difficult to resolve interests. A third party may not necessarily be an external party. In AML for example, there is the MLRO. Doctors are the third parties in the healthcare industry while internal auditors are the third parties in organisations because they sit between management on the one hand and the board on the other. Furthermore, the presence of a third party may not necessarily result in an increased cost since they already exist in the system. What is required is to identify them and treat them according to the recommendation of the approach.

Finally, the paper also provided an example of how the self-protecting theory could apply in hospitals, which demonstrates the value of the theory in organisational studies.

Reference

Aristotle, Nicomachean Ethics. *The Library of Liberal Arts,* 1962*, no.75*, 316.

Ayres, I. and J. Braithwaite, Tripartism: Regulatory capture and empowerment. *Law and Social Inquiry*, 1991, *16*(3), 435–496.

Ayres, I. and J. Braithwaite, Responsive regulation: transcending the deregulation debate. *Oxford University Press,* 1992, (Vol. 87).
http://doi.org/10.2307/2074486

Barone, R. and D. Masciandaro, Organized crime, money laundering and legal economy: Theory and simulations. *European Journal of Law and Economics*, 2011, *32*(1), 115–142
http://doi.org/10.1007/s10657-010-9203-x

Basel Committee on Banking Supervision, The internal audit function in banks. *Bank for International Settlements*, 2012.

Beaver, W., Is the stakeholder model dead? *Business Horizons*, 1999, *42*(2), 8–12.
http://doi.org/http://dx.doi.org/10.1016/S0007-6813(99)80003-2

Becker, G. S., Crime and punishment: an economic approach. *The Journal of*

Political Economy,1968, *76*(2), 169–217.

http://doi.org/jstor.org/stable/1830482

Bello, A.U. , Self-protecting theory: a classical grounded theory study of Money Laundering Reporting Officers (Unpublished doctoral thesis). *Faculty of Business and Law. Northumbria University*, 2014

Bello, A.U., Improving anti-money laundering compliance: self protec-ting theory and Money Laundering Reporting Officers. *Springer, 2017*

Boer, H. and E.R. Seydel, Protection motivation theory, 1996, 95–120. Retrieved from http://doc.utwente.nl/34896/

Bosse, D. A. and R. A. Phillips, Agency theory and bounded self-interest. *Academy of Management Review*, 2016, *41*(2), 276–297

http://doi.org/10.5465/amr.2013.0420

Broek, M. van den, The EU's preventive AML/CFT policy: asymmetrical harmonisation. *Journal of Money Laundering Control*, 2011, *14*(2), 170–182. http://doi.org/10.1108/13685201111127812

Bryant, A., Grounded theory and pragmatism: The curious case of anselm strauss. *Forum Qualitative Sozialforschung*, 2009, *10*(3)

http://doi.org/http://nbn-resolving.de/urn:nbn:de:0114-fqs090325

Collier, A., Critical realism: an introduction to Roy Bhaskar's philosophy, 1994

Collins, J. and R. Hussay, Business research. A practical guide for undergraduate and postgraduate students (2nd ed). Basingstoke: Palgrave Macmillan, 2013. Retrieved from

http://www.palgrave.com/page/detail/business-research-jill-collis/?K=9781137037480

Cooke, R.A. and D.M. Rousseau, Behavioral norms and expectations: a quantitative approach to the assessment of organizational culture. *Group and Organization Management*, 1988 *13*(3), 245–273.

http://doi.org/10.1177/105960118801300302

Corbin, J. and A. Strauss, *Basics of Qualitative Research. Techniques and Procedures for Developing Grounded Theory* (3rd ed.). Los Angeles, Calif: Sage, 1990. Retrieved from

http://prism.talis.com/northumbria-ac/items/1351468

de Catanzaro, D., Evolutionary limits to self-preservation. *Ethology and Sociobiology*, 1991, *12*(1), 13–28.

http://doi.org/http://dx.doi.org/10.1016/0162-3095(91)90010-N

Demesis, D.S., *Technology and Anti-Money Laundering: A Systems Theory and Risk-Based Approach*. Northampton, USA: Edward Elgar Publishing, 2010.

Donaldson, T. and L.E. Preston, The stakeholder theory of the corporation: concepts, evidenece, and implications. *Academy of Management Review*, 1995,

20(1), 65–91

http://doi.org/http://dx.doi.org/10.2307/258887

Doran, N., F. Fox, K. Rodham, G. Taylor and M. Harris, Lost to the NHS : a mixed methods study of why GPs leave practice early in England. *British Journal of General Practice*, 2016

http://doi.org/10.3399/bjgp16X683425

Edwards, N., Doctors and managers: poor relationships may be dama-ging patients -- what can be done ? *Quality and Safety in Health Care*, 2003, 21–25

Eisenhardt, K.M., Agency theory: an assessment and review. *The Academy of Management Review*, 1989, *14*(1), 57–74 http://doi.org/10.2307/258191

FATF., *FATF Recommendations*. Paris: Financial Action Task Force, 2012. Retrieved from http://local.crmm.ru/rosfinfatf/eng/contents/

Financial Services Authority. , Financial crime: a guide for firms. Financial Service Authority, 2011. Retrieved from

http://www.fsa.gov.uk/library/policy/policy/2011/11_15.shtml

Freeman, R.E., *Strategic management: a stakeholder approach*. Cambridge: Cambridge University Press, 2010. Retrieved from

http://books.google.com.mx/books?id=NpmA_qEiOpkC

Glaser, B.G., *Theoretical sensivity: advances in the methodology of grounded theory*. Mill Valley, Calif: Sociology Press, 1978, Retrieved from

http://prism.talis.com/northumbria-ac/items/1469902

Glaser, B,G., Conceptualization: On theory and theorizing using grounded theory. *International Journal of Qualitative Methods*, 2008, *1*(2), 23–38.

Glaser, B.G., *Getting Out of the Data: Grounded Theory Conceptualization*. Mill Valley, CA: Sociology Press, 2011. Retrieved from

https://books.google.com/books?id=qCzjZwEACAAJ andpgis=1

Glaser, B.G., *Stop, write: Writing grounded theory (Vol. 11)*. Mill Valley, Calif: Sociology Press, 2012. Retrieved from

http://scholar.google.com/scholar?hl=en   andbtnG=Search andq=intitle:Stop.Write!+Writing+grounded+theory#0

Glaser, B.G. and J. Holton, Staying open: The use of theoretical codes in grounded theory. *The Grounded Theory Review*, 2005, *5*(10), 1–20.

Glaser, B.G. and A. Strauss, *The discovery of grounded theory: strategies for qualitative research*. New York: Aldine de Gruyter, 1967. Retrieved from

http://prism.talis.com/northumbria-ac/items/268487

Glaser, B.G. and A.L. Strauss, Discovery of substantive theory: a basic strategy underlying qualitative research. *American Behavioral Scientist*, 1965, *8*(6), 5–12

http://doi.org/10.1177/000276426500800602

Guba, E.G., The alternative paradigm *dialog*. *The Paradigm Dialog, 1990* http://doi.org/10.1080/1357527032000140352

Ham, C., Reforming the NHS from within: beyond hierarchy, inspection and markets. *The King's Fund*, (June), 2014, 1–70. Retrieved from http://www.kingsfund.org.uk/

Ham, C. and G. Alberti, The medical profession, the public, and the government, *British Medical Journal*, 2002, *32*

Hyde, A. , The concept of legitimation in the sociology of law. *Wisconsin Law Review*, 1983, 4–26

Jensen, M.C. and W.H. Meckling, Theory of the firm: managerial behavior, agency costs and ownership structure, *Journal of Financial Economics*, 2008, 3(4), October, 305-60. . Retrieved from http://search.ebscohost.com/login.aspx?direct=trueanddb=edsbl andAN=RN223371217 andlang=de andsite=eds-live andauthtype=ip,uid

Jones, R. and G. Noble, Grounded theory and management research: a lack of integrity? *Qualitative Research in Organizations and Management: An International Journal*, 2(2), 2007, 84–103.

Karni, E. and D. Schmeidler, Self-preservation as a foundation of rational behavior under risk. *Journal of Economic Behavior and Organization*, 1986, 7(1), 71–81. http://doi.org/http://dx.doi.org/10.1016/0167-2681(86)90022-3

Kelle, U., Qualitative social " emergence " vs . " forcing " of empirical data ? A crucial problem of "Grounded Theory" reconsidered. *Forum: Qualitative Social Research*, 2005, *6*(2), 1–15.

Killick, M. and D. Parody, Implementing AML/CFT measures that address the risks and not tick boxes. *Journal of Financial Regulation and Compliance*, 2007, *15*(2), 210–216. http://doi.org/10.1108/13581980710744093

Mendelow, A., "Stakeholder Mapping." In *Proceedings of the 2nd Inter-national Conference on Information Systems*. Cambridge, MA, 1991.

New York District Attorney, Standard chartered bank reaches $327 million settlement for illegal transactions. (T. N. Y. C. D. A. Office, Ed.). New York, 2012. Retrieved from http://manhattanda.org/press-release/standard-chartered-bank-reaches-327-million-settlement-illegal-transactions

Nwanji, I.T. and K.E. Howell, A review of the two main competing models of corporate governance: the shareholdership model versus the stakehol-dership model. *Corporate Ownership and Control*, 2007, *5*(1), 3–158.

Oberg, H. and A. Bell, Exploring phenomenology for researching lived experience in Technology Enhanced Learning Philosophical roots of phenomenology. In *Proceedings of the 8th International Conference on Networked Learning* (pp. 1–8). Maastricht School of Management, 2012.

Peirce, C.S. , What pragmatism is, 1905.
http://doi.org/10.2307/27899577

Peirce, C.S., *A neglected argument for the reality of God, 1908*. Retrieved from
http://books.google.co.uk/books?id=13gRtwAACAAJ

POCA. , Proceeds of Crime Act, 2002.

Reasbeck, P.G., Relationships between doctors and managers in an acute NHS trust. *International Journal of Clinical Leadership*, 2008, *16*(2), 79–88.

Reuter, P. and E.M. Truman, *Chasing dirty money: the fight against money laundering, 2004*. Retrieved from
http://books.google.com/books?id=0AVwjC9TDSMC andpgis=1

Rimmer, A., Doctors' relationships with managers are being eroded by pressure on the NHS, 2016, *6502*. http://doi.org/10.1136/bmj.i6502

Rogers, R.W., A protection motivation theory of fear appeals and attitude change. *The Journal of Psychology*, 1975, *91*(1), 93–114
http://doi.org/10.1080/00223980.1975.9915803

Ryder, N., the Financial Services Authority and Money Laundering. *The Cambridge Law Journal*, 2008, *67*(3), 635–653
http://doi.org/doi:10.1017/S0008197308000706

Sadala, M.L.A. and R. de C.F. Adorno, Phenomenology as a method to investigate the experience lived: a perspective from Husserl and Merleau Ponty's thought. *Journal of Advanced Nursing*, 2002, *37*(3), 282–293
http://doi.org/10.1046/j.1365-2648.2002.02071.x

Scholz, J.T., Voluntary compliance and regulatory enforcement. *Law and Policy*, 1984, *6*(4), 385–404.
http://doi.org/10.1111/j.1467-9930.1984.tb00334.x

Shah V., HSBC Private Bank Limited, and Division, H. C. of J. Q. B. Shah V HSBC Private Bank Limited (2012). EWHC 1283 (QB).

Shehu, A. Y. , International initiatives against corruption and money laundering: an overview. *Journal of Financial Crime*, 2005, *12*(3), 221–245.
http://doi.org/10.1108/13590790510624828

Suddaby, R., From the editors: What grounded theory is not. *Academy of Management Journal*, 2006, *49*(4), 633–642

Smith, R.,Why are doctors so unhappy?, *322*(MAY), 2001, 1073–1074

Sutinen, J. G. and K. Kuperan, A socio-economic theory of regulatory compliance. *International Journal of Social Economics*, 1999, *26*(1/2/3), 174–193

Turner, J.L., T.J. Mock and R.P. Srivasta, *An analysis of the fraud triangle.*

Research Roundtable 3. Working paper, University of Memphis, University of Southern California, and University of Kansas, 2003

Tyler, T.R., *Why people obey the law.* Princeton University Press, 2006

Unger, B., Money Laundering Regulation: From Al Capone to Al Qaeda. *B. Unger and D. van Der Linde (Red.), Research Handbook on Money Laundering*, 2013, 19–32

Wright, P. and A. Mukherji, Inside the firm: Socioeconomic versus agency perspectives on firm competitiveness. *The Journal of Socio-Economics*, 1999, *28*(3), 295–307

http://doi.org/http://dx.doi.org/10.1016/S1053-5357(99)00019-0

International legal and quasi-legal approaches to combatting money laundering: an Australian perspective on norm-development

Doron Goldbarsht and *Christopher Michaelsen*[1]

Introduction

International efforts to curb money laundering have been the subject of various international treaties for almost three decades. Certain aspects of these treaties have also been taken up by the Security Council of the United Nations (UN) which has adopted several binding resolutions under Chapter VII of the UN Charter dealing with the matter. These traditional multilateral approaches have been complemented by non-conventional mechanisms, in particular the Financial Action Task Force (FATF) and its Recommendations. The FATF Recommendations do not constitute traditional formal sources of law as recognised, *inter alia*, by Article 38 of the Statute of the International Court of Justice (ICJ). In spite of this lack of normative character in the traditional (international) legal sense, the FATF Recommendations have achieved remarkable levels of implementation by states. In many cases, they have resulted in states introducing significant legislative reform at the domestic level. Yet, the arguably innovative form of international standard-setting and enforcement employed by the FATF has not been without controversy. Concerns have been raised in particular regarding the legitimacy of FATF standards and in relation to the accountability of the organisation itself (Hayes, 2013: 1).[2]

---

[1] Doron Glodbarsht is a PhD Candidate in the Faculty of Law at the University of New South Wales in Sydney. Christopher Michaelsen is an Associate Professor of Law at the same institution.

[2] Ben Hayes, for example, has called the FATF a "powerful yet unaccountable global standard–setting body (which) is helping repressive civil society regulations to spread and flourish across the globe".

The purpose of this chapter is to provide an Australian perspective on norm development in the area of anti-money laundering (AML). It examines the extent to which the development of domestic legislation to curb money laundering was influenced by international obligations and standards. The chapter will first provide a brief overview of international regulatory efforts to combat money laundering. To this end, it will distinguish between traditional legal approaches and unconventional, quasi-legal methods of norm development. It argues that the FATF standards fall into the latter category and classify as an example of informal international law-making. The analysis will then turn to an examination of the FATF's approach to standard-setting and -enforcement. In a subsequent section, the chapter will focus on the Australian experience and assess how the FATF standards on combating money laundering have affected the development of domestic AML legislation. It is argued that in spite of the fact that Australia had ratified several key international treaties prior to the FATF's Mutual Evaluation Report of 2005, the bulk of legislative reform only occurred after the FATF review. The chapter will conclude with some observations on the implications of this process of norm development and aspects of democratic legitimacy of Australia's AML legislation.

Legal and quasi-legal approaches to curbing money laundering

Legal and quasi legal approaches to international governance

The traditional approach to analysis of international governance in the realm of international law commonly takes Article 38 (I) of the ICJ Statute as a starting point (Dixon, 2013: 24-27). This article identifies three main sources of international law: (a) treaties between states; (b) customary international law derived from the practice of states; and (c) general principles of law recognised by civilised nation. In addition, Article 38 (I) refers to judicial decisions and the "*writings of the most highly qualified publicists*" as subsidiary means for the determination of rules of international law (United Nations, 1946). Strictly speaking, the ICJ Statute, as an international treaty, is only binding for those states that have ratified it. However, in light of the fact that 193 states have ratified the ICJ Statute as an annex of the UN Charter, Article 38 is generally considered to provide an authoritative list of sources of international law.

At the same time, it has been questioned whether this list continues to provide an adequate reflection of applicable norms and standards in contemporary international governance (Abass, 2013: 62-63; Boyle and Chinkin, 2007). For example, this traditional framework does not account for resolutions of the UN Security Council which, although related to an international treaty (the UN Charter), constitute administrative acts by an organ of an international organisation. As such, these resolutions do not readily fall within the ambit of Article 38 ICJ Statute. Yet, Article 25 of the UN Charter stipulates that Security Council resolutions are binding by requiring the members of the United Nations "to accept and carry out the decisions of the Security Council in accordance with the present Charter". Indeed, resolutions of the Security Council, particularly those adopted under Chapter VII of the UN Charter, play a significant role in contemporary international governance.

The traditional framework of international law-making also does not account for other recently adopted approaches to international governance. In the last two decades, states have increasingly adopted informal approaches to international cooperation addressing a variety of global issues and challenges. Indeed, there are numerous examples of states cooperating informally on a given issue in a manner which did not lead to a formal treaty or any other traditional source of international law. In some cases, trans-governmental networks serve merely as a forum for dialogue or to facilitate the exchange of information and experience. However, in other cases trans-governmental networks actually assume a regulatory role and engage in standard-setting, harmonisation, or setting of norms (Slaughter, 2004; Dilling, Herberg and Winter, 2011). Examples in the financial sector include the Basel Committee on Banking Supervision, the International Organization of Securities Commissions or the Financial Stability Board.

Joost Pauwelyn, Ramses Wessel, and Jan Wouters have described these unconventional forms of international cooperation on standard-setting as "*informal international law-making*" (Pauwelyn, Wessel and Wouters, 2012,: 34). They consider a process of norm-development "*informal*" if it "*dispenses with certain formalities traditionally linked to international law*". These formalities relate to output, process, and the actors involved. Pauwelyn, Wessel, and Wouters point out that escaping the formalities of traditional international law-making has led to claims that informal international law-making is more flexible and effective, and hence more desirable. Indeed, there is now evidence to suggest that some governments have started prioritising informal international law-making over more conventional approaches. Pauwelyn refers to the example of Germany where an internal instruction directed at all federal ministries required ministries to inquire whether an international agreement was really needed or whether the same goal could also be "*attained through other means, especially through understandings which are below the threshold of an international agreement*". At the same time, it has been acknowledged that circumventing the formalities of traditional international approaches (and related domestic procedures) may lead to an accountability gap (Kingsbury and Stewart, 2008). Deficiencies in accountability may stem from the lack of involving domestic institutions and stakeholders in the process of informal international law-making, actors which would otherwise be (constitutionally) required to participate in the process of developing binding norms and hence provide checks and balances. Further concerns relate to the fact that informal international law-making is not necessarily bound by the rules and principles that commonly apply to the traditional sources of law. For example, traditional international agreements are subject to the rules of the law on treaties as codified by the *Vienna Convention on the Law of Treaties ('VCLT')*. This convention serves as an authoritative guide regarding the formation and effects of treaties. It provides both procedural and substantive guidance on how international norms are to be applied. Moreover, it emphasises that treaty norms only apply to those states who have consented to them (*VCLT*, article 11-16, 26).

The international regulatory framework on combating money laundering

Applying the concept of traditional and informal international law making to the regulatory framework on combating money laundering, one can observe that key instruments can be found in both categories. International efforts to curb money laundering have been the subject of several international treaties dating back to the late 1980s. The first of these treaties was the *United Nations Convention against the Illicit Traffic in Narcotic Drugs and Psychotropic Substances*. Adopted in 1988 this convention was the first international legal instrument to require the criminalisation of money-laundering. About a decade later, in 1999, the UN General Assembly adopted the *International Convention for the Suppression of the Financing of Terrorism*. This instrument came into force in April 2002 and requires states parties to take measures to protect their financial systems from being misused by persons planning or engaged in terrorist activities. This Convention does not specifically mention money laundering. However, its Article 2 (1) is formulated sufficiently broad to apply to money laundering activities that are connected to a terrorism act as defined by the Convention.

In 2000, the General Assembly adopted the *United Nations Convention against Transnational Organized Crime* (also called the Palermo Convention) which entered into force in September 2003. The scope of money laundering under the terms of the Convention includes proceeds deriving from all serious crimes. The Palermo Convention was complemented by the *United Nations Convention against Corruption* which came into force in 2005. It requires states parties to take a range of measures to prevent money-laundering (article 14). What both conventions have in common is that they widen the scope of the money laundering offence beyond the application to the proceeds of illicit drug trafficking to include the proceeds of all serious crimes. Both instruments call on states to create a comprehensive domestic supervisory and regulatory regime for banks and non-bank financial institutions as well as any entities particularly susceptible to being involved in a money laundering scheme. The Conventions also call for the establishment of Financial Intelligence Units.

In addition to these conventional international efforts to curb money laundering, the UN Security Council has recognised the importance of addressing money laundering and the financing of terrorism. In the aftermath of the 9/11 attacks the Council pointed to the links between terrorism, transnational organised crime, the international drug trade and money-laundering, and called on states to become parties to the relevant international conventions. In Resolution 1373 (2001) the Council imposed certain obligations on UN Member States, such as: the prevention and the suppression of the financing of terrorist acts; the criminalisation of terrorism-related activities and of the provision of assistance to carry out those acts; the denial of funding and safe haven to terrorists and the exchange of information to prevent the commission of terrorist acts.

Aside from these traditional regulatory approaches, international efforts to combat money laundering extend into the sphere of trans-governmental networks and informal international law-making. A key mechanism in this regard is provided by the Financial Action Task Force (FATF). The FATF was established at the G-7 Summit in Paris in 1989 when the G-7 Heads of State or Government and the President of the European Commission convened the Task Force from the G-7 member states, the European Commission and eight other countries (G7 Summit, 1989: 52-53). A year later, in 1990, the FATF issued a report containing a series of "Recommendations" all of which were targeted towards providing a comprehensive action plan for combating money laundering. As the techniques, trends and methods utilised in money laundering evolved over time, these Recommendations were repeatedly revised in 1996, 2001, 2003 and 2012, to ensure that they remained up to date, relevant and capable of universal application.

The FATF has described money laundering as a three-stage process: the *placement* of funds into the financial system; the *layering* of funds to disguise their origin, perhaps by passing through several offshore or onshore jurisdictions; and the *integration* of the funds into the legitimate economy (Financial Action Task Force, What is money laundering?).Interrupting this process has been considered of critical importance as it allows individuals and entities to enjoy the profits of their illegal activities without jeopardising their source. In response, the FATF developed forty Recommendations on money laundering and an additional nine Special Recommendations on terrorism financing. Both the Security Council, in Resolution 1617 (2005) and the General Assembly, in the Annexed Plan of Action of Resolution 60/288 (2006), have stressed the importance of implementing the FATF Recommendations and Special Recommendations (in 2012 the 9 Special Recommendations were integrated into the Recommendations as part of FATF revised Recommendations). Indeed, they are now commonly recognised as the international standard for combating of money laundering and the financing of terrorism. The following section will now turn to issue of norm development by the FATF in more detail.

Norm development and enforcement by the FATF

The FATF setting the standard

As of 2017, the FATF consists of thirty-five member jurisdictions and two regional organisations, the European Union and the Gulf Co-operation Council. Its Recommendations call on states to implement the relevant international conventions on money laundering and the financing of terrorism. In particular, they call on states to criminalise money laundering and enable authorities to confiscate the proceeds of money laundering. Furthermore, states are encouraged to implement customer due diligence (*e.g.*, identity verification), record keeping and suspicious transaction reporting requirements for financial institutions and designated non-financial businesses and professions. States are also requested to establish a financial intelligence unit to receive and disseminate suspicious transaction reports, and to cooperate internationally in investigating money laundering.

In many respects, the FATF Recommendations mirror the obligations under the various international conventions discussed above. However, from the perspective of international law, there exists no binding obligation to abide by the standards established by the FATF.[3] The FATF is not an international organisation in the technical legal sense. Rather it is an informal policy-making body which works to generate the necessary political will to bring about national legislative and regulatory reforms in the areas of anti-money laundering and counter-terrorist financing. As such, the FATF approach is a prime example of informal international law-making. Nevertheless, in spite of their non-binding character, the FATF standards have attained a strong normative character. Today, FATF Recommendations, through the FSRBs, are implemented by over 180 countries well exceeding the membership of the FATF itself.

The FATF assesses compliance

In order to achieve global implementation of its Recommendations, the FATF relies on a global network of nine FATF-Style Regional Bodies FSRBs, in addition to its own thirty-seven members. These FSRBs play an essential role in promoting the effective implementation of the FATF Recommendations by their membership. Together with the FSRBs, the FATF compiles Mutual Evaluation Reports (MER) for almost every State in the world and, on an on-going basis, assesses whether a country is sufficiently compliant with the FATF Recommendations. To this end, it provides an in-depth description and analysis of each country's approach to preventing abuse of the financial system.

Over the past twenty years, the FATF has developed, used and refined rigorous compliance mechanisms to help ensure global compliance with its standards. The MER set out the specific requirements of each Recommendation as a list of criteria, which represent those elements that should be present in order to demonstrate full compliance with the substantive elements of the Recommendations. For each Recommendation, the FATF's assessors reach a conclusion about the extent to which a country complies or does not comply with the applicable standards (FATF, 2016: 5). The MER summarise the AML/CTF measures in place at the date of the FATF assessors' country visit and make recommendations on how they could be strengthened. Based on the results of the MER, and where a MER reveals a significant number of deficiencies in a country under evaluation, the case is referred to a review and, in certain circumstances, subject to enforcement measures and sanctions.

---

[3]   The UNSC has stopped short of adopting a Chapter VII resolution ordering states to enforce the FATF's recommendations, but it has "strongly urged" them to do so in resolution 1617 (SC Res 1617, UN SCOR, 60th sess, 5244th mtg, UN Doc S/RES/1617 (29 July 2005)).

There are significant differences in compliance levels in the pre- and post-2003 periods. Jackie Johnson has observed that compliance temporarily declined after the FATF updated their Recommendations in 2003 (Johnson, 2008: 47-66). She further found that there existed a significant difference between self-assessment compliance levels and compliance determined by MERs. As of 2017, however, available evidence is suggestive of impressive compliance with FATF Recommendations. Not all states have implemented the FATF Recommendations at the same time, or to the same degree, but the FATF enforcement procedures, especially the MER and FATF follow-ups, have brought reluctant states to comply. For example, by February 2016, the FATF had reviewed over 80 countries and publicly identified 59 of them as not sufficient compliant. Of these 59, 49 have since introduced the necessary reforms to address their AML/CFT shortcomings and have been removed from the review process (FATF, High-risk and non-cooperative jurisdictions).

Enforcement and sanctions by the FATF

In spite of the legally non-binding nature of FATF Recommendations, the FATF has established strict enforcement mechanisms which practically apply to members and non-members alike and has a distinctively coercive character: public warnings which are quite a sanction system. It regularly urges countries deemed to be non-cooperative to adopt measures to remove rules and practices considered to be incompatible with FATF standards (FATF, 2/2000). It also maintains a so-called "*black list*" of jurisdictions designated as non-compliant. Including a country in the 'black list' is the most drastic measure the FATF can take as part of its strategy to maximise compliance with its standards. A listed country then faces the risk that foreign investment and trade is discouraged or delayed because of enhanced due diligence, which, in turn, can damage its reputation with international organisations such as the World Bank and the International Monetary Fund (IMF, 2016; Harvey, 2004).

Specific enforcement measures in respect to countries which fail to abolish detrimental rules and practices include refusing the establishment of subsidiaries, branches or representative offices of financial institutions in the country concerned, or otherwise taking into account the fact that the relevant financial institution is from a country that does not have adequate anti-money laundering systems (Levi, 2002: 186-187). They may also include limiting business relationships or financial transactions with the identified country or persons in that country; prohibiting financial institutions from relying on third parties located in the country concerned to conduct elements of the customer due diligence process; or examination and external audit requirements for branches and subsidiaries of financial institutions based in the country concerned (FATF Recommendation 19).

The initiative to identify non-cooperative countries – the so-called Non-Cooperative Countries and Territories Initiative (NCCTs) - began in 1998, at a time when many countries around the world did not have adequate AML measures in place (FATF, 6/2001:5). The objective of this initiative was to secure the adoption by all financial centres, in jurisdictions both inside and outside of FATF membership, of international standards to prevent, detect and combat money laundering, and thereby effectively co-operate internationally in the global fight against money-laundering. The February 2000 NCCTs report laid out the basic procedure for reviewing countries and territories as part of this initiative. The FATF started by reviewing different countries and territories (selected for review based on FATF members' experience). Forty-seven jurisdictions were referred to the NCCTs process and were reviewed in two rounds (31 in 2000 and 16 in 2001). A total of 23 jurisdictions were identified as NCCTs (15 in 2000 and 8 in 2001) and added to the 'black list' (FATF, 10/2007).[4]

The FATF has not reviewed any new jurisdictions since 2001 in the framework of the NCCT initiative and as of October 2006, there were no NCCTs in the context of the NCCT initiative following the de-listing of Nigeria and Myanmar in June and October 2006 respectively. Since 2007, the FATF's International Co-operation Review Group (ICRG), which replaced the NCCTs initiative, has analysed high-risk jurisdictions and recommended specific action to address the money laundering risks emanating from them. Today, initial referral to the ICRG is based primarily on the results of the jurisdiction's MER (rather than the FATF members in the NCCTs initiative as described above) (FATF, 2009). Jurisdictions whose MER reveals a significant number of key deficiencies are referred to the ICRG for a preliminary review conducted by one of four ICRG regional review groups appointed by the FATF, covering Africa/Middle East, the Americas, Asia/Pacific, and Europe/Eurasia. Based upon the results of this review and in-depth review of the jurisdiction's key strategic anti-money laundering deficiencies, the ICRG drawn up various lists which approved by the FATF plenary meeting: the 'black list' (jurisdictions

---

[4] Jurisdictions identified as NCCTs in the year 2000 were: Bahamas, Cayman Islands, Cook Islands, Dominica, Israel, Lebanon, Liechtenstein, Marshall Islands, Nauru, Niue, Panama, Philippines, Russia, St. Kitts & Nevis, St. Vincent & the Grenadines; and in the year 2001 were: Egypt, Grenada, Guatemala, Hungary, Indonesia, Myanmar, Nigeria and Ukraine.

subject to a call for counter-measures), the 'dark grey' list (jurisdictions that have not made sufficient progress or not committed to an action plan) and the 'light grey' list (jurisdictions who have developed an action plan) (House of Lords, 2009: 246).

The significance of the regulatory approach by the FATF

The FATF's regulatory approach to curbing money laundering is significant for several reasons. First, rather than simply developing international standards to guide national legislative and regulatory reform, the FATF set up a detailed verification and compliance regime. It also employs enforcement mechanisms which exceed those available in traditional legal approaches to international governance. Taken together, the FATF's standard-setting process and its enforcement mechanisms possess a quasi-legal character in spite of the fact that pursuant to conventional international law doctrine they are without normative effect. Second, in contrast to fundamental principles of international treaty law, FATF standards practically apply to both members and non-members. The FATF essentially creates obligations for states regardless of whether states have consented to implementing them. This approach is fundamentally different from traditional approaches to international law and governance in which state consent and sovereignty constitute key defining principles. Finally, the FATF approach is significant in that the role of norm-setter, enforcer and adjudicator is largely played by the same actor. This raises concerns about transparency and accountability of the FATF itself.

Australia's implementation of international obligations and AML standards

Australia's approach to anti-money laundering

Australia has a sophisticated financial system which is generally well regulated and which exhibits a strong risk management culture (Reserve Bank of Australia, 2016). In 1998, the regulatory framework for the Australian financial system was substantially reformed in response to recommendations made as part of the Financial System Inquiry (FSI) which had been established in 1997. This FSI had been set up to evaluate the deregulation of the Australian financial system and to recommend changes to ensure an "efficient, responsive, competitive and flexible financial system to underpin stronger economic performance, consistent with financial stability, prudence, integrity and fairness" (Financial System Inquiry, 2014: 5; Hanratty, 1997: 2). The FSI Report – also known as the Wallis Report, after the Inquiry's Chairman – contained more than 100 recommendations to increase the efficiency and effectiveness of the Australian financial system and build upon the existing achievements of financial deregulation. These included recommendations that oversight of the operation of corporate law, market integrity and consumer protection be combined in a single agency (Recommendation 1); that due diligence defences apply to positive disclosure requirements (Recommendation 4); that accounting standards be harmonised with international standards (Recommendation 12), and that international standards be implemented for electronic commerce (Recommendation 92).

In addition, following the collapse of the HIH group, Australia's second largest insurance company, the Australian government established a Royal Commission to inquire into the causes of the failure (HIH Royal Commission, 2003).[5] The report of the Royal Commission was published in April 2003, and additional, measures were to strengthen financial supervision. The report also contained key recommendations in relation to greater disclosure of the scope of audit services and executive changes to the Australian Prudential Regulatory Authority; amendments to the listing rules of the Australian Stock Exchange; recommendations concerning consequential amendments and the removal of inconsistencies in a range of different Commonwealth enactments (Bailey, 2003).

In spite of these measures, money laundering is considered to present a serious risk to Australia as it undermines the integrity of its financial systems and industry sectors (AUSTRAC, 8/2011). As in other developed economies, money-laundering in Australia ranges from small scale laundering of stolen goods and funds through to highly sophisticated schemes for concealing and exploiting the proceeds of drug trafficking, people smuggling, and other organised transnational criminal activity (FATF, 2005: 15). It has been estimated that serious and organised crime costs Australia about 21 billion Australian dollars annually (Australian Crime Commission, 2015). It has also been estimated that the quantity of money laundered in Australia amounts to several billion Australian dollars each year (Schmidt, 2011). The full extent of money laundering is, of course, difficult to quantify as the authorities can only guess the amount of

---

[5] In 2001, HIH Insurance collapsed with debts of $5.3billion becoming the largest corporate collapse in Australia's history. The then Prime Minister John Howard announced that a Royal Commission would be established, under the Royal Commissions Act 1902 to inquire into the company's collapse.

laundering actually taking place (UNODC, 2011; Harvey, 2005; Van Duyne, 2003).

In response, Australia has taken a range of structural and legislative measures. In 1989, it established the Australian Transaction Reports and Analysis Centre (AUSTRAC) which is now overseeing the compliance of more than 14.000 Australian businesses ranging from major banks and casinos to single-operator businesses. The Australian government has also adopted a range of substantive laws to curb money laundering. Australian legislation in the area of anti-money-laundering can be generally divided into three separate categories (Deitz and Buttle, 2008; Walters, 2012):

- criminal offences relating to money laundering, which at the federal (Com-mon-wealth) level are contained in the *Criminal Code Act 1995* (Cth) ('*Criminal Code*')[6] and also in various state and territory Acts (e.g., *Crimes (Money Laundering) Act 2003* (VIC) and the *Crimes Act 1900* (NSW));
- proceeds of crime legislation, which is in place at the federal as well as the state and territory level;[7]
- prevention and detection measures for money laundering, which were largely established by the *Financial Transactions Reporting Act 1988* (Cth) ('*FTR Act*'), and which are now provided by the *Anti-Money Laundering and Counter-Terrorism Financing Act 2006* ('*AML/CTF Act*'),[8] and the *Anti-Money Laundering and Counter-Terrorism Financing Rules* ('*AML/CTF Rules*'), which

---

[6] Sections 400.3 to 400.8 of the *Criminal Code Act* are all similarly drafted. Each section relates to dealing with money or property which classifies as proceeds of crime or could become an instrument of crime. However, each section relates to money or property of a different amount. Sections 400.3 to 400.8 contain three different offences, each with a different maximum penalty, classified according to the state of mind (fault element) of the defendant. Whether the offence is classi-fied as being contrary to subsection (1), (2) or (3) will depend upon the classifica-tion of the fault element (intention, recklessness or negligence) associated with the circumstances that the money or other property was proceeds of crime or was a potential instrument of crime.

[7] See Commonwealth – *Proceeds of Crime Act* 2002 (Cth); Victoria – *Confiscation Act* 1997 (VIC); New South Wales - *Criminal Assets Recovery Act* 1990 (NSW); *Confiscation of Proceeds of Crime Act 1989;* Western Australia - *Criminal Property Confiscation Act* 2000 (WA); Northern Territory - *Criminal Property Forfeiture Act* 2002 (NT); South Australia - *Criminal Assets Confiscation Act* 2005 and *Serious and Organised Crime (Unexplained Wealth) Act* 2009 (SA); and Queensland - *Criminal Proceeds Confiscation Act* 2002 (QLD).

[8] Offences contained in the *AML/CTF Act* are often used in prosecuting money laundering – in particular the following sections: ss.142-143 – structuring offences; ss.53, 55 –the movement of physical currency both in and out of Australia; ss.136-138 – opening of bank accounts using false customer identification documents; ss.139-141 – use of bank accounts in false names or failing to disclose the use of 2 or more names.

are part of measures taken to ensure that Australia complies with the FATF Recommendations regarding money laundering.

Internationally, Australia has been engaged in efforts to develop and promote a regulatory framework from an early stage onward. It signed the *UN Convention against the Illicit Traffic in Narcotic Drugs and Psychotropic Substances* in February 1989 ratified the treaty in November 1992. It has been party to the *International Convention for the Suppression of the Financing of Terrorism* since September 2002, the *UN Convention against Transnational Organized Crime* since May 2004 and the *UN Nations Convention against Corruption* since December 2005. Australia is a founding member of the FATF and a member and permanent co-chair of the Asia/Pacific Group (APG) on Money Laundering. The APG is a FATF-style regional body housed by the Australian Federal Police in Sydney.

Australia's engagement with the FATF and legislative reform

Australia has been a member of the FATF since 1990. After the FATF revised its Recommendations following the 9/11 attacks, the Australian government announced that it would commit to implementing the revised Recommendations in spite of the fact that implementation required significant reform of the domestic AML regime (AUSTRAC, 2003; Jensen, 2008: 94). In October 2005, the FATF conducted a review of Australia's AML policies and found that while Australia had adopted AML legislation, there were a number of deficiencies or failures in Australia's manner of implementation of FATF standards (FATF, 2005; Deitz, 2007; Ross and Hannan, 2007: 140). The MER-2005 found that Australia was non-compliant with twenty-five percent of international AML standards, including customer due diligence, politically exposed persons, response to new technologies, reliance on third parties and others (FATF, 2005: 75). The FATF found that the number of money laundering prosecutions was too low, that the records of prosecutions indicated that money laundering was not dealt with as a separate offence, that the police did not investigate or refer money laundering as a separate charge and, in practice, cases were generally brought under the predicate offences only (FATF, 2005: 31). Consequently, only a small handful of individuals engaged in money laundering were ever prosecuted and convicted Ross and Hannan, 2007: 136; AUSTRAC, 2009: 26-28).

In 2015, a decade after the first MER, the FATF undertook a second review and published MER-2015. It found that overall, Australian authorities had a good understanding of most of Australia's main money laundering risks, but needed to develop their understanding further in certain areas (FATF, 2015). Operationally, the FATF considered national anti-money laundering coordination comprehensive and commented favourably on Australia's capacity develop and disseminate quality financial intelligence to a range of law enforcement bodies, customs, and tax authorities. Australia's legal framework to implement targeted financial sanctions was regarded as a good example for other countries (FATF, 2015). A comparison of how Australian legislation developed in order to comply with the FATF Recommendations will follow below.

a. Money-Laundering offence

Pursuant to FATF Recommendation 3, states are requested to criminalise money laundering on the basis of the applicable international conventions which require states to apply the offence of money laundering to all serious offences with a view to capturing the widest range of predicate offences (Recommendation 3). In its MER-2005, Australia was rated 'largely compliant' on Recommendation 3 (FATF, 2005: 32), because the FATF found that a lack of AML prosecutions indicated that the regime was not being effectively implemented. While the Australian criminal law appeared to be comprehensive, dissuasive and proportional, sanctions were considered to not being effectively applied.

Division 400 to the *Criminal Code* outlines AML offences and creates a range of penalties depending on the perpetrator's applicable level of knowledge (wilful with intent, recklessness, negligence), and the value of the property involved. This division was introduced into the *Criminal Code* in January 2003 (Australian Law Reform Commission, 1999; Walters, 2012: 4). It prohibits receiving, possessing, concealing or disposing of property, importing or engaging in banking transactions involving the proceeds of federal or foreign offences or property intended to be used as an instrumentality of such an offence. The definitions of "proceeds of crime and property" are broad and extend to money or other property of "every description", whether located in Australia or overseas, that has been realised directly or indirectly from the commission of an indictable offence (*Criminal Code*, 400.1).

The money laundering offences extend to proceeds of any foreign offences that, if they had occurred in Australia, would have been an offence under Commonwealth, State or Territory law. Dealing with assets located outside Australia would thus still constitute an offence under Australian law. AML offences apply to anyone who deals with the proceeds of crime, regardless of whether that person committed the predicate offence (*Criminal Code*, sections 400.1 and 400.2). The *Criminal Code* also makes it clear that the prosecution does not need to establish that an offence has been committed in relation to assets to be considered proceeds of crime (*Criminal Code*, section 400.13).

Between January 2003, when the Criminal Code was amended, and January 2008, the Australian authorities prosecuted 77 cases of money laundering in Australia, a substantial increase in comparison with the period preceding 2003. 70 per cent of these cases were prosecuted within 12 months of the MER 2005 which had rated Australia only as 'largely compliant' on the basis of a lack of prosecutions. The type of charges dealt with has also changed over the five-year period. The initial charges for offences of money laundering under the Criminal Code, dealt with in the 2003-05 period, were for summary offences when almost all of the later charges were for indictable offences (Australian Institute of Criminology, 2008; CDPP, 2003; CDPP, 2004, CDPP, 2005).[9] In contrast to the MER-2005, the MER-2015 found that FATF Recommendation 3 was effectively implemented in Australia, which was subsequently rated as 'compliant' (FATF, 2015: 18).

b. Customer due diligence

According to FATF Recommendation 10, financial institutions should be prohibited from keeping anonymous accounts, or accounts in obviously fictitious names. Financial institutions should be required to undertake so-called "customer due diligence" measures when: establishing business relations; carrying out occasional transactions above the applicable designated threshold ($15.000); there is a suspicion of money laundering or terrorist financing; or the financial institution has doubts about the veracity or adequacy of previously obtained customer identification data. The principle that financial institutions should conduct customer due diligence should be set out in law (Recommendation 10).

In its MER-2005, Australia was rated 'non-compliant' in this respect (FATF, 2005: 76). The evaluators of the MER-2005 found, among other things, that Australian customer due diligence requirements were limited in scope to certain obligations placed on "cash dealers" and did not cover the full range of financial institutions (FATF, 2005: 80). MER-2005 acknowledged that there was a complex and indirect obligation to identify and verify customer identity upon account opening although certain loans were excluded from

---

[9] Summary offences are matters that are tried by a judge alone and can also be heard in the absence of the defendant. Summary offences are usually considered to be less serious offences such as traffic offences and petty crime. Indictable offences are more serious offences that cannot be heard in the absence of the defendant, such as drug trafficking, murder and from 2005, money laundering.

customer identification requirements (FATF, 2005, 75). Furthermore, it found that there were no requirements for the identification and verification of customers making use of domestic wire transfers within Australia (FATF, 2005: 82). There were no requirements that existing clients' information be re-examined on the basis of materiality and risk, or that due diligence be conducted on existing relationships at appropriate times (FATF, 2005: 77). In addition, MER-2005 pointed out that there were no specific obligations requiring customer due diligence when there was a suspicion of Money Laundering. The 100-point check system of verification employed by Australian institutions (identity verification test under which identifying information from various sources is worth a certain number of points), involved a number of documents of questionable reliability, and for customers that were corporate entities, there were no requirements to identify the directors or provisions regulating the power to bind the entity (MER, 2005: 70).

Australian legislation was updated in accordance with the deficiencies found in the MER-2005, and today the *AML/CTF Act* prohibits the provision (*AML/CTF Act*, section 139) and reception (*AML/CTF Act*, section 140) of a "designated service", which includes opening and operating an account (*AML/CTF Act*, section 6), using a false customer name, or anonymity. The *AML/CTF Act* also requires applicable customer identification procedures to be applied prior to the provision of a designated service, including operating an account or carrying out an occasional transaction, such as wire transfers (*AML/CTF Act*, section 32), (AUSTRAC, 2009). In case of suspicion of money laundering, reporting entities are required to apply enhanced due-diligence and financial institutions are required to monitor their customers with a view to identifying, mitigating and managing Money Laundering risks (*AML/CTF Act*, section 36).

c. Politically Exposed Persons

FATF Recommendation 12 requires financial institutions to have appropriate risk management systems to determine whether the customer or the beneficial owner is a "politically exposed person" (including family members or close associates); to obtain senior management approval for establishing such business relationships; to take reasonable measures to establish the source of wealth and source of funds; and to conduct enhanced ongoing monitoring of the business relationship (Recommendation 12).

In its MER-2005, Australia was rated 'non-compliant' on Recommendation 12 as there were no specific legislative or other enforceable obligations regarding the identification and verification of politically exposed persons under the old FTR Act or other regulations (FATF, 2005: 74). The *AML/CTF Rules* provided the definition of 'politically exposed person' which is in line with the definition adopted by FATF (*AML/CTF Rules,* part 1.2). When dealing with 'politically exposed persons', reporting entities are firstly required to determine whether a customer or the beneficial owner falls under this category (*AML/CTF Rules,* part 4.13.1). In cases of foreign 'politically exposed persons' the identification procedures applicable to the customer apply as well (*AML/CTF Rules*, part 4.13.3*).* The reporting entity is also required to obtain senior management approval before establishing or continuing the business relationship and to take reasonable measures to establish the 'politically exposed person's' source of wealth and source of funds (*AML/CTF Rules*, chapter 15). Finally, it is required to comply with the obligations of ongoing customer due diligence. In light of these reforms, the MER-2015 rated Australia as 'largely compliant' with Recommendation 12 (FATF, 2015: 159).

d. New technologies and non-face-to-face business

FATF Recommendation 15 stipulates that countries and financial institutions need to identify and assess the money laundering risks that may arise in relation to the development of new products and new business practices, including new delivery mechanisms, and the use of new or developing technologies for both new and pre-existing products (Recommendation 15). In MER-2005, Australia was rated "non-compliant" in this regard (FATF, 2005: 77). In response, Australia identified and assessed the money laundering risks associated with 'electronic payment systems and new payment methods' in its national threat assessment which covers ATMs, credit and debit cards, stored value cards, online payment systems, online remittance and digital currencies. However, this assessment did not cover new business practices. The AML/CTF Rules specify the types of services provided and the methods by which services are to be delivered (*AML/CTF Rules*, parts 8.2 and 9.1). The same provisions also state that the AML programme must enable reporting entities to assess, prior to adopting them or introducing them to the market, the money laundering risk posed by all new designated services, all new methods of designated service delivery, and all new or developing technologies used for the provision of a designated service. However, other than the general obligation to assess the money laundering risk, there is no specific explicit requirement for reporting entities to take appropriate measures to manage and mitigate the identified risks in the area of new technologies. In spite of these shortcomings, the MER-2015 rated Australia as 'largely compliant' with Recommendation 12 (FATF, 2015: 162).

Concluding observations

International efforts to curb money laundering comprise both traditional legal instruments and standards which classify as informal international law making. The example of Australia's approach to combating money laundering offers interesting insights into how these two separate categories of norms impact the development of domestic legislation. It demonstrates that in the field of anti-money laundering, FATF standards have attained a normative quality which is matching, if not exceeding, the binding character of relevant conventional international law. Many aspects of the FATF Recommendations mirror substantive legal obligations under the applicable international treaties. Yet, while states have often been slow in implementing their conventional obligations – a shortcoming the UN Security Council has identified on several occasions as well – FATF standards have achieved a remarkable degree of compliance. The robust enforcement mechanisms of the FATF and potentially adverse financial and economic consequences of non-compliance provide strong incentives or, perhaps, political necessities for states to comply with FATF standards, even in cases where states are not FATF members.

Australia, however, had been party to all relevant international treaties in the field of anti-money laundering and counter-terrorist financing as well as a member of the FATF itself when its AML/CTF framework was evaluated by the FATF in 2005. At that time, it had already introduced a range to reforms to strengthen the Australian financial system. Yet, several measures it had taken domestically were found to be lacking in compliance with a number of FATF standards. This recorded lack of compliance led to further legislative reform at the domestic level. Indeed, the need to comply with FATF standards was expressly acknowledged in the introductory parts of the newly-introduced legislation itself (*AML/CTF Act*, preamble). When Australia's AML/CTF measures were reviewed again a decade later, their compliance levels had improved significantly.

While harmonising standards against money laundering is undoubtedly a worthwhile objective, concerns remain in relation to the process of norm-development at the domestic level. These concerns stem mainly from the fact that substantive legislative reform is being prescribed by an institution with little democratic legitimacy and accountability. Consequently, and as the Australian experience demonstrates, this means that domestic legislative initiatives are shaped by the executive with the legislature playing a subsidiary role at best. Indeed, one may observe that this process of norm-development reduces domestic parliaments to rubber stamping institutions with little de facto power in relation to norm-development. Ultimately this may corrupt the domestic legislative process and risk erosion of the legitimacy of the domestically adopted norms themselves. A question that remains is whether this is a worthwhile price to pay for harmonising anti-money laundering efforts.

References

Abass, A., *International Law.* Oxford University Press, 2013

AUSTRAC, 2003 'Australia endorses global anti-money laundering standards' viewed 20 April 2017,
http://www.austrac.gov.au/media/media-releases/australia-endorses-global-anti-money-laundering-standards

AUSTRAC, Customer identification requirements under the AML/CTF Act, *Public Legal Interpretation*, 2009, No. 9

AUSTRAC, Anti-money Laundering and Counter-Terrorism Financing Reporting Obligations of Legal Practitioners, *Law Society of South Australia*, 8/2011, *vol. 33*(7), 26-28.

Australian Crime Commission, The costs of serious and organised crime in Australia 2013–14, *Commonwealth of Australia*, 2015

Australian Law Reform Commission, Confiscation that counts: A review of the Proceeds of Crime Act 1987. *ALRC report* 1999, no. 87

Australian Institute of Criminology, Charges and offences of money laundering. *Transnational crime brief*, 2008, no. 4

Bailey, B., Information and Research Services, Report of the Royal Commission into HIH Insurance, *Department of the Parliamentary Library*. 2003, 32

Boyle, A. and C. Chinkin, *The Making of International Law.* Oxford University Press, 2007

CDPP, Annual Report 2003-04. Canberra: Commonwealth Director of Public Prosecutions, 2004

CDPP, Annual Report 2004-05. Canberra: Commonwealth Director of Public Prosecutions, 2005.

CDPP, Annual Report 2005-06. Canberra: Commonwealth Director of Public Prosecutions, 2006.

Deitz, A., Anti-Money Laundering and Counter-Terrorism Financing Act 2006. *Seminar Papers College of Law Sydney*, 2007, no. 2

Deitz, A. and J. Buttle, *Anti-money laundering handbook*. Sydney: Homson Lawbook, 2008

Dixon, M., *Textbook on international law*. Oxford University Press, 2013

Dilling, O., M. Herberg and G. Winter (eds.), *Transnational Administrative Rule-Making: Performance, Legal Effects and Legitimacy*. Hart Publishing, 2011

Duyne, P.C. van, Money laundering policy Fears and facts, in P.C. van Duyne, K. von Lampe and J.L. Newell (eds.), *Criminal finances and organising crime in Europe*, Wolf Legal, 2003

FATF, '*What is money laundering? Basic Facts About Money Laundering*. Viewed', 20 April 2017
   http://www.fatf-gafi.org/faq/moneylaundering

FATF, 2/2000, *NCCT Initiative: more Information about the Non-Cooperative Countries and Territories initiative*, viewed 20 April 2017
   http://www.fatf-gafi.org/media/fatf/documents/reports/Initial%20Report%20on%20NCCTs%2002_2000.pdf

FATF, 6/2001, '*Review to Identify Non-Cooperative Countries or Territories: Increasing The World Effectiveness of Anti-Money Laundering Measures*' viewed 20 April 2017,
   http://www.fatf-gafi.org/media/fatf/documents/reports/2000%202001%20NCCT%20ENG.pdf

FATF, 2005, *Third Mutual Evaluation Report on Anti-Money Laundering and Combating the Financing of Terrorism Australia*

FATF, 10/2007, *A'nnual Review of Non-Cooperative Countries and Territories 2006-2007: Eighth NCCT Review,* viewed 20 April 2017
http://www.fatf-gafi.org/media/fatf/documents/reports/2006%202007%20NCCT%20ENG.pdf

FATF, 2009, '*High-risk and non-cooperative jurisdictions*' viewed 20 April 2017,
   http://www.fatf-gafi.org/publications/high–riskandnon-cooperativejurisdictions/?hf=10&b=0&s=desc(fatf_releasedate)

FATF, 2015, *Anti-money laundering and counter-terrorist financing measures Australia*'

FATF, 2016, *Methodology for assessing technical compliance with the FATF recommendations and the effectiveness of AML/CTF Systems*', viewed 20 April 2017 http://www.fatf-gafi.org/documents/documents/fatfissuesnewmechanismtostrengthenmoneylaunderingandterroristfinancingcompliance.html

Financial System Inquiry, Financial System Inquiry Final Report, Commonwealth of Australia, c2014, 5

G7 Summit, *Economic Declaration* (Paris, 14-16 July 1989), viewed 20 April 2017, http://www.g8.utoronto.ca/summit/1989paris/communique/index.html.

Harvey, J., Compliance and reporting issues arising for financial institutions from money laundering regulations: a preliminary cost benefit study. *Journal of Money Laundering Control*, 2004, Vol. 7(4)

Hanratty, P., The Wallis Report on the Australian Financial System: Summary and Critique, P*arliament of Australia Research Papers*. 1997, 2

Hayes, B., 2013, *From countering financial crime to criminalizing civil society: how the FATF overstepped the mark,* viewed 20 April 2017 https://www.opensocietyfoundations.org/voices/countering-financial-crime-criminalizing-civil-society-how-fatf-overstepped-mark.

Harvey, J., An evaluation of money laundering policies. *Journal of Money Laundering Control,* 2005, 8(4) 339-345

HIH Royal Commission, The failure of HIH Insurance*, The HIH Royal Commission*, 2003, vol. 1

House of Lords, European Union Committee, *19th report of session 2008-09, money laundering and the financing of terrorism*, London, the Stationery Office Limited, 2009, vol. 2

IMF, *The IMF and the fight against money laundering and the financing of terrorism* (October 6, 2016), viewed 20 April 2017, http://www.imf.org/external/np/exr/facts/aml.htm.

Jensen, N., Creating an environment in Australia hostile to money laundering and terrorism financing: A changing role for AUSTRAC. *Macquarie Journal of Business Law*, 2008, 5, 93

Johnson, J., Third round FATF mutual evaluations indicate declining compliance, *Journal of Money Laundering Control*, 2008, Vol 11

Kingsbury, B. and R. Stewart, Legitimacy and accountability in global regulatory governance: the emerging global administrative law and the design and operation of administrative tribunals of international organizations. In Flogaitis, S. (ed.), *International Administrative Tribunals in a Changing World*. Esperia Publications London, 2008

Levi, M., Money laundering and its regulation. *Annals of the American Academy of Political and Social Science*, 2002, 582, 181-194

Pauwelyn, J., R. Wessel and J. Wouters (eds.), *Informal international law-making*. Oxford University Press, 2012.

Reserve Bank of Australia, *Financial Stability Review - The Australian Financial System,* April 2016, chapter 3.

Ross, S. and M. Hannan, Australia's new anti-money laundering strategy, *Current Issues in Criminal Justice*, 2007, *no. 19*, 135-150

Schmidt, J. L., *Money laundering in Australia 2011*, AUSTRAC, 2011

Slaughter, A.M., *A New world order.* Princeton University Press, 2004

United Nations, *Statute of the International Court of Justice*, 18 April 1946, viewed 20 April 2017,
http://www.refworld.org/docid/3deb4b9c0.html

UNODC, *Estimating illicit financial flows resulting from drug trafficking and other transnational organized crimes Research report*, 2011.

Walkers, J. *et al.* Anti-money laundering and counter-terrorism financing across the globe: A comparative study of regulatory action. *Canberra: Australian Institute of Criminology,* 2012, no. 83

Cannabis cultivation in the Tilburg area
How much money is involved and
where does it go?

Toine Spapens[1]

Introduction

In the Netherlands, cannabis cultivation is generally considered a serious and widespread illegal activity (Bovenkerk, 2001; Bovenkerk and Hogewind, 2003; Spapens *et al*, 2007; Emmett and Boers 2008; Jansen 2012). The origins of the problem can be traced back to the early 1990s, when indoor cultivation methods were introduced that rendered cannabis of excellent quality (Boekhout van Solinge, 2008). Cannabis cultivation is an illegal activity with a low socio-criminal threshold: one hardly needs contacts in the criminal underworld to start a plantation. So-called grow shops provide all growing equipment and advice on how to set up a nursery openly. The shops also illegally sell secretly cuttings and buy up the harvests or at the least direct the growers to others who do so (Spapens *et al.*, 2007). Although a recent change in legislation increased restrictions on grow shops, many people have over the years gained experience in the cannabis 'industry' and new growers can easily find persons who are able to give advice on how to set up and operate a nursery.

An important question is how much 'black' money cannabis cultivation generates and how this impacts on society. In this chapter I address this question focusing on the Tilburg area in particular. Tilburg is a medium-sized town of about 195.000 inhabitants in the south of the Netherlands. A key source of information is an informer who, in April 2012, walked into a police station and gave extensive information on his own criminal organisation and on the cannabis network in the Tilburg area. His job had been to manage 10 – 15 cannabis nurseries, and this position allowed him to provide a unique insight in the cannabis network. Based on this information the authorities drew up a document

---

[1]   The author is Professor of Criminology at Tilburg University, The Netherlands.

titled '*Integrated call for action*' to which I contributed as a scientific advisor (RIEC Zuidwest *et al.*, 2013; Noordanus, 2016).

Although one could argue that this is only a one person's view, it does not happen often that insiders who hold a key position in a criminal group and who maintain many contacts in the criminal underworld decide to open up. In addition, the information was checked as thoroughly as possible, and was used as a starting point for an investigation of his criminal group as well as for a search operation for money hidden in cannabis cultivators' homes. The informer had a photographic memory and was able to recall in great detail. One example is the information he gave about a shooting that took place in a cannabis nursery because the person who was assigned to guard it against thieves when the plants were almost ready to be harvested got nervous and fired his gun when he thought that someone was fumbling with the backdoor at night. No one was injured and neighbours never reported the incident to the police, but when officers visited the place they found bullet holes exactly where the informer had indicated. Generally, most of his other insights proved to be accurate or at least plausible when checked against information from other sources such as previous investigations and research.

This chapter starts with a brief history of cannabis cultivation in North Brabant. Next I address the investments and revenues associated with a cannabis nursery of 1.000 plants, followed by an estimate of the total revenues of cannabis cultivation in the Tilburg area. Then, I will focus on how the money is spent and invested in economic activities.

The history of cannabis cultivation in North Brabant

Although cannabis cultivation is an illegal activity in all Dutch regions, the problem has been more visible in the south than elsewhere. For almost a decade the police detect a disproportionally high number of nurseries in the southern provinces, and in North Brabant in particular. There is not a single explanation for this discrepancy, although the province has a long history of criminal activity. Since the beginning of the 1990s southern criminals started to focus on the production of synthetic drugs and cannabis (Spapens, 2016). As early as 1992, the police uncovered a nursery of 80.000 plants in the Tilburg area. In 1994, the Dutch police dismantled 323 nurseries, 31% of which were located in the south of the Netherlands (Weijenburg, 1996: 184-185). One of the practical explanation for the extent of cannabis cultivation in North Brabant might be the fact that from 1995 – 2005 almost all investigative efforts were focused on synthetic drugs production (Spapens, 2006). The effect was that criminal groups involved in growing cannabis could operate almost with impunity. In 1998, police intelligence showed that all known organised crime groups in one of the three police regions in North Brabant had switched from ecstasy production to cannabis cultivation or combined the two activities (Gooren and Rebel, 1998).

For a long time, the police limited itself to dismantling cannabis nurseries upon receiving information and occasionally searched known hotspots such as trailer parks and economically weak neighbourhoods where many people increased their annual income by growing cannabis themselves or by providing space to criminal groups who installed the nurseries (Bovenkerk, 2001). It was clear that the number of plantations detected represented merely the tip of the iceberg. A police officer once told the present author that "if we flew on a cold night with a helicopter equipped with infrared sensors entire city neighbourhoods and also many parts of the countryside would light up like a Christmas tree because of the warmth of the lighting used in the plantations." However, a suspicious infrared signature was (and is) insufficient cause for searching the premises and nowadays professional growers take better measures to prevent heat leaking from the plantations. Whilst going after the nurseries had some effect – particularly because growers who had installed one in social residence buildings could be evicted from their homes; something they feared very much – it hardly affected criminal structures. Furthermore, large-scale investigations of criminal groups proved to be inefficient, mainly because penalties were so low that illegal activities were hardly interrupted. According to a police officer, the 'bosses' simply kept running things from prison via messages to their wives or accomplices who had been released already.

The taskforce

Logically, all of this did not help to reduce the size of the cannabis industry. In 2011, the mayors of the five largest towns in North Brabant, together with the Minister of Safety and Justice and the King's Commissioner of the Province of North Brabant decided to establish a 'taskforce' to rein in the problem. One of the reasons was that criminals increasingly challenged the authorities. In 2010, for instance the mayor of Helmond had to be put under 24-hour police protection because of severe threats related to the fact that the municipality had allowed a second coffee shop. The shop was also attacked twice with an explosive. In 2012 criminals set fire to the town hall of Waalre which was totally destroyed. In several municipalities persons closely related to the criminal underworld succeeded in gaining political influence, mainly by sponsoring local political groups. Second, the cities of North Brabant continuously 'scored' negatively on the 'Municipal safety index.' Although the index was based on registered (petty) crime, further study revealed that these crimes were interwoven with organised crime and with cannabis cultivation in particular (Beke *et al.*, 2010).

The taskforce – first named 'B5' and later 'Brabant Zeeland' – was tasked with dismantling the criminal groups behind cannabis cultivation and trade; destroying underlying criminal structures, and the confiscation of illegally acquired assets. The taskforce started in 2012 and developed an integrated approach in which criminal investigation is combined with fiscal and administrative measures. A 'confiscation team' that was part of the Taskforce started to seize proceeds. From 2014 onwards, emphasis shifted back somewhat to traditional criminal investigation because the Ministry of Justice assigned 75 extra detectives to the taskforce. However, the public prosecution service – in the Netherlands public prosecutors formally manage criminal investigations on a day to day basis – remains a weak spot because of budget cuts and the fact that few public prosecutors are capable of handling large organised crime cases, and those who can are faced with extreme workloads and pressure.

To what extent the Taskforce has been effective is difficult to assess. Indeed, the Taskforce 'dismantled'45 criminal groups in 2015, but relatively few key figures have been arrested and convicted (Taskforce Brabant Zeeland, 2016). For a part this is the result of a policy that focuses on confiscating assets a person's legitimate income cannot account for. If the suspect agrees to renounce the money and valuables voluntarily, he will not be subjected to further criminal investigation. Such an approach is efficient because it does not burden the criminal justice system but it is also criticised by lawyers who argue that the court must always review such a 'deal.' In addition, the Taskforce focused on grow shops and suppliers of cannabis cuttings, claiming that this intervention visibly increased scarcity (Taskforce Brabant Zeeland, 2016). However, it is clear that a cannabis network that has been able develop and thrive for over a period of almost twenty years cannot be disrupted overnight. For the years to come cannabis cultivation will remain a key criminal activity in North Brabant.

Running a cannabis nursery: investments and revenues

This section addresses the question how much revenue a professional cannabis nursery brings in to the grower. Here we compare the official calculations drawn up by the confiscation bureau of the Ministry of Justice with those of the informer. It is of course difficult to produce general estimates because variables such as the size of a cannabis nursery, the type of cannabis, and the amount of lighting and fertilizers used, also impact on the quality and the size of the harvests. It was not before 2005 that national guidelines were drawn up in the report 'Standard calculation of criminal profit of an indoor cannabis nursery with artificial lighting'.[2] The report was updated in 2010 and is leading in court cases. The table below presents the official guidelines and compares these to the informer's figures.

The information presented in the next Table shows that in the informer's experience, his nurseries on the one hand produced more cannabis than the confiscation bureau uses in its estimates. Furthermore, the kilo price was at the time surpassing the authorities' assumption. On the other hand, investment costs were also much higher than the Ministry of Justice calculated. The differences can be explained in various ways. First the official estimates are an average derived from a substantial number of financial investigations of revenues gained by suspects of cannabis cultivation, whereas the informer's estimates are based on his own nurseries and to some extent on discussions with fellow growers.

---

2   *Standaardberekening wederrechtelijk verkregen voordeel bij wietkwekerijen* (Weustenraad, 2005).

Table 1

Estimates of crop and profit by the Confiscation Department and informant

	Confiscation department	Informant
Growing cycle	10 weeks	9 weeks
Number of harvests per year	4	6
Dried cannabis yield/plant	30,9 grams	40-57 grams
Wholesale price per kilo	€3.280	€4.250
Investment costs		
Construction of a 1.000 plant nursery (9 plants per square meter)	€10.000	€60.000
Cuttings	€2,85/piece	€3,50 – €5/piece (depending on cannabis species)
Water	16,35 litre/plant	30-50 litre/plant
Nutrients	€1,89/plant	€0,50 – €0,75/plant (excluding pesticides)
Electricity (600 watts lighting per m²)	614,65 Kwh per m²	720 Kwh per m²
Cutting of cannabis buds	€2/plant	€4,50 – €5,50/plant

Second, cannabis cultivation is not a transparent market and revenues as well as costs may vary across the wholesale buyers and equipment suppliers with whom the grower does business. Of course, economies of scale apply to legal growing equipments, such as lighting, nutrients, and garden mould: large-scale growers would certainly be able to receive 'volume discounts' at grow shops.

Third, the confiscation department solely calculates *direct expenses* of setting up and operating the nursery because these are deductible from the profits. Thus, criminals cannot introduce all sorts of *indirect costs* into the equation. However, for cannabis growers such costs can indeed be substantial, particularly those of measures to avoid detection. These are built-in expenses increased due to more neighbourly arwareness. In recent years, more people became aware that unusual activities in nearby dwellings and commercial buildings might be related to cannabis cultivation which may motivate them to report their suspicions anonymously.[3] Thus, professional growers must disguise the operation of a nursery in a private dwelling, for instance, by disguising measures: decorating the rooms visible from outside and maintaining the garden, all to avoid the

---

[3] In the Netherlands, people can report crimes anonymously by telephoning '*Meld misdaad anoniem*', a provision comparable to Crime Stoppers in the United Kingdom. Statistics show that most calls indeed concern cannabis cultivation.

impression that nobody lives there. Similar measures are needed when the nursery is installed in commercial property. For example, the informer told that when his group used a storage facility to grow cannabis they also had to employ a few people to pretend to pretend to 'work' there by driving around with a forklift truck; loading and unloading boxes, and having an occasional friendly chat with workers from neighbouring companies.

According to the Ministry of Justice, the informer's estimates are generally realistic. The bureau recognises that it underestimates the yield of a single plant and that informer's figures may be more accurate. However, the bureau does not acknowledge initial construction costs, even if we assume that these can be paid off over a number of crops and take into account that the informer also includes indirect costs. If we follow the informer's calculations, return on investment of the first crop would be no more than about 1:3. By comparison the confiscation bureau's calculations add up to a return on investment of 1:6, even if we take as a starting point a lower yield and kilo price. Based on interviews with growers, Spapens *et al.* (2007) estimated the investment costs of a 300-plant cannabis nursery at between €2.500 and €5.000. This would range a return on investment of between 1 : 8 and 1 : 30 depending on the yield per plant and kilo price taken as a starting point.

The above illustrates the complexity of drawing up reliable calculations of the criminal profits of a single cannabis nursery. Judges are usually reluctant to follow the prosecutor's calculations of criminal profits, which might explain why the bureau is rather conservative in its estimates. At the time the informer made his statements, he was unsure whether the authorities would try to recover his illegal assets and therefore he did perhaps exaggerate costs because these can be deducted from gross profits.

Apart from these factors, many others circumstances may affect the size of the harvest, such as the grower's proficiency and failed crops. Producing reliable estimates becomes even more complex when we try to calculate the amount of money generated through cannabis cultivation in the entire Tilburg area.

The combined revenues of cannabis cultivation in the Tilburg area

Over the past decades several researchers tried to estimate the annual amount of cannabis illegally grown in the Netherlands. Given the fact that this activity can be defined as a 'victimless' crime these estimates must primarily be based on sources such as police data on discovered cannabis nurseries and information collected during criminal investigations, and data from the energy companies on the amount of electricity leaking from their networks which can be attributed to theft. It is hardly surprising that estimates differed widely and have been the topic of debate. Estimates produced in the 1990s and early 2000s ranged from 38 tons per year to 250 tons (Korf, 2003; Bovenkerk and Hogewind, 2003). The first figure is definitely far too low because it would imply that the police seize most of the locally produced cannabis (Spapens, 2011).

In 2006, an internal police study set the estimate at a minimum of 323 tons and a maximum of 766 tons (Van der Heijden, 2006). Even with this wide margin of error the figure was politically volatile, because estimated domestic consumption was only 22 to 54 tons and the outcome implied that the larger part of the cannabis was sold to foreigners, either to drug tourists visiting the coffee shops or to dealers abroad. Drug researchers, although unable to produce better estimates, dismissed the estimate as unrealistically high.[4] A few years later Van der Heijden also distanced himself from these figures, but mainly because only 2% of the cannabis produced was intercepted and seized, which with hindsight he qualified as impossibly low. But is it?

Others argued that the methodology was inherently sound, although the limited quality and availability of data did not allow an exact estimation (Spapens *et al.*, 2007). The fact that the police in the Netherlands and other destination countries on the European continent intercepted so little Dutch cannabis could easily be explained by the 'open borders'. For a courier who transports drugs in his car the chance of being stopped if he joins the regular stream of cross-border commuters during rush hours is indeed virtually nil (Spapens, 2008). Recent information from the Dutch police indicates that criminals use on large scale small rental cars that have been modified to allow easy access to 'empty' spaces where a 'kilo shipment' can be hidden, such as the doors. Even if the car is stopped, the police often fail to detect this. And although the United Kingdom maintains its fixed border controls the volume of private cars and commercial vehicles entering the country also results in a low risk of detection.

After 2006, for a number of years only the power companies cooperating in the Platform against Energy Theft (*Platform Energiediefstal*) kept drawing up internal estimates of stolen electricity, which in 2012 amounted to 1 billion kilowatt hours of which most was attributed to cannabis nurseries. Based on its experience with discovered plantations the Platform estimated that the average annual electricity consumption of a cannabis nursery is 35.000 kilowatt hours.

---

[4] This became clear for example during a discussion at the annual conference of the International Society for the Study of Drug Policy held in Utrecht on 23-24 May 2011.

Because almost all professional growers steal electricity to cut costs and avoid detection because the power companies monitor disproportional consumption, it would imply that about 30.000 plantations of different sizes existed in the Netherlands at that time. Of course, this is a rough estimate: it does not include small nurseries that do not use stolen electricity; people may also steal electricity for other purposes; leakage of electricity cannot be measured exactly; the estimate is based on the average size of a nursery, so the total number may be lower as well as higher.

Only in 2014, the research institute of the Ministry of Justice published new official estimates. A study was commissioned because of the ongoing political debate about regulating the cultivation of cannabis destined for the Dutch coffee shops (Van der Giessen *et al.*, 2014). One of the important arguments of those who are in favour of such a step is that this would substantially reduce the number of illegal cannabis nurseries. However, this effect will hardly materialise when the larger part of the harvest never reaches the coffee shops but is trafficked abroad instead. The study adopted a more advanced mathematical method but the outcome was similar to the 2006 report. It set annual production of Dutch cannabis at 171 to 965 tons with 95% of the estimates ranging between 271 and 613 tons. Consumption was estimated at between 28 and 119 tons, with 95% of the estimates ranging between 32 and 49 tons when consumption by non-resident visitors of coffee shops was excluded and between 51 and 78 tons when it was included. The authors concluded that 95% of the export estimates ranged between 231 and 573 tons, when consumption by non-residents was excluded, and from 206 to 549 tons when consumption by non-residents was included. The government thus concluded that regulating cannabis cultivation would hardly affect illegal production.

Although criminal investigations of large-scale cannabis exporters are relatively scarce, a few examples of such criminal groups show that these alone trafficked amounts that almost equalled indigenous consumption. In 2004, the Dutch police investigated a group based at a trailer camp in the Eindhoven region that steadily sold 200 kilos of cannabis to foreign dealers every week, adding up to an annual supply of 10 tons (Spapens *et al.*, 2007). In 2012 another group operating in the same area managed to traffic 600 kilos per week mainly to the UK and Italy. This adds up to 31,2 tons per year. This case – codenamed operation Maskerbij – attracted much media attention for instance because main suspect Aran de Jong was murdered before he could stand trial.

If we assume the above estimates to be correct to the best of our knowledge, how many cannabis nurseries can we assume to be located in the province of North Brabant? The Dutch police discover about 5.000 – 6.000 nurseries per year, of which 20% are found in North Brabant. In 2012 the province accounted for 280.000 plants seized, which sets the average size of a cannabis nursery at about 260 plants.

According to the informer, wholesale buyers in the Tilburg area bought up about 20.000 kilograms of 'wet' cannabis per week. When we transpose this figure to dried cannabis at a conversion rate of 24%, annual production would measure about 250 tons, which requires at least 750.000 plants in different growing stages. At an average size of 260 plants, this would require 2.900 nurseries. Criminal groups, however, usually operate larger plantations. The informer's group permanently ran some 12 nurseries with an average size of 850 plants. He personally knew seven criminal groups in the city comparable to his own organisation. He estimated that about 60 such groups in total were supplying wholesale buyers in the Tilburg area. These groups would thus operate some 720 nurseries with 612.000 plants. This leaves 2.200 independent growers with nurseries of at least 60 plants each.[5]

It is important to notice that the informer did not exactly define the boundaries of the Tilburg area, but he certainly did not limit the area to the city of Tilburg. Furthermore, he talked about the amount of cannabis that was bought up by dealers in the area which does not mean that all cannabis is grown there too. In fact, the informer's own criminal group had some of its nurseries just across the border in Belgium.

Even with these nuances the revenues of illegal cannabis cultivation are gigantic. If we accept the estimate of the informer of 4.800 kilos of dried cannabis bought up on the regional market, weekly turnover would be €16 million based on the average kilo price of €3.280 set by the confiscation bureau of the Ministry of Justice. Annual turnover would thus add up to €818 million. The informer set the average costs of growing materials, transport and avoiding detection at €45 million so net profit would be about €773 million with a return on investment of about €17 for every euro invested.

Logically, the figures shocked the authorities. But how does it impact on society? We must take into account that cannabis cultivation is labour intensive and revenues are split over a large number of people. According to the informer the cannabis industry in the Tilburg area employed about 2.500 people in different roles. This seems to be rather conservative because if we assume that a nursery requires at least one person to operate it, some 2.200 persons are independent growers. This would leave only 300 members of criminal groups, and

---

5   Media reports on detected cannabis nurseries indeed show that most are smaller than the 260-plant average, although a 100 plants average seems to be more accurate.

facilitators working for different crime entrepreneurs, such as electricians, members of bud cutting crews, and real estate agents who search for suitable growing locations. Thus, probably more people are involved than 2.500.

How much money is then made by whom? To begin with, we can estimate the revenue generated by independent growers. Based on the information available, a 60-plant cannabis nursery renders an average annual profit of about €45.000.[6] This would add up to about €100 million for all independent growers. If we accept the estimate of 60 criminal groups operating in the Tilburg area, these would generate a profit of €11 million on average. This is in line with the revenues generated by the informer's criminal group. It produced 2,3 to 3,1 tons of cannabis annually, leaving a net profit of between €7 and €12,5 million. Unfortunately, the informer did not reveal how this money was split. However, if we assume that some 10 persons earn an average salary equal to that of an independent grower, the two 'bosses' of his group would annually cash between €3,3 and €6 million each.[7]

This analysis shows that being part of the cannabis industry does indeed bring in a substantial amount of tax-free money to a substantial number of people, but also that most of them are not 'top earners'. It is not the first observation that in terms of money 'many move few and few move very much' (Van Duyne and Miranda, 1999; Van Duyne and Soudijn, 2010). This is reflected in how the money is spent, the topic I will address in the next sections.

Spending money on the good life

Earlier Dutch research showed that criminals usually have an expensive lifestyle that costs them thousands of euros every year (Van Duyne, 1995; 1996; Klerks, 2000; Meloen *et al.*, 2003; Van Duyne and Levi, 2005). Those who operate smaller nurseries also predominantly spend the extra money on luxury. One grower interviewed by Spapens *et al.* (2007) stated that he and his girlfriend spent all of it on partying, drugs, gambling in casinos, and dinners in expensive

---

[6] This is calculated as follows: 60 plants yield 2,4 – 3,4 kilos per crop. At a kilo price of €3.280, 5 crops per year generate a turnover of €39.360 – €56.000. If we estimate profit rates at 15 to 1, annual net profit would range between €37.000 and €52.000.

[7] The informer claimed that he had hardly made money himself, mainly because the bosses held him accountable for lost profits if the police discovered a nursery or when the size of the harvest fell below expectations. Logically, we assumed that this part of his story was not very plausible although criminal groups do indeed apply this tactic to 'outsiders' who agree to install a plantation at their premises.

restaurants. Cannabis growers operating in the Tilburg area are no exception. The informer also stated that much of the income was spent on expensive designer clothing, the nightlife, parties, dinners at Michelin starred restaurants, holidays, and designer furniture and other valuables to decorate the house. According to the informer, one of the key persons in his criminal group bought clothes to the extent of €1.000 to €2.000 every week and he also possessed 80 to 100 pairs of designer shoes. He never washed his clothes, but simply threw them away after wearing them once and bought new garments. A peculiar finding is that some of the cannabis growers of Muslim origin also donated substantial sums to the mosque.

Apart from this, growers spend large sums on extensive reconstructions of their houses, as well as new kitchens and bathrooms for example. Impulsive decision-making is not uncommon. For example, after a few hot days someone decided that it would be a good idea to have an above ground swimming pool installed in his garden, including a complex tube heating system. However, after the summer season he quickly lost interest and did nothing to maintain the pool during the winter, after which it became unusable and had to be torn down.

Frequent holidays abroad are also very important, because these offer the opportunity to enjoy expensive luxury without attracting the attention of neighbours (or authorities) who might be wondering where the money came from. According to the informer, holidays with the family usually cost several ten thousand euros per week, usually paid in cash. This required some extra measures, because one can only carry €10.000 without the obligation of declaring it with the Customs. In the Netherlands, being intercepted at the airport with a substantial amount of cash money − even if the sum is below the threshold − might be a reason for further investigation. Furthermore, the person may be flagged for inspection on future travels. The criminals tried to circumvent the risk by travelling from airports in Germany and Belgium where at the time controls for cash money were less strict. They also assumed (correctly) that flying from a neighbouring country would leave the Dutch police in the dark about their movements because flight information is not shared automatically, and not requested if a person is not under investigation.

Not surprisingly, cars, motorcycles and boats are also objects of desire. Here, the members of the cannabis network had to be more careful because driving an expensive vehicle is bound to attract attention, particularly if the appearance of the driver does not seem to match the price of the car. In the Netherlands, the police and the Tax authorities regularly carry out joint inspections and discrepancies between a person's official income and his or her material possessions may lead to confiscation. Logically, criminals have thought up a number of methods to prevent this.

To begin with, some of them buy cars such as Citroën, Fiat and Toyota which do not attract as much attention as for example certain types of Mercedes, BMW and Volkswagen because the police know that those are popular in the criminal underworld. Although other brands as such were less conspicuous, the criminals did make sure to order the most powerful and full option models.

Second, because cars were also bought through cash payments, cannabis growers must also take precautions to prevent this from resulting in a suspicious transaction report. A simple method is to have another person with a large enough official income buy the car for you to become the official owner, and he is then paid back in cash. In the past the informer owned a small construction company and posed as owner of a car for another member of his criminal group who officially lived on a social benefit. The car dealer was well aware of the scheme and agreed that the car was partly paid in cash in terms that did not exceed the threshold that required to report these as unusual transactions. The boss and the car dealer knew each other from a fitness centre where both of them trained. A friendly car dealer was also essential in another case: here the car remained in the dealer's administration as in stock, which also allowed the user to regularly change it for another vehicle and thus make it more difficult for the police to track or bug him by installing a GPS-locator or a listening device.

However, the most popular option is not to own the car at all, but to lease it or rent it instead. For a criminal, this is beneficial in several ways. To begin with it requires less money to lease or rent an expensive car instead of buying it, and can be justified more easily when the police or the tax authorities start to ask questions. Second, the lease or rental company remains owner of the car and the authorities cannot seize it. Third, it allows to change cars regularly. Fourth, if the police need information about the car or on the person who is driving it, they need to contact the lease or rental company. Usually, criminals lease or rent their cars with shady businesses run by persons closely associated with the criminal underworld. These will immediately give notification when the police are interested in a specific car and its lessee. In addition, members of the cannabis network usually lease or rent their cars abroad so the police cannot immediately obtain information when for instance they stop it for a traffic inspection. Last but not least, driving a foreign car for a long time also meant that speeding and parking tickets would probably never arrive in the mailbox. The advantages for criminals to drive a rental car has had a significant impact on the sector. Based on the informer's statements the authorities started an integrated project to target rental companies. It recently revealed that of 38 companies in the Tilburg area, 36 could be qualified as *mala fide*. For example, 70-100% of their customers had criminal records and in many cases the money they spent on rental cars exceeded their official income. In February 2017, the police arrested three managers of a franchise of an international car rental company for money-laundering. They had accepted €750.000 in cash payments over a two-year period, against the company's official policy. Many customers were members of outlaw motorcycle gang *Satudarah*.

Investment in companies and in real estate

One of the authorities' primary worries is the risk that criminals use their money to acquire positions of power in the legitimate economy, for example by setting up businesses and buying real estate. They might also use the companies to facilitate illegal activities such as money laundering. Even if criminals operate their 'upper world' companies without committing any crimes, the risk remains that they will revert to threats and violence against business partners and personnel in case of conflicts.

Once criminals have managed to infiltrate in legitimate business activities it is extremely difficult to remove them from such a position. This is illustrated by experiences in the Amsterdam Red Light District where during the 1980s drug criminals invested for example in real estate, bars, gambling arcades, and coffee shops (*Project Emergo*, 2011). Logically most of them were smart enough to let figureheads with clean criminal records pose as owners or operators. From the mid-1990s onwards the Amsterdam and national authorities put great effort in developing administrative measures to tackle this problem and to prevent newcomers from acquiring operating licenses. In 2003, the Public Administration (Probity Screening) Act (*Wet bevordering integriteitsbeoordelingen door het openbaar bestuur, BIBOB*) expanded legal provisions. This so-called BIBOB-act focuses on economic sectors that have traditionally attracted criminals, such as gambling, prostitution, coffee shops, bars and restaurants but it also allows the screening of applicants for government subsidies and those who want to undertake building activities (Peters and Spapens, 2015). The BIBOB-act is a cornerstone in the Dutch administrative approach in the fight against organised crime, although it has met with criticism. An important issue is that procedures mainly seem to target 'small fry' instead of big criminals (Van der Vorm, 2016). However, in the Netherlands organised crime money does indeed materialise in

small businesses close to home and in real estate as experiences in North Brabant show.

In one case example, criminals ran a relatively small painting company and
were successful at acquisitions because they consequently underbid other firms.
The company was indeed more important for laundering money than for generating extra income. The same criminal group also provided personnel for the
harvesting of oysters in the province of Zeeland. Here they laundered money
by hiring personnel and paying them undeclared in cash whilst receiving official
payments from their customers. In another example, criminals opted for an
online money laundering scheme. They established seven gambling websites
which were registered in the Dutch Antilles and inflated the number of customers far beyond the number of actual players to fake a substantial legal income.

It remains unclear to what extent criminals set up legitimate businesses with
the aim of running it as a normal one. Some case examples show that they have
little time or motivation to operate the business themselves. They appear also to
have difficulty in finding capable staff who can manage it on their behalf. Most
criminals tend to mistrust their managers and are inclined to threaten them
when (financial) results fall below their expectations assuming – sometimes
correctly – that they are cheated. Consequently, it usually does not take managers – with a non-criminal background – long before they quit the job (Spapens,
2017; see also: Van Duyne 1996, Van Duyne *et al.*, 2009).

In several other examples the wives or girlfriends started a business. In one
case, reported in the media, suspect Humphrey D., who was the 'boss' of a
group of cannabis cultivators bought a horse riding school for his wife. She told
the local newspaper that her husband owned a very successful construction
company and that this had allowed the couple to buy the school. The premises
were also rebuilt for about €6 million and the mayor had accepted an invitation
to do the grand opening. The couple had also been active in charity – they had
sponsored for instance the Ronald McDonald house – and announced that they
would allow mentally and physically handicapped children to ride horses for
free. However, things fell apart when the police arrested the criminal group just
before the opening date. Of course, many had had their suspicions about the
origin of Humphrey D's income. Although he did own a construction company the neighbours observed that he never seemed to be doing any work.
Naturally, the wife claimed that she had had no idea what her husband's real
'occupation' was.

According to my own observations in my neighbourhood, the businesses
started by the wives or girlfriends never last very long. Without exception, they

choose an activity they are familiar with, such as a nail studio, a beauty salon or a clothing shop. Such shops face a lot of competition and usually do not attract many customers, and after a few weeks of being present in the shop from 9am to 6pm things start to get boring. Soon one can expect a note on the door that the shop is now opened from Thursday to Saturday only. A few months later the business is terminated altogether.

However, examples of difficulties and failures do not imply that criminals cannot be successful in legitimate business. For example, some seem to be quite comfortable in the real estate business (see also: Kruisbergen *et al.*, 2015). The cannabis cultivator who bought the horse riding school also had acquired over 20 premises in North Brabant. Another one managed to buy up 74 private homes in the city of Eindhoven in a period of six years with an estimated value of €12 million. He rented out most of his property to students (Spapens, 2016).

In the Netherlands, acquiring real estate is relatively easy because private homes are usually financed through mortgages. Of course, one must prove to have enough income or assets to be able to make the monthly payments to the banks. Those who are employed need a statement from their employer confirming a long-term contract and and the related income. One option is to counterfeit a declaration of employment. The aforementioned criminal who bought a large number of houses in Eindhoven for instance used this method (Spapens, 2016). Another option is to find a friendly owner of a legitimate company who is willing to 'employ' you on paper and pay out an official salary, which you then refund 'under the table' in cash. Most commonly, criminals operate a (small) company for mingling legitimate income with crime money. As in the case of Humphrey D. mentioned above, this helps (to some extent) to explain one's wealth to the outside world. Only an in-depth inspection by the tax authority would reveal discrepancies between the money-flow and actual business activities. However, this is a risk worth taking, because if no indications of tax evasion exist the chance of random inspection is about once in ten years.

The Tilburg cannabis network also comprises many persons of Turkish descent. The informer told that these mainly laundered money by smuggling it to Turkey and invest it there. These findings are consistent with earlier research (Van Duyne, 1996; Meloen *et al.*, 2003; Kruisbergen *et al.*, 2015). They used money mules who were sent to Turkey carrying amounts of cash under the threshold of €10.000. These mules usually travelled via German and Belgian airports. According to the informer, criminals for instance pushed people from the Turkish-Dutch community who travelled for a holiday or family visit to carry money. However, criminal investigation reveals that mules are also hired by offering them a free trip, a few days in a luxury hotel and some pocket money. Unfortunately, the informer did not know where Turkish-Dutch cannabis cultivators invest their money in. Earlier research mentioned above revealed that it is mostly used to buy private homes, land and sometimes to invest in hotels.

To what extent members of the cannabis network apply more sophisticated money laundering schemes remains unclear. The informer had no first-hand knowledge but stated that he heard about advices provided by several well-known lawyers who regularly defended cannabis cultivators. One told them 'hypothetically' about how he would launder substantial sums. Another lawyer provided 'for inspiration' his clients with a copy of the file of a criminal investigation regarding one of his other customers that included details of an off-shore construction. Whether they actually set up money laundering schemes on behalf of their clients is not known, although even their 'limited' services obviously conflict with the ethics of a counsellor. When confronted with the information all lawyers of course vehemently denied that any of this had ever happened.

Finally, it also became clear that money is sometimes not spent or invested at all, but hidden instead. The informer gave enough detailed information to allow an extensive search. On 21 August 2012, the police found at 13 different locations €1,4 million in cash hidden in homes and buried in plastic containers.

In sum, although it is often assumed that organised criminals use sophisticated money laundering schemes involving for example offshore constructions, most laundering activities observed in practice tend to be crude and simple. Relatively few members of the criminal underworld make so much money that they require more complex international laundering schemes (Van Duyne, 1996; Meloen *et al.*, 2003; Van Duyne and Levi, 2005; Levi, 2014). As the examples illustrate, the North-Brabant cannabis network is no exception.

Discussion

The focus on money-laundering and in its wake asset recovery is a relatively new phenomenon. First introduced in the United States in the mid-1980s at the height of the 'war on drugs', the issue of proceeds of crime quickly grew into a policy with global dimensions (Levi, 2014; Van Duyne, 2003). One important reason is the fear that large amounts of drug money would enter the legitimate economy and allow criminals a corridor to respectable positions in society, whilst at the same time undermining the integrity of the financial system, of other businesses and of government institutions, for instance by out-competing bona fide companies and by obtaining political influence. Furthermore, financially successful crime entrepreneurs may become 'untouchables' for law enforcement, because they can increasingly detach themselves from the criminal handwork.

Second, there is the moral notice that 'crime should not pay.' At the local level, most citizens have a pretty good radar for people who show financial success that is not explained by the nature and extent of their economic activities. On the one hand this annoys people: whenever the 'confiscation team' comes to seize assets such as expensive cars and immense flat-screen televisions, the neighbourhood stands around applauding. On the other hand, it may also inspire others to take the same 'easy' route for the big money. For example, a criminal in the south of the Netherlands started as a school teacher and decided to change to a life of crime because he became jealous of his delinquent friends who had all the time and money in the world to enjoy themselves (Moors and Spapens, 2017).

Money-laundering has been perceived as a global threat, and the size of the problem substantial. In 2006, it was estimated that laundered money accounted for about 5% of Dutch GDP (Unger *et al.*, 2006). However, calculations were based on an economic model and criminologists pointed out that underlying data were severely flawed (Van Duyne *et al.*, 2009; Van Duyne and Soudijn, 2010). Nevertheless, estimates such as these had a big impact on the speedy implementation of international actions against money-laundering.

In the Netherlands, studies to clarify how members of organised crime groups spend and launder their money have also been based on files of criminal investigations (Van Duyne, 1995; Klerks, 2000; Meloen *et al.*, 2003; Kruisbergen *et al.*, 2015). Just as in the present chapter, the results show that much money is spent on the good life and that investments are mostly limited to relatively small businesses and real estate, whereas criminals with immigrant backgrounds primarily invest in their country of origin. Only few who are involved in organised crime are top earners (Van Duyne and Soudijn, 2010).

Here, I took a slightly different approach by taking as a starting point the statements of an informer, who was able to oversee a larger criminal network: the cannabis network in the Tilburg area. He estimated that this network consists of 2.500 people who work in the cannabis 'industry' on a daily basis. Wholesale buyers – who need not necessarily buy from growers in the immediate area – handle about 4.800 kilos of cannabis per week. Cannabis growers generate a net profit of € 818 Million. This raises two questions. First, can this claim be substantiated and second, how does this money impact on society?

Estimating the size of any hidden criminal activity is obviously difficult, even if an insider with extensive contacts within a local criminal network provides information. Although the informer's crucial estimate of the weekly amount of cannabis bought up in the Tilburg area was based on assumptions that could not be corroborated directly, most of his other knowledge that did allow to be checked proved accurate or at least plausible. This for instance holds true for his description of the revenues and costs of a single cannabis nursery, although he did seem to exaggerate investment costs. When compared with other calculations, his estimate of the amount of cannabis traded in the Tilburg area would imply that wholesale buyers handle 30-50% of annual Dutch production. This seems to be unrealistic because we have no reason to assume that most trade is concentrated there. Moreover, the estimated number of people involved in cannabis growing seems to be too small.

The above illustrates that estimates always require crucial assumptions, such as the number of active criminal groups operating in a given area, the amount of cannabis produced and the costs. Furthermore, estimated revenues and investment costs of a cannabis nursery depend on many different parameters and it is impossible to incorporate all these variables in calculations of the total amount of money that cannabis cultivation generates locally or nationally. In any case, there is little doubt that the cannabis industry in the Tilburg area is substantial in size and that it provides a large number of people with an extra income they would otherwise be unable to acquire.

This leads to the question how the money impacts on society. Calculations also show that although estimated profits are huge, these are shared between many people and only a few make millions. This follows from the fact that criminal groups consist of 'entrepreneurs', 'workers' and 'facilitators' and as in normal business people who sell their labour may earn a decent income but they do not get rich. The same applies to independent growers: in most cases the nurseries do not generate lifestyle-changing amounts of money. Consequently, most of it is spent on clothes, luxury goods and holidays and at best invested in small businesses. The informer's insights on how the ones who do seem to make big money spend it, shows that in addition they invest in real estate, and sometimes also engage in charities and sponsoring activities. Criminals with an immigrant background tend to move the money to their country of origin and invest it there.

The findings replicate the outcomes of earlier research. There is little evidence that flows of laundered money threaten the integrity of the financial and economic system at the national or global levels. However, at the local level the life of legitimate business operators can indeed be harder when confronted with competitors who are loaded with crime money, although this is not the only circumstance that may create unfair advantages. Competitors who break the law by economising on safety or environmental regulations have a similar negative impact on the 'health' of their economic sectors. In addition, criminals do not need to own businesses to undermine entire local economic sectors, as is illustrated by what happened in the car-rental business in the Tilburg area which became seriously affected by criminal customers.

Illegal activities seem to erode primarily moral values: why work in a low-paid job if you can easily double your income even with a small cannabis nursery (see also: Van Duyne and Levi, 2005)? Or as a Turkish father once asked: "How can the government help me in guiding away my son from all this easy money?" The fact that assets are invested in small businesses is visible in local communities, as is shown by examples from my own neighbourhood I described above. It creates the impression that the authorities can do little to prevent shady persons from putting their equally shady financial assets to good use. Non-action may thus well lead to loss of legitimacy of (local) governments and negatively affect the social fabric that constitutes the first line of defence against crime in any democratic society. Although the fight against money-laundering was primarily framed in terms of global threats, and rightly criticized in that respect, we must not underestimate the fact that 'dirty money' does have a substantial detrimental effect at the local level.

References

Beke, B., E. van der Torre and M. van Duin, *Stads- en regioscan in de grootste Brabantse gemeenten. De achtergronden van de onveilige GVI-scores*. Apeldoorn, Politie en Wetenschap, 2010

Boekhout van Solinge, T., De bestrijding van de cannabisteelt in Nederland in historisch perspectief. In T. Decorte (ed.), *Cannabisteelt in de lage landen. Perspectieven op de cannabismarkt in België en Nederland*. Leuven/Voorburg, Acco, 2008

Bovenkerk, F. *Misdaadprofielen*. Amsterdam, Meulenhoff, 2001.

Bovenkerk, F. and W. Hogewind, *Hennepteelt in Nederland: het probleem van de criminaliteit en haar bestrijding*. Utrecht, Willem Pompe Instituut voor Strafrechtswetenschappen, 2003

Duyne, P.C. van, *Het spook en de dreiging van de georganiseerde misdaad.* The Hague, SDU, 1995

Duyne, P.C. van, The phantom and threat of organized crime. *Crime, Law and Social Change,* 1996, *no. 4,* p. 241-377

Duyne, P.C. van, Money laundering policy. Fears and facts. In: P.C. van Duyne, K. Von Lampe and J.L. Newell (eds.), *Criminal finances and organising crime in Europe.* Nijmegen, Wolf Legal Publishers, 2003.

Duyne, van, P.C. and M. Levi, *Drugs and Money. Managing the Drug Trade and Crime-Money in Europe.* London/New York, Routledge, 2005

Duyne, P.C. van and M. Soudijn, Crime-money in the financial system: what we fear and what we know. In: M. Herzog-Evan (ed.), *Transnational Criminology Manual.* Nijmegen, Wolf Legal Publishers, 2010

Duyne, P.C. van, M. Soudijn and T. Kint, Bricks don't talk. Searching for crime money in real estate. In: P.C. van Duyne, S. Donati, J. Harvey, A. Maljevic and K. von Lampe (eds.), *Crime, money and criminal mobility in Europe.* Nijmegen, Wolf Legal Publishers, 2009.

Duyne, P.C van and H. de Miranda, The emperor's clothes of disclosure: hot money and suspect disclosures. *Crime, Law and Social Change,* 1999, vol. 31, no. 3, 245-271

Duyne, P.C. van, F. Kristen and W. de Zanger, Belust op misdaadgeld: de werkelijkheid van voordeelsontneming. *Justitiële Verkenningen,* 2015, nr. 1, 103-119

Emmett, I and R. Boers, *Het groene goud. Verslag van een onderzoek naar de cannabissector voor het Nationaal dreigingsbeeld met een georganiseerd karakter.* Zoetermeer, Korps landelijke politiediensten, 2008

Giessen, M. van der, D. Moolenaar and M. van Ooyen-Houben, *De export van in Nederland geteelde cannabis.* The Hague, Wetenschappelijk Onderzoek- en Documentatiecentrum, 2014

Gooren, W. and J. Rebel, *Trendkaart Veiligheidsatlas georganiseerde criminaliteit in de politieregio Brabant-Noord.* Tilburg, IVA, 1998.

Heijden, A. van der, *De cannabismarkt in Nederland. Raming van aanvoer, productie, consumptie en uitvoer.* Zoetermeer, Korps Landelijke Politiediensten, 2006

Jansen, F., *Georganiseerde hennepteelt. Criminaliteitsbeeldanalyse 2012.* Woerden, Korps landelijke politiediensten, 2012

Klerks, P., *Groot in de hasj,* Antwerp, Samsom/ Kluwer Rechtswetenschappen, 2000

Korf, D., De economie van de wietkwekerij voor de Nederlandse markt: een verkenning. In: F. Bovenkerk and W. Hogewind, *Hennepteelt in Nederland:*

het probleem van de criminaliteit en haar bestrijding. Utrecht, Willem Pompe Instituut voor Strafrechtswetenschappen, 2003

Kruisbergen, E., E. Kleemans and R. Kouwenberg, Wat doen daders met hun geld? Uitkomsten van de Monitor georganiseerde criminaliteit. *Justitiële Verkenningen*, 2015, nr. 1, 84-102.

Levi, M. Money laundering. In: L. Paoli (ed.), *The Oxford Handbook of Organized Crime.* New York, OUP, 2014

Meloen, J., R. Landman, H. de Miranda, J. van Eekelen and S. van Soest, *Buit en besteding, een empirisch onderzoek naar de omvang, de kenmerken en de besteding van misdaadgeld.* The Hague, Reed Business Information, 2003

Moors, H. and T. Spapens. *Criminele families in Noord-Brabant.* Amsterdam, Reed business, 2017

Noordanus, P. Weerbaarheid tegen georganiseerde criminaliteit organiseren. *Tijdschrift voor de politie*, 2016, nr. 7, 6–10

Peters, M. and T. Spapens, The Administrative Approach in the Netherlands. In: T. Spapens, M. Peters and D. van Daele, *Administrative Measures to Prevent and Tackle Crime.* The Hague, Eleven International Publishing, 2015

Project Emergo, *Emergo. De gezamenlijke aanpak van de zware (georganiseerde) misdaad in het hart van Amsterdam.* Amsterdam, Boom, 2011

RIEC Zuidwest, Integraal Afpakteam and Tilburg University. *Integraal Appèl.* Oosterhout/Breda/Tilburg, 2013

Spapens, T., *Interactie tussen criminaliteit en opsporing.* Antwerp/Oxford, Intersentia, 2006

Spapens T., *Georganiseerde misdaad en strafrechtelijke samenwerking in de Nederlandse grensgebieden.* Antwerp/Oxford, Intersentia, 2008

Spapens, T., *The Cannabis Market in the Netherlands.* 2011. Available on SSRN https://ssrn.com/abstract=1856467

Spapens, T., *Van meerdere markten thuis?*, Apeldoorn, Politieacademie, 2017

Spapens, T., North Brabant: A Brief History of a Hotbed of Organised Crime. In: G. Antonopoulos (ed.) *Illegal Entrepreneurship, Organized Crime and Social Control.* Switzerland, Springer International Publishing, 2016

Spapens, T., H.G. van de Bunt and L. Rastovac, *De wereld achter de wietteelt.* The Hague, Boom Juridische uitgevers, 2007

Taskforce Brabant Zeeland, *Ruim 300 aanhoudingen in strijd tegen drugs Zuid-Nederland.* Press release, 2016

Unger, B., G. Rawlings, M. Siegel, J. Ferwerda, W. de Kruijf, M. Busuioc and K. Wokke, *The amounts and effects of money laundering.* Utrecht/Canberra, Utrecht University/Australian National University, 2006

Vorm, B. van der, *Ernstig gevaar. Een juridisch empirisch onderzoek naar aard, doel en toepassing van de Wet Bibob.* Oisterwijk, Wolf Legal Publishers, 2016

Weijenburg, R., *Drugs en drugsbestrijding in Nederland.* The Hague, VUGA, 1996

Weustenraad, E., *Wederrechtelijk verkregen voordeel hennepkwekerij bij binnenteelt onder kunstlicht, Standaardberekening en normen.* Leeuwarden, Bureau Ontnemingswetgeving Openbaar Ministerie (BOOM), 2005

How 'organised' is organised crime in Scotland?

Kenneth Murray MA CA[1]

Introduction

This paper is written from the perspective of a practitioner once removed. My professional role is to provide Police Scotland with professional accounting and business strategy expertise which will assist in the investigation and reporting of serious economic crime, which mostly involves what the Scottish Government refers to as 'Serious Organised Crime'.[2]

It is acknowledged that there can be a tension between how governments and law enforcement agencies engage in the discourse on this topic and how it is perceived as an object of study by criminologists. Hobbs, for example, considers that law enforcement approaches to organised crime are based on '*alien conspiracy theory*' and a phantom concept of organised crime based on a need to demonise the 'other' and posit notional criminal hierarchies that '*mirror the organisational hierarchies of policing*'.[3] If that is – or is perceived to be – the case, then the question of how that approach might be modified is surely worth addressing in a way that attempts to bridge perspectives between the practitioner and academic communities.

My aim here therefore is to outline a practical approach to this issue which harnesses criminological perspectives of the range of harmful activities that can be grouped under the description of organised crime, with a view to articulating an approach which might lead to an improved framework for tackling them. In line with this approach the sources consulted are not restricted to

---

[1] Head of Forensic Accountancy, Police Scotland. The views presented are those of the author alone and should not be taken as those of Police Scotland.
[2] Scottish Government (2015), 'Scotland's Serious Organised Crime Strategy', www.gov.scot/Resource/0047/00479632.pdf
[3] Dick Hobbs (2013), 'Lush Life – Constructing Organised Crime in the UK', Oxford p. 226.

criminology, but also consider what I believe to be relevant perspectives from the fields of economics, critical theory and business strategy.

Defining organised crime

The well aired question of what organised crime consists of is now addressed in UK legislation. According to the Criminal Justice and Licensing Act (Scotland) 2010, 'serious organised crime' is *"crime involving two or more persons acting together for the principal purpose of committing or conspiring to commit a serious offence"*. A 'serious offence' is an indictable offence committed to obtain a material benefit or an act of violence or a threat made with the intention of obtaining such a benefit.[4] In the separate legislature of England and Wales, an organised crime group, in terms of the Serious Crime Act 2015, means a group that: *"(a) has as its purpose, or as one of its purposes, the carrying on of criminal activities; and (b) consists of three or more persons who act, or agree to act, together to further that purpose."*[5]

It might be convenient to try and nail down organised crime by reference to the relevant legal definitions, but these definitions hardly cover what the public understands organised crime to be, even if that understanding is influenced and distorted by how it is imagined and portrayed in cinema and pulp fiction. In addition to legislation, the political response in the UK has been couched in the creation of special police forces to combat it, such as the now defunct Scottish Crime and Drug Enforcement Agency (SCDEA – dissolved 2013), the now defunct Serious Organised Crime Agency (SOCA – dissolved 2013) and the currently operational National Crime Agency (established in 2013).

What is it, though? If we agree it is something perhaps not best viewed through a legal prism, how else do we look at it as an experienced phenomenon? A reasonable question for openers might be: what do we mean by organised crime? According to Klaus von Lampe there is *"not one object of study but many different objects of study, comprising, for a lack of discriminating criteria, everything that in some way or another has been associated with organised crime."*[6] The key word opening things up is clearly 'organised' on the basis that no-one is likely to seriously argue that crime itself does not exist. What is the significance of this word, 'organised'?

---

4   Criminal Justice and Licencing (Scotland) Act s. 28(3)
5   Serious Crime Act 2015 s45 (6)
6   Klaus von Lampe (2016) 'Organised Crime, Analyzing illegal activities, criminal structures and Extra-legal governance', Sage, London, p. 14.

The verdict of Petrus C. van Duyne in 2006 was that it was essentially a political construct: "the word string is a core element of the word play of mainstream 'problem owners' and interested actors. Even if they all have different understandings in the way they discuss 'organised crime', they recognised a shared sing-song."[7] It is a '*sing-song*', Van Duyne implies, because when we (writing as one of these 'interested actors') talk about organised crime, we don't really know what we are talking about; and if we are essentially ignorant of the crime economy, how can we make statements about the level of threat it poses?

The same theme was reprised by Van Duyne and his collaborator Benny van der Vorm[8] in 2015: measures against 'organised crime' achieved specific aims relating to 'budget, power and legislation', but it didn't protect against a tangible threat: "*One can say there is always fear of crime, but that concerns daily street crime. Otherwise organised crime remains a matter of public entertainment: thrilling stories with a pleasant shiver.*"

The trope that organised crime does not really exist – at least as a threat that warrants any special measures (and budgets) to combat it[9] -- is encouraged by the difficulties encountered by empirical researchers to obtain data that would enable definitive measurable statements about its incidence to be made. In another paper presented in the same Cross Border colloquium volume in 2006, 'The organisation of business crime,'[10] Van Duyne asserts that, "*The 'organised crime' concept neither explains criminal conduct nor has any explanatory value*" but also posits how we should be looking at what is often perceived as such: "*What matters is to follow, map and explain the variety of organisational conduct of criminal money makers.*"

Another way of framing that is to say that what counts is the process rather than the label. The challenge then becomes one of understanding what the relevant processes are – not a straightforward challenge in a realm that is essentially clandestine; but one which is, or ought to be, a necessary pre-requisite to declamations, or 'sing-songs', regarding its incidence or threat.

---

[7] Petrus C. van Duyne (2006), 'Counting clouds and measuring organised crime', the introductory chapter to 'The Organisation of Crime for Profit – Conduct law and measurement', Petrus C. van Duyne, Almir Maljevic, Maarten van Dijk, Klaus von Lampe, James L. Newell (Eds.). Wolf Legal Publishers (WLP).

[8] Petrus C. van Duyne and Benny van der Vorm, (2015) 'From organised crime threat to nuisance control', in 'The relativity of wrong-doing', Wolf Legal Publishers, WLP.

[9] Now also a feature of popular surveys on crime, see Tom Gash (2016) 'Crime – The truth about why people do bad things', Penguin. The relevant chapter is given the title 'Organised crime is big, bad and booming' and presented as a myth, which the chapter attempts to refute.

[10] Petrus C van Duyne (2006), 'The organisation of business crime', in 'The Organisation of Crime for Profit – Conduct law and measurement', *ibid.*

Criminal organisation versus organisation of criminals

The Hell's Angels have a well-documented history as a criminal organisation,[11] but Lavigne considers the Hells Angels are 'truthful' when they claim they are not so much a criminal organisation as an 'organisation of criminals.'[12] What, if anything, is the significance of such a distinction?

Lavigne considers in respect of the Hells' Angels that the distinction manifests as an outlaw motor cycle group which is clearly bureaucratic in its authority structures but not in respect of the criminal activities conducted by its members. An organisation therefore is not necessarily indicative of a hierarchical command structure for certain activities, but still implies the existence of some form of governing authority. This might manifest itself when there are disputes between members, for example; or when members or sub-groups start operating in a way that harms the perceived common welfare or interests of the group.

Abadinsky[13] develops this to consider that the structure of organised crime is *"less like a corporation and more like a government."*[14] To pull back things to Scotland, this is a view which chimes with the viewpoint of Graeme Pearson, a prominent practitioner commentator who was the founding Direct General of the Scottish Crime and Drug Enforcement Agency (SCDEA) and, until very recently, a Member of the Scottish Parliament (MSP) and shadow spokesman for criminal justice in the Scottish Parliament. In Pearson's autobiography he re-iterates a theme which the author can vouch was the core of his approach in office. Organised crime (as practised in the West of Scotland at least) is less about profit, but more about power, influence and control: *"For those involved in serious organised crime, the provision of a profit just to maintain their living is not enough. They have lifted the 'skirt' of our society and believe that criminals can have significant power, control and influence over their environment"*.[15]

---

11 The Independent (UK), (August 14, 2007), 'Inside the biker gangs: the truth about guns, drugs and organised crime', The Independent (UK) and Julian Sher and William Marsden (2006) 'Angels of Death: Inside the Biker Gangs Global Crime Empire', Carroll & Graf, New York.

12 Yves Lavigne (1996), 'Hell's Angels: Into the Abyss'), Harper Collins, New York, p. 246.

13 Howard Abadinsky (2003) 'Organised Crime', 7th ed., Thomson Wadsworth, Belmont CA.

14 Abadinsky *ibid* p. 17.

15 Graeme Pearson (2008), 'The Enforcer', Black and White Publishing, Edinburgh, p. 208.

Anderson argues it is precisely this aspect of organised crime that carries the most worrisome threat. An ability to deploy influence in such a way that can get things done not just in criminal fields of activity but legitimate fields too: "*the capacity for forming a quasi-government*".[16] Its principal members are typically able to elude any of the adverse consequences of arrest and conviction because their status enables them to procure others to commit the offences from which they benefit. This implies a characteristic that relies on a degree of organisation that extends beyond personal charisma and influence; there must be some organisation involved in the mechanisms that convey the influence.

In Scotland, one of the ways such influence appears to manifest itself is in traditional forms of territorial control where organised crime groups compete for, and then honour, territorial borders within which it is accepted they hold domain. This allows for the taxation of criminal activities that take place within acknowledged borders.[17] Within that territorial area there also appears to be a degree of resilience to outside infiltration from other organised crime groups, implying a deeper and broader authority beyond the territory itself that supports existing power structures. This may help to at least partly explain the continuing influence of well established, dominant organised crime groups that feature frequently in Scottish organised crime mapping.[18]

In other areas of Scotland, such as Inverness and Aberdeen, local barriers to entry are less prevalent, however, and organised crime groups from Liverpool and the East Midlands are more visible as direct participants, having identified these relatively far flung territories as retail markets in which they can do business. The presence or absence of this kind of influence, or the ability to capitalise on it, is therefore a factor in determining how criminal markets are populated.

But other than offering a crude binary comparison of the effects of its presence and absence, influence on its own is not a factor of analysis which conveys much information. Where might we look for that? Where does it come from? How does it manifest itself in ways which might be measurable? The ability to participate in developed criminal markets such as cocaine and heroin imply the existence of abilities, or what I will call later *distinctive capabilities*, which enable adaptation to market parameters over which they cannot exercise primary control, and which demand interaction with other parties, whether legal or illegal. The actor groups we corral for convenience under the description of organised

---

[16] Annelise Graebner Anderson (1979), 'The Business of Organised Crime: A Cosa Nostra Family', Hoover Institution Press, p. 46.

[17] This influence is apparent from intelligence sourcing relevant to organised crime in the central belt of Scotland.

[18] Scottish Government, *ibid*.

crime groups are market participants in other words, and the characteristics of the relevant markets may offer a pathway of analysis which yields a way of understanding what organised crime is that has practical value.

Organised crime – A business or a market?

From a business perspective, the design characteristics of organised crime governance structures have to be closely affiliated with the needs of the markets in which they participate. Given Class A drug (essentially cocaine and heroin) markets continue to represent a principal criminal revenue stream worldwide, it seems reasonable to consider what characteristics are required by these markets in order to get involved in them.

These are international markets: the delivery process hinges on the ability to transport illegal commodities across borders in economically viable quantities to the target market places. The level of investment involved demands by its nature a measure of reliable governance being applied to ensure the profits realised at the retail end of the chain *i.e.* the end that ultimately funds everything, are secured and transmitted through the connect chain that forms the monetary spine of the business process. Local markets are therefore necessarily connected to the big picture involving the 'cartels' and organised crime 'brand names'(*e.g.* N'drangheta) that are becoming increasingly familiar across popular culture.

In this context, the interesting questions revolve around how the local governance structures relate to and interact with those that are more international in their scope. Participation implies a willingness and ability to be flexible and adaptive in ways that are obviously at odds with traditional concepts of organised crime groups. There is a broad diversity of type of participant that requires an approach that is capable of accommodating such diversity. The continuing apparent efficacy of these markets, however, implies there must be some basis for co-operation across different types of participants.

How does this marry with the orthodox consensus that crime itself is usually best explained in terms of opportunism?[19] Flexibility and responsiveness to opportunity are obviously necessary attributes for successful criminal enterprise.[20] It might be considered there is a tension, therefore, between the more chaotic

---

[19] For example, see Tom Gash (2016) 'Criminal – The Truth about Why People Do Bad Things'. Allen Lane, London; and von Lampe, ibid., in particular his model of the contextuality of organised crime, pp. 355-356.

[20] See Hobbs *ibid*, in particular his idea of a 'community of practice', outlined in his concluding chapter, pp. 225-235.

characteristics of organised crime with organisational attributes indicative of control and co-ordination that begin to suggest parallels with legitimate business processes, if not structures. What is required is an understanding of what enables or allows for successful participation in these markets. In considering this it might be as well to jettison the straightjacket of *a priori* structures. Structures grow out of what is required of each participant in the relevant processes in order for the market taken as a whole to be successful. What needs to be considered, in other words, is how organised crime works as a business process.

The influence of markets on organisations

In a 1991 paper entitled 'Organisations and Markets',[21] Herbert Simon set out a framework for considering the key characteristics of organisations, focussing in particular on the question of what motivated *"real people in real organisations."* There were four elements he identified as follows:

- *Authority*: within a zone of acceptance;
- *Rewards*: which Simon considered were limited in effectiveness, and that other more powerful motivations had to apply;
- *Identification*: which relates to pride in work and organisational loyalty; and,
- *Co-ordination*: the authority mechanism of organisations which provide a means for co-ordinating the activities of groups *in ways that are not always easily achieved in markets.*

This framework can readily be adapted to those traditional concepts of organised crime groups involving a continuing heritage of allegiance to a fixed group of people or ways of doing things. It can also help explain in this unregulated world how people come to agree to be and work with each other. But Simon also made an important distinction between the co-ordinating mechanisms that exists *within* organisations, and those that exists *between* them. *Within* organisations, he considered the most powerful force for subjugating personal to organisational goals to be *identification*. *Between* organisations the motivation to co-operate was almost wholly based on economic motivations and rewards. There are matters of geography, tradition and circumstance that underpin identity, but the motivating forces are those that enable commerce.

The ways in which modes of organisation develop and operate are a function of the economics of criminal co-operation within commercial markets. This does not extend only to agreeing matters such as price; it also might in-

---

[21] H. Simon (1991), 'Organisations and Markets', Journal of Economic Perspectives, Vol 5 AEA, Pittsburgh PA, pp. 25–44.

volve more encompassing methods of market control. In one of the more directly relevant passages of the Simon text to the issue of organised crime, he identifies circumstances where market price mechanisms break down, thus inhibiting the ability of actors to respond rationally to pricing signals. The extent to which groups of actors in these circumstances are open to organisational influence is indicated by the market's ability to have another signalling mechanism adopted and accepted. A relevant example is day to day co-ordination adjustment of quantity mechanisms. Scottish experience of class A drug markets indicates that variations in wholesale import prices of cocaine will tend not to affect the consistent product price offered to users on the street (as exemplified for example in the 'tenner bag'). The quantity of cocaine or heroin sold in the mix is adjusted to accommodate the wholesale price change by altering the purity levels but not the price per bag.

This implies there is another way of looking at an organisation in the context of markets. The processes which enable participation may rely upon the co-ordination of different actors within an authority framework. There is a co-ordinating force that exists between actors in a criminal enterprise that has similarities with the co-ordinating mechanisms that exists within formal organisations. The point in common is the fact of co-ordination as evidenced in the functioning of mature criminal markets.

The way in which the co-ordination is achieved, however, is obviously different. Employees within an organisation are induced into co-operative action through common goals not to mention contractual obligations as employees. Contractual obligations between criminal actors tend to rely on non-legal forms of enforcement that are usually not formalised in documentation. There are more obvious parallels, however, in the forces that combine to provide structure in economic markets.

The question therefore is how does the organising authority in the processes of criminal markets manifest itself? There is something that has to stand in place of the commonly conceived notion of 'organisation' that nevertheless delivers the minimum level of co-ordination needed for these criminal markets to function in their processes at all. What is it?

There are two factors we need to explore before we are able to get close to an answer to this question. Firstly: how do criminal markets work? Secondly, what are the essential characteristics of all the various types of participant involved in them?

The influence of organised crime on markets

One way of considering organised crime is to consider it in relation to its function. Haller considers the core business reason for the very existence of organised crime is that it satisfies needs not met in the contexts of legitimate markets: "*Organised crime . . . is best thought of as a type of organisational crime and part of a continuum between business and crime.*"[22]

Criminal markets are therefore conceived of as the driver for the activities given the description of organised crime. The Vander Beken study of Belgian organised crime of 2004 posited that organised crime was entrepreneurial in nature and that the dynamics of the market space "*provided the main environment and explanation for organised crime*".[23] An Australian study of criminal markets populated by organised crime groups articulated this idea as follows: "*organised crime becomes a function for the market of efficient goods and services rather than a function of the illegal groups providing them*".[24] Exploring how the principal criminal markets are arranged might therefore offer insights as to how organised crime manifests itself, at least as conceived through the prism of these markets.

It might be considered there will always be a demand for Class A drugs – even if these markets were to become decriminalised there would still be modes of demand for these products which would not be adequately served through points of sale and delivery involving the need for a prescription.[25] What can be learned from how these markets are organised?

A detailed description of the cocaine market was provided by Abadinsky in 2003,[26] which might serve as a useful foundation. The narrative of imported product to bags of white powder sold on the streets is made up of a short chain of discrete stages. The importation stage is managed in a way that spreads commercial risk through joint insurance arrangements between supplier and importer. Discovery risk is minimised by diversifying placements between the different commodities used as cover and the use of false documentation and nominee trading companies to confuse ownership of any seized commodity.

---

[22] M. Haller (1990), *'Illegal enterprise: a theoretical and historical interpretation'*, Criminology, 28:2, pp. 207-235, John Wiley & Sons, London.

[23] Tom Vander Beken (2004), 'Risky business: A risk-based methodology to measure organised crime', Crime. Law & Social Change 41, Kluwer Academic Publishers, Alphen aan den Rijn, pp. 471-516

[24] Projects KRISTAL, LERNA and ARKO Queensland, Australia in Black, Vander Beken (ed) (2001), 'Reporting on Organised Crime: A shift from description to explanation', Maklu, Antwerp.

[25] Philip Bean (2010), 'Legalisation Drugs – Debates and Dilemmas', The Policy Press, London.

[26] Abadinsky, ibid.

Making this supply chain work requires delivery of expertise in the core competencies concerned and also a significant measure of co-ordination. There are clear control issues arising from the need to have the commodity docked so that it can be safely secured on the destination shore. The people that perform these functions also need to know what they are doing. But the agents who arrange and control these processes, as Abadinsky points out, will typically not take part in them. They are actually unlikely to have any physical connection with what is taking place at all.

Once the commodity is ashore it requires to be cut. This implies the ability to accommodate and run what is essentially a low tech industrial process. It also involves a degree of management expertise and capital. The capital is typically provided by national class wholesalers – players who buy the product from importers in quantities of between 10 kg and 50 kgs. Given a wholesale price range of £20.000–£30.000[27], this activity implies six figure transacting. That raises the question of how to protect and manage the money for settlement and laundering purposes.

The need for organisation at the top end of this kind of process is perhaps obvious. Below the multi kilo wholesale level, however, Abadinsky contends it is an *"easy-entry business requiring only a source, clientele and funds."*[28] Even here however it should be noted the nature of the market tends to encourage some basic modes of organisation to develop: *"Transactions must be accomplished without recourse to the formal mechanisms of dispute resolution that are usually available in the world of legitimate business. This in reality leads to the creation of private mechanisms of enforcement."*[29]

An ability to inflict violence, or an ability to call on it, is recognised as an essential prerequisite for participation at all levels of the trade. Survival in economic terms, never mind physical terms, is not possible without it. This element remains therefore a dominant influence over how players in the market organise themselves. A degree of order is required, enforced by whatever discipline mechanisms are in vogue, in order that the financial returns available from participation can be realised with some degree of order.

How can we develop a model that might have some relevance to our understanding of 'order' in the context of organised crime activity? In Scotland, the intelligence picture indicates that there is a network of Serious Organised Crime Groups that exercise a degree of dominance over the territories making up the central belt (an area that can be taken for this purpose as being between

---

27 Classified Police Scotland market reports.
28 Abadinsky, ibid, p. 297.
29 Abadinsky, ibid, p. 297.

Greenock on the West coast to Dundee on the East coast). The way in which these groups are able to arrange their financial affairs implies a series of relationships and influences with specialisation of services such as money laundering and investment of accumulated funds being made available to local dominant players.

These local players can essentially outsource all their financial and business needs, concentrate on delivering the relevant revenue streams from the area markets over which they exercise dominance, and derive financial rewards in forms and locations that are resilient to asset recovery processes. The pooled resources of these various groups contribute to the relative resilience of Scottish criminal markets to outside intrusion (especially in the central belt) and represent a network of influence that operates in accordance with a hierarchy organised according to function. The arrangement of that hierarchy across different groups (and significant players who operate between groups) appears from intelligence to be a function of how they relate to each other as market participants.

The market would appear to be attractive enough to encourage these arrangements. According to UNODC[30], Scotland ranks at the top of per capita consumption rates for cocaine. It is also a market that has consistently shown higher rates of profitability than the rest of the UK in respect of all Class A drugs[31]: a market estimated in total at £1,4 billion in 2009.[32] The degree of profitability capable of being achieved within these markets in Scotland can be gauged from Gash's estimated mark up of 69% achieved on import prices of cocaine at street level (he also quotes a percentage mark up of 269% for heroin).[33]

That mark-up is not achieved in one step, however. The delivery of the drug to the end user entails a process that starts with the arrangement of the necessary importation and then proceeds through stages of wholesale distribution to sale at street or end user level. This is illustrated in Fig I below.

---

30 UN Office on Drugs and Crime, World Drug Report, 2015.
31 Classified intel sources.
32 Centre for Drug Misuse Research (2009), Assessing the Scale and Impact of the Illicit Drug Market in Scotland, University of Glasgow, www.Scotland.gov.uk/socialresearch
33 See Gash, ibid., 2015, p. 147.

Figure 1

The drug supply process in stages

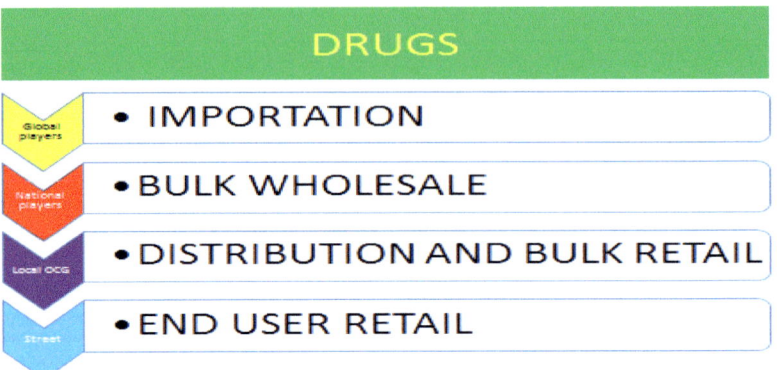

The risk attached to importation and the handling of large sized consignments are of a different order to the diversified risk attached to the sale of smaller quantities at the bottom end of the process. The rewards at the bottom end of the chain are therefore not as high as those at the top; a function of how the process is funded as much as how it is controlled.

Intelligence indicates that the earnings from Class A drug retail are used for two purposes: to earn profits and to pay suppliers. The discipline that exists in the market derives from the fact that these two processes, distribution and payment are kept separate, and also that the repeatable transactions tend to involve credit. The disciplinary mechanism within the payment chain apparent from intelligence is debt enforced by threat, or reputation allied to threat. The share of the mark-up referred to is skewed in favour of those players in charge of the higher stages of the process (as has been observed low level dealers often don't retain much money after expenses).[34] The relevant debt chain is therefore the above process reversed as shown in Figure 2 below.

---

[34] Van Duyne (2006), *ibid*.

Figure 2
The drug debt process in stages

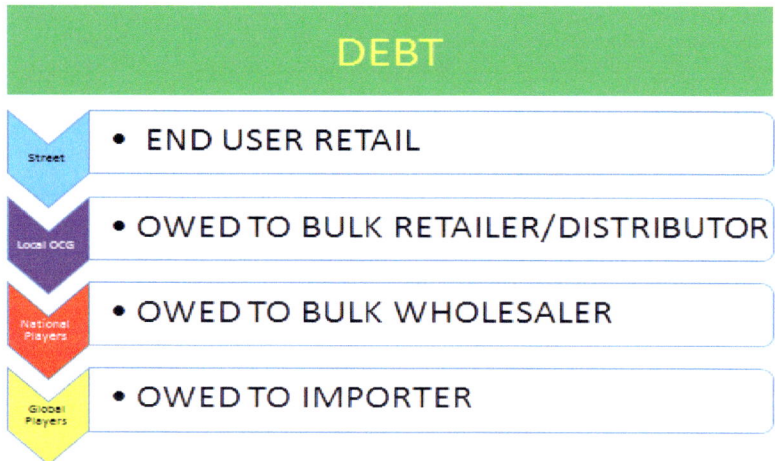

Consistent with the above, the experience of a number of high end money laundering investigations in Scotland indicates that the harvesting of criminal profits in the principal Class A drug markets often involves some kind of access to a network of international partners and processes requiring significant cross border collusion and the engagement of professional specialists in order for it to function. The efficient management of international funds through the network of offshore locations is a financial aim in itself. But the cross border characteristic can also be viewed as an evasion methodology that has developed into an organising principle. It exploits the operational advantage it has derived from the ease with which it can operate across borders. It knows that law enforcement, even within an open territory such as the EU, is still bound by cumbersome procedures if it is to move across international jurisdictions[35]. Attempting to reach definitive conclusions about the degree of organisation in these processes by referring only to the retail end of the chain is therefore like trying to explain the position of the planets in the sky without referring to gravity. The forces which forge the vertical integration necessary for the process to function have to be understood within the context of how the local market fits into the global market of supply.

---

[35] Leslie Holmes (2016), 'Advanced introduction to Organised Crime' , Edward Elgar, p. 144

The above analysis provides the backdrop for the concept of 'glocality' expounded by Hobbs: a confluence of local relationships operating within the context of a global market place.[36] Hobbs[37] describes an international crime group brought to justice in a number of different countries in 2005 where single mothers paid £10.000 to fly to the Caribbean to pick up cocaine sealed in rum bottles. They were then flown to Paris or Amsterdam where they were guarded overnight before being sent to the UK via ferry or Eurostar. Drugs were also sent by way of a parcel courier company, one of whose employees intercepted the parcels which had been sent to non-existent addresses. The cocaine in the parcels was extracted and the emptied parcels were returned as undelivered, before taking the cocaine to a local kitchen where it was turned into crack. Hobbs cites this example to support his claim that the linkages thus established between dispatching and receiving countries were consistent with the notion of 'glocality' (propounded by Robertson[38]) where, *"crime manifests itself as a tangible process of activity, deflating the mystique of globalisation by removing cross border crime from the virtual zone of transnationality, and placing it on the streets and in the suites of a class-bound, post-industrial society no longer confident of the integrity of its own borders."*[39]

Hobbs decries the notion of transnational crime because in his view it exaggerates the connectedness between individuals, yet elsewhere he concedes that a key characteristic of organised crime is the extent to which it *"mimics the everyday routine activities of 'legitimate' trade and commerce"*.[40] The connector that links the two is the way in which these routine activities are present in the legitimate world in the form of processes. The fact that they are mimicked in the criminal world does not make them any less tangible; they cannot be theorised away., '

The way crime is organised is a direct function of what arrangements and liaisons are necessary to enable the principal players to secure and enjoy the 'returns' from their industrialised criminal capabilities. This is the key dynamic in determining how modern criminal groups organise themselves; in accordance with what is necessary to survive and prosper.

---

[36] Hobbs, *ibid.*, p. 217.

[37] Hobbs, *ibid.*, p. 219.

[38] R. Robertson (1995), 'Glocalisation: Time-Space and Homogeneity - Heterogeneity', in M. Featherstone, S. Lash and R. Robertson (eds.), 'Global Modernities', Sage, London, quoted by Hobbs, p. 220.

[39] Dick Hobbs (1998), 'Going Down the Glocal: The Local Context of Organised Crime', The Howard Journal, Special Issue on Organised Crime 37(4):pp. 407-22.

[40] Hobbs (2013), *ibid.*, p. 222

Petrus C. van Duyne asserts in this context that 'managing crime-money is in essence managing information risks posed by law'[41]; a position that fits with his contention that the way most criminal organisations involved in illegal product markets organise themselves "*is to a large extent determined by the nature of the commodity and the social potential of the market.*"[42] This is the foundation for the position (also espoused by Reuter, as a 'structural consequence' of illegality[43]) that illegal markets are not conducive to the development of large organisations, owing to the element of attendant risk.

Reviews of operational intelligence from the Scottish theatre, however, indicate the means exist whereby the inherent risk factors can be accommodated in ways which exploit the control benefits of organisations at the same time as distributing risk. That being the case, the 'risk avoidance' lens might be too narrowly focussed to encompass the reality of how these organisations function and, in particular, underestimate their ability to harvest the relevant profits in the manner of a reliable economic return.

Bonding within criminal markets

The need for security encourages traditional territorial bonding within relatively well defined areas, but the fundamental requirement for success in the modern class A drugs markets is the ability to forge trading alliances with other groups. Access to new skills and opportunities of fellow crime-entrepreneurs are obtained in return for allowing access to the own home market. The criminal marketplace thus evolves into a network of flexible alliances of '*mobile marauders*', as Block puts it.[44] The pooling of talents and opportunities supports a dynamic that promotes better ways of doing things, which may or may not involve higher levels of entrepreneurial sophistication.

Within this context the apparently inchoate nature of criminal markets at the sub wholesale level derives a meaning and purpose. The apparent anarchy of criminal structures at the street retail level serves to fulfil that level's function in the context of the whole process. It is at this level, and the local wholesale level,

---

[41] Petrus C. van Duyne, (2007) 'Criminal finances and state of the art. Case for concern?' in 'Crime Business and Crime Money in Europe – The dirty linen of illicit enterprise' Petrus C. van Duyne, Almir Maljevic, Maarten van Dijk, Klaus von Lampe, Jackie Harvey (eds.), Wolf Legal Publishers (WLP).

[42] Petrus C. van Duyne (2006), 'Counting clouds and measuring organised crime', ibid.

[43] Peter Reuter quoted in Tom Gash, *ibid.*, 2006, p.131.

[44] A. Block (1983), 'East Side-West Side: Organising Crime in New York, 1930-1950, Transaction, Newark NJ, quoted by Hobbs, p. 218.

where law enforcement intrusion is likeliest. The lower the level the more expendable are the operatives. At this level the knotty problem of gathering dirty cash off the streets and tendering it in a fashion that can be laundered or stashed is a practical problem that has to be worked out. That in turn implies a different level of organisation, requiring access to skills that are essentially professional in their nature.

The process at the local wholesale level has to accommodate a diffuse branch retail network and yet enable the orderly collection of cash, and subsequent transference into bankable profits or investment assets. There is a hierarchy of functions set up to serve these practical needs of the market. It follows that it is not just the horizontal relationships between organisations that need to be considered in considering issues of criminal organisation. entire functions are hired as a criminal business service to achieve the objectives of what is a vertically integrated process.

Figure 3 below is derived from reviews of intelligence relating to a number of Serious Organised Crime Groups ('SOCG - the terms adopted by the Serious Organised Crime Task Force established by the Scottish Government). The format enables the relevant risks to be managed in ways that are appropriate to the respective roles of operatives or players in the process. The distribution and retail side is managed in a way that enables separation between principal players and the commodity, and also between harvesting of the cash returns and the commodity. The cash return process incorporates the use of safe houses to collect the funds and the use of portals within legitimate businesses networks which essentially serve as 'black banks' for SOCG personnel. The businesses concerned are therefore operating at two distinct levels side by side: the legitimate trading level, and the criminal cash management level.

Figure 3
Model of the process relationship between drug supply and proceeds

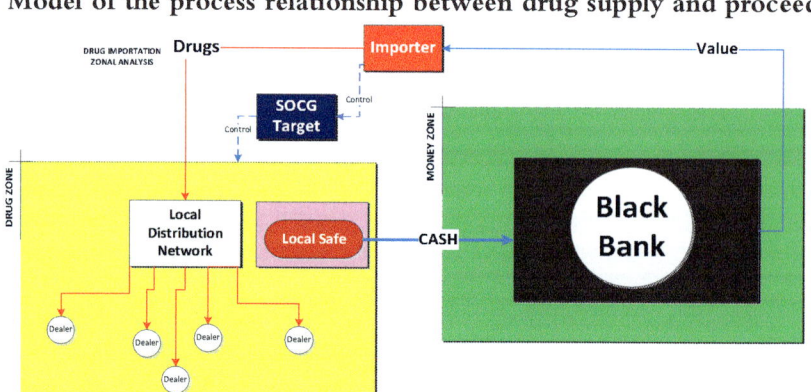

This set of arrangements is consistent with the theme of risk avoidance: it is shaped by the perceived preponderance of law enforcement to concentrate resources on the commodity rather than the money, but it also accommodates the need to treat the money in such a way that it can enter mainstream clearance systems in a way that is separated from the activity that generated it.

Risk avoidance on its own takes us only so far in explaining these arrangements. It is also about maximising economic returns and achieving them in forms that can be safely enjoyed. In the context of the Scottish theatre, the mapping process – which for nearly a decade now has provided the basis for the setting of law enforcement priorities in this field – is used to identify the service providing players as well as the customers that occupy the differentiated positions in the vertically integrated process. A deeper understanding of how these processes manage the degree of integration required between these players requires analysis of the distinctive capabilities that enable a player, or a group, to participate and maintain their role and position in these arrangements. The reasons why players deal with each other, in other words, and the way in which these relationships are conducted, need to be explored further.

The relevance of 'rhizomes'

The Scottish experience indicates that we appear to need something in addition to risk avoidance to explain the relative stability implied in the arrangements which oversee the relevant illegal markets. There is a need to also better understand the factors at play which give rise to the constituent parts of organised crime processes joining together and co-operating.

Daniel Tschofen's 2009 paper, "*Flow – The Organisation of Upper Level Drug Dealing*", [45] was founded on direct experience obtained from personal interaction with an Austrian group of drug traffickers. He concluded from this experience that the characteristics of the modern drug business were essentially nomadic and amorphous. The essential signifiers were identified as: independence, autonomy, decentralisation, informal, coalitional, reactive and an ability to shape-shift. There was, however, a unifying ethos which was heavily reliant on a code of secrecy, adherence to which was worn like a badge. The deployment

---

[45] Dr Daniel Tschofen 'Flow – The Organisation of Upper Level Drug Dealing' delivered to the sixth International Critical Management Conference in July 2009, University of Warwick, www2.warwick.ac.uk

of this nomadic culture over a competitive drug dealing territory rendered it in Tschofen's terms an "*open space that is indefinite and non-communicating.*"[46]

The conceptual framework Tschofen was using in this paper was borrowed from the critical theorists Gilles Deleuze and Felix Guattari in their seminal text, "*A Thousand Plateaus*".[47] A key distinction was drawn in that text between smooth and striated space. The nomads of Tschofen's crime group move through 'smooth space' unconfined by walls and enclosures, conceiving themselves not as an organised crime group but as a group of like-minded people under siege from the outside world. Within this space the nomads operated along relays which comprised the information networks and relationships that enabled maintenance of the criminal activity. They operated elemental modes of organisation such as the creation of a network of outstanding debts that in turn generated the necessary incentive to co-operate and bond. This set of relationships ultimately delivered mutual advantage in the form of the financial pay-off from the criminal activity.

The key concept used in 'A Thousand Plateaus', and exploited in the Tschofen paper, is the 'rhizome'. This comes into its own in considering the characteristics of decentralised networks, in particular the factors that bind them together: what it is that provides sufficient but not excessive cohesion to make them functional. The example used by Deleuze and Guattari to illustrate a rhizome was the wasp and the orchid: the orchid feeds the wasp that pollinates it. Two different species interact together to form a multiplicity, or a rhizome. The character of the rhizome is a step beyond the symbiotic element of the relationship, however: it extends to become a unity that is multiple in itself, able to connect any point in the system to any other point. How can this concept be adapted for practical effect?

Weizman[48] provides a vivid example of it being used in the context of defence. 'A Thousand Plateaus' became required reading for military officers in the Israeli Defence Force (IDF), inspiring them to think in terms of 'smoothing out space', when they were engaged in tackling the resistance of Palestinian liberation forces operating from labyrinthine urban environments – a heavily striated space in other words. What 'smoothing out space' meant in this context was the technique of 'moving through walls', destroying the streets by literally bulldozing them to the ground.

[46] Tschofen, *ibid*.
[47] Gilles Deleuze and Felix Guattari (1980), 'A Thousand Plateaus', Continuum, London.
[48] Eyal Weizman (2007,), 'Walking Through Walls', EIPCP, Vienna.

To Weizman, the value of Deleuze and Guattari concepts in military context was in how they showed that war can be conceived as 'a discourse between enemies'. There is an obvious parallel here with the establishment of specialist police forces set up to combat organised crime and the language used to justify them.[49] As noted by Holmes[50], Organised Crime is more able than these forces to operate over a smooth space (*i.e.* it is less restricted by borders) using networks which are essentially 'rhizomic' in nature. These characteristics are even more apparent in the development of criminal networks through cyberspace, but they are relevant to more traditional criminal markets too.[51] Organised crime manifests as a series of rhizomic networks able to operate across borders in ways that set significant challenges for law enforcement. It is able to operate over 'smooth space', whereas law enforcement, for most practical purposes, is condemned to negotiate the obstacles inherent in moving across striated space, represented by borders and different requirements set by different jurisdictions. This significant asymmetry can also be considered a key influence on how the organised crime processes are designed.

The concept would appear to be capable of extension to all organised crime relationships which rely on some degree of symbiosis *i.e.* all relationships which involve any form of trading activity. Each unit involved in a criminal business process has a characteristic or property that accounts for its interaction with another. The whole vista of organised crime entrepreneurial activity can therefore be conceived as the interaction of rhizomes across a smooth space. This set of characteristics, as Tschofen describes it, implies a competitive advantage over law enforcement that would seem difficult to eradicate so long as the nomadic disciplines are sustained.

Formulating a response

How can law enforcement respond to this? Contemporary organised crime, as currently experienced in the intelligence gathering functions of major law enforcement agencies, might lend support to a Hobbs' conception of it as a "*loose series of power relationships interacting seamlessly with both upper and underworlds and rooted in the class defined complexities or urban life and the subtleties of criminalisa-*

---

[49] National Crime Agency, National Strategic Assessment 2015, www.nationalcrimeagency.gov.uk

[50] Leslie Holmes (2016), 'Advanced Introduction to Organised Crime', Edward Elgar, p. 144.

[51] Marc Goodman (2015), 'Future Crimes', Transworld, London.

tions".[52] But the rhizome concept still implies there is a basis for identifying the factors or characteristics that provide the necessary cohesion to deliver a workable process however loose the relationship.

There is a force of cohesion, in other words, that criminal players themselves have to be aware of – otherwise they have no basis upon which to trade. The essential protection they require from externalities (either in the form of other criminal competition or law enforcement infiltration and action) implies the need for an organising discipline. This might be managed by consensus or diktat, or by a mixture of the two. But the intelligence dividend on offer from understanding the relevant power relationships that underpin that discipline suggests a basis for developing new initiatives of response.

Participation in criminal markets is a form of disclosure of the key characteristics that enable that participation. These characteristics are inevitably designed to enable consummation of a transaction that takes place within a business process. In a facile way, 'organisation' can be described in this context as a function of how the criminal business process is managed. All types of entity along Hagan's continuum or Smith's spectrum can be looked at this way, since all of the criminal models, however loose, require some kind of attachment to a business process to be able to survive.

Distinctive capabilities in the context of criminal markets

There is a conceptual framework that can be borrowed from business strategy analysis that may be helpful in this context. The base concept is that of competitive advantage, defined by Kay[53] as the ability to deploy *distinctive capabilities* in relevant markets. By determining the distinctive capabilities of a business process, or the structures used to exploit criminal business processes, the glue that holds them together can be analysed; the essential features of the cohesion that forms the rhizome can be identified and analysed.

A feature of organised crime, as it manifests across the central belt of Scotland, is the existence of a network of localised crime groups. These groups are dominant within their area of influence and appear able to resist infiltration into their principal markets from external organised crime groups. Assessing the

[52] J. Albini (1971), 'The American Mafia: Genesis of a Legend', Appleton-Century-Crofts, New York, quoted by Hobbs (2013), 226.

[53] John Kay (1993), 'Foundations of Corporate Success', Oxford.

typology of these local groups in terms of competitive advantage it is appears that their apparent local strength is derived from reputation and the control of local underground markets that such reputation enables.

The two identified distinctive capabilities of 'reputation' and 'strategic assets' comprise half of the quartet of such capabilities recognised by Kay as being the foundations for competitive advantage. They begin to provide an analytical framework for understanding why the organised crime groups that feature in the ranking lists of the Scottish Mapping process are on that list and why they are able to stay on it.

The first two distinctive capabilities – connected to local dominance – are augmented by the connections within the network fraternity that allows the organisation access to dominant supply channels for criminal commodities (not just class A drugs, but also illegal cigarettes and legal highs). The connections network also extends to specialist service providers that enable criminal profits to be secured. This network capability corresponds to the third distinctive capability termed by Kay as 'architecture', which relates to the network of contacts both criminal and legitimate which enable the organised crime group to function as a successful economic entity (successful in this context can be defined in terms of survival and continued influence as well as economic terms).

The most obvious way in which the value of the network existing between different organised crime groups across the central belt area manifests itself is in the collective way in which it addresses the practical problems of dirty money. The local organised crime group will typically be responsible for drug consignments issued to it for sale in their territory. They are obliged to settle the debt that comes with that commodity with the retail money earned. The collection and counting of the dirty money will typically occur on local territory, either through a series of sequenced safe houses or businesses that have been acquired to provide a legitimate screen behind which the key function of criminal cash management can be conducted 'in plain sight'. The objective of this process is to enable the money to be presented for delivery to network portals that insert the money in legitimate places.

This kind of 'architecture' is the distinctive capability that provides the link between the local and the national and international markets. On the theoretical level it is the capability that enables local dominance to be exploited in the context of developed criminal business processes. On the practical level it is the means by which criminal capital can be accumulated and deployed in a manner that has an increasing influence on markets and economies. Current experience in Scotland indicates that this is leading to participation by OCG associated businesses in an ever widening range of activities, limited only by imagination and the appetite for adventure of the principal criminal stakeholders rather than any limitation of capital. The mechanisms to transport cash are themselves up for hire; for example the exploitation of an extensive network of shell corporations to execute VAT carousel MTIC fraud by an organised crime group based in the south side of Glasgow were hired by a number of other Scottish organised crime networks to transform their criminal drugs profits into overseas funded investments in Scottish property assets.

The fourth distinctive capability identified by Kay is 'innovation'. At street level this quality equates to cleverness – a prized characteristic in criminal communities.[54] It also increasingly manifests as a collective cleverness as represented in criminal system and process design. Success is often a function of innovative ways of exploiting new opportunities in criminal markets (*e.g.* in the field of cybercrime, the exploitation of international migrated labour), the acquisition of pension assets by fraud (industrialised gambling coups) and then using the financial leverage of that success to exert increasing influence on legitimate markets (*e.g.* financial trading markets, sporting clubs and sponsorship, property and corporate investment).

A framework for analysis based on distinctive capability

The key issue is how law enforcement can adapt this thinking to practical effect. There have been a number of attempts. Project Sleipner[55] of the Royal Canadian Mounted Police was based on providing strategic intelligence analysts with a threat measurement technique for application to OCGs. The Police Scotland Mapping process is based on a matrix based scoring process based on perceptions of harm. The 2004 Vander Beken study[56] culminated in the development of a risk based methodology *"founded on the recognition that the analysis of organised crime will always depend upon imperfect information and resource limitation"*. The methodology of that study also involved a ranking of organised crime groups *"recast against the findings of an open source scan of licit and illicit markets"*. The end product included the provision a risk analysis of vulnerable sectors.[57]

---

54 Diego Gambetta (2009), 'Codes of the Underworld', Princeton University Press, New Jersey.
55 Project Sleipner, Royal Canadian Mounted Police; in Black, Vander Beken (ed) (2001), *ibid.*
56 Vander Beken (2004), *ibid.*
57 Black, Vander Beken (ed), *ibid.*

Table 1

The Jackal Matrix as a tool to identify distinctive capabilities of Organised Crime Groups

KP = KEY PARTNERS	KA = KEY ACTIVITIES	VA = VULNERABILITIES & ACTIONS	CR = CUSCUSTOMER RELATIONS	CS = CUSTOMER SEGMENTS
Accountants	Business Activity	Assessment of SOCG in terms of organisation, network or process	How do they look after their customers?	Customer markets serviced:
Lawyers	Criminal			
Surveyors			How do they keep them?	Legitimate
Logistics	Legitimate Criminal service to legitimate customer	▪ Distinctive capabilities exploited by SOCG		Criminal
Bankers			How do they get new customers?	Public Sector
Landlords		▪ Assessment of <u>Vulnerabilities</u>		
Suppliers	Criminal service to criminal customer			Private Individuals
Import/Export Agents	Legitimate service to criminal customer	▪ Actions based on options and opportunities suggested by <u>Vulnerabilities</u>		Foreign Criminal
Money Changers				Partners
Fund Managers	KR = KEY RESOURCES		CH = CUSCUSTOMER CHANNELS	
	Access to specialised expertise		Routes to market	
	commodity channels		How do they reach customer?	
	money laundering channels		Advertising and distribution channels	
CS = CASH RESOURCES – Sources of working capital; sources of loan finance; recycling of criminal funds; coinvestment of criminal partners		RS = REVENUE SPEND – Dividends; wages; cash exports; cash placements into the banking system; asset purchase; investment funds		

These methods in practice tend to provide analysis tools that function in batch process rather than real time. The reason is to do with the modes of training provided to intelligence analysts which does not equip them with basic business appraisal tools that would enable the identification of the core licit and illicit business processes identified in the intelligence and the placing of this knowledge into a context where it can identify practical options and opportunities for action. This is the approach currently being undertaken in Police Scotland through Project Jackal of which the matrix is presented above.

Project Jackal recognised that the ability to analyse was dependent upon the nature and quality of the intelligence being analysed. Developing a programme of education to encourage such capture was thus the foundation of the project. The next question was about how to use the intelligence. A matrix based on those used for business model generation was developed from business model generation science to identify the relevant distinctive capabilities of either a functioning criminal group or a criminal process (see Fig IV below). The objective of the matrix is to derive the distinctive capabilities that enable that group or process to function, in order that weaknesses can be identified and used as the basis for a programme of law enforcement action.

The distinctive capability profile that establishes organised crime groups position in a local class A drugs market relates is usually along the following lines:

- Strategic Asset – there is sufficient control over the local distribution networks that deal with the levels involved in handling; i.e. bulk retail and street retail, that they effectively decide who in that area is able to sell drugs in it.
- Reputation – The ability to maintain control is dependent upon downward looking reputation for enforcement and also upward looking reputation for delivering the settlement revenues required by wholesalers/importers.
- Architecture – the connections that enable access to the importer/wholesalers and the commodities they provide as well as the local knowledge embodied in the distribution networks
- Innovation – A capability determined by the abilities of the principles and a key factor in establishing the sustainability of positions in these processes.

The organisation as represented by process can therefore be seen as a collection of distinctive capabilities. These capabilities are brought to bear in such a way as to deliver the overall capability of being able to bring a degree of discipline and reliability to markets which because of their illegal nature are chaotic and dangerous. A retail process that is highly sensitive to environment is harnessed within a process that enables control, discipline and the harvesting of profits.

The only discipline available to stabilise these processes derives from their repeatability.[58] If you want to do business again, you make sure you perform this time. This encourages stability at the higher end of the process where the ticket prices for exchange are high, and is less important at the lower levels where they are low.

The conclusion to be drawn from Scottish experience, therefore is that the characteristics of the process are driven as much by the arrangements that must be in place in order to secure the financial settlement as the characteristics of the commodity. Apart from anything else, the financial settlement arrangements are used to deal in more than one commodity.

In the Scottish context, the notion that most laundering is self-laundering (Van Duyne 2006) tends to apply to lower level players. A noted characteristic in recent times has been the extent to which players at the wholesale level have been provided with methods of enrichment which mean that their personal financial footprint is almost non-existent. This type of facility has arisen from the development of savings and investment arrangements between SOCG players, even to the extent of providing remuneration in the form of quasi-pensions.

Approaching the process in this way enables the key 'personality' type features of organised crime to be brought into the analysis, which conventional data based studies fail to capture. Van Duyne[59] in 2006, considered these factors to be 'certainly important' but the stuff of 'pure speculation'. It is hard to see how any adequate assessment of these processes could fail to take them into account.

Conclusion

The approach outlined in this paper provides a practical framework for analysis to be developed for all contemporary depictions of what is treated as 'organised crime'. It can be used as a means of assessing a group's structure, but it can just as easily be used to assess a business process, thus acknowledging the characteristic of each crime process using different connections and different actors as the need and challenge arises. In doing so, one of the key advantages of this ap-

---

[58] Kellog Insight (2015) 'The Economics of the Illegal Drug Market', Kellog School of Management,
hhttps://insight.kellogg.northwestern.edu/article/the-economics-of-the-illegal-drug-market

[59] Van Duyne (2006, 177).

proach is in how it highlights the ways in which criminal business processes link into legitimate business processes and how relationships of dependence form between them.

The defining characteristics of the organised crime phenomenon witnessed as a business process are the deployment of distinctive capabilities that enable the capture and transmission of cash revenues derived from the criminal activity. The management of money is a process that requires access to expertise, and in Scotland's case, the intelligence points to a network of such expertise that is accessed by all established crime groups throughout the region. There is a network of criminal enablers who represent the key players providing the link ups and connections that enable the criminal business processes to function.

Organisation of this process is therefore the organisation that really matters in terms of deriving an understanding of the dynamics that apply in the conduct of the principal criminal markets. This understanding must clearly extend beyond what is perceived to happen at the low level customer facing parts of the process. The objectives of the participants at this level are of a different order to the controllers of the environments in which the activity takes place and the principal beneficiaries of the profits they generate. At these higher levels, the important functions are the maintenance of high end importer relationships, the maintenance of discipline within the distribution networks they control, and the achievement of secure and accessible profits. The Scottish experience indicates that specialist enablers able to deliver the services necessary to secure these profits can also become highly influential as mediators between different SOCGs.

The way crime is organised at this level is therefore a direct function of what arrangements and liaisons are necessary to enable the principal players to secure and enjoy the 'returns' from their industrialised criminal capabilities. This is the key dynamic in determining how modern criminal groups organise themselves; in accordance with what is necessary to service and prosper. For most practical purposes, what is necessary is what is required by the market. The market sets the challenge to be met by the business process. The business process provides a versatile and robust conception of what constitutes 'organised' in modern organised crime.

As mentioned earlier, Block (quoted by Hobbs)[60] describes the criminal market as being populated by alliances of "*mobile marauders in the urban landscape alert to institutional weaknesses in both legitimate and illegitimate spheres.*" This is not inconsistent with Varesian observations of organised crime groups continuing to be embedded in the communities where they forged their reputation such that

---

[60] Hobbs, *ibid.,* 217.

their ability to redeploy in alternative territories can rarely be achieved unless they are able to network.[61]

The fluid disorganised picture of organised crime painted by Hobbs cannot be considered as disembodied from the market processes in which they are bound to participate. You have to plug into it at some level if you wish to participate. The way in which you do that and are able to do that is your distinctive footprint which differentiates you but also identifies you as a participant. These base characteristics apply to nomadic groups as well as international drug cartels and can be used to devise meaningful programs to understand the key features of how they are able to operate and the related weaknesses that might be exploited to disrupt or contain them.

The contemporary organised crime group cannot flourish without access to the many linking arteries and processes that bind these groups to an efficiently international criminal economy. The organised crime group is therefore defined as much by the efficiency and reach of these connections as the traditional capabilities that enabled it to establish and maintain its influence in its local area. A proper conception of organised crime must also therefore take into account the existence of the 'service industry', identified through the 'architecture' distinctive capability, that is hired by organised crime clients to perform the many services that bring this international criminal economy into being. These are the facility providers that supply the essential suite of services required to transform criminal capital into a wealth resource that can be deployed in legitimate spheres.

The conception of organised crime that serves most practical use as a basis for developing effective counter strategies is therefore that offered by its consideration as a series of business processes. The inferences to be drawn from this are the need to understand such processes well enough to disrupt them. This is an international challenge for which current practices and traditions might not seem particularly suited. A core reason for this may be that law enforcement agencies feel ill equipped and fundamentally insecure to properly assess and deal with business processes. If that is the case then it is an area for priority and attention. Whether conceived as a local or international phenomenon, accumulations of criminal capital confer influence as well as wealth, in addition blueprints for others to use. There is value in paying attention to that.

There is a need, however, to develop further empirical evidence to underpin understanding of how criminal business processes work. There is a lack of relevant field knowledge, perhaps in part because law enforcement agencies draw a shroud over what they know because of its status as intelligence; perhaps

---

[61] Varese (2011), *ibid.*, quoted by Hobbs, 217.

in part because their state of knowledge is underdeveloped in respect of these business structures and processes. The reality of these processes are unlikely in any case to be adequately understood on the basis of published data alone. There is an obligation, therefore, on law enforcement to develop its capabilities in this area such that it is able to articulate more persuasively the realities of the criminal markets it is required to police, as well as developing means by which provision of empirical evidence for independent assessment can be improved. That is a prerequisite for resolving some of the obvious disconnects between practitioner experience and academic perceptions of what organised crime is that persist in the literature.

References

Abadinsky, H., *Organised Crime.* 7th ed., Thomson Wadsworth, Belmont CA, 2003

Albini, J., *The American Mafia: genesis of a legend.* Appleton-Century-Crofts, New York, 1971

Graebner Anderson, A., *The business of organised crime: A Cosa Nostra Family.* Hoover Institution Press, 1979; p 46

Bean, Ph., *Legalisation drugs – debates and dilemmas.* The Policy Press, London, 2010

Becker, G., *Crime and punishment: an economic approach*, The Journal of Political Economy 76, University of Chicago, Chicago, 1968

Black, T. Vander Beken (ed.), Reporting on organised crime: a shift from description to explanation', Maklu, Antwerp, 2001

Block, A., *East Side-West Side: organising crime in New York, 1930-1950*, Transaction, Newark NJ, 1983

Centre for Drug Misuse Research, Assessing the Scale and Impact of the Illicit Drug Market in Scotland, University of Glasgow, www.Scotland.gov.uk/socialresearch, 2009

Cevidalli, A., *Leveraging the multi – disciplinary approach to countering organised crime*, University of London, London, 2010

Deleuze, G. and F. Guattari, *A thousand plateaus*, Continuum, London, 1980

Dick, A.R., *When does organised crime pay? A transaction cost analysis*, International Review of Law and Economics 15, Elsevier B.V., Amsterdam, 1995

Duyne, P.C. van, Counting clouds and measuring organised crime. In P.C. van Duyne, A. Maljevic, M. van Dijk, K. von Lampe, J.L. Newell (eds.), *The organisation of crime for profit – Conduct law and measurement*. Wolf Legal Publishers (WLP), 2006

Duyne, P.C. van, The organisation of business crime. In The *Organisation of Crime for Profit – Conduct law and measurement*. ibid, 2006

Duyne, P.C. van and B. van der Vorm, From organised crime threat to nuisance control. In P.C. van Duyne *et al.*, *The relativity of wrong-doing*. Wolf Legal Publishers, WLP, 2015

Gambetta, D., *Codes of the underworld*. Princeton University Press, New Jersey, 2009

Gash, T., *Criminality - The truth why people do bad things*. Allen Lane, London, 2016

Goodman, M., *Future crimes*. Transworld, London, 2015

Gottschalk, P., *Criminal entrepreneurship*. Nova Science Publishers, New York, 2008

Hagan, F., The organised crime continuum. *Criminal Justice Review*, 8(2):52-57, 1983

Haller, M., Illegal enterprise: a theoretical and historical interpretation. *Criminology*, 1990, 28:2, pp 207-235

Hobbs, D., Going down the Glocal: The local context of organised crime. *The Howard Journal*, Special Issue on Organised Crime 37(4):pp. 407-22, 1998

Hobbs, D., Lush life – constructing organised crime in the UK. Oxford, 2013

Holmes, L., *Advanced introduction to organised crime*. Edward Elgar, 2016

The Independent (UK), (14 August 2007), 'Inside the biker gangs: the truth about guns, drugs and organised crime'

Kay, J., *Foundations of corporate success*. Oxford, 1993

Lavigne, Y., *Hell's Angels: Into the abyss*. Harper Collins, New York, p.246,1996

National Crime Agency, National Strategic Assessment 2015 www.nationalcrimeagency.gov.uk

Pearson, G., *The enforcer*. Black and White Publishing, Edinburgh, p.208., 2008

Robertson, R., Glocalisation: time-space and homogeneity-heterogeneity. In M. Featherstone, S. Lash and R. Robertson (eds.), *Global Modernities*. Sage, London, quoted by Hobbs p 220, 1995

Saviano,R., *Zero Zero Zero*. Allen Lane, London pp 189-193, 2015

Schilling, T.C., *Economic analysis of organised crime*. In President's Commission on Law Enforcement and Administration of Justice, '*Organised Crime*', US Government Printing Office, Washington DC, 1967

Scottish Government, 'Scotland's Serious Organised Crime Strategy www.gov.scot/Resource/0047/00479632.pdf, 2015

Sher, J. and W. Marsden, *Angels of death: inside the biker gangs global crime empire.* Carroll & Graf, New York, 2006

Simon, H., Organisations and markets. *Journal of Economic Perspectives*, Vol 5 AEA, Pittsburgh PA, pp 25-44, 1991

Smith, D.C., Paragons, pariahs and pirates: a spectrum-based theory of enterprise. *Crime & Delinquency*, Vol 26, No. 3, 1980

Tschofen, D., Flow, The organisation of upper level drug dealing. Delivered to the sixth International, 2009 Critical Management Conference in July 2009, University of Warwick, ww2.warwick.ac.uk, 2009

UN Office on Drugs and Crime, World Drug Report, 2015

Vander Beken, Tom, Risky business: A risk-based methodology to measure organised crime. *Crime. Law & Social Change*, 41, pp 471-516, 2004

Varese, F., *Mafias on the move.* Princeton, New Jersey, 2011

von Lampe, K., Organised crime: analyzing illegal activities, criminal structures and Extra-legal Governance' pp356-360, 2016

von Lampe, K., *The use of models in the study of organised crime.* Papers presented at the 2003 conference of the European Consortium for Political Research (SCPR), Marburg, Germany, 2003

Weizman, E., *Walking Through Walls.* EIPCP, Vienna, 2007

Organised crime and cybercrime in Romania

Radu Nicolae[1]

Introduction

There had been an increase in the number of cyber attacks originating from Romania reaching media headlines. At the same time, Romania still lacks independent criminological research on cybercrime. While the criminal justice system in Romania pursues more and more cases of cybercrimes, new criminal activities such as ransomware, for instance, are a reality that is acknowledged but not combated with commensurate means. This is not only the case in Romania as cybercriminals enjoy structural advantages against law enforcement: many incidents are not reported; criminals have access to knowledge and expertise of a wider community on the Internet; criminals are specialised in using specific tools while law enforcement lacks the experience or knowledge for all specific types of attacks; criminals act across borders while law enforcement have limited jurisdiction; cybercrimes are regarded by the justice system more as 'white-collar crimes' and receive lenient sentences.[2] Also, complaints about inadequate law enforcement resources are heard in most countries[3]. Given the wide diversity of types of cybercrime (or cyber related crime) [4], the imprecise delineation

---

[2] SANS Institute, An Uneven Playing Field: The Advantages of the Cyber Criminal vs. Law Enforcement-and Some Practical Suggestions (white paper), 2002
https://www.sans.org/reading-room/whitepapers/legal/uneven-playing-field-advantages-cyber-criminal-vs-law-enforcement-and-practica-115

[3] USA: "*law enforcement officials lack the manpower, training, technical resources and political support necessary*"
(http://www.cio.com/article/2402264/security0/why-law-enforcement-can-t-stop-hackers.html); France:
http://en.rfi.fr/economy/20131003-france-has-highest-cybercrime-rate-europe;
UK: https://krebsonsecurity.com/2016/07/cybercrime-overtakes-traditional-crime-in-uk/

[4] Some types of cybercrime are done exclusively online (ex. phishing) while other require also 'real world' structures and activities (ex. skimming).

of its meaning and the emergence of new technologies it is not easy to decide how much and in what type of law enforcement capacities to invest.

Recent interference by hackers (allegedly masterminded by the Kremlin) in the US presidential election campaign has raised the awareness of the deficiencies in the defence against cyberattacks.

In this area of crime, Romania has benefited by intensive cooperation and collaboration with Western law enforcement agencies: exchange of information with over 50 countries, institutional cooperation with FBI since 2000s, prosecutors trained by private sector entities like eBay (Kshetri, 2010: 65-66). Starting with primitive methods of attacks in 1998, Romanian scammers and hackers have become more and more sophisticated over the years (Wittkop, 2016: 164).

According to the literature (Hill and Marion, 2016: 96; Wittkop, 2016) cybercrime in Romania has a transnational character and it is conducted by organised crime groups specialising in information and communications technologies. Groups that were previously disbanded or individuals convicted for cybercrimes, tend to regroup and pursue similar activities. Like the international fraudsters described two decades earlier by Van Duyne (1996), they are like a flock of crows: opportunistically coming together, scattering if felt endangered, and coming together again in adapted composition.

Cybercrime and cybersecurity literature contains little mention of the usual 'instruments' of serious or organised crime, such as corruption and physical violence.[5] Several reasons may be advanced why these 'instruments' are less researched by scholars or less needed by cybercriminals. First, the concept of violence in the context of cyber-attacks is less understood.[6] Second, corruption and physical violence are more related to the control of a real world territory while cybercriminals are ubiquitous. Then, cybercriminals are very mobile and part of loose networks, with less intense relationships and less control, thus less opportunity or reasons for physical violence. Nevertheless, we have to see if these reasons are backed by data.

This chapter aims to address the cybercrime challenge in Romania and research the types of offenders and *modi operandi* of organised crime groups (OCGs) involved in cybercrimes. Besides the 'cold' statistics, questions will be addressed regarding the profile of individuals involved, cross-border implications, usage (or not) of corruption and physical violence, and the business mod-

---

[5]   Child pornography may be an exception as it is generally classified as a potentially violent crime – Shinder (2002).

[6]   A disscution on what is violence in the context of cybercrime is advanced by Gillespie (2015).

els developed by cybercriminals. I will analyse criminal cases in which the cybercrime related offences have been determined in final judgements. In addition the chapter considers the concerns by stakeholders.

Overview of main organised-crime related offences indicted

Romania is one of the EU countries with the highest rates of corruption and organised crime (Gounev and Bezlov, 2010: 150). In the context of the European integration and the use of information and communications technologies, Romanian crime groups expanded into new areas and joined international crime structures (Rusev *et al.*, 2016: 5). Academic studies on organised crime in Romania are mainly available in Romanian language and are written by scholars affiliated to police or national security universities.[7] Issues related to organised crime in Romania are mentioned in different international studies which focus on specific crimes[8] or in general organised crime compendiums.[9] In this chapter we will focus on cybercrime, whether direct or related to organised crime.

Before beginning to address cybercrime in the context of organised crime in Romania, a short overview of legislation, institutional structures and statistics is needed.

In the Romanian legislation, an organised criminal group is defined as "*a structured group formed of three or more persons that exists for a period of time and acts in a coordinated manner for the purpose of committing one or more offences*".[10] The Romanian Criminal code also defines terms such as computer system, computer data and electronic payment instruments.[11] Computer-related offences are sanctioned by the Criminal code.[12] Romania is part of the Convention on Cybercrime of the Council of Europe and has established in 2014 the Cybercrime

---

[7] Search of the phrase "*crimă organizată*" on google Scholar finds studies conducted by scholars affiliated to Romanian Police, Alexandru Ioan Cuza University - Police Academy, Ministry of Internal Affairs or National Prosecutors Office.

[8] For instance Corrin (2005) on human trafficking.

[9] Paoli (2014).

[10] Criminal Code, art. 367, alin. 6

[11] Criminal Code, art. 180 and 181

[12] Criminal Code, Title II, Chapter IV - Fraud committed through computer systems and electronic payment instruments: art. 249 - Computer Fraud, Art 250 - Fraudulent financial transactions, Article 251 - Accepting fraudulent transactions, Article 252 - Sanctions for attempt.

Programme Office (C-PROC) to assist countries worldwide in responding to cybercrimes on the basis of the standards of the Convention.

The main institution having the legal mandate to investigate and prosecute organised crime offences in Romania is the Directorate for Investigating Organised Crime and Terrorism (DIICOT). The Directorate is an autonomous structure (having legal status and its own budget) within the Prosecutor's Office attached to the High Court of Cassation and Justice (PICCJ). DIICOT has the mandate to investigate: human trafficking; drug trafficking; deprivation of liberty; harassment; cybercrime; counterfeiting of money; stamps or other valuables; and smuggling.

Official statistics on the prosecution of organised crime offences compiled for the last five years is organised below with a view on the number of persons prosecuted by type of crime (Figure 1), and number of files sent to the Courts by type of crime (Figure 2). Both types of database organisations have their limitations in grasping trends in prosecuting.

First, although the Romanian criminal code sanctions *per se* the crime of participating in an organised crime group, each of such files is related to a more specific crime and not to a 'mafia type' organisation. So, even though the statistics give the impression that this offence is the most relevant and the prosecution target OCGs, while in fact all the numbers in this category may be allocated to the listed underlying offences (many of which are cybercrimes).

Second, as it will be later emphasisedl, the numbers do not reflect in any way the number of groups or persons involved in organised crime because the same perpetrator may appear in different files for different crimes.

Considering these limitations, the statistics report an increase prosecution of cybercrimes, with the number of files sent to Courts having doubled in the span of five years (Figure 1). If taking into consideration all the cybercrime files registered and investigated by the prosecution service[13], not only those indicted, in the period 2010-2015, the number of cybercrime cases saw a threefold increase, from 2.210 files in 2010 to 6.309 files in 2015.[14]

---

[13] Prosecution service in Romania has powers to investigate all crimes; few of the files open being finalized with indictment/prosecution.

[14] DIICOT 2015 report, page 24.

Figure 1

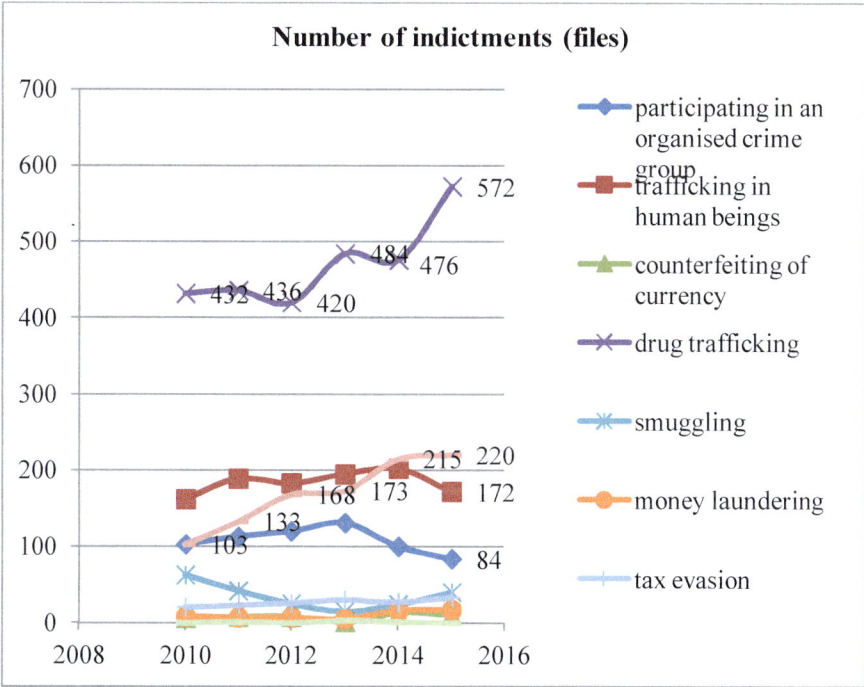

Figure 1: Main crime markets in the last 5 years by no. of indictments (data compiled from DIICOT annual reports)

Also the number of persons prosecuted for cybercrime increased by 100 individuals compared to five years ago (Figure 2). However, if we look only at the number of individuals prosecuted (Figure 2), cybercrime is not even in the top four offence categories, but rated according to the number of indictments (Figure 1), it is on the second place after drug trafficking. Nevertheless, such a rating must be interpreted cautiously. Most of the drug indictments involve low level dealers, couriers and users/addicts (especially of Cannabis). The assets recovered from these cases are negligible compared with those recovered from corruption, for instance. Compared to the level of crime for profit[15], it seems that, at least from a prosecution point of view, cybercrime is most challenging issue in Romania, and this is also true from a criminological point of view.

---

[15]   Centre for Legal Resources, 2015.

Figure 2
Main crime markets in the last 5 years
by no. of persons prosecuted

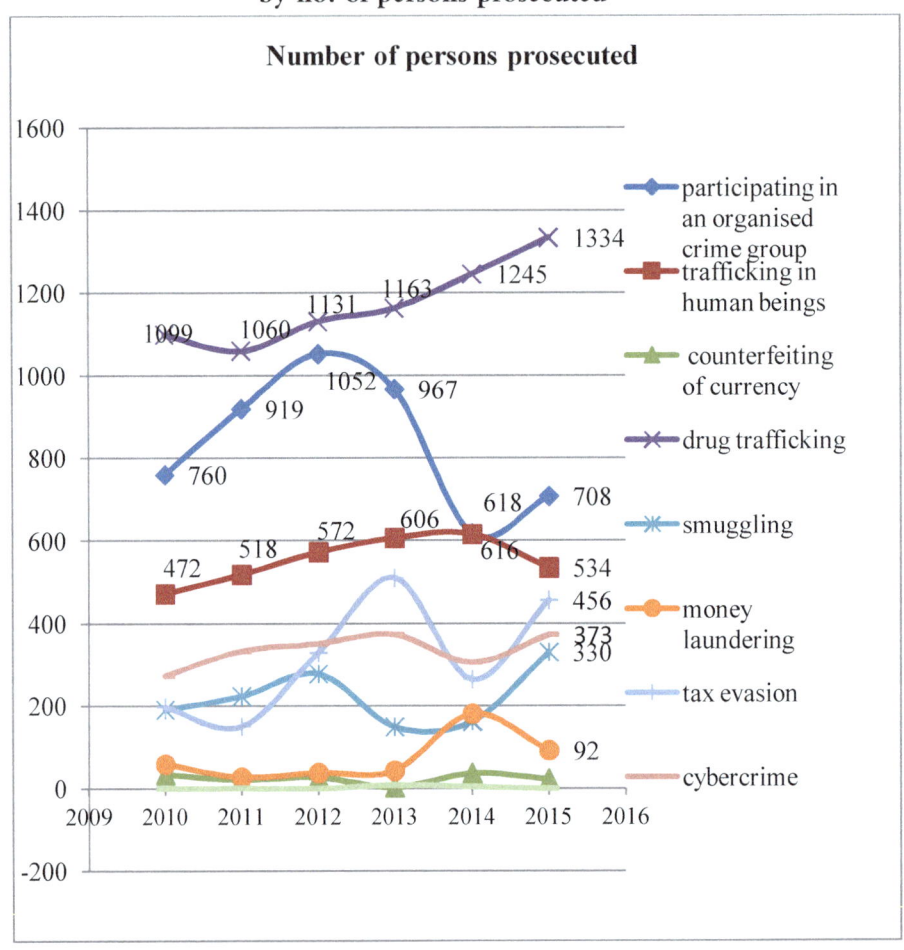

Data compiled from DIICOT annual reports.

Methodology

In order to map the cybercrime characteristics in Romania, I drew on 30 case studies collected from final court decisions issued in the period 2014-2016. The court decisions were selected from Rolii Foundation database.[16] In the initial

---

[16] The database was launched in December 2015 and it contains the full anonymised text of all court decisions issued in Romania. The database is managed and updated by Rolii - Romanian Legal Information Institute which was established as a

search a total number of 509 court decisions were taken into consideration. After removing false positives, including decisions related to pre-emptive arrests and lower courts decisions[17], 50 court decisions were further analysed. Of these, decisions related to child pornography or hate-crimes were eliminated so that in the end 30 cases were included in the final analysis, more specifically 3 cases relating to court decisions taken in 2016, 19 cases with decisions taken in 2015 and eight cases with decisions dating back to 2014. The information gleaned from the court files is put in context and supplemented with other data from official statistics and reports.

Nevertheless, the research has several limitations. In the analysed final court decisions the cybercrime activities of OCGs are documented only partially. So, the research reflects only what was established in court documents. Thus, the cybercrime activities of OCGs may in reality be more diverse. The court files were hard to trace and follow through the justice system because a criminal group is not treated only in one court case. In practice, different activities of the same group of individuals are treated in separate judicial files or individuals from the same criminal group figure in different files: cases can be split or conversely fused into one case. Thus judicial statistics based on the number of files or the number of perpetrators may be misleading.

Cybercrime: concerns and typologies

The European Commission (2013) defines cybercrime as "*a broad range of different criminal activities where computers and information systems are involved either as a primary tool or as a primary target. Cybercrime comprises traditional offences (e.g. fraud, forgery, and identity theft), content-related offences (e.g. on-line distribution of child pornography or incitement to racial hatred) and offences unique to computers and information systems (e.g. attacks against information systems, denial of service and malware)*".

In order to fight against organised crime, the European Union has set up a four-year policy cycle which includes a serious and organised crime threat as-

---

private foundation having as founders Superior Council of Magistracy, Wolters Kluwer Romania, National Institute of Magistracy, National Union of Bars in Romania, National Institute of Professional Training of Lawyers, National Union of Public Notaries in Romania, Romanian Notarial Institute and a natural person.

[17] Some of these decisions were removed because they referred either to the cases already taking into consideration or to controversial cases sent by upper courts for retrial. The rest were removed from the analysis because they may be appealed and an upper court may decide cassation. Thus, there is a probability that the facts established by the lower courts to prove inaccurate in the end.

sessment (SOCTA) and a European multidisciplinary platform against criminal threats (EMPACT). One of the nine EMPACT priority crime areas is cybercrime. SOCTA 2013 finds that cybercrime is linked primarily to financial fraud offences, key threats being infecting devices with malicious software, child sexual exploitation and card payment fraud. In this policy framework, Europol produces yearly the Internet Organised Crime Threat Assessment (IOCTA). IOCTA 2016 reports on the new developments in cybercrimes, the top listed being: cryptoware (encrypting ransomware), card fraud, including contactless cards and targeted phishing. Law enforcement and justice systems have to face a rapidly changing landscape in cybercrime as criminals constantly adapt to emerging technologies.

Regarding the situation in Romania, concerns have been raised internationally about the level of cybercrime as Romanians have a high level of IT expertise.[18] The U.S. Embassy in Bucharest has estimated that Romanian cybercriminals steal $1 billion every year by hacking American computers as 80% of the cyberattacks originating from Romania target US citizens and companies.[19] The media made a small Romanian town named Râmnicu-Vâlcea famous by calling it "Hacker-Ville," or "Cybercrime Central," or "The Most Dangerous Town on the Internet".[20] Federico Varese (2015) emphasises the local ties of the OCGs involved in cybercrimes and the local factors that facilitate the growth of cybercrime in Romania: corruption; few economic opportunities; weak law enforcement and a particularistic culture. He finds the following characteristics of Romanian cybercriminals: strict division of labour, leaders are criminal minds that recruit young computer enthusiasts, local protection from politics and police, low-level intermediaries used for most exposed activities.

Choo (2008) proposes three types of groups developing illegal activities in the cyberspace:

1. traditional organised criminal groups (OCGs) that use ICT to enhance their regular criminal activities conducted in the 'real world';
2. OCGs which operate exclusively online[21] and

---

[18] For the reasons explained by Varese (2015).

[19] Vlad Odobescu, USA TODAY - U.S. data thefts turn spotlight on Romania, 13-01-2014
http://www.usatoday.com/story/news/world/2014/01/13/credit-card-hacking-romania/4456491/

[20] Lorenzo Franceschi-Bicchierai, Inside 'Hackerville', Romania's Infamous Cyber Crime Hub, 17.06.2015 / http://motherboard.vice.com/read/inside-hackerville-romanias-infamous-cyber-crime-hub

[21] Choo (2008) exemplifies with a group formed by individuals who had never met in person and knew each other only online, p. 277.

3. ideologically and politically motivated individuals which use ICT to facilitate their objectives[22] (hacktivists groups).

In the case studies developed, all three instances have been identified but also a fourth category emerged, OCGs that have cybercrime as core activity but large parts of operations are done offline – ex. ATM fraud.

There are numerous distinctions regarding organised cybercrime groups based on criteria such as level of cooperation between individuals, the degree of activities routed in the cyberspace, the ways of using cyberspace or the level of interactions of the members in the real world.[23]

Focusing on the relational patterns between criminals and their victims, von Lampe (2016) classifies organised crime activities in three main categories:
1. market-based crimes (those concerning voluntary transactions, provision of illegal goods or services by suppliers to customers, the victims being somehow remote),
2. predatory crimes (concerning transfer of resources by force, perpetrator threatening the victim) and
3. illegal-governance crimes (concerning government resembling activities by crime syndicates).

In connection with these organised crime activities, von Lampe (2016) defines three types of organised crime structures not necessarily mutually exclusive:
1. entrepreneurial (markets, networks or illegal firms),
2. associational (social structures such as outlaw gangs or mafia type) and
3. quasi-governmental structures.

According with this theoretical perspective, markets tend to be the predominant coordinating mechanism in the cyberspace, cybercrime being a hybrid form of market-based and predatory crime. At the same time, online forums foster associational criminal structures (online communities of cybercriminals) while forums administrators take the task of governance in cyberspace underworld.[24]

---

[22] Such an example may be the group *Anonymous* - David Kushner, The Masked Avengers. How Anonymous incited online vigilantism from Tunisia to Ferguson, 2014,
http://www.newyorker.com/magazine/2014/09/08/masked-avengers
[23] Von Lampe (2016), p. 325 gives a brief account of all these distinctions.
[24] Von Lampe (2016), p. 332.

Findings

The analytical distinctions above prove relevant when applied to the 30 analised organised crime groups in Romania. Thus, following Choo's (2008) distinctions, two groups may be considered 'traditional' organised criminal groups engaged also in cybercrime (cases no. 10 and 15), 27 groups may be considered organised cybercrime groups, and one case refers to a member of a 'hacktivist' group (case no. 2). Although, there is only one case in the sample of ideology motivated hacking, the potential threats of such activities cannot be underestimated. Romania became famous because the Romanian hacker named *Guccifer* released several emails addressed to the Secretary of Clinton in 2013[25] exposing the existence of Clinton's private email accounts. As an irony or a threat, it seems that Russian military intelligence used the so called *Guccifer 2.0* persona to release data obtained in cyberattacks in order to influence 2016 US presidential election.[26]

Regarding the analytical distinctions proposed by von Lampe (2016), almost all groups display entrepreneurial criminal structures, while in one case an associational structure, Anonymous Romania, is on focus. Except illegal activities in *case no. 2*, all the activities analysed may be considered market-based and predatory crimes. As *cases no. 21* and *27* highlight, cybercriminals act on a market and offer stolen bank data for sale or buy it through the Internet.

Based on analyse, three main predatory cybercrimes seem mostly punished by the justice system in Romania:

- Data theft through email scams – *phishing (*5 cases – no. 1, 8, 13, 14, 21*)*;
- Card fraud through – *skimming (*23 cases – no. 3, 4, 6-12, 15-18, 20, 22-30*)*;
- Shopping and auction fraud (3 cases – no. 1, 19 and 22).

In the jurisprudence cases related to data-stealing / ransomware could not be identified although it appears to be a growing problem.[27] According to a report issued by the cyber-security company, Symantec, in 2016[28] *"the perfection of the ransomware business model has created a gold-rush mentality among attackers, as growing numbers seek to cash in. Infection numbers are trending upwards, with the number of new ransomware families discovered annually reaching an all-time high of 100 in 2015. Today, the average ransom demanded by attackers has jumped to $679"*. An expert

---

25 https://www.rt.com/news/362417-hacker-guccifer-clinton-romania/
26 Intelligence Community Assessment, 2017 report available online: https://www.dni.gov/files/documents/ICA_2017_01.pdf
27 Interview with an expert from an IT company in Romania.
28 Symantec, 2016, p. 3. Symantec Corp. is global software and cybersecurity company, established in 1982. Symantec's well-known technology is Norton™ brand.

from an IT company in Romania, who was interviewed for this research, suggested that Romanian businesses have also been victimised by ransom ware.

Group profile

Each grouped analysed has its own peculiarities: context of establishment and profile of the members. Based on the nationalities of the perpetrators, three types of groups may be identified: *local groups* (formed by Romanians only), *foreign groups* (formed by individuals of other nationalities) and *mixed groups* (Romanians and other nationalities). Groups also differ on level of structuring and membership or the dimension of online vs. 'real world' activities. On one end this dimension there are groups acting almost exclusively online (case no. 21) and on the other end we have groups acting mainly in the 'real world' (case no. 7).

Local groups: there are two main subcategories: groups that have local ties and reduced mobility in the real world and extremely mobile groups that act primary abroad. From the first subcategory, cases 1 and 7 are detailed below.

In the *case no. 1*, the group was established in 2005 in Bucharest, having also members in Galati city. The members of the group originally met through Internet communication channels such as Yahoo Messenger, Skype and mIRC, then got to know each other personally and started working together to organize fake auctions on eBay. The group was structured having a *command level* acting online and an offline *implementation* level, the members of the offline team being called *arrows*. The personal data of the *arrows* were used to build the profiles of the eBay sellers so that the victims were to send the money in the name of the *arrow*. The group actions were supported by Western Union employees who were bribed in order to fill-in the forms with inconsistent data about the identity of the persons (*arrows*) receiving money. The group was disbanded in 2011. During this period, the criminal group defrauded more than 600 victims in the USA, Canada, Australia and Western Europe, causing proven damages amounting to over $ 750.000.

In *case no. 7*, the crime group was composed of nine members, all from Romania (Bucharest and Ploieşti), age 20 to 50 years old. The group was active during 2012, mainly in Romania, the activities being skimming, cash-trapping, and forking.

For local groups that are active abroad, *cases no. 8, 10, 15-18, 23-27* are relevant. In *case no. 8*, the group was formed by 8 individuals from Romania. The group was active in the period 2010-2011. Some of the members were specialised in assembling and installing abroad skimming devices on ATMs and phishing in order to capture data from bank cards, other were specialised in withdrawing cash using cloned bank cards. In *case no. 10*, a similar pattern was used: the group was also established and based in Romania but the activities were undertaken abroad in cooperation with other criminal networks.

Another peculiarity of some local groups is that the perpetrators involve their family members (spouses or brothers and sisters) in illicit activities and put them to execute low-level assignments – *cases no. 14* and *21*.

Foreign groups: different groups in the sample were composed of Bulgarian citizens (*cases no. 3, 4, 6* and *29*). In all these cases the Romanian authorities were unable to find the links in Bulgaria and only the persons caught red-handed in Romania were prosecuted. In case no.2, two Bulgarian citizens were caught installing skimming devices in Constanţa. Although only these members faced criminal charges in Romania, it is reasonable to assume that the group had several other higher profile members in Bulgaria. In *case no. 4*, the group was composed of five Bulgarian citizens in their 30s and it was specialised in ATM skimming. Two of the group members had been previously caught by police using skimming devices. Data copying at ATM's was followed by fraudulent cash withdrawals from banks in Indonesia, Peru and the USA. The group was visiting Bucharest for short periods of time in order to install skimming devices. They had a violent way of reaction and physically strongly resisted their arrest by the police officers. The police found in their possession falsified bank cards issued by a bank in Ukraine.   In *case no. 6*, two Bulgarian citizens in their 20s were caught installing skimming devices on 7 ATMs in Cluj-Napoca in 2015. As in the *case no.2*, it is reasonable to presume that they were not acting alone and they were part of a larger structured network.

In the sample of cases researched, there is only one case regarding perpetrators having different nationalities (*case no. 25*). In this case, a Dutch citizen recruited, transported and trained criminals from Romania in order to conduct skimming activities in the Netherlands. The Dutch leader could not be identified by law enforcement.

Most of the groups analysed had cybercrimes as the sole activity (see Annex). Nevertheless, in two cases, the group's main criminal activity was burglary (*case no. 15*) and drug trafficking (*case no. 10*).

According to the information available from the verdicts, there are only two cases (*cases no.1* and *28*) in which corruption was involved. In the first case, the perpetrators bribed the Western Union employees and in the second case, public servants received bribe in exchange for personal data. In a single case (*case no. 19*) an official, employee of the intelligence services is mentioned as involved in the criminal network. Another separate case (*case no. 2*) reflects ideological motives for the cyberattack.

Modi operandi

Based on the sample of cases, depending on the main type of cybercrime pursued by the crime group, three types of business models may be discerned: online auctions, phishing and skimming.

The first type of business model is focused on selling non-existent goods on e-commerce websites. In *case no. 1*, group members posted fictitious online auctions for goods at below market prices on e-commerce websites (especially eBay, Amazon, Craiglist, Alibaba and Secundamano), managing the communication with potential victims and collecting the cash through low level members acting offline (*arrows*). In order to secure a good online profile, the command level group created or bought false registration pages on eBay or Paypal websites, used '*phishing*' to extract authentication information from legitimate e-commerce users, acquired databases of user names and passwords of legitimate users of e-commerce portals, used predefined texts in foreign languages with which they contacted and misled victims and used pictures in digital format of fictional products offered for sale (mobile phones, motorcycles, laptops, *etc.*). In a typical situation, a potential buyer asking about an auction is persuaded by email to negotiate directly the sale of goods. Thus, it begins an exchange of emails on the selling price of goods, their performance, guarantees, ways of delivery and payment of the price, finally settling the delivery of goods and payment by Western Union or MoneyGram money transfer system. Later, criminal group members send messages to the purchasers containing falsified electronic documents such as delivery of goods statements, creating the misconception that such documents were issued by the e-commerce websites guarantying the accuracy of online transactions. Messages are dispatched apparently from e-commerce websites but in reality they are created by the criminal group members and sent from dedicated servers using the same name as the name of the e-commerce website. In these messages prospective buyers are asked to pay for the goods via Western Union money transfer service. Potential buyers are assured that in the case of delivery failure they will be fully compensated by e-ecommerce websites, falsely stating that guarantee deposits are in place. Following these assurances, the buyer sends the money through money transfer services. A command group member informs the *arrow* about the name of the buyer (victim) and the reference number of the transaction.[29] She fills-in the

---

[29] For instance: MTCN - Money Transfer Control Number.

Western Union or MoneyGram form, collects the money, pays the bribe to the Western Union employee, retains the agreed part of the money for herself and gives the rest to the command member. A similar business model was employed in *cases no. 19* and *22*.

The second type of business model is focused on copying data from bank cards at ATMs and cloning them in order to extract cash or buy online. In *cases no. 3 and 4*, the perpetrators used "skimmer" type devices to copy and store data in order to falsify electronic payment instruments (bank cards). During 2014, the group from *case no.3* installed "skimmer" type devices on 30 ATMs in Constanța, a major economic centre at the seaside, near Bulgarian border. During 2011, members of the group from case no.9 travelled abroad (Finland and Germany) to install skimming devices on ATMs and obtain confidential bank data (copying data from the magnetic stripe and capturing the PIN code). The data were rewritten on blank cards, money being withdrawn abroad (from Jordan, Colombia, Japan, Mexico, United States) and then divided among group members (using Western Union). Only in Germany, did the police register a damage of € 125.000. Damage figures in other affected countries are unknown. The group from *case no. 10* also acted abroad installing skimming devices in different European countries and withdrawing the cash in Latin America (Colombia, Mexico, Venezuela). The same modus operandi was employed by the groups from *cases no. 6, 7, 11-12, 15-18, 23-27*, and *28-30*.

A third type of business model involves phishing for bank data using spam emails. In the *case no. 8*, the criminal group had two ways of obtaining bank account data: skimming and phishing. In the first instance, some group members assembled and installed skimming devices on ATMs in Australia. They passed the data by email to other group members that imprinted the data from the compromised bank cards on blank magnetic cards. They used the cloned cards to withdraw in less than four months more than 165.000 of Australian dollars in cash from ATMs in Australia, Malaysia and United Kingdom. In the second instance, one of the group members built software able to send thousands of emails simultaneously to the email addresses of a multitude of citizens, especially the UK, containing links to a fake version of the Internet website that appeared to belong to HM Revenue & Customs (UK website that collects and administers taxes). In this way, the group obtained and used personal information and card numbers of more than 360 UK citizens. Mostly, the data were used in fraudulent Internet transactions, with a total damage of 20.000 euros being identified.

The same modus operandi can be identified in the *case no.13*. The group was divided into a command group and an implementation group. The command group created false web pages resembling the webpages of different banks and extracted an impressive number of confidential data from Romanian and foreign citizens (name, address, credit card number, e-mail, bank card CVV number, date of validity, internet banking passwords, etc.). The data were thoroughly inspected, distributed among group members and used to carry out payments using services such as Western Union or on-line purchases of goods / services, payment of invoices, purchase of rechargeable cards or goods (clothing, electronics, jewellery, watches, etc.) from on-line retailers, especially outside the borders of Romania.

In *case no.14*, the perpetrators also used phishing. Using specialized software the group send e-mails that appeared to be sent by banks in which users were notified that there was an error with their online account and must fill in identification data about their cards and account. The card data were used in Austria to buy goods that were resold in Romania. Also, the card data were used for online purchases. A similar method was employed in *case no. 21*.

Besides these three main *modi operandi*, several cases display other creative methods for using cyberspace to obtain quick but illegal profits.

In the *case no. 5*, the criminal group behind could not be identified due to the complex transnational links. The group acted through a Romanian intermediary. He was involved in an affair with an employee of a Romanian company and asked her to install against company regulations on her office computer the application TeamViewer and leave the computer open during weekend. Immediately after, using the TeamViewer application, unidentified persons accessed the company's computer system[30] without right and initiated unauthorized transfers of money via MoneyGram, being transferred € 289.922. The money was transferred in the names of different Romanian citizens whose personal data were stolen, while none of the persons involved were aware of such transfers. The TeamViewer application was accessed from an IP belonging to an USA Internet service provider. According to the response from the USA provider the IP address is administered by another customer of the company from UK, London. The checks led to a certain natural person who could not be identified by UK authorities.

In the *case no. 7*, the group used three methods to extract approximately 70.000 euros in cash: *skimming, cash trapping* and *forking*. After getting data from *skimming* devices, blank cards were imprinted and used for cash withdrawals. The second method involved plugging a metallic device in the money hatch of the A.T.M. The device was unnoticeable from the outside after being placed inside. Once an order was given to withdraw from the card a sum of money by

---

[30] Delta Works application.

an unaware user, the ATM automatically starts to expel normal banknotes but money remained stranded in the A.T.M., trapped in the device previously placed by the criminals. The operation appears to have been executed, but the banknotes remained trapped until the criminals took the device out along with the money. The third method involved buying valid bank cards from different persons. Those persons were instructed to declare the cards lost after couple of days. The criminals placed in the ATM the valid card after previously feeding it with more than 1.000 US dollars. After typing the valid PIN code and ordering a cash withdrawal, usually a small amount of money, during the release of this amount, the criminals placed a device resembling forks on slot. While the device was inside, the perpetrators ordered cash withdrawal at maximum amount allowed by the bank. While the ATM prepared the amount of money, they cancelled the transaction, while the requested amount remaining physically locked into the slot. The money was withdrawn by forcing ATM's slot but because of the cancellation the money remained also in the account of the cardholder.

In *case no. 20*, the perpetrators were specialized in manufacturing hardware and software components of skimming equipment which they sold to other crime groups.

Operational mobility

All these models of crime require resources for recruiting, training and organising the group members: buying equipment, shipping goods, covering communication, transport and accommodation costs, or bribing officials. In some cases the costs were paid with cloned bank cards (especially low-cost flights) but to preserve secrecy, perpetrators still incur high operational costs. For instance, in case no. 30, the group leader claimed an investment of 170.000 euros for several operations. Most of the skimming cases exhibit a tremendous operational mobility and cooperation: the cards compromised in the Netherlands and cash withdrawn in South Korea[31] or bank cards from Czech Republic are used to withdraw cash from ATMs in Columbia, Ecuador and Jamaica[32] in a matter of hours or days. Such speedy mobility requires good organisation and strong discipline that cannot be achieved by loose networks. For instance, in *case no. 13* specialised personnel is instructed to inspect and recommend use of the bank data obtained through phishing.

---

[31] Case no. 25
[32] Case no. 16.

Most studied groups have internal structures and well trained members. The command group is more stable as low level agents tend to change across time. With only two groups having other core activities, cybercrime in Romania is conducted by ICT specialised OCGs. The group leaders use youngsters with ICT skills and most of the perpetrators convicted are in their 20s or 30s.

These models require also a good business plan in order to maintain economic viability. According to a Europol report from 2012, card payment fraud only is a very profitable and low risk crime producing a yearly income of around 1,5 billion Euros to organised crime groups. Also, from the cases analysed, it can be noticed that authorities are unable to track all the damages, a good share of profits still remaining in the hands of the perpetrators even after a conviction. This is a good incentive to continue the criminal activity after release from prison. Previously convicted criminals are in fact regrouped in *cases no. 11, 12 and 17.*

Despite Varese's (2015) highlighting of the local context, case studies prove that perpetrators do not need to have local ties were they act, but they have to have local ties somewhere. For instance, *cases no. 3, 4, 6* and *29* refer to Bulgarian citizens acting on Romanian territory without local ties. In the same way, many Romanian skimmers go to Western European countries on specific missions not relating to OCGs in the respective countries. For cash withdrawals traveling around the world is less likely to involve local connections. Local ties are still needed because the criminal group researched tend to have a stable basis for its operations which at the same time mostly requires an elaborate mobility.

Discussion and conclusions

With only one case involving ideological motives, cybercrimes in Romania are profit oriented. Proved damages in many cases amount to hundreds of thousands of euro or dollars. Nevertheless, in some cases[33], assets could not be confiscated because of the lack of evidence of the damages. Evidence gathering procedures through *letters rogatory* are slow and expensive. Such circumstances may encourage criminals and lower the overall risk for such offences. While money remains in their pockets, they face higher incentives to regroup after released from prison to pursue similar activities.

---

[33] For instance case no. 18

Three crime models have been identified: online auctions, phishing and skimming. In practice these models are interweaved because the groups involved in copying data from bank cards at ATMs may expand in online phishing for bank data or selling non-existent goods on e-commerce websites. Cybercriminal are also engage in exchanging, selling and buying bank card data. Despite the operational costs, these models are economically viable. The amount of officially identified damages ranges from $1 million to €3 million in just nine cases[34] while the real numbers remain hidden in the complexity of cyberspace. The perpetrators exploit systemic vulnerabilities of the banking, data protection and law enforcement systems making easier and safer profits that some traditional organised crime.

Some groups are based on family ties, while other involves members from different cities or of different nationalities.

The perpetrators tend to communicate between them through mobile phones and internet applications such as Skype, as references to Darknet forums[35] were not identified during the research.

Corruption does not seem to be a common instrument for such groups; in only in two cases has bribery been reported. Nevertheless, as *case no. 19* suggest, a form of protection form state officials may be needed in order to enable the group to expand and flourish. It may be a lead to be followed by investigators as in many cases perpetrators admit the accusations but do not admit other elements of their operations. The perpetrators only try to lower the level of prison sentence and seem comfortable about the basic charges as long as many of their additional deeds remain unmentioned.

Violence does not seem to be an issue, only in one case the perpetrators having a violent reaction while taken into custody. Violence against persons was not reported during their operations. Compared with other type of crimes the cybercriminals do not exercise control over a physical territory. For instance the Bulgarian perpetrators installing skimming devices in Bucharest, Constanța or Cluj-Napoca did not meet resistance from other OCGs.

With the exception of *case no. 2*, all of the cases have a trans-national character because either victims or the compromised systems are from abroad or some

---

[34] Cases no. 1, 5, 8, 9, 21, 23, 24, 26 and 30
[35] Darknet often refers to "*anonymising peer-to-peer networks such as Tor, I2P and Freenet. These tools are used by criminals operating online in order to escape identification and [...] to hide the hosting location of criminal websites, forums and online markets*". (Europol, IOCTA, 2016)

illegal activities are carried out abroad. Some of the groups become specialised in conducting activities only in some countries or target only a few types of information systems, financial institutions or types of ATMs. But once an opportunity closes, they prove to have a high capacity to adapt identifying new methods, equipment or vulnerabilities. The perpetrators travel large distances (to Asia, Africa or Latin America) in short periods of time making tracking in real time hardly possible. In most cases, the prosecutors retrace itineraries and money flows long after it actual happened. Perpetrators target also financial institutions, business and individuals in Romania.

The statistics and cases studied may suggest a slow improvement in the law enforcing capacity but innovative methods and trends in cybercrimes still wait to be uncovered by Romanian prosecutors. The threats may have for the moment only a profit-oriented profile but Romanian criminal groups continue to build their cybercrime expertise. The grim perspective is that such expertise may be used by internal or external actors for political motivated attacks undermining democracy and rule of law in a sensitive part of the European Union.

References

Centre for Legal Resources, *Reuse of confiscated criminal assets for social purposes*, Hamangiu Publishing House, 2015

Choo, K.K.R., Organised crime groups in cyberspace: a typology. *Trends in Organised Crime*, September 2008, Volume 11, Issue 3, pp 270–295

Corrin, C., Transitional Road for Traffic: Analysing Trafficking in Women From and Through Central and Eastern Europe, Europe-Asia Studies, Vol. 57, No. 4 (June, 2005), pp. 543-560

Directorate for Investigating Organised Crime and Terrorism, *Annual report 2015*, Bucharest: 2016

European Commission, *Joint communication to the European Parliament, the Council, The European Economic and Social Committee and the Committee of the Regions - Cybersecurity Strategy of the European Union: An Open, Safe and Secure Cyberspace*, Join (2013) 1 final, Brussels: 2013

European Police Office - Europol, *Payment Card Fraud in the European Union - Perspective of Law Enforcement Agencies*, 2012

European Police Office - Europol, *EU Serious and Organised Crime Threat Assessment (SOCTA)*, 2013

European Police Office – *Europol, Internet Organised Crime Threat Assessment (IOCTA)*, 2016

Gillespie, A. A., *Cybercrime: Key Issues and Debates*, Routledge, 2015

Gounev, P. and T. Bezlov, *Examining the links between Organised Crime and Corruption*, Centre for the Study of Democracy, 2010

Hill, J.B and N.E. Marion, *Introduction to Cybercrime: Computer Crimes, Laws, and Policing in the 21st Century*. Praeger Security International, 2016

Intelligence Community: Central Intelligence Agency (CIA), Federal Bureau of Investigation (FBI), and National Security Agency (NSA), *Assessing Russian Activities and Intentions in Recent US Elections*, 2017

Kshetri, N., *The global cybercrime industry: economic, institutional and strategic perspectives*, Springer, 2010

Paoli, L., *The Oxford Handbook of Organised Crime*, Oxford University Press, 2014

Rusev A., L. Garofalo, C. Jorda, R. Nicolae, I. Stamouli and M. Gasparinatou, *Extortion Racketeering in the EU: Vulnerability Factors*, 2016

Shinder, D.L, *Scene of the Cybercrime: Computer Forensics Handbook*, Syngress 2002

Symantec - ISTR special report, *Ransomware and Businesses*, 2016

Van Duyne, P.C., Organised crime in a turbulent Europe. *European Journal on Criminal Policy and Research*, 1993, no. 3, blz. 10-31

Van Duyne, P.C., M. Scheinost, G.A. Antonopoulos, J. Harvey and K. von Lampe (eds.), *Narratives on organised crime in Europe criminals, corrupters & policy*, Nijmegen, Wolf Legal Publishers, 2016

Varese, F., The local Dimension of Cybercrime: Report from a Trip to Ramnicu Valcea (Romania). In Tottel, Ursula, Bulanova-Hristova, Gergana and Flach, Gerhard (eds.), *Research Conferences on Organised Crime at the Bundeskriminalamt in Germany*. Vol. Ill, Transnational Organised Crime, 2013 – 2015, pp. 163-169, 2015

von Lampe, K., *Organized Crime: Analysing Illegal Activities, Criminal Structures, and Extra-legal Governance*, SAGE Publications, 2016

Wittkop, J., *Building a Comprehensive IT Security Program: Practical Guidelines and Best Practices*, Apress, 2016

Annex:

Overview of the cases with main characteristics

Case No	Identified seize of the group	Main type of offence	Nationality of perpetrators	Affected countries[36]	The recorded damage/loot	Online vs. real world
1	16 persons	Phishing and Auction fraud	Romanian	USA, Canada, Australia, Western Europe	$750.000	Both
2	N/A (one perpetrator identified)	Hacking	Romanian	Romania	€2.000	Exclusively online
3	N/A (two identified)	Skimming	Bulgarian	Romania	N/A (only crime instruments confiscated)	Both
4	N/A (five identified)	Skimming	Bulgarian	Romania	N/A (only crime instruments confiscated)	Both
5	N/A (one identified)	Hacking	N/A	Romania	€289.922	Exclusive-ly online
6	N/A (two identified)	Skimming	Bulgarian	Romania	N/A (only crime instruments confiscated)	Both
7	9 persons	Skimming	Romanian	Romania	€70.000	Predominately real world
8	8 individuals	Skimming and Phishing	Romanian	UK, Australia. Romania	AUD $165.000 (€117.000) €20.000	Both

---

[36] Citizens from these countries were targeted or bank data were stolen from them. The cash withdrawals were initiated in other counties, especially Latin America.

9	8 persons	Skimming	Romanian	Finland, Germany	€125.000 only in Germany	Both
10	5 persons	Skimming	Romanian	Romania, Czech Republic, Ukraine	N/A (only crime instruments confiscated)	Both
11	3 persons	Skimming	Romanian	USA	N/A (only crime instruments confiscated)	Both
12	N/A (two identified)	Skimming	Romanian	Netherlands	€3.409,60	Both
13	13 persons	Phishing	Romanian	Romania, Italy, USA,	€10.000 $12.500	Both
14	8 persons	Phishing	Romanian	Switzerland, Austria, USA	€20.000	Both
15	N/A (14 persons identified)	Skimming	Romanian	Netherlands	€340.847, 5 / €648.362, 2	Both
16	27 persons	Skimming	Romanian	Czech Republic, Netherlands	$28.817 CZK 557.701,5 (€21.658)	Both
17	5 persons	Skimming	Romanian	Hungary and Netherlands	N/A (only crime instruments confiscated)	Both
18	18 persons	Skimming	Romanian	Australia	AUD $30.000	Both

					LEI 125.402,50 (€27.867)	
19	23 persons	Auction fraud	Romanian	USA and UK	$131.000 and £7.200	Both
20	4 persons	Skimming	Romanian	N/A	N/A €3200	Both
21	3 persons	Phishing	Romanian	USA	$400.000	Exclusive-ly online
22	5 persons	Skimming and auction fraud	Romanian	Germany, Italy, Japan, Hungary	$74.875, AUD 8.489, €29.893, 4.934 GBP	Both
23	6 persons	Skimming	Romanian	Germany and Netherlands	€150.000	Both
24	5 persons	Skimming	Romanian	Germany	€352.342	Both
25	12 persons	Skimming	Dutch, Romanian	Netherlands	€15.600 and Jewellery	Both
26	22 persons	Skimming	Romanian	Germany, Italy	€1.884.315	Both
27	N/A (one identified)	Skimming	Romanian	Sweden and Denmark	N/A (only crime instruments confiscated)	Both
28	7 persons	Skimming	Romanian	Romania	5.669 lei (€1260)	Both

29	N/A (three identified)	Skimming	Bulgarian	Romania	N/A (only crime instruments confis-cated)	Both
30	24 persons	Skimming	Romanian	Portugal, Spain, Germany, Switzer-land, Cy-prus, Ja-pan, New Zealand, Australia, Dubai.	€163.262,78 (in Spain); €477.567,38 (in Germany);	Both

Fraud victims or unwary accomplices? An exploratory study of online communities supporting quack medicine

Anita Lavorgna and *Anna Di Ronco*[1]

Introduction

An increasing number of patients and their families are turning to untested therapies and unregulated practitioners, according to Offit (2013). Questionable practices not based on rigorous scientific testing, but rather on anecdotes and theories (Angell and Kassirer, 1998), are labelled by some as pseudoscience, quackery and frauds, and by others as Complementary and Alternative Medicine (CAM).[2] The medical research community has repeatedly clarified that

"There cannot be two kinds of medicine – conventional and alternative. There is only medicine that has been adequately tested and medicine that has not, medicine that works and medicine that may or may not work" (Angell and Kassirer, 1998: 841).

While certain complementary approaches can have a role in addressing specific patients' physical, psychological and spiritual needs (Ernst *et al.,* 2006; Bausell, 2007; Singh and Ernst, 2009; Deng and Cassileth, 2013), countless outright fraudulent practices abound. These lack any biological plausibility and may cause harmful side effects have been widely used and supported, with patients enticed to seek fraudulent "life-saving" treatments, which are completely unsupported by scientific evidence (Munsie and Hyun, 2014; Zettler, 2015). There are many individual reasons to turn to untested medical treatments: desperation with some patients (and physicians) being no longer prepared to wait and pursue treatments that are still untested; others look for interventions that are marketed as "natural" and "no risk" and that, therefore, are perceived

---

[1] The authors are, respectively, lecturers at University of Southampton (UK) and University of Essex (UK).

[2] Complementary (or integrative) treatments are those used alongside conventional medical treatments. Alternative treatments are used instead of conventional medical treatment.

as safer than conventional treatments (Munsie and Hyun, 2014).

The promotion and use of fraudulent therapies is not something new (Lerner, 1984; Offitt, 2013). However, the rising commercialisation of medical products through the Internet and the increasing dissemination of (medical or pseudo-medical) information through online social media constitute a new and worrying development and provide a whole new range of criminal opportunities for health frauds. For example, new opportunities have been created for fraudsters who present themselves as health gurus, while being in reality moved by the search for profit and social prestige (or a combination), while some may be under a self-delusion of having found the 'real' treatment and wisdom. Belief and (self-)deceit may go hand-in-hand.

In several countries, including Italy, a number of court trials and journalistic reports have provided evidence of the social harm of these types of frauds, *in primis* for the health of people but also for the confidence in the professional scientific and medical norms. This notwithstanding, this issue has so far been overlooked in criminological research. The existing criminological literature on health frauds has tended to focus mainly on the harm caused to patients by the deceitful conduct of pharmaceutical companies, which have been framed as economic (organised) criminals (see, for example, Punch, 1996; McFadden *et al.,* 2007; Gøtzsche, 2012; Braithwaite, 2013). Sociological literature on religious sect (see, for example, Wallis, 1975; Robbins and Anthony, 1979; Lewis, 2012) can be helpful to understand the sect-like nature of some of the health groups developed around certain gurus (Gunther Brown, 2013); however, to our knowledge, this literature neither does look specifically on health-related sects nor does it frame them in terms of fraud.

In our exploratory study we aim to provide a first criminological analysis of the worrisome, but still understudied, phenomenon of fraudulent medical treatments as furthered by the use of internet. Specifically, in this study we aim to investigate the behaviour of participants of a major online forum promoting non-traditional medical treatments that have been proved fraudulent (www.luogocomune.net), and to unpack their fuzzy role as both victims and unwary accomplices in the promotion of these health frauds.

As highlighted in the literature (*e.g.,* Pedersen, 2013), supporters of fraudulent treatments play an ambivalent role: on the one hand, they are interested in health issues and try to help/be helped, on the other hand, they have a moral responsibility as they facilitate the dissemination and adoption of dangerous practices by lending their support to practitioners with near-guru status. *Uncovering the role of these supporters* is crucial to the understanding of the popularity of fraudulent pseudo-medical treatments. This is a question that has so far been overlooked, not only by criminologists, but also by social scientists in general.

Methodology[3]

a. Case studies selection

For this exploratory study we selected through convenience sampling (a non-probability sampling method (Patton 1990)) three case studies, which have been recognised as *health frauds* by the Italian courts and have consequently been subject of a media debate and of individuals' and groups' reactions in online fora. To be able to look at different dimensions of this phenomenon of health frauds scams, after a pilot stock taking through media articles and broadcasts, blogs and social networks, we selected the following cases covering different types of health fraud. They refer to the deceitful actions of three health fraud-sters, who are:

1. *Simoncini*, a former physician claiming that cancer is caused by a fungus and needs to be treated with injections of sodium bicarbonate;
2. *Hamer*, a German former physician, who claimed that what accounts as "disease" in medicine is a meaningful program of nature, which is to be addressed by resolving a pre-existing conflict; and
3. *Vannoni*, an entrepreneur promoting a contested stem-cell "therapy" mainly aimed at neurodegenerative diseases.

The first two cases (*Simoncini* and *Hamer*) concern quack remedies offered primarily to treat *cancer*. Unluckily, the promotion and use of fraudulent remedies to cure cancer has a long history, which reached a first peak with the laetrile (also known as amygdalin or vitamin B17) movement in the US in the 1970s, which had no other effect than cyanide poisoning of the patient (Lerner 1984). Already three decades ago, Lerner (1984) suggested that a lack of confidence in the public institutions, a public panic towards cancer or "the big C", and a general feeling of frustration with the official medicine for not finding a "cure", created a fertile soil for fraudsters,

> "*who regularly refer to surgery, radiation, and chemotherapy as mutilation, burning, and poisoning. Surely, fear of them has been a powerful force in driving patients to the unorthodox*" (Lerner, 1984: 816).

---

[3] This research design was approved by the University of Southampton Ethics and Research Governance online (ERGO), submission no. 19705.

The third case (*Vannoni*) concerns a major scandal about a fraudulent *stem-cell* therapy. This type of therapy had a lot of international resonance and caused, in Italy, a firm resistance of people against governmental attempts to restrict access to this unproven treatment. This case is important because it touches upon the so-called "right to try"[4] and the inherent tension between patients, providers, scientists and regulators as regards the development and commercialisation of new cellular therapies (Munsie and Hyun, 2014). Stem cells have, indeed, long been announced as the next revolution in medicine and as a 'repair kit' for life-threatening diseases (despite the current presence of only few established stem cell-based treatments). However, such high expectations are unlikely to be met in the near future, which is something that will likely lead many patients and their loved ones to get in touch with those offering stem-cell treatment outside clinical trials, and to look for unorthodox stem-cell treatments online (Munsie and Hyun, 2014).

b. Data gathering

We identified through keyword searches all the relevant threads in the popular online forum *www.luogocomune.net* (hereafter LC), which, after a preliminary online search, appeared as the most active forum covering all the selected case studies. During the pilot, we started checking the "official" websites of the gurus and of the "therapies" considered in this study. These websites, however, were either no longer in use in Italian[5], no longer reachable[6], or did not have full open access to the blog section.[7]

In LC, both the old forum (active until 28 November 2015) and the new forum were considered. If no numbers were available accounting for the users of the old forum, they were available for the new one, which counts 17167 users. The choice of this specific forum was also guided by the fact that for ethical reasons we wanted to consider an 'open' forum, where registration is not needed to access the content of online posts and conversations. In line with

---

[4] So-called 'right to try' movements (and the laws it inspired) generally intend to expand terminally ill patients' access to experimental treatments that have not been approved by regulatory agencies. Similar cases were recently debated in, among others, Australia, USA, and Japan (Adriance, 2014; Munsie and Hyun, 2014; MacGregor *et al.*, 2015).

[5] As in the case of Simoncini's webpage curenaturalicancro.org.

[6] As the ones of ALBA, the Italian association dedicated to Hamer's theories, that once hosted a virtual forum (no longer reachable) and that now mostly refer to offline contacts.

[7] As for Vannoni's websites, which are movimentostamina.it and staminafoundation.org.

previous criminological research on online communities in the open web (see, among others, Mann and Sutton, 2010; Sugiura *et al.*, 2012; Lavorgna, 2015; Pink *et al.*, 2016), in carrying out this type of online data gathering there is no need to approach participants, given that participants in online activities are aware that their postings and conversations are being watched by people who do not reveal themselves (*e.g.*, general public, law enforcement, researchers). This approach avoids the risks related to deceiving participants in virtual communities or of interfering with unknown law enforcement operations taking place on the selected communities (Holt and Lampke, 2010). Overall, we identified nine relevant discussion threads (that is, a collection of posts on a specific topic) on LC, covering a period of about nine years (from January 2006 to November 2014) (see Appendix A for details).

It should be noted that the dates of the posts analysed were not as updated as we initially expected, which suggests that popular social media (such as Facebook) may now be extensively used for this type of discussions. We suggest that further research should consider an analysis of additional online platforms, first and foremost Facebook groups. From a quick key-word search on Facebook, in fact, we easily identified at least 14 pages and "open" groups whose posts might be of great interest to researchers. Unluckily, such an analysis would have been too ambitious for our small-scale exploratory study.

c. Data analysis

NVivo, a data analysis software package that allows one to manage and arrange unstructured information, was used to systematically organise and analyse the data collected from LC. In the light of the exploratory nature of the analysis, we used open coding (Glaser and Strauss, 1967) for the nodes construction and refinement, and categorised relevant passages in the text in 3 main content codes or, in the language of NVivo, "nodes" (Who, Attitude and Support), and a total of 32 sub-codes or sub-subcodes ("child nodes" and "grandchild nodes") as summarised in Table 1 on the next page.

Firstly, the use of NVivo for the computer-assisted data analysis allowed us to obtain descriptive statistics of the different codes and sub-codes. Particularly, the number of references (that is, the number of selections within our sources that have been coded with any node) provided us with insights into the recurrence of certain themes in the discourse of the online community analysed (see tables 2 to 13 in the "Findings" below).

Table 1

Codes and sub-codes

Codes	Sub-codes	Sub-sub-codes
Who		
	Patient him/herself	
	Friend, family member	
	External, unclear	
	Actor in the fraudulent network	
Attitude		
	Sense of belonging	Online community identity
		We open mind
		Us v them
		Moral support
	Proactive support role	Online
		Offline
		General
	Conspiracy	
	Motivation	Information-provider role
		Inquiring role
		Looking for a specific info
		Last hope
		Request for monetary contribution
		Redeeming role
	Self-representation	Survivor
		Sceptic
		Somehow expert
		Non-expert
Support		
	Against the system	Against medical establishment, BigPharma
		Against official research, universities
		Against the State, general economy
		Against the media
	Against opponents	
	Evidence of effectiveness	
	It makes sense	
	No harm in trying	
	Freedom of choice	

Secondly, codes and sub-codes were used to guide and assist the qualitative part of the content analysis. We acknowledge that a certain degree of overlap exists between the different identified sub-codes. The proposed categorisation, however, does not aim to pigeonhole behaviours into a certain category, but only to guide a systematic analysis.

The three cases

a. Simoncini

Tullio Simoncini is a former doctor known for promoting the idea, in Italy and abroad (as he promotes himself online in English), that every cancer is an infection caused by a fungus (*Candida Albicans*), which can be best treated by bringing it into contact with sodium bicarbonate (baking soda), as closely as possible. Consistently over time, this idea has been considered physiologically implausible by the medical research community. Further, there is no evidence supporting it.[8] Since he treated his patients with bicarbonate, Simoncini was expelled from the Italian Medical Association in 2003 for unethical human experimentation (Di Grazia, 2015). He was prosecuted and found guilty of serious fraud and manslaughter in Italy.[9] He is also under investigation for other deaths in Albania, the Netherlands, the US, UK, and France (Di Grazia, 2015). The regulator and competition authority for the communication industries in Italy (Autorità per le Garanzie nelle Comunicazioni or AGCOM), condemned Simoncini for misleading advertising in 2011 and banned him from further advertising his "treatments".[10]

Nonetheless, together with his brother and other collaborators, he kept working in private practices in different countries and still openly advertises his ideas online, asks for donations and can be easily contacted offline. Although he still presents himself as a published expert applauded at international conferences, he has only presented his ideas in pseudo-science arenas and has completely been discredited by the international medical community. After

---

[8] Among some websites that are doing some debunking activity on Simoncini's claims are
http://www.123hjemmeside.dk/cancer_is_not_a_fungus,
http://www.cancertreatmentwatch.org/reports/simoncini.shtml,
http://www.kwakzalverij.nl/nieuws/de-kankertherapie-van-dottor-tullio-simoncini-uit-rome/and
http://medbunker.blogspot.nl/2015/06/il-cancro-il-bicarbonato-i-medici-i.html.

[9] Appeal Court of Rome, decision no. 1255/2007; Italian Supreme Court, decision no. 1432/2012.

[10] PS6458 document no. 22300
(http://www.agcm.it/component/joomdoc/bollettini/15-11.pdf/download.html).

being relatively neglected by the media, Simoncini resurfaced the mainstream Italian news in mid-2015, as he was (again) indicted for unauthorised practice of the medical profession and manslaughter in Italy, as well as for the death of a young Italian patient in Albania in 2012 (*Il Corriere della Sera* 2015a). His website in English still attracts an international audience.

b. Hamer

Ryke Geerd Hamer is a German theologian and a former doctor. After the sudden death of his son in 1978, Hamer was diagnosed with testicular cancer and postulated a relationship between the two events. He funded the so-called German New Medicine (GNM), a set of principles, or the so-called "Five Biological Laws"[11], that holistically base the nature of diseases on the interaction between the mind and the body. According to this view – which has constantly been considered by the international medical research community a blatant and dangerous cancer quackery (Gorsky, 2009; Barrier and Yarett, 2012) – all cancer forms have a psychosomatic cause and arise from an emotional trauma that impacts on the brain. Therefore, his treatment focuses on resolving the initial trauma and on overcoming the new trauma caused by a cancer diagnosis, which (according to the GNM) impairs one's possibilities to heal naturally. In a way, victims are blamed for having developed cancer or for not overcoming it (Barrier and Yarett, 2012). The stress of receiving a cancer diagnosis would be often enough to deprive a person of his/her life force, and conventional cancer treatments would tend to accelerate the downward spiral (Gorsky, 2009). The GNM approach promises a 95 per cent or more chance of curing any cancer, no matter how advanced it is (Gorsky, 2010).

Hamer was convicted by several courts. He was prohibited from practicing medicine by a German court already in 1986.[12] In 1997, he was arrested and sentenced to 19 months in prison for failure in the duty of care and for unauthorised practice of the medical profession (see D'Amato (2010) for further details). In 2004, Hamer was arrested in Spain and, following a European extradition order, was extradited to France and sentenced to three years in prison

---

[11] (1) Every disease is initiated by a shock, an unanticipated event; (2) every disease has a phase when the disease begins and a phase when the disease resolves (healing phase); (3) the development of every disease follows a system of symbolic transformation from the psyche to the brain and the organs; (4) bacteria and virus are controlled by the body and help the body in the process of healing; (5) all diseases are rational and for the benefit of the patient.

[12] Köln, 34 Js 85/86.

(without probation) for the deaths of a number of French citizens.[13] After that he moved to Norway (D'Amato, 2010; *La Stampa*, 2016).

GNM is obviously neither supported by any empirical testing nor by medical literature other than Hamer's own delusional writings. As an anti-Semite and Holocaust denier, he claimed that Jewish doctors secretly practised GNM on Jewish patients but denied it to others. He also claimed that AIDS is a consequence of the trauma of being diagnosed with HIV, that vaccinations are of no use except to implant you with a chip, and denied the moon landing and the 9/11 attacks. Despite the danger of Hamer's ideas and the years in jail he was sentenced to, he enjoys international support, up to the point that other cancer quackeries were inspired by his nonsense (Gorsky, 2010). The death of at least 140 GNM patients has been documented in several countries including Germany, Austria, France and Spain (Gorsky, 2009; D'Amato, 2010).

In Italy the GNM was "imported" already in the 1980s and, since then, it has spread like a sect especially through the promotional activities of the Association ALBA (Associazione Leggi Biologiche Applicate) – led by a former bartender – which organises expensive courses and sells expensive material to its adepts (D'Amato, 2010).[14]

c. Vannoni

Davide Vannoni is a communication scientist, who has turned into medical entrepreneur. As such, he lacks any training as a scientist or physician, and has no publications in the medical peer-review literature (Abbott, 2013; Cattaneo and Corbellini, 2014). Vannoni was the president of the Stamina Foundation, created in 2009 as a private organisation in Italy (even if linked to a multinational commercial company, Medestea, which had been fined for misleading advertisement of dietary supplements) (Cattaneo and Corbellini, 2014). He claimed (his last public post was in late 2015) that he could cure a wide number of neurological diseases with an unproven stem cell therapy that was allegedly developed after he received a successful treatment for a facial paralysis in Russia.

For many years the Stamina Foundation had been "treating" patients, including children. He moved his laboratory around and outside Italy, searching for less strict regulations (Cattaneo and Corbellini, 2014). For instance, when in 2007, the EU ruled that stem-cell therapies have to follow the same safety and

---

13   FB/EC, Cour d'Appel de Chambéry, dossier no 02/00261, arret no 04/515, 01 July 2004.
14   While the Association ALBA and its website were formally shut down, it is extremely easy to find with a simple Google search the contacts of the new associative realities that originated from them and of their key actors.

efficacy rules of pharmaceuticals, Vannoni moved his lab from Turin to the republic of San Marino. His work, however, drew the attention of a public prosecutor whose investigations concluded that his work could be dangerous for public health. Consequently, from San Marino he moved again to Italy (to Trieste and then to Brescia), where in 2011 he founded the Stamina Foundation in a public hospital (Abbott, 2013)[15].

In 2012 the Italian Medicines Agency (the Agenzia Italiana del Farmaco or AIFA) inspected the facilities and stopped its activities due to serious concerns about how the cells were prepared and the lack of detailed protocols or patient follow-up (Abbott, 2013; Munsie and Hyun, 2014). After these enforcement actions, which had the effect of shutting down the premises, patient groups responded with lawsuits, demanding that terminal patients would be granted access to the "Stamina method" and that its costs would be covered by the Italian public health service. Many courts, despite the lack of scientific evidence, ruled in favour of the treatment and, for example, ordered its administration in the Brescia hospital as a "compassionate use" (Cattaneo and Corbellini, 2014). In May 2014, the European Court of Human Rights (ECtHR) ruled that patients have no right to receive therapies for which there is no scientific evidence (Durisotto v. Italy, appeal n. 62804/13, 6 May 2014)[16]. However, before the "compassionate use" of Stamina was stopped by the ECtHR, more than 100

---

[15] During the scandal he announced his intention to move abroad. Although the compassionate use of the Stamina therapy should not have been permitted under Italy's legal framework, judges granted access to it, arguably because they were pressured by the public opinion (Zettler, 2015). In the past few years, in fact, compassionate therapies were permitted in Italy only when supported by published data justifying their use (this, according to the Decree 5 December 2006 "Decreto Turco", which was in place at that time). After the Stamina outbreak, the Decree 21 January 2015 ("Decreto Lorenzin") was introduced with more stringent rules. These newly-introduced rules state that, for instance, non-industrial "advanced therapy medicinal products" (like stem-cells) must be produced "in compliance with the European standards of Good Manufacturing Practices", that therapies not yet tested will be offered "only in a public hospital, university hospital or institution or in-patient care in a scientific sites in the national territory", and that the administration of these medical treatments must take place "under the exclusive professional responsibility of a physician"; further, they also limit the discretion of courts, and entrust AIFA all the powers of authorization and control over the advanced therapy.

[16] The Court declared the application inadmissible (manifestly ill-founded) under Article 8 (right to respect for private and family life) and under Article 14 (prohibition of discrimination) taken in conjunction with Article 8 of the European Convention on Human Rights (ECHR). In its judgement, however, the court did not consider the negative opinion on the "Stamina method" issued by a scientific committee set up by the Italian Ministry of Health, nor the fact that the scientific value of the therapy had not been clearly established.

patients had received it, with many paying thousands of Euros for that (Rial-Sebbag and Blasimme, 2014; Zettler, 2015).

These facts fostered a heated public exchange in the media between those demanding caution in using new untested treatments and respect for existing regulations and the scientific method, and those calling for the "compassionate use" of Vannoni's therapy (Munsie and Hyun, 2014). As complained by, among others, Cattaneo and Corbellini (2014), those objecting the Stamina method were being vilified by some media outlets and accused of contributing to keeping children from life-saving treatments. By contrast, the media largely ignored the scientific evidence relating to this method. Even in the popular satirical television program *Le Iene*, celebrities and even politicians came out in support of activists and requested that the ban on the Stamina therapy should be overturned. Supporters of the therapy put forward a "right to life" narrative in their campaign, and adopted the slogan "*Sì a Stamina, sì alla vita*" ("yes to Stamina, yes to life") (MacGregor et al., 2015).

As a result, the government passed in 2013 an *ad hoc* legislation providing 3 million Euros for the treatment to undergo a clinical trial. In the same year, the Minister of Health ordered the Stamina Foundation to release its scientific data and treatment protocols to undergo examination by an expert committee. This committee soon rejected the scientific basis of the Stamina therapy and did not let it proceed to the clinical trial. As the impartiality of the expert scientific committee was questioned in a lawsuit, it was replaced by a second panel of experts in 2014, which (again) recommended not proceeding with the trial (Margottini, 2014). In April 2014, after a 4-year investigation, a public prosecutor accused Vannoni of fraud and (together with others) of criminal conspiracy: Vannoni was considered the head of a criminal organisation, which, since 2006, defrauded about a thousand patients by administering a dangerous and unapproved treatment in exchange for money. The judge for the preliminary investigations defined the Stamina method as "an enormous scientific fraud" (*Il Corriere della Sera* 2015b). Meanwhile, the Italian Supreme Court, which was also tasked with judging other related "stem-cells treatment" cases, stated that the Stamina method had no scientific validity and that the procedure was risky.[17] This notwithstanding, Vannoni received no penalty for the fraud case, as it was ruled that the statute of limitations had been exceeded. He was only found guilty in the conspiracy case, and negotiated a suspended sentence on the condition that he would no longer treat patients (*La Stampa* 2015a, b).

---

[17] Italian Supreme Court, judgments no. 24242/2015, 24243/2015, and 24244/2015.

Findings

This section presents the results of our research. To answer the research questions of this study, we decided to employ a mixed-method approach (based on both quantitative and qualitative methods), which allowed us to investigate our area of enquiry with both breadth and depth. By using NVivo, for example, we obtained descriptive statistics of the different themes that were fleshed out in the forum by its members (which we measured in terms of 'codes' and 'sub-codes'). Specifically, the number of references (that is, the number of coded entries in the forum) provided us with insights into the type of actors that were more active in the forum, their attitudes, and the themes that were raised by them in the online discussion when supporting the fraudsters or the fraudulent treatments. Codes and sub-codes were also used to guide and assist the qualitative part of the content analysis, whose results are also included in the sections below (in the form of short quotes).

1. Who

In 92 references, the forum users identified themselves as *friends or family members* of current and/or former patients. In other cases (103 references), the context suggested that they were *external* to a specific situation but nonetheless interested in the discussed topic. Only in a minority of cases, the members of the online community participating in the discussions were *patients* (20 references). However, it was generally unclear whether they were suffering specifically from one of the diseases discussed in the forum thread, or from other (generally less serious) diseases. Finally, some fraudulent *actors* (for instance, Simoncini and practitioners offering Hamer-inspired treatments) also occasionally participated in the discussions (54 references).

Table 2

Codes	Sub-codes	Sub-sub-codes
Who		
	Patient him/herself	20
	Friend, family member	92
	External, unclear	103
	Actor in the fraudulent network	54

2. Attitude

Different types of attitudes were identified in the narratives used by the members of the online community.

Sense of belonging

In many cases (131 references), the language used suggested a *sense of belonging* to a certain social group – that is, the LC forum. More specifically, in the majority of cases (79 references) a clear sense of *community identity* emerged. Consider for instance the following examples: "Could we do something, we people from Luogocomune? [. . .] We are 4196"[18]; "We are all in the same boat"[19]; "Here there are no enemies [. . .], they are elsewhere, not here [. . .]. Here we are all fragile"[20]In other cases (23 references), as exemplified in the following representative fragments, the sense of identity was specifically built around an '*open mind*' *narrative*: "[LC] ADRESSES ALL THOSE WHO WANT TO THINK"[21]; "Thanks to everyone [. . .] because this forum is a sign that there is still people who think and search for [the truth]".[22] In 22 cases, the participants of this online forum also relied on an '*us versus them*' narrative, where 'them' were usually the deceitful doctors and the other representatives of the official medicine (*e.g.*, "We are our best doctors [. . .] This is our health, we feel the pain and WE suffer the consequences and not THEM!!!!"[23]). Only in 7 cases, the sense of group identity translated into a feeling of *moral support* towards a fellow-member experiencing pain or discomfort (for instance, for the death of a beloved one, as in this case: "My best wishes, even if we don't know each other, and all my solidarity to you"[24]).

Table 3

Codes	Sub-codes	Sub-sub-codes	
Attitude			
	Sense of belonging	Online community identity	79
		We open mind	23
		Us v them	22
		Moral support	7

---

18 Thread Simoncini&HamerLC1.
19 Thread Simoncini&HamerLC1.
20 Thread Simoncini&HamerLC1.
21 Thread Simoncini&HamerLC1, capitalised in the original file.
22 Thread Simoncini&HamerLC1.
23 Thread Simoncini&HamerLC1, capitalised in the original file.
24 Thread Simoncini&HamerLC1.

Proactive support role

We also identified a total of 69 references where members of the online community were *proactively supporting* one of the fraudsters considered in this study, by promoting *online support campaigns* (19 references), *offline actions* (22 references), or by offering a *general active support* (27 references). Typical examples are offered by the following fragments: "Given that I am convinced that Simoncini is right, I insert information about his website in every forum I bump into"[25]; "Why don't we establish an Association [. . .]?"[26]

Table 4

Codes	Sub-codes	Sub-sub-codes	
Attitude			
	Proactive support role	Online	19
		Offline	22
		General	27

Conspiracy

Certain members of the online community also adopted a *conspiracy-led narrative* (49 references): they suggested the existence of clandestine governmental plans and other supposed schemes behind certain major historical events, which include governmental opposition to alternative medicine. Consider the following examples: "I read the links . . . they are shocking. This [situation] is so rotten that in comparison [what happened in New York on] September 11 was a fairy-tale for children"[27]; "Maybe they want to kill us on purpose [. . .] to control the population [growth]? Do you still remember about the terrible avian flu?"[28]

Table 5

Codes	Sub-codes	Sub-sub-codes
Attitude		
	Conspiracy	49

Motivation

We also identified different types of *motivations*, which were indicated by online community members as reasons behind their engagement in the online forum.

---

[25] Thread Simoncini&HamerLC1.
[26] Thread Simoncini&HamerLC1.
[27] Thread Simoncini&HamerLC1.
[28] Thread Simoncini&HamerLC1.

In a majority of cases, active members of the online community embraced an *information-provider role* among their peers (98 references): they posted links, texts, contact details, and other types of information to promote the knowledge and the implementation of the fraudulent treatments (*e.g.*, "I signal you this very interesting link [. . .]"[29]). In many other cases (97 references), they were explicitly *inquiring about a specific medical approach*, in an effort to better understand its reliability or to expand their knowledge on a specific treatment (in cases where they were already convinced about its validity). Consider, for example, the following representative fragment: "I will continue to follow [. . .] Luogocomune, where the truth, whatever it is, must emerge".[30] In many cases (45 references), moreover, forum members were *looking for specific information*, including contact information (*e.g.*, "I kindly ask your advice on how to contact MD Simoncini, as we would like to entrust a family member to his care [. . .]".)[31] Only in a minority of cases (5 references) the narrative used suggested that they approached the online forum as a *last hope,* when facing a desperate medical situation (*e.g.*, "Should I get a treatment from some doctor who says 'there is nothing else to do', or should I go to someone who gives me a way out, despite the fact that it is difficult?")[32] Only in one isolated case, there was an explicit *request for a monetary contribution* to sustain the ALBA Association.

In a relatively high number of cases (23 references) the narrative used by the forum members reflected their self-perceived *redeeming role*, as it shows in the following examples: "We count on you [. . .] to sustain us so that all patients, [good] doctors, and parliamentarians [. . .] can be properly informed about this immense opportunity for the whole humanity!"[33]; "I had the chance to meet MD Hamer in person [. . .] The New Medicine belongs only to him. Only he is up to it. To kill the New Medicine was easy, they just had to kill him. But he will resurrect with the resurrection of mankind [. . .], when men will be able to recognise again the spiritual nature of everything that exists."[34]

---

29   Thread Simoncini&HamerLC1.
30   Thread Vannoni LC1.
31   Thread Simoncini&HamerLC1.
32   Thread Simoncini&HamerLC1.
33   Thread Simoncini&HamerLC1.
34   Thread Simoncini&HamerLC2.

Table 6

Codes	Sub-codes	Sub-sub-codes	
Attitude			
	Motivation	Information-provider role	98
		Inquiring role	97
		Looking for a specific info	45
		Last hope	5
		Request for monetary contribution	1
		Redeeming role	23

Self-representation

Finally, in 57 cases, we could appreciate the specific *self-representations* of members of the online community, who explicitly described themselves or their role on the forum as survivors, sceptics, somehow experts, or *non-experts*. Only in a very limited number of cases the members described themselves as a cancer-*survivor* (2 references) or as '*sceptic*' (8 references) towards traditional and/or alternative treatments (e.g., "[. . .] this [approach] is much more appealing also for a sceptic like me").[35] By contrast, in a relatively high number of cases (24 references), the person interacting in the forum presented him/herself as *somehow expert* on the topic. This number is of great relevance if we consider that in 23 cases members of the online community were explicitly presenting themselves as *non-experts*, looking for expert advice. Consider for instance this example: "Of course I am not a MD, but from what I read I think that the research is valid".[36]

Table 7

Codes	Sub-codes	Sub-sub-codes	
	Self-representation	Survivor	2
		Sceptic	8
		Somehow expert	24
		Non-expert	23

3. *Support*

The members of LC have supported the alternative treatments under investigation in different ways.

---

35 Thread Simoncini&HamerLC1.
36 Thread Simoncini&HamerLC1.

Against the system

In a majority of cases, the participants of the forum supported the fraudulent therapy or the related 'guru' as a way of being "*against the system*" (479 references). More specifically, the forum members heavily criticised (235 references) the *medical establishment* (for instance, doctors, for their incompetence, ignorance or their lack of empathy) *and/or* '*Big Pharma*'. These narratives are especially evident in the following representative fragments: "Oncology is just one of the areas where it is EVIDENT the incompetence of official doctors!"[37]; "I believe instead that this might work ONLY if there are possibilities for profit for the pharmaceutical industry."[38] These aspects are in line with the antagonistic attitude towards physicians, which was also observed during the laetrile movement (Sampson, 1996), and displays the presence of a deeply rooted feeling of distrust towards the medical profession. As urged by, among others, Munsie and Hyun (2014), both the medical establishment and the public should be reminded of the social importance of medical professionalism, and commit to the reinforcement of the fiduciary ties between doctor and patient.

Interestingly, in many cases the critique towards the system was directed towards "*official*" *research* (medical and non-medical), including universities and private research centres (119 references). This result does not really come as a surprise: after all, scientific illiteracy and denialism have already been emphasised as key factors in shaping patients' perceptions of diseases, leaving them susceptible to medical frauds (Offitt, 2013: 251). Consider, for example, the following fragments: "The medical science, contrary to what one could normally think, is not an exact science and therefore it often relies on opinions"[39]; "Maybe it is not clear to you how modern science is in fact experienced and treated nowadays as a religion, as the Religion, with all its hierarchies, liturgies and symbolism. Or you are aligned, or you are out. For good. It took 500 years to rehabilitate Galileo".[40] Furthermore, several critiques (74 references) were raised, more broadly, *against the State and the capitalistic economic system*, as demonstrated by the following examples: "Unluckily we live in a foolish world where the only thing that matters is money! [. . .] I have no doubts that these statistics have been 'adjusted' [. . .] Our world (or, at least, the Western society) is currently and collectively linked to one economic system: capitalism [. . .] does not care about the health of people".[41] Finally, harsh criticism was directed *against the media* and its allegedly distorted way of reporting medical information regarding alterna-

---

[37] Thread Simoncini&HamerLC1, capitalised in the original file.
[38] Thread Simoncini&HamerLC1, capitalised in the original file.
[39] Thread SimonciniLC4.
[40] Thread SimonciniLC1.
[41] Thread Simoncini&HamerLC1.

tive therapies (51 references) (*e.g.*, "On TV and in the press they have been telling us just lies"[42]).

Table 8

Codes	Sub-codes	Sub-sub-codes	
Support			
	Against the system	Against medical establishment, Big Pharma	235
		Against official research, universities	119
		Against the State, general economy	74
		Against the media	51

Against opponents

In many cases, the discourse of supporters was directly framed *against specific opponents*, who raised critiques against them and/or against the "gurus" (244 references). Consider, for instance, these examples: "If Simoncini's enemies were straight-arrows and not villains in a white coat, they would attack his ideas and not his person"[43]; "[. . .] he had the courage to go against the current, to risk everything he had in order to follow an ideal"[44]; "I am sorry dear, but you need MUCH MORE to argue that [his] medical report is unreliable."[45]

Table 9

Codes	Sub-codes	
Support		
	Against opponents	244

Evidence of effectiveness

Furthermore, the members of this online community also supported the fraudulent treatments by offering some sort of *evidence of effectiveness*, for instance by reporting successful cases or statistics (226 references) (*e.g.*, "The 98% of therapeutic success of the German New Medicine [. . .]"[46]; "The evidences he brings are international studies, they do not live on air!"[47]; "One of his patients, with a stomach cancer, is still alive (and she is fine) after 17 years!!!"[48]).

---

42   Thread Simoncini&HamerLC1.
43   Thread Simoncini&HamerLC1.
44   Thread Simoncini&HamerLC1.
45   Thread Simoncini&HamerLC1, capitalised in the original file.
46   Thread HamerLC1.
47   Thread Simoncini&HamerLC1.
48   Thread Simoncini&HamerLC1.

Table 10

Codes	Sub-codes	
Support		
	Evidence of effectiveness	226

It makes sense

In addition, in some fragments (54 references) the alternative therapy was supported as "*it makes sense*": it sounded "*simple and logical*"[49], also from a layman point of view.

Table 11

Codes	Sub-codes	
Support		
	It makes sense	54

No harm in trying

The forum participants also supported the fraudulent therapies by arguing that there is generally *no harm in trying* them (85 references): they at least can provide hope to patients. Consider, for example, the following fragment: "The truth can be found only by trying [. . .] I believe that there are many cases where the treatment based on baking-soda cannot do anything terrible to a person, and therefore the famous saying 'there is no harm in trying' would be applicable".[50]

Table 12

Codes	Sub-codes	
Support		
	No harm in trying	85

Freedom of choice

Quite surprisingly, only in 21 cases there was a reference to the "*freedom of choice*" narrative, which should have been a major theme raised by supporters according to the (scarce) existing literature on the topic (Sampson 1996). Illustrative are the following examples: "I don't know yet what to think about this baking-soda solution, but the person involved in my opinion should be left free to choose"[51]; "Can I cure myself with the GNM if I believe in it? With Simon-

---

49   Thread Simoncini&HamerLC1.
50   Thread Simoncini&HamerLC1.
51   Thread Simoncini&HamerLC1.

cini's approach? To not cure myself, if I don't want to? Or would I go behind the bars if I do not do the chemo?"[52]

Table 13

Codes	Sub-codes	
Support		
	Freedom of choice	21

Discussion and conclusions

In this exploratory study, we aimed to investigate the behaviour of participants of a major online forum (www.luogocomune.net), which promotes fraudulent medical treatments. The gathered data suggests the people who mostly participate in this forum are externals who have an interest in the topic, as well as individuals whose friends and family are seriously ill. As shown in the Findings section of this chapter, the online forum is mostly perceived by them as a tool to discuss together (as within a community, although a virtual one) alternative therapies and health-related issues. Members in the online community pivot around a few guru-like persons; some of them, or their disciples, have an active presence in the forum. Interestingly, the online community is considered as the most reliable tool to get 'real' information about non-conventional methods and therapies, which are otherwise – according to the forum's participants – disguised by the state, the pharmaceutical industry and the medical establishment, acting in a sort of conspiracy. The active forum members mostly participate in the forum discussion to provide or receive specific information on the relevant therapies, but some of them also are motivated by the bigger aim to 'redeem' and 'save' the society.

The active forum members mostly support the guru as a way of being against the medical establishment and the pharmaceutical industry, academic research, as well as the state and the capitalist society. More concretely, they support the health gurus by directly challenging their opponents, by providing some sort of evidence supporting the effectiveness of their methods or by arguing that "*there is no harm in trying*". This last approach, however, is not unproblematic, as the *caveat emptor* ("let the buyer beware", a contract law principle) position and the implication that it would be better to legalise all possibilities, as many might otherwise be tempted by 'the forbidden fruit', which is not always

---

[52] Thread Simoncini&HamerLC1

sustainable. As already stressed by Lerner (1984), not only some of these products are not safe; they are also, when used in lieu of effective conventional
therapies, likely to cause physical, emotional and financial harm. In addition,
they impair the trust in the scientific method and, more generally, in the medical therapeutics. Interestingly, only in a very limited number of cases a reference
was made to the "*freedom of choice*", which (according to the (scarce) existing
literature on the topic (Sampson 1996)) should have been a major theme present in the narratives of supporters.

In conclusion, in this explorative study we described the attitudes and behaviour of health fraud supporters. More broadly, we addressed the topic of
alternative medicine-related scams – which has been under-studied in criminological scholarship and has received relative little attention in both medical and
policy-making circles – as health frauds. As Offitt (2013: 240ff) pointed out,
there is a line between valuable placebos and dangerous quackery that can be
crossed in four ways by:

1. recommending against conventional therapies that are helpful;
2. promoting potentially harmful therapies without adequately warning;
3. draining patients' bank accounts; and
4. promoting magical thinking.

All these patterns lead to both short and long term sorrowful consequences. We
do not want to deny the potential benefits of valuable placebos, but rather urge
the criminological research community not to ignore the social dangerousness
of this "hope business" (Offitt, 2013: 161). After all, to borrow Cattaneo and
Corbellini's (2014: 335) words, "*desperate patients will always be vulnerable to exploitation*".

We believe that further research in this domain is timely and necessary, and
in this conclusive part we would like to suggest potential research agendas. First
of all, the criminological literature on deviant *subcultures* could be useful here, as
it could provide a theoretical framework to guide additional research on both
online and offline communities of health fraud scams supporters. Given the
cross-border nature of many of these frauds, comparative research would be
particularly needed to better understand the specificities and commonalities of
these subcultures in different countries.

Secondly, from the analysis of the results, it appears that online supporters of
health frauds do not recognise their current or potential status as victims, which
derives from the normative definition of crime as crystallised in the criminal
code (Walklate, 1989; Mawby and Walklate, 1994; Rock, 2002; Mythen,
2007). By contrast, it appears that they rather feel victimised by the State for
being denied the "right to try" – that is, the possibility to try new therapies,

which have, in their opinion, some potential to cure them or their beloved ones from tremendous diseases. The literature on *victimology* already recognises that people may have different and subjective perceptions of victimisation (Spalek, 2005; Mythen, 2000.[53] Victimological approaches could therefore further investigate the perceptions of people involved in health fraud scams, especially to uncover whether supporters ever come to recognise their factual status as victims. This is much relevant as the recognition of being a victim of a crime has an impact on the level of and attitudes towards reporting these frauds to the law enforcement agencies.

Thirdly, the obtained data suggest that the media conveys ambivalent messages on these particular frauds, causing confusion among the general public: the media can either support the fraudster and the fraud (as in the case described at footnote 12) or oppose to them (as indicated by the above sub-code "against the media"). Hence, the results of the analysis suggest the importance of studying *media representations* of health guru-frauds. More accurately, what we argue here is that a more in-depth analysis of the media discourse and media framing would be needed in order to gain a better grasp of supporters' attitudes.

In addition, research is required into the possibilities for a better dissemination of scientific research via mainstream media and for improving outreach activities by scholars, which could have an impact towards an increased awareness of the harms caused by health frauds (Nerlich and McLoad, 2016).[54] In the long run, an enhanced awareness may lead to a reduced number of people supporting health frauds scams, and to an increased recognition of the status of victim of these frauds. Ultimately, this may also lead to an increase in fraud reporting and to a more systematic and accurate gathering and processing of data on victimisation (which is currently very scarce).

---

[53] With this respect, see also chapter by Herkes and Vander Beken in this volume.

[54] There is much literature written on 'news making' criminology (*e.g.*, Barak, 1988, 2007) and on Science and Technology Studies (e.g., Sismondo, 2010) that can assist criminologists and scientists more in general, in their effort to communicate more effectively their research findings to the public through the media. These efforts, however, can be "blocked" or discouraged by journalists and editorial boards, who have the power to decide over (among others) the "newsworthiness" of crime-related news (on this point, see, for example, Jewkes, 2004). The authors of this chapter, for example, have made a few attempts to disseminate information on quack medicine through the print and online media. So far, however, our attempts have failed as these health fraud scams have not been considered as a 'news' by news-making journalists (one of the editors of one international online newspaper, for example, has answered to us as following: "Everybody knows that people all over the world give up their chemo and take up coffee enemas because some quack told them to, and people die needlessly. I just don't think this is news. Sorry.").

Fourthly, a research direction could be sketched with respect to issues of responsibility of different actors. As stressed already by Nerlich and McLoad (2016), the complex relationship between science, media and communication raises a series of questions, which also relate to issues of *responsibility* of the media sector, research communities, and public actors. In other words, it suggests the need for social sciences and humanities scholars to look more in detail at the ethical and moral challenges of science-media interactions, and for legal scholars to clarify the boundaries of legal responsibilities in this complicated research domain. In Italy, the Italian Republic Senate Health Commission, after assessing the so-called Stamina method, developed guidelines (Senato della Repubblica, 2015). Besides calling on the legislator to enact a new updated legislation on untested medical treatments, the Commission has recommended:

a. to develop specialists and multi-disciplinary community-based networks to support individuals and families affected by non-treatable diseases;
b. to initiate institutional informative campaigns, supported by the Ministry of Health, aimed at better informing citizens;
c. to introduce in the Italian judicial system the so-called "standard Dubert", which is used in the US by a trial judge to preliminarily assess whether an expert's scientific testimony relies on a scientifically valid reasoning or a methodology that can be properly applied to the facts at issue;
d. to adopt guidelines informing the media on how to properly convey public scientific and medical information; and
e. to strengthen the independence of ethical committees.

It is too soon to assess the medium- and long-term impact of these guidelines and to assess the extent to which they are to be implemented in practice. However, they can be considered as a first step towards the raising of awareness on the health fraud scams problem by the government, and are certainly very much welcomed.

More broadly, we argue that research on the attitudes of the medical world itself and its malpractices (Gøtzsche, 2012) is much needed, especially as the reported lack of transparency and the accusation of not standing up to sector-based misconducts give fertile ground to health fraudsters and expose the general public to fatal hazards.

References

Abbott, A., Italian stem-cell trail based on flawed data. *Nature News*, 2013, 02 July

Adriance, S., Fighting the "Right to Try" Unapproved Drugs: Law as Persuasion. *Yale Law Journal Forum*, 2014, 124/148

Angell, M. and J.P. Kassirer, Alternative medicine: the risks of untested and unregulated remedies. *New England Journal of Medicine,* 1998, 339, nr. 12, 839-41

Barak, G., Newsmaking criminology: Reflections of the media, intellectuals, and crime. *Justice Quarterly,* 1988, 5, nr. 4, 565–587

Barak, G., Doing newsmaking criminology from within the academy. *Theoretical Criminology*, 2007, 11, nr. 2, 191–207

Barrier, C.R., and I.R. Yarett, Cancer quackery: The persistent popularity of useless, irrational "alternative" treatments. *Oncology,* 2012, 26, nr. 8, 754-8

Bausell, R.B., *Snake oil science. The truth about complementary and alternative medicine*. Oxford, Oxford University Press, 2007

Braithwaite, J., *Corporate Crime in the Pharmaceutical Industry (Routledge Revivals)*. First published in 1984. London, Routledge, 2013

Cattaneo, E. and G. Corbellini, Taking a stand against pseudoscience. *Nature*, 2014, 510, pp. 333-335

D'Amato, I., *Dossier Hamer. Una valutazione critica basata sui documenti* (http://www.dossierhamer.it/index.html), 2010

Deng, G., and B. Cassileth, Complementary or alternative medicine in cancer care – myths and realities. *Nature Reviews Clinical Oncology*, 2013, 10, nr. 11, 656–664

Di Grazia, S. La cura Simoncini: una bufala pericolosa. *MedBunker* (http://medbunker.blogspot.co.uk/p/la-cura-simoncini-non-cura-nessuno.html), 2015

Ernst, E., M.H. Pittler and B., Wider, *The desktop guide to complementary and alternative medicine: an evidence-based approach*. London, Mobsy, 2006

Glaser, B.G., and A.L. Strauss, *Discovery of grounded theory: strategies for qualitative research*. Chicago, Aldine, 1967

Gorski, D., The "Iron Rule of Cancer": The dangerous cancer quackery that is the "German New Medicine". *Science-Based Medicine* (https://www.sciencebasedmedicine.org/the-iron-rule-of-cancer-the-new-german-medicine-and-cancer-quackery/), 2009

Gorski, D., Biologie Totale and other bastard offspring of Ryke Geerd Hamer's German New Medicine. *Science-Based Medicine* (https://www.sciencebasedmedicine.org/biologie-totale-the-french-cousin-to-the-cancer-quackery-known-as-the-german-new-medicine/), 2010

Gøtzsche, P.C., Big pharma often commits corporate crime, and this must be stopped. *The BMJ* 2012, 345 doi: http://dx.doi.org/10.1136/bmj.e8462

Gunter Brown, C., *The Healing Gods. Complementary and alternative Medicine in Christian America.* Oxford, Oxford University Press, 2013

Holt, T.J., and E. Lampke, Exploring stolen data markets online: products and market forces. *Criminal Justice Studies*, 2010, 23, nr. 1, 33-50

Jewkes, Y., *Media and Crime.* London, Sage, 2004

La Repubblica, Vannoni, lo stregone di Stamina: "Nessuna truffa, vado all'estero" (http://www.repubblica.it/salute/medicina/2013/12/27/news/vannoni_lo_stregone_di_stamina_nessuna_truffa_vado_all_estero-74555568/), 2013

Il Corriere della Sera, Malato di tumore: muore dopo cura con il bicarbonato. Medico a giudizio (http://roma.corriere.it/notizie/cronaca/15_luglio_16/malato-tumore-muore-cura-il-bicarbonato-medico-giudizio-56746808-2bdf-11e5-a01d-bba7d75a97f7.shtml), 2015a

Il Corriere della Sera, Stamina, il gup: "Il metodo è un'enorme truffa scientifica" (http://www.corriere.it/salute/15_giugno_16/stamina-gup-il-metodo-un-enorme-truffa-scientifica-af6cefe6-1435-11e5-896b-9ad243b8dd91.shtml), 2015b

La Stampa, Truffa per Stamina: Vannoni si salva con la prescrizione (http://www.lastampa.it/2015/10/20/italia/cronache/truffa-per-stamina-vannoni-si-salva-con-la-prescrizione-24SVvgYMPSPrH4li5IlN2O/pagina.html), 2015a

La Stampa, Caso Stamina, Vannoni e Andolina patteggiano Guariniello: "Giustizia e scienza hanno trionfato" (http://www.lastampa.it/2015/03/18/cronaca/caso-stamina-in-mattinata-la-decisione-sul-patteggiamento-GKKF873ry5LSUZOe0cyqOM/pagina.html), 2015b

La Stampa, Nel cottage blindato dove Hamer "cura" il cancro con le vitamine (http://www.lastampa.it/2016/09/08/italia/cronache/nel-cottage-blindato-dove-hamer-cura-il-cancro-con-le-vitamine-QMCH4cEJVEvpd4kT8rM8IO/pagina.html), 2016

Lavorgna, A., The social organization of pet trafficking in cyberspace. *European Journal on Criminal Policy and Research*, 2015, 21, *no. 3*, 353-370

Lerner, I.J., The whys of cancer quackery. *Cancer,* 1984, 53, 815-819

Levi, M., Regulating fraud revisited. In: P. Davies, P. Francis and T. Wyatt (eds.), *Invisible Crimes and Social Harms*. Basingstoke, Palgrave Macmillan, 2014, pp. 221-243

Lewis, J.R., *Cults. A reference and guide*. New York, Routledge, 2012

MacGregor C., A. Petersen and M. Munsie, Patient access to unproven stem cell treatments: a human right issue? *EuroStemCell* (http://www.eurostemcell.org/commentanalysis/patient-access-unproven-stem-cell-treatments-human-rights-issue), 2015

Mann, D. and M. Sutton, Netcrime: more change in the organization of thieving. *British Journal of Criminology*, 1998, 38, nr. 2, 210–229

Margottini, L., Italy blocks use of controversial stem cell therapy. *Science* (http://www.sciencemag.org/news/2013/10/italy-blocks-use-controversial-stem-cell-therapy), 2014

Mawby, R. and S. Walklate, *Critical victimology: international perspectives*. London, Sage, 1994

McFadden, D.W., E. Calvario and C. Graves, The devil is in the details: the pharmaceutical industry's use of gifts to physicians as marketing strategy. *Journal of Surgical Research*, 2007, 140, nr. 1, 1-5

Munsie, M. and I. Hyun, A question of ethics: Selling autologous stem cell therapies flaunts professional standards. *Stem Cell Research*, 2014, 13, nr. 3, 647-653

Mythen, G., Cultural victimology: Are we all victims now? In S. Walkate (ed.), *Handbook of Victims and Victimology*. Abingdon, Routledge, 2007

Nerlich, B. and C. McLeod, The dilemma of raising awareness "responsibly". *EMBO Reports. Science & Society*, 2016 (online first)

Offit, P., *Killing us softly. The sense and nonsense of alternative medicine*. London, Harper Collins, 2013

Patton, M.Q., *Qualitative evaluation and research methods*. Thousand Oaks, CA, US: Sage Publications, 1990

Pedersen, I.K., "It can do no harm": Body maintenance and modification in alternative medicine acknowledged as a non-risk health regimen. *Social Science and Medicine,* 2013, 90, 56-62.

Pink, S., Horst, H., Postill, J., Hjorth, L., Lewis, T. and J. Tacchi, *Digital ethnography. Principles and practice*. London, Sage, 2016

Punch, M., *Dirty business: Exploring corporate misconduct: Analysis and cases*. London, Sage, 1996

Quinney, R., Who is the crime victim? In: P. Rock (ed.), *Victimology*. Aldershot, Dartmouth, 1972/1994

Rial-Sebbag, E. and A. Blasimme, The European Court of Human Rights' Ruling on unproven stem cell therapies: a missed opportunity? *Stem Cells and Development*, 2014, 23, nr. 1, 39-43

Robbins, T. and Anthony, D., Cults, Brainwashing, and Counter-Subversion. *The Annals of the American Academy of Political and Social Science, 1979,* Vol. 446, pp. 78-90

Rock, P., On becoming a victim. In: C. Hoyle and R. Young (eds.), *New Visions of Crime Victims*. Oxford, Hart, 2002

Sampson, W., Antiscience trends in the rise of the "alternative medicine" movement. *Annals of the New York Academy of Sciences*, 1995, 775, nr. 1, 188-197

Senato della Repubblica, *Indagine conoscitiva su origine e sviluppi del cosiddetto caso Stamina.* 12a Commissione Permanente Igiene e Sanità. XVII Legislatura, Resoconto Stenografico no. 20, 2015

Singh, S. and E. Ernst, *Trick or treatment? Alternative medicine on trial.* London, Corgi Books, 2009

Sismondo, S., *An introduction to science and technology studies.* Malden, Blackwell, 2010

Spalek, B., *Crime victims: theory, policy and practice.* Basingstoke, Palgrave Macmillan, 2005

Sugiura, L., C. Pope, M.J. Weal and C. Webber, Observing deviancy online. Paper presented at *Digital Research,* Oxford, GB, 10-12 September, 2012

Wallis, R., Scientology: Therapeutic Cult to Religious Sect. *Sociology*, 9(1), 89-100

Zettler, P.J., Compassionate use of experimental therapies: who should decide? *EMBO Molecular Medicine. Perspectives*, 2015, 7, nr. 10, 1248-1250

Trafficked, smuggled or exploited: Ignore the labels, they all involve abuse

Rob Hornsby, Jackie Harvey and *Deborah Booth*[1]

Introduction

This chapter reports on research in relation to child trafficking; specifically, from the viewpoint of the professionals located within the various organisations whose remit includes efforts to either counter child trafficking or coping with its aftermath. These organisations are structured in a way that reflects national legislative frameworks and in the UK, this tends to be predicated on the assumption that trafficking is organised, large scale and international in nature. The presumption of an 'international dimension' is important as it implies that those 'being trafficked' might very well be brought into the UK from elsewhere by criminal organised gangs. Our research reveals a different scenario in which trafficking and abuse of children is not recognised because it presents in ways that are different.

There has been greater awareness raising and data made available regarding the incidence of trafficking in the UK, although this is not specifically in relation to minors. For example, Wake and Reed (2016) draw attention to increased efforts following from the 2015 Modern Day Slavery Act that have seen a rise in prosecutions in the UK. In part this might also have been prompted by recent press coverage in the UK in response to official enquiries about trafficking and sexual exploitation of children. It is interesting that these press reports pointed more towards a localised and opportunist activity. Thus, Hobbs (2013) talked of the commodities of organised crime being very much a part of the local criminal social order. Such exploitation is far from being a recent phenomenon, one only has to think back to the time of Dickens and his vivid portrayal of Fagin's exploitation of street children in Victorian London and from real, rather than fictional, accounts of activists at the time who were chal-

---

[1]   Respectively Senior Lecturer, Professor and Researcher at Northumbria University, UK

lenging church and society to take action to deal with the large numbers of children on the streets of London.[2]

Legislative framework

The organised movement of people against their will for labour is far from being a new phenomenon. One only has to think of the history and longevity of the European Slave Trade. The United Nations Fourth World Conference on Women identified trafficking as a form of violence against women and called for countries to *"Adopt specific preventive measures to protect women, youth and children from any abuse - sexual abuse, exploitation, trafficking and violence"*.[3] The subsequently produced United Nations Protocol to "Prevent, Suppress and Punish Trafficking in Persons, especially Women and Children, Supplementing the United Nations Convention Against Organised Crime,"[4] provides the following widely used definition:

> "Trafficking in persons" shall mean the recruitment, transportation, transfer, harbouring or receipt of persons, by means of the threat or use of force or other forms of *coercion*, abduction, of fraud, of deception, of the abuse of power or of a position of vulnerability or of the giving or receiving of payments or benefits to achieve the consent of a person having control over another person, for the purpose of *exploitation*. Exploitation shall include, at a minimum, the exploitation of the prostitution of others or other forms of sexual exploitation, forced labour or services, slavery or practices similar to slavery, servitude, or the removal of organs." (UN General Assembly 2000 Article 3 (a)) (our emphasis added).

As noted by Harvey *et al.* (2015), the definition contains three distinct areas: the activity that takes place; the means of perpetration; and the final area that explains the purpose of the activity. Two things are apparent from this definition.

---

[2] Refer to the Guardian 'Age of Innocence' 24th May, 2000 by Ian Sparks, Chief executive of The Children's Society. Available at:\
https://www.theguardian.com/society/2000/may/24/childrensservices.guardiansocietysupplement (accessed: 6/2/17)

[3] United Nations Report of the Fourth World Conference on Women Beijing, 4-15 September 1995, p 44, available at
http://www.un.org/womenwatch/daw/beijing/pdf/Beijing%20full%20report%20E.pdf (accessed 10/2/17)

[4] Annex II of The United Nations Convention against Transnational Organized Crime, signed in Palermo, Italy, in December 2000. Annex III is the "Protocol against the Smuggling of Migrants by Land, Sea and Air", entering into force in December, 2003.

Firstly, although there is no mention of the perpetrators of the activity of trafficking, its positioning as part of the UN Convention against Organised Crime (hereinafter OC), frames it in this context. Indeed, the preamble at the start of the Annex is clear in stating that its inclusion arose from growing concern over the increased activity by organised criminals (p .53) and that the measures would help states to combat its occurrence. This duality has, therefore, been translated into the national legislative frameworks of member states adopting this protocol. It has, to date, been signed by 117 countries.[5] This slowness in take up has been explained by the resource implications associated with policing and enforcing the required national legislation. Where resources are limited the problem is easier to manage by using a less expansive definition, or indeed by not acknowledging the problem at all (Dempsey *et al.*, 2012).

For clarity, although contained within the same UN Protocol, 'trafficking' is distinct from 'smuggling' (as covered in Annex III). Some have argued (Pearce *et al.* 2013; ECPAT 2007) that trafficking contains both exploitation and coercion, setting it apart from smuggling. Recent events in the Mediterranean illustrate an evident crossover between the two with reports of OC groups moving into the lucrative supply of smuggling services.[6] Desperate people 'pay' to receive a service (being smuggled); sadly as migrants are 'price takers'[7] OC are increasingly able to impose terms and conditions particularly skewed to their advantage. There are, for example, reports of setting the overcrowded inflatable boats off with only enough fuel to take them to international waters.

Besozzi (2004) and Bales (2005) pointed to a symbiotic relationship between illegal migration, trafficking in human beings (including minors) and organised crime, although, not all academics adhere to this view (see for example, Spencer, 2010). Aronowitz (2001) distinguishes between trafficked and smuggled persons, arguing that for the former, a continuing inter-dependency builds up between trafficked person and the OC-group whereas the relationship with

---

[5] Information retrieved
   from:https://treaties.un.org/Pages/ViewDetails.aspx?src=IND&mtdsg_no=XVIII
   -12-a&chapter=18&lang=en (accessed 10/6/16)

[6] Financial Times 'Organised crime moves in on migrant smuggling trade in Turkey' December 13th 2015 available at
   http://www.ft.com/cms/s/0/17cf4fc0-9ffa-11e5-8613-
   08e211ea5317.html#axzz4BMXDCivQ (accessed 12/6/16); Europol 'Europol and Interpol takes steps against Organised Crime behind Migrant Smuggling' The Hague, the Netherlands, 23 February 2016, available at
   https://www.europol.europa.eu/content/europol-and-interpol-take-steps-against-organised-crime-behind-migrant-smuggling (accessed 12/6/16).[5]

[7] 'Price taking' refers to asymmetry in the relationship between buyers and sellers in the market place that accords great power to one party to influence price to its advantage.

the smuggled person is more transactional in nature. Although not the focus of our research, some of our respondents[8] commented that agents often maintain control over the people they have brought to the UK and these people, although claiming asylum, will remain debt bonded and may, in consequence, suffer further abuse.

The link from OC to trafficking

Penna and Kirby (2012:488) highlight the entrepreneurial criminal as facilitating human trafficking activities: "profits from buying and selling women and children have attracted organized crime networks" (also see Hughes and Denisova, 2002; Liu 2011; Webb and Burrows 2009). Europol (2011:4) similarly observes "*highly mobile and flexible groups operating in multiple jurisdictions and criminal sectors*". According to Europol (2004), criminal organisations are becoming ever more involved in human trafficking, and this has resulted in the methods of transit becoming more sophisticated (also see, Coene, 2001; Tailby, 2001; Schloenhardt, 2001; David, 2000; United States General Accounting Office, 2000; Koser, 2001; NCIS, 2003), and as a result, their vulnerability to investigation and prosecution has actually decreased (Schloenhardt, 2001). While this 'official' view talks of the enhanced skill and organisation of illegal traffickers, this does not diminish the contribution of less 'organised' criminals (Di Nicola, 1999; Siron and Van Beaveghem, 1999). Much of the evidence points to foreign-nationals increasingly becoming involved within such markets, however, these cross-boundary collaborations often require involvement of home-grown criminal entities (Besozzi, 2004; Hobbs, 1998). What is evident is that trafficking organisations seem to have flexible structures, consisting of several loosely interconnected and competitive networks where the available 'business' is continuously being 're-shared' within the marketplace (Salt, 2000; Juhász, 2000; Içduygu and Toktas, 2002; Skeldon, 1997).

Furthermore, little is known beyond that available from professionals involved with trafficked children (see for example, Somerset, 2001), regarding the market composition and organised criminal network *modus operandi* of trafficking children especially for purposes of prostitution. Family, friends, friends of friends, boyfriends, have all been identified as key-players in facilitating the supply of trafficked children for sexual purposes to this market. Yet, due to the 'market specialisation' of this 'business' and the necessity of those involved in

---

8   Reported by our interviewees N7 and N4.

such specialist trading to remain unknown, detailed insights of this significant 'hidden criminal population' continue to be elusive.

Child trafficking

It has long been acknowledged that there is little in the way of empirical data to assist in providing in-depth understanding of the criminal markets in the trafficking of children for exploitation (Bruckert and Parent 2002; UNODC, 1999; Morrison and Crosland 2000; Kelly 2002, 2005; Shelley, 2010; and Kleemans, 2011). Undoubtedly this has been compounded by victims' unwillingness to seek help from those in authority, with the result that they remain 'hidden' from official databases (IOM, 2001; Joint Committee on Human Rights, 2007; SOCA, 2009; Jackson *et. al.*, 2010; and Helfferich *et al.* 2011). In addition, there are pressing (conflicting) concerns regarding political issues and approaches to security (potential terrorist threats); humanitarian issues (victim awareness), and organised crime (a rapidly developed market and activities aiding and exploiting illegal entry) that diverts resources. It further diverts attention from the victims of such organised criminal activities to concerns, perceived or real, of the threats posed to security and/or immigration policies by unwarranted migration (Geddes, 2005; Young and Quick, 2005; Capdevila and Callaghan, 2008; Maas, 2010; Korsell *et al.,* 2011, O'Connell Davidson, 2013). It is imagined that, in the UK in particular, the rising tide of moral panic in relation to immigration cannot help in this regard.[9]

To be effective, any intervention or counter-measures to curb child-trafficking must, therefore, extend globally (Penna and Kirby 2012), requiring an increase of awareness of trafficking issues amongst police forces (and others) to avoid an emergent culture of tolerance (Markovska and Moore, 2008). As observed by a spokesperson for ECPAT UK[10]: "*Many front line police and local authority workers are just not aware of child trafficking and do not identify victims*" (*The Telegraph* 2013). Often the exploitation experience is identified as domestic servitude, forced marriage, indentured or slave labour and/or sexual exploitation. Whilst some identify these as typologies of child trafficking (Hope for Justice, 2012; Home Office, 2012; Webb and Burrows 2009), others have

---

[9] See, for example "Secret report warns of migration meltdown in Britain" http://www.dailymail.co.uk/news/article-398232/Secret-report-warns-migration-meltdown-Britain.html#ixzz4TTuvhNlg (accessed 21/12/16)

[10] ECPAT UK - End Child Prostitution, Child Pornography and the Trafficking of Children for Sexual Purposes

pointed towards the lack of clarity within the trafficking protocol definitions themselves (Pearce *et al.* 2013:11) as possibly explaining the under-reporting of child trafficking and of trafficking victims being misclassified as a result (Bokhari 2008). This misclassification is important as a theme that arose from our own research in the UK, which will be elaborated in the next sections.

The UK situation

The Council of Europe Convention on Action against Trafficking in Human Beings entered into force in the UK in April, 2009.[11] This required the UK to implement measures enabling the identification of and support for the victims of trafficking, giving rise to the National Referral Mechanism (NRM) frame-work to recognise "potential victims of trafficking" (PVoT). However, despite these efforts, recent research within the UK on 'caring services' exposes a lack of awareness and understanding "*about the signs and consequences of the trade in human beings*" (Eccleston, 2013:40). Indeed, within our study, the majority of practitioners questioned about the NRM (National Referral Mechanism), had either no knowledge or very sketchy knowledge of the reporting strategy. As will be discussed in the section '*not trafficking*', although examples of suspected cases of child trafficking were shared with us by respondents, there was no *framework* within which these cases could be officially reported and hence re-corded as trafficking cases. This was corroborated by the Competent Authority at UKBA (UK Border Agency) who confirmed there had been no child traf-ficking cases reported through the NRM for the city during 2011, the year of our study.

Furthermore, in May 2013 a review of the UK's Sexual Offences Act 2003 (referred to as the *Davies Review*), stated that the myriad of policies and proce-dures aimed at eradicating trafficking in the UK, essentially hindered efforts to prevent the sexual abuse of children in both the UK and abroad. From 31 July 2015 the NRM was extended to all victims of 'modern slavery' in England and Wales following the implementation of the Modern Slavery Act 2015. Statistics from National Crime Agency's NRM relating to 2013 (most recent available)[12]

---

[11] A copy is available at:
https://www.gov.uk/government/uploads/system/uploads/attachment_data/file/236093/8414.pdf

[12] Link to the PDF report 'most recent statistics' is available at:
http://www.nationalcrimeagency.gov.uk/about-us/what-we-do/specialist-capabilities/uk-human-trafficking-centre/national-referral-mechanism (accessed 21-12-2016)

revealed there were 609 victims of child trafficking, compared with 549 in 2012, (United Kingdom Human Trafficking Centre [UKHTC] 2013:21-26). For girls, the most common form of trafficking was for sexual exploitation (see also, Pearce, 2011; Jobe, 2008; Dowling *et al.*, 2007). This increase may reflect higher levels of illegal activity or, equally, greater awareness and thus reporting of the problem. The most common form of exploitation for boys was recorded as being for criminal activity, which was then followed by exploitation for labour purposes, followed by a smaller number for the purposes of sexual exploitation (NCA 2014:25-32). At this time, the majority of children trafficked into the UK and identified by organisations are Vietnamese and Albanian, with the next largest group being internal from the UK.[13] Of course exploitation of one child is one too many, however, despite these rising numbers, it is difficult to gauge the scale of operations, the countries involved and the extent to which such activity is '*organised*'.

In so far as domestic protocols are based on the presumption that trafficking *is* organised, large scale and international in nature it would be expected that internal operating procedures and mandates are set up assuming that trafficking involves minors being brought into the UK. However, Hobbs (2013) draws attention to the fact that 'commodities of OC' are very much a part of the *local* criminal social order. Indeed, our study indicated that much activity is internal and more 'local' in nature with children moved across the country for begging, benefit and other fraud activities. These findings appear consistent with Candappa, (2007) and with recent press coverage in UK that suggests activity to be more local and opportunistic especially in regards to sexual exploitation.

Method

Our contribution is based on the results of a series of interviews conducted with a range of organisations whose mandates included responsibility for prevention of child exploitation and included trafficking as part of their organisational remit. Data was collected over a five month period in 2011 during which time we conducted 17 semi-structured interviews each lasting approximately one and a half hours, augmented by attendance at an organisational workshop in-

---

[13] National Crime Agency Human Trafficking: National referral mechanism statistics, October to December 2013 available at http://www.nationalcrimeagency.gov.uk/publications/210-ukhtc-nrm-statistics-oct-dec-2013/file (accessed 12/6/16)

volving child protection agencies.[14] The 17 respondents represented 14 difference organisations and for analytical purposes we have categorised the respective agencies under 'statutory' and 'community and voluntary' groupings.[15] The interviews generated 25 hours of recordings and 233 pages of transcript which were analysed to generate overarching themes. Given the sensitivity of the subject, access often proved difficult and a snowballing technique was employed in which respondents were asked to identify other organisations that we should contact. In line with our ethics approval, all respondents and the corresponding agencies have been provided with an anonymous identity.

Findings

The Definition of trafficking

The research identified confusion amongst all agencies and individuals with regards to the definition of trafficking. There was only a single respondent (who had formerly worked with UKHTC) who could speak with confidence about what constituted trafficking. The agencies *drew different boundaries around what fell within or out* with the trafficking agenda (N17). Lack of knowledge on the definition of trafficking was identified by two respondents (N17 and N4) as severely hampering the anti-trafficking agenda in the UK. They commented that if people didn't know what constituted trafficking it becomes impossible for agencies ever really to engage with identifying and reporting cases, supporting victims and targeting the perpetrators.

N4 additionally argued that there was contention around the (then) current international debate to establish a single definition of trafficking. The original definition had been broadened beyond its original emphasis on sexual exploitation to a much wider agenda encompassing bonded labour, labour exploitation and trafficking for organs. The respondent stated that it is almost unhelpful to use 'trafficking' as a term at all and it might be more useful to move to talking about a more general term 'exploitation'. This term was supported by N5 and N12.

---

[14] 13 were tape recorded, the remainder requested not to be taped but consented to notes being taken.
[15] The Statutory Agency respondents are coded as: N1, N2, N3, N4, N5, N8, N9, N10, N11, N14, N15 and N17. The Community and Voluntary Agency respondents are coded as: N6, N7, N12, N13 and N16.

Trafficking Cases Identified

During the research there were examples of child trafficking confidently identi-fied and discussed by respondents.

'The Chinese Girls'

Everyone interviewed cited the case of, as almost everyone described it, 'the Chinese girls' who were identified as having been trafficked in the ECPAT[16] research in 2007. From this report it is evident that the respondents were aware that trafficking had been identified within the region. Further, this trafficking case was identified by respondents as the 'only' case of trafficking in the city.

Sexual Exploitation – Trafficking from Outside the UK

During the course of the research there seemed to be a general identification of child trafficking being mostly associated with trafficking for the purpose of sex-ual exploitation. However, during the research there were two brothels raided, one in the city and one in an adjacent city. The press reported that Chinese women, ages undisclosed, were found in the city brothel. Respondents inter-viewed following this raid all suggested that these women would most likely have been trafficked into the country on an organised basis.[17]

The cases *not* identified as trafficking

None of the following were identified officially within the agencies as trafficking and in consequence were not recorded as part of the statistics although those agency workers that we interviewed clearly regarded these cases as involving some dimension of trafficking.

Child Sexual Exploitation - Internal 'Trafficking'

---

[16] ECPAT UK - End Child Prostitution, Child Pornography and the Trafficking of Children for Sexual Purposes

[17] These raids follow on from Operation Caspian in 2009 and Operation Pentameter 2 in 2007 and Operation Pentameter in 2006.
(http://www.soca.gov.uk/about-soca/library/doc_download/122-uk-pentameter-2-statistics.pdf). Women and children were identified in all these raids as having being trafficked for sexual exploitation; some of the brothels targeted were in the North East.

The majority of internal trafficking cases identified were with regards to sexual exploitation. During the research respondents shared very disturbing accounts of young people, mainly girls being targeted and exploited sexually in the city (N1, N6, N8, N9, N10, N11, N12, N14, N15, N17). It was very interesting to note that three agencies who work very closely together on sexual exploitation of young people in the city, (N6, N11, N12, N13,) had differing definitions of what internal trafficking comprised. Two organisations stated that if a person was moved even from street to street for the purpose of sexual exploitation then this amounted to internal trafficking. They reported that in contrast, their partner organisation did not view such local movement as internal trafficking lacking sufficient 'severity' to justify the trafficking label.

A key feature of the cases shared by a majority of the participants involved with our research were that the girls had suffered problems at home or were or had been in the 'Looked After' system[18], with the majority of these composed of emotionally vulnerable White British girls. The perpetrators of this grooming and subsequent sexual exploitation were all identified, by professional workers, as being from a specific sector of the asylum seeking community in the city. "*These people know where the most vulnerable in our community are and they are only too eager to exploit these vulnerable people*" (N1) This feature of internal trafficking of minors for purposes of sexual exploitation corresponds with other studies where "*Fieldworkers describe a hidden but widespread problem with far-reaching implications*" (Cockburn, Brayley and Laycock, 2012:144) and more recently following the media exposure of the 'Rotherham case' (see Jay, 2014 and more generally OFSTED, 2014).

Children and Benefit Fraud

Five respondents identified cases of Eastern European families using children for suspected benefit fraud, (N5, N8, N9, N10, N12). The examples given were of families moving children around different addresses, registering children with GPs and other services and moving young people across regional boundaries to claim benefits. There was a detail, here noted, that the families 'disappear' very quickly to other areas of the country if agencies try to investigate the fraud or concerns are raised around child protection issues. Each respondent identified such cases of as difficult to both control and monitor given the movement of these families and the difficulty in being able to prove what was happening. One respondent, a health visitor, (N5), identified a case of visiting a family to make a health assessment and being met by a young person who had just

---

18   This term is used within the UK and refers to children in state provided care.

'appeared' at the house and whom the respondent had never seen before on previous visits. The family claimed that this child was their daughter but the respondent stated that the child looked unlike any other member of the family.

In our study of child trafficking this transposable commodification of young children for monetary gain was referred to as 'child swapping', where agencies often came across unknown children residing in 'known' properties. As one of the agency respondents revealed:

"... *children swapping was going on, for claiming asylum support purposes; people were lending children to claim more money, we turn up and there are supposed to be four children and we then need to add a couple of children on to the claim because there's no proof. We don't routinely use finger printing . . . Whenever you tried to meet with the whole family there was never the right amount of people . . . I mean ever*". (N 13)

Using Children to Beg and Commit Petty Crime

A number of cases of children being moved throughout the city and then trafficked to other areas of the country for begging and to commit theft were highlighted by respondents, revealing similarities with other localised child trafficking studies (see also BBC, 2011[19]). One mentioned children from Eastern Europe being used to steal from people on trains and stations (N17). While a health worker raised the complexities involved with the tracking and tracing of Diaspora minorities providing the example of a young child being forced to beg:

"*I mean some people disappear for no reason untoward, but we have to know where they are and then eight months later we have a message from Great Ormond Street hospital informing us she had been picked up on the streets in London severely sun burned, dehydrated and emaciated. So they were trafficked for child labour whether they were also trafficked for sexual exploitation we don't know, they had moved to the south east and they didn't come back so they were clearly trafficked to work . . . you know a three year old begging. . .*' (N5).

---

[19]   BBC (2011) *Panorama: Britain's Child Beggars*. [Accessed 19/10/11]. http://www.bbc.co.uk/programmes/b0169lg6

Forced Marriage

Although no one introduced forced marriage as an example of child trafficking, ECPAT UK, (2007, 2009) and Bhokari, (2009) both identified forced marriage as significant in the child trafficking debate. When questioned regarding their experience of having worked with people subject to forced marriage, 8 respondents identified it as an issue in city and the North East and gave examples of cases (N1, N2, N5, N8, N9, N10, N12, N16).

Cannabis Farms

One respondent (N12) stated that there had been cases of cannabis farms (in the region) having been found in residential houses and of young people, ages unknown, having been arrested. The young people were from either Vietnam or China (see also ECPAT UK, 2010).

Trafficking for Domestic Service

Consistent with Kapoor (2007) and Hynes (2010), examples were given by three respondents of people being trafficked to work as domestic servants (N5, N12, N17). In one of these cases (N12,) a young woman from the Philippines was trafficked to work in the home of a wealthy Middle Eastern family. When the family had come over to the UK for an extended period bringing her with them, she had fled the house and with the help of another person had been put on the bus to a nearby city. Here, she had been supported by the respondent to talk about her experience. However, she was fearful of sharing her case with UKBA and potentially of having to return to the Philippines. From her perspective this would prevent her from being able to earn money to send home to her family. The consequence was that she 'voluntarily' returned to the family.

Another case identified young women who were coerced into marriage with young men in the city. On arriving in the UK, however, they found themselves forced to do all the domestic tasks in the home; the respondent identified this as 'modern slavery' (N5). The final case was of British South Asian families having children trafficked over from India to act as servants in their homes. This was identified as a new phenomenon in child trafficking across the UK (N17).

'Dropped off the radar'

To the extent that these forms of trafficking were often not recognised as such, they were for the most part, not recorded within records retained by any of the organisations. As previous localised studies have suggested, this failure in recognition leads to a significant underreporting of child trafficking cases (Sillen and Beddoe, 2007; ECPAT, 2009; Pearce, 2011). This means that decisions over where (increasingly limited) resources are best targeted may result in child trafficking slipping further down the agenda as an issue. By far the most repeated phrase or inference made by respondents was that child trafficking was "*off the agenda*" with regard to organisations and agencies within the North East, although all respondents stated that they felt that child trafficking was still happening in the city. A number of reasons were offered as to why the child trafficking agenda in the city had been downgraded. However, the lack of a firm definition of trafficking and, allied to this, a lack of an understanding of what constitutes a trafficking case, are major themes emerging from this research.

a.   Hidden numbers

First, was that there were insufficient recorded cases of child trafficking in the city to keep it as organisational priority, despite concerns from frontline agency workers that this was not the case. For those at the vanguard of children's services, child trafficking activities continued within the city. It was also suggested that within the local remit of children's services provision and of potential child protection issues that the fragmented approach to identifying and reporting suspected child trafficking had created a situation where agency workers had concerns of potential trafficking cases but failed to report them.

> "*They say well I worked with a child who raised significant issues related to trafficking . . . but when I ask . . . 'Did you do anything or register the case?' They say no because they weren't sure or, they don't know where to go to in the reporting process*". N4

Almost all respondents stated that "the numbers just weren't there". There weren't sufficient recorded cases of child trafficking in the city to keep it an organisational priority. One possible explanation was the suggestion from one respondent (N11) that there had been a new protocol introduced at the regional airport to deal with young people:

> "*So now they are actually taken to the police station their prints taken and placed in a safe place . . . The police developed the protocol and maybe you see that could have worked – traffickers aren't stupid they know what is happening . . . I mean well that could be chance or is it because they have heard of these procedures and moved their*

operations to another less organised airport . . . So I am not saying trafficking in [city] isn't happening, not at all but that it has dropped off the radar because of cases we can work with. You know [airport] is certainly not the main airport in the country for trafficking and so it isn't that a far up professionals' agendas not the everyday.

b. 'The buzz has gone'

Numerous respondents stated that there was a 'buzz' about child trafficking following the launch of the ECPAT Research in 2007. This resulted in a number of high profile regional initiatives. One such initiative was the Regional Anti Trafficking Group (N11). This partnership grouping was comprised of the police, UKBA, Children's Services, health, education, local authority and community and voluntary sector organisations. The group was chaired by one of the participants of this case study, who stated he had recently disbanded the group because there was a lack of identifiable cases of trafficking being recorded in the city and the group was *"meeting for meetings sake"* (N11). With a lack of reported cases the general reaction expressed in the research was that organisational priorities placed around child trafficking had been significantly reduced.

c. 'Funding'

Almost all of the respondents stated that given the current spending review and the devastating impact on the public sector, community and voluntary sectors, which had severely impacted within the region, services had to prioritise and streamline their work. Where large numbers of cases of 'need' were not being recorded, funding could no longer be given to support work in these areas – with child trafficking identified as one such area.

d. 'Don't pick up the stone'

A number of professionals stated that due to the complex and sensitive range of factors involved with child trafficking cases for many of the agencies, it was often organisationally viewed as an unfeasible concern to deal with. A number of the participants from law enforcement and child welfare agencies (five in total) suggested that organisations prefer not to highlight it as an issue, as this means they avoid responsibility for intervention and in so doing cannot be criticised for dealing with such a difficult issue inappropriately (N1, N2, N4, N11, N12.) One respondent stated that there was a significant scarcity of knowledge with regards to trafficking amongst all organisations in the city and that this lack of awareness was perpetuated by *"professionals and organisations being too worried of what they might find . . . so it's best not to look"* (N13). And, such problems were not isolated incidents and were further supported by a number of respondents who believed that even within local organisations providing services and expertise within child trafficking agendas there exist extensive internal gaps in knowledge and information sharing strategies.

"*I mean child trafficking is a difficult one – unless we force it as an issue and flag it up then people will be less likely to identify cases but without any cases identified it is going to slip off focus so it's a catch 22 situation*". (N11)

e. "They go quiet don't they"

The reluctance on the part of agencies to even talk about child trafficking has led to it no longer having a voice on the organisational agenda in the city, (N12, N2). Recently, the shift of emphasis by both policing and the UKBA towards security (real and/or perceived terrorist threats) and unsolicited immigration agendas has had a damaging bearing upon trafficking priorities and service provision. This was clearly stated by one respondent who argued that there was a deficiency of knowledge with regards to trafficking amongst all organisations within the region, and that this deficit was replicated nationally (Solace, 2009).

Within the city it became evident that there was a lack of coordinated organisational commitment by agencies either to identify potential trafficking cases or to raise awareness of trafficking issues amongst organisational agendas. Even for well-established organisations with experience and practice in tackling child (and adult) trafficking there were apparent gaps in knowledge; and human trafficking *per se* appears to have been lost amongst the long-grass of other organisational priorities.

Further concerns are raised regarding the current coalition Government's overhaul of law enforcement within England and Wales and its implementation in 2013 of the National Crime Agency and the subsequent closure of the UK Human Trafficking Centre. As one law enforcement official claimed: ". . . *nationally and locally this has led to a very serious reduction of expertise in the trafficking field*" (N14), and stated that knowledge and expertise had been built up over a number of years and that ". . . *it was criminal that it was now so fragmented*".

Discussion on the evidence of 'organisation'

The forgoing suggests that, under various guises but without a formal label, trafficking of children is taking place. However, whilst evidently, 'organised' there was little mention of the extent to which the activity was associated with OC activity in the minds of our respondents. In particular, the use of 'internal' trafficking of children within the UK is a poorly understood phenomenon, due largely to its context of a hidden population of victims. Yet, such internal trafficking movements within the UK are known to occur, and while this is known to happen to overseas children trafficked into the UK, it is also an issue that occurs to indigenous British children (UKHTC 2009). The exploitative activities that those children encounter are diverse, ranging from an assortment of sexually abusive exploitation where "*young people who had been sexually exploited were often being moved by coercers and exploiters to locations other than their place of residence; the most common experience was of being taken to a nearby city, town or borough where sexual exploitation occurred*" (Barnados, 2007, 1).

Furthermore, little is known, beyond that of professionals involved with trafficked children regarding the market composition and organised criminal network *modus operandi* of trafficking children for prostitution (see, Somerset, 2001). Elsewhere, family, friends, friends of friends, boyfriends, and increasingly sophisticated exploitative organised crime networks have all been identified as key-players in facilitating the supply of trafficked children for sexual purposes to this market (Dowling, *et al.*, 2007). Globally, the majority of convicted traffickers are male, replicating virtually every other form of crime. Yet due to the important role of initial victim trust towards perpetrators, female offending rates are significantly higher than for other crimes as females play a significant role in recruitment and the supervision of victims (UNOCD, 2010). This may be due in part to the importance of initial "trust" between the victim and the perpetrator, and additionally, in some markets, victims may become exploiters over time, as this may be the only way to escape further exploitation (Dowling *et al.*, 2007).

Currently, what appears to be one of the most pressing issues and more overtly related to OC, is that traffickers are training children to present themselves as "*unaccompanied asylum seekers*" at UK points of entry, therefore meriting local Social Services intervention in order to house them in care facilities including in some instances Bed and Breakfast lodgings (Pearce, 2012). These 'insecure' facilities are often in close proximity to the children's port of entry into the UK, thus it is relatively straightforward for their traffickers to coerce or persuade these children to leave such hostels or local authority care homes. Indeed, the latter are viewed as "holding pens" by the traffickers (Home Affairs Committee, 2009). Our research suggested that measures at the airport to intervene and identify unaccompanied minors might have removed the 'organised' element out of the region. However, rather than eliminating it completely there is every chance that it merely relocated to another port of entry.

Interestingly, we found that exploitation applied equally to smuggled as well as trafficked persons in the region. Thus the same exploitation with regards labour exploitation and sexual exploitation is also experienced by asylum seekers, failed asylum seekers and refugees. Examples were given by nine respondents (N1, N4, N7, N8, N9, N10, N11, N13, N12) of some of these individuals who have been exploited, both on their way to the UK and also when living in the UK. Respondents stated that these people were extremely vulnerable and exploiters where aware of this vulnerability. Further they were aware of where these people were housed (N1, N7). Examples were given of asylum seekers being sexually exploited and of labour exploitation.

One of our respondents reported on what they felt was a very moving interview with former asylum seekers that explored the trauma and abuse often experienced by people who are being transported by agents to the UK. Forced to flee trauma in their own home country they have to put trust in people who can assist their transit to safety. The respondent stated that she felt their situation was very similar to trafficking victims as they are not aware of the abuse they will suffer on the way to the UK nor what awaits them on arrival. She also stated that the agents often maintain control over the people they have brought to the UK and these people, although claiming asylum will be debt bonded to these agents suffering further abuse (N7). Clearly this activity appears to fall within the scope of being 'organised' but lacks identification in the minds of our respondents with being 'OC'.

Another respondent stated that he has interviewed many young unaccompanied asylum seeker children and they are very reluctant to share any information, (N1). He was concerned that at the point at which they were interviewed these young people were in shock and traumatised and had little understanding of where they were or how they had got to the UK. He stated that these young people may have been trafficked but would not yet know it; their traffickers would only appear once the young person was 'safely' away from service interventions.

Conclusion

Our findings point to confusion about the use and application of the label 'trafficking'; to prevalence of internal rather than international trafficking (within the city, region and country); and to exploitation that is far wider than sexual abuse. This suggests that attention should be paid to domestic 'home grown' criminal gangs as orchestrators as much as to those operating transnationally. Respondents were all keen to do the right thing but there seemed to be a disconnect between their front line experience that we have discussed above and the priorities of the various agencies. In consequence we draw attention to the mislabelling and thus underreporting of the scope of activity by these organisations. The result appears to be that scarce resources within the agencies tasked with supporting and helping the victims of trafficking have been moved to other areas of need. Further, those agencies charged with countering OC, have moved resources away from the trafficking domain.

If the label of 'trafficking' is a pre-requisite for funding, then in light of the experience of the practitioners that we interviewed we would suggest that organisations revisit their own internal protocols and policies to update their guidance to reflect these broader types of exploitation. For irrespective of the label applied, exploitation is taking place from which others have been and will continue to be able to profit. Finally, our findings suggest that those in the front line need to be given a greater 'voice' through further academic studies or newspaper reporting to elevate the issues they have raised in the minds of both the public and the policy makers.

References

Aronowitz A., Smuggling and trafficking in human beings: the phenomenon, the markets that drive it and the organisations that promote it. *European Journal on Criminal Policy and Research,* 2001, 9: 163–195, 2001

Bales, K., *Understanding Global Slavery: A Reader.* CA: University of California Press, 2005

Barnardos (2007) *A summary report mapping the scale of internal trafficking in the UK based on a survey of Barnardo's anti-sexual exploitation and missing services.* [Accessed 01/15/12]

http://www.barnardos.org.uk/internal_trafficking_final_report_aug07.pdf

Besozzi, C., Illegal markets and organised crime in Switzerland: Critical assessment. In C. Fijnaut and L. Paoli (eds.), *Organised Crime in Europe: Concepts, Patterns and Policies in the European Union and Beyond,* Dordrecht: Springer, 2004

Bokhari, F., Falling through the gaps: Safeguarding children trafficked into theUK. *Children and Society,* 2008, 22(3) :201-211

Bruckert, C. and C. Parent, *Trafficking in human beings and organized crime: a literature review,* Royal Canadian Mounted Police, 2002

www.rcmp-grc.gc.ca.

Candappa, M., *Child trafficking in Newcastle. A report on the evidence and agency responses to child trafficking*, ECPAT UK, 2007

Capdevila, R. and J. Callaghan, "It's not racist. It's common sense": A critical analysis of political discourse around asylum and immigration in the UK'. *Journal of Community and Applied Psychology*, 2008, (18) 1: 1-16

Cockbain, E., H. Brayley and G. Laycock, exploring internal child sex trafficking networks using social network analysis. *Policing*, 2012, 5 (2): 144-157

Coene, G., Human smuggling and human trafficking. In: Ronald Commers and Jan Blommaert (eds.), *Het belgische asielbeleid. Kritische perspektieven*, Uitgeverij EPO, Antwerp, Uitgeverij EPO, 2000

David, F., *Human smuggling and trafficking: an overview of the response at the federal level*, Australian Institute of Criminology Research and Public Policy Series, 2000

Dempsey, M., C. Hoyle and M. Bosworth, Defining sex trafficking in international and domestic law: mind the gaps. *Emory International Law Review*, 2012, 26(1): 137-162

Di Nicola, A., Trafficking in immigrants: a European perspective. paper presented at the *Colloquium on Cross-border Crime in Europe*, Prague, 27-28 September 1999

Dowling, S., K. Moreton and L. Wright, *Trafficking for the purposes of labour exploitation: a literature review*. London: The Home Office, 2007

Eccleston, D., Identifying victims of human trafficking. *Community Practitioner,* 2013, 86(5): 40-42

ECPAT, Missing Out: A study of child trafficking in the North-West, North-East, and West Midlands. London: ECPAT. 2007

The ECPAT, Report 'Stolen Futures: Trafficking for forced child marriage in the UK 2009' (http://www.ecpat.org.uk/sites/default/files/stolenfutures_ecpatuk_2009.pdf)

Europol, *EU Organised Crime Threat Assessment*. 2011 www.europol.europa.

Europol, *Trafficking in human beings for sexual exploitation in the EU: a Europol perspective*, Europol: The Netherlands. 2004

Geddes, A., Chronicle of a crisis foretold: the politics of irregular migration, human trafficking and people smuggling in the UK. *The British Journal of Politics and International Relations*. 2005, 7 (3): 324-339

Harvey J, R. Hornsby and Z. Sattar, Disjointed service: an English case study of multi-agency provision in tackling child trafficking. *British Journal of Criminology*, 2015, 55 : 494-513

Helfferich, C., B. Kavemann and H. Rabe, Project Management BKAWiesbaden: C. Toll and G. Flach, Determinants of the willingness to make a statement of victims of human trafficking for the purpose of sexual exploitation in the triangle offender–police–victim' *Trends in Organized Crime* 2011, 14: 125–147

Hobbs, D., *Lush life: constructing organised crime in the UK.* Oxford: Oxford University Press, 2013

Hobbs, D., "Going Down the 'Glocal'": the local context of organised crime. *The Howard Journal*, 1998, 37, 4: 407– 22

Hope For Justice, *Hope for Justice.* Retrieved from http: hope justice.org.uk, 2012. [Accessed: 20/12/13]

Home Affairs Committee, *The trade in human beings: human trafficking in the UK: Sixth Report of Session 2008-09*, 14th May 2009

Home Office, *An evidence assessment of the routes of human trafficking into the UK.* 2012,
http://www.homeoffice.gov.uk/publications/science-research-statistics/research-statistics/immigration-asylum-research/occ103?view=Binary [Accessed 19/03/12]

Hughes, D.M. and T. Denisova, *Trafficking in women from Ukraine.* Final report to the National Institute of Justice, NCJ 203275, 2002

Hynes, P., Global points of "vulnerability": Understanding the processes of the trafficking of children into, within and out of the UK'. *International Journal of Human Rights.* 2010 14 (6): 952-970

Içduygu, A. and S. Toktas, How do smuggling and trafficking operate via irregular border crossings in the Middle East - Evidence from fieldwork in Turkey', *International Migration*, 2002, 40, (6): 25-54

International Organisation for Migration (IOM) *Deceived migrants from Tajikistan: A study of trafficking in women and children.* Geneva, Switzerland: IOM, 2001

Jackson, K., J. Jeffery and G. Adamson, *Setting the record. The trafficking of migrant women in the England and Wales off-street prostitution sector.* Association of Chief Police Officers, Regional Intelligence Unit for the South West, 2010. http://www.acpo.police.uk/documents/crime/2010/201008CRITMW01.pdf [Accessed 09/04/11]

Jobe, A., Sexual trafficking: a new sexual story? In F. Alexander and K. Throsby (eds.), *Gender and interpersonal violence: language, action and representation.* Basingstoke: Palgrave, 2008

Joint Committee on Human Rights, *Human Trafficking Update*. London: House of Commons. 2007, http://www.statewatch.org/news/2007/oct/uk-jhrc-human-traff-rep.pdf.[Accessed 18/11/11]

Juhász, J., Migrant trafficking and human smuggling in Hungary. In: F. Laczko and D. Thompson (eds.), *Migrant trafficking and human smuggling in Europe: A review of the evidence with case studies from Hungary, Poland and Ukraine, International Organisation for Migration*, Geneva: 2000, 167-232

Jay, A., Independent inquiry into child sexual exploitation in Rotherham 1997 –2013, 2014 file: www.C:/Users/Guest/Downloads/Independent_inquiry_CSE_in_Rotherham.pdf [Accessed: 4/10/14]

Kapoor, A., *A scoping project on child trafficking in the UK*. CEOP, 2007. http://ceop.police.uk/Documents/child_trafficking_report0607.pdf   [Accessed 18/11/11]

Kelly, E., *Journeys of jeopardy: a review of research on trafficking in women and children in Europe*, IOM. 2002

Kelly, E., "You can find anything you want": A critical reflection on research on trafficking in persons within and into Europe. In IOM, *Data and research on human trafficking: a global survey*, IOM: Geneva, 2005.

Kleemans, R., Expanding the domain of human trafficking research: introduction to the special issue on human trafficking. *Trends in Organized Crime*, 2011, 14 (2-3): 95-99

Korsell, L., D. Vesterhav and J. Skinnari, Human trafficking and drug distribution in Sweden from a market perspective –similaries and differences. *Trends in Organised Crime,* 2011, 14(2-3) : 100-124

Koser, K., The smuggling of asylum seekers into Western Europe: contradictions, conundrums and dilemmas. In D. Kyle and R. Koslowski (eds.), *Global Human Smuggling*, Baltimore and London: The Jones Hopkins University Press, 2001

LCPC, *London procedure for safeguarding trafficked and exploited children*, London Child Protection Committee, 2006

Lui, M., *Migration, prostitution and human trafficking. The voice of chinese women*. New Brunswick: Transcation Publishers, 2011

Maas, W., Unauthorized migration and the politics of regularization, legalization, and amnesty. In G. Menz and A. Caviedes (eds.) *Labour Migration in Europe* . Palgrave Macmillan, 2010

Markovska, A., and C. Moore, 'Stilettos and steel toe-caps: legislation of human trafficking and sexual exploitation, and its enforcement in the UK and the Ukraine. (In van P.C. van Duyne, J. Harvey, A. Maljevic, K. von Lampe and M. Scheinost, (eds.) *European crime-markets at cross-roads: Extended and extending criminal europe*. (121-150) Nijmegen,Wolf Legal Publishers, 2008

Morrison, J. and B. Crosland, *The trafficking and smuggling of refugees: the end game of European asylum policy*. UNHCR Policy Research Unit, Centre for Documentation and Research, 2000

National Crime Agency (NCA), *UK Human Trafficking Centre*. National Crime Agency, 2014 www.nationalcrimeagency.gov.uk/about-us/what-we-do/specialist-capabilities/uk human-trafficking-centre, [Accessed: 20/6/14].

National Crime Intelligence Service (NCIS), *UK Threat Assessment*, London: National Criminal Intelligence Service, 2013

O'Connell Davidson, J., Telling tales: child migration and child trafficking. *Child Abuse and Neglect*. 2013, 37(12): 1069-1079

Office for Standards in Education, Children's Services and Skills (Ofsted), 'The Sexual Exploitation of Children: It couldn't happen here, could it? 2014, Retrieved at//www.ofsted.gov.uk/resources/sexual-exploitation-of-children-it-couldnt-happen-here-could-it. [Accessed: 29/11/14]

Pearce, H., Safe accommodation for separated children. In E. Kelly and F. Bokhari (eds) *Safeguarding children from abroad: refugee, asylum seeking and trafficked children in the UK*. Jessica Kingsley Publishers, 2012

Pearce, J., Working with trafficked children and young people: complexities in practice. *British Journal of Social Work*, 2011, 41 (8), 1424-1441.

Penna, S. and S. Kirby, Bridge over the river crime: mobility and the policing of organised crime. *Mobilities*, 2012, 8(4): 487-505

Salt, J., Trafficking and human smuggling: a European perspective', *International Migration*, 2000, 1: 32-54

Schloenhardt, A., Trafficking in migrants: human smuggling and organised crime in Australia and the Asia Pacific Region. *International Journal of the Sociology of Law*, 2001, (29) 331 - 378

SOCA, *The United Kingdom Threat Assessment of Organised Crime 2009/10*, 2009 http://www.soca.gov.uk/threats/humantrafficking [Accessed 22/11/11].

Shelley, L., *Human trafficking: a global perspective*. Cambridge: Cambridge University, 2010

Sillen, J and C. Beddoe, *rights here, rights now: recommendations for protecting trafficked children*, London, ECPAT UK, 2007

Siron, N. and P. Van Baeveghem, *Trafficking in Migrants through Poland: Trafficking in migrants through Poland: Multidisciplinary Research into the phenomenon of transit migration in the Candidate Member States of the EU, with a view to the combat of traffic in persons*, University of Ghent Research Group [in] Drug Policy, Criminal Policy, International Crime, Antwerp/Apeldoorn, Maklu, 1999, (10): 326

Skeldon, R, Trafficking: A perspective from Asia. *International Migration.* 2000, Special Issue 1. 38 (3) : 7–30

Solace, *The role of local authorities in addressing human trafficking*: report of the Solace Study Group. 2009, www.solace.org.uk/library_documents/SOLACE_on_trafficking3.pdf [Accessed: 11-13⁻11]

Somerset, C., *What the professionals know: the trafficking of children into, and through, the UK for sexual purposes*, ECPAT UK, 2001

Spencer, J., The illicit movement of people across borders: The UK as a destination country and the disorganisation of criminal activity' Chapter in P.C. van Duyne and J. Spencer (eds.), *Flesh and money. trafficking in human beings.* Wolf Legal Publishers, Nijmegen, 2010

Tailby, R., Organised crime and people smuggling/trafficking to Australia: Trends and Issues. *Australian Institute of Criminology*, 2001, 208: 1-6

UKHTC, *A strategic assessment on the nature and scale of human trafficking in the UK 2012.* August, 2013 available at: http://www.nationalcrimeagency.gov.uk/publications/15-ukhtc-strategic-assesssment-on-human-trafficking-in-2012/file. [Accessed:27/10/14]

United States General Accounting Office, *Alien smuggling: management and operational improvements needed to address growing problem.* Report to Congressional Committees, May 2000.

United Nations Office on Drugs and Crime (UNODC), *Global illicit drugs trend.* New York., 1999

UNOCD, The globalization of crime: a transnational organized crime threat assessment. UNOCD.2010 http://www.unodc.org/documents/data-andanalysis/tocta/TOCTA_Report_2010_low_res.pdf//[Accessed 23/11/11]

Wake, N. and A. Reed, reconceptualising the contours of self-defence in the context of vulnerable offenders: a response to the New Zealand Law Commission. *The Journal of International and Comparative Law* 2016, 195-247

Webb, S. and Burrows, J., Organised Immigration Crime: A post-conviction study: Research report No 15, London: Home Office, 13th July, 2009

Rob Hornsby, Jackie Harvey and Deborah Booth

Young, W. and D. Quick, *The struggle between migration control and victim protection: The UK approach to human trafficking*. New York: Women's Commission for Refugee Women and Children, 2005

The criminalisation of legal prostitution
The Dutch Zandpad case

Dina Siegel[1]

Introduction

On July 31, 2013 an article appeared in the Dutch newspaper *Trouw* with the headline: "Many women from Zandpad have disappeared". The article's main question was simple: where were the women who had been working on the 'sex boats' along Zandpad, now that Utrecht City Council had closed down the facilities? The answer, however, turned out to be far from simple. Immediately after the closure rumours started circulating that some women had moved to other cities to work in 'window prostitution', while others were supposed to have found jobs in sex clubs, escort agencies, legal or illegal brothels, or were now working from home. There were also indications that 'Zandpad women' had turned up in Utrecht's street prostitution areas. There were rumours that some women had moved abroad or had left the sex industry altogether. On October 13, 2013, the Geisha Foundation reported that many of the prostitutes who had lost their jobs in July were now working in worse circumstances, for lower wages and in constant fear and insecurity (Stichting Geisha, 2013). Allegedly, many of the Zandpad women had fallen into the hands of criminal gangs of human traffickers who exploited, sold and abused them (*ibid.*).

The Dutch and international media's interest in the events at Zandpad focused mainly on the relations between sex workers, operators and local government officials. Questions were raised as to why the facilities had been closed down and inevitably 'the problem of human trafficking' in Utrecht came up.

As is obvious with partly covered phenomena in the margin of society, it is difficult to get an accurate picture. Those who have access to information about sex workers, such as police officers, social workers and government officials, create a specific reality. Their presentation of the facts provides a general, abstract story, a certain image of prostitution and human trafficking, and creates a

---

[1] The author is Professor of Criminology at the Willem Pompe Institute, Utrecht University, the Netherlands.

sense of urgency that problems related to prostitution must be solved quickly. Given that on the one hand prostitution is a legal occupation in the Netherlands, and on the other hand, that the Dutch government invests a great deal of effort in police investigations into human trafficking in the legal prostitution sector, the Zandpad acase provided criminologists with a 'natural experiment' as part of an extended case study evoking various questions. What were the reasons for the closure: was human trafficking going on at the Zandpad prostitution zone, and if so, how and to what extent? Who were responsible for the decision? Finally, did closing all the windows contribute to the fight against human trafficking?

In our research we studied the consequences of this decision for the women involved. We examined the Zandpad case in terms of the potential effects of a (temporary and local) ban on prostitution within the wider context of sex work as a legal occupation in the Netherlands.

The past ten years have seen a tendency among politicians in the Netherlands to look for alternatives to the supposedly failed policy of legal prostitution. Scientific studies and government reports such as the WODC's evaluation reports (Daalder, 2007), the police report *Schone Schijn* (KLPD, 2008) and *Emergo* (Emergo Project Group, 2011) all paint a negative picture of the effects of the lifting of the brothel ban. Despite the legalisation of sex work in 2000, a great deal of abuse is, allegedly, still taking place in the licensed prostitution sector, including the red-light districts of Amsterdam (Emergo Project Group, 2011), Arnhem, Emmen and Vlaardingen (NRM, 2012), and other cities. The fight against human trafficking has become the main topic in the debate on prostitution and combating abuse.

Most of the heated media debates about measures to deal with prostitution revolve around the question as to whether prostitution is a 'normal occupation' practised voluntarily or, by definition, 'a modern form of slavery'. Can sex workers be seen as full citizens with all of the corresponding rights and obligations and are they sufficiently able to take care of themselves? (Oude Breuil and Siegel, 2012). Those who place a negative value judgement on prostitution find it hard to believe that there are sex workers who have freely chosen to work as prostitutes. Such an approach only serves to blur the line between prostitution and human trafficking impeding a non-moral look. Is it still possible to have a positive or even neutral image of sex workers in today's society? If 'no', the Dutch policy of legalisation may be built on wishful thinking by equating sex work with regular occupations which proved be at odds with the prevalent moralist perception with its persistent negative stereotypes eventually prevail.

The stereotypes are repeated in the media: prostitution can never be a voluntary occupation and is therefore an evil that must be eradicated. Dutch politicians keep coming up with new proposals to criminalise clients and pimps (NOS, 20 January 2015).

On the other hand, numerous scientific publications have shown that reality is more complicated and there is no clear dichotomy between 'naive abused victims' and 'ruthless criminal exploiters' (cf. O'Connell Davidson, 2005; Kempadoo, 2005; Davies, 2009). Various authors have concluded on the basis of their empirical studies that human trafficking and prostitution must not be conflated (Oude Breuil et al., 2011; Zhang, 2009). According to Ronald Weitzer, who conducted a decades-spanning comparative study of commercial sex locations in cities across Europe, statements by politicians and policymakers about forced prostitution are often not based on facts, if not on insufficiently substantiated or poorly conducted research. Conclusions are drawn on the basis of incomplete or incompatible data sets, collected by 'armchair' academics who have never talked to a prostitute or a pimp or visited a sex worker's place of work and who often rely in their reports on the information and moral judgements provided by 'second-hand' experts. This has led to a paradox. "*What we have, in sum, is a very mixed picture – a lucrative industry that employs many individuals and attracts numerous customers but is regarded by many people as immoral or harmful and in need of either stricter control or total elimination*" (Weitzer, 2012: 6).

Methodology

In our research we listened to the life stories of Zandpad sex workers. Our 31 respondents came from the Netherlands, West, Central and Eastern Europe and Latin America. Their life stories gave us insight into what made them decide to work as prostitutes, why in the Netherlands and why in Utrecht in particular. We also discussed their past, their relationships with relatives, experiences in other European countries and bureaucratic procedures in Utrecht. They told us about the practical aspects of working in Utrecht, such as rent, working hours and rates for sexual services, but they also discussed their sense of security, interaction with colleagues from other ethnic groups and the role of operators, police officials and welfare organisations during and after the closure of the Zandpad prostitution zone. The sex workers expressed their emotions about the loss of their work, their fears, anger, expectations and hope of returning to Zandpad. They also always spoke about human trafficking and other abuses and gave us their own views and interpretations. The experiences of these women were central to our research.

The research was carried out between July 2013 and February 2015, but relationships with many respondents had already been established during previous studies (Oude Breuil *et al.*, 2011; Siegel, 2009; Oude Breuil and Siegel, 2012; Goderie *et al.*, 2014). The data for the Zandpad case study were gathered through desk research, including a literature and media analysis, cyber research, open and semi-structured interviews with sex workers, clients, lawyers, representatives of the police, the justice system and welfare organisations. We interviewed 31 sex workers and 13 clients, some of them several times. Almost all of these interviews were conducted face-to-face at different locations, varying from pubs to their workrooms 'behind the window' or at the informants' residences. We collected our field data in various cities in the Netherlands and Belgium: Groningen, Alkmaar, Amsterdam, Rotterdam, Eindhoven, Tilburg, The Hague and Antwerp. We also carried out observations in sex clubs, sex shops, the Zandpad neighbourhood, the street prostitution area ('*tippelzone*') on the Europalaan in Utrecht, and the red-light districts in other cities. Observations also were conducted during city council meetings and demonstrations by sex workers. We also spoke with policy makers, law enforcers, representatives of different relevant NGO's, clients and escort clubs' owners.

Prostitution in Utrecht in its historical perspective

The Utrecht prostitution is almost as old as the existence of the city. Two additional factors facilitated prostitution in Utrecht during the 14th and 15th Century: the bustling urban environment and the annual fair, which attracted many visitors from the neighbouring villages. Prostitution was not illegal during this period and brothels were allowed to operate in several neighbourhoods. Nevertheless, the authorities tried to keep the affluent city centre (Oudegracht, de Trans, de Bochtbrug) 'free of whores'. Prostitution was concentrated in Wittevrouwen, Achter Sint Pieter, Kromme Nieuwe Gracht and beside the Weerthaven harbour. Public bath houses also served as clandestine locations where prostitutes could receive their clients (Stemvers, 1985: 19). In the 15th Century, prostitutes worked mainly in brothels and bath houses where they brought their clients after soliciting them in an inn or on the street (Wurf-Bodt, van der, 1988: 15). Although prostitution was not a punishable offence in Utrecht, pimping was. Stringent measures were enforced against '*poytiers*' or '*putiers*', as they were known (*ibid.*, 9).

Prostitution was made illegal after Utrecht's transformation from a Catholic diocese to a centre of Calvinism. On 8 November 1586 the city authorities issued an ordinance in which all 'public women', pimps and bawds were given 24 hours to leave Utrecht (*ibid.*: 19). This ordinance had no effect, despite the threat of corporal punishments, such as the pillory or stocks (*ibid.*: 22). Prostitutes continued to work in houses run by pimps and madams. Under the influence of the Reformation, punishments became harsher, and all forms and expressions of 'immoral living', including dancing, public baths and comedies, were forbidden. There was also an outbreak of syphilis, a hitherto unknown disease that could have been introduced to the Netherlands by the Spanish army. Syphilis was seen as a 'plague sent by God', a punishment for lechery and prostitution (*ibid.*: 25).

In the 17th Century, the city government relaxed these harsh measures. Brothels were not only frequented by men from the lower social classes, but were mainly popular with travellers (*ibid.*: 28-29). Secret private houses, known as the '*stille knip*' became popular among men from the higher social classes; 'expensive women' received clients at their home.

In 1713, approximately fifty diplomats from various European countries travelled to Utrecht to participate in the congress to negotiate the Peace of Utrecht. In the same year, Augustus Freschot, a teacher living in Utrecht, wrote a book, *Histoire amoureuze & badine du congres & de la ville d'Utrecht*, which described the debauchery indulged in by almost all of the diplomats − including elderly diplomats and a papal envoy − in the brothels of Utrecht. Apparently, there was so much work for the prostitutes of Utrecht that they had to call in colleagues from other cities to cope with demand. After the congress, the local authorities tried to curb prostitution, but their efforts were in vain (Freschot, 2013).

During the French period, all brothels, including the secret '*stille knip*' houses were registered with the police. In 1813 there were fifty registered prostitutes in Utrecht, and in 1850 there were between one hundred and one hundred and fifty women working in nine rendez-vous houses and fourteen brothels (Van der Wurf-Bodt, 1988: 37). Other sources reveal more 19th Century statistics: in 1842 there were fourteen public houses in Utrecht (Stemvers, 1985: 67); in 1862 there were twelve brothels and the number continued to decline: in 1885 Utrecht had only three brothels left and by 1912 only one (in Lollestraat) remained (*ibid.*: 68).

Sexually transmitted diseases were usually blamed on prostitution. In the 19th Century, medical examinations of 'public women' were justified by the necessity to protect public health, which was an important government task (De

Vries, 1997: 58). After medical examinations of prostitutes were introduced in Rotterdam, Utrecht followed in 1858. 735 prostitutes were registered for these medical examinations (Van der Wurf-Bodt, 1988: 45). In 1880, Van Goudoever, a prominent Utrecht professor who had conducted such inspections for many years, described the problems and shortcomings of the inspection system and statistics in an article entitled "A much discussed topic" (*Een veelbesproken onderwerp*). He concluded that it is necessary to tolerate public houses in order to enable strict monitoring and medical examinations. He also concluded, however, that medical examinations could not prevent sexually transmitted diseases (*ibid.*: 58). What is more, only prostitutes were examined, not soldiers.

Another problem found time and time again in the historical literature is the nuisance caused by prostitution. From the second half of the 19th Century, the contrast between rich and poor in Utrecht widened. "*Two worlds collided head-on: as the old city centre became more crowded with new inhabitants and increasing numbers of prostitutes, who plied their trade ever more openly, so did the frustration of the established citizens increase*" (Bossenbroek & Kompagnie, 1998: 20). These wealthy citizens felt threatened in their status, intimidated in their own environment and convinced that their norms and values regarding decent behaviour and morality were being insulted. Despite their complaints, the police were not prepared to close or relocate the brothels. They feared that if they clamped down on the problem, that prostitution would move to other locations and they would lose a grip on it altogether (*ibid.*: 87).

Hence, in 19th Century Utrecht, prostitution was practised in the same forms as in other cities: regular brothels existed alongside a host of other clandestine sex establishments and street prostitution. There were, however, more protests against prostitution and the accompanying nuisance in Utrecht than in other cities. The residents of Mariaplaats in particular, protested against 'public women' and their inebriated clients, who often started fighting among each other. The houses in Mariaplaats declined in value and businesses there lost customers (*ibid.*: 101). Residents of Zadelstraat and Buurkerkhof also complained that their children could see the dealings between prostitutes and their clients from their houses and gardens, something which flew in the face of their norms and values with which they were raised their children ('t Hart, 2005: 51; De Bruin, 2000). Opposition to prostitution was not only founded on financial arguments, but was largely fuelled by moral objections. "*That prostitution must exist, we agree, so be it; but not where we live. They should ply their trade elsewhere*", was an often-heard argument ('t Hart, 2005: 102).

Brothels were at last banned in 1890. The man behind this prohibition was De Louter, a law professor in Utrecht who persuaded six members of the city council to submit a proposal to close the city's brothels. Their argument was to make it impossible to "tempt people into immorality". Despite opposition from some who considered that such a prohibition would not be legally feasible and furthermore in conflict with articles 250 and 452 of the Criminal Code, in which brothels are considered as a business, the motion was passed in the city council. On 25 July 1890 'houses of immorality' were prohibited. (Van der Wurf-Bodt, 1988: 93).

The enemies of prostitution, however, were not content with just a ban on brothels, but wanted prostitution to be banned altogether ('t Hart, 2005: 50). Prohibition was based upon moral objections: human trafficking, which would dominate the arguments used by policy makers for closing sex windows and sex boats in 21st Century Utrecht, was not yet an issue in the 19th Century. In the 19th Century, the emphasis lay on bringing up girls and boys, whereby a strict line was drawn between decent women, who would go on to be wives and mothers, and loose, 'fallen' women, who were devoid of standards or moral values, and 'dirty' or infected with a venereal disease. Once more we can see that the notorious 'Madonna/whore' dichotomy is of all times.

This brief historical overview of prostitution in Utrecht also shows us the consequences of banning brothels. The closure of the legal brothel in Zandpad in July 2013 is nothing new. We have been able to clearly observe the consequences that banning regulated prostitution in previous centuries has had for the women involved, their clients and their surroundings. Two phenomena in particular stand out: the relocation of prostitution to different locations and settings and the flourishing of illegal prostitution.

In the 19th Century prostitution shifted from regulated brothels to the street (Van der Wurf-Bodt, 1988: 94). At the time of closing the brothels, the police estimated the number of prostitutes at 25 but this number increased following the ban (*ibid.*: 98). This proves that prohibition and relocation do not necessarily lead to a reduction in prostitution.

The other consequence of closing the brothels was that brothels which had previously been legal continued their business operations illegally and that new, illegal brothels opened alongside. The police did not have sufficient manpower to enforce strict controls. Prostitution continued to be practiced in 'milk salons', cigarette shops, and at the yearly fair ('t Hart, 2005: 50). Some prostitutes found work as waitresses in cafés and tea houses, and had regular sexual contacts with clients there (Van der Wurf-Bodt, 1988: 94). This phenomenon illustrates the creative solutions and alternatives that prostitutes sought out.

Against this historical background one may wonder whether opinions and stereotypes about prostitution in Utrecht in 2013 were any different than they had been in the 19th Century. It is as if history is repeating itself: since the closure of the sex boats on Zandpad and the prostitution windows in Hardebollenstraat, the city council has been looking for a new location for sex workers. So far, their attempts have been unsuccessful, due to protests from local residents who are worried about nuisance and possible other 'dangers', such as drug-related crime and human trafficking. These societal reactions are not unique to the Netherlands: the argument that prostitution has to exist, but preferably not anywhere near one's own home is known all over the world and is sometimes referred to as the NIMB (Not In My Backyard) principle. This is partly the reason why the decision on a new fixed location for prostitution in Utrecht has been continuously postponed.

In 2013, exactly the same two phenomena – relocation and illegality (or 'hidden' prostitution) – could be observed following the closure of Zandpad. Sex workers moved to other cities where window prostitution had not yet been forbidden, either in the Netherlands or in neighbouring countries, such as Belgium and Germany (geographical relocation). Some ended up in Utrecht's streetwalking zone, or in sex clubs and escort agencies (generic relocation). Others found work in massage salons, bars or saunas, while yet other women received clients at home, in hotels or in other private premises.

Opposing views on prostitution in Utrecht in past and present

There is a great deal of academic literature on regulating and combating prostitution in the Netherlands. These studies reveal that there are nuances within and differences between each city, due to the specific nature of the local authorities, the church and the populace. Most literature from previous centuries sought to explain prostitution by focusing on psychological factors (Stemvers, 1985: 64). Later on, poverty was generally viewed as the most important reason, along with unmarried motherhood and 'deviating sexual preferences' (*ibid.*). According to generally accepted 19th Century wisdom, "entrance into a brothel heralded the start of a downward trajectory for the prostitute, which would inevitably lead to her death in the gutter" (*ibid.*: 65). Archive material, however, shows that the average life expectancy of prostitutes in Utrecht and Amsterdam in the period between 1860 and 1870 was 54, which was high in those days (*ibid.*: 65-66).

Utrecht had several institutions and organisations working to regulate prostitution. In the 19th Century, these initiatives were inspired by two main schools of thought: on the one hand, prostitutes were regarded as 'fallen women' who had to be saved. On the other hand, prostitution was perceived as an 'evil' that had to be totally eradicated.

In 1853, the Association for the salvation of penitent fallen women (*Vereniging tot behoud van boetvaardig gevallen vrouwen*) was set up in Utrecht. Its main objective was to re-educate prostitutes, because the prevailing wisdom held that, "laziness, vanity and the desire for pleasure" had led these women into prostitution. These 'saviours' of public women placed the blame firmly on the prostitutes and viewed them as 'contemptible creatures' (Van der Wurf-Bodt, 1988: 81).

In 1878 the Dutch Association to Combat Prostitution (*Nederlandse Ver-eeniging tot Bestrijding van de Prostitutie*) was founded by Hendrik Pierson following a conference on prostitution that was held in Utrecht on 27 May 1878. A division of the organisation was set up in Utrecht six years later, led by members of the higher social classes and orthodox Protestants. Its president, Dr. Mounier, believed that the only way to extirpate prostitution was to prosecute prostitutes, including those working in clandestine brothels (*ibid.*: 85).

In the same period, a 'Midnight Mission' was started in Utrecht by a few evangelicals, who stood in front of brothels to admonish clients for their immoral conduct and organised information, neighbourhoods meetings and prayer sessions. In contrast to other cities, campaigners could count on full support from the police in Utrecht (*ibid.:* 85-86).

In 1901 a 'stop the fair' movement began in Utrecht to abolish the fair, which according to the campaigners, was the scene of much immoral behaviour. This movement was founded by the Midnight Mission and supported by several Christian organisations. The city council turned down their petition, however, as there was no proof to substantiate their allegations (*ibid.*: 88).

The anti-prostitution movement, the Women's Union to Raise Moral Awareness (*Vrouwenbond tot Verhoging van het Zedelijk Bewustzijn*) eventually achieved a major victory, together with other Christian organisations, when brothels were banned in 1890. The language used by the members of the Women's Union is striking: they speak of 'fallen sisters' or 'daughters'. These terms served to emphasise their own identity as mothers and older sisters in contrast to prostitutes who were viewed as the vulnerable, defenceless and sometimes infantile victims of male sexual needs. This pity and 'collective' motherhood meant that it was necessary to rescue and protect prostitutes (De Vries, 1997: 121). Concepts such as 'fall', 'guilt', 'sin', and 'temptation' were central to the discourse of the Women's Union. "*The woman's will was irrelevant, absent"* (*ibid.*: 127). Today, we would call this "denying the agency" of sex workers (Oude Breuil, 2011: 24; Ham and Gerard, 2014).

The church's vision on regulating prostitution was not the only view taken in the 19th and early 20th Century. Other ideologies had their own stand on the issue. The socialist and feminist movements were mainly concerned with the social position and rights of women. According to Marxist-socialist ideology, prostitution is a capitalist phenomenon, caused by poverty, inequality and the vulnerable economic position of women (De Vries, 1997: 148). Socialists saw prostitutes as 'one of us', belonging to the proletariat, providing that they allowed themselves to be rescued from their 'bondage' (ibid.: 277).

Feminists campaigned for the complete abolition of all laws and regulations that 'gave women fewer rights than men' (*ibid.*: 161). Radical feminists viewed prostitution as a product of male domination, and spoke of 'slavery' and 'the trade in women' (*ibid.*: 220, 224). Feminists acted against this trade in women, which mainly consisted of recruiting woman in foreign countries by using deception and coercion (*ibid.*: 244), engaging in 'social work', operating rescue homes for women and by warning girls of the dangers. This abolition movement led to social work and the rehabilitation of prostitutes (Stemvers, 1985: 73). Today, providing information and emergency shelters for women who have become the victim of human trafficking are among the most important tasks of support organisations in Utrecht.

Throughout the 20th Century, prostitutes were regularly targeted and put under pressure to change their way of life, but as it turned out, most of them were well able to resist this moral pressure (*ibid.*: 105). On the contrary, it was precisely this type of pressure from various agencies trying to combat immorality, which led to the development of a new type of prostitute, one who was strong and much more professional than her predecessors (*ibid*).

The history of prostitution in Utrecht from the Middle Ages until the 1980s can thus be typified as a continuous cycle in which toleration is followed by repression and prohibition, which in turn is followed by milder attitudes and the lifting of the stringent restrictions of the past.

Regarding window prostitution two phenomena resulting from the ban on this sex business recur throughout the history of prostitution in Utrecht: 1) physical relocation to different locations in the city and 2) the emergence of clandestine and/or illegal prostitution. There has never been a period in history when strict measures and repression have managed to eradicate prostitution. Sexually transmitted diseases and other miseries have also failed to lead to its disappearance. These problems do not seem to deter clients. Prostitution is of all eras and survives all obstacles, whether they are of a bureaucratic or medical nature.

Utrecht has always had a host of organisations working to solve the 'problem' of prostitution. There are still many aid organisations working there. Even to this day, they are still driven by conflicting ideas about sex workers: one the one hand is the view that sex workers are actual or potential victims of human trafficking who need to be saved. The other point of view sees sex workers as 'bad girls' or 'happy hookers' who have chosen prostitution, becoming a source of nuisance and criminality and setting a bad example. According to these views, it is necessary to combat prostitution. Both were expressed in the case of the closure of Zandpad.

In comparison to other cities, where accessibility was not always optimal, the Zandpad had a very favourable location: it was situated in a quiet, green natural area which was nonetheless close to the city centre, and easy to reach. This set Zandpad apart from the noisy, crowded prostitution zones in other cities. There was scarcely any public nuisance, at least according to the official complaints. In this study we have tried to analyse why Zandpad nevertheless came to be considered as a problem.

Closing window prostitution in Utrecht in 2013

In 2000, the ban on brothels was lifted in the Netherlands. The purpose of the new act was to remove sex work from the illegal circuit in order to organise better supervision of potential abuses and to grant independent and voluntary sex workers a legal status with all the corresponding rights and obligations.

The act was the result of a long period of public debate. The legislator formulated six main goals: regulating the exploitation of voluntary prostitution (local licensing policy); combating involuntary prostitution; preventing the sexual abuse of minors; protecting and strengthening the position of prostitutes; separating prostitution from criminal activities; and combating illegal prostitution (and prostitution by illegal aliens).

Eight years later, in 2008, the report *Schone Schijn* showed that large-scale human trafficking was taking place within the licensed prostitution sector. The infamous Sneep investigation into the criminal activities of the *Durdan group* (KLPD, 2008) and the criminal investigation *Ablak*, which targeted a Hungarian network of human traffickers, have since served as evidence of the involvement of organised crime in the sex industry.

The *Sneep* investigation in particular can be seen as a turning point in the views on prostitution held by official bodies. How could human trafficking take place in the supervised licensed sex industry? (KLPD, 2008; Kiemel and Ten Kate, 2007; Van de Bunt, 2007). In 2010, a parliamentary document stated the following: "the sex industry is vulnerable to criminality: it is a criminogenic sector" (Parliament, Session year 2009-2010, 3211, no 3, p. 6). Organised crime in particular is mentioned in relation to the sex industry.

Since then, illegal (unlicensed) sex work as well as licensed window, escort and club prostitution has been associated with organised criminality. Increasingly, the agencies concerned are making a connection between sex work and human trafficking. The *National Rapporteur* on Trafficking in Human Beings underlined the vulnerability of the prostitution sector in her reports. In 2013, she concluded "Human trafficking is all around us" (NRM, 2013: 18). Other reports (Arrondissementsparket Groningen and Leeuwarden, 2010; Emergo Project Group, 2011; Heuts *et al.*, 2012) also confirm the image that human trafficking is taking place within licensed and unlicensed prostitution. The Dutch prostitution policy is often regarded, both domestically and abroad, as pragmatic and tolerant. The question is whether these characterisations are still appropriate. Worries about criminality and moral concerns regarding prostitution are being expressed increasingly. Our 'risk society' (Beck, 1999; Boutellier, 2002), with its 'culture of control' (Garland, 2001), demands strict regulation, prevention and an emphasis on security, as the result of a process of 'securitization' (Aas, 2007) whereby all kinds of social concerns are 'framed' in terms of 'security'. In this context one of the original goals of lifting the brothel ban, *i.e.* combating the stigmatisation of sex workers, seems to have been abandoned.

During previous research on prostitution policies in other cities we observed how '*risk thinking*' and a *culture of fear* can influence the municipal decision-making process (Oude Breuil & Siegel, 2011; Siegel, 2009). In Utrecht, these factors played a major role in determining the city's policy on prostitution.

In the spring of 2013 the City Council faced a major dilemma. The licences that had been granted to the five operators in Utrecht's window prostitution sector were about to expire and it was expected that the operators would apply for an extension. In the meantime, the council had received 'signals', varying in seriousness and reliability, indicating abuses in window prostitution. In a number of cases criminal investigations found solid evidence of serious abuses. The data from investigations, administrative inspections, contacts with support agencies etc. were recorded in administrative reports that were not made public, to protect the privacy of the prostitutes concerned, but were only made available to the operators. Disclosing certain information on human trafficking in the

Zandpad area would also allegedly jeopardise investigations by police teams elsewhere in the country. The city decided to move ahead and not wait for the expiration date of the licences.

On 28 March 2013, the council sent a letter to the operators announcing its intention to "withdraw their licence" and "refuse an extension of their licence" to operate a window prostitution business. The grounds mentioned by the council included "a threat to public order" and "indications of human trafficking". The strongly worded letter told the operators where they had failed in the eyes of the city (letter from the City Council, 28 March 2013).

The problem was that, together, these five operators controlled all the prostitution windows in Utrecht. The withdrawal of their licences meant that all prostitution windows would be closed down within a short space of time (June/July 2013) without there being any 'plan B' or 'evacuation plan' for the approximately 300 prostitutes about to be evicted without notice. The paradox of this policy was that the city wanted to protect the women from abuse but instead created a situation where they found themselves on the street without any support or protection.

Many of the signs or suspicions of human trafficking in Utrecht were based on 'soft facts'. It should be noted that 'soft facts' can be important, intuitive and well-informed notions of people who are directly involved – but they can also be 'gut feelings', influenced by the current public debate, societal anxiety, and indignation about prostitutes becoming victims of human trafficking. Estimates were made, but the way in which quantifications were achieved was never made clear. The methodology used and the foundation of the figures are still unclear, and the considerable margin between the lower and upper limit of the estimated figures on involuntary prostitution (between 5 and 95%) makes the numbers unreliable and of no use.

Nevertheless, these figures took on a life of their own and could not be verified or nuanced after the closure of the Zandpad. They reinforced existing stereotypes of human trafficking and prostitution and led to an escalation in the definition of the problem. Estimates, conjecture, signals and a limited number of actual victims of human trafficking (between 4 and 8 in the period between 2000 and 2014, according to various sources) shaped the 'narrative' and, in the end, led to the elimination of window prostitution in Utrecht.

The time of the closure of all of the windows in Utrecht was, in a sense, determined by accidental circumstances. All of the licences expired in the same period, which meant that the decisions to withdraw the licences and not wait for their renewal dates were taken in quick succession and that all the windows in Utrecht were closed down almost simultaneously. The argument of 'human trafficking' was used because a more substantial reason was needed to convince the public.

Sex work, prostitution, human trafficking: the same?

The past decades have seen the publication of numerous books, scholarly articles, biographies, novels and official reports on prostitution, human trafficking, victims, perpetrators *etc*. Sex work has become a sexy subject for academics, students, NGO activists and journalists, as well as for politicians engaged in national and international debates on legalisation, criminalisation, decriminalisation, condoning and other types of policy. The 'rescue industry' for victims of human trafficking is flourishing and punitive and preventive methods and models are being designed and implemented. One example of this is the 'barrier model', which is particularly popular with the Dutch police and justice system. Different services (police, municipal control, tax authorities etc.) are increasingly working together to combat human trafficking. This is known as the integral or 'programmatic' approach. The emphasis is not on criminal investigations, but on tackling situational circumstances that enable human trafficking to exist. According to this approach, raising the barriers to human trafficking can be effective. Barriers to human trafficking are, for example, the transport of victims from their countries of origin, better border checks, better inspections of places of work *etc*. (Kiemel & Ten Cate, 2007).

The language and professional jargon regarding various aspects of sex work vary between countries and ideological streams. For example, what radical feminists see as 'liberating' or 'saving' women is considered by sex workers in the Netherlands (and in other countries) as a form of oppression and a violation of their right to make their own choices with respect to their occupation, contacts and mobility. They also do not want the government to dictate what they can or cannot do with their own bodies and from what age. Some interpret this as a form of 'infantilisation' and contempt, while what social workers are actually trying to effect is 'protection' and 'emancipation'.

There are three mainstream approaches to analysing prostitution and human trafficking: safety, migration and human rights. The first approach focuses on feelings of safety and the risks of the occupation: women who are potential victims of exploitation and coercion are seen either as the 'other' or as 'risky individuals' (Aradau, 2004; Muftic, 2013; Berman, 2003). To protect its citizens against these dangerous 'others' the state takes repressive and preventive measures (Meshkovska *et al.*, 2015).

In the second approach the mobility and migration of sex workers are central (Mai, 2013; Andrijasevic, 2007; Pickering and Ham, 2014). Illegal migration, transnational criminality and the informal economy are all topics that often accompany sex work. In this approach, sex work can be analysed as a type of informal labour (Agustin, 2006; Andrijasevic, 2007).

The third approach focuses on the vulnerability inherent in the profession and on ways of assisting and protecting prostitutes (Saunders, 2005; Fitzpatrick, 2002).

These approaches do not address a number of other aspects, such as the socio-economic position and reputation of the profession, ethnic differences, shame, anonymity, professional confidentiality and friendship versus business relationships with operators and clients, and the power relations between the 'powerful' (in our research: the city council and the police) and the sex workers.

The lives of the Zandpad sex workers, who are always on the look-out for new opportunities and places of work, are analysed here from the perspective of social exclusion. Given the negative image of prostitution, sex work is still not accepted in our society, even after legalisation and the assumed 'normalisation' of the profession. Like other marginal groups (such as refugees, drug addicts or the homeless) prostitutes are seen as 'criminogenic', and this leads to stigmatisation and social exclusion. In such a context prostitutes are forced to develop survival strategies. Their constant mobility in search of better prospects, is part of this. However, mobility does not guarantee an improvement of their situation. This raises the question whether sex work can really be a normal profession,

Prostitution – a 'normal' profession?

In the social science and legal literature the sex industry is regarded as a large economic sector (Agustin, 2002; Weitzer, 2012; Chin and Finckenauer, 2012). Prostitution is a form of labour, but the question remains whether or not it can ever be an 'ordinary occupation'. Despite the fact that 'prostitution' and 'sex work' cover the same sexual services, the terms have different connotations. In history, we find various images, myths and stereotypes about prostitution, from shameless temptresses to spreaders of syphilis, 'fallen women' or victims of violent pimps. The term 'sex worker' derives from the above-mentioned human rights approach and emphasises the connection between sex and work. This means: agreed-upon terms of employment and compliance with fundamental human rights, such as physical integrity and equal treatment (Janssen, 2007: 31).

The concept of 'agency' focuses on the difference between naïve and deceived victims and independent strong women who regard prostitution as work and a way of life chosen of their own accord. Ethnographic studies on sex workers in particular underline the importance of agency (Kempadoo and Doezema, 1998; O'Connell Davidson, 1998; Nencel, 2001; Brennan, 2004; Janssen, 2007).

According to the NRM, however, 'the "romantic image" of a prostitution sector with only Dutch, articulate prostitutes working behind the windows and in brothels and "students moonlighting as escorts" (. . .) no longer corresponds to reality' (NRM, 2013: 55). The 'real image' is that the prostitution sector is dominated by non-Dutch, mainly Central and East European prostitutes (who are, supposedly, not 'articulate'). "Many of these women come to the Netherlands at a young age, do not speak Dutch or another western language such as English and are insufficiently aware of their rights and obligations in the Netherlands. These circumstances make this group vulnerable to exploitation" (ibid). We question the assumption that these women must be considered victims of exploitation if they cannot speak Dutch or English; elsewhere in the report we learn that Dutch women (who do speak more than one language) can also be victims. "*In any case it would appear that part of the group of Dutch girls are recruited at a young, sometimes very young, age and are groomed to start working in legal prostitution as soon as they reach eighteen*" (*ibid.*: 56). Here, both age and language are mentioned. These two aspects (young age and a lack of language skills) have been included as 'signs of human trafficking' in the official lists used by police and social workers to detect victims.

These views are based on stereotypes of East European women as helpless and dependent. Such stigmatisation puts them in the category of potential victims and can be seen as discrimination. It also counteracts the idea of sex work as a legal occupation and fails to take sex workers seriously (Oude Breuil and Siegel, 2012: 156). In the Zandpad case, these stereotypes of 'victims' and the city council's plan to protect them from exploitation and human trafficking led to a situation that only further damaged their reputation and socio-economic position. They were not consulted on the actual state of affairs at Zandpad, neither were they invited to participate in the policymaking process on window prostitution in Utrecht or to discuss the development of possible alternatives to closure.

Researchers on prostitution and human trafficking often point to the lack of an empirical basis (Sanghera, 2005; Zhang, 2009). According to Sheldon

Zhang, "*imagination seems to have taken the place of sound empirical studies*" (Zhang, 2009: 185). Bovenkerk *et al.* noted that a media hype occurs when "all media focus on the same subject and journalists print snap judgments on facts that have not been verified" (2006: 67). The media hype has its own dynamics, whereby political and legal developments are followed and lots of statistics are bandied about. Despite its 'hype status' in media and policy, little is actually known about the phenomenon of human trafficking, the connection between prostitution and human trafficking, and the actors involved (Oude Breuil *et al.*, 2011).

This lack of fact based knowledge and in-depth analysis has not stopped some researchers and interest groups from making policy recommendations (Zhang, 2009:185). Other authors criticise the fact that policy and practice with regard to suspected perpetrators and victims of human trafficking are usually based on an oversimplified image of naïve and innocent victims versus violent perpetrators (see O'Connell Davidson, 2005; Sanghera, 2005; Agustín, 2007; Janssen, 2007). According to Zhang (2009: 191), the empirical data show a much more nuanced picture, where sex work involves negotiation instead of coercion or violence.

The definition of human trafficking is constantly being changed and extended. In the 19th Century it addressed the problem of 'white slavery': European girls who were sold against their will to brothels in Western Europe (Haveman, 1998; Segrave et al., 2009). May 1904 saw the signing of the International Agreement for the Suppression of the White Slave Traffic (Paris, 18 May 1904), which criminalised the recruitment of women for sex work by use of coercion (Oude Breuil et al., 2011). In 1949, the definition of victims of human trafficking was expanded in the UN Convention for the Suppression of the Traffic in Persons and of the Exploitation of the Prostitution of Others, according to which the victim's consent was no longer a criterion. Under the influence of radical feminists, who regarded prostitution as 'sexual slavery' and the result of patriarchal oppression (the 'sexual domination discourse'), all women in the sex industry were seen as victims of human trafficking (Kempadoo, 2005; Segrave *et al.*, 2009). Therefore, prostitution ought to be prohibited.

About the same time, the view emerged that prostitution should be recognised as a legitimate occupation. Today, we recognise the polarisation between the two positions. The stereotypes are still being repeated (the victims are women and children, the perpetrators are men) and emotions still play a major role. However, from a historical perspective, the comparison between victims of human trafficking and victims of the white slave trade in previous centuries stands in the way of an objective scientific analysis of the phenomenon (Kempadoo, 2005: xix; O'Connell Davidson, 2005: 42).

The stereotypical image of human trafficking with its clearly recognisable victims and perpetrators reflects the enduring dichotomy between the repressive approach and the human rights approach. Various authors describe these positions as contradictory (Kempadoo, 2005: xiv; O'Connell Davidson, 2005: 69; Mertus & Bertone, 2007). Other studies show that most prostitutes do not see themselves as victims, and certainly not as naïve, innocent or passive (Siegel & Bovenkerk, 2000; Siegel & Yesilgoz, 2003; Siegel, 2005; Agustín, 2007; Janssen, 2007; Brunovskis & Surtees, 2008; Davies, 2009). These studies also show that the women's decision to move to another country was taken freely and well-considered. In most cases they knew in advance that they would be working in the sex industry. Other research tells us that the women's high expectations, such as working for an upmarket escort agency, were not always fulfilled. Many of these women had already been working as prostitutes in their country of origin or elsewhere in West Europe (Aronowitz, 2009; Agustín, 2007; Janssen, 2007).

The stereotype that all victims come from the lower social classes or from extreme poverty is not valid either. According to Europol, the victims are '. . . not limited to the poorly educated or desperately impoverished' (Europol, 2006: 18). Other reasons for emigrating, such as a thirst for adventure, new opportunities and "following successful friends", appear to provide enough motivation to go and work abroad in the sex industry (Agustín, 2005; Corrin, 2005; Europol, 2006).

The question as to whether prostitution can be regarded as a 'normal occupation' in this context is, therefore, ambivalent. Sex workers themselves ask this question in interviews and on internet blogs. An article was published on the website *zondares.nl* ("sinner.nl" popular among sex workers and clients) that expressed the frustrations of sex workers about current opinions and the treatment of prostitutes by the authorities: "*The rest think of us as shady people in a dirty little world*", "*If we were treated like a normal profession, we wouldn't have to worry about anonymity like paranoid lunatics. Once you come out as a whore, you're a social outcast . . .*"; "*The banks treat us like criminals and want nothing to do with us*"; "*The government . . . should be protecting us against injustice, but they are protecting the public from us, from having to treat us like normal people.*"

In our research we often encountered the current negative images of prostitution, whether or not in connection to human trafficking. Attempts, including legal efforts, to promote prostitution as a regular occupation are being met with resistance from politicians, the media and the public. It would appear that the good intentions underlying the lifting of the brothel ban and the legalisation of prostitution with all corresponding rights and obligations cannot be realised in the current climate of fear and insecurity. "*The signs of danger need not to be crime itself or the threat of it, but more subtle perceptions of possible risk and the escalation of danger*" (Young, 1999: 72).

All over the world, prostitution has become a metaphor for urban disintegration and decay. Prostitutes evoke all sorts of conflicting feelings. "*Symbolic of urban encounters and fantasies, the prostitute was desired and feared, degraded and threatening, and regarded with disgust and fascination*" (Scott *et al.*, 2015: 82). She was seen as the deadly seductress of the men in the city streets. One solution to the problem was to reduce the visibility of prostitution by banishing prostitutes to the margins of the cities. However, creating prostitution-free inner cities turned out to be impossible. ". . . *The city is not an inherently a sexualised space; nor can they* [policy makers, DS] *expect to create such a space*" (Maginn and Steinmetz, 2015: 264). The Zandpad area is a perfect example of how prostitution was kept out of the city centre. Its location was advantageous for policymakers as well as for sex workers and their clients. It was easy for the city council and the police, as they only had to monitor one street where window prostitution was concentrated, while the women and their clients benefited from guaranteed anonymity and easy accessibility.

In recent years, however, we have seen that the prostitution areas in various cities in the Netherlands have been reduced in size (Korf *et al.*, 2005; Wijk, van, 2009). The legalisation of prostitution in 2000 was accompanied by a flood of new rules and measures pertaining to the sex industry. Media research seems to suggest that new regulations and programmes (often inspired by the image of prostitution as 'criminogenic') are regularly being introduced at the municipal or national level.

These regulations are aimed at clearly distinguishing between ordinary prostitution (accepted and normalised) and the abuses that often accompany prostitution (prohibit and criminalise). Excesses such as human trafficking, 'lover boy' practices, public nuisance and citizens' feelings of unsafety are given high priority. In the context of accepting and normalising, the (hazardous) occupation of sex worker is regulated and operators are subject to a number of conditions. These regulations cover age, nationality (since 2000, only EU citizens are allowed to work as prostitutes), practical aspects such as registration, working hours, premises, and opening hours. The municipality checks whether or not operators and sex workers are complying with the conditions imposed on them. The police's primary focus is on the other side of the prostitution policy: the fight against abuses such as the employment of underage girls or forced prostitution (human trafficking). However, it would appear that this prostitution policy has lost its sense of direction. The line between normalising prostitution on the one hand, and a tough approach to abuses on the other, has become blurred. Within the context of regulating an 'ordinary occupation', municipalities have become ever more demanding. When, in 2010, Utrecht city council ordered the operators to put stronger measures in place to ensure safety on the Zandpad, a great deal of money had already been invested in video surveillance, security checks, number plate registration, alarm systems in the women's rooms and other practical measures. Clearly, more than what is demanded of any other entertainment sector.

These continuing and far-reaching policy changes can be seen as a sign of late modernity. In the social sciences, constantly changing policy rules are known as 'liquid policies' (Bauman, 2006), fitting in with our 'liquid life' (Bauman, 2000). The closure of the Zandpad prostitution zone could be interpreted as an example of liquid policies. Some say that the 'days of tolerance in the Netherlands are over and that there is no way back' (Schuilenburg and Van Swaaningen, 2013: 109). An alternative interpretation might be that the two-track approach has not been strictly adhered to and experiences gained from tackling abuses and the display of moral 'righteousness' have had a spill-over effect on ordinary regulation. In Utrecht, a relatively small number of abuses determined the fate of the entire prostitution sector.

In spite of the city's two-track approach, the police used to share their information about abuses with the city council and even though Zandpad was regarded as a safe environment by sex workers and clients alike – no doubt partly as a result of more stringent regulation – the city nevertheless decided to close down all prostitution windows in 2013.

In his *Culture of Fear* (1997), Frank Furedi describes how social problems can be magnified and taken out of context by the media and the world of politics, the effect of which is to make people feel insecure and fearful. In the Zandpad case, the arguments adduced by the city regarding criminality (human trafficking) and the suspected involvement of operators and pimps in criminal activities should be understood within the context of a culture of fear, where facts no longer matter. A culture of fear and the negative stereotypes it creates can emphasise various aspects of the perceived problem, such as fear of foreigners, fear of globalisation, fear of transnational organised crime etc. In response, a 'neo-conservative administrative rationality' emerges in which 'order and discipline are the core values' (Schuilenburg and Van Swaaningen, 2006: 118).

The culture of fear cannot be viewed separately from the 'risk society' (Beck, 1992), which is characterised by early risk evaluations and rapid government responses. In the Netherlands, we are seeing that preventive policies are being pushed aside by 'punitive populism', despite a great number of studies showing that prevention rather than repression produces the best results when it comes to safeguarding security (Rosenbaum et al., 1998; Van Swaaningen, 2013).

The decision to close Zandpad can be understood as the culmination of a period of 'moral panic' about human trafficking in the licensed sex industry, which began after the Sneep case (KLPD, 2008). The term 'moral panic' is used in the social sciences to describe a disproportionate and usually negative social response to deviance. Such a response leads to stigmatisation, exclusion or, in the words of Stanley Cohen, who introduced the concept in 1972, the 'amplification' and worsening of the problem (Cohen, 1972). Some authors argue that the concept of moral panic has become more relevant in recent years with the emergence of new threats and dangers (Goode and Ben-Yehuda, 2013; Krinsky, 2013) and the call for severe action. According to Cohen, the media, the police and politicians adopt a negative attitude when certain situations, groups or individuals are identified as a threat to social norms, values and interests. 'Moral entrepreneurs', *i.e.* policymakers, the police and the media, 'diagnose' the seriousness and extent of the problem and offer treatment to cure the 'disease' (Cohen, 1972: 9). When the majority of the population agrees on the threat posed by certain persons or groups, these 'folk devils' are labelled as the 'enemy', who must be removed or eliminated (Goode and Ben-Yehuda, 1994; Cohen, 1972).

The consequences can vary from repressive measures and criminal prosecutions to exclusion of the marginalised groups. Sometimes a problem appears to have been solved, but the moral panic repeats itself when certain events take place (criminal trials) or new scandals come to light (Furedi, 2013). In other cases, the problem disappears from a particular setting but re-emerges somewhere else (a phenomenon known as the 'waterbed' effect). According to Howard Becker, public dissatisfaction can also take the shape of a 'moral crusade'. Moral crusaders do not accept the solution to the problem and will always find new issues to rail against (Becker, 1963: 149-155).

Despite the fact that the sex workers and their clients at the Zandpad provided little evidence for human trafficking; despite the steps that already had been taken to combat human trafficking; and despite the fact that both women and clients felt safe at this location, the city council went looking for a new 'villain' and pointed to the operator as the suspected facilitator of 'abuses'. The council's decision illustrated the deep mistrust and fear that had developed between the different social groups (policymakers and those involved in the sex industry). Needless to say, a combination of mistrust, fear and moral panic is not likely to result in effective solutions or contribute to social cohesion (Furedi, 2013).

Sex workers' views on the Zandpad and the consequences of its closure

As it turned out, there was a serious discrepancy between the city council's stated policy goals (safety and a 'clean' sector) and the actual effects of the closure of window prostitution on the Zandpad. There was also a major difference of opinion between the city and the prostitutes. The women and their clients refused to believe the official reasons given for the closure. Because the city and the police never provided any evidence of human trafficking (all the evidence was in the 'secret report'), speculation began to circulate among the women about other possible motives, such as plans for new construction projects, a national (or even international) agenda to suppress prostitution, personal motivations on the part of the former mayor or the previous community police officer *etc.*

The process of closing down the windows on the Zandpad was met with resistance and a great deal of emotion; the women demonstrated twice and organised several petitions. To date, the promise that window prostitution would soon be made possible again in Utrecht, has not been fulfilled.

The case attracted a great deal of attention, both positive and negative, from politicians and academics. The positive responses praised the decisiveness of the city council in its "war against human trafficking". Most of the criticism was directed at the fact that the city, despite its good intentions to combat human trafficking and protect its potential victims, ended up endangering and harming hundreds of women by not offering them an alternative.

After the closure of Zandpad, there was a marked increase in mobility among the sex workers. They relocated to other cities where window prostitution is still allowed, in the Netherlands, Belgium or Germany. Some ended up in Utrecht's street prostitution area or in sex clubs and escort agencies. Others found work in massage parlours, bars and saunas, or meet their clients at home, in hotels or private residences. The consequence for the authorities was a loss of overview.

All our respondents (women, clients and welfare organisations) remarked that the majority of women are worse off since the closure of the Zandpad, financially, mentally and physically. They are finding it more difficult to pay their mortgage, provide for their children and support their families abroad, which means that they have to work longer hours and for lower wages. They are now faced with considerable travelling expenses (many still live in Utrecht) and spend many hours travelling to other cities, in some cases three hours a day. By moving to another town many women have lost their regular clients, who were at first willing to follow them to their new place of work but eventually stopped doing so.

The Zandpad women also found themselves in competition with the local sex workers in other cities. Coming from a location associated with human trafficking, they were sometimes seen as 'tainted' and treated with suspicion by operators and other sex workers.

For their part, the newcomers from Utrecht found it difficult to adapt. In their new places of work, prices were often lower than they were used to and there was less privacy. All of our respondents who had found work in window prostitution elsewhere in the Netherlands described their new circumstances as less favourable and not as safe as Utrecht. We also interviewed women who were now working in sex clubs and private residences and they, too, were earning less than before. They all looked back with nostalgia to the time they worked at the Zandpad.

For some women, working from home allowed them to stay in Utrecht, but this too was a last resort rather than a first choice. Some of them mentioned their sense of insecurity, which they tried to manage by constantly 'screening' their clients, mostly by telephone. Others had had unpleasant experiences with neighbours or were worried about their children. On the Zandpad they were able to work openly and legally, but working from home as a prostitute is prohibited in Utrecht and the women knew that what they were doing was illegal.

In our search for the Zandpad women we approached various official bodies. We found that there was no central registration of the sex workers' mobility. The women we interviewed told us that they had little to no contact with social workers, either in Utrecht or anywhere else. Some social workers tried to stay in touch with 'their women' if they had their phone numbers, but most numbers were no longer in use. It also became obvious that neither the city nor the police, nor any other government agency maintained regular contact with the sex workers after the closure of the Zandpad. Most of them had no idea of the women's whereabouts. This lack of personal contact, commitment and central registration obscured the problems facing these women from view. Some agencies appeared to take a resigned attitude toward this loss of oversight, even though the literature tells us that when a brothel is closed down, the sex workers are forced to relocate to more hazardous environments and become an easier prey for pimps. Although Utrecht's prostitution policy was meant to protect women from human traffickers, there was no agency tasked with reducing or at least keeping track of the harmful consequences of the closure of the Zandpad. One can speak of a serious discrepancy between moral righteousness and proclaimed care.

Conclusions

"*It is much easier to condemn and exclude rather than to explain in depth and do justice to all sides*" (Sumner, 2014: 98). Prostitution and human trafficking are not one and the same phenomenon. In 2000 the ban on brothels was lifted in the Netherlands. This change in legislation was intended to send a clear signal that on the one hand working as a prostitute or operating a prostitution business must be considered as a normal occupation. On the other hand, it acknowledged that there are risks attached to prostitution and that robust action must be taken against excesses such as exploitation, forced prostitution and prostitution involving minors. Making a distinction between ordinary sex work and forced prostitution lies at the heart of the Netherlands' legalisation policy.

But how did we get to the point where prostitution – the oldest profession in the world – has become synonymous with a relatively modern phenomenon – human trafficking – despite considerable criticism of this viewpoint in the public debate, politics and academic research? Why has the alleged connection between sex work and human trafficking become so widely accepted and embedded in Dutch society? How did we reach the situation we find ourselves in today, in which paid sex is talked about almost exclusively in terms of the dangers it represents?

In this study, we show how the 'human trafficking hype', namely the over-exaggerated and extreme propagation of negative images of prostitution, has led to policy decisions that have made existing problems worse, rather than better. Hundreds of sex workers who had nothing whatsoever to do with the problem of human trafficking, became the victims of the irresponsible and hasty decision taken by Utrecht city council to close the Zandpad prostitution zone.

We have analysed the consequences of this policymaking, focusing on the fate of the women who lost their place of work in Utrecht. This study shows what happened to these women after the closure of Zandpad and the consequences for them, their clients, welfare organisations and other parties involved.

The history of prostitution in the Netherlands in general and in Utrecht in particular shows us the consequences of banning regulated sex services for sex workers, their clients and the surrounding area. In every era, we can observe two effects of restrictive policy changes: the relocation of prostitution to other locations and settings, and the flourishing of illegal prostitution. This should not be a surprise to the responsible policy makers: there has never been a period in history when strict policy measures and repression have succeeded in eradicating prostitution.

Utrecht has always had a host of organisations working to solve the 'problem' of prostitution. This is still the case today, as many welfare organisations in Utrecht are working on this issue. There are two competing points of view regarding prostitution: the first one considers that sex workers need to be rescued ("*prostitution is not a normal job, no one ever chooses to do it of their own accord*"); the second point of view sees sex workers as people who have made a conscious decision to work as an entrepreneur. If the latter viewpoint is taken, policy is mainly focussed on rooting out abuses (long working hours, feelings of unsafety *et cetera*).

We conclude that the decision to close Zandpad was taken too hastily. No real alternatives for the sex workers were proposed at the time – and to this date, none have been put forward. The reason given for closing down the area – 'human trafficking in Zandpad' – was considered 'unfounded' by all of the sex workers, their clients, lawyers and some of the welfare organisations.

The generalised label 'human trafficking' is being used as an excuse to combat prostitution in Utrecht, in the same ways as in previous centuries. The decision to close the Zandpad prostitution zone was taken within the current policy framework of legalised prostitution, yet its effect has been to worsen the position and reputation of sex workers.

Obviously, it is necessary to take proportional tough action against excesses and the city council, police and the courts need to take appropriate measures. But an opposing logic also holds: by no means is all prostitution connected with human trafficking. Utrecht's policy did not take this second argumentation into account. Their failure to do so resulted in a policy based on a broad generalisation; a policy that has affected every window prostitute in Utrecht, even though human trafficking only affected a limited number of victims over a wide time span. Utrecht's policy of closing down window prostitution was intended to 'protect' prostitutes against abuse, but paradoxically it has only served to increase the risks to which they are exposed. It seems, however, that this is of little interest to those in favour of closing the zone: closing brothels means closing your eyes to real problems wrapped in a display of righteousness.

References

Aas, K. F., *Globalization and crime*. Los Angeles: Sage, 2007

Agustin, L., The disappearance of a migration category: Migrants who sell sex. *Journal of Ethnic and Migration Studies*, 2006, 29–47

Andrijasevic, R., Beautiful dead bodies: Gender, migration, and the representation in anti-trafficking campaigns. *Feminist Review*, 2007, 24–44

Aradau, C., The perverse politics of four-letter words: Risk and pity in the securitization of human trafficking. *Millenium Journal of International Studies*, 2004, 251–277

Aronowitz, A., *Human trafficking, human misery: The global trade in human beings*. Westport/Conneticut/London: Praeger, 2009

Bauman, Z., *Liquid modernity*. Cambridge: Polity Press, 2000.

Bauman, Z., *Liquid times: Living in an age of uncertainty*. Cambridge: Polity Press, 2007.

Beck. U., *World risk society*. Cambridge: Polity Press, 1999

Becker, H., *Outsiders: Studies in the sociology of deviance*. New York: The Free Press, 1963

Berman, J., (Un)popular strangers and crises (un)bounded: Discourse of sex trafficking, the European political community, and the panicked state of the modern state. *European Journal of International Relations*, 9, 37–86

Bossenbroek, M. and J. Kompagne, *Het mysterie van de verdwenen bordelen. Prostitutie in Nederland in de negentiende eeuw*. Amsterdam: Bert Bakker, 1998

Boutellier, H, *De veiligheidsutopie: hedendaags onbehagen en verlangen rond misdaad*. Den Haag: Boom Juridisch Uitgever, 2002

Bovenkerk, F., M. van San, M. Boone, T. Boekhout van Solinge & D. Korf, *Loverboys of modern pooierschap*. Amsterdam/Antwerpen: Augustus 2006

Brennan, D., *What's love got to do with it? Transnational desires and sex tourism in the Dominican Republic*. Durham/London: Duke University Press, 2004

Brunovskis, A. and R. Surtee, R., Untold stories: biases and selection effects in research with victims of trafficking for sexual exploitation. *International Migration*, 2008, 4, 1–38

Chin, K. and J. Finckenauer, *Selling sex overseas. Chinese women and the realities of prostitution and global sex trafficking*. New York/London: New York University Press, 2012

Cohen, S., *Folk devils and moral panics. The creation of Mods and Rockers*. Oxford: Martin Robertson, 1972.

Daalder, A., *Het bordeelverbod opgeheven. Prostitutie 2000-2001*. Den Haag: WODC, 2007

Davies, J., *'My name is not Natasha'. How Albanian women in France use trafficking to overcome social exclusion (1998-2001)*. Amsterdam: Amsterdam University Press, 2009

De Vries, P., *Kuisheid voor mannen, vrijheid voor vrouwen. De reglementering en bestrijding van prostitutie in Nederland, 1850-1911*. Hilversum: Verloren, 1997.

Europol, *Trafficking of women and children for sexual exploitation in the EU. The involvement of Western Balkans organized crime 2006. Crimes against persons unit.* Den Haag, 2006

Freschot, A., *Amoureuze en pikante geschiedenis van het congress en de stad Utrecht.* Hilversum: Verloren, 2013

Furedi, F., *Culture of fear: Risk-taking and the morality of low expectation.* London/Washington: Cassell, 1997

Goderie, M., *Controle van de prostitutie door de politie.* Apeldoorn: Politie en Wetenschap, 2014

Goode, E. and N. Ben-Yehuda, *Moral panic: the social construction of deviance.* Oxford: Blackwell, 1994

Haveman, R., *Voorwaarden voor de strafbaarstelling van vrouwenhandel.* Deventer: Gouda Quint, 1998

't Hart, P., *Leven in Utrecht 1850-1914. Groei naar een modern stad.* Hilversum: Verloren, 2005

Heuts, l., E. Tromp and G. Homburg, *Doublestraat sluiten? Een marktonderzoek naar de seksuele dienstverleningsbranche in Den Haag.* Amsterdam: Regioplan, 2012.

Janssen, M.-L., *Reizende sekswerkers. Latijns-Amerikaanse vrouwen in de Europese prostitutie.* Apeldoorn/Antwerpen: Het Spinhuis, 2007

Kempadoo, K. (ed.), *Trafficking and prostitution reconsidered: New perspectives on migration, sex work, and human rights.* Boulder: Paradigm Publishers, 2005

Kempadoo, K. and Doezema, J. (eds.), *Global sex workers: Rights, resistance, and redefinition.* New York/London: Routledge, 1998

Kiemel, J and W. Ten Kate, De programmatische aanpak van mensenhandel en mensensmokkel. *Justitiële verkenningen*, 2007, 7, 97-106

KLPD, *Schone Schijn. De signalering van mensenhandel in de vergunde prostitutiesector.* Driebergen: KLPD, 2008

Mai, N., Embodied cosmopolitanism: The subjective mobility of migrants working in the global sex industry. *Gender, place, and Culture*, 107-124, 2013

Muftic, L., Attitudes regarding criminal justice responses to sex trafficking among law enforcement officers in Bosnia and Herzegovina. *Journal of Criminal Justice and Security*, 2013, 2, 177-189

NRM, *Nationaal Rapporteur Mensenhandel en Seksueel Geweld tegen Kinderen. Mensenhandel in en uit beeld II. Cijfermatige rapportage* 2008-2012. Den Haag: BNMR, 2012

O'Connell Davidson, J., *Prostitution, power and freedom*. Cambridge: Polity Press, 1998

Oude Breuil, B. and D. Siegel, De autonome sekswerker: mythe of blinde vlek? Stereotypering en 'deresponsibilisering' in het Nederlandse prostitutie-beleid. In F. de Jong and R. Kool (eds.), *Relaties van gezag en verantwoorde-lijkheid: strafrechtelijke ontwikkelingen* (139-157). Den Haag: Boom Lemma uitgevers, 2012

Oude Breuil, B., D. Siegel, D., P. van Reenen, A. Beijer and L. Roos, Human trafficking revisited: The legal, law enforcement and ethnographic narratives on sex trafficking to Western Europe. *Trends in Organized Crime*, 2011, 1, 30-46

Rosenbaum, D., A. Lurigo and R. Davies, *The Prevention of crime: Social and situational strategies*. Belmont: Wadsworth 1998

Saunders, P., Traffic violations determining the meaning of violence in sexual trafficking versus sex work. *Journal of Interpersonal Violence*, 2005, 343-360

Schuilenburg, M. and R. van Swaaningen (2013) Veiligheidin een laatmoderne cultuur. *Tijdschrift over Cultuur en Criminaliteit*, 2013, 2, 109-122.

Siegel, D., Recent trends in women trafficking and voluntary prostitution: Russian-speaking sex workers in the Netherlands. *Transnational crime*, 2005, *1*, 4-23

Siegel, D., Human trafficking and legalised prostitution in the Netherlands. *Temida*, 2009, 5-16

Siegel, D. and F. Bovenkerk, Crime and manipulation of identity among Rus-sian-speaking immigrants in the Netherlands. *Journal of Contemporary Crimi-nal Justice*, 2000, 4, 424-444

Siegel, D. and Y. Yesilgoz, Natashas and Turkish men: new trends in human trafficking and prostitution. In D. Siegel, H.G. Van de Bunt and D. Zaitch (eds.), *Gobal organized crime. Trends and developments*, (73-84). Dordrecht: Kluwer academic Publishers

Stemvers, F., *Meisjes van plezier. De geschiedenis van prostitutie in Nederland*. Weesp: Fibula-Van Dishoeck, 1985

Van de Bunt, H.G., In het hart van de vergunde sector. *Justitiële Verkenningen*, 2007, 7, 78-81

Van der Wurf-Bodt, C., *Van lichte wiven tot gevallen vrouwen. Prostitutie in Utrecht vanaf de late middeleeuwen tot het einde van de negentiende eeuw*. Utrecht: Kwadraat, 1988

Weitzer, R., *Legalizing Prostitution. From illicit vice to lawful business.* New York/London: new York University Press, 2012

Young, J., *The Exclusive society.* London: Sage Publications, 1999

Zhang, S., *Beyond the 'Natasha story'. A review and critique of current research on sex trafficking.* Global Crime,2009, 3, 178-195

A 'virtuous circle' of illicit markets? Smuggling and colonial state building in the Italian interwar Dodecanese

Georgios Papanicolaou and *Filippo Espinoza*[1]

Introduction

Can illegal markets play a role in a state's conscious strategies and efforts to establish and further order? Are there conditions under which law enforcement takes second place to wider considerations of national interest? The relationship between state policy and illicit economic activity is typically understood as an oppositional one: beyond a sense of lawlessness, illegal markets exist as a threat to the state's economic and fiscal interests. In fact, our contemporary understanding of illegal markets is underpinned by the understanding of 'organised crime', which is often equally seen as inherently oppositional to a state's claim on law and order over its territory. Contemporary discourses leave very little margin for a consideration of the relationship between state policy makers and regulators as anything other than conflictual.

Nevertheless, the idea that state administrators or agents may collude with agents of the underworld, under circumstances and considering the pursuit of a state's strategic aims, is not unheard of and unprecedented. There no lack of historical examples indicating that state agents will collude with underground elements in so far as such collusion is understood as beneficial to those strategic aims, particularly in the sphere of international relations and as means to interfere with domestic or regional situations abroad (*e.g.* Thomson 1994; Campbell 1977). It is far less clear, however, whether, with specific regard to economic activity, state administrators would be inclined to approach illegal markets as less of a problem to be addressed and more as an opportunity to be exploited than legal ones.

[1] Georgios Papanicolaou, Reader in Criminology, Teesside University UK. Filippo Espinoza, Doctoral student, University of Trento, Italy.

In this chapter,[2] building on our investigation of archival sources in Rhodes and Rome with regard to the situation and the policies of the Italian Administration of the Dodecanese (the 'Government of the Italian Islands of the Aegean') (Espinoza and Papanicolaou, 2016) we will offer an example and discussion of precisely this latter possibility. Specifically, we interrogate the policy and practical approach of the Italian Administration between its early phase up until the mid-1930s towards two key areas of illegal economic activity, namely, the smuggling of goods and the smuggling or currency. We argue that the geopolitical situation and internal economic conditions of the Dodecanese, marked by extensive and intensive presence of illegal economic activity, became both a tool for the articulation of the Italian rule over the population of this region and a lever for the promotion and pursuit of Italian expansionist plans in the wider region of Anatolia and Eastern Mediterranean. The two illegal markets we examine were not only synergistic to each other, as we shall see soon, but were also conducive to the Italian aim of social pacification in the fledging colony.

The structure of this chapter is straightforward. We begin with a brief interrogation of the relationship between state and illicit economic activity, aiming to situate the Dodecanesian context among other instances of upperworld and underworld convergence. We then proceed to explain in some detail the particularities of that context, particularly in the light of the geopolitical changes it was exposed to around the beginning of the 20th Century and during the early days of the Italian annexation in the 1920s. We provide an account of both areas of illicit activity, the smuggling of goods and the smuggling of currency and explain how the local Italian government approached them as means to pacify the wider local populations and to co-opt the local elites. We conclude with a few reflections on the significance of our findings.

---

[2] Work for this project has been supported by a British Academy Small Research Grant (SG132031). We would also like to thank Ioannis Papageorgiou, the Rhodes Centre for Historical and Social Research (Rhodes Project) SCE, and Irene Toliou, Director of the Greek General State Archives of the Dodecanese, for their generous support of our work. The translation in English from the Italian originals is ours.

The state and illicit economic activity: always conflictual

The purpose of this section is to situate what we found most interesting in our material within the wider theoretical debates and insights about the relationship between state and illegal markets. The Italian authorities of the Dodecanese had unambiguous knowledge of the extensive and emphatic presence of illegal markets. Our material suggests that the function of illegal markets appears to have been taken into account, if not integrated, in the articulation of Italian political strategies to pacify and co-opt local populations. We reserve for the concluding section some qualifications arising from the particularities of the Dodecanesian regime and its relation with the general policies of Rome and fascism during the period. However, the nature and extent of the considerations regarding illicit economic activities in a range official documents and reports leave little doubt that the Italian administration engaged directly and uniquely with these activities.

This is already an intriguing starting point, as in the literature on illicit markets there is a very wide consensus regarding the oppositional nature of the relationship between illicit economic activity and state policies. Much of the literature has focused on the association of illegal markets and the underground economy with 'organised crime'. Firstly, it was thought that the former constitutes an important source of income for the latter at the expense of legitimate business and of the fiscal interests of the state. And secondly, importantly, to the extent that the connection between illegal markets and 'organised crime' is present, the organisational element in illegal entrepreneurship represents a challenge to the state's territorial control and authority (for an overview, see von Lampe, 2016). The possibility of (quasi-)governmental structures accounts for the understanding of state and illegal markets as an oppositional relationship in the discussions of organised crime ever since the latter emerged as an important social issue (e.g., Cressey, 1969; Albini, 1971; Arlacchi, 1998). In fact, the very notion of sovereignty, which is associated with the modern state, would alone account for the designation of underground economic activity as 'illegal' and undesirable. Nonetheless, the informal economy, escaping the regulatory claim of the state, is in itself a widespread reality of economic activity (see Portes *et al.*, 1989).

It is not the case that there is rigid separation and a clear line of demarcation between the underworld of illegal markets and the upperworld of the formal economy and of the state. Legitimate economic actors may engage in illicit economic activity, just as illegal entrepreneurs (and 'organised crime') may operate from within licit economic structures, entities and institutions. There is some consensus today that the delineations established by early discussions of illegal markets and 'organised crime', particularly ones that typically reflect policy concerns, are not necessarily helpful for understanding the reality of these phenomena (Antonopoulos and Papanicolaou, 2014; Fiorentini and Peltzman, 1997; Naylor, 2004; Reuter, 1983; Ruggiero, 1996; Van Duyne, 1996; Woodiwiss and Hobbs, 2009), as they tend to underestimate the overlap, interchange and interdependency between underworld and upperworld. This of course only serves to underscore that from a state administrator's viewpoint, illicit economic activity is viewed as a political challenge and issue by default (see, *e.g.*, Kerry, 1998), and that the state's effort to regulate and suppress such activity is a genuine and serious expression of its claim to sovereignty. Thus, their default position would be the firm denial of any hint or suspicion of such interdependency.

Once the question of illegal markets has been transposed into lines underscoring the political nature of the problem – and much of the literature is very much aware of and keen to highlight this aspect (Cressey, 1969; Shelley, 1999), then it rather becomes a matter of analytical candour to acknowledge that the national interest may always colour the state's approach and thus mitigate any understanding of that approach on absolute terms. That a state's policy may involve some extent of complicity with the underworld is not unheard of, as means of furthering a strategic pursuit, particularly in the domain of international politics. For example, McCoy (2003) has provided a very robust account of how the CIA played a role in the trafficking of heroin as part of its cold war strategy and of the US intervention in Southeast Asia. Earlier on in the same region, the French colonialists tapped into the tribal opium economy and relied to some extent on opium revenues to fund the development of French Indochina. An equally interesting account emerges from the context of the Philippines, where the early 20th Century policies of the US colonial regime can be seen to have contributed to the 'creation of regulatory framework for the later rise of a thriving vice economy' (McCoy, 2009, p. 234). This development in its turn is understood by McCoy (2009) to have furnished a tool of political rule for both the colonial power and the local political elites. It is of course highly doubtful that such phenomena could be part of mainstream politics and policy making, certainly not as part of domestic politics. The reason for this is that they are much more likely to be subject to opposition and to cause scandal. They are typically seen as instances of 'parapolitics' (Wilson and Lindsey, 2009) rather than conventional politics, and they seem to be residing predominantly in the domain of foreign policy. Admittedly, however, the study of such cases remains limited.

Our interest for the Italian treatment of illegal markets in the Dodecanese stems precisely from this latter consideration: what we understand as a policy of tolerance towards illegal markets is situated in the domain of domestic policy. In this case the Italian concern with consolidating their sovereign claim over people and territory with a view to developing an "ubi consistam" (Lago, 1924a) of Italian imperial power in the region. In fact, the colonial context makes this stance even more paradoxical, as it runs counter to other experiences of colonial rule, including the Italian one in Africa, which was marked by prolonged and violence efforts to suppress resistance and to pacify the population (Calchi Novati, 2011; Cresti, 2011; Labanca, 2002). While the question of illegal markets does not emerge clearly, if at all, in the histories of the Italian expansionism, colonial pacification, more than military campaigns to suppress resistance, involves an economic aspect and a project with a view to reorganising production and economic relationships. Its quintessence is to create conditions conducive to economic exploitation (see Neocleous, 2013). In studies of other contexts, when the question of illegal markets emerges, it is clear that the suppression of economic activity outlawed by the colonial authorities is a key concern and a primary goal (*e.g.*, Tagliacozzo, 2005).

In the remainder of this chapter we aim to document in some detail the situation in the Dodecanese and the coordinates of the Italian approach, particularly by investigating the conditions under which the existence and function of illegal markets in that region came to be understood as a peculiar political opportunity for the Italian authorities.

Between geopolitical change and economic decline: the emergence of illegal markets in the Dodecanese

The task we aim to accomplish in this section is to situate the emergence of illicit economic activity in the Dodecanese as a general reality in the final quarter of the 19th Century and into the period of the Italian occupation of the region that commenced in mid-1912. As we have provided a more detailed account of the historical context elsewhere (Espinoza and Papanicolaou, 2016), we focus here on those aspects that we consider the key for the development of illegal markets in the Dodecanese.

Most students and commentators of the region's situation seem to identify the growth of illegal markets with the latter's economic decline following domestic political change in the Ottoman Empire and the introduction of taxes and duties aiming primarily to service the Ottoman public debt. Not much is known about illicit activity in the period prior to that point and up to the first thirty years of the 19th Century, but it is certain that the economic significance of the Dodecanese had remained marginal as economic growth itself had been very limited. The 'barren islands' of the archipelago (Desio, 1924) did not lend themselves well to the development of agriculture. This geography and other related circumstances contributed to the development of a preponderantly subsistence economy. Such limitations meant that for primary subsistence goods such as foodstuff, cattle and other basic provisions, the region depended heavily on the Anatolian coast and the port of Izmir, located a stone's throw away from the islands of the Dodecanese (Ameglio, 1913). Equally adverse had been the conditions for the growth of naval commerce of some significance, as even the largest islands such as Rhodes or Kos lacked suitable locations for the development of significant ports. At any rate, the region's production had been of limited, if any, interest to export markets.

Clearly, therefore, up to the mid-19th Century there was little to support significant economic activities, including illicit activities, except piracy. It is, of course, conceivable that some activity may have occurred following the establishment of the independent Kingdom of Greece in the early 1830s. The creation of a new border opened the possibility that Dodecanesian entrepreneurs could take advantage of the difference in the customs regimes of Greece and Ottoman Empire to undercut licit markets. The reason for such a development could have been – eventually, it became a factor – the special taxation and customs regime, known as 'privileges'. These were granted to the islands, except Rhodes and Kos, by the Suleiman the Magnificent following the conquest of the region in 1522, and which remained in place until the late 19th Century. The islands enjoyed extensive self-government and their only tax obligation to the Empire consisted in a yearly lump tribute, a regime, which may have functioned as an assymetry (Passas, 2001) conducive to the growth of illicit activities.

A complementary factor, benefitting the region's economy in all aspects, emerged in the course of the 19th Century, as the growth of industry and trade internationally, and technological developments such as steam navigation, gave the Dodecanese a new economic significance. On the one hand, a local product, sponge, became an industrial resource of significance and thus boosted sponge fishing to the status of a key and sizeable local industry. On the other hand, the development of trades route via the Suez Canal underscored the significance of the region as a commercial crossroads in the Eastern Mediterranean. The surplus of wealth thus generated gave a decisive boost to the local economy in its entirety. It firstly made possible significant investment in infrastructure, such as public works and education. Secondly, it encouraged the growth of other local industries, such as the tobacco industry – one that also developed into a mass scale production in the course of the 19th Century.

In the off-season the women made cigarettes from imported tobacco, many of which were smuggled into Greece. With their wealth, settlers from Calymnos bought farms on the mainland, and sold European goods in Budrum and up the gulfs. There were similar settlers from Cos. Like Calymnos also, Symi had farms and small settlements on the mainland and on the peninsula of Cnidus to the north, where there are both cattle pastures and plantations of olives and almonds. There was a flourishing yard for building sponge-trading boats and small vessels, and for prompt and skilful repairs. Cos established a "lucrative trade in fresh fruit and vegetables with Egypt, carried till recently in its own spacious and speedy sailing vessels" (Myres, 1941, p. 147).

The islands were successful in prolonging the conditions for economic growth up until the late 19th Century, by resisting the administrative and fiscal policy changes introduced by the Ottomans during the *tanzimat* reform period (Inalcik and Quataert, 1997)[3], which also involved greater uniformity across the territory of the Empire. But this implied the abolition of the 'privileges'. During this period the Ottoman reform efforts were resisted by the local populations, often in strong and vocal forms (Doumanis, 1997, p. 29). A more decisive development was the establishment of the Ottoman Public Debt Administration (OPDA) in 1881, which was accompanied by the policy measures such as the introduction of monopolies on tobacco, salt, alcohol and a license fee for sponge fishing. As the purpose of the OPDA was to administer the servicing of the Ottoman public debt towards European creditors, taxes and duties were intended to be collected and administered centrally, ultimately meaning that a key factor for the economic growth of the region, fiscal autonomy, was to be removed. While at an initial stage the very purpose of this development, servicing foreign debt, entailed a rather lax approach by the Ottoman authorities, the reform programme of the Young Turks brought formally all privileges to an end, without exception (Alhadeff, 1927).

At that time, however, certain local industries had already grown to significant size. For example, the manufacturing of cigarettes and cigarette paper by numerous small workshops, had become a key source of employment and income in islands such as Kalymnos. The attrition and finally the removal of the regime of privileges meant that ultimately such businesses had to seek ways to

---

3   The Tanzimat ("reorganization") of the Ottoman Empire, was a period of reform spanning the mid-19th century. The reforms aimed to modernize Ottoman administration. Their thrust was towards administrative centralization, entailing a removal of the autonomies granted by the preceding "millet" system.

secure their survival and engaging in illegal trade turned out to be one of them. This is reflected in retrospective discussions of the situation by Italian officials: one of the military commanders of the Dodecanese noted in 1918 that *"under the Ottoman regime, smuggling constituted the only and true profession of Calymnos, Symi and Chalki, that specialised in this industry"* (Elia, 1918).

The descent of the local economic circuits into the domains of the underground was to be consolidated further with the beginning of the Italian occupation of the Dodecanese during the Italo-Turkish war of 1912. While the domestic policies of the Ottoman Empire had triggered the onset of larger scale illegal trading, the Italian war in Libya and then WWI brought geopolitics to the foreground as the preponderant factor underpinning the economic fates of the region. The dependence of the islands for vital subsistence goods on the Anatolian coast was dictated by geography and their geophysical outlook. It became a major issue during the war as the Ottomans closed the newly established Italian possession's access to these markets. This entailed that not only goods intended for export but also subsistence goods had to be traded illicitly, the alternative being rapid and radical economic and social decline. It was not the case that the region completely escaped this fate—due to the Ottoman embargo, economic conditions deteriorated significantly. It became so serious that the Italian military authorities had to organise a supply chain for food directly from Italy to rescue local populations from the spectre of famine (Doumanis, 1997). At the same time, the Italian occupation authorities, aiming to maintain their hold over the population of the Dodecanese, had been reluctant to impose a new order on the region's socio-political life. Thereby they acknowledged and retained the Ottoman era privileges as the prevailing administrative status quo of the Dodecanese. Under this regime, the very same factor that accelerated the growth of the region's economy, became, as we shall see in the next section, a factor for the consolidation and accelerated the expansion and growth of illegal markets up until the early 1930s, when Italo-Turkish relations began to improve.

Two complementary illicit markets and the Italian stance towards them

We have already identified a combination of factors underpinning the emergence and operation of illicit economic activity in early 20th-Century Dodecanese: firstly, the productive limitations of the islands themselves, which entailed heavy dependence for subsistence goods and other trade on the neighbouring coast of Anatolia; secondly, the declining economic position of the region triggered by the removal of aspects of domestic Ottoman policies upholding its trade position; and thirdly, the subjection of this activity to the implications of the geopolitical position of the islands and the ebb and flow of Italo-Turkish relations.

The newly acquired territory came to be seen by the Italians as another opportunity for colonial expansion during the 1910s and the course of WWI. and then during the onset of the fascist rule in metropolitan Italy as a potential strategic lever for the Italian ambitions in Anatolia (Espinoza and Papanicolaou, 2016). They, however, were thus presented with a double challenge, namely, sustaining on the one hand, the strategic relevance of the Dodecanese towards Anatolia despite the Ottoman embargo and then the continuing mistrust and protectionism of the Turkish Republic. On the other hand, the Italians also had to address the irredentism of the Greeks (Zervos, 1919). This was the dominant ethnic group among the region's diverse population, and thus it was important to formulate an approach towards pacifying these populations, and, given the region's traditionalist sociopolitical structure, co-opt the local elites to the Italian rule.

Following the annexation of the Dodecanese to Italy with the Treaty of Lausanne in 1923, the new regime in Rome under Mussolini bestowed the Dodecanese with an administrative framework (Royal Decree of 8 August 1924) that provided the colonial-style role of the Governor with ample autonomy and powers. However, it remained accountable directly to the Ministry of Foreign Affairs and thus the Duce himself. The appointed Governor, Mario Lago proved to be precisely the kind of office holder that would make full use of such autonomy and power. Himself a career diplomat and a politically astute individual, Lago was among the most zealous proponent of Italian expansion in Anatolia, an idea that he held on to even after the conclusion of the 1928 Neutrality and Reconciliation Treaty and the gradual normalisation of Italo-turkish relations. As Lago saw the newly established Turkish Republic as a precarious and transient reality, his policies were unambiguously animated precisely by a vision of the Dodecanese as a bastion of Italian power.

"I believe I am not exaggerating when I state that on the resumption of regular commercial relations between Rhodes and the Anatolian coast depends greatly the valorisation of our splendid Possession, which must become the *ubi consistam* of Italian power in the Levant" (Lago, 1924a).

Alongside an Italian programme of gradual modernisation of the Possedimento's productive base that was seen as ambitious and perhaps well-received by the Dodecanesians at the time (Doumanis, 1997), Lago pursued policies that on one hand, aimed to neutralise the sources of potential agitation among the wider population, and on the other hand, to co-opt the local commercial and financial elites that controlled much of the economic activity in the region. With regard to the illicit economy, this strategy of social pacification practically translated into an approach of 'relative tolerance', as we call it, towards illegal markets, aspects of which we will document in the following sections. Of course, it is not the case that the Italian law and customs agencies did not establish a degree of activity, which from their own viewpoint may have appeared difficult but substantial nevertheless (*e.g.*, for the Guardia di Finanza's deployment and record see Cecini, 2014). But as Lago ultimately embodied and acted as the final authority in the Possedimento, his communications to Rome (and also his practice) reflect considerations and intentions of strategic importance for the view of the Italian management of the colony's affairs.

The smuggling of goods

While analytically the examination of the generic category 'goods' would appear to confound different illegal markets, our purpose in this section is to document the Italian Administration's approach towards the goods that could be considered as the prime mover of Dodecanesian society. It is with regard to these goods that the dependency of the islands' economy on the Anatolian coast is exhibited best. The closing of the border by the Turkish authorities during WWI, which had devastated the region during WWI, presented the Italian colonial authority with a key policy double challenge in the early 1920s and after. On the one hand, it had to prevent severe disruptions in the rhythm of the wider population's everyday life, such as the provisioning of the islands with vital food supplies and the other day-to-day small trade with the Anatolian coast. . . . . On the other, it had to address the potentially devastating effect of the Turkish policy on the commercial routes to Anatolia. The latter were seen as an important component of Italian expansionist policies in Asia Minor, but at the same time, important commercial agencies depended on these routes; legal as well as illegal: by the time of Lago's arrival in Rhodes, the growth of illegal trade with the coast had become endemic, and the new Governor himself was acutely aware of that reality.

"[T]he reopening of the east coast is a matter of life or death for the commerce of Rhodes [. . .] The local effects of this crisis are intuitive. A large part of the Dodecanesian population that used to live on the Anatolian trade, currently suffers from the darkest poverty. Rather, in order to survive, it throws itself into riskier smuggling. Naturally, even though they know it is not the Italian regime's fault that such disaster has befallen them, the Dodecanesians do not hold a high opinion of our authority. Which helps create a widespread mood, if not of hostility, at least of distrust, very harmful to the order of our regime. Smuggling becomes every day more organised in almost regular form with the collaboration of the Turks from the coast, who suffer from the uneconomical situation created by the Turkish government as much as our subjects" (Lago, 1924a).

The situation described by Lago in 1924, was to be prolonged throughout the 1920s due to the protectionist policies and the Turkish deep mistrust of the Italian presence in the region. For example, in 1929 the inspector of the Bank of Italy, Arturo Paladini, was reporting that in the past Rhodes was an important supply centre of the nearby lands, and of Anatolia more particularly, which is only a few hours of sailing away. However, this commercial function that gave reason for private banks and a good number of merchants to exist in this city has been deteriorating gradually. According to Paladini trade became ever more difficult due to the tendency of the neighbouring nations to eliminate from their territories every form of foreign penetration, whether commercial or industrial. Despite this, the local commerce, which depends much on the smuggling on the Anatolian coast, remained sufficiently active, as demonstrated by the increased traffic of the port and the very low number of bankruptcies (Paladini, 1929).

The early realisation of the problem and the persistence of the trade barriers to Anatolia throughout the 1920s, gave rise to a unique understanding of the situation by Governor Lago. He thought smuggling was impossible to suppress because Italy as "*a great power, cannot leave a population which she has taken under its guardianship to suffocate, without her prestige being profoundly damaged throughout the Levant*" (Lago, 1924b). Apart from that, smuggling was taking place "*completely to our advantage and at the expense of Turkey*". This stance also led Lago to be very cautious of and to even resist Turkish demands towards Italy to suppress contraband in the Dodecanese. He commented:

"I insist, however, that I must indicate the risks of [any] agreements entailing turkish interference towards the suppression of contraband. Firstly, whichever concessions we made in this area to the Turks for Kastellorizo, we may have to extend them to other islands, thus creating obstacles and situations of conflict that are difficult to foresee; and secondly, we must admit frankly that the exercise of smuggling will be inevitably one of the activities of the Italian islands of the Aegean" (Lago, 1923).

As a result, smuggling became quasi-institutionalised throughout the 1920s in the Dodecanese; even to such an extent that it came to represent a primary economic activity of the smaller islands, and also a significant part of commercial flows through Rhodes. This was not a well-hidden secret, as it were: as the journalist Virginio Gayda, an individual very close to Rome's fascist regime, noted

"[u]nder the pressure of these four negative elements, but, above all, of the increasing distrust and resistance of the Turkish authorities, the commerce of the Dodecanese has been driven back from the Turkish coast, and, therefore, it has been cut off from its vital base. There is no more commerce except contraband. Defying storms and the darkness of the night in order to survive, Greek and Turkish sailors brought their boats and sails towards the coast, furtively loading and unloading goods with the complicity of the indigenous population" (Gayda, 1928, p. 149).

But why exactly was Governor Lago adamant that smuggling took place entirely at the expense of Turkey? "Our customs authorities", he noted, *"are charged with the task of ensuring that the goods do not enter* [our territory] *as contraband. Once they have landed, whether they arrive or not to their destination, I do not believe it is our duty to oversee"* (Lago, 1927). From his point of view, as long as the low customs duties of the Possedimento had been paid, anything went – the goods were free to move in whichever way the involved merchants and entrepreneurs saw fit. This being the official stance, even very established companies began in the 1920s not only to import but also to produce goods destined to be smuggled.

Take for example the firm Alhadeff, perhaps the most important and sizeable commercial entity in Rhodes, which was also connected with the Alhadeff Bank belonging to the same family. The firm produced, in association with the Benosiglio firm in Kos, two types of cigarette paper (Memphis and Tebriz) which were destined to be traded in large quantities on the black market in Turkey exclusively. Vittorio Alhadeff himself, commenting on this type of activity, remarked in his memoirs that *"our commerce was fully legal. We were selling to the Anatolian merchants who came to and went from Rhodes on their caïques. How do they enter the goods in Anatolia? That's their business"* (Alhadeff, 1998; 174).

Awareness of the idea that contraband was taking place "to the advantage of Italy" was also shared by members of the law enforcement agencies in the Dodecanese. Reporting in the 1930s on two "influential" individuals of Greek ethnic origin form Patmos, the local commander of the Carabinieri noted

"how in the past [the first individual] practiced effectively and notoriously, and on a large scale, the smuggling of alcohol and other goods at the expense of Greece and Turkey, activity that was seen favourably by the Government of the time [. . .] also because it did not do any harm to our treasury, as he had always declared the merchandise which bought in order to smuggle it subsequently . . . [the other individual] managed to attain a solid financial position, particularly with profits he made by exercising, as is well known to us, the smuggling of cigarette paper in our favour and at the expense of Greece and Turkey" (Grassini, 1937).

The tolerance towards smuggling persisted beyond the 1920s and the normalisation of Italian-Turkish relations after 1928. Whether the Italians felt confident enough to intervene in the operation of illegal markets is a moot point. To be sure, the removal of the key geopolitical consideration meant that smuggling could perhaps be seen more clearly as an activity detrimental to the fiscal interests of the colony. At the same time, Rome had undertaken a effort to modernise Italian customs legislation and that brought about a wholesale strengthening of sanctions against smuggling, and also the introduction of additional offences relating to this activity. Nevertheless, with the local economy still damaged by the prolonged economic decline and hardship and with Lago retaining ultimate authority in the Dodecanesian affairs, policies of tolerance remained in place. For example, there was official support for appeals, leniency towards convicted smugglers and even pardons and amnesties. This policy was practiced consciously in the Possedimento's territory, precisely on individual grounds of poverty and inability to pay fines and so on.

In 1932, for example, the local commander of the Guardia di Finanza in Rhodes was still reporting that the inhabitants of the island [Halki, in this instance], not having other local resources, dedicate themselves exclusively to the clandestine trade of tobacco: they import it as leaves from Greece or Turkey, process it and then they export it in the most convenient mode, especially to the nearby island of Rhodes (Spinelli, 1932). The task of the Guardia di Finanza section itself was to merely report to Rhodes the departure of any "suspicious boat".

Overall, we see why, in our view, there are good reasons to call the relative tolerance of the Italian authorities towards smuggling a 'strategy'. Under the overarching aim of keeping alive the Italian expansionist ambitions in Anatolia, by means of commercial infiltration, the Italian authorities appear to have pursued two important goals domestically in the Possedimento. On one hand, by not actively disrupting the circuits of illicit trade in the region, the Italian authorities ensured that latter's economic life, which involved illicit trading to a remarkable and vital extent, was not itself disrupted. Smuggling in this sense would be seen as a cushion, absorbing the local population's economic distress and consequently, any political implications that such distress would entail, preponderantly Greek irredentism. At the same time, Lago's regime seems to have been able to take advantage of this circumstance to co-opt and integrate the commercial and also other local elites in the emerging system of colonial rule, in so far as illicit markets represented an opportunity for good business for everyone involved.

The smuggling of currency

The extent to which the above three aspects of the Italian approach had been very closely interwoven, is illustrated by an equally widespread illicit activity which may be regarded as complementary to the smuggling of goods, the smuggling of currency. Again, the activity can be understood to be of importance for the liquidity of both legal and illegal markets. For the illicit market it is a condition for its operations; it is particularly in this circuit that the regime's relation with the local commercial elites can be seen more crisply.

The Dodecanese under the Ottoman rule had featured a rather anarchical banking system, featuring a handful of powerful local family banks and commercial firms that could finance the local population's commercial activity. As most of the currency circulating in the region was absorbed in trade and currency speculation, the figures of banker, merchant and money changer were often indistinguishable. These banks and commercial firms were able to take advantage of wartime conditions in the 1910s to consolidate their dominant position in the operation of local economic circuits. Salomon Alhadeff and Fils, for example, which was mentioned previously, had by the mid-1920s successfully brought most of the region's trade under its control: it has a powerful organisation which was reinforced by the credit and prestige of the Bank Alhadeff. The two agencies were distinct legally and operate in different and well separated fields, yet as both are constituted by elements connected by the ties of kinship, they are emotionally and financially solidary. That means they acted to mutually complement each other in a form of moral and financial cooperation that represented a force that was formidable in relation to the modest potential of the market. In fact, there was no undertaking or business of any importance in which one did not find the name of Alhadeff, just as there is no nice property that does not belong to any of them (Paladini, 1926).

As these local bourgeois elites were integral to the region's economic life in its totality, Governor Lago's policy tended to protect and maximise their liberty even if that meant a range of exceptions from metropolitan legislative requirements and regulations applicable to banking. Such a stance can be understood again by means of the interpretative scheme we propose. That is, the strategy towards the pacification of local populations – cooptation of the elites – to support of the Italian ambitions in Anatolia.

In the circuit of the currency trade in 1920s and early 1930s Dodecanese, Lago's maximisation of liberty approach translated into an exceptional regime that placed no restrictions on the movement of currency in the region, and lacked any regulatory provisions regarding the trade in foreign currency. To justify his policy, the Governor again referred to the "normal movement of business that takes place here with special characteristics and exigencies", in the light of the need to maintain active the trade flows between the Dodecanese and Anatolia. To that end, he resisted any possibility of interfering with the trade of currency, legal and, not explicitly, illegal:

"Prior to the detachment from Turkey, the natural market of the islands had been Anatolia. These markets constituted a centre for the collection and distribution of overseas trade just as their transit commerce was booming, from which the islands drew most of their wealth. Such commerce ceased almost completely after the territorial political separation of the Possedimento from the Continent [Asia].

The Dodecanesian merchants, aiming to maintain the traffic in their hands, while it could easily turn towards the major centres of Turkey, particularly Smirna and Adalia, finance [instead], via local banks, the producers of the goods in the form of advances.

Hence a movement of Turkish currency towards current account operations, a movement, which cannot be documented in the ways prescribed by the current regulations in the Kingdom [of Italy].

Another field of commercial activity particular to these transactions is constituted by the importation from Anatolia of goods, above all goods of first necessity (cattle, vegetables, eggs and many other alimentary goods), which are transported here by boat in noticeable quantity, but in small batches, by modest Turkish merchants, who, once they've sold their goods in Italian lire, must convert the proceeds into Turkish money in order to re-enter their country.

"It is a daily and small-scale traffic, which in its totality represents one of the cornerstones of the commercial activity of the islands; and it is easy to understand, from the very same way it is conducted, that it could not be practically subjected to the rule of the normal trade of currency" (Lago, 1932; 2).

The situation that Lago does not explicitly acknowledge, and thus obscures in his report, is that most of the flows of Turkish currency in and out of the Dodecanese had been illegal, precisely because Turkey prohibited either the exportation or the importation of its currency. Consequently, in so far as commerce with the Anatolian coast required liquidity in Turkish currency, it relied to a considerable extent on contraband money, made available to the Dodecanesians by small sellers or more established commercial actors, such as the banking firms of Rhodes, which would also rely on the informal currency market for liquidity in Turkish money. Practically, the course of historical events of the early 20th Century *"created the particular situation, where a large majority of the population itself is in possession, more or less, of foreign currency, credit abroad and foreign securities"* (Gigli, 1934b: 404). As a result, the trade of currency could spread widely and informally, and was very open to speculation.

This "special' situation in the Possedimento was not unknown to banking regulators, whose internal communications usually comment on and document very clearly both the anarchical order of things and the Governor's protective approach towards it. On several occasions, attempts to enforce some of the standards required by the metropolitan banking system proved to be a frustrating failure, due to the extent of informality that characterised the trade of currencies. Reports of the local inspector of the Bank of Italy in Rhodes, Fortunato Gigli, director of the local branch, acknowledge clearly the challenges posed by the specific configuration of the currency market.

"The Turkish banknotes form the most important base of the coastal trade with the neighbouring coasts. Here, far from the great centres and without any banking equipment, what counts is not the cheque that is difficult to cash, but only the banknote. The small sailing boats, motorboats etc. depart, equipped with banknotes, for the ports of Anatolia. They make their purchases and return with the provisions necessary to the population (primarily cattle, coal, wood, coffee etc.)" (Gigli, 1934a, p.411).

"With Turkish banknotes (in Rhodes there is a very active exchange of this currency which is smuggled in and out of Turkey) advances are given for the production in Anatolia of beams, which are then exported to Egypt and sold in sterling with a conspicuous profit margin" (Gigli, 1934b, p. 405).

"Such activity is very difficult to control in so far as, thanks to the intermediaries, everything takes place without documents, without contracts, with some bills and a lot of trust, which arises from habit" (Gigli, 1934b, p.406).

While in the 1920s this particular outlook was seen by Lago as critical to the survival of the Dodecanesian trade flows with Anatolia, in the early 1930s informality in the currency market still retained its relevance for the bigger local commercial players, who, as seen previously, were typically combining merchant activities and banking operations. These players, would still tap into the informal currency market to secure a sufficient supply of Turkish currency. As Governor Lago, arguing against calls for regulation, remarked:

> "[i]t must be observed that some local firms have branches abroad, above all in Turkey and Greece. Now, it would prove very difficult for these firms to finance their agencies with the necessary foreign currencies, for which it would not be possible to present invoices to prove the corresponding acquisition of goods" (Lago, 1932).

In the course of the early 1930s these local banks also took advantage of the local situation to engage more actively in speculation in the currency trade, an endeavour, which in some cases proved extremely lucrative and strengthened considerably the position of these firms. Around the time, Italian regulators moved more aggressively to impose discipline on the foreign currency trade, by requiring that all remittances in Italian or foreign currency and all foreign credit by the "bankers, money changers, companies, firms and institutions" be declared, and that all operations in exchange currency must demonstrate their relevance to the real needs of the industry and commerce or to the needs of those travelling abroad. Essentially, this was an effort to both formalise and "moralise" (Poli, 1949) the foreign currency trade.

The authority of the Possedimento, however, still resisted these efforts and secured for the Dodecanese exceptions from this regime, so as "not to embarrass the trade patterns in the region" (Gigli, 1934c). Governor Lago appeared determined to defend the interests of the pro-Italian local bourgeoisie, this time by resisting greater transparency in the conduct of their business in the name of not disrupting the status quo in the region and by refusing to differentiate between population and the big local commercial actors. Unsurprisingly, this policy ultimately benefited the latter more than the former, since the defence of the practices of the wider population were a defence of subsistence economy, whereas the defence of the practices of the bigger local commercial interest facilitated an enormous accumulation of wealth.

> "It is at any rate a fact that under the auspices of the Italian administration [this bank] . . . benefited . . . from the most complete liberty of action with regard to the movement of currency, which flowed abundantly to it . . ."

And:

"What is certain is that the company developed after the Italian occupation [1912-1923], and its fortune, which was well limited in 1912, was estimated in 1938, indeed with great approximation, around 80 million lire in Rhodes and abroad" (Poli, 1949: 2, 8)

In sum, once again it is possible to see how the Italian colonial administration consistently approached legal and illegal markets and practices as a unity, firmly integrated and attuned to the region's economic reality. This approach was not a concession, or a confession of weakness: rather it appears to be the result of a conscious concern to use the functions of the local economic circuits in order to further consolidate the Italian rule on the Dodecanese and develop a new system of power, suited to Italy's enduring expansionist ambitions in Anatolia.

Concluding reflections

Can illegal markets play a role in a state's conscious strategies and efforts to establish and reproduce order, and are there conditions under which law enforcement takes a second place to wider considerations of national interest? It would appear that, in the light of the Dodecanesian experience under the Italian colonial administration, the possibility must be affirmed. In fact, what would lend unity to the policies of the Italian administration is precisely such considerations of higher national interest, namely the development of a support platform for the pursuit of wider foreign policy ambitions of fascist Italy. Tolerance of illicit economic activity involving the wider population provided a cushion absorbing the tensions emerging from economic hardship and thus their political implications with regard to the stability of the regime domestically in the Dodecanese. At the same time, a similar policy of tolerance via the acceptance of illicit practices and the avoidance of regulation, helped the regime articulate a vital bond with the local financial and commercial elites, which maintained a dominant position over the islands' economic life. Ensuring domestic stability in the colony was seen as key to the development of the lever for imperialist expansion that Governor Lago saw as the Possedimento's ultimate purpose.

Whether the story of the Dodecanese offers any lessons that are of wider relevance in our understanding of the relations between state and the illicit economy is a moot point. There are important elements of the Dodecanesian experience that would not be readily transferable to other contexts and contemporary situations. For example, Governor Lago's quasi-absolutist position (sanctioned by the Dodecanese's 'constitutional' arrangement) or perhaps the particularities of Lago's relationship with the fascist regime in Rome. Intuitively, such an experience would not lend itself easily to conditions prevailing in a true liberal democratic polity. In fact, Lago's policies, particularly those towards the local economic elites, would be more likely to be seen as generalised corruption, rather than rational policy. Nevertheless, the bureaucratic compartmentalisation of the modern state could notionally be seen as conducive to a situation in which, with regard to illegal markets and their political uses, some parts of the state may recognise opportunities where others perceived unqualified threats.

Our main point is that this possibility cannot be abstractly excluded. Particularly under the label of 'organised crime' illegal markets are seen as absolute threats and the content of any policy cannot be other that of active opposition and suppression. What our account offers, is precisely a glimpse of the view from the heights of state administration: our explanatory scheme is derived from the reports and communications from the highest echelons of the Italian administration in Rhodes and in Rome: Lago to Ministry of Foreign Affairs and Mussolini, head of local branch to the directors of Bank of Italy, and so on. These kinds of strategic deliberations are not always and easily accessible to students of contemporary realities. The possibility, however, that policy and enforcement gaps do not necessarily represent merely 'technical problems' suggests – as our story shows – that such strategic considerations are highly relevant even if well hidden in archives.[4]

References

Albini, J.L., *The American mafia: genesis of a legend.* New York, Meredith, 1971

Alhadeff, V., *L'ordinamento giuridico di Rodi e delle altre isole Italiane dell'Egeo.* Milano, Istituto Editoriale Scientifico, 1927

Alhadeff, V., *Le chêne de Rhodes: saga d'une grande famille sépharade.* Paris, Méditerranée, 1998

Ameglio, G., *Contributo monografico per lo studio politico ed economico dell'isola di Rodi.* Rhodes, Tipo-litografia del Comando della 6a Divisione Speciale, 1913

---

[4] Archival materials would allow broader access and thus the construction of much richer overviews.

Antonopoulos, G.A. and G. Papanicolaou, *Unlicensed capitalism, Greek style: illegal markets and 'organised crime' in Greece*. Nijmegen, Wolf Legal Publishers, 2014

Arlacchi, P., Some observations on illegal markets. In V. Ruggiero, N. South, and I. Taylor (eds.), *The new European criminology. Crime and social order in Europe* (pp. 203-215). London, Routledge, 1998

Calchi Novati, G. P., *L'Africa d'Italia: una storia coloniale e postcoloniale*. Roma, Carocci editore, 2011

Campbell, R., *The Luciano project: the secret wartime collaboration of the Mafia and the U.S. Navy*. New York, McGraw-Hill, 1977

Cecini, G., *La Guardia di Finanza nelle isole italiane dell'egeo 1912–1945*. Roma, Gangemi Editore, 2014

Cressey, D. R., *Theft of the nation: the structure and operation of organised crime in America*. New York, Harper and Row, 1969

Cresti, F., *Non desiderare la terra d'altri: la colonizzazione italian in Libya*. Roma, Carocci editore, 2011

Desio, A., *La potenzialità agricola delle isole del Dodecaneso e i suoi rapporti con la constituzione geologica*. Florence, Istituto Agricolo Coloniale Italiano, 1924

Doumanis, N., *Myth and memory in the mediterranean: remembering fascism's empire*. Basingstoke, MacMillan, 1997

Duyne, P.C. van, The phantom and threat of organised crime. *Crime, Law and Social Change*, 1996, *24*, 341-377

Elia, V., Rapporto a MAE. [Report to the Ministry of Foreign Affairs, 6 October 1918, signed Elia]. Archivio di Gabinetto 1915–1918 (box 56, file 4). Diplomatic Historical Archive of the Ministry of Foreign Affairs, Rome, 6 October 1918

Espinoza, F.M., and G. Papanicolaou, Smuggling in the Dodecanese under the Italian administration. In G. A. Antonopoulos (ed.), *Illegal entrepreneurship, 'organised crime' and social control: essay in honour of Prof. Dick Hobbs* (pp. 189-203). New York, Springer, 2016

Fiorentini, G. and S. Peltzman, Introduction. In G. Fiorentini and S. Peltzman (eds.), *The economics of organised crime* (pp. 1-30). Cambridge, Cambridge University Press, 1997

Gayda, V., L'economia del Dodecaneso. *L'Oltremare*, 1928, 4, 146-149

Gigli, F., Commercio dei cambi. CPL Riservato (b. 95). Historical Archive of the Bank of Italy, Rome, 29 December 1934a

Gigli, F., Commercio dei cambi: nuove disposizioni. [E. Gigli a Roma]. CPL Riservato (b. 95). Historical Archive of the Bank of Italy, Rome, 22 December 1934b

Gigli, F., Decreto Ministeriale 26/5/934/XII. [Ministerial Decree of 26/5/1934 Report of Inspector Gigli to the Bank of Italy]. CPL Riservato (b. 95). Historical Archive of the Bank of Italy, Rome, 21 July 1934c

Grassini, G., Situazione del comune di Patmo. [Report on the situation of the community of Patmos, from Grassini to De Vecchi, 18 March 1937]. Affari Politici 1931–1945, Dodecaneso-Egeo (box 13, file 7). Diplomatic Historical Archive of the Ministry of Foreign Affairs, Rome, 16 March 1937

Inalcik, H. and D. Quataert (eds.). *An economic and social history of the Ottoman Empire, volume 2: 1600–1914.* Cambridge, Cambridge University Press, 1997.

Kerry, J., *The new war: the web of crime that threatens America's security.* New York, 1998

Labanca, N., *Oltremare: storia dell'espansione coloniale italiana.* Bologna, Il mulino, 2002

Lago, M., Castelrosso. [Castellorizo. Re the Report of the High Commisioner in Constantinople no.4175 of 11th April]. Direzione Generale Affari Commerciali, Egeo 1924–1926 (box 986, f. Isolotti di Castelrosso). Diplomatic Historical Archive of the Ministry of Foreign Affairs, Rome, 1 May 1923

Lago, M., Commercio del porto di Rodi. [Report to the Ministry of Foreign Affairs, telespresso n. 8227, 7 September 1924, signed Lago]. Direzione Generale Affari Commerciali, Egeo 1924–1926 (category 4, fiile 2). Diplomatic Historical Archive of the Ministry of Foreign Affairs, Rome, 7 September 1924a

Lago, M., Il regime doganale Turco e il Dodecaneso. [Report of Mario Lago to the Ministry of Foreign Affairs and the Italian Embassy in Constantinople, Telespresso n.1473, 1924, signed Lago]. DGAC 1924-1926 (cat. 4 f. 2). Diplomatic Historical Archive of the Ministry of Foreign Affairs, Rome, 22 February 1924b

Lago, M., [Lago to the Italian Diplomatic Mission of Italy in Athens]. DGAC 1927 Egeo (cat. 9 f. 2). Diplomatic Historical Archive of the Ministry of Foreign Affairs, Roma, 29 December 1927

Lago, M., Situazione bancaria nel Possedimento. [Situation of banking in the Possedimento, telespresso n. 1993, 23 December 1931, signed Lago]. Direzione Generale Affari Commerciali, Egeo 1934 (cat. 28, file banchi). Diplomatic Historical Archive of the Ministry of Foreign Affairs, Rome, 23 December 1932

McCoy, A.W., *The politics of heroin. CIA complicity in the global drug trade* (Revised ed.). Chicago, Lawrence Hill Books, 2003

McCoy, A.W., Covert netherworld: clandestine services and criminal syndicates in shaping the Philippine state. In E. Wilson, and T. Lindsey (eds.), *Government of the shadows. Parapolitics and criminal sovereignty* (pp. 226-255). New York, Pluto Press, 2009

Myres, J. L., The islands of the Aegean. *The Geographical Journal*, 1941, 97(3), 137-156

Naylor, R.T., *Wages of crime. Black markets, illegal finance and the underworld economy* (Revised ed.). Ithaca, Cornell University Press, 2004

Neocleous, M., The dream of pacification: accumulation, class war and the hunt. *Socialist Studies*, 2013, 9(2), 7-31

Paladini, A., [Inspector Arturo Paladini to His Excelency the Governor of the Bank of Italy, Rome]. Affari Coloniali (prat. 34). Historical Archive of the Bank of Italy, Roma, 22 December 1926

Paladini, A., Succursale di Rodi Regenza della direzione. [Inspector Arturo Paladini to His Excelency the Governor of the Bank of Italy, Rome]. Affari Coloniali (prat. 34). Historical Archive of the Bank of Italy, Roma, 6 December 1929

Passas, N., Globalization and transnational crime: effects of criminogenic assymetries. In P. Williams, and D. Vlassis (eds.), *Combatting transnational crime. Concepts, activities and responses* (pp. 22-56). London, Frank Cass, 2001

Poli, E., Ex Banca Salomon Alhadeff Figli. sua attività a Rodi. [Ex Banca Salomon Alhadeff Figli: sua attività a Rodi]. Vigilanza sulle Aziende dfi credito (box 9947 f.4 Alhadeff). Historical Archive of the Bank of Italy, Roma, 25 June 1949

Portes, A., M. Castells, and L. A. Benton (eds.). *The informal economy: studies in advanced and less developed countries*. Baltimore, John Hopkins University Press, 1989

Reuter, P., *Disorganised crime. Illegal markets and the Mafia*. Cambridge, Massachusetts, The MIT Press, 1983

Ruggiero, V., *Economie sporche. L'impresa criminale in Europa*. Torino, Bollati Boringhieri, 1996

Shelley, L., Transnational organised crime: the new authoritarianism. In H. R. Freeman, and P. Andreas (eds.), *The illicit global economy and state power* (pp. 25-51). Lanham, Maryland, Rowman and Littlefield Publishers, 1999

Spinelli, [Report to the Genral Command of the Guardia di Finanza]. 1919-1939 (box 546 f.3). Archive of the Historical Museum of the Guardia di Finanza, Roma, 3 February 1932

Tagliacozzo, E., *Secret trades, porous borders: smuggling and states along a southeast Asian frontier, 1865–1915*. New Haven, Yale University Press, 2005

Thomson, J. E., *Mercenaries, pirates, and sovereigns. State-building and extraterritorial violence in early modern Europe.* Princeton, Princeton University Press, 1994

von Lampe, K., *Organized crime: analyzing illegal activities, criminal structures and extra-legal governance.* Los Angeles, Sage, 2016

Wilson, E., and T. Lindsey (eds.). *Government of the shadows. Parapolitics and criminal sovereignty.* New York, Pluto Press, 2009.

Woodiwiss, M. and D. Hobbs, Organised evil and the Atlantic alliance: moral panics and the rhetoric of organised crime policing in America and Britain. *British Journal of Criminology*, 2009, 49(1), 106–128

Zervos, S., *The Dodecanese: the history of the Dodecanese through the ages, its services to mankind and its rights.* London, A. Page, 1919

German-Polish cross-border
Police cooperation: A brief overview

Klaus von Lampe and *Aleksandra Zurakowska*[1]

Introduction

In recent years there has been a *"sudden surge in police and judicial cooperation around the world"* (Fijnaut 2012:2). Driven by the idea that increasing cross-border crime demands increasing interaction between law enforcement agencies across borders, manifold forms of legal, institutional and operational collaboration have emerged, building on long-standing instruments such as Interpol, originally established in 1923, and a host of mutual legal assistance treaties such as the European Convention on Mutual Assistance in Criminal Matters of 1959 (Deflem and McDonough 2014; Joutsen 2014a). Yet, cross-border police cooperation is far from being perfect. Even within the European Union, often considered to set an example for other world regions, *"cooperation between Member States is still fragmented"* (Hufnagel 2012:178) and *"nobody seems to have a plan of what the arena of police cooperation should look like in the future and what the level of institutionalisation in this field should be"* (den Boer 2015: 115). In the end Europe continues to encounter the same obstacles for police cooperation found elsewhere. These include fundamental issues of sovereignty, cleavages such as historically rooted tensions between countries, cultural and language barriers, but also obstacles specific to the law enforcement arena, such as differences in the prevalence and perception of crime threats, differences in substantive and procedural law, differences in institutional structures and cultures, and a lack of

---

[1] Klaus von Lampe is Associate Professor at John Jay College of Criminal Justice in New York. Aleksandra Zurakowska is a doctoral student at European University Viadrina in Frankfurt (Oder). The authors would like to thank their interview partners for the willingness to participate in this research project and Silke Wilberg from the Landeskriminalamt Brandenburg for arranging the interviews on the German side. The first author is also grateful for the support he received from the Brandenburg Police College in Oranienburg, Germany, and in particular from Jochen Christe-Zeyse. Major parts of the study have been funded by PSC-CUNY Research Award TRADA-46-523.

resources available for cooperation and mutual assistance (Casey 2010:107-108; Fijnaut 2012; Joutsen 2014b; Lemieux 2010:2).

Given these various factors there are some border regions that appear to be more and some to be less favourable to cross-border police cooperation. Neighbouring countries with well-developed ties and great similarities in language, culture and socio-economic conditions can be expected to also have established close cooperative relations between their law enforcement agencies. Such is the case with the Scandinavian countries and with the Benelux countries (Belgium, Netherlands, Luxembourg) where close cooperation has a long tradition preceding the emergence of the current EU framework (Heeres 2012; Kleiven 2012). In contrast, many of the factors that tend to hamper police cooperation are salient in the relationship between Germany and Poland, not least the historical baggage of centuries of abuse suffered by the Polish nation at the hands of German rulers, culminating in the brutal occupation of Poland during World War II.

What is the nature of cross-border police cooperation under such less favourable circumstances? The purpose of this chapter is to provide a rough assessment of the current state of cross-border police cooperation between the two countries, and more specifically between the German state of Brandenburg and the neighbouring district of Lubus on the Polish side. We draw on an ongoing research project and provide preliminary findings obtained from open sources, unpublished law-enforcement data, and semi-structured interviews with nine German and three Polish law enforcement officers conducted in late 2015 and early 2016.

The border between Germany and Poland and history

German-Polish police cooperation is an interesting object of study not only because international law enforcement cooperation is a fascinating and dynamic phenomenon, but also because for various reasons the German-Polish border is a rather unlikely place to find international police cooperation working.

The German-Polish border is 460 km in length, running from the Baltic Sea coast to the Czech border (Fig. 1). On the German side, there are three *Länder* (states) bordering Poland (Mecklenburg-Hither Pomerania, Brandenburg and Saxony) with the largest part of the border, some 60 % or 280 km, shared by the state of Brandenburg, the site of the present study. Importantly, each of the German *Länder* has its own police force. In contrast to the federal system in

Germany, Poland is a unitary state governed from the capital of Warsaw, which is also true for the police. Poland has one national police force which is subdivided into branches corresponding to the country's 16 provinces (voivodeships). Three voivodeships are situated along the western border to Germany (West Pomerenia, Lubus and Lower Silesia). West Pomerenia in the north and Lubus in the centre, each roughly take up two-fifths of the border. This means that the *Länder* and voivodeships are not neatly paired. Instead, Brandenburg has a common border with West Pomerenia and Lubus, and Saxony has a common border with Lubus and Lower Silesia.

Figure 1
The German-Polish border region

The border is largely marked by two rivers, the Oder River which flows into the Baltic Sea and its southern tributary, the Neisse River. There are only relatively few bridges that connect both countries. For example, there is a bridge across the Oder River, the so-called *Stadtbrücke*, connecting the town of Frankfurt (Oder) on the German side with the town of Slubice on the Polish side, and similarly a bridge across the Neisse River between the towns of Guben and Gubin. An important lifeline of cross-border travel and trade is the E30 highway from Berlin to Warsaw which crosses the Oder River in Frankfurt and Slubice parallel to the *Stadtbrücke*.

German-Polish history

Germany and Poland share a common history full of conflict and trauma. The history of Poland has for centuries been a history of foreign annexation and occupation, largely at the hands of its German neighbours to the west and its Russian neighbours to the East. In the late 1700s, Poland was divided up between Russia, Prussia and Austria and ceased to exist as an independent state until 1918 (Lukowski, 2014). In September 1939, Nazi-Germany and shortly thereafter the Soviet Union invaded Poland in accordance with an agreement reached by the two dictatorships as part of the Molotov-Ribbentrop non-aggression treaty that had been signed the previous month. Subsequently, from 1939 until 1945 Poland had to endure a merciless occupation regime with the German forces actively pursuing a genocidal agenda. It is an important fact, but one that is little known outside of Poland that this agenda was not only directed against Jews but against the entire Polish population. The atrocities systematically directed against the non-Jewish Poles included mass killings, mass deportations and the enslavement of some one million workers into forced labour in Germany. The ultimate goal of the Nazi leadership was to remove the Polish population and to replace it by Germans. According to plans drafted by the SS in 1942, this would eventually have entailed a policy of deliberate starvation and the deportation of millions of people to Siberia (Kochanski, 2012).

In 1945, Poland was shifted westward, losing almost half of its territory to the Soviet Union while gaining previously German territory in the West. As a result of this westward shift, the Oder-Neisse line became the new western border of Poland. In the process, the German population east of the Oder-Neisse line was replaced by Poles that were relocated from other parts of the country, including formerly Eastern Poland. This means that as of the late 1940s there were no historically grown ties between the German and Polish populations along the border. Significantly, in the following years few efforts were made to bring both sides closer together. On the contrary, in response to the Solidarnosc movement the East German government effectively closed the border to Poland in December of 1981 (Stoklosa, 2011: 149, 474).

Current Differences

German-Polish relations on all levels have greatly improved and intensified since the end of the Cold War. With strong German support, Poland has become a member of NATO in 1999, a member of the European Union in May 2004, and a member of the Schengen System in December 2007 so that the German-Polish border has lost much of its separating character (Ruchniewicz, 2006; Ulatowski, 2016). What remains are socio-cultural and economic differences, and also reservations and stereotypes that seem to be slow to disappear. In a survey conducted in April 2016, only 53 % of Polish respondents voiced positive feelings about Germany, and an even smaller share (28 %) of German respondents reported a positive attitude towards Poland. 36 % of German respondents expressed an outright dislike for their Eastern neighbour and 14 % of Poles stated that they had ill feelings about Germany (Lada 2016). However, the results on the German side seem to have been heavily influenced by current developments, namely the new conservative Polish government that came into office in 2015 with an anti-European platform and the refusal of Poland to participate in the German-led effort to give shelter to large numbers of Syrian refugees (see Lada, 2016: 46). In a similar survey in 2013, only 22 % of Germans had indicated that they disliked Poland (Lada 2016: 22). Negative sentiments are primarily tied to the Nazi-era with respect to Germany and to crime with respect to Poland. In 2016, 21 % (2013: 25 %) of Polish respondents associated Germany primarily with the Third Reich, World War II and the occupation of Poland, while 11 % (2013: 16 %) of German respondents connected Poland to crime and disorder, particularly with the theft of automobiles, often citing the slogan *"kaum gestohlen, schon in Polen"* (just barely stolen, already in Poland) (Lada, 2016: 5-8).

Socio-cultural factors

Against an overall positive trend in neighbourly relations there are a number of long-term cleavages separating Germany and Poland. Perhaps the least divisive of these differences is that the German side of the border is predominantly protestant while the Polish side is predominantly catholic.

A much more substantial barrier is created by language differences. German is a Germanic language while Polish is a Slavonic language and both languages are considered to be difficult to learn, expressed in the notion that the German-Polish border is the *"hardest language boundary in Europe"* (Wilkinson, 2009: 73). More efforts are made on the Polish side than on the German side to mitigate the language barrier. In Polish schools, German is the second most popular foreign language after English. 35,5 % of school students in Poland take German classes (Glowny Urzad Statystyczny, 2015:103). This share is even higher, up to 54,9 %, in the voivodeships along the border to Germany (Glowny Urzad Statystyczny 2015:105). In comparison, Polish as a foreign language is only of marginal importance in Germany. Even in the eastern *Länder* Mecklenburg-Hither Pomerania, Brandenburg and Saxony, less than 1 % of school students take Polish classes (Kultusministerkonferenz, 2012).

Socio-economic factors

In terms of the economy, there continues to be a large wealth gap between both countries even though Poland's economic growth has exceeded that of Germany over the past 25 years (Gomulka, 2016). For example, the per-capita gross national income, as of 2015, is more than three times higher in Germany ($ 45.790) than it is in Poland ($ 13.370) (World Bank, 2016). Such discrepancies in socio-economic conditions constitute what Nikos Passas calls *"criminogenic asymmetries", defined as "structural disjunctions, mismatches and inequalities in the spheres of politics, culture, the economy and the law [that] generate or strengthen"* incentives and opportunities for crime (Passas, 2002: 26). Differences in economic strength, however, are not only potential drivers of crime. Importantly, looking at cross-border police cooperation, one effect at the institutional level is that there are marked differences in the compensation of public servants. Polish police officers receive a pay that nominally is only about one-fourth of what German police officers take home. In other words, cross-border cooperation implies that Polish police officers are expected to collaborate, and at times work side-by-side with their German colleagues, performing the same tasks but being paid significantly less.

Cross-border crime between Germany and Poland

German-Polish police cooperation has to be examined against the backdrop of cross-border crime. Given the wealth differential between Germany and Poland and between the former West and the former Soviet Bloc more generally, it would not be surprising to see Germany targeted by cross-border offenders from the East. Indeed, in public perception, this is what characterises the current crime situation. The narrative promoted in the media is that cross-border crime has dramatically increased since Poland's accession to the Schengen System in 2007 as a result of criminals from Poland and other Eastern European countries liberally taking advantage of the removal of permanent border controls (Höhn, 2015; Schwers, 2012; Siegel, 2014).

Figure 2
Crime trends along the border

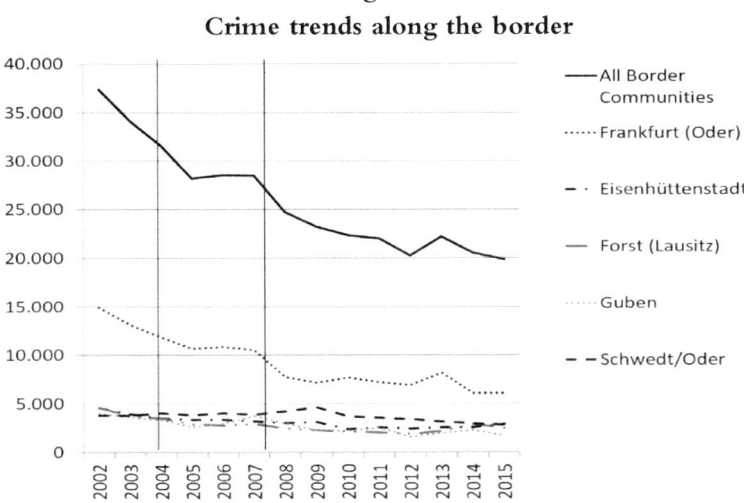

Figure 2 presents the total number of reported crimes in the communities in the Land Brandenburg situated along the border to Poland and in select border towns. The two vertical lines mark Poland's accession to the EU on May 1st, 2004 and Poland's accession to the Schengen System on December 21st, 2007. Source: Landeskriminalamt Brandenburg

Upon closer inspection, however, a much more complex picture emerges (Lada 2014). The crime statistics for the border region show an overall trend in the opposite direction. Reported crime has been *declining* more or less consistently since the 1990s and, contrary to expectations, neither Poland's accession to the EU in 2004 nor accession to Schengen in 2007 have triggered spikes in the crime rate (Fig. 2). Likewise, data provided by the Brandenburg police show that most offenders (2015: 80,9%) in the border area are Germans. At the same time, crime rates along the border are higher than the average for the *Land* Brandenburg as a whole and there have been increases locally and with respect to certain types of crime. For example, there has been a manifold increase in the number of cars stolen after 2007, especially in border towns like Frankfurt (Oder), and many of these crimes are attributed to Polish gangs or to gangs from Eastern European countries like Lithuania or Ukraine (Blankennagel 2015; Funke 2013; Metzner 2011). In recent years, localised spikes in property

crimes have occurred parallel to a decreasing police presence in the border region, particularly as a result of organisational reforms and staff reductions within
the Brandenburg police force (Fröhlich 2015).

These developments help explain why despite an overall decrease in crime
rates crime continues to be perceived as a major problem in the border region
and why even cases of vigilantism have occurred. This, in turn, has created
political pressure towards improving police cooperation between Germany and
Poland. There is an expectation on the German side in particular that the border should not be an obstacle for effective law enforcement.

German-Polish Police Cooperation

German-Polish police cooperation takes place within a framework that is partly
multilateral and partly specific to the bilateral relations between Germany and
Poland. The multi-lateral framework encompasses three sets of instruments:
1. international and EU instruments such as Interpol, Europol and the Schengen Information System (SIS) which are primarily relevant for the exchange
   of data across borders,
2. EU instruments regulated in the Schengen Implementation Agreement that
   pertain to operational cooperation such as cross-border surveillance and
   cross-border hot pursuit, and
3. international and EU-level regulations on mutual legal assistance, namely the
   EU Convention on Mutual Assistance in Criminal Matters of 2000.

The bilateral framework consists of treaties and agreements between Germany
and Poland at the national and sub-national levels. For routine police business
the bilateral framework appears to be much more important than the multilateral framework, while criminal investigations largely rely on the European
framework of mutual legal assistance.

The key facets of German-Polish police cooperation

The main element of the bilateral framework is the German-Polish Treaty on
Police- and Customs Cooperation which was signed in May 2014 and which
went into effect in July 2015. In part the treaty has simply consolidated previous
agreements, including a treaty on police cooperation from 2002, and adapted
them to the new situation that was created by Poland's accession to the EU and
to the Schengen area. In part it has broadened the scope of cross-border coop-

eration and has gone further beyond the minimum standards that are set by the Schengen Convention (Bavendamm, 2016; Bode, 2015).

Below the level of international treaties there are cooperation agreements at the sub-national level that regulate the interaction between regional police agencies. For example, in 2006, the Chief of Police of Frankfurt (Oder) and the Chief of Police in Gorzow Wielkopolski, the main city in the voivodeship Lubus, signed an agreement on joint patrols in the border area (Stolpe and Buschmann, 2014: 151).

Cross-border police cooperation ranges from support for unilateral police action to carrying out joint police operations. A key aspect of police cooperation is the sharing of information, be it in the most mundane day-to-day policing or in complex criminal investigations. A typical scenario is, for example, that a Polish driver is stopped in Germany at a routine traffic check and realises that he or she has left the driver's license at home. In Germany, driving without a license is a criminal offense which means that under the legality principle the police officers making the stop have to start a criminal investigation into whether or not the individual does hold a valid driver's license. All the ensuing inconveniences for the driver can be avoided because the police officers on site are legally and technically in a position to quickly obtain information from Poland on the driving privileges of a Polish citizen. The issue is then reduced to an administrative offence of not being able to show a valid driver's license, which in Germany carries a fine of 10 Euros.

Compared to assistance in unilateral police activities, with thousands of information requests going in both directions across the border every year (Lada, 2014:30), cooperation in the narrow sense of the word, *i.e.* the pursuit of shared goals in a collaborative way, is a rather rare occurrence. In the area of public order policing, joint patrols and joint traffic checkpoints on both sides of the border on land or on water take place on a more or less regular basis, for example once a month or, at best, once a week. In addition, German and Polish police officers cooperate directly at large events like football matches or the annual "Przystanek Woodstock", an open air music festival that attracts hundreds of thousands of visitors to the Polish border town of Kostrzyn.

In the area of criminal investigations, so-called parallel or mirror investigations where law enforcement agencies on both sides of the border investigate the same offenders appear to be the most common form of joint operations, although it is not clear how many parallel operations are actually carried out. According to our respondents, it may not be more than a handful in any given year involving the Brandenburg police.

The most comprehensive direct cooperation, as far as criminal investigations are concerned, is attained with Joint Investigation Teams (JITs) under Article 13 of the EU Mutual Legal Assistance Convention of 2000. JITs are composed of law enforcement officers from two or more countries to investigate a specific criminal case for a limited period of time. So far, three German-Polish Joint Investigation Teams have been set up with the active participation of the Brandenburg police. The first of these JITs was formed in 2013 and targeted Polish car thieves who operated in Brandenburg and other parts of Germany but also inside Poland. The second JIT was launched in 2015 to investigate a Polish gang of thieves specializing in the theft of Mercedes Sprinter vans. A third JIT was established in January 2016 to track down an offender group specializing in the theft of trucks.

Permanent bi-lateral police cooperation between Germany and Poland is institutionalised in the form of the Joint Centre for Police and Customs Cooperation in Swiecko, housed in the former Polish customs and border checkpoint on the E30 highway. Broadly modelled after the French-German Police and Customs Cooperation Centre (PCCC) in Kehl, set up in 1999 (Nogala, 2001:139), the Centre in Swiecko became operational with Poland's accession to the Schengen area in December 2007 and is charged with facilitating the communication between German and Polish law enforcement agencies. It is staffed by officers from the police, border guard and Customs services from both sides of the border and connects national databases through human-to-human interfaces. The main component of the Centre is the *operations room* where the representatives of the German agencies sit on one side and representatives of the Polish agencies on the other side of a long table with access to their respective databases. The Centre is staffed around the clock seven days a week, similar to the PCCC in Kehl but different from other joint centres, namely those with Luxembourg and with Denmark (Stolpe and Buschmann, 2014).

The German-Polish treaty on police cooperation

With the German-Polish police treaty of 2014 that went into effect in 2015 an attempt has been made to comprehensively regulate the cooperation between police agencies on both sides of the border. As already indicated, in various respects it goes beyond the 2002 police treaty and the Schengen framework.

· For example, with respect to the exchange of information, the German-Polish police treaty (Article 7) broadens the substantive scope of the information that can be shared to include not only information about criminal offences but also on administrative offences. This facilitates the sharing of information on petty transgressions that are criminalised in Germany but not in Poland, such as petty thefts and certain traffic violations which fall under the category of contraventions (*wykroczenie*). The German-Polish treaty is also supposed to make it easier to use shared information in criminal proceedings, because judicial consent is no longer required as long as the police agency providing the information agrees to its use in court. However, differences in interpretation limit the practical importance of this clause.

Another example is cross-border surveillance. The new treaty (Article 22) broadens the substantive scope beyond the investigation of crimes that have been committed to also include the *prevention* of crimes. In addition, the police agency conducting cross-border surveillance is given more time in urgent cases to obtain the consent of the host country to continue the surveillance operation. Under the Schengen Implementation Agreement (Article 40) a surveillance operation has to be discontinued five hours after crossing the border at the latest if no consent by the host country is obtained. Under the new German-Polish treaty the limit is an additional seven hours for a total of twelve hours that cross-border surveillance can be continued without the consent of the host country. Finally, officers conducting cross-border surveillance are also authorised to make preliminary arrests if the observed person is committing a crime while under surveillance.

The authorisation to apprehend a person on foreign soil not only applies to cross-border surveillance but also to *cross-border hot pursuit* (Article 25). In contrast to the Schengen Implementation Agreement (Article 41), the pursuing officers are explicitly authorised to stop a vehicle. There are also no limits in terms of time and geography for cross-border hot pursuit. Theoretically, a suspect may be pursued all the way to the Eastern border of Poland, or all across Germany. This, however, only confirms the previous status quo established by the declarations of Germany and Poland to the Schengen Convention (Bavendamm, 2016:39). Perhaps most significantly, the German-Polish treaty of 2014 not only permits cross-border hot pursuit on land. It now makes pursuit possible on water and by air as well, so that, for example, a suspect fleeing by car across the border can be pursued by helicopter.

German-Polish police cooperation in practice

Overall, the framework for German-Polish police cooperation is fairly far reaching, even in comparison to police cooperation between Germany and some of its western neighbours (Stolpe and Buschmann, 2014). But how do things play out in practice? To shed light on the day-to-day realities, we examine three aspects in more detail: the language barrier, institutional differences, and the asymmetry in the degree to which Germany and Poland are affected by cross-border crime.

The language barrier

Arguable the greatest challenge faced by German and Polish police officers in cross-border cooperation is the language barrier. The two sides do not share a common language. We do not have exact data, but from our interviews it has become obvious that there are only few Polish police officers who speak German. Lada (2014: 34) provides an estimate of 10 %. And there are even far fewer German police officers who speak Polish. English language skills, it seems, are not sufficiently prevalent and sufficiently developed for communication at a professional level. Reportedly, only some of the younger officers converse in English. Likewise, Russian did not emerge as a working language in the 1990s even though it was taught as the first foreign language in East Germany and Poland during the Cold War.

For some official meetings, professional interpreters are hired while otherwise cross-border communication hinges largely on those officers on the respective police forces who are fluent in German and Polish. To increase their number, the Brandenburg police has been eager to hire native Polish-speakers. This includes second generation immigrants from Poland and the children of mixed German-Polish parents who are fluent in Polish, although, because they have only attended school in Germany, may not be able to read and write well in Polish. The Brandenburg police also actively seeks to recruit Polish citizens who do not need to give up their Polish citizenship in order to become police officers in Germany. As of June 2016, three Polish citizens were enrolled at the Brandenburg Police College. One German respondent mentioned a colleague who is a sworn officer on the Brandenburg police force who has retained his Polish citizenship and also continues to live in Poland, something that appears to be regarded as entirely unproblematic.

In practice, those officers who are bi-lingual disproportionally share in the burden of cross-border communication and cooperation. They are tasked with establishing and maintaining contacts across the border on behalf of their superiors and colleagues, they participate in meetings to serve as interpreters, they are assigned to Joint Investigation Teams, and they are the points of first contact for new inquiries from the other side. In effect, bi-lingual officers assume a position that does not necessarily correspond to their formal position in the police hierarchy, and the tasks they perform may be different from their official job description. One senior German police officer noted:

> "We see that our native-speaker is being accepted as a partner in negotiations, and we see how intimately he is dealt with."

Some efforts have been made to broaden the language skills and cross-cultural competence of police officers. One example is the EU-funded "Tandem" program which has provided joint training for German and Polish police officers since 2012 (Lada 2014:33-34; Stolpe and Buschmann, 2014:151). Up to 12 officers from each side are paired in bi-weekly courses that are held annually over a three-year period. The third-year course is organised as an exchange program where each officer is interning for a week at the place of work of his or her Tandem-partner.

Brandenburg police officers also have the opportunity to take Polish (or other foreign language) classes as part of their official duties. However, these courses do not seem to fundamentally lower the language barrier because too few officers participate and because the courses fall short of what would be needed to reach true language proficiency. One German respondent suggested that it would require assigning officers to a partner agency on the other side of the border for half a year or a full year to accomplish that.

Institutional differences

A second challenge for German-Polish police cooperation, apart from the language barrier, is presented by institutional differences. As indicated, Poland has a centralised system of government with one national police force, leaving aside the border guard and also some other branches of government that fulfil some limited policing tasks. Germany, in contrast, has a federalist system with 16 states (*Länder*) that each have their separate and autonomous police force. These state level police forces are supplemented on the federal level by the federal police agency BKA (*Bundeskriminalamt*) and the former border guard which has been reorganised into a federal police force (*Bundespolizei*). Needless to say, the structure of German policing looks rather diffuse from the Polish point of view and it is a challenge to determine who within the federalist structure of the German police has jurisdiction over a particular matter. In a typical case of trafficking in stolen motor vehicles, for example, which involves the theft of cars in several German *Länder*, the Polish national police has to deal with the BKA, and possibly the *Bundespolizei*, and the police agencies in the affected *Länder*. At the same time, German police officers have to get used to the fact that because of the centralisation of the Polish police their direct counterparts at the regional level may in some instances need to seek prior approval from Warsaw.

Closely connected to the issue of centralisation vs. decentralisation, another salient difference between German and Polish police lies in the institutional culture. In Poland, according to the observations of German officers, the police adhere to a more top-down management style whereas in Germany a more cooperative management style is prevalent. As a result, in cross-border interactions German police officers feel that they individually have more leeway in making decisions than their Polish counterparts.

There is also an important institutional difference between both countries in the relations between police and prosecution. In Poland, most criminal offences are first investigated by the police independently from the prosecutor. In Germany, criminal investigations, as a matter of principle, are conducted under the supervision and guidance of the prosecutor. This means that in criminal cases the Polish police is always faced with two stakeholders on the German side, police and prosecutor. On the other hand, it is difficult for the German side to determine whether to contact the police or the prosecution service in Poland. Inquiries and requests for mutual legal assistance made to Polish prosecutors are fruitless as long as an investigation is still in the hands of the police. At the same time, intelligence collected by the Polish police independent from the prosecutor is subject to special restrictions with respect to the cross-border sharing of information.

Against the backdrop of these complications, our respondents stressed the importance of trust-based, informal relations to make optimal use of the possibilities for cross-border cooperation that the current framework allows. A German respondent explained the importance of informal links in the following way:

> "Informal contacts are very important because that way more background knowledge is shared than through official letters. When I sit down face-to-face with the colleague in Poland I simply learn more than from sending him three requests and getting three responses."

A Polish respondent likewise stressed the value of informal relations:

> "I work directly with German agencies. These direct contacts are very important. The official channels we also need, but direct contacts are more important, of course within the limits of the law."

416

That these informal contacts are crucial but are not ubiquitous is highlighted in the following statement by a German respondent, who also highlights that for use in court, information has to be shared through formal channels:

"Formal and informal contacts are at least of equal importance. Without informal contact, information often cannot be obtained. (. . .) When you need information quickly, you get it informally. Through formal channels it would be too time-consuming so that the information will no longer be needed. But informally obtained information is of no use either when you cannot put it into the dossier later on. You need both: formal and informal. 'Formal' means in writing through the LKA [state level police] - BKA - Warsaw - Gorzow - specific unit, and back the same way. You sometimes have speedy processing when you know the people. There are voivodeships that have not come as far with respect to cooperation compared to Szczecin, Gorzow or Lodz. Then you get the response: no information available, even though we know that there is information. The Poles experience it the same way. We in Brandenburg try very hard to respond in a timely manner, but there are other *Länder* who are very spartan in the way they react to requests from Poland."

Aside from the network of informal contacts across the border, some of the problems that arise from institutional differences are also alleviated by formal arrangements, namely by the Joint Centre for Police and Customs Cooperation in Swiecko and by Joint Investigation Teams. The Joint Centre supports officers on one side of the border in finding partners for cooperation on the other side of the border. This helps Polish officers, for example, in cutting through the maze of multiple police agencies in Germany. The Joint Centre also lowers the language barrier in that it makes it possible to quickly obtain information from the other side of the border without having to bother with translating a request or having to involve a bi-lingual officer.

Joint Investigation Teams are seen to be particularly valuable in that they help overcome the difficulties that arise from differences in the role of police and prosecutor in criminal proceedings. Through the integration of prosecutors into JITs the information that is collected in the course of an investigation can be directly used by both sides in court so that issues of data exchange do not arise in the first place. The downside is that JITs require months of preparatory work in negotiating the underlying agreement. Setting up the first German-Polish JIT with Brandenburg participation in 2013 reportedly even took one and a half years of preparation. That is why there are plans to set up a permanent joint investigative unit in the medium and long run. Several German respondents mentioned this as the single most important measure to further improve German-Polish police cooperation.

Asymmetry in German-Polish police relations

An important aspect of German-Polish police cooperation is that the relationship is asymmetric. Overall, as a result of differential patterns of cross-border crime there is more at stake for the German side than for the Polish side. Cross-border hot pursuit is a case in point.

Cross-border hot pursuit means that police officers from one country follow an individual into a neighbouring country who has either been caught in the act of committing a crime or has escaped from custody (see Article 41 Schengen Implementation Agreement).

Since 2008, the first year after Poland joined the Schengen area, there has been an upward trend in the annual number of hot pursuits from 8 in 2008 to 55 in 2015 (Tab. 1). However, this instrument has largely been used by the German side while there have only been few cases, 13 in all, when Polish officers pursued suspects across the border into Germany. Still, the instrument of hot pursuit is viewed by both sides as routine, with about half of the pursuits leading to the apprehension of a suspect. Also, in about 50 % of the cases, officers from both sides of the border are involved.

Table 1. Cross-border hot pursuit

	2008	2009	2010	2011	2012	2013	2014	2015	total
Germany → Poland	7	18	16	20	33	42	34	54	224
Poland → Germany	1	2	–	3	1	1	–	5	13
Total	8	20	16	23	34	43	34	55	237

Source: Polish Police; Brandenburg Police

There has been a similar asymmetry in the sharing of information through the Joint Centre for Police and Customs Cooperation in Swiecko. However, in recent years the number of requests for information that go to the Centre from Poland has approximated the number of requests for information from Germany (Lada, 2014: 29). Most inquiries pertain to minor cases while for major criminal investigations the role of Swiecko is limited to brokering cross-border working relationships and providing logistical support for mutual legal assistance.

Discussion and Conclusion

All of our respondents, irrespective of their nationality, shared a generally positive outlook on German-Polish police cooperation. There appears to be a genuine commitment on both sides to mutual assistance and collaboration despite the various obstacles that do exist; and there is some sense of pride certainly among senior police officials that collaboration between Germany and Poland is in some respects more advanced than between Germany and some of its other neighbours. At the same time it cannot be ignored that there is an asymmetry in the German-Polish police relations in that Germany is more affected by cross-border crime than Poland, at least as far as the Oder-Neisse border is concerned. Germany, overall, also seems to be somewhat more enthusiastic about further developing cross-border cooperation. In contrast, the Polish side has shown greater concern for maintaining national sovereignty.

As has been noted for international policing generally, informal relations play a crucial role in the day-to-day functioning of German-Polish police cooperation. The picture that emerges from our interviews is that the German and the Polish sides are connected through a network of informal contacts characterised by strong ties, marked by frequent, trust-based interaction, connecting immediately neighbouring agencies, for example the police forces in the twin cities of Frankfurt (Oder) and Slubice, or the Brandenburg LKA and the office of the national police in Gorzow. The ties weaken with distance even within the border region. For example, the contacts the Brandenburg police maintains to the office of the national police in Szczecin (Western Pomerania) up north by the Baltic coast do not seem to be as strong as those to Gorzow. Finally, cross-border informal ties are the weakest or are even non-existent to *Länder*, respectively voivodeships further inland. In these cases, cooperation has to rely on the institutional framework of cross-border cooperation which appears to work far less efficiently without underlying informal network ties and may in many instances be too slow for practical purposes.

The key positions in the informal cross-border network are occupied by *bilingual* officers. In fact, especially in the case of the Brandenburg police, the main burden of communication and cooperation with Poland is apparently borne by a small number of Polish-speaking officers, which is partly a reflection of the imbalance in language training between the two countries. In Poland, considerable resources are invested at the school level for teaching German, and arguably, Poles have greater incentives to learn German than Germans have for learning Polish because of the business and job opportunities Germany provides. In this light, efforts by the Brandenburg police do make sense to recruit Polish citizens. However, it should be noted that this approach is not without caveats because it potentially fuels discontent on the Polish side given the markedly lower salaries police officers receive in Poland.

The language barrier will continue to be the greatest obstacle for cross-border police cooperation between Germany and Poland in the foreseeable future. It seems questionable whether the language barrier can be overcome by the means that are currently in place, namely language courses and recruitment of bilingual officers. Stolpe and Buschmann (2014:129) suggest that in the medium and long run it may make more sense to promote English since it is already the official language in international policing. Pragmatically speaking, English may also be a foreign language that is easier to learn for Poles and Germans alike, and anecdotal evidence suggests that German and Polish police officers already draw at an increasing rate on English in cross-border communication. However, it would require novel efforts to bring English-language skills to a level comparable to that of the current German-Polish bilingual speakers on the German and Polish police forces. It should also be noted that English-language skills are still of rather limited use in communication with the population along the German-Polish border.

It is difficult to assess the effectiveness of German-Polish police cooperation in terms of measureable outcomes with respect to cross-border crime. The continuous decline in crime rates on the German side of the border may be an indicator that police cooperation does curb crime. Recent increases in the clearance rates of crimes in the border region have also been attributed to the functioning of German-Polish collaboration (Lada 2014:59). Likewise, in the case of Germany and Poland, Joint Investigation Teams have proven to be a potent tool, leading to the dismantling of internationally active criminal gangs. A comprehensive assessment, however, would require a detailed analysis of spatial and temporal crime patterns to see, for example, to what extent improvements in cooperation or specific successes in cross-border police cooperation such as those attained by Joint Investigation Teams have suppressed, deterred or at least displaced cross-border crime. Such an analysis has yet to be carried out.

In conclusion, the German-Polish border region encompassing the *Land* Brandenburg and the voivodeship Lubus sets a positive example for cross-border police cooperation. It shows how against many odds law enforcement agencies can collaborate effectively based on a shared sense of professionalism and mutual trust in a generally conducive political climate.

References

Bavendamm, M., Grenzüberschreitende Nacheile. *Kriminalistik*, 2016, 70(1): 38-43

Blankennagel, J., Autodiebe haben's schwerer. *Berliner Zeitung*, 28 May 2015

Bode, T., Deutsch-polnisches Polizeiabkommen tritt in Kraft: Zusammenarbeit als Chance. *der Kriminalist*, 2015, 48(9): 10-12

Casey, J., *Policing the world: the practice of international and transnational policing.* Durham, NC: Carolina Academic Press, 2010.

Deflem, M. and S. McDonough, International law enforcement organizations. In: S. Kethineni (ed.), *Comparative and international policing, justice, and transnational crime*, 2nd ed. (pp. 79-101). Durham, NC: Carolina Academic Press, 2014

den Boer, M., Police cooperation: A reluctant dance with the supranational EU institutions. In: F. Trauner and A. Ripoll Servent (eds.), *Policy Change in the Area of Freedom, Security and Justice: How EU institutions matter* (pp. 114-132). Milton Park, UK: Routledge, 2015.

Fröhlich, A., Bedingt einsatzbereit. *Potsdamer Neueste Nachrichten*, 7 July 2015

Funke, R., Autodiebe sind schnell in Polen. *Neues Deutschland*, 3 June 2013

Gomulka, S., Poland's economic and social transformation 1989-2014 and contemporary challenges. *Central Bank Review*, 2016, 16(1): 19-23

Glowny Urzad Statystyczny (2015). *Oswiata i wychowanie w roku szkolnym 2014/2015.* Warsaw: GUS. Available at:
http://stat.gov.pl/download/gfx/portalinformacyjny/pl/defaultaktualnosci/5488/1/9/1/oswiata_i_wychowanie_w_roku_szkolnym_2014-2015.pdf (last accessed 14 December 2016)

Höhn, S., Auf Streife gegen Autodiebe. *Berliner Zeitung*, 20 March 2015.

Joutsen, M., International instruments on cooperation in responding to transnational crime. In: P. Reichel and J. Albanese (eds.), *Handbook of Transnational Crime and Justice*, 2nd ed. (pp. 303-322). Thousand Oaks, CA: Sage, 2014a

Joutsen, M., A view from the trenches: the reality of international cooperation. In: P. Reichel, J. Albanese (eds.), *Handbook of transnational crime and justice*, 2nd ed. (pp. 419-423). Thousand Oaks, CA: Sage, 2014b

Kochanski, H. *The eagle unbowed: Poland and the Poles in the Second World War*. Cambridge, MA: Harvard University Press, 2012

Kultusministerkonferenz. *Zur Situation des Polnischunterrichts in der Bundesrepublik Deutschland*. Bericht der Kultusministerkonferenz vom 22.08.1991 i.d.F. vom 4.10.2012. Available at:

http://www.kmk.org/fileadmin/veroeffentlichungen_beschluesse/1991/19 91_08_22-Situation_Polnischunterricht.pdf (last accessed 14 December 2016)

Lada, A., *Floskeln oder Fakten? Die Deutsch-Polnische Zusammenarbeit bei der Bekämpfung der Grenzkriminalität*. Warsaw: Instytut Spraw Publicznych, 2014

Lada, A., *Deutsch-Polnisches Barometer 2016: Gegenseitige Wahrnehmung der Polen und Deutschen 25. Jahre nach der Unterzeichnung des Nachbarschaftsvertrages*, Bertelsmann Stiftung, 2016 Available at:

http://www.isp.org.pl/barometr2016/de/runterladen.pdf (last accessed 14 December 2016)

Lemieux, F., The nature and structure of international police cooperation: an introduction. In: F. Lemieux (ed.), *International police cooperation: emerging issues, theory and practice* (pp. 1-22). Cullompton, UK: Willan, 2010

Lukowski, J., *The partitions of Poland 1772, 1793, 1795*. Milton Park, UK: Routledge, 2014

Metzner, T., An der Grenze steigt Kriminalität stark an. *Der Tagesspiegel*, 10 March 2011. Available at: http://www.tagesspiegel.de/berlin/brandenburg-polen-an-der-grenze-steigt-kriminalitaet-stark-an/3933108.html (last accessed: 14 December 2016)

Polizei Brandenburg. Festnahmen in Polen - Deutsch-polnischer Einsatz gegen Bande von Fahrzeugdieben. 10 December 2015

https://polizei.brandenburg.de/pressemeldung/festnahmen-in-polen-deutsch-polnischer-e/108278 (last accessed: 21 June 2016)

Ruchniewicz, K., Versöhnung - Normalisierung - Gute Nachbarschaft. In: A. Lawaty, H. Orlowski (eds.), *Deutsche und Polen: Geschichte, Kultur, Politik* (pp. 95-107). 2nd ed. Munich: C.H. Beck, 2006.

Schwers, O., Forderung nach harten Strafen. *Märkische Oderzeitung*, 3 January 2012

Siegel, J. Immer mehr Täter: Die Polizei fährt meist nur hinterher. *Lausitzer Rundschau*, 13 March 2014

Stoklosa, K., *Polen und die deutsche Ostpolitik 1945-1990.* Göttingen: Vandenhoeck and Ruprecht, 2011

Stolpe, I. and U. Buschmann, *Forschungsbericht zum Projekt Weiterentwicklung der polizeilichen Zusammenarbeit zwischen Brandenburg und Polen - Reflexionen unter Berücksichtigung der Erfahrungen anderer Bundesländer.* Unpublished manuscript, 2014

Ulatowski, R., German-Polish Relations: Polictical and economic aspects. *UNISCI Journal,* 2016, 40: 43-56

Wilkinson, J. In: J. Carl and P. Stevenson (eds.), *Language, discourse and identity in Central Europe: The German language in a multilingual space* (pp. 73-95). Houndsmill, UK: Palgrave Macmillan, 2009.

World Bank. *Gross national income per capita 2015, Atlas method and PPP,* 2016. Available at: http://databank.worldbank.org/data/download/GNIPC.pdf (last accessed: 13 December 2016)

The European Union
Rule of Law Mission in Kosovo:
a capsized flagship?

Joschka J. Proksik[1]

Introduction

The European Union Rule of Law Mission in Kosovo (EULEX) has been widely labelled as the 'flagship mission' of the EU's Common Security and Defence Policy. The purpose of the EULEX mission has been to strengthen the rule of law in Kosovo. To this end, the mission has been mandated to assist and support Kosovo's authorities in the areas of police, customs and the judiciary. In addition, EULEX has enjoyed executive powers in the areas of war crimes, organised crime, large-scale corruption and in other (politically) sensitive cases. The mission was launched in 2008 against the backdrop of an unsatisfactory rule-of-law situation in Kosovo, characterized by widespread corruption, organised crime, weak law enforcement and a dysfunctional justice system prone to political and criminal interference.

With an initial strength of more than 3.000 international and local civilian staff, an average annual budget of more than €100 million and an operational duration of hitherto more than nine years, EULEX is by far the largest and most ambitious civilian mission that the EU has ever deployed. Consequently, the mission has often been perceived as a 'test case' for the EU's ability to enact its foreign policy goals (see Bancroft, 2007; Pond, 2008; Wittkowski and Kasch, 2012). Yet, nine years after its deployment, the EU's 'flagship mission' has attracted widespread criticism. Many observers consider EULEX's overall performance as feeble, if not an outright failure (see Bajrami, 2011; Borger, 2014; Capussela, 2015; European Court of Auditors [ECA], 2012; Jaqué, 2015; Kursani, 2013; Llaudes and Sánchez Andrada, 2015; Radin, 2014). Notably, this perception is also shared by a number of (former) staff members (see *Spiegel*

---

[1]   The author is research fellow and programme coordinator at the University of Konstanz in the Department of Politics and Administration [joschka.proksik@uni-konstanz.de].

Online International, 2012).[2] However, EULEX has defended its performance against critics by pointing to its accomplishments while stressing the difficult operating environment, the complexity of its tasks and the high expectations (see, for example, EULEX, 2012a, 2016a; Hawton, 2012).[3]

This chapter sets out to assess EULEX's overall performance record. It is analysed to what extent EULEX has been effective in achieving the key objectives set out in its (original) mandate and how efficient the mission has been in this regard. By means of a qualitative case study the available evidence is analysed, drawing primarily on academic literature and reports of international organisations active in Kosovo. The analysis also draws on a number of personal interviews and background talks with (former) EULEX personnel and other relevant local and international interlocutors conducted between June 2009 and December 2016. In addition, qualitative data found in local and international media reports is included to complement the picture.

Assessing EULEX's performance in terms of strengthening the rule of law in Kosovo, particularly in the areas of corruption and organised crime, may also shed some light on the broader question to what extent international missions can and should be employed to enact the rule of law in (volatile post-conflict) environments characterised by precarious security, weak statehood and a high prevalence of corruption and (organised) crime. In many diverse cases, a lack of the rule of law and the influence of criminal networks have been identified as major obstacles for the successful conduct of international peace (support) operations (see Cockayne and Pfister, 2007; Cockayne and Lupel, 2011; Dziedzic, 2016; Kemp, Shaw and Boutellis, 2013). As a consequence, international missions have been increasingly confronted with the demand to employ countermeasures against organised crime and corruption and to add respective capacities to their 'peace-building toolboxes.' As Mark Shaw and Walter Kemp (2012, p. 6) claim: "[. . .] *organized crime is a threat to security, justice and development. Therefore, it should be tackled as part of the mainstream of any peace operation or development plan.*" It is argued that EULEX constitutes a 'show case' in this regard, as the mission's special focus on the rule of law, its powerful, intrusive mandate and its capacities in terms of expertise, resources (human and financial) and operational time frame are unparalleled in many regards.

---

[2]   Author's interviews with (former) EULEX staff members between June 2009 and August 2014.

[3]   Nicholas Hawton has served as EULEX's Chief Spokesperson.

EULEX: purpose, mandate, structure and resources

The overarching political purpose of the EULEX mission has been to increase public security in Kosovo in accordance with the premises of a liberal peace (see, for example, Altwicker and Wieczorek, 2015). After more than eight years under UN administration (1999-2008), Kosovo was left with weak rule-of law institutions and, in particular, with a largely dysfunctional justice system. Under UN administration, (informal) wartime power structures intertwined with organised crime had been co-opted into the internationally-guided state-building process (see Hansen, 2013; Proksik, 2013; Strazzari, 2008). As a consequence, a high prevalence of corruption and organised crime and widespread impunity, particularly for criminal members of the local elite, characterized the rule-of-law situation at the eve of Kosovo's independence. This state of affairs was regarded as a persistent threat to public security in Kosovo, the Western Balkans and, ultimately, EU countries (cf. Radin, 2014). Accordingly, the EU could not allow Kosovo to become a "*black hole*" in the EU's immediate neighbourhood as Olli Rehn the former EU Enlargement Commissioner stated (cited in Musliu, 2009).

To this end, the EU has created the EULEX mission to assist Kosovo's authorities to improve the rule of law, particularly in the areas of corruption, organised crime and other criminal activities. The core objective of EULEX as outlined in the "*Mission Statement*" has been to strengthen and assist Kosovo's judicial system and law enforcement agencies while ensuring that the relevant institutions remain "*free from political interference*" and adhere to "*internationally recognised standards and European best practices*" (Council of the European Union [CEU] 2008, art. 2).[4] To achieve this, the EU has mandated EULEX to carry out two categories of tasks:

- strengthening local institutions through capacity-building;
- taking up direct rule-of-law responsibilities in areas where there is reasonable cause to suspect that local authorities lack the capacity and/or the willingness to act impartially and in conformity with the law.

To fulfil these tasks, EULEX's mandate spells out a dual set of responsibilities or functions: in the field of capacity-building, EULEX is requested to "*mentor, monitor and advise the competent Kosovo institutions on all areas related to the wider rule of law* [. . .]" (ibid., art. 3, lit. a), and, in particular, to "*contribute*" to the fight against corruption, fraud, financial and organised crime (ibid., art. 3, lit. e, f, g);

---

[4] COUNCIL JOINT ACTION 2008/124/CFSP of 4 February 2008 on the European Union Rule of Law Mission in Kosovo (EULEX KOSOVO).

in the field of direct rule-of-law responsibilities, the mission is explicitly tasked to "*ensure that cases of war crimes, terrorism, organised crime, corruption, inter-ethnic crimes, financial/economic crimes and other serious crimes are properly investigated, prosecuted, adjudicated and enforced* [. . .]" (ibid., art. 3, lit. d).

In order to fulfil these tasks, EULEX has been endowed with far reaching executive powers. These include the power to "[. . .] *revers*[e] *or annu*[l] *operational decisions taken by the competent Kosovo authorities*" (*ibid.*, art. 3, lit. b) and for international investigators, prosecutors and judges to become active "*as appropriate*" either in cooperation with local authorities or independently (ibid., art. 3, lit. d). In practice, this means that EULEX's law enforcement and judicial personal has been authorized, in accordance with the applicable law, to deal with all (sensitive) civil and criminal cases at their own discretion. In an even more general way, the mission has been tasked to "*assume other responsibilities, independently or in support of the competent Kosovo authorities, to ensure the maintenance and promotion of the rule of law, public order and security* [. . .]" (*ibid.*, art. 3, lit. h).

Figure 1:
EULEX staff composition, May 2010

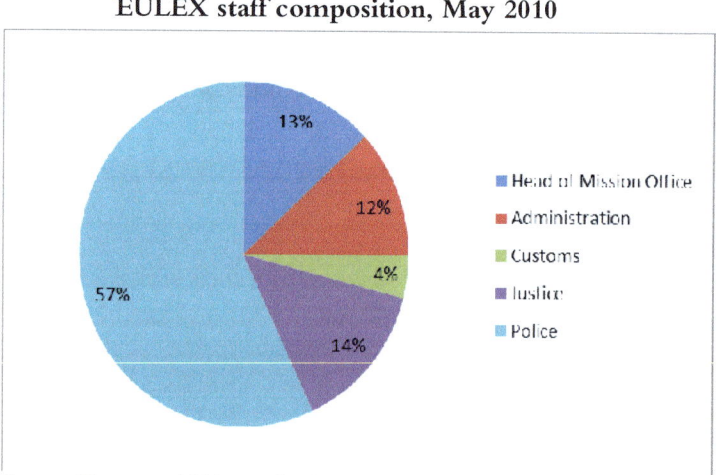

Source: Kormoss, 2010; see also Janssens, 2015

The mission has been staffed by local and international personnel of whom the majority has been seconded by EU member states and other contributing nations such as Canada, Norway, Switzerland, Turkey and the United States. As of May 2010, the mission's staff target was 1.900 international and 1.100 local staff, out of which 1.712 international and 1.097 local positions were actually filled, totalling 2.809 staff (Kormoss, 2010). As indicated in Figure 1, in May 2010, the vast majority of EULEX personnel were police officers (1.601), making up 57% of the entire EULEX staff, followed by the justice component of 228 staff members or 8,1% (*ibid.*).

During the first mandate period (April 2008 - June 2010) EULEX had a budget of some 265 million Euros (CEU, 2009). After 2010, the mission has been gradually downsized both in terms of staff and budget. During the first two mandate periods (April 2008 – June 2012),[5] EULEX's internal structure reflected the three main rule-of-law areas which the mission has set out to strengthen: the police, customs and the judiciary (including the corrections system). In summer 2012, the organisational structure of the mission was revised and its international staff was reduced by some 25% whereby the largest reduction occurred among the international police forces (Kursani, 2013).[6] The new organizational structure replicated the above-mentioned 'dual' set of objectives which lays out functions in the field of local capacity-building and in the field of direct rule-of-law responsibilities as stipulated in the mandate. Accordingly, since 2012, EULEX's organisational structure consists of a 'strengthening' and an 'executive division' (EULEX, 2012b).

After another extension of EULEX's mandate in June 2014, the mission was further downsized to 800 local and 800 international staff members with a reduced budget of approximately 90 million Euros (CEU, 2014). The two-pronged structure of an 'executive' and a 'strengthening division' was maintained, however. Yet, with the new mandate also the mission's target objectives were modified: an important change was that thenceforth EULEX "[. . .] *would not take on new cases and would gradually hand over competencies to the Kosovo judicial system*" (EULEX, 2016c). Thus, since June 2014, EULEX restrained itself from investigating and adjudicating new cases, except "*under extraordinary circumstances*", but would only process on-going cases from the previous years (EULEX, 2016d). Furthermore, as a part of the intended transfer of competencies, the composition of mixed court panels (panels in cases where EULEX judges are involved) was modified such that all court panels would consist of a majority of local judges (EULEX, 2016c). In practice this means that EULEX basically gave up its previous authority to overrule local judges by majority vote. However, also here, the mission has retained itself the authority that "*in*

---

5   The mandate of EULEX covers a period of two years after which the mandate must be extended by legal decision of the Council of the European Union. So far, EULEX's mandate has been extended four times. The current mandate lasts until 14 June 2018 (see EULEX, 2016b).
6   EULEX's structure was changed twice, in the summers of 2012 and 2014. Both times the re-configuration of the mission came along with a reduction in staff and budget.

extraordinary circumstances" a mixed panel can be composed with a majority of EULEX judges (EULEX, 2016b).

It follows that by mid-2014, the mission has begun to purposefully curtail its executive competences by diminishing its direct rule-of-law responsibilities in terms of investigating and adjudicating cases (EULEX, 2015a). In the latest mandate period (June 2016 - June 2018), the policy of reducing EULEX's executive role and transferring competences to Kosovo's domestic rule-of-law institutions has been further pursued (EULEX, 2016e). An exception consti-tutes the mostly Serbian-inhabited northern part of Kosovo "[. . .] *where EULEX will remain in charge of judicial proceedings until the EU Facilitated Dialogue between Pristina and Belgrade brings a solution for the judiciary*" (EULEX, 2016c). The special situation in the Serbian-held North, however, will not be covered in the analysis, as EULEX's deployment was stalled for several years and the mission could not operate as planned due to local opposition and a volatile security environment (see, for example, ICG, 2011; 2013).

Evaluating EULEX's performance

At first, it needs to be clearly stated that this chapter does not intend to deliver a fine-grained evaluation of EULEX: in this limited context not all areas can be covered. To that end EULEX is a too complex and multi-dimensional under-taking encompassing several layers of analysis. Only by analysing the mission's interacting constituent elements EULEX's performance on various levels of management can be evaluated against the background of the operating envi-ronment. Moreover, EULEX does not only consist of various operational units performing different capacity-building and/or executive functions but is under-pinned by a bureaucratic apparatus which in turn is linked to an even more compound political and bureaucratic body: the European External Action Ser-vice (EEAS) of the EU. This chapter limits itself to focus on the mission's per-formance with regard to its overarching goal of improving the rule of law in Kosovo by fulfilling its two main objectives of strengthening local institutions through capacity building and implementing the law in critical areas through executive action. It is argued that the mission's performance can best be gauged by analysing both the *efficiency* and the *effectiveness* of the mission in terms of fulfilling its core objectives (cf. ECA, 2012).

The mission's efficiency can be assessed by analysing the mission's (average) *outputs* in conjunction with the mission's (average) staff size, costs and opera-tional duration, i.e. the inputs. However, it is not analysed whether the mission has been cost efficient. As EEAS has not gathered information on the payments that EU member states have made to their seconded staff, the total expenditure for EULEX, cannot be established. Thus, it is "[. . .] *not possible to assess how cost-effective* [i.e. efficient] *EULEX is compared with other forms of EU capacity building assistance*" (ECA, 2012, p. 32). Although a (rough) estimation of EULEX's total costs could be made, the analytical focus is placed on assessing the mission's *efficiency* in terms of its rule-of-law performance in the fields of capacity-building and executive action. The mission's *effectiveness* can be assessed by estimating the actual *outcomes* with regard to the evolvement of Kosovo's rule-of-law situation.

A special focus is placed on EULEX's activities and achievements in tackling high-level corruption and organised crime as these areas had been defined as "*key priorities of the mission*" (CEU, 2009). However, the assessment of the mission's outputs and outcomes in terms of both strengthening local institutions and enacting the rule of law through executive actions is subject to a range of limitations, the most important of which shall be presented below.

EULEX has tried to fulfil its strengthening objective mainly through so called "*Monitoring, Mentoring and Advising*" (MMA) activities which are commonly referred to as the 'MMA approach' (EULEX, 2016f). The MMA approach provides that individual EULEX personnel train, council and supervise their local counter-parts in their respective fields of expertise (*i.e.* police, customs and the judiciary). Given the inter-personal, consultative nature of MMA actions it is highly difficult to measure them in terms of quantifiable mission outputs, particularly as the efficiency/effectiveness of MMA actions depends largely on the quality of interaction between individual EULEX and Kosovar officials.[7] Moreover, the efficiency/effectiveness of individual MMA-actions is likely to differ across various fields of capacity-building. Particularly, the overall efficiency of EULEX's MMA actions is difficult to assess as (by late 2012) "*EULEX does not have an adequate system to monitor and analyse the amount of time staff spend on MMA actions and on executive functions*" (ECA, 2012, p. 32). Due to a lack of quantifiable data, the analysis of the efficiency of EULEX's MMA actions needs to rely on qualitative data found in existing studies and on (anecdotal) evidence obtained from personal interviews and media reports.

Moreover, the general efficiency levels of EULEX's executive actions in the areas of police and customs are difficult to assess, particularly as internal monitoring of the performance of the mission's various units has generally been poor (cf. Jaqué, 2015) and respective data is not (publicly) available. Therefore, the

---

[7] Author's interviews with EULEX judge, 2011; senior EULEX police officer, 2011.

mission's executive outputs in these areas can often not be adequately quantified and do not allow for a systematic, comparative analysis.

EULEX's executive outputs in the field of the judiciary, however, are somewhat better assessable. Here, the mission's outputs can be sufficiently quantified in terms of (high-profile) cases processed and solved (cf. Capussela, 2015; Gashi, cited in Bajrami, 2011; Kursani, 2013). By analysing the number of case proceedings/verdicts in conjunction with the resources spent in terms of staff and time, the efficiency of EULEX's executive actions in the field of the judiciary can be assessed.

In contrast to efficiency levels, it is argued that the overall effectiveness of EULEX's capacity-building efforts through MMA-activities can be gauged by analysing the outcomes in terms of the general (capacity) development of Kosovo's domestic rule-of-law institutions. Likewise, the effectiveness of EULEX's executive actions can be approached by assessing Kosovo's prevailing rule-of-law situation in general and with regard to corruption and organised crime in particular. However, a cautionary note is due as the prevalence of corruption and organised crime is difficult to estimate, let alone the trends. Given the clandestine nature of these criminal activities, their estimation often relies on *perceptions*, rather than on established facts. This also applies to the case of Kosovo (cf. Jaqué, 2015). Thus, uncertainties concerning the measurement of the prevailing levels of corruption and organised crime in Kosovo reflect on the ability to assess the mission's effectiveness in repressing these two phenomena.

EULEX: mission outputs

While acknowledging the difficulties in quantifying and systematically assessing EULEX's combined outputs in the field of MMA activities, there are numerous indications which suggest that efficiency levels of EULEX's MMA activities have been highly uneven and in many cases rather low. In its 2012 audit report, the ECA evaluated a sample of eight MMA actions conducted by EULEX.[8] Out of the sample of eight audited MMA actions, only three received a decidedly positive review (two in the field of customs and one in the field of police) (ECA, 2012). While the report indicates that the level of efficiency (and effectiveness) has varied with regard to different MMA measures and across different operational areas, the overall (fragmentary) evidence obtained from field inter-

---

[8]   Four MMA actions in the field of the police, two in the field of the judiciary and two in the field of customs (cf. European Court of Auditors, 2012).

views suggests that EULEX efficiency in conducting capacity building through MMA has been rather 'limited', particularly in the judicial sector.

In the following, a number of frequently mentioned problems that negatively affected the efficiency of EULEX's MMA actions are presented. According to a EULEX judge the dual task to 'monitor, mentor and advise' local counter-parts while simultaneously dealing with serious crime cases in an executive capacity has been difficult and 'exhausting.' As a consequence, many international judges tended to work on their own, neglecting their MMA function. Over time, this neglect effectively facilitated the emergence of a 'parallel justice system' run by internationals.[9] Two years later, in 2011, the judge stated that the intended weighing of using 70% of one's working time for MMA and only 30% for executive actions had effectively become inverted, leaving MMA measures in many areas disregarded due to a lack of time.[10] Another EULEX judge recalled that, at the beginning of the mission, no guidelines were in place that defined how MMA should actually be enacted leaving it largely to the judges how and to what extent they practise MMA.[11] Consistently, the 2015 Jaqué mission review cites an unnamed official as stating that "[t]*here was a lack of management oversight or interest by EULEX in judges' activities over and above reaching and publishing verdicts*" (Jaqué, 2015, p 19). Notably, in 2011, a senior UNMIK official outright opined that EULEX does not take its MMA approach serious.[12]

One of the interviewed EULEX judges also pointed to the different national backgrounds of EULEX judicial staff and to respective differences of legal work practices as a factor that negatively affected the efficiency of MMA actions in the judicial sector (cf. Jaqué, 2015).[13] Similarly, a high-ranking EULEX police officer noted that while the main objective was to bring the Kosovo Police to 'EU standards', individual standard operating procedures of various EU police officers often differed markedly.[14] Accordingly, the efficiency of MMA actions suffered from such incoherencies. Moreover, many MMA actions have been found to suffer from the high turnover of international staff, particularly in the field of the police and the judiciary (cf. ECA, 2012; Kursani, 2013; Jaqué, 2015).[15]

---

[9] Author's interview with EULEX judge, 2009.
[10] Author's interview with EULEX judge, 2011.
[11] Author's interview with EULEX judge, 2013.
[12] Author's interview with senior UNMIK official, 2011.
[13] Author's interview with EULEX judge, 2011.
[14] Author's interview with senior EULEX police officer, 2011
[15] Author's interviews with senior EULEX police officer, 2011; EULEX prosecutor, 2012; EULEX legal officer, 2013; EULEX legal officer, 2014

More generally, in 2011, a EULEX spokesperson highlighted the problem of constantly requiring translators for the communication between international and local counter-parts as a source of inefficiency since communication was often cumbersome and time consuming. The requirement that all documents had to be issued in Albanian, Serbian and English further added to the situation. The official also stressed inadequate recruitment processes of staff from member states as one of the main problems hampering the mission's efficiency often leading to long vacancies or the recruitment of unqualified staff (cf. Jaqué, 2015).[16] This criticism was re-affirmed by a EULEX legal officer who criticized the 'secondment system' through which contributing states send national staff to EULEX as inefficient and inadequate.[17]

Most, if not all, of these problems have also been identified in the ECA's (2012) auditing report which, by and large, provides a rather sobering résumé with regard to the efficiency of EULEX's capacity-building efforts and EU's rule-of-law assistance to Kosovo in general. In fact, the mission's re-organisation in 2012 appears to have (at least partly) been driven by a lack of efficiency in the field of capacity building through MMA. Notably, in 2014 a EULEX legal officer claimed that despite the mission's re-structuring in 2012 EULEX's MMA actions have remained highly inefficient and that nearly all problems highlighted in the ECA's audit report continue to exist.[18] Three years later, Jaqué (2015, p. 23) recommends in his mission review that "[a]*t all events, a form of strengthened MMA [...] should be put in place.*"

EULEX's executive output in field of the judiciary is somewhat better assessable by identifying the number of cases solved by EULEX, i.e. cases in which verdicts have been delivered through EULEX judges. By comparing the number of cases with the number of international judges and the mission's operational duration, a rough estimation of EULEX's overall efficiency can be made (cf. Kursani, 2013; Capusella, 2015). According to information provided by EULEX, as of January 2015 (after 6,75 years of operation),[19] "*EULEX judges have delivered over 566 verdicts, including 423 verdicts on criminal cases such as corruption organized crime and war crimes*" (EULEX, 2015b). Thus, by January 2015, EULEX judges have delivered, on average, 'over' 83,85 verdicts per year, with a yearly average of 62,66 verdicts on criminal cases. As the number of international judges working in the mission has been fluctuating it is not possible to enter the average number of verdicts into a direct comparison with the number

---

[16] Author's interview with EULEX spokesperson, 2011
[17] Author's interview with EULEX legal officer, 2014
[18] Author's interview with EULEX legal officer, 2014
[19] From April 2008 to January 2015

of EULEX judges. However, the given reported numbers of judges at different times allow for an approximation: Capussela (2015) reports a total of 49 EULEX judges; Kursani (2013) reports that the mission included 36 EULEX judges whereas Qosaj-Mustafa (2010) reports a total of 37 EULEX judges. On the basis of these numbers, one can construct an estimated average of 40,66 EULEX judges. Based on this estimation, by January 2015, EULEX has, on average, delivered 'over' 2,06 verdicts per judge and year – a quota that, by all standards, cannot be regarded as efficient.[20] However, EULEX's judicial staff also includes international prosecutors that work together with their local counter-parts in Kosovo's Special Prosecution Office (SPRK). Thus, comparing the estimated average number of judges with the average number of verdicts per year may misrepresent EULEX's executive output in the judiciary as the work of EULEX's prosecutors remains disregarded. In June 2016, EULEX's Press and Public Information Office (PPIO) stated that "*[s]ince the beginning of the mission, EULEX SPRK was involved in different stages of the proceedings 1.350 cases – 800 backlog cases (backlog cases include cases from all categories), 213 war crimes cases, 16 counter terrorism* [cases], *16 financial crime* [cases], *75 corruption* [cases], *143 organised crime* [cases].*"[21] Thus, as of May 2016 (after 8,08 years of operation),[22] EULEX prosecutors were 'involved' in the proceedings of, on average, 167,07 cases per year. Again, if one divides this figure through the estimated average number of international prosecutors working in the mission (23,66)[23] then each prosecutor was, on average, 'involved' in 7,06 cases per year – again, a quota that must be regarded as inefficient.[24] Consistently, Jaqué (2015, p 19) notes in his mission review that when (internal) statistics on EULEX's judicial work finally became available they revealed "*low levels of performance.*"

As others have pointed out (see Capussela, 2015; Gashi, cited in Bajrami, 2011; Kursani, 2013), these quotas decline even further when one focuses exclusively on serious crime cases and on corruption and organised crime cases in particular. According to a EULEX spokesperson, as of November 2014, "*[t]he*

---

[20] If one enters the lowest provided number of 36 EULEX judges into the equation the quota slightly increases to an average of 2,3 verdicts per judge and year.

[21] Cited from author's email conversation with EULEX PPIO, 9 June 2016; 'backlog cases' are cases that EULEX inherited from UNMIK.

[22] From April 2008 to May 2016.

[23] Also the number of international prosecutors has fluctuated during the mission. Capussela (2015) provides the of number 27 EULEX prosecutors; Kursani (2013) reports 24 EULEX prosecutors; Qosaj-Mustafa (2010) reports 20 EULEX prosecutors.

[24] If one enters the lowest provided number of 20 EULEX prosecutors into the equation, the quota would slightly increase to an average of 8,35 yearly case proceedings per prosecutor.

mission has obtained 20 verdicts in the fields of organised crime, trafficking in human beings and trafficking in human organs and 43 verdicts in the field of anti-corruption, such as fraud, accepting or giving bribes, or abuse of official position" (cited in Borger, 2014). It follows that, as of November 2014 (after 6,14 years of operation),[25] EULEX delivered, on average, 3,25 verdicts per year in the field of organised crime (or 0,07 yearly verdicts per judge)[26] and, on average, 7 verdicts per year in the field of corruption (or 1,05 yearly verdicts per judge).[27]

Moreover, it needs to be pointed out that EULEX's special focus on corruption and organised crime is owed to the perceived high-level of intertwining, if not symbiotic relation, between politics, organised crime and corruption in post-war Kosovo. Already years ago, a range of Kosovar senior officials (including two former prime ministers), political party members and prominent businessmen have been branded as key figures in Kosovo's organised crime landscape in several Western intelligence assessments (see Bundesnachrichtendienst, 2005; KFOR, n. d.; NATO/KFOR, 2004). These (and other) allegations have been prominently rehearsed in a Council of Europe (2011) report produced by the former Swiss Senator Dick Marty and were echoed by a stream of media reports and high-lighted in a number of academic publications (see Capussela, 2015; Carvajal and Simons, 2011; Dziedzic, 2016; Lewis, 2011; McAllester, 2011; Phillips, 2010; Proksik, 2013, 2015; Strazzari, 2008). As a consequence, among many (including high-ranking Western officials), the independent Republic of Kosovo has earned the reputation of a 'mafia state' (see, for example, Arlacci, cited in *b92*, 2011; Marzouk, 2011; Naím, 2012; Sudetic, 2015).

It is against this background that EULEX has pledged to take on high-profile cases of organised crime and corruption in Kosovo and, in 2009, boastfully announced its hunt for 'big fish' (see Bajrami, 2011; Qosaj-Mustafa, 2010; Radin, 2014). Thus, from the outset, EULEX was widely expected to break with the legacy of UNMIK under whose auspices several local potentates were treated as 'untouchable' and where, in some cases, their prosecution was effectively obstructed by UN and NATO officials (see Borger, 2014; Deliso, 2007; King and Mason, 2006; McAllester, 2011; Proksik, 2013; Strazzari, 2008; Wood, 2000). Hence, the mission's executive output (as an indicator of its efficiency) must also be measured in terms of the number of verdicts it delivered in so called 'high-profile' cases in the field of corruption and organised crime.

---

[25] From April 2008 to October 2014.

[26] Using an estimated average number of 40,66 international judges working in the mission.

[27] Using an estimated average number of 40,66 international judges working in the mission.

That means that disregarding the number of staff, one has to look at how many members of Kosovo's post-war elite have been investigated, charged and convicted (or acquitted) by EULEX after years of impunity under UNMIK (see Qosaj-Mustafa, 2010).

Already in late 2011, EULEX was criticized by several members of the European Parliament for failing to deliver on high-profile cases. As the local Kosovo newspaper *Koha Ditore* (as reported by UNMIK, 2011) states:

> *"While diplomats of EU member states express their dissatisfaction in private meetings, the number of critics in the European Parliament about the work of EULEX is constantly growing. Some members of the European Parliament note that EULEX has conducted 'very few or no' investigations on high-level corruption cases in Kosovo and on the suspected connection between political structures and organized crime."*

Relying on data provided by the EU's Civilian Planning and Conduct Capability, Kursani (2013, p. 14) states that, as of December 2012, EULEX delivered 51 verdicts in cases of "*high level*" organised crime and corruption. However, taking the mission's operational duration and the number of international judges into account, Kursani (2013, p. 14) criticizes that "[. . .] *the number and quality of cases that have to do with 'high profile' organized crime and corruption remain at disappointing levels.*"

Other observers have been more explicit in their criticism of EULEX's prosecution record. Capussela (2014), for example, claimed that the "[. . .] *mission did not convict one single 'big fish'.*" Based on a taxonomy which ranks the elite status of those implicated in 15 selected criminal cases[28] that were opened by EULEX, Capussela (2015, p. 117 ff.) infers that (as of August 2014) not a single high-profile member of Kosovo's elite had been convicted but only "*secondary figures.*" Consistently, several local and international observers have attested EULEX a "*lack of results*" in terms of prosecuting high-profile criminal figures (McKinna, 2014; see also Capussela, 2015; Jannsens, 2015; Llaudes and Sánchez Andrada, 2015; Rettman, 2012).[29] The arrest and indictment of the former Kosovo Liberation Army (KLA) commander and Member of Parliament, Azem Syla, in April 2016, for allegedly running an organised crime ring involved in a large-scale land scam has been EULEX's latest notable attempt to prosecute a high-profile figure in Kosovo (see for example, Bytyci, 2016; Govori, 2016).

---

[28] Cases which according to Capussela (2015, p. 117) "*have more than negligible political or economic importance.*"

[29] Author's interviews with senior UNMIK official, 2013; EULEX legal officer, 2014.

Arguably, EULEX has been somewhat more successful in prosecuting high-level figures for war crimes. In 2013, members of the so called 'Llapi group' were found guilty of war crimes, among them the former KLA commander Rrustem Mustafa (EULEX, 2013). In 2015, the two influential former KLA members Sulejman Selimi and Sami Lushtaku were found guilty of war crimes in the so called 'Drenica group' case and were sentenced to years-long prison terms (EULEX, 2015c, 2015d). Moreover, in spring 2011, EULEX decided to establish the EU Special Investigative Task Force (SITF) to investigate the organised crime and war crimes charges put forward in the above-mentioned 2011 Council of Europe report by Dick Marty (SITF, 2016). In September 2016, the SITF was transferred to The Hague where an internationally staffed Special Prosecutor's Office has been set up to prosecute former KLA figures for (war) crimes committed between 1998 and 2000. In 2014, former SITF Chief Prosecutor, Clint Williamson, stated that "*[i]nvestigative findings are largely consistent with the Council of Europe (CoE) report 2011* [the report by Dick Marty]" and that "*SITF has found compelling evidence to file an indictment against certain former senior officials of the Kosovo Liberation Army (KLA)*" (SITF, 2014). The first indictments are expected in 2017. Thus, it remains to be seen whether high-level figures will be indicted and, ultimately, convicted.

Nevertheless, as of December 2016, there is little denying the fact that EULEX has been highly inefficient in prosecuting high-level figures among Kosovo's post-war elite circles. Given the presumed close inter-linkages between organised crime and parts of Kosovo's post-war elites and the vast amounts of unaccounted wealth that many of its members have amassed (see Qosaj-Mustafa, 2013, 2016), precious few have been inconvenienced by EULEX. In response to such criticisms, former EULEX spokesperson Nicholas Hawton (2012: 20) criticized that "[t]*he highly complicated issue of measuring success in the 'rule of law' is reduced to the simple equation of whether or not high profile people have been jailed*" and further stressed that while "[t]*he pace of improvement may be slow for some* [. . .] *progress is being made.*" The section below seeks assess to what extent "progress has been made" and analyses whether the general rule-of-law situation in Kosovo has improved since the mission's inception and, in particular, whether the (perceived) prevalence of organised crime and high-level corruption has decreased.

EULEX: mission outcomes

According to the World Bank's Worldwide Governance Indicators (as of 2016), the general rule-of-law situation on Kosovo has seen only little improvement over the last nine years since EULEX's deployment in 2008 (see Figure 2). Moreover, in comparison with its direct neighbours Kosovo not only remains the country with the weakest rule of law but has also made the least improvements since 2008 (cf. World Bank, 2016a). This finding is further supported by Freedom House's Nations in Transition Ratings: over the past nine years (2007-2016) Kosovo's average score in the category Judicial Framework and Independence has seen no improvement at all (Freedom House, 2016). If the evolvement of Kosovo's general rule-of-law situation is accepted as an indicator of the quality of the local justice system, then Kosovo's justice system has seen at best marginal improvements despite EULEX's presence.

The annual 'Kosovo progress reports' issued by the European Commission (EC, 2007-2016) document the apparent lack of positive development in Kosovo's justice system. EC Kosovo progress reports from 2007 to 2011 have uniformly described the overall performance of Kosovo's justice system as 'weak'.

The 2012 EC report on a 'Feasibility Study for a Stabilisation and Association Agreement' between the EU and Kosovo notes that, in practice, the impartiality and independence of the judiciary remains limited and that the "[e]*nforcement of judgements, in both civil and criminal cases, is weak*" (*ibid.*).

Figure 2:

Worldwide Governance Indicators, Rule of Law:
Percentile Rank

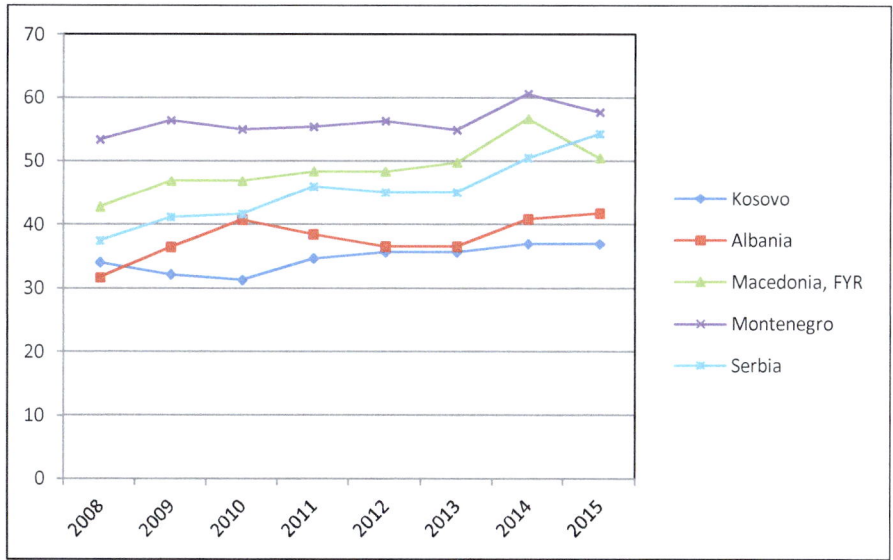

Source: World Bank, 2016

The report further notes that "[a]*llegations of threats and intimidation are frequent and continue to persist in the judiciary*" and that Kosovo's prosecutors and judges are reluctant "[…] *to prosecute and try politically sensitive or high-profile cases against influential defendants*" (EC, 2012: 9). Moreover, the report stipulates that "[a]*ppropriate security measures should also be provided for prosecutors, witnesses and complainants*" which implies that by late 2012 such measures were not in place (*ibid.*). In 2013, these deficits have largely been rehearsed in different wordings (cf. EC, 2013). While in 2014, the EC notes that *"some progress in the judiciary"* has been made, it nevertheless states that, besides other challenges, "[…] *there continue to be serious concerns regarding the independence, accountability, impartiality and efficiency of judges and prosecutors*" (EC, 2014, p. 14). Similarly, the 2015 report finds that *"Kosovo's judicial system is at an early stage of developing a well-functioning justice system"*[30] and that "[j]*udicial structures are still prone to political interference*" (EC, 2015: 12). The 2016 report reiterates these findings (EC, 2016).

While the later EC reports (2013-2016) positively comment on the evolvement of Kosovo's legal framework and the enactment of several reforms, they also point to the lack of progress with regard to the actual implementation of laws. Thus, although in many areas adequate legislation has been put in place, the government of Kosovo has displayed little efforts to enable local institutions to enact the law in practice. Hence, there is a rather stark discrepancy between progress on the formal, legal level and actual, notable achievements in practice, particularly in terms of prosecuting and repressing corruption and organised crime (cf. EC, 2013-2016; see also, Capussela, 2015; Jaqué, 2015). Crucially, the fundamental problem of political interference in Kosovo's rule-of-law institutions persists (EC, 2015, 2016). Overall, the EC Kosovo progress reports (2007-2016) clearly document that progress in the judicial sector has been very limited.

The situation with regard to witness protection can be considered as emblematic for the lack of progress in Kosovo's justice system. The 2008 EC Kosovo progress report states that "[w]*itness protection continues to be weak, if not absent* [. . .]. *Due to Kosovo's size, close-knit social fabric and limited possibilities for relocating witnesses outside Kosovo, few witnesses are willing to participate in sensitive cases* [. . .]" (EC, 2008, p. 13). Six years later, the 2014 EC Kosovo progress report acknowledges that "[w]*itness protection is still a major concern.*" The 2016 report states that although the capacities for local witness protection have been im-

---

[30] Emphasis in original.

proved, "[. . .] *there are no witnesses under the witness protection programme, as citizens have little trust in the locally run protection system*" (EC, 2016, p. 69). The fact that local and international witness protection programmes have largely failed to reassure locals to come forward and testify in serious crime cases must be considered a key problem that prevents Kosovo's justice system from functioning effectively. That precarious security and intimidation of witnesses and local law enforcement officials constitute serious problems in Kosovo has been public knowledge since more than a decade (see European Union Planning Team for Kosovo, 2006; UNMIK, 2004). Over and over again, international law enforcement practitioners in Kosovo have stressed that without witnesses willing to testify, an effective prosecution of high-level organised crime and corruption is largely impossible (see Diemer, 2014; Proksik, 2015; United Nations Development Programme [UNDP], 2002).[31]

Citizens' lack of trust is not limited to the local witness protection programme, however. A survey conducted in 2015 by the Kosovar Centre for Security Studies (KCSS) indicates that the local judiciary (including EULEX) is the least trusted institution in Kosovo. According to survey results, in 2015, 51% of respondents have no trust in Kosovo's courts while another 26% declared that they only "*somehow*" trust in the court system (KCSS, 2015, p. 12). The survey results for Kosovo's prosecution are only slightly better with 40% of respondents stating that they do not trust Kosovo's prosecution while another 32% declared that they trust "*somehow*" in the prosecution (ibid.). However, the authors note that the slightly higher trust rating for the prosecution may be due to the fact that "[. . .] *citizens very often mistakenly link the judiciary only with the courts, leaving the prosecution, to a certain extent, outside public opinion scrutiny*" (ibid.). The author's also point out that citizen's trust ratings for the courts and the prosecution have improved only marginally compared to previous surveys conducted by the KCSS. Notably, the levels of trust in the Kosovo Police (KP) are higher with 56% of respondents stating that they trust the KP and only 21% and 23% indicating respectively that they do not or only 'somehow' trust the KP (ibid.). For Kosovo customs there are no survey results available from KCSS. Consistently, as of September 2015, UNDP opinion polls that measure citizen's 'satisfaction level' with Kosovo's institutions show that "[. . .] *the citizen's highest dissatisfaction remains with the performance of the judiciary* [. . .]" with

---

[31] Author's interviews with (former) UNMIK and EULEX judges, 2009, 2011, 2012.

only 13,9% and 12,8% of respondents being satisfied with Kosovo's courts and the prosecution office respectively (UNDP, 2015, p. 2). Thus, the survey results from the KCSS and the UNDP indicate that trust and satisfaction levels of Kosovar citizens with their judicial institutions remain low.

The low levels of trust in Kosovo's judicial institutions are likely to be directly related to the high perceptions of the prevalence of corruption, including in law enforcement institutions. According to the World Bank's Worldwide Governance Indicators (as of 2016), 'control of corruption' in Kosovo has seen only little improvement over the past eight years (see Figure 3). Moreover, in comparison with its direct neighbours Kosovo has not only the lowest score in 'control of corruption' but has also made the least progress since 2008 (cf. World Bank, 2016b). In Transparency International's (2015) Corruption Perception Index, Kosovo shares rank 103 (out of 167)[32] with the Dominican Republic, Ethiopia, and Moldova, and has only marginally improved its score from 33 in 2012 to 34 in 2015.[33] Semi-annual opinion polls conducted by UNDP between November 2010 and September 2015 further show that local perceptions of the prevalence of large-scale corruption in the three rule-of-law institutions that EULEX was mandated to strengthen continue to be worrisome: as of September 2015, 46,9% of respondents perceived the courts as corrupt, 41,3% customs and 19% the KP (UNDP, 2015). Moreover, between November 2010 and September 2015, perceptions have, on average, only slightly improved for Kosovo's courts and customs but deteriorated for the KP; however, perceptions of the prevalence of large-scale corruption in the KP have been consistently and significantly lower than in the other institutions (cf. UNDP, 2015).

---

[32] The lower the rank, the higher the perception of corruption.
[33] On a scale from 0 (highly corrupt) to 100 (very clean).

Figure 3:
Worldwide Governance Indicators, Control of Corruption:
Percentile Rank

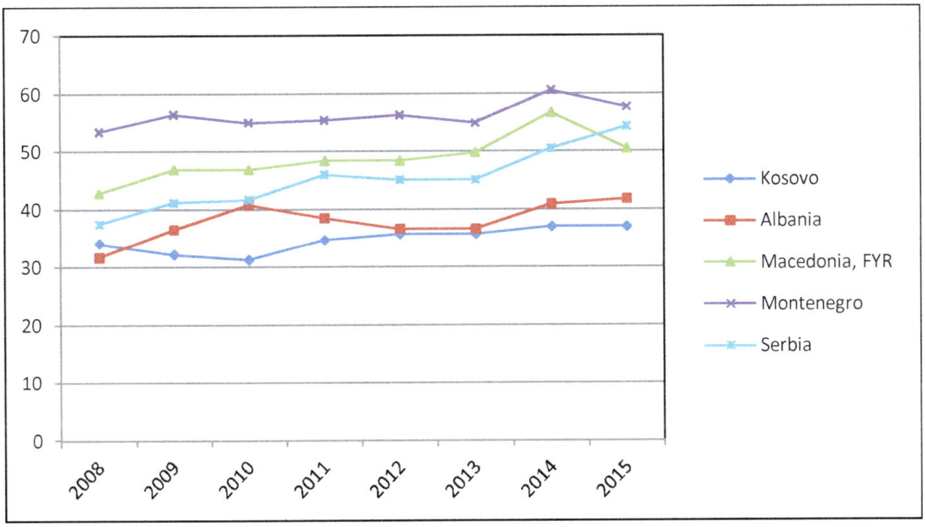

Source: World Bank, 2016

KCSS (2015, p 17) survey results on citizens' perceptions of the extent of corruption in security and judicial institutions paint an even bleaker picture with 62% of respondents viewing the courts, 57% the prosecution and 27% the KP as "*corrupted.*" Likewise, Jaqué (2015, p. 16, 22) states in his review of EULEX that corruption in Kosovo remains "*omnipresent*" and that "[t]*he Mission has not yet achieved its main objective as regards the fight against corruption.*"

The consistently better results for the KP are in line with the frequently encountered perception that the KP has been a (relative) success story in terms of state- and institution-building (see, for example, Greene, Friedmann and Bennett, 2012). This view was also reaffirmed in a 'background talk' (2016) with a senior EULEX police officer who stated that most local police officers are generally capable, professional "*police officers by heart*".[34] Yet, while the 2013 EC progress report notes that the

"[. . .] *Kosovo Police has established good capacities for providing general public safety and security*" it nevertheless points out that the "[c]*apacities in the Kosovo Police to investigate complex criminal activities remain limited and need to be considerably enhanced. Political leaders in Kosovo need to establish an environment conducive to independent professional investigations* (EC, 2013, p. 29).

---

[34] Background talk with senior EULEX police officer, 2016.

The 2016 EC Kosovo progress report reiterates this finding and states that "[. . .] *police is still subject to corruption and political pressure hindering investigation on organised crime*" (EC, 2016, p. 69). Consistently, the above-cited EULEX police officer stated political control of the KP remains tight and that KP officers are regularly prevented from effectively investigating cases of corruption and organised crime, particularly when it comes to investigations against influential figures.[35] Thus, to a certain extent, the KP appears to be rather a force that ensures public order than one that enforces criminal law. Moreover, the fact that political control over the higher ranks of the KP remains tight and is exercised by some of the very elite circles which have been widely accused of being involved in large-scale corruption and organised crime, raises doubts whether the KP can be considered a success story. Even though many local police officers may be capable and motivated, it seems unlikely that they are able improve the rule of law in Kosovo when they are antagonized by the political and executive leadership or intimidated by (overlapping) criminal power structures.

As regards the fight against organised crime, there is little, if any, evidence that would suggest that the organised crime situation in Kosovo has improved notably under EULEX's presence. However, the available evidence from opinion polls on organised crime in Kosovo is scanty and often inconclusive (cf. Proksik, 2013, 2015). Therefore, the assessment of Kosovo's organised crime landscape is to large degree based on perceptions and anecdotal evidence obtained from personal interviews and (media) reports.

According to the Gallup Balkan Monitor (2010, p. 37) survey from 2010, 47% of respondents declared that the level of organised crime in Kosovo is the "*about same*" than it was five years ago, while 27% stated that the level is "*higher*"; only 11% perceived the level of organised crime to be lower than five years ago. Although the number of respondents that felt either "*daily*" or "*occasionally*" affected by organised crime decreased significantly, from 67% in 2009 to 43% in 2010, even the last percentage must nevertheless be regarded as high (Gallup Balkan Monitor, 2010, p. 36). In 2011, the Riinvest Enterprise Barriers Survey indicated that 64% of respondents regarded "*organised crime/mafia*" as the 6th in a list of 22 most intense business barriers (UNDP, 2012, p. 44). However, according to a UNDP (2013, p 27) opinion poll, only 0,8% of Kosovo Albanian respondents regarded "*organized crime/mafia*" as the biggest security threat to families in Kosovo; the item was ranked 9th out of a list of 16 predefined security threats to families. Yet, it needs to be pointed out that the low figure of 0,8% may be misleading as respondents were asked to identify the "*most threatening*" (UNDP, 2013, p. 27) item in a predefined list of security threats towards

---

[35] Background talk with senior EULEX police officer, 2016.

444

families and not to indicate whether they constitute threats at all.[36] Notably, a survey conducted by the KCSS (2015, p 22) found that "[a]*ccording to respondents, organized crime is the third highest internal threat in Kosovo. More precisely, 92 percent of them stated that organized crime represents a high threat for Kosovo. The result is slightly more negative compared to last years.*" While the authors argue that this increase is partly attributable to "*more publicity*" on organised crime, they also point to the widespread perception that state "[. . .] *institutions have shown weak performance in combating organized crime*" (KCSS, 2015, p. 21). Overall, the available data from opinion polls does not point to a decreasing prevalence of organised crime in Kosovo since EULEX's deployment.

Anecdotal evidence obtained from (media) reports and personal interviews equally does not suggest that Kosovo's organised crime situation has changed for the good. In 2012, an international police officer with a long-time work experience in Kosovo opined that EULEX is ineffective and that the organised crime situation in Kosovo is worsening.[37] Consistently, in November 2012, a former EULEX police officer stated that EULEX is incapable of penetrating local criminal networks and that high-level criminal figures remain undisturbed by law enforcement:

"*The major criminals are already out of reach, protected by traditional clan structures and the old-boys' networks within the former Kosovo Liberation Army (KLA), from which many police officers were recruited. [. . .] A wall of silence [. . .] protects these networks. In reality, we hardly have any idea what's going on here. [. . .] The only thing that's clear is that Kosovo is firmly in the grip of organized crime*" (*Spiegel Online International*, 2012).

In 2014, a EULEX legal officer suggested that the only thing that has changed is that organised crime has become much more sophisticated vis-à-vis law enforcement: nowadays, everything would be run behind a myriad front men and shell companies while money is effectively laundered through all kinds of legal businesses.[38] Consistently, the EC progress reports (2007-2016) confirm that, in practice, the progress of Kosovo's institutions in fighting organised crime has been marginal. Moreover, Jaqué's (2015, p. 16, 23) conclusions with regard to the prevailing levels organised crime (and corruption) are unambiguous:

"*In the complete absence of any respect for the rule of law in Kosovo over the years, crimes of this type* [corruption and organised crime] *have abounded. The situation has remained deeply worrying since the Mission began. [. . .] In the current*

---

[36] Respondents of Kosovo's minorities indicated higher figures with 9,6% for Kosovo Serbs and 3,5% for other ethnicities.
[37] Author's interview with a senior international police officer, 2012.
[38] Author's interview with EULEX legal officer, 2012.

scheme of things, Kosovo's judicial system does not yet seem capable of meeting the challenges posed by corruption and organised crime."

However, based on counter-factual reasoning, it could be argued that without EULEX's presence the rule-of-law situation in Kosovo would have been worse than it is today. As Kursani (2013, p. 14) states: "[. . .] *EULEX's presence in some of Kosovo's institutions has had a significant impact on protecting the independence of the institutions."* As an example, he refers to Kosovo customs officials who reported that "[. . .] *political pressure on the institution was made much less likely because the high ranking officials in Kosovo Customs feared that they may be prosecuted by EULEX"* (ibid.). In fact, as the country's biggest source of revenue Kosovo's customs service had long been the target of criminal interests (see Acda, 2016).[39] In 2014, a EULEX legal officer stated that local judicial staff continues to feel threatened by informal power structures, admitting in private meetings what they could not state in public: that they want EULEX to stay because, the mission still causes powerful criminal networks to act with some restraint. Consequently, the EULEX official opined that EULEX, although largely ineffective, *"keeps the situation under check."*[40] Likewise, Kursani (2013, p. 14) claims that "[n]*ot only was EULEX's staff presence important on 'the receiving end of pressure' (i.e Customs), but also on the 'sending end of pressure' (i.e. higher officials in the GoK* [Government of Kosovo]*) – all on the basis of caution that EULEX may launch investigations against them."* Therefore, it can be assumed that the mission has, to some extent, functioned as a deterrent, shielding local rule-of-law institutions from undue interference and criminal infiltration. Due to EULEX's executive mandate, criminal actors may have acted with less impudence, shying away from the most blatant forms of corruption or organised crime. However, by mid-2014, EULEX has started to strip itself off its executive competencies and has generally pledged not to take on new (criminal) cases. Hence, it can be presumed that the mission, although still on the ground, has diminished its 'deterrent potential.'

Conclusion

The analysis of EULEX's performance finds that, by and large, the mission has been both inefficient and ineffective in terms of achieving the main goals set out

---

[39] Paul Acda is the former Director General of UNMIK customs and former Head of EULEX's Customs Component.
[40] Author's interview with EULEX legal officer, 2014.

its (original) mandate. Over the past eight years, the general rule-of-law situation in Kosovo has improved only marginally. World Bank (2016a) data suggests that, in a regional comparison, Kosovo, not only remains the country with the weakest rule-of-law but has also made the least improvements during the past eight years. The same observation applies to 'control of corruption' (cf. World Bank, 2016c). Likewise, the European Commission (2007-2016) Kosovo progress reports indicate that progress in improving Kosovo's domestic justice system has been limited. While the Commission reports point to improvements in Kosovo's legal framework, or in the capacity-development of local rule-of-law institutions, such improvements pale against the persisting problems: continuing reports about threats against witnesses and law enforcement personnel, aggravated by largely dysfunctional witness protection and precarious security for local law enforcement; ongoing political interference and undue pressure on local rule-of-law institutions; persistently high (perception) levels of corruption, including in the judiciary; a general lack of trust among citizens in domestic rule-of-law institutions, particularly in the judiciary. These (and other) grave deficits are complemented by a diagnosed *lackof political will* among large segments of Kosovo political leadership to enable local law enforcement institutions to function effectively (cf. EC, 2007-2016, ICG 2010). Given the well-known and lengthy record of criminal allegations that surrounds many of Kosovo's post-war elites and all the illegally amassed wealth (see Qosaj-Mustafa, 2013, 2016) the diagnosed lack of political will to move support for the rule of law beyond symbolical action, can hardly surprise.

EULEX was endowed with an executive mandate and the authority to investigate and adjudicate high-profile criminal cases because no one expected Kosovo's political-criminal networks to prosecute themselves, and because it was acknowledged that local law enforcement was not in the position to take on such networks. However, as the analysis has shown, the mission has largely failed to prosecute high-level figures, particularly for crimes committed in areas of corruption and organised crime. Unsurprisingly, perceptions on the prevalence of corruption and organised crime in Kosovo remain as high as ever since the mission's deployment. Given the lack of political will and ongoing interference with local law enforcement, one cannot escape the conclusion that the Kosovar 'fish is rotting from its head': the persistence of "*criminalized power structures*" (Dziedzic, 2016) in and above the very institutions that are supposed to enact the rule of law, that prevent any significant local progress in this area.

As EULEX's prosecution record shows, the mission has clearly not been successful in dismantling Kosovo's 'criminalized power structures.' Some may argue that, for various reasons, it was unrealistic to assume that EULEX would be able (or even willing) to do so. However, by failing to do so and by instead shifting all emphasis on capacity-building, EULEX has been trying to square the circle. Whatever the mission achieved in terms of local capacity-building and executive action, it is unlikely that these (limited) achievements will yield sustainable results as it is argued that EULEX has failed to ensure the *necessary conditions* under which capacity building can bear fruit. As long as Kosovo's criminal power networks pose a (perceived) security risk to local witnesses and law enforcement personnel, such networks wield coercive power and can issue credible threats. Thus, no matter how well-trained, motivated and capable local police officers, prosecutors and judges may be, without robust (international) backing they will be easy prey for Kosovo's criminal forces which, after all, have successfully outlived the presence of UNMIK, and EULEX. In fact, many observers have opined that Kosovo's criminal power networks will simply 'sit out' the international presence (cf. Cheng and Zaum, 2012).[41] Although EULEX is likely to have contributed to the rule of law in Kosovo by keeping Kosovo's politico-criminal networks somewhat in check (if only through the mere spectre of its executive mandate), it has not contributed to solving the underlying problem of state capture. Consistently, none of the interviewed EULEX staff believed that Kosovo's rule-of-law institutions will be 'seaworthy' on the day the EU's 'flagship mission' is finally scrapped.

References

Acda, P., Customs and border control. In Dziedzic, M. J. (ed.): *Combating criminalized power structures: a toolkit.* London: Rowman & Littlefield, 2016

Altwicker, T. and N. Wieczorek, Bridging the security gap through EU rule of law missions? Rule of law Administration by EULEX. *Journal of Conflict & Security Law*, 2015, 1-19

b92, Kosovo is "mafia state", says Italian MEP. 24 February 2011. http://www.b92.net/eng/news/politics.php?yyyy=2011&mm=02&dd=24&nav_id=72906 . Accessed 15 December 2016.

Bajrami, S., The rule of law in Kosovo: mission impossible? *BalkanInsight*, 17 November 2011. http://www.balkaninsight.com/en/article/the-rule-of-law-in-kosovo-mission-impossible. Accessed 29 November 2016

---

[41] Author's interview with EULEX legal officer, 2014; KFOR official, 2011.

Bancroft, I., The Kosovo test. *The Guardian*, 17 November 2007. www.theguardian.com/commentisfree/2007/nov/17/thekosovotest. Accessed 04 November 2016

Borger, J., EU accused over its Kosovo mission: corruption has grown exponentially. *The Guardian*, 6 November 2014 http://www.theguardian.com/world/2014/nov/06/eu-accused-over-kosovo-mission-failings. Accessed 17 November 2014

Bundesnachrichtendienst, *BND-Analyse vom 22.02.2005*, 2005 http://file.wikileaks.info/leak/bnd-kosovo-feb-2005.pdf Accessed 6 May 2014

Bytyci, F., Six arrested, lawmaker sought, over alleged Kosovo land scam. *Reuters*, 27 April 2016. http://www.reuters.com/article/us-kosovo-crime-idUSKCN0XO1UG Accessed 2 December 2016

Capussela, A.L., EULEX's Legacy: A response to a flawed analysis. *Kosovo 2.0*, 6 November 2014. http://archive.kosovotwopointzero.com/en/article/1457/imazhi-i-eulex-reagim-ndaj-nje-analize-defektive Accessed 30 November 2016

Capussela, A.L., *State-building in Kosovo: democracy, corruption and the EU in the Balkans*. I.B. Tauris, 2015

Carjaval, D. and M. Simon, Report Names Kosovo Leader as Crime Boss. *The New York Times*, 15 December 2010. http://www.nytimes.com/2010/12/16/world/europe/16kosovo.html Accessed 30 November 2016

Cheng, C. and D. Zaum, *Corruption in post-conflict peace-building: selling the peace?* London/New York; Routledge 2012

Cockayne, J. and A. Lupel (eds.), *Peace operations and organized crime: enemies or allies?* London/New York: Routledge, 2011

Cockayne, J. and D. R. Pfister, *Peace operations and organized crime*. Geneva Centre for Security Policy and International Peace Institute, 2007

Council of Europe, Inhuman treatment of people and illicit trafficking in human organs in Kosovo⋆. Doc. 12462, 7 January 2011.

Council of the European Union, COUNCIL JOINT ACTION 2008/124/CFSP of February 2008 on the European Union Rule of Law Mission in Kosovo, EULEX KOSOVO. *Official Journal of the European Union,* 16 February 2008

Council of the European Union, EULEX Kosovo: EU Rule of Law Mission in Kosovo. Mission Facts and Figures. December 2009.

Council of the European Union, EULEX Kosovo: EU Rule of Law Mission in Kosovo. Mission Facts and Figures. October 2014

Deliso, C., Political 'interests' saved Kosovo's thugs. Interview with detective Stu Kellock, *Balkanalyses*, 13 January 2006 www.balkanalysis.com/blog/2006/01/13/political-interests-saved-kosovos-thugs-interview-with-detective-stu-kellock/ Accessed 12 May 2014

Diemer, C., Ruling Kosovo: The dilemma of legitimacy of European engagement in Kosovo, *Europe & Me Magazine*, No. 9, July 2010 http://www.europeandme.eu/9brain/485-kosovo-politics-unmik-and-albin-kurti Accessed 14 June 2014

Dziedzic, M. J. (ed.): *Criminalized Power Structures: The Overlooked Enemies of Peace*. Lanham, Rowman & Littelfield, 2016

EULEX (2012a), 'EULEX is doing nothing.' 12 June 2012. http://www.eulex-kosovo.eu/en/pressreleases/0298.php Accessed 10 November 2016

EULEX (2012b), EULEX Mission extended until June 2014. 6 June 2012 http://www.eulex-kosovo.eu/en/news/000368.php Accessed 10 November 2016

EULEX (2013), Llapi group found guilty of war crimes. 7 June 2013. http://www.eulex-kosovo.eu/en/pressreleases/0452.php Accessed 12 December 2016

EULEX (2015a), EULEX's Rorschach test. 24 April 2015 http://www.eulex-kosovo.eu/?page=2,11,210 Accessed 23 November 2016

EULEX (2015b), Implementation of Rule of Law. http://www.eulex-kosovo.eu/eul/repository/docs/mission accomplishments_2.pdf Accessed 23 November 2016

EULEX (2015c), Drenica 1 Verdict. 27 May 2015 http://www.eulex-kosovo.eu/?page=2,10,228 Accessed 23 November 2015

EULEX (2015d), Drenica 2 Verdict. 27 May 2015. http://www.eulex-kosovo.eu/?page=2,10,228 Accessed 23 November 2016

EULEX (2016a), Want to know what EULEX is doing? Our infographic will tell you everything you need to know. http://www.eulex-kosovo.eu/?page=2,13,44 Accessed 14 December 2016

EULEX (2016b), What is EULEX?. 2016 http://www.eulex-kosovo.eu/?page=2,16 Accessed 12 November 2016

EULEX (2016c), Short history of EULEX. 2016 http://www.eulex-kosovo.eu/?page=2,44,197 Accessed 14 November 2016

EULEX (2016d), Executive Division. 2016
http://www.eulex-kosovo.eu/?page=2,2 Accessed 16 November 2016

EULEX (2016e), EULEX New Mandate. 21 June 2016
http://www.eulex-kosovo.eu/?page=2,10,437 Accessed 16 November 2016

EULEX (2016f), The Strengthening Division. Monitoring, Mentoring, Advising. 2016 http://www.eulex-kosovo.eu/?page=2,3 Accessed 21 November 2016

European Commission, Kosovo under UNSR 1244 2007 Progress Report. SEC(2007) 1433, Brussels, 6 November 2007

European Commission, Kosovo (under UNSR 1244/99) 2008 Progress Report. SEC(2008) 2697, Brussels, 5 November 2008

European Commission, Kosovo under UNSR 1244/99 2009 Progress Report. SEC(2009) 1340, Brussels, 14 October 2009

European Commission, Kosovo 2010 Progress Report. SEC(2010) 1329, Brussels, 9 November 2010

European Commission, Commission Communication on a Feasibility Study for a Stabilisation and Association Agreement between the European Union and Kosovo★. SWD(2012) 339 final/2, Brussels, 23 October 2012.

European Commission, Kosovo★ 2013 Progress Report, SWD(2013) 416 final, Brussels, 16 October 2013

European Commission, Kosovo★ 2014 Progress Report. SWD(2014) 306 final, Brussels, 8 October 2014

European Commission, Kosovo★ 2015 Progress Report. SWD(2015) 215 final, Brussels, 10 November 2015

European Commission, Kosovo★ 2016 Progress Report. SWD(2016) 363 final, Brussels, 9 November 2016

European Court of Auditors, European Union assistance to Kosovo related to the rule of law. Special Report No. 18, Luxemburg, 2012

European Union Planning Team for Kosovo, September Assessment Report. Doc. 3206/06, 2006

Freedom House, Kosovo. 2016. https://freedomhouse.org/report/nations-transit/2016/kosovo Accessed 12 December 2016

Govori, S., Kosovo crime group led by former KLA commander & politician indicted. *Prishtina Insight*, 25 October 2016. http://prishtinainsight.com/kosovo-crime-group-led-former-former-kla-commander-politician-indicted/. Accessed 2 December 2016.

Greene, M., J. Friedmann and R. Bennet, Rebuilding the police in Kosovo. *Foreign Policy*, 18 July 2012.

http://foreignpolicy.com/2012/07/18/rebuilding-the-police-in-kosovo/
Accessed 13 December 2016

Hansen, W., *Mehr Interaktion als geplant: Friedenseinsätze und organisierte Kriminalität in fragilen Staaten*. Wissenschaftliche Schriften der WWU Münster, Reihe
VII, Band 12, 2013

Hawton, N., In defence of EULEX. *Prishtina Insight*, April 13-26, 2012, p 20.

Janssens, J., *State-building in Kosovo: A plural policing perspective*. Antwerpen/
Appeldorn/Portland, Maklu, 2015.

International Crisis Group, The Rule of Law in Independent Kosovo. Europe
Re   port No. 204, 19 May 2010.

International Crisis Group, North Kosovo: Dual Sovereignty in practice.
Europe Report No. 211, 14 March 2011.

International Crisis Group, Serbia and Kosovo: The Path to Normalisation.
Europe Report No. 223, 19 February 2013.

Jaqué, J.-P., Review of the EULEX Mission's Implementation of the Mandate
with a Particular Focus on the Handling of Recent Allegations. Brussels,
Council of the European Union, 31 March 2015

KFOR, Organised crime in Kosovo.
http://www.globalpost.com/dispatch/news/politics/world-
eaders/110325/presentation-criminal-networks-kosovo Accessed 12 May
2014

King, I. and W. Mason, *Peace at any price. How the world failed Kosovo*. New
York, Cornell University Press, 2006

Kormoss, S., EULEX Rule of Law Mission in Kosovo. NATO Committee on
Gender Perspectives Annual Meeting. 25 May 2010

Kosovar Centre for Security Studies, Kosovo Security Barometer, Fifth Edition.
December 2016.

Kemp, W.; Shaw, M. and A. Boutellis, *The elephant in the room: how can peace
operations deal with organized crime?* New York, International Peace Institute,
2013

Kursani, S., A comprehensive analysis of EULEX: What next? Policy Paper
No. 1/13, *Kosovar Institute for Policy Research and Development (KIPRED)*,
Prishtina, 2013

Lewis, P., Report identifies Hashim Thaci as 'big fish' in organised crime. *The
Guardian*, 24 January 2011.
https://www.theguardian.com/world/2011/jan/24/hashim-thaci-kosovo-
organised-crime Accessed 30 November 2016

Llaudes, S. and F. Sanchéz Andrada, EULEX: a mission in need of reform and
with no end in sight. Real Instituto Elcano, ARI 41/2015, 25 July 2015

Marzouk, L., Dutch Minister: 'Kosovo is run by criminals.' *Balkan Insight*, 29 January 2011 http://www.balkaninsight.com/en/article/dutch-minister-kosovo-is-run-by-criminals Accessed 14 August 2014

McAllester, M., Kosovo's Mafia: How the US and allies ignore allegations of organized crime at the highest levels of a new democracy. *Global Post*, 27 March 2011 http://www.globalpost.com/dispatch/news/regions/europe/110321/kosovo Accessed 13 May 2014

McKinna, A., EULEX mandate extended amid reports of corruption investigations into EULEX judges and prosecutors. *Transconflict*, 23 April 2014 http://www.transconflict.com/2014/04/eulex-mandate-extended-amid-reports-corruption-investigations-eulex-judges-prosecutors-234/ Accessed 2 December 2016

Musliu, V., Kosovo not to become a 'black hole'. *BalkanInsight*, 26 March 2009 http://www.balkaninsight.com/en/article/kosovo-not-to-become-a-black-hole Accessed 5 November 2016

Naím, M., Mafia States: Organized crime takes office. *Foreign Affairs*, May/June 2012 issue, 2012 https://www.foreignaffairs.com/articles/2012-04-20/mafia-states Accessed 21 March 2015

NATO, KFOR, Secret Rel USA KFOR and NATO: J2 Special Projects. 10 March 2004 https://wikispooks.com/w/images/8/8f/SECRETFOR_Dossier_on_Xhavit_Haliti.pdf Accessed 12 May 2014

Phillips, D.L., The Balkan's underbelly. *World Policy Journal*, vol. 27, no. 3, 2010, 93-98.

Pond, E., The EU's test in Kosovo. *The Washington Quarterly*, Volume 31, Issue 4, 2008, 97-112

Proksik, J.J., Organised crime and dilemmas of democratic peace-building in Kosovo. *International Peacekeeping*, vol. 20 (3), October 2013, 280-298

Proksik, J.J., Organised crime in post-war Kosovo: Local concerns vs. International responses? In P. C. Van Duyne, A. Maljevic, G. A. Antonopoulos, J. Harvey and K. von Lampe (eds.): *The relativity of wrongdoing: Corruption, organised crime, fraud and money laundering in perspective.* Wolf Legal Publishers, Nijmegen, 2015, 73-104.

Qosaj-Mustafa, A., Strengthening the rule of law in Kosovo: The fight against corruption and organised crime. *Kosovar Institute for Policy Research and Development*, Policy Paper 2010/8, Prishtina, November 2010

Qosaj-Mustafa, A., The impunity in Kosovo: Inexplicable wealth. *Kosovar Institute for Policy Research and Development*, Policy Paper No. 5 /13, Prishtina, November 2013

Qosaj-Mustafa, A., Impunity in Kosovo: The Fight against High Profile Corruption. *Kosovar Institute for Policy Research and Development*, Policy Paper No. 1 /16, Prishtina, January 2016

Radin, A., Analysis of current events: "towards the rule of law in Kosovo: EULEX should go." *Nationalities Papers*, 42:2, 2014, 181-194

Rettman, A., Organised crime problem dogs EU record on Kosovo. *EUobserver*, 25 January 2012. https://euobserver.com/foreign/115010 Accessed 5 November 2016

Shaw, M. and W. Kemp, *Spotting the spoilers: a guide to analyzing organized crime in fragile states.* New York, International Peace Institute, 2012

Special Investigative Task Force, Statement by the Chief Prosecutor Clint Williamson. 29 July 2014
http://sitf.eu/index.php/en/news-other/42-statement   -by-the-chief-prosecutor-clint-williamson Accessed 13 December 2016

Special Investigative Task Force, About SITF. 2016
http://www.sitf.eu/index.php/en/about-sitf Accessed 14 December 2016

Spiegel Online International, An Insider's View of EU Efforts in Kosovo. 7 November 2012. http://www.spiegel.de/international/europe/veteran-insider-provides-grim-account-of-eulex-efforts-in-kosovo-a-865650.html Accessed 4 November 2016

Strazzari, F., *L'oeuvre au noir.* The shadow economy of Kosovo's independence. *International Peacekeeping*, Vol. 15, Issue 2, 2008, 187-205

Sudetic, C., The bullies who run Kosovo: Political elite frustrates murder, kidnap and organ trafficking probe. *Politico*, 21 June 2015
http://www.politico.eu/article/kosovo-hashim-thaci-un-special-court-tribunal-organ-trafficking-kla-serbia-milosevic-serbia-ramush/ Accessed 30 November 2016

Transparency International, Corruption Perceptions Index 2015.
https://www.transparency.org/cpi2015/ Accessed 12 December 2016

UNDP, Early Warning Report Kosovo #2. September – December 2002

UNDP, Kosovo Human Development Report 2012.

UNDP, *Public Pulse Report.* Pristina, 6 August 2013

UNDP, *Public Pulse -X-.* Pristina, October 2015

UNMIK, Media Monitoring Headlines, Division of Public Information, 26 December 2011

UNMIK, Pillar I Police and Justice Presentation Paper. June 2004

Wittkowski, A. and H. Kasch, Test Case Kosovo: A Preliminary Stocktaking of European Conflict Management. Berlin, Center for International Peace Operations (ZIF), 2012

Wood, N., US 'covered up' for Kosovo ally. *The Observer*, 10 September 2000 http://www.theguardian.com/world/2000/sep/10/balkans.international crime Accessed 13 May 2014

World Bank, *Worldwide Governance Indicators, Rule of Law: Percentile Rank*, 2016a

World Bank, *Worldwide Governance Indicators, Control of Corruption: Percentile Rank*, 2016

The Newcastle Cross-border Crime Colloquium 2016